BOTTOM LINE YEAR BOOK 2014

BY THE EDITORS OF

Bottom Line
PERSONAL

www.BottomLinePublications.com

Contents

PART TWO: YOUR MONEY

7 • MONEY MANAGER

8 • INSURANCE INSIGHTS

PART THREE: YOUR FINANCIAL FUTURE

12 • RETIREMENT REPORT

PART FOUR: YOUR LEISURE

13 • TRAVEL TIME

14 • FOCUS ON FUN

PART FIVE: YOUR LIFE

15 • AUTO ADVISER

16 • HAPPY HOME

17 • HOUSEHOLD HINTS

18 • LIFE LESSONS

19 • BUSINESS BULLETIN

20 • SAFETY SURVEY

Preface

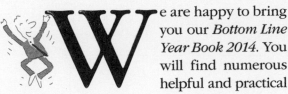We are happy to bring you our *Bottom Line Year Book 2014*. You will find numerous helpful and practical ideas for yourself and for everyone in your family.

At Bottom Line Publications, it is our mission to provide all of our readers with the best information to help them gain better health, greater wealth, more wisdom, extra time and increased happiness.

The *Year Book 2014* represents the very best and the most useful *Bottom Line* articles from the past year. Whether you are looking for ways to get the most from your money or land a job in this tough economy…reduce your blood pressure naturally or assert your rights in the hospital…revive the romance in your marriage or break a bad habit, you'll find it all here…and so much more.

Over the past 30 years, we have built a network of thousands of expert sources.

When you consult the *2014 Year Book*, you are accessing a stellar group of authorities in fields that range from natural and conventional medicine…to shopping, investing, taxes and insurance…to cars, travel, security and self-improvement. Our advisers are affiliated with the premier universities, financial institutions, law firms and hospitals. These experts are truly among the most knowledgeable people in the country.

As a reader of a *Bottom Line* book, you can be assured that you are receiving reliable, well-researched and up-to-date information from a trusted source.

We are very confident that the *Bottom Line Year Book 2014* can help you and your family have a healthier, wealthier, wiser life. Enjoy!

The Editors, *Bottom Line/Personal*
Stamford, CT

1

Health Hotline

Watching Sports Can Cause a Heart Attack— and 4 More Triggers You Should Know About

We've all seen dramatic scenes in movies in which a person suffers a heart attack following an angry outburst…after hearing of the death of a loved one…or while having sex.

But that's just Hollywood melodrama, right? Well, actually no.

An ever-increasing body of scientific evidence shows that some emotional and physical "stressors" can temporarily increase the risk for a heart attack, stroke or sudden cardiac death.

While these dangers are highest in people with heart disease, elevated cholesterol, high blood pressure or cardiovascular risk factors, such as smoking, obesity and/or a lack of exercise, even seemingly healthy people can be affected.

How to protect yourself: If you do aerobic or endurance exercise, such as brisk walking, jogging or walking up a treadmill incline, for 45 to 60 minutes, five days a week, you'll be much less susceptible to cardiovascular triggers than people who get less exercise or are mainly sedentary, according to research. It's believed that moderate-to-vigorous exercise increases the body's ability to adapt or safely respond to bursts of *sympathetic stimulation* (the body's reaction to stress, such as a faster heartbeat or a spike in blood pressure), which

Barry A. Franklin, PhD, director of preventive cardiology and cardiac rehabilitation at William Beaumont Hospital in Royal Oak, Michigan. He has served as president of the American Association of Cardiovascular and Pulmonary Rehabilitation and the American College of Sports Medicine. He is coauthor, with Joseph C. Piscatella, of *Prevent, Halt & Reverse Heart Disease* (Workman) and coauthor, with Robert Sweetgall, of *One Heart, Two Feet* (Creative Walking). *www.CreativeWalking.com*

1

can trigger cardiac events. *Cardiac dangers you should know about...*

Danger #1: **Getting angry.** When you get extremely angry, your risk for a heart attack in the next two hours is two to nine times higher than it was before. Extreme anger can trigger *arrhythmias* (heartbeat irregularities), constriction of the arteries and an increase in blood clots.

Important: Mere annoyance does not have the same effect—the risks are associated with physiological changes that can occur when a person is enraged.

Self-defense: Consider therapy if you are prone to extreme anger—for example, during arguments or when someone cuts you off in traffic. In therapy, you'll learn to respond appropriately to stressful situations and not to overreact.

Also helpful: If you're unable (or unwilling) to get your emotions under control, ask your doctor if he/she recommends taking a daily aspirin to help prevent blood clots and/or a beta-blocker such as *atenolol* (Tenormin) to slow heart rate. The risk for an emotionally triggered heart attack may be lower in patients who use these medications.

Danger #2: **Receiving very bad news.** Suppose you've just learned that a loved one has died or that you have cancer. Your immediate risk for a heart attack is six to 21 times higher than it was before you heard the bad news.

Two recent studies reported in *Circulation* and *The New England Journal of Medicine* discovered that the risk of having a heart attack is highest on the day that you receive bad news, but the risk remains higher than normal for at least the next four weeks.

Self-defense: Regular exercise and certain medications (such as a beta-blocker or aspirin) may reduce this cardiovascular risk. I also advise patients who have experienced emotional trauma to spend more time with family and friends. Staying socially active and maintaining close emotional ties have been shown to lower cardiovascular risks.

Danger #3: **Having sex.** Some people may find it hard to believe that having sex could trigger a heart attack in a man.

What's risky: Sex with an extramarital lover. According to one widely cited report, about 80% of heart attack deaths during or after sex take place in hotel rooms when people are not with their spouses.

Extramarital sex can cause higher-than-normal levels of arousal, which can produce an abrupt and sustained rise in heart rate and tax the heart. Also, these encounters are more often accompanied by increases in smoking or excessive alcohol use—both of which increase heart attack risk—than sexual relations with a spouse or steady partner.

Self-defense: Sex is safer if you exercise regularly. In general, sexual activity increases the heart rate by about 20 to 30 beats per minute. Extramarital sex may produce a considerably higher increase in heart rate. If you are not in good physical shape, start walking. Regular walking appears to prevent the triggering of a heart attack during or immediately after sex. Sex with a regular partner or spouse isn't risky for people who are physically active.

Danger #4: **Watching sporting events.** If you're passionate about sports—and really care who wins—your heart could pay the price.

For example, during the World Cup soccer matches in Germany in 2006, there were 2.7 times more cardiac emergencies on the days when the German team played. When sports fans get excited, the heart rate can increase from about 70 beats a minute to 170 beats in some cases. In people with existing (sometimes undiagnosed) heart disease, this can trigger life-threatening clots or arrhythmias.

Self-defense: Try not to get carried away at sporting events...and don't let the excitement of big games lead you into unhealthy practices —for example, forgetting to take your heart medications...drinking excessively...and/or smoking.

Danger #5: **Shoveling snow and other strenuous activities.** Every winter, we read about people who die from a heart attack while shoveling snow. Even though cold temperatures usually are blamed, the main reason is overexertion of a diseased or susceptible heart.

When habitually sedentary people engage in unaccustomed, vigorous physical activity, they may be 50 to 100 times more likely to have a cardiovascular event, such as a heart attack, than those who don't exert themselves.

Shoveling snow can cause increases in heart rate and blood pressure that are comparable to maximum exertion on a treadmill. The upper-body movements involved in shoveling are more taxing on the heart than movements involving only the legs. And breathing cold air can constrict the arteries that supply the heart. Holding one's breath, muscle straining and mainly standing still while shoveling, all of which impair blood flow to the heart, also can create excessive cardiac demands.

Skiing, especially cross-country (and downhill, to a lesser extent), can tax the heart, too. At higher altitudes, the relatively low pressure of oxygen in the air makes the heart work harder.

Self-defense: Do not shovel snow if you're generally sedentary or have been diagnosed with cardiovascular disease or have risk factors (such as high blood pressure or a family history of heart disease). Hire someone to do it for you. If you must shovel, work slowly and for only a few minutes at a time. If possible, push the snow or sweep it rather than lifting it or throwing it. Consider buying an automated snowblower, which decreases demands on the heart.

If you are an amateur skier and mostly sedentary, gradually increase your activity levels for at least four weeks before a ski trip.

When outdoors in cold weather, wear layers of clothing, a hat, gloves and a scarf to cover your mouth and nose. This helps prevent constriction of the arteries.

Are You Really Doing *Everything* You Can to Prevent a Heart Attack?

Steven Nissen, MD, chairman of the Robert and Suzanne Tomsich Department of Cardiovascular Medicine at the Cleveland Clinic main campus. He is editor of *Current Cardiology Reports* and senior consulting editor to the *Journal of the American College of Cardiology.* Dr. Nissen is also coauthor, with Marc Gillinov, MD, of *Heart 411* (Three Rivers). *www.Heart411Book. com*

You already know the best ways to prevent a heart attack—give up cigarettes if you smoke…get regular exercise…lose weight if you're overweight…and prevent (or control) high blood pressure (hypertension), elevated cholesterol and diabetes.

Yet millions of Americans continue to jeopardize their cardiovascular health by not fully understanding how to address these key risk factors.

Example: One common misconception is that you need to do hard aerobic exercise to protect the heart. While it's true that people who increase the intensity and duration of their exercise may have greater reductions in cardiovascular disease, that doesn't mean you have to run on a treadmill or work up a sweat on a stair-climber to help your heart. A daily brisk walk (ideally, 30 minutes or more) will provide significant improvements in blood vessel function and heart-muscle efficiency.

Other misconceptions…

Misconception #1: **Reducing dietary fat is the best way to control cholesterol.** In the 1960s, the average American consumed about 45% of calories from fats and oils. After decades of warnings that a high-fat diet increased cholesterol, that percentage has decreased to about 33%.

That sounds like good news, but it's not. Research clearly shows that the best diet for improving cholesterol is not a low-fat diet.

Reason: People who cut back on fat tend to reduce all fats in the diet, including healthful monounsaturated fats such as olive and canola oils. These fats improve the ratio of LDL "bad"

3

cholesterol and HDL "good" cholesterol—a critical factor in reducing heart disease.

What to do: Cut back on saturated fat (ideally, less than 7% of total calories)—this fat does increase cholesterol.

But make sure that your diet includes healthful monounsaturated and polyunsaturated fats. In addition to olive and canola oils, foods that are high in monounsaturated fats include avocados, almonds, pecans, and pumpkin and sesame seeds. We get most of our polyunsaturated fats from sunflower, corn, soybean and other oils. Foods containing polyunsaturated fats include walnuts, fish and flaxseed.

Important: Of course you should avoid trans fats—engineered fats that are commonly used in commercially made cookies, crackers and other baked goods, as well as in deep-fried fast food. It's been estimated that for every 2% of calories that are consumed daily in the form of trans fats, the risk for heart disease rises by as much as 23%!

Misconception #2: **Blood pressure medication should be stopped if it causes side effects.** Everyone knows that hypertension is a very strong risk factor for heart disease and a subsequent heart attack. Yet studies show that many patients who have been diagnosed with hypertension don't achieve adequate control.

Blood pressure drugs are usually effective—but only if taken as directed. The problem is that these medications often cause uncomfortable side effects, including fatigue, dizziness or even fainting.

As a result, many patients—consciously or not—find excuses to skip doses or stop the medications altogether. It has been estimated that only about 60% of patients follow all of the instructions for taking these medications.

But reducing or stopping blood pressure medications abruptly can cause a rebound, in which blood pressure suddenly spikes to dangerous levels.

What to do: Don't suddenly stop medications because of side effects. And do your best not to forget doses or neglect to fill a prescription on time. Even if you do experience side effects when you first start a blood pressure medication, try to be patient and speak to your doctor, if necessary. Side effects typically go away on their own within a few weeks as your body adjusts to the lower blood pressure.

Important: If a side effect is severe (fainting, for example), seek immediate medical attention.

With good control, people with high blood pressure can dramatically reduce their risk for heart attack and stroke. Studies have shown, for instance, that people who lower their systolic (top number) pressure by just five points can reduce heart attacks by 15% to 20% and strokes by 25% to 30%.

Misconception #3: **There's nothing you can do about your family history.** We all know that heart disease "runs in the family." If a close sibling or either of your parents developed heart disease before age 55, your risk of developing it is approximately one and a half to two times as high as someone without the family link. And if you have a first-degree relative (a parent or sibling) who developed atrial fibrillation (an irregular and often rapid heartbeat) at any age, your chance of developing heart disease is increased two to three times.

What to do: Even though family history is considered a nonmodifiable risk factor, you still can take precautions that will reduce your risk. If you have a family history of atrial fibrillation, for example, ask your doctor if you should have a yearly EKG. It can be included as part of an annual exam.

You should also be particularly vigilant about managing other risk factors for heart disease. Multiple risk factors—say, family history plus high cholesterol or hypertension—increase your risk far more than any one factor alone.

Misconception #4: **Stress isn't a danger once you've calmed down.** It's widely known that acute emotional stress caused by a near accident or some other frightening situation causes a momentary spike in blood pressure and heart rate that can cause harmful consequences. Anger, one of the most common stressful emotions, has been found to precede 2% of all heart attacks.

However, ongoing stress (due to financial or health worries, for example), which triggers chronically high levels of the stress hormone *cortisol*, is an often underrecognized threat to one's heart and blood vessels.

What's more, even though obesity is a factor in about 90% of patients with diabetes, some research suggests that chronic stress also may increase risk for diabetes—a known risk factor for heart attack and stroke.

What to do: Do whatever it takes to avoid chronic stress. Exercise, including yoga, is among the best ways to reduce stress while also protecting the heart. But find whatever works specifically for you to defuse stress—for example, listening to relaxing music and reading are also helpful.

Calcium Supplement Alert

According to a recent study, people who took calcium supplements were more than *twice* as likely to have heart attacks as people who did not take these supplements. (Foods with added calcium were not studied.)

Best: Get calcium naturally from foods such as dairy products, sardines and kale.

Sabine Rohrmann, PhD, MPH, head of cancer epidemiology and prevention at Institute of Social and Preventive Medicine, University of Zurich, Switzerland, and coauthor of a study of 23,980 people, published in *Heart*.

You Can Get Too Much Vitamin D

Even though vitamin D supplements can *reduce* blood levels of *C-reactive protein* (an indicator of inflammation linked to heart disease), after vitamin D levels exceed 21 nanograms per milliliter (ng/mL), any additional vitamin D *increases* C-reactive protein. If you take the supplement regularly, have a blood test to check your C-reactive protein levels.

Study by researchers from Johns Hopkins University, Baltimore, published online in *The American Journal of Cardiology*.

Aspirin as Effective as Clot-Prevention Prescription

Aspirin is as effective as *warfarin* (Coumadin) for preventing blood clots in congestive heart failure patients.

Recent finding: There were no significant differences in the number and severity of heart attacks between patients who took warfarin and those who took aspirin. Patients who took warfarin were significantly less likely to have a stroke, but they were more likely to have gastrointestinal bleeding and other hemorrhages.

And: Aspirin is simpler to take—warfarin requires a blood test every month and may cause people to restrict activities because of the risk for bleeding.

Six-year study of 2,305 people by researchers at Columbia University, New York City, published in *The New England Journal of Medicine*.

Aspirin Can Increase Risk for Vision Loss

Taking aspirin routinely (adult- or baby-size, at least twice weekly for more than three months) nearly doubles the risk for *"wet" age-related macular degeneration* (AMD)—but not until 10 or more years later, according to a recent study.

Important: If you are on daily aspirin therapy, don't stop on your own. See your doctor to discuss the pros and cons.

Barbara Klein, MD, MPH, professor of ophthalmology and visual sciences, School of Medicine and Public Health, University of Wisconsin, Madison, and author of a study published in *The Journal of the American Medical Association*.

Hidden Causes of Heart Disease: 6 Little-Known Risk Factors

Stephen Sinatra, MD, board-certified cardiologist and assistant clinical professor of medicine at University of Connecticut School of Medicine in Farmington and a fellow in the American College of Cardiology and the American College of Nutrition. In addition, he is founder of HeartMDInstitute.com, an informational Web site dedicated to promoting public awareness of integrative medicine. Dr. Sinatra is author or coauthor of numerous books, including *The Healing Kitchen* (Bottom Line Books). *www.BottomLinePublications.com/HealingKitchen*

There are well-known risk factors for heart disease, such as high blood pressure, diabetes, being overweight and a family history of early heart attacks. But some little-known risk factors are as threatening to your heart as those you're familiar with—in some cases, doubling your risk for disease.

Here are six of these "secret" risk factors, revealed by recent scientific studies—and how to reduce your risk...

BISPHENOL A (BPA)

BPA is a chemical frequently found in food and beverage containers, such as plastic bottles and the lining of metal cans. It can harm your arteries.

Recent research: In a study of 591 people published in *PLOS One*, those with the highest urinary levels of BPA were the most likely to have *advanced coronary artery disease*—severely narrowed arteries ripe for the blockage that triggers a heart attack.

What happens: BPA sparks the chronic inflammation that drives arterial damage and heart disease.

My recommendation: Reduce your exposure to BPA. Avoid canned foods as much as possible because cans may have an epoxy liner that leaches BPA into food. Or look for cans labeled BPA-free. Drink water out of glass or stainless steel bottles that don't have a plastic liner. Don't microwave food in plastic or use plastic containers for hot foods or liquids—the heat can cause BPA to leach out.

Exception: Soft or cloudy-colored plastics typically do not contain BPA—they usually are marked on the bottom with the recycling labels #1, #2 or #4.

SHIFT WORK

Dozens of studies have linked shift work—an ongoing pattern of work that is not roughly 9 am to 5 pm—to higher heart disease risk, but the link has always been speculative. The latest study—a so-called "meta-analysis" of previous research—changes the shift work/heart disease hypothesis into scientific fact.

Recent research: The study, published in *BMJ*, analyzed data from 34 studies involving more than two million people and found that shift work was linked to a 23% increased risk for heart attack. It was concluded that 7% of all heart attacks—about one out of every 14—are directly attributable to shift work.

What happens: Shift work disrupts the normal sleep-wake cycle, throwing every system in your body out of balance, including the *autonomic nervous system,* which regulates heartbeat. An irregular heartbeat (*arrhythmia*) can cause a type of heart attack.

My recommendation: A key way to balance your autonomic nervous system is to increase your intake of foods rich in omega-3 fatty acids, such as wild-caught fatty fish (salmon, sardines, mackerel, tuna), grass-fed red meats, free-range poultry, walnuts and flaxseed oil. Also, take a daily fish oil supplement that delivers 1 gram (g) to 2 g of the essential fatty acids EPA and DHA.*

If your work schedule includes shift work, pay attention to other heart disease risk factors and go for regular screenings.

DIABETES DRUGS

The generic, low-cost class of antidiabetes drugs called *sulfonylureas* (*glipizide, glyburide* and *glimepiride*) help control type 2 diabetes by stimulating the pancreas to produce insulin, which regulates blood sugar levels, but these drugs can be dangerous to your heart.

Recent research: Researchers at the Cleveland Clinic analyzed data from nearly 24,000 patients who had taken either a sulfonylurea

*Check with your doctor before starting new supplements—especially if you take a blood thinner or other medication or have a chronic health condition.

drug or *metformin*, another generic, low-cost drug used to control diabetes. Compared with metformin, the sulfonylureas were linked to a 50% greater risk for death.

What happens: It's likely that sulfonylurea drugs are toxic to the body's mitochondria, the energy-generating structures in every cell that are crucial to health and longevity.

My recommendation: If you're taking a sulfonylurea drug, ask your doctor to switch you to metformin.

Even better: In a major, multiyear study, losing weight and exercising outperformed metformin in regulating blood sugar.

FATTY DEPOSITS AROUND THE EYES

Recent research: In a 35-year study involving nearly 11,000 people, researchers found that those with three out of four signs of visible aging had a 39% increased risk for heart disease and a 57% increased risk for heart attack. The four signs (in both men and women) are receding hairline at the temples...crown top baldness...earlobe creases...and fatty deposits around the eyes.

Important: Of these four signs, fatty deposits around the eyes were the strongest predictor of heart attack and heart disease.

My recommendation: If your doctor finds at least three of these risk factors—or just fatty deposits around your eyes—he/she should schedule you for regular screenings for heart disease.

EARLY MENOPAUSE

Menopause, and its accompanying drop in heart-protecting estrogen, increases the risk for heart disease. So it's no surprise that early menopause (starting at age 46 or younger) is a risk factor.

Recent research: In an eight-year study published in *Menopause*, researchers found that women who enter menopause early are twice as likely to suffer from heart disease and stroke.

My recommendation: There are several ways menopausal women can lower their risk for heart disease...

●**Eat more noninflammatory foods,** such as fresh, organic vegetables and fruits and wild-caught fatty fish.

●**Minimize your intake of inflammatory simple sugars** (white bread, pastries, cookies, pastas, candies, etc.).

●**Exercise regularly,** such as a daily 30- to 60-minute walk.

●**In addition to a multivitamin, take daily supplements** that strengthen the heart and circulatory system, including CoQ10 (60 milligrams [mg] to 100 mg)...fish oil (1 g to 2 g)...vitamin C (1,000 mg)...and magnesium (400 mg to 800 mg).

●**Decrease stress with meditation, yoga and/or tai chi.** Other ways to reduce stress include socializing with friends and doing hobbies you enjoy.

PSORIASIS

The chronic inflammatory disease of psoriasis causes patches of dry, itchy skin. A new study shows that it also damages arteries.

Recent research: In a study in *Journal of Investigative Dermatology*, researchers found that chronic inflammation of the skin is accompanied by chronic inflammation in blood vessels. And in a study published in *Circulation: Cardiovascular Imaging*, researchers found that treating psoriasis patients with the anti-inflammatory drug *adalimumab* decreased inflammation in the arteries (carotid and ascending aorta) often involved in heart attack and stroke.

My recommendation: All psoriasis patients should go on a gluten-free diet, eliminating inflammation-sparking grains such as wheat, rye and barley. They also should take inflammation-reducing omega-3 fatty acids (three to four grams daily). In addition, people with psoriasis should be screened regularly for heart disease.

The Cholesterol Myth: Why Lowering Your Cholesterol Won't Prevent Heart Disease

Jonny Bowden, PhD, CNS, a nutritionist and nationally known expert on weight loss, nutrition and health. Based in Los Angeles, he is board-certified by the American College of Nutrition and a member of the American Society of Nutrition. He is author, with Stephen Sinatra, MD, of *The Great Cholesterol Myth: Why Lowering Your Cholesterol Won't Prevent Heart Disease—and the Statin-Free Plan That Will* (Fair Winds). *www.JonnyBowden.com*

Many people believe that managing cholesterol is key to preventing heart disease. That's not necessarily so. *Here are six common misconceptions…*

Not true: **Most heart attack patients have high cholesterol.**

About half of heart attack patients turn out to have perfectly normal cholesterol. When Harvard researchers analyzed data from the Nurses' Health Study, they found that about 82% of heart attacks and other "coronary events" were linked to smoking, excessive alcohol consumption, obesity, a lack of exercise and poor diet—not high cholesterol.

Not true: **All LDL "bad" cholesterol is dangerous.**

Some forms of LDL are harmful, but others are not. The standard cholesterol test doesn't make this distinction. You can have sky-high LDL with a low risk for heart disease. Conversely, even if your LDL is low, your risk for heart disease could be high.

Scientists have identified several subtypes of LDL that act in totally different ways. For example, subtype A is a large, pillowy molecule that does not cause *atherosclerosis*, the underlying cause of most heart attacks. Subtype B, a small, dense molecule, is dangerous because it is prone to oxidation and can penetrate artery walls, one of the first steps in heart disease.

What to do: Ask your doctor for an expanded cholesterol test. It will measure the different types of LDL particles and the number of particles as well as triglycerides, HDL and other substances. The test probably won't be covered by insurance, but it's reasonably priced—usually around $100.*

Not true: **Cholesterol should be as low as possible.**

It doesn't matter if your total cholesterol is above or below 200 milligrams per deciliter (mg/dL). What matters is your size pattern, the ratio of small-to-large LDL molecules.

Suppose your LDL is high, with a large concentration of fluffy, subtype-A particles. This is known as *Pattern A*. Your cholesterol-associated risk for heart disease is negligible.

You do have to worry if you have *Pattern B*. It means that you have a lot of the artery-damaging subtype-B particles and that your risk for heart disease is elevated. The expanded cholesterol test can help determine this.

Not true: **You need a statin if you have high LDL.**

The statin medications, such as *simvastatin* (Zocor) and *atorvastatin* (Lipitor), can help some patients with high LDL. If your LDL is Pattern B, a statin could save your life. You probably don't need a statin, or any other cholesterol-lowering drug, if you have Pattern A.

There's good evidence that statins are effective for secondary prevention—they help prevent subsequent heart attacks in patients (especially middle-aged men) who already have had a heart attack. This is not because of a cholesterol-lowering effect but because statins stabilize plaque, thin the blood and are anti-inflammatory.

Overall, however, statins don't do much for primary prevention (preventing a heart attack in patients who do not have existing heart disease).

If you're generally healthy and your only "symptom" is high cholesterol, you probably don't need a statin or any other cholesterol-lowering drug.

Not true: **Saturated fat is dangerous.**

Forget what you've heard—the saturated fat in red meat, butter and eggs does not increase your risk for heart disease.

*Price subject to change.

Researchers from Harvard and other institutions analyzed 21 previous studies that looked at the relationship between saturated fat and heart disease. Their meta-analysis included nearly 350,000 subjects who were followed for between five and 23 years.

Conclusion: Saturated fat did not cause an increase in heart disease or stroke.

Not true: **Carbohydrates are healthier than fats.**

The conventional advice to substitute carbohydrates for dietary fat is misguided—and dangerous.

A Harvard study compared the progression of heart disease in postmenopausal women who changed their intakes of certain foods, including carbohydrates and saturated fat. Researchers found that women who consumed more saturated fat had less disease progression. Those who ate more carbohydrates got worse.

Another study found that the risk for a heart attack was higher in patients who replaced saturated fat with refined carbohydrates.

Not all carbohydrates are bad. People who eat healthy carbs—such as whole grains, legumes and vegetables—will probably do better, regardless of their fat intake. What people tend to consume, however, is *refined* carbohydrates—white bread, white rice, desserts.

Sugar is particularly bad because it increases arterial inflammation, insulin levels and blood pressure. It also elevates triglycerides, one of the main heart disease risk factors.

What helps: The best ways to reduce your risk for heart disease include maintaining a healthy weight, exercising regularly and not smoking.

Skip the Stent?

Stents are not the best initial therapy for stable *coronary artery disease* (CAD). Medicines such as *beta-blockers*, *ACE inhibitors*, *statins* and daily aspirin are just as effective as stents at preventing chest pain, heart attack and death in CAD patients. Patients who already have stents should be sure to continue taking their medicines as prescribed—it is the medications, not the stents, that prevent a future heart attack.

David L. Brown, MD, professor of medicine, division of cardiology, Stony Brook University, New York, and leader of an analysis of eight clinical trials, published in *Archives of Internal Medicine*.

Quit Smoking and Get Benefits in *Minutes*!

Former smokers have reduced heart rates and blood pressure *just 20 minutes* after having their last cigarette. Twelve hours later, their blood levels of carbon monoxide drop to normal. And one year later, their risk for coronary heart disease is half that of a smoker.

Study by researchers at Gottlieb Memorial Hospital, Loyola University Health System, Melrose Park, Illinois, announced in celebration of the Great American Smoke Out, sponsored by the American Cancer Society.

Last Resort to Quit Smoking

The drug Chantix, used to help smokers quit, is known to cause mood changes that can lead to depression and even suicide. And recent research shows that Chantix users are more likely than nonusers to suffer major cardiac events, including heart attacks and strokes.

Best approach: Use behavior modification, support groups, nicotine patches and other techniques to stop smoking.

Sonal Singh, MD, MPH, assistant professor of medicine at Johns Hopkins University School of Medicine, Baltimore.

Stroke: It's on the Rise Among Younger People

Brett M. Kissela, MD, professor and vice-chair of the department of neurology at the University of Cincinnati College of Medicine. He was the lead researcher of the National Institutes of Health–funded study, published in *Neurology*, that documented increasing strokes in younger adults. He specializes in stroke treatment and prevention and the role of diabetes and elevated glucose on stroke risks and outcomes.

Few people in their 40s or 50s can imagine having a stroke, particularly if they are generally healthy. But the risk is higher than you might think—dispelling the common belief that stroke is a risk for only the elderly.

An unexpected trend: Over the last several years, there has been an increase in strokes among adults in their 40s, 50s and 60s. What's most alarming about this development is that doctors don't expect to see strokes in these relatively young patients, so the diagnosis sometimes gets overlooked.

Important finding: One in seven young stroke patients was initially misdiagnosed as having another problem, such as a seizure or alcohol intoxication, researchers at Wayne State University–Detroit Medical Center found in a recent study.

What to do: First and foremost, be alert. Stroke can occur at any age, so it's important for all adults to pay close attention to symptoms (see page 11). If you are diagnosed and treated within about four hours of having a stroke, you are far more likely to recover than someone whose diagnosis and treatment are delayed. Unfortunately, only about 20% to 30% of young patients with stroke symptoms go to the emergency room, according to research. The others are likely to shrug off the symptoms (especially if they were relatively minor and/or short-lived) and do not learn that they have suffered a stroke until a subsequent problem is detected later on.

WHAT'S CAUSING EARLIER STROKES?

Many of the so-called "age-related" diseases that greatly increase stroke risk, such as high blood pressure (hypertension), diabetes and high cholesterol, are now appearing in patients who are middle-aged or younger—primarily because so many Americans are eating more junk food, gaining too much weight and not getting enough exercise. Family history is also a risk factor for stroke.

But even if you don't have any of these conditions (or a family history of stroke), you are in good physical shape and generally eat a well-balanced diet, do not be lulled into a false sense of security. Anyone can suffer a stroke. That's why it's very important for all adults to be on the lookout for red flags that could signal a stroke.

PREVENTION WORKS

Stroke is the fourth-leading cause of death in the US. Those who survive a stroke often face a lifetime of disability, including paralysis and speech and emotional difficulties.

Fortunately, younger patients, in general, are more likely to recover than older ones because their brains have greater plasticity, the ability to regain functions after stroke-related trauma. Even so, many young stroke patients will have permanent damage.

Important: Regardless of your age, fast treatment is critical if you experience stroke symptoms. The majority of strokes are ischemic, caused by blood clots that impair circulation to the brain. Patients who are given clot-dissolving drugs, such as *tissue plasminogen activator* (tPA), within the first few hours after a stroke are far more likely to make a full recovery than those who are treated later.

Up to 80% of strokes can be avoided by preventing or treating the main risk factors, according to the National Stroke Association. For example, not smoking is crucial—people who smoke are twice as likely to have an ischemic stroke as nonsmokers. *Also important…*

•**Do not ignore hypertension.** Like stroke, hypertension is often viewed as a problem only for the elderly. But there's been an increase in hypertension in younger patients, who often go undiagnosed.

Warning: Uncontrolled high blood pressure damages the brain—even in patients who haven't had a stroke, according to a new study published in *The Lancet Neurology.*

If your blood pressure is high (normal is below 120/80), you are two to four times more likely to have a stroke than someone with normal blood pressure.

What to do: All adults should always have their blood pressure taken during routine doctor visits (at least once every two years if your blood pressure is normal…and at least annually if you've been diagnosed with hypertension or prehypertension). You can reduce both blood pressure and the risk for stroke by maintaining a healthy body weight…eating a healthful diet…getting regular exercise…and taking medication if your blood pressure remains elevated despite lifestyle changes.

•**Manage diabetes.** It's second only to hypertension as a risk factor for stroke. Diabetes increases the risk for all cardiovascular diseases, including hypertension. Individuals who have diabetes are up to four times more likely to have a stroke than those without the condition.

What to do: Get tested. The American Diabetes Association recommends that all adults age 45 and older get screened for diabetes every three years.

If you already have diabetes, do everything you can to keep your blood sugar stable—for example, eat properly, get exercise and lose weight, if necessary.

•**Keep an eye on your cholesterol.** It's the third most important stroke risk factor because LDL ("bad") cholesterol can accumulate in the arteries, impede circulation to the brain and increase the risk for blood clots.

What to do: Beginning at age 20, get your cholesterol tested at least every five years. If your LDL is high (less than 100 milligrams per deciliter [mg/dL] is optimal), you'll want to get the number down by eating less saturated fat…getting more vegetables and other high-fiber foods…and possibly taking a statin medication, such as *simvastatin* (Zocor). Depending on the drug and dose, statins typically lower cholesterol by about 25% to 50%.

•**Pay attention to your alcohol consumption.** People who drink heavily (three or more alcoholic beverages daily for men and two or more for women) are more likely to have a stroke earlier in life than moderate drinkers or nondrinkers.

In fact, in a study of 540 stroke patients, French researchers found that heavy drinkers suffered their strokes at age 60, on average—14 years earlier than patients who drank less or not at all.

Warning: Heavy use of alcohol is also associated with increased risk for hemorrhagic stroke, which is caused by bleeding in the brain (rather than a blood clot). This type of stroke can occur even in patients without a history of serious health problems.

What to do: If you drink, be sure to follow the standard advice for alcohol consumption—no more than two drinks daily for men…or one for women.

SURPRISING RED FLAGS FOR STROKE

Stroke symptoms aren't always dramatic. If you've had a minor stroke or a transient ischemic attack (a brief interruption of blood flow known as a "ministroke"), the symptoms might be fleeting and easy to miss. What's more, in rare cases, symptoms may occur that you may not think of in relation to a stroke. For example, you may initially feel disoriented or experience nausea, general weakness, face or limb pain, chest pain or palpitations—all of which typically come on suddenly. Depending on the part of the brain that's affected, you may not be aware of your symptoms and must rely on someone else to call for help. Do not take chances. Get to the emergency room if you have these and/or the classic symptoms below—FAST (Face, Arm, Speech and Time) is a helpful guide.

•**Face.** The most common stroke symptom is weakness on one side of the body, including on one side of the face. You may have difficulty smiling normally.

•**Arm.** One-sided weakness often affects one of the arms. Hold both arms out to your sides. You could be having a stroke if one of your arms drops down.

•**Speech.** Your words could sound slurred, or you might be unable to say a simple sentence correctly.

• **Time.** In the past, the "window" to receive clot-dissolving medication was considered to be three hours. New research indicates that stroke patients can benefit if they get treated within 4.5 hours after having their first symptom.

Loud Traffic Increases Stroke Risk

Previous studies have linked traffic noise with heart attack risk and increased blood pressure, and a new study shows that persistent exposure to loud traffic can significantly increase the risk for stroke in people older than 64½. Every 10-decibel increase in traffic noise increased the risk for stroke by 27%. Researchers theorize that persistent road noise disrupts older people's sleep patterns (which already tend to be more fragmented) and in turn increases stress hormones, blood pressure and heart rate.

Mette Sørensen, PhD, senior researcher, Institute of Cancer Epidemiology, Danish Cancer Society, Copenhagen, Denmark, and lead author of a study of 57,053 people, published in *European Heart Journal*.

Poor Sleep Can Trigger Stroke

Adults with normal body weight who regularly slept less than six hours per night were four times more likely to have a stroke than those who slept seven or eight hours a night. Researchers monitored stroke symptoms (such as weakness on one side of the body) for three years in 5,666 people (age 45 and older) with no history of stroke or sleep apnea.

Theory: Poor sleep triggers more established stroke risk factors, such as high blood pressure and high cholesterol.

If you regularly sleep less than six hours per night: Talk to your doctor.

Megan Ruiter, PhD, postdoctoral fellow, psychology, The University of Alabama at Birmingham.

So Long, Soda!

Karen Larson, editor, *Bottom Line/Personal*, 281 Tresser Blvd., Stamford, Connecticut 06901. *www.BottomLine Publications.com*

I used to have a diet soda with my lunch every day. I switched to water a few years back when it was reported that the phosphoric acid in soda might cause bone loss.

Now I'm really glad I did. A recent study by researchers at Harvard University and Cleveland Clinic's Wellness Institute has linked the regular consumption of soda—both sugar-sweetened and diet—with increased risk for stroke. The study analyzed the soda consumption of more than 100,000 men and women over more than 20 years and concluded that drinking soda on a daily basis increases stroke risk by about 16%.

The fact that sugar-sweetened sodas increase stroke risk should come as no surprise, says Adam Bernstein, MD, one of the authors of the study. Earlier studies had already linked consumption of sugar-sweetened sodas to coronary artery disease, high blood pressure, high cholesterol, weight gain and increased risk for diabetes. But Dr. Bernstein and his coauthors were surprised to learn that low- and no-sugar diet sodas appear to produce the same increased stroke risk. "We don't have a good biological mechanism to explain this finding," Dr. Bernstein says. A recent study suggests that a widely used caramel coloring might be one contributing factor, though Dr. Bernstein cautions that this finding is very preliminary.

Rather than soda, Dr. Bernstein recommends that we drink water, tea, coffee or skim milk, beverages that do not increase stroke risk. In fact, the study found that drinking coffee—caffeinated or decaf—actually decreases stroke risk, perhaps because of the antioxidants that coffee contains.

That's welcome news! I gave up my lunchtime diet soda for the sake of my health, but it looks like I get to keep my morning coffee.

Better Care After a Stroke...

After a stroke, the patient's blood sugar should be carefully monitored. *Hyperglycemia*—high blood sugar—has been linked to poorer outcomes after a stroke. Also, the patient's temperature should remain between 95.9°F and 99.5°F. For each 1°C (approximately 1.8°F) increase in body temperature, risk for death or severe disability more than doubles. Finally, the patient should lie flat for 24 hours. Sitting upright decreases blood flow to the brain. If the person has difficulty breathing when lying prone, keep the head of his/her bed at the lowest elevation that he can tolerate.

Study of stroke patients by researchers at Loyola University Medical Center, Maywood, Illinois, published in *MedLink Neurology*.

What Your Eyes Reveal About Your Health: Valuable Early Warning Signs

Emily Y. Chew, MD, medical officer and deputy director in the division of epidemiology and clinical applications at the National Eye Institute, part of the National Institutes of Health, Bethesda, Maryland. She is chair of the Age-Related Eye Disease Study 2, which is testing supplements for preventing advanced age-related macular degeneration. She also chairs the Action to Control Cardiovascular Risk in Diabetes Eye Study. She is on the editorial board of *Investigative Ophthalmology & Visual Science* and other major journals.

The eyes may be the windows to the soul, but they also are the windows to the body. Via the eyes, doctors can view internal structures, including nerves and blood vessels. What they learn can provide important clues about your whole body—and your current and future health.

Regular eye exams are obviously important for visual health. But they also can detect conditions that you might not know you have—and that your primary care doctor might have missed. *Important clues...*

Clue: **Damaged blood vessels.**

Could mean: **Diabetes.**

Patients with diabetes have a high risk for diabetic retinopathy, a diabetic eye disease in which blood vessels in the retina are damaged, causing vision loss and blindness. During an eye exam, your doctor will look for microaneurysms, areas where blood vessels are swollen or leaking, a sign of *diabetic retinopathy*. Your doctor also might notice the growth of new, abnormal blood vessels, which could indicate advanced diabetes and diabetic retinopathy.

Most diabetics get regular eye exams because they know about the risk for eye damage. But in some cases, patients who don't know that they have diabetes—or who have it but aren't controlling their blood sugar—first learn there's a problem during a routine eye exam.

Clue: **Thickened blood vessel walls.**

Could mean: **High blood pressure.**

High blood pressure damages artery walls and causes them to thicken. It also promotes the accumulation of fatty buildups. Artery changes can be detected during an eye exam.

Your doctor also will look for damage to the optic nerve. This often occurs in patients with impaired circulation and poorly controlled hypertension. It can lead to hypertensive retinopathy, damage to the retina that is a common cause of vision loss.

Patients with severe hypertension can develop copper wiring and/or silver wiring, damage to the retinal arteries that gives the arteries a coppery or silvery hue.

Clue: **Clots in the retinal blood vessels.**

Could mean: **Increased stroke risk.**

Most strokes are *ischemic*, caused by blood clots that reduce or stop circulation to parts of the brain. As with other cardiovascular diseases, patients may not suspect that anything is wrong until it's too late.

Your doctor might detect tiny blood clots in the arteries in the retina. Clots in these blood vessels could indicate that there is a similar problem elsewhere in the body, including in blood vessels in the head or neck. Your doctor also might see yellow flecks that indicate high cholesterol, an important stroke risk factor.

Important: See your primary care doctor immediately if you realize a sudden change in your visual field—if, for example, the right side of your field of vision is dark or blurry. Changes in the visual field could mean that you've already had a stroke.

Regular eye exams are critical if you have any stroke risk factors, including diabetes, hypertension, smoking or a family history of cardiovascular disease. The same strategies that can protect you from heart disease also will reduce your risk of having a stroke.

Clue: **Inflammation.**

Could mean: **Autoimmune diseases.**

Patients with an autoimmune disease don't always know that they have one because the symptoms—such as joint pain from rheumatoid arthritis or leg weakness from multiple sclerosis—might not appear until the disease progresses.

Signs of ongoing inflammation could include swollen blood vessels in the retina or blood vessels with an inflammatory coating. Other immune-related eye symptoms include blurring, dryness, itching and red, watery eyes.

A significant percentage of multiple sclerosis patients will have optic neuritis, inflammation of the optic nerve that temporarily can cause eye pain, hazy vision and sometimes blindness in one eye. *Optic neuritis* is an early symptom of multiple sclerosis.

Clue: **Bulging eyes.**

Could mean: **Graves' disease.**

Having an excess of thyroid hormones—known as *Graves' disease*—can cause tissues around the eyes to swell. This makes the eyes bulge outward. You can distinguish this from naturally prominent eyes by the amount of white that is visible—in patients with high thyroid levels, you will see an unnatural amount of white all around the eyes.

About half of patients with Graves' disease will develop Graves' ophthalmopathy. Along with bulging eyes, the symptoms may include eye irritation, immobility of the eye muscles and/or visual changes (such as light sensitivity).

Your doctor may recommend surgery and/or medications to reduce the production of thyroid hormones. You also might be given medications to reduce the effects of thyroid hormones.

Hidden Diabetes: You Can Get a Clean Bill of Health...but Still Be at High Risk

Mark Hyman, MD, founder and medical director of The UltraWellness Center in Lenox, Massachusetts, *www.DrHyman.com*. A leading expert in whole-systems medicine that addresses the root causes of chronic illness, he is chairman of the Institute for Functional Medicine in Gig Harbor, Washington. Dr. Hyman also is author of several books, including *The Blood Sugar Solution: The UltraHealthy Program for Losing Weight, Preventing Disease, and Feeling Great Now!* (Little, Brown).

With all the devastating complications of diabetes, such as heart disease, stroke, dementia and blindness, you might assume that most doctors are doing everything possible to catch this disease in its earliest stages. Not so.

Problem: There are currently no national guidelines for screening and treating diabetes before it reaches a full-blown stage.

Research clearly shows that the damage caused by diabetes begins years—and sometimes decades—earlier, but standard medical practice has not yet caught up with the newest findings on this disease.

Fortunately, there are scientifically proven ways to identify and correct the root causes of diabetes so that you never develop the disease itself.

WHEN THE PROBLEM STARTS

Diabetes is diagnosed when blood sugar (or glucose) levels reach 126 milligrams per deciliter (mg/dL) and above. "Prediabetes" is defined as blood sugar levels that are higher than normal but not high enough to indicate diabetes. Normal blood sugar levels are less than 100 mg/dL.

What most people don't know: Although most doctors routinely test blood sugar to detect diabetes, it's quite common to have a normal level and still have diabesity, a condition typically marked by obesity and other changes in the body that can lead to the same complications (such as heart disease, stroke and cancer) as full-fledged diabetes.

Important: Even if you're not diabetic, having "belly fat"—for example, a waist circumference of more than 35 inches in women and more than 40 inches in men—often has many of the same dangerous effects on the body as diabetes.

Important finding: In a landmark study in Europe, researchers looked at 22,000 people and found that those with blood sugar levels of just 95 mg/dL—a level that's generally considered healthy—already had significant risks for heart disease and other complications.

AN EARLIER CLUE

Even though we've all been told that high blood sugar is the telltale sign of diabetes, insulin levels are, in fact, a more important hallmark that a person is in the early stages of the "diabetes continuum."

High blood sugar is typically blamed on a lack of insulin—or insulin that doesn't work efficiently. However, too much insulin is actually the best marker of the stages leading up to prediabetes and diabetes.

Why is high insulin so important? In most cases, it means that you have insulin resistance, a condition in which your body's cells aren't responding to insulin's effects. As a result, your body churns out more insulin than it normally would.

Once you have insulin resistance, you've set the stage to develop abdominal obesity, artery-damaging inflammation and other conditions that increasingly raise your risk for prediabetes and diabetes.

A BETTER APPROACH

Because doctors focus on prediabetes and diabetes—conditions detected with a blood sugar test—they tend to miss the earlier signs of diabesity. *A better approach…*

• **Test insulin as well.** The standard diabetes test is to measure blood sugar after fasting for eight or more hours. The problem with this method is that blood sugar is the last thing to rise. Insulin rises first when you have diabesity.

My advice: Ask your doctor for a two-hour glucose tolerance test. With this test, your glucose levels are measured before and after consuming a sugary drink—but ask your doctor to also measure your insulin levels before and after consuming the drink.

What to look for: Your fasting blood sugar should be less than 80 mg/dL…two hours later, it shouldn't be higher than 120 mg/dL. Your fasting insulin should be 2 international units per deciliter (IU/dL) to 5 IU/dL—anything higher indicates that you might have diabesity. Two hours later, your insulin should be less than 30 IU/dL.

Cost: $50 to $100 (usually covered by insurance).* I advise all patients to have this test every three to five years…and annually for a person who is trying to reverse diabetes.

STEPS TO BEAT DIABESITY

With the appropriate lifestyle changes, most people can naturally reduce insulin as well as risk for diabesity-related complications, such as heart disease.

Example: The well-respected Diabetes Prevention Program sponsored by the National Institutes of Health found that overweight people who improved their diets and walked just 20 to 30 minutes a day lost modest amounts of weight and were 58% less likely to develop diabetes. *You can reduce your risk even more by following these steps…*

• **Manage your glycemic load.** The glycemic index measures how quickly different foods elevate blood sugar and insulin. A high-glycemic slice of white bread, for example, triggers a very rapid insulin response, which in turn promotes abdominal weight gain and the risk for diabesity.

*Prices subject to change.

My advice: Look at your overall diet and try to balance higher-glycemic foods with lower-glycemic foods. In general, foods that are minimally processed—fresh vegetables, legumes, fish, etc.—are lower on the glycemic index. These foods are ideal because they cause only gradual rises in blood sugar and insulin.

• **Eat nonwheat grains.** Many people try to improve their diets by eating whole-wheat rather than processed white bread or pasta. It doesn't help.

Fact: Two slices of whole-wheat bread will raise blood sugar more than two tablespoons of white sugar. If you already have diabetes, two slices of white or whole-wheat bread will raise your blood sugar by 70 mg/dL to 120 mg/dL. Wheat also triggers inflammation… stimulates the storage of abdominal fat…and increases the risk for liver damage.

These ill effects occur because the wheat that's produced today is different from the natural grain. With selective breeding and hybridization, today's wheat is high in *amylopectin A*, which is naturally fattening. It also contains an inflammatory form of gluten along with short forms of protein, known as exorphins, which are literally addictive.

Best: Instead of white or whole-wheat bread and pasta, switch to nonwheat grains such as brown or black rice, quinoa, buckwheat or amaranth. They're easy to cook, taste good—and they don't have any of the negative effects. Small red russet potatoes also are acceptable.

• **Give up liquid calories.** The average American gets 175 calories a day from sugar-sweetened beverages. Because these calories are in addition to calories from solid food, they can potentially cause weight gain of 18 pounds a year. The Harvard Nurses' Health Study found that women who drank one sugar-sweetened soft drink a day had an 82% increased risk of developing diabetes within four years.

Moderation rarely works with soft drinks because sugar is addictive. It activates the same brain receptors that are stimulated by heroin.

My advice: Switch completely to water. A cup of unsweetened coffee or tea daily is acceptable, but water should be your main source of fluids.

Bonus: People who are trying to lose weight can lose 44% more in 12 weeks just by drinking a glass of water before meals.

Important: Diet soda isn't a good substitute for water—the artificial sweeteners that are used increase sugar cravings and slow metabolism. Studies have found a 67% increase in diabetes risk in people who use artificial sweeteners.

Best Breakfast for Diabetes Protection

Skipping breakfast raises diabetes risk for type 2 diabetes by 21%. And the best breakfast is a combination of low-saturated-fat protein and low-glycemic-index carbohydrates.

Example: A western omelet with peppers, low-fat cheese and ham.

Eating fruit is common at breakfast but not ideal—it contains too much sugar and may leave you hungry again within as little as an hour.

Other ways to avoid type 2 diabetes: Increase physical activity and intake of omega-3s and vitamin D.

Frederic J. Vagnini, MD, a cardiovascular surgeon at the Heart, Diabetes and Weight Loss Centers of New York, Lake Success.

Could Your Moisturizer or Soap Raise Diabetes Risk?

Phthalates are chemicals that are found in some personal-care products such as moisturizers, nail polishes, soaps, hair sprays and perfumes.

Recent finding: Women who had the highest concentrations of certain phthalates in their bodies had twice the risk for diabetes, compared with women who had the lowest levels of those chemicals.

Phthalates also are found in adhesives, electronics, toys and other products. They are known to disrupt the body's endocrine system, which may cause a change in insulin resistance that leads to diabetes.

Study of urinary concentrations of phthalates in 2,350 women, ages 20 to 80 years old, by researchers at Brigham and Women's Hospital, Boston, published online in *Environmental Health Perspectives*.

Some Diabetes Drugs Linked to Vision Loss

Macular edema—a swelling in the central retina that can cause blindness—is more common among patients who take Actos or Avandia. But these medicines, known as *thiazolidinediones*, generally have more benefits than risks, and the risk for macular edema is small. Patients taking the medications should have more frequent eye examinations to detect early signs of the condition.

Joel Zonszein, MD, FACE, FACP, a certified diabetes educator, professor of clinical medicine and director of the Clinical Diabetes Center, University Hospital of the Albert Einstein College of Medicine, Montefiore Medical Center, Bronx, New York.

New Warning for Diabetes Patients

There have been reports of insulin-delivery pumps and glucose-monitoring devices being potentially damaged after they passed through full-body or X-ray scanners used by airport security.

If you use one of these devices for diabetes care: Get a letter from your doctor that will allow you to bypass the scanners and be hand-screened instead.

H. Peter Chase, MD, clinical director, Barbara Davis Center for Childhood Diabetes, University of Colorado, Aurora.

Little-Known Cancer Risk Factors: Fruit Juice, Alarm Clocks, Heavy Traffic and More

Keith I. Block, MD, medical director of the Block Center for Integrative Cancer Treatment in Skokie, Illinois, which combines advanced conventional medicine with research-based complementary therapies. He is the founding editor-in-chief of *Integrative Cancer Therapies*, a peer-reviewed journal. In 2005, he was appointed to the National Cancer Institute's Physician Data Query (PDQ) Cancer CAM Editorial Board, on which he continues to serve. He is author of *Life Over Cancer* (Bantam). *www.BlockMD.com*

What if you were told that your bedside alarm clock—or even your morning glass of orange juice—could possibly increase your risk for cancer?

That would sound pretty far-fetched, right? Believe it or not, scientists in many parts of the world are now making intriguing new discoveries about such surprising and little-known factors that may increase your likelihood of developing, or dying from, cancer.

For example…

FRUIT JUICE

Fruit is loaded with cancer-preventing antioxidants and fiber. But when you remove the fiber and drink the juice, which is high in sugar, you trigger greater spikes in blood sugar (or glucose) and the glucose-regulating hormone insulin. High levels of glucose and insulin, acting as a growth stimulant, can promote more rapid cellular growth and division, which may increase one's risk of developing cancer or promote existing disease.

Scientific evidence: In a study of nearly 1,800 people, those who drank the most fruit juice (more than three glasses a day) were 74% more likely to develop colorectal cancer than those who drank the least, reported researchers in the October 2011 issue of the *Journal of the American Dietetic Association*.

Cancer self-defense: This research, which was based on responses to food-frequency questionnaires, is not definitive, but I believe that the evidence is strong enough to advise people to avoid fruit juice and eat the whole fruit instead. If you don't want to give up fruit juice, mix three ounces of pure fruit juice with three ounces of water. Drink no more than two to three servings of the diluted fruit juice mixture a day.

Also avoid other fast-digesting, glucose-spiking carbohydrates (such as sugar and white flour). Emphasize foods that stabilize blood sugar and insulin, such as whole grains, legumes and vegetables. If you regularly eat pasta, cook it al dente (to minimize blood sugar increases). Choose whole-wheat pasta or brown rice pasta.

LIGHT AT NIGHT

Some interesting research is now being conducted on possible cancer risks associated with a phenomenon known as *"light at night"* (LAN)—that is, any type of light exposure at night…even from a bedside alarm clock.

Research on the health effects of light exposure began more than two decades ago when scientists first identified an increased risk for breast, prostate, colorectal and other cancers in night-shift workers. Researchers theorize that night-shift work can disrupt the body's natural *circadian rhythm* of daytime activity and nighttime rest, leading to imbalances in the hormones *melatonin*, *estrogen* and *cortisol*, which may play a role in triggering cancer. Now the research extends far beyond night-shift work.

Scientific evidence: Researchers at the University of Haifa in Israel measured light levels in the "sleeping habitats" of 1,679 women. They found that those with the highest "bedroom-light intensity" had a 22% higher risk for breast cancer. A 2009 study discovered that risk for prostate cancer increased as the exposure to LAN increased.

To help protect yourself…

• **Use an alarm clock with a red light.** An alarm clock that's too close to your head and illuminated with any color other than red generates light in the blue spectrum, which may be associated with disruption in sleep and cut the production of melatonin, the circadian-regulating hormone.

In addition, if you need a light to help you find your way to the bathroom, use a dim nightlight. Avoid direct exposure to light.

Helpful: Use a sleep "mask" to cover your eyes when you're sleeping.

HEAVY TRAFFIC

It's logical that breathing air pollution from traffic might increase the risk for lung cancer.

Recent unexpected finding: Research published in various peer-reviewed journals in the last year links air pollution from traffic to a higher risk for ovarian, cervical, brain and stomach cancers. Researchers are still studying the association, but it may be due to *volatile organic compounds* (VOCs), *polycyclic aromatic hydrocarbons* and other toxic substances in car exhaust that cause cellular damage not just in the lungs but throughout the body. *To avoid exposure to pollution from automobiles…*

• **When driving, maintain a reasonable distance from the car in front of you.** Use the rule of thumb from safety experts—at least one car length for every 10 miles per hour (mph) of speed. So if you're driving 60 mph, there should be at least six car lengths between your car and the one in front of you. And in stop-and-go traffic or at a stoplight, leave one car length of space between your car and the one in front of you.

• **Turn on the air-recirculation system in your car**—and leave it on when you are in heavier traffic. This helps ensure that no outdoor air is circulating in your car.

• **If you live near a busy road, close your home's windows during peak traffic hours** and place one or two air filters in appropriate locations in your home.

• **Avoid driving, bicycling or walking in or near rush-hour traffic whenever possible.**

• **Wear a breathing mask,** often used by motorists, joggers and cyclists to filter out noxious odors and fumes, if you can't avoid areas with high levels of pollution from traffic.

Two examples: Filt-R Reusable Neoprene Commuter Pollution Mask (about $30*) and Respro Techno Face Mask (about $40)—both

*Prices subject to change.

are available on the Web. Or, if you can't wear a mask, breathe through your nose instead of your mouth. Breathing through the nose helps filter out particles that get trapped in the mucous membranes. When breathing through your mouth, pollutants may directly enter the lungs.

•**Eat an antioxidant-rich diet with leafy greens, melons and dark-colored fruits** such as plums and berries (for example, blueberries and blackberries)—these protect your body's cells from harmful pollutants.

Check the Web site *www.AirNow.gov* for air quality in your area, and avoid going outside when the air-quality index is higher than the "moderate" range.

VITAMIN E

Research investigating vitamin E's effect on prostate cancer has been mixed. At one time, it was reported that vitamin E could reduce men's risk for prostate cancer.

However, a recent study published in *The Journal of the American Medical Association*, which analyzed existing data, found that men who took vitamin E alone had a 17% increase in prostate cancer compared with men who took a placebo. Men who took vitamin E and selenium (a supplement with cancer-suppressing properties) had no increased risk for prostate cancer.

What's now been discovered: In the research linking vitamin E use with increased prostate cancer risk, men took a form of vitamin E called *alpha-tocopherol*, which has several drawbacks.

For example, it is synthetic (not natural), and it does not include the vitamin's seven other compounds—three tocopherols (gamma, beta and delta) and four tocotrienols.

Numerous experts now think that *gamma-tocopherol*—not alpha-tocopherol, which was shown in research to increase prostate cancer risk—is the type of vitamin E with the greatest cancer-fighting activity.

Cancer self-defense: If you take vitamin E, look for a supplement that contains mixed tocopherols (including gamma-tocopherol) and tocotrienols.

All people, especially those with a history of cancer, should consult a doctor who is experienced in nutrition and the use of dietary supplements before starting a supplement regimen. Also, eat a varied antioxidant-rich diet as part of your cancer-fighting defense.

Dental Plaque Cancer Danger

In a recent study, scientists tracked almost 1,400 healthy adults (average age 40) for 24 years.

Findings: Of the 58 people who died prematurely, cancer was the most common cause of death. Additionally, those who died of cancer had more dental plaque on their teeth and gums than those who did not die prematurely. Dental plaque was found to increase risk for premature death due to cancer by 79%—perhaps due to a systemic inflammatory response.

Birgitta Söder, PhD, professor of odontological prophylaxis, department of dental medicine, Karolinska Institutet, Stockholm, Sweden.

Cell Phone Alert!

Rebecca Shannonhouse, editor, *Bottom Line/Health*, 281 Tresser Blvd., Stamford, Connecticut 06901. *www.BottomLinePublications.com*

Now that so many Americans have smartphones, it's more important than ever to do whatever you can to use them safely. These phones rely on multiple antennae that produce radiation—every time you use Wi-Fi or GPS navigation, for example.

While experts disagree on the risk associated with *radiofrequency radiation* from any cell phone—some studies have linked their use to an increase in head cancers—everyone agrees that hands-free systems are one of the best ways to reduce exposure.

The lowest levels of radiation exposure occur when you place the phone on a table and use the speaker mode, explains Magda Havas, PhD, an expert in radiofrequency radiation and associate professor of environmental and resource studies at Trent University in Peterborough, Ontario.

However, some cell phone users find this practice inconvenient. A wired headset is a popular alternative, but most people do not realize that the wire itself emits radiation.

Other choices…

• **"Blue Tube," a type of headset in which the tube is hollow.** The wire closer to the phone can expose the body to radiation, but the head receives minimal exposure.

• **Bluetooth allows your cell phone to "talk" wirelessly to the earpiece.** Since the phone can be several feet away, the radiation level (including small amounts from the earpiece)may be lower than with a wired or handheld device.

Also helpful: Switch the phone to "airplane mode on" when it's not in use—this way, it does not receive or transmit radiation.

When a Minor Head Injury Turns Deadly

E. Sander Connolly, Jr., MD, vice-chairman of neurosurgery, the Bennett M. Stein Professor of Neurological Surgery, director of the Cerebrovascular Research Laboratory and surgical director of the Neuro-Intensive Care Unit at Columbia University Medical Center in New York City. Dr. Connolly is the author or coauthor of more than 300 scientific papers that have appeared in leading medical journals.

Everybody knows about the devastation of a major head injury. This may occur, for example, during a car accident that fractures the skull and damages the brain, leaving the victim in a coma.

An often-overlooked threat: You also can die from a minor head injury, a bump on the noggin seemingly so slight that you may not even remember it happened. Perhaps you banged your head on the door frame of your car as you got out. Or maybe you stood up in a small garden shed and hit your head.

This type of supposedly harmless injury can sometimes tear tiny veins in the thin space between the brain and the skull (the *dura*). And in the days and weeks that follow, a thick, oil-like mixture of blood and water (a *hematoma*) can slowly pool beneath the dura and begin pressing on the brain.

Called a *chronic subdural hematoma (CSDH),* this problem can cause a range of symptoms from minor to serious—and even can become life-threatening. The condition is not common, but it's not rare, either—particularly in people in their 70s and 80s.

ARE YOU AT RISK?

People at greatest risk are…

• **Age 70 or older.** The brain shrinks with age, stretching the veins draining into the dura so they are more easily torn by a bump on the head. And blood doesn't clot as well, so it's more likely to form a hematoma.

• **Taking one or more anticoagulant or antiplatelet drugs,** which prevent clotting. So-called blood-thinning drugs include aspirin, *warfarin* (Coumadin) and *clopidogrel* (Plavix).

• **Male.** No one really knows why men are at higher risk for a CSDH.

• **At increased risk of falling.** People who have osteoarthritis, mild cognitive impairment or neuropathy, are more likely to fall. Hearing loss, impaired vision and balance problems also increase fall risk.

In addition, some medications can put you at greater risk for falling. These include sleeping pills, antidepressants, antianxiety drugs, anticonvulsants, antipsychotics and drugs that normalize heart rhythm. You are also at increased risk for a fall if you are taking four or more of any medications. And, if you are a heavy drinker, you are more likely to fall.

• **Diagnosed with liver disease.** Liver problems can slow or impede blood clotting, increasing risk for a CSDH.

RED FLAGS TO WATCH FOR

The symptoms of a CSDH, described below, usually develop slowly, occurring in the days and weeks after a head injury. Over time, they can become more pronounced.

Main symptoms include a worsening headache…unusual fatigue, lethargy or excessive drowsiness...dizziness...subtle alterations in mental status, such as confusion or poorer memory...changes in personality, such as apathy...nausea and vomiting...strokelike symptoms, such as weakness in an arm or leg or slurred speech...and/or seizures.

Important: If you experience one or more of the above symptoms (whether you remember a recent head injury or not), go to a hospital emergency department or call 911. In most cases, you will receive a CT scan for diagnosis. An MRI also can diagnose a CSDH, but it is more expensive and time-consuming. The earlier a CSDH is diagnosed, the less likely it will cause any long-term effects (such as cognitive impairment) or that it will become life-threatening.

BEST TREATMENT OPTIONS

In many cases, a small-sized CSDH with minor symptoms (such as mild dizziness) does not require medical treatment—it simply goes away on its own. The blood often is reabsorbed without causing further brain damage. Your neurologist may choose to monitor your CSDH with regular CT scans.

However, if you have a larger CSDH with significant symptoms, a neurologist will probably recommend surgery to drain the accumulated blood.

Main surgical treatment: Burr hole drainage—a hole is drilled in the skull over the area of the hematoma, and the fluid is suctioned out.

Most operations are successful, with no recurrence of the CSDH. However, 15% of patients develop progression or recurrence of their CSDH despite drainage.

WHAT TO DO AFTER SURGERY

Get seven to eight hours of sleep every night...do not drive or participate in recreational sports without your doctor's permission...check with your doctor before taking any new medication...and do not drink alcohol until you have a normal CT scan. If you previously took a blood-thinning drug, your doctor will advise you when to resume it.

Need a New Joint? Check Out "Pre-Hab" to Improve Results

Karen Pechman, MD, medical director of the department of physical medicine and rehabilitation at Burke Rehabilitation Hospital in White Plains, New York. She is an assistant professor of rehabilitation medicine at Weill Cornell Medical College in New York City.

Joint-replacement surgery may be a good solution if your joint pain interferes with everyday activities.

Secret to getting better results: A targeted form of physical conditioning known as "pre-hab" can dramatically reduce the often-painful recuperation period that follows joint-replacement surgery.

Even though surgeons have encouraged pre-hab for as long as they've been doing joint replacements, not enough patients take advantage of it.

When performed for six weeks before your surgery, pre-hab can reduce your recovery time by up to 73% for common joint-replacement surgeries such as those for the knee and hip—and even less common replacement procedures, including those for the ankle and elbow. *What you need to know...*

WHY PRE-HAB?

With pre-hab, a physical therapist coordinates an exercise program that helps build the physical "reserves" you'll need to recover from surgery.

To accomplish this, pre-hab focuses on specific exercises that strengthen multiple muscle groups without stressing the affected joint... improves balance and flexibility...and increases stamina and coordination.

But is pre-hab really worth the effort?

Consider these facts: Pre-hab not only results in shorter hospital stays, but also shorter stints in inpatient and outpatient rehab...and a quicker return to the activities and lifestyle that had to be put on hold due to unbearable joint pain. What's more, there's significant scientific evidence that supports the use of pre-hab for people undergoing joint replacement.

For example, participation in pre-hab has been found to greatly increase your chances of having a successful surgical outcome—that is, having little or no pain and regaining full joint mobility and functional capacity—according to research published in *Physiotherapy Theory and Practice, Clinical Orthopaedics and Related Research* and *The Journal of Strength and Conditioning Research*.

Although pre-hab is not a substitute for rehab that's done after joint replacement, there are several advantages to strengthening one's body before surgery. A faster recovery is perhaps the most important benefit.

Someone who undergoes a few weeks of pre-hab prior to a hip replacement, for example, might complete a postsurgery rehabilitation program in only five to seven days, while another person who hasn't undergone pre-hab and isn't in the best of health could require several weeks in rehab.

With pre-hab, you will exercise to strengthen the muscles around the joint that is going to be replaced. While this is done in several ways to avoid straining the joint, you may experience some discomfort.

If you're planning to undergo a knee replacement, for example, you might do exercises that strengthen muscles around the knee, rather than flexing the knee itself. In rare cases, patients are in so much pain that pre-hab isn't possible.

Helpful: Doing pre-hab at the same facility handling your rehab creates a seamless pre- and postsurgical "program."*

WHAT TO EXPECT IN PRE-HAB

In general, the therapist will choose exercises that strengthen—but don't overly stress—the affected joint. Pre-hab is usually done two or three times a week for 45 minutes to an hour. Patients are also given a program to do at home for 30 to 45 minutes on the days they are not in pre-hab. *Some examples…*

•**Straight-leg raises are often used for patients who are about to undergo a knee replacement.**

*To find a physical therapist or pre-hab program near you: Ask your surgeon…or check with the director of the rehabilitation clinic at the hospital where your surgery and/or rehab will take place.

What to do: While lying down (with the pain-free knee slightly bent), the patient raises and lowers his/her painful leg. This strengthens muscles around the knee, such as the quadriceps in the thigh. Those who are preparing for joint-replacement surgery in both knees perform the exercise on each of their legs.

•**Side leg raises are exercises commonly used for a hip replacement.**

What to do: While standing upright (and holding on to the back of a chair for balance), the patient slowly raises his leg out to the side, then slowly brings it back to the starting position. This strengthens side hip muscles.

•**Isometric shoulder extensions help prepare patients for shoulder surgery.**

What to do: The patient stands with his back against a wall and arms straight at his sides. Keeping arms straight, he pushes his arms into the wall, holds for five seconds, relaxes and repeats.

Also important: Pre-hab optimally includes exercises done in a swimming pool, where there is virtually no direct impact on the joints and minimum pain during workouts.

Important: Because some pre-hab exercises increase heart rate, anyone with high blood pressure, heart disease or any other significant health issues should consult his physician before beginning this type of program.

WHO PAYS FOR PRE-HAB?

Pre-hab is usually covered by insurance, but you may be responsible for some out-of-pocket expenses. Your insurer may cover a specific number of sessions, which include both pre-hab and rehab. Pre-hab can cost as little as $10 for a group class** or up to $200 for an initial consultation with a physical therapist. Check with your insurer.

**Prices subject to change.

Sitting Is Bad for the Kidneys

In a recent finding, women who sat a total of eight hours or more daily were about 30% more likely to develop chronic kidney disease than women who sat for three hours or less. Men who spent the most hours sitting had 19% increased risk.

Thomas Yates, PhD, senior lecturer at University of Leicester, Leicester, England, and lead researcher on a study of 6,379 people, published in *American Journal of Kidney Diseases.*

Antibiotics for Appendicitis *Not* Surgery!

According to a recent analysis, a nine-day course of antibiotics—including two days of intravenous drugs while in the hospital and seven days of oral drugs—had a 63% success rate in patients with uncomplicated appendicitis. Treating appendicitis with antibiotics has been practiced in Europe for a long time, but it is slowly catching on in the US.

Dileep Lobo, MD, professor of gastrointestinal surgery at University of Nottingham, England, and lead researcher for an analysis of four studies of appendicitis patients, published in *BMJ.*

Ugly Truths About Plastic Surgery

Anthony Youn, MD, a plastic surgeon in private practice in Troy, Michigan, and an assistant professor of surgery at Oakland University William Beaumont School of Medicine in Rochester, Michigan. Certified by the American Board of Plastic Surgery and a fellow of the American College of Surgeons, Dr. Youn has published scientific papers and lectured at professional meetings. He is author of *In Stitches: A Memoir* (Gallery).

Americans set a new record in 2012 for the number of cosmetic procedures performed. All told, there were about 14.6 million face-lifts, nose jobs, liposuctions, Botox injections and other elective procedures done for beauty's sake. But some of these quick fixes aren't what they're cracked up to be, and not every potential patient is well-suited for a nip, tuck, implant or injection. What's more, some of these procedures carry little-known—and often serious—risks.

What you need to know…

Secret #1: **You can't stop the clock.** Some patients assume that a face-lift is a long-term fix. But that's a myth.

What most people don't realize: It's true that a good face-lift (with a typical cost of $8,000 to $15,000)* can take several years off of your appearance and last for 10 or more years. But the moment surgery is over, the clock starts ticking again, and droopy jowls, wrinkles, etc., eventually will return.

There are, however, alternatives to going under the knife. For example, a laser procedure ($2,000 or more) can, to a somewhat lesser extent than a face-lift, tighten skin for the short term (about one to three years).

Secret #2: **Fillers can make you go blind.** Among the fastest-growing cosmetic treatments are soft-tissue fillers that can plump up lips, soften facial wrinkles and minimize folds around the nose and mouth. The most popular of these—used 1.3 million times last year in the US—is *hyaluronic acid,* better known as Juvéderm or Restylane. This substance is extracted from rooster combs or derived from bacteria in a laboratory setting.

What most people don't realize: Injecting hyaluronic acid between the eyebrows to diminish furrows that make an individual look angry (at about $600 a pop) can, in rare cases, cause instant, incurable blindness.

The *ophthalmic artery*—part of the internal carotid artery that supplies the eyes with blood—can accidentally be injected with filler, irreversibly clotting the artery. Even an experienced plastic surgeon can make this mistake. That's why I advise patients to avoid any between-the-brow fillers.

*Elective cosmetic procedures that do not correct a functional defect are usually not covered by insurance. Prices subject to change.

Hyaluronic acid can, however, be safely injected into the lips and *nasolabial folds* (laugh lines).

The best treatment for correcting eyebrow furrows is Botox (about $325 per treatment), which does not carry the same risk for blindness as hyaluronic acid. Headache commonly occurs after the procedure but it is only temporary. Receiving Botox injections every three to four months will eliminate "angry" furrows without potentially robbing you of your eyesight.

Secret #3: **A brow wax is often as effective as a surgical "brow lift."** More than 28,000 Americans received brow lifts (also called forehead lifts) last year at an average cost of about $5,000.

With this procedure, the surgeon makes an incision along the front of the scalp so that he/she can peel back and "lift" the forehead in order to give the patient a more youthful, well-rested appearance.

However, a far less invasive and less expensive procedure can provide similar—or even better—results.

What most people don't realize: A simple brow wax ($15 to $30) reshapes the arc of the eyebrow, which gives the appearance of "lifting" the eyebrow several millimeters, just as surgery does. The trick?

A good brow wax removes hair from the lower area of the eyebrow, not from the top. The beneficial effect is especially noticeable if the person starts out with bushy eyebrows and goes to a professional aesthetician for the service.

To find a qualified aesthetician, consult Associated Skin Care Professionals at *www.ASCP SkinCare.com*. The aestheticians referred by ASCP have completed appropriate training and have met state requirements.

Secret #4: **Fat sucked out during liposuction may come back.** Some plastic surgeons tell their patients that body fat removed during liposuction—a surgical procedure that can "sculpt" problem areas such as the thighs and buttocks by removing up to 12 pounds—is gone for good.

What most people don't realize: The jury is still out on the long-term results of liposuction, the third most popular plastic surgery in the US, with a cost of up to $10,000.

A 2011 study, published in *Obesity*, concluded that with liposuction the body merely redistributes fat to untreated areas—especially the abdomen, shoulders and arms, which leads to a top-heavy "Popeye effect."

Meanwhile, a 2012 study, published in *Plastic and Reconstructive Surgery*, found that fat sucked away during liposuction had not returned one year later—perhaps living up to the promise of permanence (barring any significant weight gain).

Of course, diet and exercise are ultimately the best ways to lose weight and shape your body.

Secret #5: **Some people should see a therapist instead of a surgeon.** Cosmetic surgery is simply not advisable for some individuals who have it.

What most people don't realize: Up to 15% of individuals seeking cosmetic enhancements have a condition known as *body dysmorphic disorder* (BDD), sometimes called "imagined ugliness" because its sufferers obsessively fixate on perceived physical defects that do not seem prominent to others. To a person who has BDD, a small, hardly noticeable bump on the nose, for example, could, in his mind, be a real deformity.

Some opportunistic plastic surgeons view BDD patients as "cash cows." That is because there is seemingly no end to the flaws these patients notice on their faces and bodies, and they are usually willing to pay big bucks to "fix" these supposed defects.

In my practice, I'd estimate that one of every six or seven people I see has BDD. I won't treat these patients but, rather, gently suggest that they'd be better off seeing a psychiatrist or other mental-health professional. This is often a difficult message for these patients to receive because they have a skewed perception of reality. But it's the right thing to do!

Sleep Apnea Could Be Killing You While You Sleep…Millions Have It and Most Don't Even Know It

Chris Meletis, ND, former chief medical officer for the National College of Naturopathic Medicine and currently the executive director of the Institute for Healthy Aging and a physician on the staff of Beaverton Naturopathic Medicine in Oregon. He is author of 18 books on health and healing, including *The Hyaluronic Acid Miracle* (Freedom Press). *www.DrMeletis.com*

Twenty-eight million Americans have *sleep apnea*, a sleep disorder in which breathing repeatedly stops and starts. More than 80% of these people don't know they have it. And every year, an estimated 38,000 Americans die in their sleep because sleep apnea has exacerbated a circulatory problem, causing a fatal heart attack or stroke.

Bottom line: Diagnosing and treating sleep apnea can save your life. And now there's an exciting new treatment that's available. *What you need to know…*

THE DANGER

For people with sleep apnea, nighttime levels of blood oxygen can plummet from an optimal saturation of 100% to below 65%. This oxygen-robbing disorder can contribute to extreme daytime sleepiness, as well as high blood pressure, heart attack, stroke, congestive heart failure, type 2 diabetes, Alzheimer's disease, erectile dysfunction, depression, anxiety and *gastroesophageal reflux disease* (GERD). In fact, if you have sleep apnea, you have a nearly five times higher risk of dying overall.

What happens: During sleep, the muscles at the back of the throat relax, which relaxes the soft palate and the uvula, a small, triangular piece of tissue hanging from the soft palate.

When you have obstructive sleep apnea, the most common kind, this tissue doesn't just relax, it sags, plugging the airway—and breathing stops. You may snort, grunt, gasp or cough as the body rouses itself—and breath-ing restarts. Then you fall back to sleep, never remembering that you woke up.

This mini-suffocation and awakening can occur over and over—from as few as five times an hour (the criteria for being diagnosed with "mild" sleep apnea) to dozens of times each hour.

Risk factors for obstructive sleep apnea include snoring (a sign of a thickened soft palate), being male, being 65 or older (for women, risk rises after menopause) and obesity. But some people with sleep apnea have none of those risk factors.

DO YOU HAVE IT?

Several daytime symptoms are possible signs of sleep apnea. You might wake up with a headache and a dry mouth. You could be intensely tired during the day—even falling asleep at a red light. You might be irritable and depressed and find it hard to think clearly.

If your doctor suspects sleep apnea, he may recommend a "sleep study" conducted in a sleep disorder center. This overnight test—*polysomnography*—monitors and measures breathing patterns, blood oxygen levels, arm and leg movement, and heart, lung and brain activity. *But there are several downsides to a study in a sleep center…*

• **It's expensive,** costing $1,500 to $2,500* —which could be out-of-pocket if your insurance has a high deductible.

• **It's inconvenient.** You are spending the night in a strange place with a video camera focused on you and personnel walking in and out.

Instead, I often recommend a sleep study at home. Using a portable device, it provides the same information as a study at a center—for a fraction of the cost ($450 to $650). It is becoming the preferred method of testing for many doctors and often is covered by insurance. I prefer the home test by SleepQuest.

For more information: 800-813-8358, *www.SleepQuest.com.*

EXCITING NEW TREATMENT

Up until now, the standard treatment for sleep apnea has been a *continuous positive airway pressure* (CPAP) machine. This device

*Prices subject to change.

uses tubing and a mask worn over the nose… over the nose and mouth…or directly in the nose (via what is called a nasal pillow). The mask continuously pumps air into the airway, preventing the soft palate from sagging. But the mask often is uncomfortable. In one study, nearly half of people prescribed a CPAP device stopped using it within one to three weeks.

The exciting news is that there's a convenient treatment for sleep apnea called Provent. A small, disposable patch fits over each nostril. The treatment uses your own breathing to create *expiratory positive airway pressure* (EPAP)—just enough to keep the throat open.

Recent scientific evidence: In a three-month study involving 250 people with sleep apnea, 127 used Provent and 123 used a fake, look-alike device. The people using Provent had a 43% decrease in nighttime apnea events, compared with a 10% decrease for those in the fake group. Over three months, there was also a significant decrease in daytime sleepiness among Provent users.

A 30-day supply of the patches costs about $70. They are prescription-only and currently are not covered by insurance or Medicare.

My perspective: Provent is an excellent new option for many people with obstructive sleep apnea, but it is not for mouth breathers, people with nasal allergies or those with severe apnea.

Information: 888-757-9355, *http://Provent. ActiveHealthCare.com.*

CUSTOMIZED MOUTH GUARD

If the nasal patch is not an option for you, a customized oral appliance may be best. It moves the lower jaw forward, opening the throat. It usually is covered by insurance, either partially or totally.

I was diagnosed with severe obstructive sleep apnea six years ago—and I've had very good results with a customized oral appliance. In a recent sleep test, I used CPAP half the night and my oral appliance the other half— my blood oxygen levels were higher while using the appliance.

Red flag: Over-the-counter oral appliances for snoring are available, but for optimal results, you need an oral appliance created for

your mouth and jaw by a dentist trained to make such a device.

Important: No matter which device you use, you need to get tested first and then retested after you start using the device to make sure that you are getting the oxygen you need.

LIFESTYLE CHANGES

Self-care strategies…

• **Sleep on your side.** This helps keep airways open.

• **Lose weight,** because extra pounds mean extra tissue in the throat. Just a 10% weight loss can decrease apnea events by 26%. However, thin people and children can have apnea, too.

• **Don't drink alcohol within three hours of going to bed.** It relaxes the airway.

• **Sing some vowels.** In a study by UK researchers, three months of singing lessons helped decrease snoring, which could in turn decrease apnea.

What to do: Sing the long vowel sounds a-a-a-e-e-e, taking two or three seconds to sing each vowel. Do this once or twice every day for five minutes a session.

Smoking Speeds Memory Loss

Smoking speeds memory loss in men according to a recent finding. On cognitive tests, male smokers performed at a level about 10 years older than their chronological age. And they had increased risk for dementia. The more cigarettes smoked, the more severe the cognitive decline.

Good news: After 10 or more years of no smoking, men's bodies can repair themselves.

Smoking affects not only the brain but also organs vital for survival, such as the heart, lungs and blood vessels, which, in turn, affect the amount of oxygen these organs receive. Cognitive decline did not vary with smoking status in women.

Study of 5,099 men, ages 44 to 80, by researchers at University College London, England, and Pierre and Marie Curie University, Paris, published in *Archives of General Psychiatry.*

Alzheimer's Linked to Restless Sleep

People who wake up frequently (more than five times in an hour) or who are awake for more than 15% of the time that they are in bed are significantly more likely than better sleepers to show physiological changes associated with early Alzheimer's disease.

Not yet known: Whether it is poor sleep that causes the brain changes—or vice versa.

Yo-El Ju, MD, assistant professor of neurology and a sleep medicine specialist at Washington University School of Medicine, St. Louis, and leader of a study presented at the American Academy of Neurology's 2012 annual meeting.

Sharks and Alzheimer's?

Scientists took tissue samples from the fins of seven species of sharks to measure their levels of the neurotoxin *BMAA*, which is linked to human neurological disorders such as Alzheimer's disease and *amyotrophic lateral sclerosis* (ALS), also known as Lou Gehrig's disease.

Result: The average single shark fin contained a similar level of BMAA as that found in the brains of humans with Alzheimer's or ALS.

Implication: Eating shark fin soup, an Asian delicacy, or taking shark cartilage supplements, used by some people as an unproven cancer treatment or for osteoarthritis, may pose a risk for degenerative brain diseases.

Neil Hammerschlag, PhD, research assistant professor, University of Miami, Florida.

Surprising Help for MS Tremors

An injection of *botulinum toxin* (Botox) lessened arm tremors by two points (on a 10-point scale), reducing moderate tremor to mild in *multiple sclerosis* (MS) patients. It also improved patients' ability to write and draw by one point.

Study of MS patients by researchers at The Royal Melbourne Hospital and University of Melbourne, both in Australia, published in *Neurology*.

Trouble Sleeping? Watch Out for Depression

In a recent finding, men with *sleep apnea*—a condition characterized by snoring and interruptions in breathing while sleeping—were twice as likely to be depressed as men who did not have the condition. Women with sleep apnea were five times as likely to be depressed. Depression was most likely in people who had difficulties five or more nights a week.

Study of 9,714 men and women by researchers at the Centers for Disease Control and Prevention, Atlanta, published in *Sleep*.

Fast Food Is a Downer!

In one recent finding, people who ate the most fast food were 37% more likely to become depressed during a six-year period than those who ate the least. People who ate large amounts of commercially baked goods, such as muffins and doughnuts, also were more likely to become depressed. Those eating the most fast food and commercially baked goods tended to be single, younger and less active, with worse overall eating habits, so it is not known whether depression is caused by lifestyle or the specific foods consumed.

Study of 8,964 people by researchers at University of Las Palmas, Gran Canaria, and University of Navarra, Pamplona, Spain, published in *Public Health Nutrition*.

Feeling Crabby? Check Your Diet

Trans fats, found in margarines, shortenings and many processed foods, inhibit the body's synthesis of omega-3 fatty acids, which tend to reduce irritability and aggression.

Result: Eating trans fats can make you more angry, impatient and aggressive.

Study of dietary data on 945 adults by researchers at University of California, San Diego, reported in *PLOS ONE.*

Facebook Postings May Indicate Depression

In a recent finding, 30% of the Facebook updates studied suggested that the person posting the update had a symptom of depression, including feelings of worthlessness…insomnia or sleeping too much…or difficulty concentrating. Facebook works with the National Suicide Prevention Lifeline to identify postings with suicidal thoughts.

Megan A. Moreno, MD, assistant professor of pediatrics, University of Wisconsin-Madison, and a principal investigator in a study of 200 Facebook profiles, published in *Depression and Anxiety.*

Get Online Help for Depression

Therapists using Skype and other computer-based connection methods can talk with patients anywhere. *Telemedicine* is becoming more accepted among doctors and can be as effective as in-person therapy. Private insurers generally will not pay for it, although Medicare will in some circumstances.

To find an online therapist: Go to *www. Breakthrough.com* or *www.ETherapyWeb.com.*

Lynn F. Bufka, PhD, American Psychological Association, Washington, DC.

Millions Die from Sepsis: But It Can Be Cured If Detected *Quickly*

Derek C. Angus, MD, MPH, the Mitchell P. Fink Endowed Chair in Critical Care Medicine and professor of critical care medicine, medicine, health policy and management, and clinical and translational science at University of Pittsburgh School of Medicine.

Sepsis is the tenth-leading cause of death in the US. It doesn't have to be. *The challenge:* There isn't a single test that can diagnose sepsis. Because its symptoms can be very similar to those caused by the original infection, the diagnosis sometimes is overlooked—and even a brief delay in treatment can be deadly.

Every year, at least 750,000 Americans develop severe sepsis and about 40% of patients with severe sepsis will die from it. The death rate approaches 50% in patients who develop *septic shock* (a dangerous drop in blood pressure that can lead to organ failure), which can't be reversed by the administration of intravenous (IV) fluids.

WHO'S AT RISK

Sepsis often is triggered by a bacterial infection. It also can be caused by viral or fungal infections. Pneumonia is the infection most likely to lead to sepsis.

The risk for sepsis is highest among adults age 65 and older, particularly those in the hospital who get IV lines, urinary catheters or other invasive devices. But you don't have to be elderly or seriously ill or be in a hospital to develop sepsis. About half of all cases occur in nonhospital settings. If you have any type of infection—an infected cut, a urinary tract infection, the flu—it can progress to sepsis.

Examples: Many of the 18,000 deaths that were linked to the swine flu outbreak in 2009 actually were caused by sepsis. Last fall, a New York sixth-grader cut his arm during a basketball game and got an infection. He died from sepsis three days later.

WARNING SIGNS

For reasons that still aren't clear, some infections are accompanied by an exaggerated immune response. It's normal for the body to respond to an infection with local inflammation. In patients with sepsis, the inflammation is systemic—it spreads throughout the body and often causes a loss of fluids that leads to plummeting blood pressure and shock. It also triggers microscopic blood clots that can block circulation to the heart, kidneys and other organs.

Warning signs...

•**You're sicker than expected.** Suppose that you have a bladder infection or an infected cut. If the severity of your symptoms seems to be out of proportion to the illness, call your doctor.

Go to the emergency room if you or a loved one also has two or more of the following symptoms...

•**Rapid heartbeat.** Patients who are developing sepsis usually will have tachycardia, a rapid heartbeat that exceeds 90 beats/minute.

•**High or low temperature.** Both hypothermia (a body temperature below 96.8°F) and fever (above 100.4°F) can indicate sepsis.

•**Rapid breathing, or tachypnea.** Patients with sepsis may have a respiration rate of 20 breaths/minute or higher.

•**Mucus.** The common cold is unlikely to cause sepsis, but it's not impossible. Call your doctor if a cold or other respiratory infection is accompanied by foul-smelling, discolored (rather than clear) mucus. This could indicate that you have developed a more serious infection.

•**Mental confusion.** When sepsis starts to interfere with circulation, it often will cause mental confusion.

•**Mottled skin.** There may be blue patches on the skin. Or if you press on the skin, there might be a delay before it returns to its normal color. Both of these changes indicate that circulation is impaired—a sign of severe sepsis.

Important: When patients begin to develop signs and symptoms suggesting that vital organ function is compromised, sepsis already is an emergency. For example, altered mental status, falling blood pressure, difficulty breathing or mottled skin all suggest that the inflammatory response intended to help is now, in fact, causing life-threatening harm.

WHAT COMES NEXT

Sepsis always is treated in the hospital. To confirm that you have it, your doctor will do a variety of tests, including a blood pressure check and a white blood cell count. You also will need blood cultures to identify the organism that is causing the infection so that your physician can choose the most effective treatment.

•**Treat first, diagnose later.** A study in *Critical Care Medicine* reported that the risk of dying from sepsis increases by 7.6% for every hour that passes without treatment. If your doctor suspects that you have sepsis, he/she will immediately start treatment with an antibiotic—usually a broad-spectrum antibiotic that's effective against a wide variety of organisms. Later the drug may be changed, depending on what the blood cultures show.

•**Intravenous fluids.** They often are needed to counteract the capillary leakage that causes blood pressure to drop.

•**Vasopressor treatment.** Depending on the severity of sepsis, you might be given *dopamine* or *norepinephrine*—medications that increase blood pressure and improve circulation to the heart, kidneys and other organs.

Other treatments may include supplemental oxygen, anti-inflammatory steroids and sometimes kidney dialysis.

PREVENTING SEPSIS

Don't watch and wait if you suspect sepsis. Call your doctor. *And to build up your defense against sepsis in the future...*

•**Get a pneumococcal pneumonia vaccination if you're 65 years old or older...**have chronic health problems...take medications that lower immunity...or you are a smoker. Most people should get a pneumonia vaccination every five years.

•**Get an annual flu shot.** The rate of sepsis increases by about 16% during flu season. Getting an annual flu shot—along with washing your hands several times a day—reduces your risk for sepsis.

•**Clean wounds thoroughly.** If you have a cut, scrape or burn and are taking care of it yourself, wash it several times a day with soap and water, and apply an antibacterial ointment.

Call your doctor immediately if there is pus, increased or streaking redness, or if the wound feels warm.

New Pneumonia Protection for People Age 50 and Older

The vaccine Prevnar was recently approved by the FDA to protect people age 50 and older against infection by *Streptococcus pneumoniae* bacteria, which can cause pneumonia, meningitis, and blood and middle-ear infections. Prevnar lasts longer than the older vaccine, Pneumovax, and has been given to children for several years. Now it is approved for older adults as well.

University of California, Berkeley Wellness Letter. www.BerkeleyWellness.com

Before You Flush...

Close toilet lids before flushing. *C. difficile bacteria*—which can cause diarrhea and life-threatening colon inflammation—have been found nearly 10 inches above the toilet seat when lidless toilets are flushed and can remain there for up to 90 minutes after flushing.

Study by researchers at Leeds Teaching Hospitals, UK, reported in *Journal of Hospital Infection*.

Cookware That Helps Prevent Food Poisoning

The oxidation of copper in copper-alloy pots and pans produces a residue that kills *salmonella* and some other bacteria that cause food poisoning. Stainless steel cookware has no effect on salmonella at all.

Study by researchers at University of Arizona, Tucson, reported in *USA Today Magazine*.

Watch Out for Meat Glue!

A common meat additive may make you sick. Meat glue, also called *transglutaminase* (nothing to do with so-called pink slime), binds together bits of meat into what looks like a prime cut.

But: When not handled properly, meat glue can seal in *E. coli* and other bacteria present on raw meat.

Self-defense: Check package labels—glued meats must include the words "formed" or "reformed." Glued meats are commonly used in high-volume restaurants and banquet facilities. To be safe, eat meat cooked well-done.

Suzanne Havala Hobbs, DrPH, RD, a clinical associate professor in the departments of health policy and management and nutrition in the Gillings School of Global Public Health, University of North Carolina at Chapel Hill.

Surprising Source of Sodium

Did you know that the top source of sodium in our diet is bread?

Recent study: When researchers studied the diets of 7,227 American adults and children, nearly half of the total amount of sodium consumed came from 10 foods—and bread was the biggest contributor to daily sodium intake. On the list, bread was followed by less surprising foods, such as cold cuts, canned soups and salty snacks.

Explanation: One slice of bread typically contains only 80 milligrams (mg) to 230 mg of sodium, but because many Americans eat it often, it is the top source of sodium.

Mary E. Cogswell, DrPH, senior scientist, epidemiology and surveillance branch, division for heart disease and stroke prevention, Centers for Disease Control and Prevention, Atlanta.

Medical Matters

Is Your Doctor a Bully? How to Tell and What to Do

When my neighbor Kendall went to a well-known surgeon to discuss a tricky elective surgery she was considering, she was appalled at his manner. He answered her questions brusquely (even calling one of her queries "insipid") and seemed to barely listen to her concerns about the procedure's risks. After 10 minutes, he abruptly announced that their time was up and left the room.

As Kendall told me the tale, she was angry and confused. "He has a reputation as a great surgeon, but he treated me like trash. Why would he do that? And should I overlook his nasty personality because his work is good... or go elsewhere?"

What really seemed to strike my neighbor as odd was to find a bully in a "helping profession" such as medicine. Yet this is not uncommon, I heard when I contacted Ronald Schouten, MD, JD, an associate professor of psychiatry at Harvard Medical School and co-author of *Almost a Psychopath: Do I (or Does Someone I Know) Have a Problem with Manipulation and Lack of Empathy?* In fact, Dr. Schouten told me that he has evaluated a number of physicians, male and female, whose patients complained about their lack of empathy.

What should you do if you're dealing with such a doctor? *First, consider which of the following categories he or she falls into...*

• **The unintentional bully.** Least worrisome is the doctor who basically does want to help

---

Ronald Schouten, MD, JD, an associate professor of psychiatry at Harvard Medical School and director of the Law and Psychiatry Service at Massachusetts General Hospital, both in Boston. He also is coauthor of *Almost a Psychopath: Do I (Or Does Someone I Know) Have a Problem with Manipulation and Lack of Empathy?* (Hazelden).

others but who is unintentionally bullying at times. He may be insensitive…feel overly rushed…get caught up in a sense of his own importance…or be so stressed out from the demands of his practice that he does not always behave appropriately.

What to do: If you trust this doctor and aren't overly disturbed by his brusqueness or egotism, you're probably fine sticking with him if you want to.

• **The true psychopath.** This type of person shows a profound lack of empathy, extreme egocentricity and a willingness to engage in immoral and antisocial behavior for his own gain. Psychopaths are rare in medicine but not unheard of. "History reveals that medicine has had its share of con artists, white-collar criminals, sex offenders, even serial killers," Dr. Schouten said.

What to do: If you have even the slightest inkling that a doctor may fall into this category, clearly you must leave his care immediately…and if you have any evidence (for instance, of sexual misconduct or other criminal behavior), alert the authorities.

• **The "almost psychopath."** Between those two extremes lies the type of bully that Dr. Schouten calls an almost psychopath. Such people are self-centered, egotistical, controlling, shallow and indifferent to the needs of others. A physician who exhibits such traits may have excellent technical skills yet nonetheless do significant damage—for instance, by manipulating vulnerable patients or by making decisions based on the belief that he is more important than the people he is meant to take care of.

What to do: If you suspect that your doctor is this kind of bully and you live in a large city or near a university hospital, it's probably easy enough to change doctors. However, in a smaller community with a limited number of physicians, you'll want to weigh the objectionable traits of your current doctor against the inconvenience of traveling far afield to see someone else.

Examples of red flags to watch for include a doctor who…

• **Refuses to answer your questions or provide you with information about your condition.** (Do be reasonable, though—if you have booked a 15-minute appointment, it's not fair to arrive with 60 minutes' worth of questions.)

• **Is arrogant**—for instance, if you ask how many procedures of a particular type he handles each year and he replies, "Do you know how famous I am for this?"

• **Is insensitive to modesty and privacy issues.** You deserve a doctor who knocks before entering the room if you have been told to disrobe…warns you of what he is about to do during an exam…and does not leave you in an exposed position.

• **Handles you roughly.** Yes, some procedures are painful—but you should not sense a lack of regard for your comfort or any unnecessary prodding.

If you experience scenarios such as those above, step one is to discuss your concerns with the doctor. Be frank—"It makes me uncomfortable when you act this way." Bring a friend or family member along if you want moral support…or write the doctor a letter if that is easier for you.

Many physicians recognize that they have been inappropriate once a patient points it out to them, Dr. Schouten said, and they try to mend their ways.

But what if the problem persists? It's time to say good-bye to the bully and find yourself a doctor who truly has your best interests at heart.

Medical-Alert Tattoos

In lieu of medical-alert jewelry, some patients are now getting tattoos that tell doctors, nurses and other health-care professionals about their medical conditions, such as diabetes, or indicate their health-care directives, such as "do not resuscitate."

AARP. *www.AARP.org/bulletin*

The Epidemic of Overdiagnosis: How the Pursuit of Health Could Be Making You Sick

H. Gilbert Welch, MD, MPH, professor of medicine at The Dartmouth Institute for Health Policy and Clinical Practice and general internist at the White River Junction VA in Vermont. His research has been published in *The New England Journal of Medicine, The Journal of the American Medical Association* and many other major medical journals. He is author of *Overdiagnosed: Making People Sick in the Pursuit of Health* (Beacon) and *Should I Be Tested for Cancer? Maybe Not and Here's Why* (University of California).

There's a dangerous epidemic out there. It is called overdiagnosis—when you are diagnosed with a condition that will never hurt your health.

Overdiagnosis can lead to potentially harmful medical care, as you undergo invasive tests, take medications or have surgery—all for a condition that is harmless. Medical care also can be expensive, time-consuming and anxiety-producing. *Here, the conditions that are frequently overdiagnosed…*

HIGH BLOOD PRESSURE

There is tremendous value in treating moderate-to-severe hypertension—a reading of 160/100 or higher—because it can prevent heart attack, heart failure, stroke and kidney failure. But below that range (very-mild-to-mild hypertension), overdiagnosis is likely. In statistical terms, almost everyone treated for severe hypertension will benefit, but 18 people with mild hypertension have to be treated for one person to benefit.

And all that unnecessary treatment can involve added expense, hassle (doctor appointments, lab tests, refills, insurance forms, etc.) and drug side effects such as fatigue, persistent cough and erectile dysfunction.

My viewpoint: Don't automatically take medication to lower mild high blood pressure. Losing weight and getting more exercise generally are the way to go.

TYPE 2 DIABETES

More than 20 million Americans have type 2 diabetes, which can cause heart disease, kidney failure, blindness, nerve pain and leg infections that lead to amputation.

However: Like high blood pressure, type 2 diabetes has a range of abnormality, from the asymptomatic to the severe. Some people with diabetes will never develop complications.

That's even more likely nowadays because the medical definition of type 2 diabetes—and therefore, the criteria for who should and should not be treated—has changed. The definition of type 2 diabetes used to be a fasting blood sugar level higher than 140 milligrams per deciliter (mg/dL). Today, it is a fasting blood sugar level higher than 126 mg/dL—turning millions of people into diabetics. A newer test—hemoglobin A1C, a measurement of long-term blood sugar levels that detects the percentage of red blood cells coated with glucose (blood sugar)—defines diabetes as a level of 6.5% or higher.

My viewpoint: Physicians should use medication to reduce blood sugar in patients with an A1C of 9% or higher…discuss treatment with patients between 8% and 9%…and typically not treat patients under 8%.

In a randomized trial designed to test the effect of aggressive blood sugar reduction, more than 10,000 people with type 2 diabetes and A1C levels above 8% were divided into two groups. One group received intensive glucose-lowering therapy aimed at reducing A1C to less than 6%. The other group received standard therapy, targeting a level of 7% to 7.9%. After three years, the intensive-therapy group had about 25% increased risk for death, and because of that, the trial was stopped.

PROSTATE CANCER

In 2012, the US Preventive Services Task Force recommended against screening for prostate cancer with the *prostate-specific antigen* (PSA) test, concluding that "many men are harmed as a result of prostate cancer screening and few, if any, benefit."

Recent research shows that 1,000 men need to have a PSA test annually for a decade to prevent one death from prostate cancer. However, between 150 and 200 of those men will have a worrisome PSA test (a level higher than 4) that will lead to a biopsy of the prostate—an invasive procedure that can cause blood in the urine, infections and a high rate of hospitalization in the month after the procedure. Of those biopsied, 30 to 100 will be treated for a cancer that was never going to bother them. As a result, between one-third and one-half of those men will become impotent and 20% to 30% will become incontinent.

My viewpoint: I am a 57-year-old man—I have not had a PSA test, nor do I intend to. I understand that I may develop symptoms of prostate cancer (such as trouble urinating and bone pain), that I may die from prostate cancer (as about 3% of men do) and that lifelong screening might reduce my risk (maybe down to as low as 2.5%). But I also recognize that most men (about 97%) will die from something else, and I don't want to spend my life looking for things to be wrong. Most prostate cancers found by the PSA test are slow-growing and not life-threatening, but because there is no way to determine which prostate cancers are dangerous and which are nonthreatening, most of them are treated. Given the limited benefits in saving lives and the terrible risks of overtreatment, I don't recommend PSA testing.

BREAST CANCER

Diagnostic mammography—testing a woman when a new breast lump is found to see if she has cancer—is an absolute must. Screening mammography—for early detection of breast cancer—is not.

New scientific research: A study I coauthored, published in *The New England Journal of Medicine* last November, links three decades of mammographic screening for breast cancer to a doubling in the number of cases of early-stage breast cancer, from 112 to 234 cases per 100,000 women. Our study estimated that over those 30 years, 1.3 million American women have been overdiagnosed—tumors that were detected on screening would never have led to clinical symptoms.

The result is more tests…more anxiety from "suspicious" findings…and more harsh anticancer treatments, including more mastectomies.

My viewpoint: It is probably true that some women will die of breast cancer if they don't get screened for it. But it is much more com-

mon to be hurt by screening than helped by it. Mammography is a choice, not an imperative.

When Doctors Get It Wrong: Conditions Most Commonly Misdiagnosed…

Joe Graedon, MS, and Teresa Graedon, PhD, consumer advocates whose first book, *The People's Pharmacy*, was published in 1976. Since then, they have written "The People's Pharmacy" syndicated newspaper column, which discusses various issues related to drugs, herbs and vitamins. Their most recent book is *Top Screwups Doctors Make and How to Avoid Them* (Crown Archetype). *www.PeoplesPharmacy.com*

As the recent outbreak of fungal meningitis has so clearly shown, certain medical conditions are notoriously difficult to diagnose. The first of these patients suffered vague symptoms—including headache, fever, nausea and stiffness of the neck—that were initially misdiagnosed. Fortunately, doctors have now identified the tainted medication that caused the outbreak.

But mysterious symptoms are not always unraveled so quickly.

Startling statistic: Every year in the US, an estimated 40,000 to 80,000 hospital deaths are caused by diagnostic errors, according to a report in *The Journal of the American Medical Association*. When researchers use autopsies to discover discrepancies between diagnosed and actual causes of deaths, the error rate can be as high as 40%.

Conditions often misdiagnosed…

•**Alzheimer's disease.** It is impossible to diagnose this condition with 100% certainty because the only definitive "test" is an autopsy of the patient's brain after death. Even though there are fairly accurate ways to determine that a patient *might* have Alzheimer's (see below), mistakes are common.

Examples: Depression is one of the most common causes of Alzheimer's-like symptoms, but doctors often fail to recognize it. Other problems, including nutritional deficiencies and medication side effects—for example, from anticholinergic drugs, such as antihistamines, incontinence medications and tricyclic anti-depressants—also can cause symptoms that mimic Alzheimer's.

Surprising fact: It's estimated that 10% to 25% of patients with symptoms of dementia (such as memory problems and/or peculiar behavior) may have a non-Alzheimer's condition that could be reversed with the proper treatment.

What to do: Don't accept a diagnosis of Alzheimer's disease after a single office visit or after taking a simple questionnaire. Specialists (such as neurologists) take a very detailed personal and family history…conduct neurological and mental-status tests…and order a variety of blood and imaging tests to determine whether other conditions might be involved.

•**Deep vein thrombosis (DVT).** A blood clot anywhere in the vascular system can be deadly. Those that form in the deep veins in the legs are particularly risky because the symptoms—if there are any—can seem minor. For that reason, some people don't even seek medical care, or doctors may assume that the symptoms are caused by a leg strain or sprain.

The risk: A clot can break free and enter a lung, creating a deadly *pulmonary embolism.* About 20% of DVT patients who develop pulmonary embolism will die from it.

What to do: If you have leg pain, leg cramps or a sense of tightness in one leg that you can't explain (discomfort in both legs probably is *not* caused by DVT), speak to your doctor right away. If he/she is unavailable, go to an urgent-care center or hospital emergency department. It's particularly important that you get medical attention if you have DVT symptoms and are at increased risk for the condition due to cardiovascular risk factors, such as smoking or high blood pressure.

You are also at higher risk for DVT for at least three months after knee/hip replacement or if you've recently been immobile for hours at a time, as may occur on a long airplane flight. Other DVT symptoms may include swelling, tenderness or a reddish or bluish tint on part of the leg. DVT is easy to diagnose with an ultrasound or a CT or MRI scan.

Important: Call 911 if you experience any symptoms of pulmonary embolism—such as sudden shortness of breath or sudden, sharp chest pain that may worsen when you breathe deeply or cough.

•**Hypothyroidism.** Patients who produce too little thyroid hormone (*hypothyroidism*) may have the condition for years before it is diagnosed because the symptoms are usually vague and seemingly minor.

Common scenario: A doctor might assume that a patient who complains of fatigue, recent weight gain or apathy is suffering from stress or depression and write a prescription for an antidepressant.

What to do: Insist on a blood test to check your thyroid hormone levels if you have any of the above symptoms. Fatigue that's accompanied by an increased sensitivity to cold often is a sign of hypothyroidism. So is hair loss (but not that due to male-pattern baldness). For unknown reasons, thinning of the outer one-third of the eyebrows is also a red flag for hypothyroidism.

Experts disagree on the optimal range for *thyroid stimulating hormone* (TSH). Current guidelines suggest that it should fall somewhere between 0.45 milli-international units per liter (mIU/L) and 4.49 mIU/L. (The specific values will depend on the laboratory that your doctor uses.) If your TSH is normal but symptoms persist, ask your doctor about other blood tests, such as *free T3/T4* or *anti-thyroglobulin.* In some patients, these tests are useful in detecting hypothyroidism.

Most people do well with a thyroid replacement regimen. Some will benefit from *levothyroxine* (Levoxyl, Levothroid, Synthroid, etc.), while others find that natural desiccated thyroid hormone, such as Armour Thyroid, Nature-Throid or Westhroid, provides a better balance of T3 and T4 hormones.

•**Celiac disease.** More than three million Americans have this intestinal disease in which the immune system reacts to a protein (*gluten*) found in wheat, barley and rye.

Because this used to be considered a rare disease, physicians—particularly older doctors who went to medical school decades ago—don't always look for it. In addition, some of the most common symptoms, such as fatigue, abdominal pain, anemia and headaches, can be caused by dozens of other conditions.

What to do: Get tested. A blood test that looks for abnormal immune activity and other factors, perhaps followed by an intestinal biopsy, can detect celiac disease. If you test positive, you will need to follow a gluten-free diet. Web sites such as *www.Celiac.org* specify foods/products that are gluten-free. Patients who eliminate all gluten will usually make a full recovery.

Don't eliminate gluten before testing—the partial recovery of the intestinal lining will make it harder to get an accurate diagnosis.

• **Lyme disease.** If a person has Lyme disease and it's missed, he/she may go on to develop joint inflammation, heart-rhythm disturbances and even problems with concentration and memory.

Lyme disease, the most common tick-borne disease, now has been reported in most US states, but doctors often do not look for it outside the Northeast, where the disease originated. The initial symptoms, such as muscle aches and fatigue, are often confused with the flu, particularly when patients don't even know that they were bitten.

What to do: Look for a rash. About three-quarters of patients will develop a "bull's eye" rash along with the flulike symptoms that last for weeks. Sadly, there are no symptoms that are especially diagnostic for Lyme if the rash is missing. In these cases, symptoms may include stiff neck, headache, swollen glands, Bell's palsy (usually temporary facial paralysis), sore throat, fever and/or tingling or numbness in the extremities.

Lyme disease can be diagnosed with a blood test. Patients who are treated with oral antibiotics at the onset of symptoms almost always make a full recovery. The longer someone goes untreated for Lyme, however, the more challenging the course of recovery may be.

Check Your Medical Records for Mistakes

Karen Larson, editor, *Bottom Line/Personal*, 281 Tresser Blvd., Stamford, Connecticut 06901. *www.BottomLine Publications.com*

My doctor recently asked me about a medication I was taking. Trouble was, I wasn't taking it and had never been prescribed it. It was a mistake in my medical records.

I was lucky to find out. Medical errors that remain in our files can cause health insurance companies to reject our applications for coverage or, worse, cause doctors to make inappropriate diagnoses that could endanger our health.

Deborah Peel, MD, a practicing physician for more than 30 years and founder of Patient Privacy Rights, a health information privacy watchdog organization, says that mistakes in medical records are distressingly common.

The frightening truth, according to Dr. Peel, is that "you have to check your records yourself—your life could depend on it." Healthcare providers are required to give you copies of your medical records upon request. Patients historically have had to pay a per-page fee for retrieval and copying of their records, but the digitalization of medical records means that retrieving records now is easy and copying is unnecessary. Ask to have a digital copy of your files e-mailed to you, rather than a printed copy mailed to you. If you have many files, start with the most recent.

When you get your records, scan them for mistakes. If you find anything that you don't understand, call the health-care provider's office and ask for assistance. If you find a mistake, ask the provider to amend the inaccurate information.

It's worth having a copy of your records even if you don't spot mistakes. You can give them to doctors when you seek second opinions or see a specialist for the first time.

Stop Waiting So Long at Your Doctor's Office

Charles B. Inlander, a consumer advocate and health-care consultant based in Fogelsville, Pennsylvania. He was the founding president of the nonprofit People's Medical Society, a consumer advocacy organization that is credited with key improvements in the quality of US health care in the 1980s and 1990s, and is author or coauthor of more than 20 consumer-health books. He is also a featured columnist in *BottomLine/Health, www. BottomLinePublications.com.*

I once sent a doctor a bill for $50 after I was forced to wait for more than an hour to see him. He called and apologized and said his office would contact me if he were ever running that late again when I had an appointment. I waived my bill, and I never again waited for more than 10 minutes when I was scheduled to see him. If you're not comfortable billing your doctor for your time, consider these tried-and-true techniques for cutting down your wait times…

• **Can you do it by phone or e-mail?** In the US, the average wait time for a doctor's appointment is 23 minutes. So it's smart to handle whatever issues you can over the phone or via e-mail. Some insurers now pay doctors for these communications. Phone or e-mail contacts are especially useful for discussing test results, changing a medication or following up on an earlier treatment.

At your next appointment: Ask your doctor when phone and/or e-mail exchanges are useful and if there are certain hours when you can call in with questions or concerns.

• **Request the right day.** When you do need an appointment, you're likely to experience the longest delays on Mondays and Fridays, because lots of people like to get things taken care of early in the week or just before the weekend. For this reason, Tuesday, Wednesday and Thursday are usually better options. To confirm whether this is the pattern at your doctor's office, always ask which days are the slowest and try to book one of them. Also try to avoid school holidays.

• **Be smart about time of day.** You probably already know to ask for the first appointment of the day, but that appointment time typically gets booked quickly. In that case, ask for the first appointment right after the office lunch break (most practices do not book during lunchtime so the staff can eat and doctors can catch up on any backups from the morning). If that time is taken, ask for the last appointment of the day. Why is this a good time? Doctors' offices close at a certain time of day, and appointments are typically back on schedule by then so everyone can go home on time.

Also helpful: Call an hour ahead of your appointment time to find out if the doctor is running late. That way, you can adjust your arrival time or reschedule if a long delay is anticipated.

• **Do your paperwork in advance.** When booking an appointment, ask that all the forms you need to fill out be mailed or e-mailed to you in advance. Fill them out and bring them with you to the office about 20 minutes prior to your appointment time. You may think that you're not really saving time if you have to arrive early. But that's not true. That fact is, you will be delayed if you have to fill out forms at the office. People with completed paperwork usually move to the front of the line!

• **Watch the clock.** No matter what you do, there will be times when you'll have to wait more than you would like at your doctor's office. Don't just sit there. If you are waiting 15 minutes after your scheduled time, go to the desk and ask how much longer it will be. Do it again every 10 minutes until you are seen. The squeaky wheel does get the grease!

More from Charles B. Inlander…

Health Coaching: Just a Phone Call Away

Health coaching is a term that we're hearing more often these days, but few people fully understand what it entails—or how it can help you. Often offered by hospitals, large employers and insurance companies, health coaching involves regular contact (in-person, online or on the phone) with a health professional who gives personalized medical advice. You can work with the same coach for the duration of the program (which can last from days to months). Health coaching is especially helpful for people with chronic conditions, such as heart disease, diabetes, Parkinson's disease and various types of cancer, but it can be used for disease prevention as well.

A friend of mine who was recently diagnosed with diabetes used a health-coaching program offered by her local hospital. The program, which was covered by her health insurance, included *unlimited* telephone coaching by a nurse specializing in diabetes care as well as classes on such topics as nutrition and the importance of taking medication properly. My friend's blood sugar levels have remained stable, and she has found it easy to maintain her new diet. But not all health coaching is this effective. There are a lot of so-called "health coaches" out there who have virtually no training or credentials. *What you need to know…*

• **What health coaching is—and isn't.** The most effective health-coaching programs assign a nurse, social worker or, in some cases, a physician who works directly with you to serve as an expert consultant in managing your care and overall health. The best coaches act as health partners and help recommend medical approaches that are appropriate for you based on your condition, age and health status.

• **How to find a good health coach.** I advise first checking with your health insurer. Most health insurance companies offer health-coaching programs to their members either directly or through their employers as a benefit of coverage. If your insurer or employer doesn't offer health coaching, check with your local hospital or a major advocacy group that focuses on your condition (such as the American Heart Association if you have heart disease). Most of these health-coaching programs will be covered by your insurer or Medicare if your doctor orders it.

• **Traps to watch out for.** Because there are no national accrediting standards for health coaching, anyone can claim to be a health coach. So be careful! If insurance does not cover your health coaching, it will likely cost $50 to $150 per hour* (in some cases, this may

*Prices subject to change.

be covered by a flexible-spending account, but check first). Before signing on to work with a health coach, ask about the person's credentials. If he/she claims to be a nurse, for example, ask which state granted the person's license and check with that state's nurse-licensing board to verify. In addition, ask for at least five references whom you can contact directly—online testimonials are suspect. Health coaching can be very helpful if your coach is well-qualified!

Also from Charles B. Inlander…

How to Deal with Medical Obsessions: 4 Helpful Strategies

At a recent social gathering I attended in Washington, DC, the hostess, who had just completed an extensive round of chemotherapy for cancer, welcomed everyone by saying how wonderful she felt and that the evening was not about illness but happiness. She asked all her guests to enjoy themselves, and we had a delightful evening without talking about her health or our own.

When I was younger, my parents seemed *obsessed* with their medical problems and drove many of their friends away by letting their health challenges take over their lives. I swore that I would never be like that. And I try not to be. But I am now at the age that my parents were when I used to duck out of the room just as they began rattling on about some medical problem. And many of my friends are beginning to sound a lot like my parents.

While this may appear to be nothing more than a minor annoyance, it can be bad news for the person who can't stop talking about his/her health. Research shows that medical obsession can lead to depression and isolation—both of which can worsen one's overall health.

Here's what I do to keep my health-obsessed friends—and my sanity…

• **Issue a five-minute rule.** When we get together with friends, I usually start by saying, "OK, we have five minutes to talk about medical issues, and that's it!" Everyone laughs, but it works. This tactic recognizes that we care about one another and allows for a brief chat about a problem, but people quickly turn to another topic of conversation.

• **Go ahead and talk about a "taboo" subject.** This great tactic came from a psychologist I know. She suggested starting the conversation with what has been historically a "taboo" social topic, such as religion. Her theory is that people have such strong opinions on taboo subjects that they forget about their medical issues and cannot stop themselves from expressing their views.

• **Find an enjoyable distraction.** My wife and I know a couple who just cannot stop talking about their medical problems when we go out with them for dinner or they come to our home. So we stopped seeing them in those settings and instead make dates with them to go to the movies, the theater or a sporting event. This approach has worked like a charm! Their attention is diverted most of the time we're together, and, on the way home, we make sure we talk about what we have just seen or done.

• **Focus on the "good news."** There is nothing wrong with talking about a friend's health matters, but it's wise to keep the conversation focused on whatever *good* there is in his situation. Telling someone that he looks great or is lucky to have such a good doctor can help anyone who is obsessed by his medical situation to feel better—at least psychologically. And as studies point out, the more positive that people with serious medical problems feel about themselves, the better their chances of living more normal and happier lives.

What Your Breath Says About Your Health

Cristina E. Davis, PhD, a professor in the department of mechanical and aerospace engineering and director of the Bioinstrumentation and BioMEMS Laboratory at the University of California, Davis. She specializes in strategies for identifying disease biomarkers and the use of breath analysis for detecting and monitoring diseases. She was awarded a 2010 Hartwell Individual Biomedical Research Award from The Hartwell Foundation, an organization that funds innovative biomedical research that benefits children.

E ven in this age of high-tech tests, doctors can learn crucial information about a patient's health just by smelling his/ her breath. For example, breath that smells fruity may indicate the presence of acetone due to uncontrolled diabetes, while a fishy odor may be a red flag for kidney failure.

Latest development: Highly sensitive electronic sensors can now diagnose and monitor certain illnesses by testing for chemical compounds in the breath.

This breakthrough technology, which is still in its early stages of development, is based on the principle that biochemical changes in the body that are caused by illness produce a characteristic *breath signature.*

Breath analysis is already being used to diagnose and/or monitor common diseases, including stomach ulcers and asthma, and researchers are developing tests for such conditions as tuberculosis (TB) and lung cancer.

To learn more, we spoke with Cristina E. Davis, PhD, a professor at the University of California, Davis, and a leading specialist in chemical and biological sensing technologies...

• **Why is breath analysis considered an advance over the current tests that are used to diagnose diseases?** One advantage is that breath analysis is completely noninvasive. You don't have to tolerate a stick from a needle or even urinate into a cup. You simply breathe into a device. The accuracy of breath analysis is about the same as blood, urine and other types of medical tests.

Unlike tests that involve blood or other body fluids, breath testing can be performed and analyzed right in your doctor's office instead of at a laboratory. You do not have to wait for days (or weeks) to get lab results. Right now, you can get results from some tests in about 10 minutes. In the future, the information will most likely be available almost instantaneously.

I do not expect breath testing to replace other tests, but it will undoubtedly be combined with blood-work and other tests to gather more information.

●**How does breath analysis work?** Every time you exhale, your breath carries thousands of different molecules. Many of these molecules are *volatile organic compounds*, substances that evaporate and potentially produce odors. These compounds can be detected with highly sensitive electronic sensors.

Some molecules in the breath are present only when you have a particular disease. With breath analysis, we can detect these molecules and also measure their concentrations. This information can be used both to diagnose a disease and to monitor some types of illness over time. Several tests are FDA-approved and sometimes covered by insurance.

●**Which breath tests can be used to diagnose medical conditions?** Doctors are routinely using breath analysis to diagnose stomach ulcers and lactose intolerance.

Most stomach ulcers are caused by a bacterial infection. The organism, *Helicobacter pylori* (*H. pylori*), naturally breaks down *urea*, a chemical comprised of nitrogen and carbon, into carbon dioxide.

To diagnose this infection, the patient is first given a capsule that contains urea with an isotope for detection. Then, the patient's breath is tested for the presence of carbon dioxide—a positive result means that there is an H. pylori infection present, and antibiotic treatment is required. The test is repeated after treatment to make sure that the bacteria have been eradicated.

Lactose intolerance is diagnosed with a *hydrogen breath test*. Patients who have this condition can't digest *lactose,* a sugar found in milk and other dairy foods, and experience gas, cramps and other digestive symptoms. To diagnose lactose intolerance, a patient consumes a lactose-containing solution. Then, the

patient's breath is tested every 15 minutes for two hours. High levels of hydrogen, produced by the fermentation of undigested lactose in the colon, could mean that the patient is lactose intolerant.

●**Are there any other breath tests now available?** Yes. The *Heartsbreath* test is an important advance for patients who have received heart transplants. This test measures *alkanes,* substances that are elevated when there's a risk for organ rejection in someone who has had a heart transplant.

Heartsbreath is used with a biopsy of the heart muscle to monitor signs of rejection. Signs of organ rejection are traditionally monitored by biopsy, imaging tests and blood tests.

●**How is breath analysis being used to monitor disease?** Breath testing is now a key element in the treatment of asthma. Doctors can use levels of *nitric oxide*, a molecule that can be detected with a breath test, to determine whether medications and/or dosages need to be adjusted. Breath analysis, used with conventional asthma tests, such as spirometry and peak flow—both of which involve blowing into devices to measure airflow—gives a more complete picture of the lung inflammation that causes asthma symptoms.

●**Which breath tests are still in development?** Tests to diagnose TB and lung cancer are being studied, and the results so far are quite promising. For example, the bacterium that causes TB produces a distinctive pattern of volatile organic compounds. One study found that breath testing can identify TB with about 80% accuracy. (The TB skin test, which takes 48 to 72 hours, often provides a false-negative result.)

Also, tests at the Cleveland Clinic have shown that breath analysis is about 81% accurate at detecting lung cancer. That's comparable to the accuracy of a CT scan. The devices can also distinguish between different subtypes of lung cancer. Other tests are being developed for diabetes, kidney disease and colorectal cancer.

Breath analysis is one of the most exciting areas of medical research, with many new tests expected to be available over the next several years.

Tattoos? Why You Must Tell Your Doctor Before an MRI

Anything that contains metal may cause a burn during *magnetic resonance imaging* (MRI), and permanent tattoos sometimes are done using ink that contains iron oxide. If you have a tattoo, talk to your doctor before an MRI.

Other things that contain metal and should be removed before an MRI: Body piercings, hearing aids, removable dental work, medication patches and makeup that contains metallic particles.

Health After 50. www.JohnsHopkinsHealthAlerts.com/health_after_50

New Dental X-Ray Danger

Rebecca Shannonhouse, editor, *Bottom Line/Health*, 281 Tresser Blvd., Stamford, Connecticut 06901. *www.BottomLinePublications.com*

Does your dentist take X-rays every time you get a checkup? If so, there's a new study that you should know about.

Researchers from Yale and Brigham and Women's Hospital found that people (mean age 57) who received "bitewing" exams (using X-ray film held in place by a tab between the teeth) yearly or more frequently over their lifetimes were 50% more likely than a control group to develop a *meningioma*, a noncancerous brain tumor that can cause headaches, vision problems and loss of speech, during a five-year period. People who had been given "panorex" exams (X-rays that show all of the teeth on one film) one or more times a year had triple the risk.

It is true that modern dental X-rays use less radiation than in the past, but any exposure is risky.

"I go to the dentist two or three times a year, but haven't had an X-ray in probably 10 years," says Keith Black, MD, chairman of the department of neurosurgery at Cedars-Sinai Medical Center in Los Angeles. *Dr. Black's advice...*

• **Refuse "routine" X-rays.** If your dentist has examined your teeth and deemed them healthy, don't allow him/her to take an X-ray "just to be safe." Risk for a brain tumor increases with every X-ray.

• **Limit the exposure.** If you have a cavity or other problems, ask your dentist to X-ray only that area.

• **Less is more.** The American Dental Association recommends that adults get their teeth X-rayed every two to three years (children—one X-ray every one to two years). Unless your dentist needs to evaluate a specific problem or plan a procedure, you don't need an X-ray.

Don't Just Say "Yes" When a Doctor Tells You to Take a New Drug

Marianne Legato, MD, a professor of clinical medicine and founder and director of The Partnership for Gender-Specific Medicine at Columbia University in New York City. She also is editor of the textbook *Principles of Gender-Specific Medicine* (Academic) and author of numerous books, including *Eve's Rib: The Groundbreaking Guide to Women's Health* (Three Rivers). She has received numerous awards, including a Research Career Development Award presented by the National Institutes of Health.

You're wise enough to take your doctor's advice to eat right, watch your weight and get screened for cancer—but if you also take every medication he or she mentions without question, you may be too compliant. Sure, you need to trust your physician...but blind faith could leave you vulnerable to drug-related dangers.

The truth is that many medications are much riskier than people generally recognize. A recent article in *Archives of Internal Medicine* reported that 25% of people surveyed mistakenly believed that the FDA approves only drugs without serious side effects...39% wrongly believed that only "extremely effective" medications get FDA approval.

Reality check: The FDA does require manufacturers to demonstrate that new medications are "safe" and "effective," but those terms are far from precise. And in spite of "scientific testing," the extent of risks for a given drug are generally not known until after the drug has been used by far more people and for longer periods of time.

What's more, until about two decades ago, researchers routinely excluded women from clinical trials of drugs, fearing possible harm to women of childbearing age and assuming that what worked for men would work in the same way for women, too.

What we know now: Women have a 50% to 70% greater risk of developing an adverse drug reaction than men, according to the Society for Women's Health Research (SWHR).

Why are women are greater risk? Marianne Legato, MD, founder and director of The Partnership for Gender-Specific Medicine at Columbia University in New York City, explained that women and men often have disparate reactions to drugs due to differences in hormones, metabolism, biochemistry and anatomy—and even factors such as oral contraceptive use or where a woman is in her menstrual cycle can make a difference.

Unfortunately, some problems become evident only after a drug has been in use for a while. For instance, Dr. Legato pointed out that the antihistamine *terfenadine* (Seldane) was on the market for years before it was found to cause potentially fatal disruptions in cardiac rhythm, especially in women, and was banned by the FDA. This was not an isolated event. According to the SWHR, of the 10 prescription drugs withdrawn from the US market between 1997 and 2000, eight caused statistically greater health risks for women than men. What's more, even when information is available on a drug's dangers, you can't assume that every doctor is aware of all potential side effects, especially the gender-specific ones.

More than half of all adverse drug reactions treated in hospitals and emergency facilities are preventable, according to the International Pharmaceutical Federation. Such prevention requires patients to be proactive in assessing the pros and cons before using a prescription or over-the-counter drug that is new to them. *So when your doctor says, "Take this," be sure to ask…*

•**Why do I need to take this drug?** Your doctor should be able to pinpoint your medical problem…describe what the medication is intended to do…clarify why this drug is better than any other…and explain why medication is more appropriate for you than any non-drug treatment available. A full explanation is particularly important if the drug is being prescribed "off-label"—meaning that it is being used in a way that has not been formally tested or approved by the FDA—as 21% of prescriptions written by US doctors are.

•**What are the possible side effects?** There is no such thing as a drug with zero potential adverse effects, Dr. Legato noted. Your physician should review not only the most common side effects, but also the warning signs of a dangerous reaction (no matter how rare) and outline what to do (call the doctor, go to the emergency room) if problems arise.

•**Did the clinical trials for this drug include women?** If the answer is yes, find out how well the drug worked for women specifically and whether females were more prone to problems. If the answer is no, ask what is known about how women react to this drug.

•**How long has this drug been on the market?** Unless absolutely necessary, try to avoid taking a brand new medication until its full effects are better known.

•**What is your doctor's own experience in prescribing this drug?** For instance, has your doctor received any complaints about side effects from his other patients? It is best if your doctor has firsthand knowledge of the medication, rather than prescribing it based solely on its reputation.

•**Could this drug interact with other medications?** The average American is prescribed medication 12.6 times per year, according to a recent report from the Kaiser Family Foundation. Women consume more medications than men, and the use of multiple medications is higher in women, the SWHR reports. Obviously, the more drugs you take, the higher the risk for potentially dangerous interactions. With your doctor, review all prescription and nonprescription drugs—as well as supplements—that you take regularly or even occasionally. If there is a potential for interaction, discuss alternatives to the new medication or needed alterations to your current regimen.

Once you get home, it's prudent to do further research using a reliable Web site such as the National Library of Medicine Drug Information Portal (*http://druginfo.NLM.NIH.gov*). Or try the new interactive online tool called the Question Builder (*www.AHRQ.gov*) from the Agency for Healthcare Research and Quality, designed to help patients ask questions that will optimize their care, including safe and appropriate medication use. If you learn something about your new drug that concerns you, call your doctor to discuss it.

You May Not Need All the Drugs You're Taking: 5 Overprescribed Medications

Armon B. Neel, Jr., PharmD, a certified geriatric pharmacist and founder of the Georgia-based Medication-Xpert, LLC, a private practice focused on pharmaceutical care for outpatients and institutional geriatric patients. He is author of *Are Your Prescriptions Killing You? How to Prevent Dangerous Interactions, Avoid Deadly Side Effects, and Be Healthier with Fewer Drugs* (Atria). *www. MedicationXpert.com*

Nearly 60% of the prescription medications taken by patients aren't needed. That is what researchers discovered in a study published in *Archives of Internal Medicine*. The study also revealed that 88% of patients said they felt healthier when taking fewer drugs.

The fact is that adverse effects from medications are the fourth-leading cause of death in the US (after heart disease, cancer and stroke). About 6% of patients who take two medications daily will experience a drug interaction. If you're taking five medications a day, the risk rises to 50%.

As a geriatric pharmacist, I have evaluated the drug regimens of thousands of patients. *Here are the medications that often are overprescribed…*

STATINS

The cholesterol-lowering statins, such as *atorvastatin* (Lipitor) and *simvastatin* (Zocor), are among the highest-selling prescription drugs in the US. They are not as effective as you might think…and the potential side effects, including muscle pain and memory loss, can be serious.

One recent study, published in *Pharmacotherapy*, found that 75% of patients who took statins reported memory loss or other cognitive problems. The same study found that 90% of patients who stopped their medication had rapid mental improvements.

Statins can be lifesaving drugs for patients who have high cholesterol and existing heart disease or other cardiovascular risk factors. But generally, they are not effective for primary prevention (preventing a heart attack in healthy patients with few risk factors).

Before starting to take a statin, ask your doctor about the drug's *Number Needed to Treat* (NNT). The NNT for Lipitor is 168. This means that 168 patients would have to take it (for 4.1 years) to prevent one cardiovascular event. Those are impressively bad odds, particularly when the risk for muscle pain/memory loss can be as high as one in 10.

My advice: Try to lower your cholesterol with nondrug approaches. These include taking fish-oil supplements…and eating less saturated fat and more fiber. Take a statin only if you have high cholesterol and other cardiovascular risk factors, such as a family history, high blood pressure and/or diabetes.

BLOOD PRESSURE DRUGS

About 40% of the patients I see are taking at least four different drugs to control hypertension. Some patients need this many drugs to lower blood pressure, but they are the exceptions. If you are taking more than two drugs for blood pressure, you probably are taking the wrong drugs.

Example: Beta-blockers for hypertension. Millions of older Americans take these drugs, even though the drugs often cause fatigue, dizziness and other side effects. In addition, doctors often prescribe both an ACE inhibitor (such as *captopril*) and an angiotensin receptor blocker (such as *losartan)*, even though they work in similar ways. Patients using this combination are 2.4 times more likely to have kidney failure—or die—within six months as those taking just one of them.

My advice: If you are like most patients with hypertension, you probably need to take only a diuretic (such as *chlorthalidone*) and perhaps a calcium channel blocker (such as *diltiazem*). Don't assume that you need additional drugs if your blood pressure still is high—you might just need a higher dose—though some patients do need other medications.

Important: Some patients who reduce their salt intake, exercise and lose weight can take lower doses of medication. A study published in *The New England Journal of Medicine* found that salt restriction for some people has about the same effect on blood pressure as medication does.

PAINKILLERS

Ibuprofen and related analgesics, known as the *nonsteroidal anti-inflammatory drugs* (or NSAIDs), are among the most commonly utilized medications in the US. People assume they're safe. They're not.

One study found that 71% of patients who used NSAIDs experienced damage to the small intestine, compared with just 5% who didn't take them. These medications also increase the risk for stomach bleeding, ulcers and hypertension.

My advice: Take an NSAID only if you need both the painkilling and anti-inflammatory effects—for a flare-up of knee pain, for example. Take the lowest possible dose, and take it only for a few days at a time.

If you're 60 years old or older, you may need to avoid these drugs altogether. The risk for stomach or intestinal damage is much higher than in younger adults. A safer medication is *tramadol* (Ultram), a prescription analgesic that doesn't cause gastrointestinal irritation.

SEDATIVES

Valium and related drugs, known as *benzodiazepines*, are among the most dangerous medications for older adults.

Reason: They are not efficiently broken down (metabolized) in the liver. This means that high levels can accumulate in the body.

Patients who take these drugs daily for conditions such as insomnia or anxiety are 70% more likely to fall—and 50% more likely to have a hip fracture—than those who do not take them. Also, patients who use them regularly have a 50% chance of experiencing memory loss.

Sedatives such as *diazepam* (Valium), *triazolam* (Halcion) and *zolpidem* (Ambien) should never be taken for extended periods.

My advice: If you're going through a stressful time, ask your doctor to write a one- or two-week prescription for a short-acting medication such as *lorazepam* (Ativan). It is eliminated from the body more quickly than other drugs.

For long-term insomnia/anxiety, ask your doctor about *venlafaxine* (Effexor). It's good for depression as well as anxiety, and it's safer than sedatives for long-term use.

ANTIDEPRESSANTS

Doctors routinely prescribe SSRI antidepressants, such as *fluoxetine* (Prozac) and *paroxetine* (Paxil), to patients who don't really need them.

One study, based on data submitted to the FDA, concluded that these and other antidepressants are no more effective than a placebo for most patients. Yet the risks, including falls, bone fractures and even seizures, are high, particularly in older patients.

Important: Depression often is episodic. Patients who have suffered from a traumatic event—the loss of a job, divorce, the death of a spouse—will often have a period of depression that eventually clears up without treatment.

My advice: Start with nondrug approaches. If you're going through a rough patch, see a psychologist or meet with a pastor or another type of counselor. For many patients, talk therapy is as effective as medication.

What You May Not Know About Grapefruit and Drugs...

Joe Graedon, MS, and Teresa Graedon, PhD, consumer advocates whose first book, *The People's Pharmacy*, was published in 1976. Since then, they have written "The People's Pharmacy" syndicated newspaper column, which discusses various issues related to drugs, herbs and vitamins. Their most recent book is *Top Screwups Doctors Make and How to Avoid Them* (Crown Archetype). *www.PeoplesPharmacy.com*

Most people know that grapefruit and grapefruit juice can interfere with various medications, possibly triggering dangerous reactions. But did you know that you might have to wait as long as 24 to 48 hours before taking a drug after having the fruit? Grapefruit inhibits the important intestinal enzyme *CYP3A4*, which is required to break down many medicines properly. Different people have differing amounts of the enzyme and so are affected to a greater or lesser degree. *Medicines known to be affected by grapefruit include...*

- **Calcium channel blockers,** including *nifedipine* (Adalat CC or Procardia), *verapamil* (Calan, Covera-HS, Verelan) and others.
- **Cholesterol-lowering medicines,** including *atorvastatin* (Lipitor), *lovastatin* (Mevacor) and *simvastatin* (Zocor)—but not *pravastatin* (Pravachol).
- **Sleeping pills and antianxiety drugs,** such as *buspirone* (Buspar), *diazepam* (Valium) and others.
- **Heart medicines,** such as *amiodarone* (Cordarone, Pacerone) and *quinidine*.
- **Transplant drugs,** such as *cyclosporine* (Neoral, Sandimmune) and *tacrolimus* (Prograf).
- **Estrogen,** including birth-control pills.
- **HIV/AIDS drugs.**
- **Epilepsy drug** *carbamazepine* (Tegretol).

Studies of grapefruit's effects on medicines are continuing. Many other drugs may be affected to a greater or lesser degree.

Medication Timing Does Matter

If the directions instruct you to take medicine in the morning or evening, do just that. Certain drugs interact with chemicals in your body that may be most active during daytime or nighttime. For best results, time your dose based on label instructions and keep it consistent.

Roshini Rajapaksa, MD, medical editor of *Health*, board-certified gastroenterologist and assistant professor of medicine at the NYU School of Medicine, New York City.

Surprising Dangers in the Hospital...and How to Protect Yourself

Marty Makary, MD, MPH, a surgeon at Johns Hopkins Hospital and an associate professor of health policy at the Johns Hopkins School of Public Health. He was one of the researchers who helped pioneer the surgical checklists that have greatly reduced infection and other complications. He is author of *Unaccountable: What Hospitals Won't Tell You and How Transparency Can Revolutionize Health Care* (Bloomsbury). *www.UnaccountableBook.com*

When you're admitted to a hospital, you probably don't stop and wonder what your chances are of getting out alive. But the odds are worse than you might imagine—and you can literally save your own life (or that of a loved one) by knowing how to investigate a hospital's record *before* you're checked in.

Some frightening statistics: An estimated 98,000 hospital patients die from medical errors in the US annually. That's more than *twice* the number of Americans killed in car crashes each year. Additionally, many other hospital patients suffer from serious—and preventable —complications.

Examples: About one of every 20 hospital patients will develop an infection...and surgeons operate on the wrong body part up to 40 times a week.

Getting the information you need: Because few hospitals publish statistics about their performance, it's difficult for patients to know which ones are worse—in some cases, *much* worse—than average.

For advice on avoiding the most common threats to hospital patients, we spoke to Marty Makary, MD, MPH, one of the country's leading experts on hospital safety.

WHAT YOU CAN FIND OUT

When I've asked patients why they chose a particular hospital, they typically say something like, "Because it's close to home." Others might say, "That is where my doctor has privileges." But those are bad answers. Before you get any medical care in a hospital, you should find out everything you can about the track record of the hospital. *Five clues to consider…*

Clue #1: **Bounceback rate**. This is the term that doctors use for patients who need to be rehospitalized within 30 days. A high bounceback rate means that you have a higher-than-average risk for postsurgery complications, such as infection or impaired wound healing. Patients also can look up bounceback rates for conditions such as heart attacks and pneumonia. The rate for a particular procedure should never be higher than the national average.

Why this matters: A high bounceback rate could indicate substandard care or even a lack of teamwork in the operating room. It could also mean that the hospital is discharging patients too soon or that patients aren't getting clear discharge instructions that tell them what to do when they get home.

What to do: Check your hospital's rating on the US Department of Health and Human Services' Web site Hospital Compare (*www. HospitalCompare.HHS.gov*), where the majority of US hospitals are listed. You can see if the bounceback rate is better than, worse than or the same as the national average for the procedure you need.

Hospitals that are serious about reducing readmissions go the extra mile. For example, they will provide patients with detailed instructions on such issues as medication use and proper wound-cleaning procedures. Some even give patients a 24-hour hotline number to call if they have symptoms that could indicate a problem.

Clue #2: **Culture of safety.** My colleagues and I at Johns Hopkins recently surveyed doctors, nurses and other hospital employees at 60 reputable US hospitals and asked such questions as, "Is the teamwork good?" "Is communication strong?" "Do you feel comfortable speaking up about safety concerns?"

We found a wide variation in the "safety culture" at different hospitals—and even within different departments at the same hospital. At one-third of the hospitals, the majority of employees reported that the level of teamwork was poor. Conversely, up to 99% of the staff at some hospitals said the teamwork was good.

Why it matters: Hospitals with a poor safety culture tended to have higher infection rates and worse patient outcomes.

What to do: Few hospitals that have conducted this type of survey make the findings public. Patients have to find other ways to get similar information. To do this, I suggest that before you choose a hospital you ask employees—including nurses and lab technicians—if *they'd* feel comfortable getting medical care where they work. Even if some hospital employees put a positive spin on their answers, you can generally tell a lot from their demeanor and comfort level when they respond.

Clue #3: **Use of minimally invasive procedures.** Compared with "open" surgeries, the minimally invasive procedures—such as knee arthroscopy and "keyhole" gallbladder surgery—require shorter hospitalizations. They're also less painful, less likely to result in an infection and less likely to lead to the need for subsequent surgery.

In spite of this, some surgeons still prefer open procedures. During my training, for example, I worked with a surgeon who was not skilled at minimally invasive surgery. His procedures were always open and involved large incisions—his wound-infection rate was about 20%. But his colleagues, who had trained in the newer minimally invasive techniques, had infection rates that were close to zero.

Why it matters: For these reasons, you should usually choose a minimally invasive procedure if it's appropriate for your condition.

What to do: When discussing surgery, ask your physician if there is more than one approach…the percentage of similar procedures that are done in a minimally invasive way…and the percentage that *he/she* does that way versus the percentage done each way nationwide.

Important: Get a second opinion before undergoing any ongoing or extensive treatment, including surgery. About 30% of second opinions are different from the first one.

Clue #4: **Volume of procedures.** "See one, do one, teach one" is a common expression in medical schools. The idea is that new doctors have to start somewhere to learn how to perform medical procedures. Don't let them start on *you.*

Why it matters: Surgical death rates are directly related to a surgeon's experience with that procedure. The death rate after pancreas surgery, for example, is 14.7% for surgeons who average fewer than two procedures a year. It is 4.6% for those who do four or more. A survey conducted by the New York State Department of Health found that hospitals with surgeons who did relatively few procedures had patient-mortality rates that were *four* times higher than the state average.

What to do: Ask your doctor how often he does a particular procedure. For nonsurgical care, ask how many patients with your condition he treats.

Helpful: If 50% or more of a doctor's practice is dedicated to patients with exactly your condition, he will probably be a good choice.

Clue #5: **The availability of "open notes."** Doctors make detailed notes after every office visit, but many patients have never seen these notes. Hospitals may not make them easily available, or the office/hospital might make it difficult (or expensive) to get copies.

Why it matters: Transparency builds trust. Patients who know what's in their medical records will not have to wonder what the doctor is writing about them.

Patients who read the notes will remember the details about treatment advice…ask

questions if they are confused…and often correct errors that can make a difference in their diagnosis and/or treatment. Also, these records are needed for a second opinion.

I purposely dictate notes while my patients are still in my office sitting next to me. Once, I was corrected when I said that a prior surgery was on the left side—it was actually on the right side. Another patient corrected me when I noted a wrong medication dose. Another reminded me to mention a history of high blood pressure.

What to do: Get copies of all of your medical records, including test results. If your doctor or hospital refuses to share them, ask to speak to an administrator. The records are yours—you have a right, under federal law, to see them and get copies. Fees range from a few dollars for a few pages to hundreds of dollars for extensive records.

The Hospital Patient's Packing Checklist

Hospital supplies you might not think to bring for a stay…

• **A sleep mask**—the lights are never out in a hospital.

• **Extra socks** to improve blood circulation in your feet by keeping them warm.

• **Mouthwash and facial wipes** for a quick refresher if you cannot get up to brush your teeth or wash your face.

• **A large container of hand sanitizer** for your bedside table—patients can pick up germs from food trays, medical equipment, TV remotes and elsewhere.

• **A family photo** to remind you of life outside the hospital.

• **Earplugs** to shut out the noise of loudspeakers, carts, conversations and TV.

Elizabeth Bailey, student in the Masters in Health Advocacy program at Sarah Lawrence College, Bronxville, New York, and author of *The Patient's Checklist: 10 Simple Hospital Checklists to Keep You Safe, Sane & Organized* (Sterling).

Surgery Preparation Myth

Does the "nothing by mouth after midnight before surgery" rule still hold true?

Decades of research have shown that having a light breakfast, such as black coffee and dry toast, six or more hours before surgery is *safe* for most healthy patients. So is drinking clear liquids two or more hours before surgery. In fact, surgical patients who drink clear liquids are less thirsty and hungry, less worried about surgery and less likely to get a headache from forgoing their morning coffee. Surgical patients should just be sure to first check with their doctors.

Those facing surgery should also ask their doctors about carbohydrate loading. Several European health organizations now recommend drinking a carbohydrate-rich, clear liquid, such as Clearfast, the evening before and the morning of surgery. It can ease recovery by reducing some of the negative side effects of surgery, such as nausea, vomiting and impaired insulin response.

Jeannette T. Crenshaw, DNP, RN, assistant professor of nursing, Texas Tech University Health Sciences Center, Lubbock, Texas.

Blood Test Warning

Drawing blood too many times may cause hospital-acquired anemia in patients with *acute myocardial infarction.*

Recent finding: For every 50 milliliters of blood drawn, the risk for anemia rises by 18%. Drawing just under one-half pint of blood can lead to moderate-to-severe anemia.

Self-defense: Ask your doctor if the amount of blood drawn can be reduced or if pediatric-sized blood tubes can be used.

Mikhail Kosiborod, MD, associate professor of medicine at the University of Missouri–Kansas City School of Medicine, and coauthor of a study of 17,676 people, published in Archives of Internal Medicine.

Common Surgery Increases Risk for Blood Clots

In a recent finding, one of every 100 patients who had knee-replacement surgery and one of every 200 patients who had hip-replacement surgery developed a potentially deadly blood clot before leaving the hospital. But the risk actually may be higher because the threat of developing a blood clot persists even after the patient leaves the hospital.

A blood clot can be fatal if it travels to vital organs, such as the lungs. Doctors typically prescribe anticlotting medicine for six weeks or more after surgery to reduce the risk for blood clots.

Study of 47 previously published studies by researchers at Lausanne University Hospital, Lausanne, Switzerland, published in The Journal of the American Medical Association.

Free Apps That Are Good for Your Health

Lose It! monitors food and fitness—log meals into the database, and the app gives you a target calorie count based on how much you exercise. *RunKeeper* gives you a personalized fitness plan based on your current weight and your goal. *GoodRx* offers comparative pricing for medicines—just enter the specific medication you are looking for. *ZocDoc* finds a dentist or doctor who takes your insurance in more than 1,600 cities—important if you need help while traveling. *SpotCheck* lets you snap a picture of a mole and have it analyzed for skin cancer by a board-certified dermatologist within 24 hours.

Money. www.Money.CNN.com

3

Common Conditions–
Fast Help!

Rev Up Your Immunity...
To Fight Colds, Flu
and Pneumonia
All Winter Long

Colds are potentially more dangerous than most people realize. That's because they often weaken an already compromised immune system, which makes the sufferer more vulnerable to the flu and pneumonia.

A nutritional deficiency is the most common cause of depressed immunity, but even people who make a real effort to eat a well-balanced diet often fall short when it comes to getting enough key nutrients. For this reason, many Americans turn to dietary supplements for extra protection.

But which ones really work?

For answers, we spoke to Michael T. Murray, ND, a leading naturopathic physician who

has spent more than 30 years compiling a database of more than 60,000 scientific articles on the effectiveness of natural medicines, including supplements.

Here are some of the most effective supplements for preventing and treating colds and related upper-respiratory ailments. Start with the first supplement and add others (all are available at health-food stores), based on specific symptoms...*

•**Mixed antioxidants.** When it comes to fortifying your body to fight off colds, it is wise to start with a high-potency multisupplement. I recommend one that combines zinc,

*Consult your doctor before trying these supplements —especially if you have a chronic medical condition and/or take medication. Some of these remedies may interact with medication. Most supplements need to be taken for at least six weeks to reach their full effect.

Michael T. Murray, ND, one of the country's best-known naturopathic physicians. He serves on the Board of Regents of Bastyr University in Seattle and has written more than 30 books, including *The Encyclopedia of Natural Medicine* (Atria) with coauthor Joseph Pizzorno, ND. *www.DoctorMurray.com*

selenium, beta-carotene (or other carotenes) and vitamins C and E. This antioxidant mix helps prevent oxidative damage to the *thymus gland*—a robust thymus is needed to produce *T lymphocytes*, a type of white blood cell that recognizes and attacks viruses and other infectious agents.

Typical daily dose: 20 milligrams (mg) to 30 mg zinc…200 micrograms (mcg) selenium… 25,000 international units (IU) beta-carotene… 500 mg vitamin C…and 200 IU vitamin E. You'll find roughly these amounts in any high-potency multisupplement. Many people take a multisupplement year-round.

•**Astragalus.** Few Americans know about this herb, although it's a standard treatment in Traditional Chinese Medicine (TCM). It is getting more attention these days because scientists have learned that it contains *polysaccharide fraction F3* and other substances that stimulate different parts of the immune system.

Test-tube and animal studies have found that astragalus has potent antiviral effects—important for preventing colds and the flu. In one study, 115 patients who took the herb for eight weeks showed significant improvement in their counts of white blood cells, which help to fight infection.

Typical daily dose: 100 mg to 150 mg of powdered extract combined with any liquid, three times daily, whenever you have a cold or the flu or throughout the winter months if your immunity is low (for example, due to extra stress).

Caution: If you have rheumatoid arthritis or some other autoimmune disease, use astragalus only under a doctor's supervision— the increase in immune activity could worsen your autoimmune symptoms.

•**South African geranium.** Also known as *umckaloabo*, this herbal remedy is commonly used for bronchitis, an upper-respiratory infection that often follows colds, particularly in winter.

In a study of 205 patients with bronchitis, those taking it had reduced bronchitis-related symptoms, such as a cough and shortness of breath. Other studies have shown similar effects.

Although doctors who specialize in herbal medicine typically recommend this supplement for patients who have been diagnosed with bronchitis or sinusitis, I advise taking it if you have a cold because it reduces symptoms and helps prevent a *secondary* bronchial infection.

Typical daily dose: 20 mg, three times daily, until the symptoms subside.

•**Beta-glucan.** This class of compounds is found in baker's yeast, medicinal mushrooms (such as maitake) and a variety of grains. Supplemental forms have been shown to stimulate the activity of immune cells. They also stimulate *immune signaling proteins*, which help the body fight viral infections.

In a study of 54 firefighters (who are susceptible to colds because of frequent exposure to smoke and other fumes), those who took a beta-glucan supplement had 23% fewer upper-respiratory infections compared with participants who took a placebo.

Typical daily dose: 250 mg to 500 mg daily. This dose is effective for treatment of viral infections as well as prevention (for example, when you feel a cold coming on). I recommend Wellmune WGP (it contains a substance derived from yeast that has been shown to strengthen immune cells) or Maitake Gold beta-glucan supplements—the research is more solid with these than with other products.

•**Echinacea.** This herb has been the subject of more than 900 studies. A few years ago, researchers reported that it was not effective for colds—probably because these scientists were using products that had insufficient amounts of active compounds. In my experience, echinacea is very effective both for prevention and treatment.

Example: One study that involved 120 patients who had just started to experience cold symptoms, found that only 40% of those taking echinacea went on to develop a full-fledged cold compared with 60% of those not taking the herb. When patients in the echinacea group did get sick, their symptoms started to improve after four days versus eight days in those taking placebos.

Typical daily dose: One-half to one teaspoon of liquid extract, which can be added to a glass of water or taken straight, three times daily, when you have a cold or feel one coming on. Buy a product that is made from the *fresh aerial portion* of the plant. This information will be printed on the label. You will receive a higher concentration of active compounds. People who have allergies to plants in the daisy family (which includes ragweed) should not take echinacea.

ADD A DOSE OF STRESS RELIEF

It's important to remember that virtually everyone is more likely to get sick during times of stress.

Reasons: Stress increases blood levels of adrenal hormones, which suppress the immune system. In addition, stress triggers the release of *cytokines* and other substances that decrease the activity of white blood cells and inhibit the formation of new ones.

What to do: In addition to getting regular exercise and sleeping at least seven hours a night, make a habit of doing activities that improve your mood. Deep breathing, meditation or simply having a good time with friends will all help you stay healthier.

DITCH THE SUGAR!

If you want to stay healthy this winter, cut way back on sugar. This is important because the simple sugars in sweets and sweet beverages (including fruit juices) diminish the ability of lymphocytes to fight off viruses. When you consume sugar, the immune system weakens within just 30 minutes—and it remains in a depressed state for more than five hours.

It's not clear why sugar has such serious effects on immunity. It's possible that elevated blood sugar prevents vitamin C from attaching to and entering white blood cells, which makes the immune system less effective.

My advice: Have no more (and preferably less) than 15 grams (g) to 20 g of sugar in any three-hour period. Sugar-content information is, of course, found on food labels. A four-ounce glass of fruit juice, for example, will have about 12 g of sugar.

Don't Catch a Cold on the Plane!

Air travelers have a 20% increased risk for catching a cold. Viruses thrive in the extremely dry environment and low humidity of airplanes. Also, the air filters often are shut down while people are boarding or exiting, as well as during long waits on the ground.

To protect yourself: Use alcohol-based sanitizers if you must use airplane bathrooms… disinfect tray tables…and don't use seat-back pockets because prior sick passengers may have used these pockets to store their tissues or magazines.

The Wall Street Journal. www.WSJ.com

"Starve a Fever"? Think Again

Even if you are not hungry, eat a normal number of calories if possible when you have the flu. The flu comes in new strains every year, so the body must make new antibodies. To do that, it requires fuel to produce natural killer cells. Eating fewer calories slows recovery. Eat fresh fruits and vegetables—they help create an alkaline environment in which viruses cannot survive.

Caution: Limit sweets while you are ill—sugar feeds viruses.

Study by researchers at Michigan State University, East Lansing, published in *The Journal of Nutrition*.

Better Flu Recovery

Researchers divided 154 healthy adults (age 50 and older) into three groups—one that was trained to meditate daily for 45 minutes, one that exercised daily for 45 minutes and a control group that did neither.

Result: During a single flu season, the meditation and exercise groups had similarly fewer acute respiratory infections than the control group, but the meditation group's symptoms were far less severe than those of the other two groups.

Theory: Daily meditation decreases stress, which may protect against infection.

Bruce Barrett, MD, associate professor of family medicine, University of Wisconsin School of Medicine and Public Health, Madison.

How to Get Over a Stomach Virus *Fast!*

Andrew L. Rubman, ND, founder and director of the Southbury Clinic for Traditional Medicine, Southbury, Connecticut. *www.SouthburyClinic.com*

To get over a stomach virus quickly, the best strategy is to combine *repletion* with *palliation*...

Repletion means restoring crucial nutrients that your body loses in gastrointestinal distress. One way to do that is with egg drop soup from any Chinese restaurant—it combines water-based chicken stock with whole egg. It also contains salt, which a depleted body needs.

In addition, try taking Larix, the trade name for the inner bark of the *Western larch*—this sweet-tasting white powder, very soluble in water, calms mucous membranes.

Palliation means making the stomach and large intestine feel better. For the stomach, sip a tea made with *gentian* and *slippery elm bark*. The herbs are available at *www.TeaHaven. com*. Use a mixture of two-thirds gentian and one-third slippery elm with a teaspoon of the combination in each cup. Steep for eight minutes. For the intestine, try Thorne Research's Formula SF374, which includes *deglycyrrhizinated licorice root* and *berberine* in a base that is mainly *bismuth citrate*—it effectively calms the large intestine.

Do Antibiotics Really Speed Sinus Infection Recovery?

In a new study, doctors administered either a 10-day course of *amoxicillin* or a placebo to 166 adults (ages 18 to 69) suffering from acute sinus infections.

Result: There were no significant differences between the antibiotic and placebo groups in reported symptoms, days missed at work, and relapse or recurrence. Eighty percent of patients in both groups experienced significant improvement within 10 days.

Caution: Taking antibiotics for conditions for which they are ineffective could actually be harmful—it gives bacteria the chance to develop resistance to the drugs.

If you have an acute sinus infection: Talk to your doctor about treating pain, cough and congestion with bed rest and painkillers instead of antibiotics. Your doctor may reevaluate your need for antibiotics if symptoms have not improved after 10 days.

Jane Garbutt, MD, research associate professor of medicine, Washington University School of Medicine in St. Louis.

Pets Provide *Protection* from Allergies

In a recent finding, children younger than age one who lived with a cat were 50% less likely to become sensitive to cats later in life. (Exposure to pets after the age of one is not associated with allergy risk.)

Theory: Being exposed to pet allergens and bacteria at a young age may allow infants' immune systems to develop in such a way as to avoid being sensitive to pets.

Study of 566 children by researchers at Henry Ford Hospital, Detroit, published in *Clinical & Experimental Allergy*.

Are You Allergic to Your Cell Phone?

Cell phones containing nickel and cobalt may cause allergic reactions in individuals sensitive to these metals. About one-third of BlackBerry phones contain nickel, and many flip phones contain nickel and cobalt. iPhones and Android phones don't have either component. Symptoms of allergies include redness, swelling, itching, blistering and skin lesions. People who develop symptoms should consider using plastic cell phone cases, wireless earpieces and clear film screens to prevent reactions.

Study of 72 cell phones by researchers at Winthrop University, Mineola, New York, presented at a recent meeting of the American College of Allergy, Asthma and Immunology.

Surprising Asthma Symptoms

Itching at the front of the neck or an itchy feeling in the chest may indicate asthma. These unusual symptoms may precede the more common symptoms, which can include coughing, chest tightness, shortness of breath and wheezing.

Stephen J. Apaliski, MD, an allergist and immunologist, Allergy & Asthma Centres of the Metroplex, Arlington, Texas, and author of *Beating Asthma: Seven Simple Principles* (Salveo Media).

Clean Your Carpets for Better Allergy and Asthma Care

In a recent study, researchers tested nine carpets, sampling for airborne allergen particles before and after deep-cleaning the rugs.

Result: Airborne particles were reduced more than fourfold after proper cleaning (scrubbing with hot water and a carpet-cleaning solution or a professional cleaning), while surface cat allergens dropped 37-fold and dust mites dropped 10-fold.

The study did not result in a specific recommendation, but it's wise for asthma or allergy patients to vacuum carpets at least twice a week and deep-clean monthly.

Angela Southey, PhD, technical manager of Airmid Healthgroup, Dublin, Ireland.

Natural Migraine Therapies That Work Just as Well as Drugs— Without Side Effects

Jay S. Cohen, MD, the author of MedicationSense. com, an online newsletter that provides information about medications and natural therapies, and an adjunct associate professor of psychiatry and family and preventive medicine at the University of California, San Diego. Dr. Cohen is also author of the book *15 Natural Remedies for Migraine Headaches* (Square One).

Anyone who has ever had a migraine knows that the excruciating pain will drive you to do almost anything to get relief.

Case in point: Powerful migraine medications, including *triptans*, are rife with side effects, such as dizziness, drowsiness and nausea, but these drugs are among the most widely prescribed for migraine sufferers.

Latest development: Important new research just completed in Great Britain has found that painkillers, including *nonsteroidal anti-inflammatory drugs* (NSAIDs) and triptans, often *worsen* headaches due to overuse (defined as 15 or more days of NSAID use per month or 10 or more days of a triptan or opiate-based painkiller). So what's the solution?

POWERFUL NONDRUG THERAPIES

Increasing scientific evidence now supports the use of natural therapies that, in many instances, are just as effective—and sometimes

53

even *more* effective—in preventing migraines than the standard medications.

Important: Unlike prescription medications, which usually reach high concentrations in the body almost immediately, natural remedies work more slowly and, as a result, rarely cause side effects. It may take about three months before a particular remedy is fully effective.

My advice: Start with *riboflavin* (see below) and take it for about one month. This may be all that you need. If migraine frequency and severity don't seem to be subsiding, keep taking riboflavin and add one (and then another) of the other supplements below every month or so until symptoms improve. If you require more than one supplement, take them individually rather than in a manufactured combination product for optimal therapeutic effect. *Three of the following supplements are the most anyone should require...* *

• **Riboflavin.** This B vitamin is believed to improve oxygen metabolism within the energy-producing *mitochondria* of nerve cells. Researchers now speculate that a dysfunction in oxygen metabolism is an underlying cause of migraine headaches.

Scientific evidence: When researchers studied patients who averaged four migraine attacks a month, the number dropped to two per month after three months of taking riboflavin. It also reduced the duration of the attacks by an average of 44%.

Typical dose: 400 milligrams (mg) daily.

Side effects: Very rarely, patients who take high-dose riboflavin will experience nausea or other gastrointestinal side effects. These can be avoided by splitting the dose—take 200 mg at breakfast and another 200 mg with dinner.

Note: In some people, riboflavin turns the urine an iridescent yellow color. Don't worry —it's harmless.

*Consult your doctor before trying these supplements if you have a chronic medical condition and/ or take prescription medication—some remedies may interact with commonly used medications. If you use migraine medication, you'll need advice on tapering off that drug while adding these therapies.

• **Magnesium.** Estimates show that 70% to 80% of the US population is deficient in magnesium. In some people, low magnesium triggers spasms in the cerebral arteries that lead to migraines.

Scientific evidence: A study that looked at 81 migraine patients found that supplemental magnesium, taken for three months, decreased the frequency of migraines by 42%. It also reduced the duration and severity of the attacks.

Typical dose: Start with 100 mg in the morning and 100 mg at night. Every few weeks, increase the dose until you're taking 400 mg daily, in divided doses.

Side effects: About 40% of patients who take magnesium experience loose bowel movements. Experiment with different forms of this supplement until you find one that doesn't cause this.

For example, the *magnesium hydroxide* form used in Milk of Magnesia is more likely than most to cause diarrhea at high doses. This is less likely to occur with *magnesium citrate, magnesium lactate* or *magnesium malate*.

Important: Drink plenty of water—about eight glasses daily—when taking magnesium. This prevents excessive levels from accumulating in the body, which can lead to diarrhea.

• **Co-enzyme Q10 (CoQ10).** This supplement is a strong antioxidant that reduces the release of inflammatory substances that have been linked to migraines.

Scientific evidence: One study reported that 94% of patients who took CoQ10 had at least a 25% reduction in the frequency of their migraines.

Typical dose: Start with 150 mg once daily. If needed, you can increase the dose to 300 mg, divided into three daily doses.

Side effects: Less than 1% of people who take CoQ10 will experience stomach upset or other side effects. Dividing the dose usually prevents this.

• **5-HTP (5-hydroxytryptophan).** This is a naturally occurring substance that's produced from an amino acid (*tryptophan*) in foods. The body uses 5-HTP to produce *serotonin*, a neurotransmitter with paradoxical effects—

that is, in some patients, elevated serotonin dilates the blood vessels, while in others it causes constriction. This is why 5-HTP prevents migraines in some patients, but not in everyone.

Scientific evidence: In one study, more than half of migraine patients taking 5-HTP reported less pain and frequency of headaches after two months.

Typical dose: 50 mg to 100 mg daily. Take the lower dose for several weeks, then gradually increase it if your migraines aren't improving. Don't take more than 400 mg daily.

Side effects: In rare cases, sedation and/or strange dreams will occur. 5-HTP should not be taken with an antidepressant and may interact with other medications.

• **Butterbur.** This powerful herbal medicine is considered a natural product in the US but requires a doctor's prescription in Germany. Butterbur has compounds that are thought to reduce arterial spasms. It also inhibits the body's production of *leukotrienes*, inflammatory substances that can trigger migraines.

Scientific evidence: A double-blind study of 202 migraine patients found that a twice-daily dose of 75 mg of butterbur decreased the frequency of migraines by an average of 48%.

Typical dose: 50 mg to 75 mg twice daily.

Side effects: In rare instances, patients may experience burping or stomach upset when taking butterbur.

Important: Use a butterbur extract labeled PA-free (free of the harmful chemicals *pyrrolizidine alkaloids*). Butterbur may cause allergic reactions in people who are sensitive to plants in the ragweed family.

Start Treating a Migraine *Right Away*

Start treating a migraine as soon as symptoms appear. Migraine sufferers often wait for the pain to become severe, even unbearable, before taking any medication—because they believe they should not take it until they absolutely must.

But: Migraine treatment is much more effective when started as soon as possible—preferably within the first 20 minutes.

Study by researchers at Beth Israel Deaconess Medical Center, Boston, presented at the American Neurological Association annual conference, held in Boston.

The Natural Cures I Prescribe Most Often (Because They Really Work)

C. Norman Shealy, MD, PhD, founding president of the American Holistic Medical Association, a leading advocate for the use of holistic and integrative medicine by health-care providers. A neurosurgeon, Dr. Shealy is director of the Shealy Institute, Springfield, Missouri, a center for comprehensive health care and pain and stress management. His most recent book is *The Healing Remedies Sourcebook* (Da Capo). *www. NormShealy.com*

Americans take an astonishing number of medications—an average of 26.5 million pills per hour. Medications do ease symptoms, but they do little to correct the root cause of most illnesses.

I have found that most patients do significantly better when they use natural therapies that restore physical as well as emotional balance. Of course, always check with your doctor before trying any new remedy.

Problem: **High blood pressure.**

Remedy: **L-arginine.**

L-arginine is an amino acid found in meats, grains, fish and other foods. When you take higher, supplemental doses, it increases blood levels of *nitric oxide*, which dilates arteries and reduces blood pressure. Recent studies have shown that patients who take L-arginine can reduce their blood pressure by 20 points or more. Also, L-arginine appears to reduce *atherosclerosis*, buildups in the arteries that lead to most heart attacks.

How to use it: Take 1,000 milligrams (mg) twice a day. Use a timed-release form—it will stay active in the body throughout the day.

Caution: L-arginine can interact with some medications, including high blood pressure medications and nitroglycerin.

Problem: High cholesterol.

Remedy: Sustained-release niacin.

The cholesterol-lowering statin medications, such as *atorvastatin* (Lipitor) and *simvastatin* (Zocor), are very effective at reducing LDL (bad) cholesterol and reducing the risk for heart disease. But they're rife with side effects, including memory loss and muscle pain.

Better: Sustained-release niacin. Available over-the-counter, it is less likely to cause flushing than immediate-release niacin. It lowers LDL by about 20 points—the same as some statin doses. It also increases levels of HDL (the protective form of cholesterol), which is just as important for preventing a heart attack.

How to use it: Take 500 mg of sustained-release niacin with each meal—don't exceed 2,000 mg daily.

Caution: Patients who take niacin should get their liver enzymes tested before taking niacin to establish a baseline liver function and again after about six months. Liver complications are rare, and if the tests are normal, you need to repeat the test only once a year. Never stop taking a statin without your doctor's OK.

Problem: Poor memory.

Remedy: Lecithin granules.

Lecithin is the common name for a group of related chemical compounds known as *phosphatidylcholine*. It's converted in the body into *acetylcholine*, a *neurotransmitter* that plays a critical role in many brain functions, including memory. One study found that participants who took two tablespoons of lecithin daily for five weeks had fewer memory lapses and performed better on memory tests than those who took a placebo.

How to use it: Take two heaping tablespoons of the granules twice daily. I put it in water, but it can be mixed in food, juice or milk. There are no side effects associated with this dose.

Problem: Stomach discomfort, muscle aches, poor immunity.

Remedy: Castor oil application.

Castor oil (a vegetable oil from the castor bean) is an effective remedy for abdominal discomfort—including bloating, constipation and cramps. It's equally effective for joint and muscle pain. You also can use it to improve the immune system.

How to use it: Saturate a large gauze pad with castor oil. Place the pad directly over the area that hurts—on your abdomen, over your knee, etc. Cover it with a few layers of plastic food wrap, and then leave it in place overnight for about eight hours or you can apply a heating pad during the day for one hour.

To strengthen your immune system when you are feeling sick, take a castor oil bath. Fill the tub with warm water, add about one-half cup of castor oil and soak for 20 to 30 minutes. Then pour about one cup of inexpensive shampoo into the water to dissolve the oil. Slosh well, and rinse off before getting out. Studies have shown that a castor oil bath increases lymph flow and boosts white blood cells, which are needed to resist infection.

Problem: Colds and flu.

Remedy: Vitamin D-3.

The "sunshine vitamin" is critical for immunity. The majority of Americans don't get enough vitamin D, largely because they don't get enough exposure to the sun. I recommend taking a vitamin D-3 supplement because it will strengthen your immune system without the risk of getting too much sun.

How to use it: I often advise 50,000 international units (IU) of vitamin D-3 once a week (there are no risks or side effects at this dose). Ask your doctor what dose is best for you. A weekly supplement can reduce the incidence of colds and flu by at least 80%. Also, combine vitamin D-3 with a supplement that contains 100 micrograms (mcg) of vitamin K-2. The nutrients work together to improve immunity.

Caution: Do not take K-2 supplements if you are taking an anticoagulant such as *warfarin*.

Problem: Low energy, low libido.

Remedy: Magnesium lotion spray.

Many foods contain magnesium, but levels of dietary magnesium have dropped because the mineral has been largely depleted from soil. In the US, magnesium deficiencies are very common. This mineral is involved in about 350 enzymatic reactions, so even a slight deficiency can cause various health problems, including weakness and low energy.

How to use it: Use a skin lotion spray that contains 25% magnesium. Apply 10 sprays twice a day to any part of your skin (except your face). It's readily absorbed through the skin—and it's easier for the body to utilize than oral supplements. Most patients will achieve optimal intracellular levels of magnesium within six weeks.

Bonus: Supplementing with magnesium increases levels of *DHEA* by about 60%. DHEA is a precursor hormone used by the body to manufacture testosterone and estrogen. Increases in these hormones can improve libido as well as energy in men and women.

Take a Coffee Break to Ease Neck and Shoulder Pain

Researchers asked 48 volunteers (average age 36) to perform a series of physically awkward computer tasks and measured the pain in their shoulders, necks and forearms.

Result: Volunteers who drank just one cup of coffee about an hour before these tasks reported significantly lower levels of pain—even if they were chronic pain sufferers.

Theory: Caffeine is an *adenosine receptor antagonist*, a molecule that inhibits pain signals in the nervous system.

If you suffer from aches and pains: Try drinking a cup of caffeinated coffee or tea.

Vegard Strom, PhD, researcher, National Institute of Occupational Health, Oslo, Norway.

For Back Pain Relief— Wear Wool Undies!

In a recent finding, men with lower back pain who wore merino wool underwear for two months reported 89% less pain and needed fewer pain medications than men who wore cotton underwear. Wool's heat-retaining properties help keep back muscles flexible, reducing pain. Merino wool is comfortable to wear.

Study by researchers at Atatürk University, Erzurum, Turkey, published in *Collegium Antropologicum*.

For Faster Workout Recovery: *Ginger*

Ginger eases muscle pain and inflammation caused by exercise.

Recent finding: Exercisers who consumed 2 grams (g) (about one teaspoon) of raw or heated ginger had 23% to 25% less pain after exercise than those who did not consume ginger. Volunteers consumed the ginger daily for eight days prior to exercising and three days afterward.

Recommendation: Add some fresh ginger to your diet for faster workout recovery.

Christopher D. Black, PhD, assistant professor, department of kinesiology, Georgia College and State University, Milledgeville, and leader of a study published in *The Journal of Pain*.

Stop Nighttime Leg Cramps Tonight!

To prevent nighttime leg cramps, stay hydrated—drinking water and other liquids throughout the day helps muscles contract and relax more easily. Also, wear shoes with proper support during the day. Do light exercise before bed, such as riding a stationary bike for a few minutes, and before going to sleep, stretch out your leg muscles. Finally, be sure to loosen or untuck sheets and other covers at the foot of the bed.

Mayo Clinic Health Letter. www.HealthLetter.Mayo Clinic.com

3 Ways to Keep Heartburn at Bay

To avoid heartburn, chew sugar-free *non-sorbitol* gum for a half hour after eating a meal likely to cause this ailment—chewing produces saliva that coats the esophagus. Avoid sorbitol because it can make you gassy.

Also, try using a wedge pillow when sleeping. It uses gravity to help keep stomach acid where it belongs. Incline the portion of your body from the Adam's apple to the breastbone—or even to the belly button.

Deglycyrrhizinated licorice (DGL) relieves heartburn without causing high blood pressure and low potassium levels—side effects of chewing on licorice root. Chew 400 milligrams (mg) to 800 mg of DGL slowly for 20 minutes before meals or bedtime, up to three times a day.

Consensus of doctors who treat heartburn, reported in *Vegetarian Times*.

Stem Bloat with Lavender

Bloating and poor digestion can be caused by an overgrowth of certain bacteria—this can happen when you take antibiotics. Lavender contains antioxidants called *polyphenols* that can reduce these unwanted bacteria.

Try sprinkling dried culinary lavender onto Greek yogurt, which also helps your gut.

Christine Gerbstadt, MD, author of *Doctor's Detox Diet* (Nutronics) and spokesperson, Academy of Nutrition and Dietetics, Chicago.

Don't Ignore These "Trivial" Complaints

Jamison Starbuck, ND, a naturopathic physician in family practice and a guest lecturer at the University of Montana, both in Missoula. She is past president of the American Association of Naturopathic Physicians and a contributing editor to *The Alternative Advisor: The Complete Guide to Natural Therapies and Alternative Treatments* (Time Life). She is also a featured columnist in *BottomLine/Health, www.BottomLinePublications.com.*

Do you know when to go to the doctor? Even though this seems like a simple question, plenty of people either don't really know when a health problem warrants a visit to the doctor—or they simply put it off. They think their health concerns are trivial...or they tell themselves they don't have time to go. But that can be a mistake. *Seemingly trivial complaints that do require medical evaluation...*

• **Constipation.** Because millions of Americans suffer from constipation, we often consider it an insignificant condition. However, constipation can indicate something far more serious than a missed bowel movement. On many occasions, a patient's report of constipation has been my only clue to give an exam or order tests that led to a diagnosis of colon cancer, rectal prolapse, anal fissure, gallbladder disease or hypothyroidism. If you fail to have a daily bowel movement for three to four consecutive days, see your doctor for an evaluation before you use laxatives or fiber formulas to treat your condition.

• **Fatigue.** This is tricky because everyone feels tired some of the time. Report fatigue to your doctor when you notice a change in your energy level or a significant difference in your energy compared with that of similarly aged peers of your gender. Common causes of fatigue include anemia...thyroid, adrenal or reproductive hormone disorders...cancer...prescription drug overdose...insomnia...poor diet...and inadequate or excessive exercise. If everything checks out well with your doctor, ask him/her about adding a vitamin B-complex (with at least 75 milligrams [mg] of B-5 and 800 micrograms [mcg] of B-12) as well as

1,000 mg of vitamin C to your daily regimen. This simple protocol can pep up a tired but otherwise healthy body.

• **Indigestion.** Inflammation, stomach ulcers and cancers of the liver, pancreas, stomach and digestive tract often show up as vague, dull painful indigestion. If you have abdominal pain throughout the day or find yourself reaching for an antacid after most meals, see your doctor. If your physician doesn't find any illness, consider botanical remedies. Pancreatic enzyme tablets made from pineapple and papaya are available at natural-food stores and promotes better digestion by breaking food into smaller molecules. Use the dosage found on the label at the end of each meal. A cup of peppermint or chamomile tea will also help digestion.

• **Nosebleeds.** Though most often associated with dry air, colds, allergies or a nose injury, some nosebleeds, particularly in older adults, signal hypertension, leukemia, a bleeding disorder or heart disease. If you get nosebleeds once a month or more, see your doctor. If he/she doesn't find an underlying condition, using homeopathic Phosphorus 30C (two pellets under the tongue) will reduce the bleeding time associated with most nosebleeds. If the bleeding doesn't stop within 15 minutes, take a second dose.

Also: Pinch your nostrils closed and lean forward (for example, while seated, hold your head roughly at the level of your waist) for about 10 minutes to help stop a nosebleed. Leaning your head backward may cause you to swallow blood.

helping to stop the spasms that cause an episode of hiccups.

Luc Morris, MD, surgical oncologist at Memorial Sloan-Kettering Cancer Center, New York City, quoted in *Woman's Day. www.WomansDay.com*

Natural Treatment for Acne Works Better Than Prescriptions

Researchers performed lab tests comparing prescription acne creams that contained up to 10% *benzoyl peroxide*, which can irritate the skin, with tinctures made from thyme, marigold or myrrh.

Result: The thyme tincture killed more of the *Propionibacteria* that infect the skin's pores than marigold, myrrh or prescription creams.

Theory: Thyme offers more effective antibacterial properties than the other herbs or benzoyl peroxide, the main ingredient used in most prescription and over-the-counter (OTC) creams.

If you have adult acne: Ask your doctor about using a thyme tincture, which is available at health-food stores.

Margarita Gomez Escalada, PhD, senior lecturer in microbiology, Leeds Metropolitan University, UK.

Got the Hiccups? Quick Cure...

First, take the deepest breath you can and hold it for 10 seconds. Second, without exhaling, breathe in again and hold for five more seconds. Third, take in a little more air and hold it for another five seconds. Then breathe normally. This exercise calms the diaphragm,

To Relieve Common Summer Ailments...

The lactic acid in milk reduces inflammation from sunburn. Dip a washcloth into a bowl of cool whole milk, then gently place it on the burned areas for about 20 minutes. Rinse off with cool water. Use apple cider vinegar for insect bites and athlete's foot. Dab vinegar onto each bite with a paper towel—it will relieve the itching and reduce swelling. If you have athlete's foot, soak the infected foot/

feet for 20 minutes in a mixture of three parts water and one part vinegar to kill fungi. This can be done twice daily.

Men's Health. www.MensHealth.com

For Fast Burn Relief, Grab an Onion!

After applying cold water or a cold compress, apply a slice of raw onion to a burn. Leave it on for 15 minutes, off for five minutes and then put a fresh piece on for another 15 minutes. Repeat as necessary.

Joan Wilen and Lydia Wilen, authors of *Bottom Line's Treasury of Home Remedies & Natural Cures* (Bottom Line Books). To get the Wilens' free e-letter, *Household Magic Daily Tips*, go to *www.BottomLine Publications.com/free-e-letters*.

What Works for Wounds

To speed healing of a wound, take 500 milligrams (mg) to 1,000 mg of vitamin C twice a day. To reduce pain and lessen bruising, dissolve homeopathic *arnica* (12c to 30c) under your tongue several times a day. Take 500 mg to 1,000 mg of *bromelain* between meals to increase healing enzymes. And to prevent infection, take 825 mg of olive-leaf extract, an antioxidant, three times a day.

Alan Dattner, MD, holistic dermatologist, New York City, writing in *Natural Health Magazine. www.Natural HealthMag.com*

Natural Way to Control Dandruff

Wet hair with warm water and towel dry. Mix 15 drops of lavender essential oil in two tablespoons of olive or almond oil. Microwave for about 10 seconds. Massage the

oil into your scalp, put on a shower cap, let set for an hour, then wash out. It may take several treatments to see benefits. Lavender essential oil is available online and at some health-food stores and specialty markets.

Francesca Fusco, MD, dermatologist, New York City, quoted in *Health* magazine. *www.Health.com*

Surprising Dry-Eye Reliever: Caffeine

When adults were given either caffeine tablets or a placebo in a recent study, tear production increased threefold within 45 minutes in the caffeine group. For participants taking the placebo, tear production did not increase.

Theory: Caffeine's stimulating effect on secretions, such as saliva and digestive juices, also extends to tears.

If you have dry-eye syndrome: Consider drinking coffee, tea or other caffeinated beverages to help relieve dry-eye symptoms.

Reiko Arita, MD, clinical researcher, University of Tokyo School of Medicine.

Simple Trick for Eye Twitch

To get rid of an annoying eye twitch, soak a clean washcloth in cold water and place it over both eyes for 20 minutes. The cold constricts blood vessels, reducing muscle response and easing the twitch, which often is brought on by stress or fatigue.

Caution: If the twitching continues for several days or the skin on your face feels numb or you notice that your pupils are different sizes, see your doctor.

Cristina Schnider, OD, senior director of professional communications for Vistakon, maker of Acuvue contact lenses, Van Buren Township, Michigan, quoted in *Natural Health*.

Don't Let Your Bed Partner Ruin Your Sleep: Simple Solutions for the Most Common Problems

Jeffry H. Larson, PhD, a licensed marriage and family therapist for more than 25 years and a professor of marriage and family therapy at the School of Family Life at Brigham Young University in Provo, Utah. He is the author of *Should We Stay Together? A Scientifically Proven Method for Evaluating Your Relationship and Improving Its Chances for Long-Term Success* and *The Great Marriage Tune-Up Book* (both from Jossey-Bass). Dr. Larson also is editor of the *Journal of Couple & Relationship Therapy.*

Sooner or later, one in every four American couples ends up sleeping in separate beds. Maybe it's your spouse's tossing and turning or TV watching in bed. Whatever the reason, it may seem easier just to turn that spare bedroom into a nighttime sanctuary of your own. But is that arrangement healthy?

New thinking: Even with the challenges that can come with sharing a bed, the net effect is usually positive for your health. While the exact mechanism is unknown, scientists believe that sleeping with a bed partner curbs levels of the stress hormone *cortisol* and inflammation-promoting proteins known as *cytokines*...while boosting levels of the so-called "love" hormone *oxytocin.*

Sleeping in the same bed also cultivates feelings of intimacy and security, which can strengthen a relationship and promote better sleep—factors linked to living a longer life. *Here, six common challenges and how to overcome them...*

• **You like to keep the room dark, while your partner prefers it light.** Sleep experts recommend keeping the room dark to help stimulate the production of the naturally occurring sleep hormone *melatonin.*

My advice: Room-darkening shades or light-blocking curtains help create the darkness we need for a good night's rest. But if your partner insists on having some light in the room, consider placing a dim night-light near his/her side of the bed. The person who prefers darkness may want to wear a sleep mask.

• **You're always cold, but your bed partner is too warm.** Sleep experts agree that a cooler room is generally more conducive to sleep and complements the natural temperature drop that occurs in the body when you go to sleep.

My advice: Optimal room temperature for the best sleep varies from person to person—most insomnia experts recommend a range of 60°F to 68°F. To help achieve your personal comfort level, use separate blankets so you can easily cover yourself or remove the blanket during the night without disturbing your bed partner. If you like to use an electric blanket during the winter, choose one with separate temperature controls.

• **You're a night owl, but your partner is a lark.** If the two bed partners prefer different bedtimes, this can cause both of them to lose sleep and can be a major contributor to marital strife. In a study involving 150 couples, which I conducted with several colleagues at Brigham Young University, the University of Nebraska–Lincoln and Montana State University, those who had mismatched body clocks argued more, spent less time doing shared activities and had slightly less sex.

The first step in trying to resolve conflicting bedtimes is to understand that one's circadian rhythm, the internal body clock that regulates sleep and wakefulness as well as other biological processes, dictates whether you are a natural early riser or a night owl. One's particular *circadian rhythm* is determined by genetics but can be influenced by sunlight, time zone changes and work schedules. Bedtime tendencies also can be socially learned.

My advice: Have a conversation with your partner. Avoid blaming the other party for having a different sleep schedule—we can't control our circadian rhythms or such factors as work schedules. Then, like everything else in a partnership, you'll need to compromise.

For instance, say your partner likes to go to bed at 10 pm and get up at 6 am, while you're rarely in bed before 1 am and sleep until 10 am. As a compromise, you might agree to get in bed with your partner at 9:30 pm to talk, snuggle, relax, read together, etc. Then, when your partner is ready to go to sleep, you can get up and continue with your night. Alternatively, you and your partner could agree to go to bed at the same time two or three nights a week. A night owl could also lie in bed and listen to music or an audiobook with headphones while his partner sleeps.

•**Your bed partner wants to watch TV, but you want peace and quiet.** Watching TV—or looking at any illuminated screen, such as a laptop or smartphone—promotes wakefulness and can interfere with sleep. So it's not really something *anyone* should do just before lights out. However, if one partner wants to watch TV or use a laptop before bed, he should do it in another room.

•**Your partner thrashes all night long.** Some individuals are naturally restless sleepers, tossing and turning throughout the night. Other people may have *restless legs syndrome* (RLS) and/or *periodic limb movement disorder* (PLMD)—two related but distinct conditions.

RLS causes unpleasant sensations, such as tingling and burning, in the legs and an overwhelming urge to move them when the sufferer is sitting or attempting to sleep. PLMD causes involuntary movements and jerking of the limbs during sleep—the legs are most often affected but arm movements also can occur.

With RLS, the sufferer is aware of the problem. Individuals with PLMD, on the other hand, frequently are not aware that they move so much.

My advice: To help ease symptoms, you may want to try natural strategies such as taking warm baths, walking regularly and/or using magnesium supplements, which also promote sleep. But be sure to check with a doctor. If you have RLS or PLMD, it could signal an underlying health condition, such as iron deficiency.

If symptoms persist, you may want to talk to the doctor about medications such as *ropinirole* (Requip) and *pramipexole* (Mirapex), which can help relieve symptoms. Side effects may include nausea and drowsiness.

•**Your partner snores a lot—and loudly.** This is not only a nuisance, it also makes it hard for you to sleep.

My advice: In some cases, running a fan, listening to music through earbuds or using a white-noise machine can help.

If the snoring occurs almost every night, however, your partner may need to see an *otolaryngologist* (ear, nose and throat doctor) to determine whether there's an underlying medical condition.

Loud snoring that is accompanied by periods in which the person's breathing stops for a few seconds and then resumes may indicate *sleep apnea*, a serious—but treatable—disorder usually caused by a blocked or narrowed airway.

Beware: OTC Sleep Aids Cause Side Effects

Over-the-counter (OTC) sleep aids—such as *diphenhydramine* (found in Tylenol PM) and *melatonin*—should not be taken for more than five consecutive days. Taking them longer can cause side effects, such as dry mouth and dizziness.

Best approach: Lifestyle changes—cutting back on caffeine and alcohol…exercising…and going for therapy if stress and anxiety are disturbing your rest.

Health. www.Health.com

Better Way to Fall Asleep

Fifty-one adults who had difficulty falling asleep (sleep-onset insomnia) were divided into two groups. Both groups were taught good sleep practices (maintaining a standard wake-up time, using the bed only for sleeping, etc.). One group, however, also received *cognitive refocusing therapy* (CRT)—which involves thinking about something interesting but unexciting, such as song lyrics or recipes, when preparing for sleep or upon wakening during the night. After one month, the CRT group fell asleep much faster than the group that didn't do CRT. If you try CRT but insomnia persists, see a sleep medicine specialist.

Les A. Gellis, PhD, assistant professor of psychology, Syracuse University, New York.

For Sweet Dreams, Drink This Tart Juice

In a recent finding, people who drank two ounces of tart cherry juice concentrate a day slept an average of 39 minutes longer and spent less time awake in bed than those who drank a noncherry fruit drink.

Reason: Cherry juice significantly increases levels of the sleep-regulating hormone *melatonin* in the body. Try drinking cherry juice concentrate 30 to 60 minutes before bedtime. Available in health-food stores.

Study by researchers at Northumbria University, Newcastle upon Tyne, UK, published in *European Journal of Nutrition*.

Foods for Better Sleep

Try salmon and spinach salad for dinner at 7 pm—omega-3s in the fish help you relax, and magnesium in spinach can calm your nerves. For dessert at 7:30, eat tart cherries—they contain the sleep hormone *melatonin*—or drink tart cherry juice. For a bedtime snack at 9 pm, make warm milk part of a soothing ritual—it is the routine, not the *tryptophan* in the milk, that is calming.

Health. www.Health.com

For More Restful Sleep...

Prevent upsetting thoughts from waking you at night by adding more physical stillness into your day.

Examples: Take a walk without checking electronics...eat lunch alone in a sunny area

By doing this while awake, you will feel less anxious, making it less likely that your mind will seize on middle-of-the-night stillness to fret.

Brené Brown, PhD, author of *The Gifts of Imperfection* (Hazelden).

To Combat Daytime Drowsiness...Let the Sun Shine In!

Blue light from the sun suppresses *melatonin*, the hormone that causes sleepiness.

Easy ways to get more sun: Eat your lunch outside, walk to work and do not habitually wear sunglasses because they may block the blue light that you need.

To prevent insomnia: Avoid watching TV and using your computer right before bedtime—both emit blue light.

Psychology Today. www.PsychologyToday.com

Fatigue-Buster for Women

In a recent study, women who took 80 milligrams (mg) of iron a day for 12 weeks reported a 47% decrease in fatigue, compared with a 28% decrease among women given a placebo.

Caution: Iron deficiency is only one cause of fatigue. If a woman is experiencing fatigue, she should see her doctor to determine if there are other underlying causes.

Study of 198 women by researchers at University of Geneva, Switzerland, published in *Canadian Medical Association Journal*.

2 Steps to Enhance Memory

For enhancing memory, the combination of *computer use* and *exercise* is better than mental or physical activity alone. The exact reason is not yet known, but it may be that physical activity improves blood flow to the brain and therefore delivers more nutrients... while mental activity works at the molecular level to boost synaptic activities.

Yonas E. Geda, MD, MSc, a neuropsychiatrist at Mayo Clinic, Scottsdale, Arizona, and leader of a study of 926 people, ages 70 to 93, published in *Mayo Clinic Proceedings*.

Chew Your Way to a Better Mood

In a recent finding, people who chewed gum for at least five minutes twice a day for two weeks showed improved levels of anxiety, mood and fatigue. Their scores on tests of depression and mental fatigue were 47% better than the control group.

Possible explanation: Chewing may increase blood flow to the brain and lower levels of stress hormones.

Chifumi Sato, MD, department of analytical health science, Tokyo Medical and Dental University, quoted in *Men's Health*.

Just 2 Minutes of Exercise Boosts Mood

Two minutes of activity raises your heart rate and increases the body's production of neurotransmitters such as *norepinephrine*, *dopamine* and *serotonin*—the same substances increased by antidepressants.

John J. Ratey, MD, associate clinical professor of psychiatry, Harvard Medical School, Boston, and author of *Spark: The Revolutionary New Science of Exercise and the Brain* (Little, Brown), quoted in *Prevention*.

Diet & Fitness Finds

To Lose Weight...Eat More! And Other Proven Ways to Drop Pounds

There is a science to weight loss, but the facts often are obscured by many myths. For example, the calories-in, calories-out theory says that for every 3,500 calories you lose, you drop a pound of fat. If you follow this logic, a 150-pound woman who reduced her daily caloric intake by 100 calories (the amount in less than one cup of reduced-fat milk) for 10 years would give up 365,000 calories—and would weigh only 46 pounds!

Despite what you've heard, calories are not all that matter...they're not all the same...and the government's dietary guidelines are not effective for weight control.

What really works...

• **Eat more to lose weight.** It's true. People who consume more food gain less weight than those who cut calories—but only as long as the calories come from the right foods.

Example: When researchers at the University of Pennsylvania compared the effects of higher- and lower-calorie diets, they found that people who ate more lost 200% more weight.

A diet high in high-quality foods (such as protein-rich seafood, nuts and seeds and non-starchy vegetables, such as celery, asparagus and salad greens) increases satiety, the ability of calories to fill you up and keep you full. The same foods are less likely to be stored as body fat than, say, processed foods, and they're more likely to be burned off with your normal metabolism.

Individuals who eat less to lose weight usually fail because the body interprets calorie

Jonathan Bailor, a health-and-fitness researcher located in the Seattle area, who analyzed more than 10,000 pages of academic research related to diet, exercise and weight loss for his book *The Smarter Science of Slim: What the Actual Experts Have Proven About Weight Loss, Dieting & Exercise* (Aavia). *www.TheSmarter ScienceofSlim.com* restriction as starvation. For self-protection, it hangs on to body fat and instead utilizes muscle tissue for energy. Up to 70% of the weight that people lose on a low-cal diet actually is muscle tissue, not fat.

When we eat more—but smarter—we are satisfied…eat only the number of calories that we really need…and provide our body with an abundance of nutrition. This enables us to sustainably burn body fat.

•**Focus on protein.** Protein is a high-satiety nutrient that triggers the release of hormones that send "I have had enough" signals to the brain. In one University of Washington study, participants were allowed an unlimited amount of calories as long as 30% of those calories came from protein.

Result: They consumed 441 fewer calories a day—without feeling hungry.

Protein is less likely to be converted to fat. When you eat an egg omelet or a chicken breast, about one-third of the protein calories are burned during digestion…another one-third are burned when the liver converts protein to glucose (a process called *gluconeogenesis*).

Compare this to what happens when you eat bread or other starchy foods. About 70% of those calories can be stored as fat.

Recommended: Get one-third of your calories from protein—in the form of seafood, poultry, meat or nonfat dairy, such as plain Greek yogurt or cottage cheese.

•**Don't neglect fiber.** This isn't new advice, but most people still don't get enough fiber—or understand why it helps.

The fiber in plant foods isn't digested or absorbed. Instead, it takes up space in the digestive tract…and makes you fill up faster and stay full longer. This is why you will feel more satisfied when you eat, say, 200 calories worth of celery instead of 200 calories worth of candy. The celery takes up about 30 times more space.

You don't have to "count" fiber grams. As long as you get about one-third of total calories from nonstarchy vegetables (discussed previously), you'll get enough.

Do not believe the claims about grains. Whole-wheat bread, oatmeal, brown rice and other grains will not help you lose weight.

Reason: The calories in grains are aggressive, which means that they're more likely to be stored as fat than the calories that you get from protein or nonstarchy carbohydrates. Grains—even whole grains—are rapidly converted to glucose (blood sugar) in the body. The rapid rise in glucose is followed by an equally rapid drop-off. This stimulates the appetite and causes you to crave more calories.

Also, fast-rising glucose is hard for the body to handle. It responds by attempting to rid itself of glucose—by storing it in fat cells.

•**Eat fat.** It's true that fat has about twice as many calories as protein or carbohydrates, but that would matter only if the calories-in, calories-out equation had anything to do with weight loss—which it doesn't.

Decades ago, doctors encouraged Americans to consume fewer calories from fat.

Result: The average person got heavier, not leaner. Experts now agree that people who consume more fat are no more likely to be overweight or obese than those who eat less—if anything, the people who eat less fat are more likely to gain weight.

Recommended: Get about one-third of your calories from fats, including olive and canola oils (monounsaturated fats that lower your risk for heart disease) and the fats in meats, poultry and fish.

•**Drink a lot of green tea.** You will naturally burn more fat when you drink more water. If you get much of this water in the form of green tea, you will do even better. The polyphenols in green tea are among the healthiest antioxidants ever discovered. These compounds, along with the caffeine in tea (about one-fifth the amount in coffee), increase fat metabolism. If you drink decaffeinated tea, you still will burn more fat than you would just by drinking water.

Recommended: Between five and 15 cups of green tea daily. For maximum efficiency, put all the tea bags you need for the day in hot water. Let the tea brew for a few minutes, and then drink the tea throughout the day like iced tea…or put it in the microwave if you prefer hot tea.

Food Portion Alert

Did you know that food portions are four times bigger today than they were in the 1950s?

Examples: The average hamburger was 3.9 ounces in the 1950s, versus 12 ounces now. A serving of french fries is now just under seven ounces, up from 2.4 ounces. And the average soda today is 40 ounces, compared with only seven ounces previously.

Centers for Disease Control and Prevention, Atlanta. *www.CDC.gov*

Change Your Plates to Eat Less

A recent study shows that you eat more if your plate is the same color as your food. Buffet lunch guests were assigned to either a line where only white Alfredo-sauce pasta was served or a line with only red marinara-sauce pasta. Each was randomly given a red or white plate. Those with plates that matched the color of their food helped themselves to much more than those who had plates of the different color.

Study done by researchers from Cornell University, Ithaca, New York, published in *Journal of Consumer Research.*

Fragrant Foods May Lead to Weight Loss

In a recent finding, people tended to take smaller bites of foods that were accompanied by strong smells. Researchers believe that making foods more aromatic could decrease the amount of food people eat per bite, aiding weight loss.

Study by researchers at Wageningen University and Research Centre, the Netherlands, published online in *Flavour.*

Sweet Smells May Suppress Appetite

In a recent finding, volunteers who smelled 30 grams (g) of dark chocolate with 85% cocoa content had just as much suppression of the appetite-stimulating hormone *ghrelin* as people who actually ate the chocolate.

Study by researchers at Reinier de Graaf Group of Hospitals, Delft, the Netherlands, reported in *Health Revelations.*

Watch How You Talk If You're Trying to Lose Weight

How you talk during a diet affects how well you stick to it.

Recent finding: 80% of women who used the phrase "I don't eat that" were able to resist foods that were not on their plans...but only 10% of those who said, "I can't eat that," resisted.

Bottom line: Talking as if you are in control of what you do is more effective than talking as if you are being deprived.

Vanessa M. Patrick, PhD, associate professor, C.T. Bauer College of Business, University of Houston, and leader of a study published in *Journal of Consumer Research.*

Sleep Away the Pounds!

When well-fed but sleep-deprived men were shown images of high-calorie foods, activity in areas of the brain that control appetite was higher than in the same men after they had slept for seven hours. When well-rested, the men found the images far less appetizing.

Study by researchers at Uppsala University, Uppsala, Sweden, and King's College London, published in *The Journal of Clinical Endocrinology & Metabolism.*

Popular Diet May Increase Heart Disease Risk

In a recent finding, eating a diet similar to the Atkins diet—with low carbohydrate intake and more protein intake—was linked to an increased risk for cardiovascular disease in women ages 30 to 49.

Study of data from the Swedish Women's Lifestyle and Health Cohort (43,396 women ages 30 to 49) by researchers at University of Athens, Greece, published in *BMJ*.

The Truth About Calories: New Research Shows Why So Many Americans Are Packing on the Pounds

Marion Nestle, PhD, MPH, Paulette Goddard Professor in the department of nutrition, food studies and public health and professor of sociology at New York University in New York City. She is author of several books, including *What to Eat* (North Point), and recently coauthored, with Malden Nesheim, PhD, *Why Calories Count* (University of California).

More than 60% of Americans are classified as overweight or obese. What's going wrong?

For answers, we spoke with Marion Nestle, PhD, MPH, one of the country's leading nutritionists and coauthor of *Why Calories Count*.

•**Instead of focusing on calories, the most popular diets these days focus on eating less of certain food groups such as fats and carbohydrates—or more of foods rich in, say, protein or fiber. Is this a good idea?** Numerous studies have compared popular diets such as Atkins, Ornish, The Zone and South Beach—all of which promote eating one type of food over others or eliminating certain food types. And the studies have concluded that *all* low-calorie diets help people lose weight, regardless of how much protein, fat and carbohydrates are included. Some people do find higher-fat diets, such as Atkins, to be more satisfying, so they aren't so hungry all the time.

•**What's the best way for a person to determine his/her individual daily caloric needs?** "Calorie" is such a widely known term, you might assume that most people would already know their daily caloric requirements. But research suggests there's a widespread "calorie oblivion" in which consumers are clueless about the number of calories they should be eating and how many they actually are eating. A study conducted last year found that only 9% of respondents even came close to estimating the number of calories they should consume each day.

The average number of calories required for healthy living, according to guidelines, is 2,000 to 2,500 calories per day for adult males and 1,800 to 2,300 for adult females.

The formula used to accurately determine an individual's exact calorie requirements is complicated and requires a professional to help calculate. It involves your *basal metabolic rate* (BMR), the heat effects of food and the energy expended in physical activities.

Of course, energy expenditure levels decline with age—by as much as 20% by age 50 and by 30% for those over age 70. Also, men of all ages expend more energy than women, on average, and people with more lean muscle burn more calories doing the same activity than those with more fatty tissues.

•**If it is as simple as counting calories, then why do so many people have such problems maintaining normal body weight?** The truth is, nobody wants to think about calories. They are too abstract. You can't see them, smell them or taste them. You can only see their effects on your weight and waistline. It's impossible to know exactly how many calories are in many foods unless you identify and weigh every ingredient. Plus, Americans have no idea of proper serving sizes.

So it's not very surprising that virtually everyone significantly underestimates the number of calories eaten each day—typically by about 30%, according to research. Even when calorie information is available (for example, on labels or posted at restaurants), people still are shocked to find out that a bagel, for instance, can contain up to 600 calories…and the supersized 64-ounce sodas sold at convenience stores have nearly 800 calories each.

•**What's the best way to figure out how many calories one needs to cut daily to lose weight?** It takes approximately 3,500 extra calories to put on a pound of body fat. So cutting back by 500 calories a day is reasonable and should result in losing about one pound a week—but it varies a lot with individuals. To lose weight, you need to balance your caloric intake with your physical activity…eat more fruits, vegetables and whole grains…eat less meat and dairy (and choose low-fat)…and stay out of the center aisles of supermarkets—that's where junk food is found. To see how well you're doing at maintaining a healthy body weight—or even dropping a few pounds—simply weigh yourself on a household scale. The most successful dieters do that routinely and compensate for small increases by eating less.

•**Why do some people lose weight more easily than others—even when they consume the same number of calories?** Some of it has to do with metabolic rate and some with so-called "spontaneous non-exercise activity," also known as fidgeting, which can account for as much as 100 to 800 calories a day. There are also factors that remain unknown. Studies on overeating demonstrate that all people gain weight if they overeat calories, but some gain a lot more than others.

•**Is that due to genetics?** A genetic propensity to obesity can be a factor—especially when there is food around all the time and it's served in big portions. People must learn to manage that environment to control their weight.

•**Does chewing food slowly help with weight loss?** It might. The research is mixed, but when Chinese researchers recently counted the number of times that obese and lean people chewed their food, they found that those who chewed each bite 40 times before swallowing consumed 12% fewer calories than those who chewed only 15 times. The number of calories burned during the act of chewing is trivial, so it could be that slow eaters simply feel more satisfied than fast eaters or get bored with eating so slowly.

•**What about so-called "calorie-restricted" diets that limit people to, say, 25% fewer calories than the recommended daily intake. Do you consider these diets healthful?** No. Research shows that sustained calorie restriction improves the lives of fruit flies, rats, mice and other animals. But it's not at all clear that it extends human life. The lowest rates of mortality occur among people who have a "normal" *body mass index* (BMI) of 18.5 to 24.9. When a person's BMI is considered "underweight" (less than 18.5), which often occurs in those who are practicing this form of calorie restriction, mortality rates *increase*. This isn't a healthful approach to eating—and it can't be much fun.

•**How can we ensure that we're getting adequate amounts of the various nutrients that we need in our diets?** Unless you restrict many different types of foods, you can take care of your nutrient needs by eating a variety of nonprocessed foods—that is, ones that don't come in packages with "Nutrition Facts" labels. Whole foods contain many different nutrients in varying proportions—and all of them complement each other. Even people who want to, or must, restrict certain foods should vary the foods they do eat.

Common Beverages That Have More Calories Than Junk Food!

A recent study showed that a breakfast smoothie (470 calories) has more calories than a double cheeseburger (450). Also, an average glass of wine (165) has more calories than three mini powdered sugar donuts (157)…one 12-ounce soda (152) is almost the same as a small bag of nacho cheese chips

(150)…and a large sweetened iced tea (291) is higher in calories than a small order of fries (271).

Study by researchers at Purdue University, West Lafayette, Indiana, reported in *Glamour* and Glamour.com.

Just *One* Reduced-Calorie Meal a Day May Keep Pounds Away

Eating just one reduced-calorie meal a day could be an effective dieting technique. When, over a two-week period, participants ate a 200-calorie lunch, then ate whatever they wanted at other meals, they consumed an average of 250 fewer calories per day, which resulted in a loss of 1.1 pounds.

David A. Levitsky, PhD, professor of psychology and nutritional sciences, Cornell University, Ithaca, New York, and leader of a study published in *Appetite*.

Dieting? Why It's Best to Have Dessert with Breakfast

Have dessert with breakfast when dieting to boost your willpower.

Recent finding: Overweight people who ate dessert in the morning had fewer cravings later in the day and were more likely to stick to their diets.

Possible reason: A morning dessert may suppress production of the hunger hormone *ghrelin*.

Try to have a small dessert, such as two ounces of dark chocolate, as part of a 600-calorie breakfast.

Study of nearly 200 people by researchers at Wolfson Medical Center and Tel Aviv University, both in Holon, Israel, published in *Steroids*.

It's True! Chocolate Lovers Weigh Less

A recent study found a five-to-seven-pound difference between people who ate chocolate five times a week, compared with those who didn't eat any.

Study of 1,018 healthy adults, ages 20 to 85, by researchers at University of San Diego, published in *Archives of Internal Medicine*.

Food Swaps: All the Pleasure… None of the Guilt

Dawn Jackson Blatner, RD, a registered dietitian in private practice in Chicago. She is author of *The Flexitarian Diet: The Mostly Vegetarian Way to Lose Weight, Be Healthier, Prevent Disease, and Add Years to Your Life* (McGraw-Hill). She is also the nutrition consultant for the Chicago Cubs and writes a food and nutrition blog for *The Huffington Post. www.Dawn JacksonBlatner.com*

The next time you're craving a less-than-healthful treat, such as a plate of pasta or a bowl of ice cream, don't assume that it's off-limits.

There are plenty of good-for-you cooking and baking swaps that don't significantly alter the food's flavor and texture but will up the nutritional ante and save you calories. *My favorites…*

What to skip: **Bread crumbs.**

Try instead: **Seeds.** *Good choices:* Sesame seeds, chopped pumpkin seeds or chopped sunflower seeds.

Most bread crumbs are nothing more than refined white bread. Coating fish or chicken with seeds delivers more flavor and a satisfying crunch along with healthful types of fat, satiating fiber and protein.

What to do: Sprinkle the seeds on a plate, and dip your fish or chicken in to coat it.

What to skip: **Butter.**

Try instead: **Avocado.**

When baking, you can substitute some—but not all—of the butter with puréed avocado. Try a ratio of 70% butter to 30% avocado at first. If the taste and texture are good, work toward a half-and-half mixture. Avocado has the same creamy texture as artery-clogging butter, but one tablespoon of avocado purée has far fewer calories (23 versus 100 calories) and is a good source of heart-healthy fat and fiber, cancer-fighting folate and blood pressure–regulating potassium.

***What to skip:* Pasta.**

***Try instead:* Spaghetti squash.**

A typical plate of pasta (about three cups) can easily cost you 600 calories, and that's before topping it with butter, oil or sauce. One cup (a more appropriate serving size) of spaghetti squash "pasta" has just 42 calories plus fiber and 9% of your daily requirement of vitamin C.

What to do: Slice a spaghetti squash in half, remove the seeds and place flesh side down on a baking sheet with a little water in it. Bake at 375°F for 40 minutes. Remove it from the oven, then with an oven mitt still on to protect your hands from the hot squash, run a fork through the flesh lengthwise—it will naturally separate into pastalike strands. Top it with a marinara sauce and lean ground turkey or chicken.

***What to skip:* Sour cream.**

***Try instead:* Greek yogurt.**

Greek yogurt is essentially yogurt that has been strained to remove much of the liquid and sugar. It has twice as much protein as regular yogurt (for almost the same amount of calories) and less than half as much sugar as regular yogurt. In fact, a six-ounce cup of nonfat Greek yogurt packs in 18 grams (g) of protein—almost as much as a small chicken breast! Greek yogurt has a similar look, taste and consistency to sour cream, which is typically high in saturated fat and low in protein.

***What to skip:* White or brown rice.**

***Try instead:* Cauliflower "rice."**

One cup of medium-grain white rice contains 242 calories with very little fiber (brown rice has 218 calories). The same amount of cauliflower has only 14 calories, plus 22% of your daily need for vitamin K, which helps with blood clotting and bone health. As a cruciferous vegetable, cauliflower is thought to help protect against cancer of the mouth, pharynx, larynx, esophagus and stomach.

To make cauliflower "rice": Pulse fresh, raw cauliflower in a food processor until it resembles rice grains. Briefly steam or sauté it.

***What to skip:* Ice cream.**

***Try instead:* Frozen banana soft serve.**

Frozen bananas, when thoroughly blended, achieve a creamy, ice cream–like consistency.

What to do: Chop a ripe banana into small pieces and freeze in a plastic bag (spread pieces out flat to avoid a large frozen clump.) The colder the bananas are, the thicker the dessert. Toss frozen pieces in a blender, and add a splash of low-fat milk. Start the blender on low, then do high pulses until the mixture is thick and creamy.

You'll save hundreds of calories (a medium banana has 105 calories…a cup of premium ice cream has 369), plus it's fat-free and rich in potassium and vitamins C and B-6. Toss in antioxidant-rich blueberries. Or sprinkle with cinnamon—it helps to stabilize blood sugar… unsweetened cocoa powder, which is low in calories…or chopped walnuts to add a dose of heart-friendly fats.

Can You Be Fit and Fat?

C. Noel Bairey-Merz, MD, professor of medicine, Women's Guild Chair in Women's Health and director of the Barbra Streisand Women's Heart Center and the Preventive and Rehabilitative Cardiac Center at Cedars-Sinai Medical Center, Los Angeles. She is chair of the National Institutes of Health–sponsored Women's Ischemic Syndrome Evaluation.

Good news if you're overweight—you still can be fit, as long as you're physically active.

THE RESEARCH

Researchers at Dallas's Cooper Institute recruited 22,000 men in a study designed to look at the relationship between body fat and fitness. First, they measured the participants' body compositions and gave them treadmill tests. Then they tracked the men for eight years.

Result: Men who were overweight but fit were two times less likely to have died than those who were lean but unfit. Those who were lean and exercised were healthier than fat people who exercised, but the difference was small.

Being fit does not require high-level athletic training—it simply means that you should aim for a cumulative 30 minutes of moderate-intensity daily activity such as walking.

Other studies, including one that utilized findings from the long-term Harvard Nurses' Health Study, had similar results. In the Harvard study, published in *The New England Journal of Medicine*, those who were physically active had lower death rates—regardless of whether they were lean, overweight or obese—than lean people who exercised less than one hour a week.

Also, studies have shown that people who are thin, whether or not they exercise, tend to have higher mortality rates than those who are heavy. This is partly because very lean people lack the physical reserves to keep them going during times of stress, such as when they have a serious illness. Additional research shows that overweight heart attack patients tend to have better outcomes, including higher survival rates, than patients who are not overweight.

THE GOAL THAT COUNTS

If you have to pick a single health goal, it's generally better to get fit than to lose weight. *To begin…*

•**Check your fitness.** If you are fit, you should be able to walk 30 minutes without stopping…and climb a flight of stairs without gasping for breath. If you can't, you'll want to see a doctor and ease into an exercise plan. Heart attacks often occur when sedentary people suddenly face a cardiovascular stressor, such as overly vigorous exercise.

•**Exercise consistently.** You do not need hard-core exercise to stay fit. The duration of exercise—and doing it regularly—is more important.

•**Exercise without workouts.** You can achieve fitness as you go about your day. *Examples…*

•Walk. Every hour of walking can increase your life expectancy by two hours. At work, take the stairs instead of the elevator…go for a walking break instead of a coffee break…make walking tours part of your vacations.

•Squeeze in exercise. Bring a resistance band to work, and do short workouts at your desk. At home, stand up rather than sit when watching TV or talking on the phone. When reaching for something on a high shelf, stretch up on your toes to get it. Squat down to pick up something low.

Get More from Your Workouts! Leading Fitness Guru Tells How

Tom Holland, CPT, a certified personal trainer and exercise physiologist located in Darien, Connecticut. *Women's Health* magazine named him one of the top 10 fitness professionals in the country. He is author of *Beat the Gym* (William Morrow) and *The Marathon Method* (Fair Winds).

Anyone who sticks to an exercise program knows that the commitment involves a lot of time and, in some cases, money if you belong to a gym or fitness center.

Trap: All too often, people follow ineffective routines that cause them to waste their time and money. *Here are my secrets for getting the most from your workout…**

Secret #1: **Do the right amount of cardio.** If you don't do enough cardiovascular exercise, you won't get the maximum benefits. But, if you do too much, you'll increase your risk for injury. So how much cardio should you do?

My advice: Follow this simple formula—for every pound you weigh, do one minute of cardio each week. For example, if you weigh 150 pounds, you should do 150 minutes of

*Consult your doctor before beginning or significantly changing an exercise regimen.

cardio (incorporating a variety of exercises) per week.

Because women in general will end up doing less cardio than men with this formula, it's wise for them to spend more time doing strength training (see below). Genetically, women have less muscle than men, and as a woman ages, the preservation of lean muscle becomes vital.

Secret #2: **Understand what the programs on cardio machines really mean.** Let's say that you opt for a "fat-burning" program on a treadmill because you want to lose (or maintain) body weight. Based on the "calories burned from fat" percentages given with these programs, it appears that you will burn more fat if you work out at a lower intensity. But that's not true. Because these fat-burning calculations are based on percentages—not total calories burned—they are easily misunderstood. *For example…*

Easier Workout: A 30-minute cardiovascular workout at an easy intensity burns 250 calories and 20 grams (g) of fat. With this workout, 72% of calories burned are from fat.

Intense Workout: A 25-minute intense cardio workout burns 330 calories and 25 g of fat. That's the equivalent of 68% of calories burned from fat.

The easier workout burns a larger percentage of fat, *but the more intense workout burns more fat and calories in total—*and in less time. The more calories and fat burned, the more weight you will lose.

Secret #3: **Skip the heart-rate zone charts.** The most widely used maximum heart-rate zones are calculated by subtracting the exerciser's age from 220. For example, if you are age 50, your maximum heart rate would be 170 (220 − 50 = 170). This is supposed to be the highest heart rate you should reach during a workout. However, research has found that in most cases the number is too low.

My advice: Whether you choose to use a treadmill, StairMaster, stationary bike, elliptical trainer, etc., simply focus on *varying the intensity of your workout.* Use a scale of one to 10, with 10 being the most intense. On some days do a lower intensity workout (around a

five or six), and on other days bring it up to a seven or eight. Mix in short intervals (10 to 60 seconds) of high-intensity (nine to 10) exercise.

Important: Always get your doctor's approval before following any maximum heart-rate formulas.

Secret #4: **Do not slight your strength-training regimen.** Many individuals complain that, as they age, they eat and exercise the same amount but still gain weight. One of the main causes of this is loss of muscle mass. The more muscle mass you have, the more calories you burn. Strength training preserves and even increases muscle mass, keeping metabolism at a high level.

Strength training also increases bone density and functional strength and preserves joint health.

My advice: As with cardio workouts, vary your strength-training routines. Some days use machines, others use dumbbells or stretch bands. You also could do squats, push-ups and lunges. If you have trouble incorporating separate strength-training sessions into your workout, an efficient method is to do circuit training. This approach involves strength exercises with short bursts of cardio in between.

Important: Don't spend too much time on ab crunches. The appearance of abs is largely due to diet. The best way to reduce abdominal fat is with healthful eating and cardio exercise. Spend only 10% of your strength-training sessions on ab exercises. This will *define* the abdomen once you have decreased abdominal fat.

Secret #5: **Start with an exercise you hate.** Because you're less likely to perform exercises you hate, doing them will have a big impact on your body.

My advice: Do just one exercise you don't like at the beginning of a workout—if you put it off until the end of your exercise session, chances are you won't do it. Incorporate one exercise you hate for a few weeks, then switch to another you dislike. This prevents your body from getting used to the hated exercise.

Treadmill Tips

For a better workout on a treadmill or elliptical, use an interval program that alternates high and low intensities. Do not lean on the handrails—that reduces your muscles' workout. And push and pull the handlebars on an elliptical machine to give extra work to your triceps, chest, biceps and back. To work quadriceps and buttocks on an elliptical, exercise in a squatting position. Also keep your chest upright and your back flat, and don't let your knees extend past your toes. Finally, don't sink out of your target heart-rate zone while exercising while reading or watching TV.

Consumer Reports. www.ConsumerReports.org

Lighter Weights Work, Too

Lifting lighter weights more times is just as effective at building muscle as lifting heavy weights.

Recent finding: After 10 weeks of training three times a week, participants who lifted light weights for more repetitions gained as much muscle as people who lifted heavy weights but with fewer repetitions.

Study from McMaster University, Hamilton, Ontario, Canada, published in *Journal of Applied Physiology.*

Boost Your Calorie Burn

Edward Weiss, PhD, an exercise physiologist and assistant professor of nutrition and dietetics at Saint Louis University in Missouri. Dr. Weiss is certified as a health/fitness specialist by the American College of Sports Medicine, has coauthored dozens of research studies on exercise and diet and serves as a peer reviewer for numerous journals.

We all know that a walk can be a nice workout—but if it's too leisurely, it isn't exactly super-duper in terms of the calories it uses up. Given the time crunch we're all under (not to mention the desire to keep weight under control), wouldn't it be great to jack up the calorie burn our walks provide?

Well, that's actually quite simple to do, says Edward Weiss, PhD, an exercise physiologist and associate professor of nutrition and dietetics at Saint Louis University. *Here's how…*

• **Listen to fast music.** You'll subconsciously pick up your pace to match the tempo of the music. This can make a significant difference! For instance, according to the Mayo Clinic, during a one-hour walk, a 160-pound person walking at 2 mph (a 30-minute mile) uses 204 calories…but speeding up to 3.5 mph (a 17-minute mile) burns off 314 calories.

• **Head outdoors.** When you walk on a naturally uneven surface, such as grass, snow or sand, your body has to work harder and thus uses up more calories than on a treadmill. Remember the 160-pound walker in the example above? If she hikes for one hour instead, she increases her calorie expenditure to 438—more than double the amount burned during her 2-mph walk.

Bonus: The change of scenery and extra sunlight can boost your mood, enhancing your enjoyment and encouraging you to walk even farther.

• **Get your arms into the action.** Swinging your arms as you walk can increase the calories used by 5% to 10%, according to research from the University of California, Berkeley.

What to do: With elbows bent at a 90° angle, wrists straight and hands unclenched, let your arms swing from your shoulders in opposition to your legs.

• **Stick with it.** Consistency is key, so you don't want to burn yourself out. "Long, intense workouts like those shown on television may burn a lot of calories in a single session—but they also can make exercise difficult to stick with. You'll burn more calories in the long run if you do a daily 30-minute walk than if you do so much exercise that you quit the routine after the first week or two because it's too demanding," Dr. Weiss said.

• **Buddy up.** Walking with a partner—preferably one who's a bit more fit than you—challenges you to keep up and take your workout to the next level. Also, knowing that your buddy is counting on you to show up makes it less likely that you'll bail out.

Benefits of Running *Slower* and *Less Often*

In a recent finding, people who jogged no more than 20 miles a week at a relatively slow pace of 10 to 11 minutes per mile tended to live longer than people who ran more miles at a faster pace of seven minutes per mile.

Reason: Most of the cardiovascular and health benefits of exercise are obtained in the first 35 to 40 minutes. After that, runners burn more calories and get better at their sport—but there may be long-term negative changes to their hearts.

Good news: People who do any jogging—a little or a lot—have a 19% lower risk of dying within a given time period than those who do not jog at all.

Study of 52,656 people by researchers at Ochsner Medical Center, New Orleans, presented at a recent meeting of the American College of Sports Medicine in San Francisco.

Yoga for Men: Shed Belly Fat, Get a Healthier Heart and Have Better Sex

Timothy McCall, MD, a board-certified internist, medical editor of *Yoga Journal* and author of *Yoga as Medicine* (Bantam). His articles have appeared in dozens of publications, including *The New England Journal of Medicine* and *The Journal of the American Medical Association*. He teaches workshops on yoga as medicine. *www.DrMcCall.com*

About 16 million Americans regularly practice yoga for health and healing—but four out of five are women.

What few people realize: Despite its reputation as a "soft" exercise that's more suited to women, yoga can provide special health benefits for men—even helping to slow the growth of prostate cancer.

What all men need to know…*

BENEFITS FOR MEN

Hundreds of scientific studies on yoga have shown that it can improve health conditions ranging from sleep problems and sinusitis to high blood pressure and schizophrenia. Many of these benefits are particularly relevant for men. *For example, yoga has been shown to…*

• **Slow prostate cancer.** In a study published in *The Journal of Urology*, some men with prostate cancer did 60 minutes daily of gentle yoga (stretching, breathing, meditation, guided imagery and relaxation) for one year while others did not. Those who didn't do yoga had eight times more growth of cancer cells than those who performed yoga daily.

• **Reduce abdominal fat.** Stress is behind many "spare tires," because it triggers high levels of the hormone *cortisol,* which stimulates appetite and overeating and then plays a key role in turning extra calories into extra belly fat. For unknown reasons, visceral fat, which releases disease-causing inflammatory chemicals, is more prevalent in men than in women.

Good news: Yoga reduces cortisol, which helps control abdominal fat.

• **Help prevent a heart attack.** Each year more than 900,000 Americans have heart attacks, and the majority of them are men.

New research: Yoga can reduce many of the heart attack risk factors in people who have heart disease, including high blood pressure, elevated total and LDL "bad" cholesterol and high triglycerides.

• **Improve sexual performance and satisfaction.** In a study of 65 men reported in *The*

*Before starting yoga, check with your doctor if you have severe osteoporosis, problems with your spine or artificial joints—you may be at greater risk for injury. Also consult your doctor if you have any chronic health conditions or recent injuries. If you develop pain, dizziness or other symptoms while doing yoga, stop the pose and tell your teacher immediately.

Journal of Sexual Medicine, practicing yoga an hour a day for three months improved every dimension of sexual functioning—libido... erections...ejaculatory control...satisfaction with performance, intercourse and orgasm...and sexual confidence.

HOW TO START

Many middle-aged men make the mistake of thinking that because yoga looks easy, it is easy. While there are some easy versions that anyone can do, faster, more vigorous yoga styles require a fair degree of fitness and strength to even start. Even though yoga is generally safe for most people of all ages, if you're middle-aged or older and have never practiced yoga, it's best to start with a slower, less vigorous style. *My advice...*

• **Start with a yoga class, not with a book or DVD.** Taking a class led by a skilled yoga teacher is invaluable because the teacher can *look* at you, review what you're doing and guide you to the best injury-free experience. Expert instruction, mindfulness and not pushing too hard during practice can prevent most injuries, such as muscle spasms and ligament strains.

Helpful: If you do use a book or DVD to learn yoga, have a skilled yoga teacher look over your routine now and then to help you correct any mistakes.

• **Find a good class for men.** Ask a male family member, friend or colleague who practices yoga for his recommendation. If you don't know any men who practice yoga, ask a woman, or visit the Web site of the International Association of Yoga Therapists, *www. IAYT.org.*

• **Don't rush results.** Men are often achievement-oriented and want fast results. That's a mistake. Yoga is not about performance or competition—it's about how the poses *help you.*

• **Just do it!** This is the secret to success with yoga—simply doing a yoga routine, 15 to 20 minutes a day, every day.

For overall fitness, yoga is a good complement to cardio exercise and strength training. But remember, yoga also provides stress reduction, flexibility and mental focus.

WHAT YOGA ISN'T...

Misconceptions about yoga can keep some men from trying it. *Yoga is not...*

• **A religion.** It is practiced by Christians, Jews, Muslims and atheists.

• **Just stretching.** Yoga includes stretching poses (*asanas*), as well as other techniques, such as breathing exercises and meditation.

• **A single style of exercise.** There are many styles of yoga, from slow and gentle (such as *Ananda* or *Kripalu*) to fast and vigorous (such as Power Yoga or *Vinyasa Flow*).

The Ultimate Knee Workout: You Can Be Free of Pain *Without* Surgery

Steven P. Weiniger, DC, a postgraduate instructor at Logan College of Chiropractic, outside of St. Louis, Missouri, and a managing partner of BodyZone.com, a national online health information resource and referral directory to chiropractors, physical therapists and Certified Posture Exercise Professionals (CPEPs). He is author of *Stand Taller, Live Longer: An Anti-Aging Strategy* (BodyZone). *www.StandTallerLiveLonger.com*

Most people over age 50 can expect to live longer than their parents or grandparents, but many are doing so *without* their original knees.

What's happening: Knee-replacement procedures, known as *total knee arthroplasty*, have become one of the most commonly performed surgeries in the US.

Each year, more than 600,000 Americans undergo knee replacement to help relieve the pain associated with knee osteoarthritis, rheumatoid arthritis or other forms of degenerative joint disease—and the numbers just keep rising. This trend is due largely to an aging population and obesity, a leading cause of joint damage.

But is surgery really the right solution for all these people? Not necessarily.

Here's the catch: Many people who receive knee replacements could have avoided surgery—along with the risk for infection and the painful weeks of postsurgical rehabilitation—with simple exercises that strengthen the knee and help prevent deterioration of the tendons, ligaments and bones.

A HEALTHY-KNEE PROGRAM

In addition to exercise, normal body weight is critical for long-term knee health. If you're overweight or obese, your knees are subjected to unnecessary force. Research has shown that losing as little as 11 pounds can cut the risk of developing knee arthritis by 50%.

But if you're overweight, losing any amount of weight can help. One study, published in the journal *Arthritis & Rheumatism*, found that every pound of lost weight translates into a four-pound reduction in knee stress—with each and every step.

Why exercise helps: Patients who stretch and strengthen the muscles around the knees have better joint support. There is also an increase in *synovial fluid*, a gel-like substance that keeps the joints moving smoothly.

What's more, exercise increases bone density in these patients and results in better range of motion.

4 MUST-DO EXERCISES

Everyone can benefit from knee exercises. Even if you don't suffer from knee pain now, the following exercises may help prevent problems from developing. People who have received surgery to replace or repair a knee also can benefit by strengthening their muscles to help guard against future knee injuries.

The goal of knee exercises is to work the muscles *around* the joint. These include the quadriceps (muscles on the front of the thigh)... the hamstrings (back of the thigh)...and the muscles in the calves. Strength and flexibility in these areas support the knees and help keep them aligned. Alignment is critical because asymmetry can increase pressure and joint damage.

Perform the following regimen daily—it can be completed in about 15 to 30 minutes. If you have an advanced knee problem due to a condition such as rheumatoid arthritis, your doctor may also prescribe additional exercises that are targeted to address your specific issues.

Important: All of the exercises described in this article should be performed within a range of motion that does *not* cause pain. If a slight strain occurs with the first repetition, that is acceptable, as long as the pain diminishes with subsequent repetitions. If the pain worsens with subsequent repetitions, stop the exercise.

Four must-do knee exercises...

• **Knee-to-Chest Stretch.** This exercise improves flexibility in the lower back, hips and hamstrings. People who do this stretch will notice an opening of their hips, allowing them to stand taller. This improvement in posture is important for reducing knee stress.

Bonus: You can use this movement to diagnose knee problems. If the knee you are bending does not come straight toward your shoulder and stay in line with your foot, you'll know that you have an alignment problem that needs to be corrected.

This knee exercise can be performed in bed if that is more comfortable than doing it on a carpeted floor or on a padded surface.

What to do...

• Lie on your back with your knees bent and your feet flat on the floor (or bed).

• Using both hands, slowly pull one knee toward your chest. (To avoid straining the knee, grip behind it, not on the front.) Go as far as you can without discomfort—you should feel a stretch in your lower back, but no pain. Hold the position for 15 to 30 seconds, then slowly lower the leg.

Perform the movement eight to 12 times. Repeat with the other leg.

• **Knee-to-Chest Stretch with Resistance.** This is similar to the exercise described above, except that you use a latex exercise band (such as Thera-Band) to increase resistance and strengthen muscles.

• Lie on your back with your legs straight. Loop the latex band around the bottom of one foot. Grip the loose ends of the band with both hands.

• Use the band to pull your knee toward your chest. Hold the position for 15 to 30 seconds, then straighten the leg while pushing against the band—hold the band taut to increase resistance.

Do this eight to 12 times, then repeat with the other leg.

•**Standing One-Leg Balance.** This move is more challenging than it looks because you're using the weight of your body to strengthen your legs as well as the "core" muscles in the abdomen. These muscles, which connect the torso and pelvis, help control motions in your whole body. Core weakness is a common cause of asymmetric motion, which often leads to knee problems.

•Stand next to a wall, with your right shoulder just touching the wall.

•Lift your left knee until the foot is off the floor. If you can, keep raising it until the thigh is about parallel to the floor. Make sure that your posture is upright at all times. Hold the position for about 15 seconds, then lower your foot.

Repeat eight to 12 times, then turn around and do the same thing with the other leg.

Important: If you can't balance for 15 seconds—or if you find yourself using the wall for support or moving your arms or dancing around to balance on one foot—your legs are weaker than they should be. This means you should definitely also do the next exercise.

Note: Even if you can easily perform the one-leg balance above, it's a good idea to do the one below to maintain your strength.

•**Standing One-Leg Balance with Resistance.** This is similar to the exercise that's described above, except that you use a latex band to strengthen muscles in the thighs and hamstrings.

•Stand with your right shoulder barely touching a wall. Loop a latex band under your left foot. Hold the loose ends of the band in each hand.

•With your hands at waist level, raise your left foot until your thigh is about parallel to the floor. Shorten the band by wrapping it around your hands to keep some tension on the band.

•While holding the band taut and your knee elevated, slowly press your foot forward, as though you're taking a big step.

Keep the band taut to increase resistance. Maintain your balance!

•Now, pull on the band to return to the bent-knee position.

Repeat eight to 12 times, then turn around and repeat with the other leg.

Exercise with a Cold?

Most people can continue to exercise if they have a cold but no fever. As a general rule, if symptoms are "above the neck" (runny or stuffy nose, sneezing or sore throat), exercising should pose little or no risk. In fact, mild-to-moderate exercise, such as brisk walking, has been shown to help boost immune system function. However, if symptoms are "below the neck" (chest congestion or tightness, hacking cough, upset stomach or diarrhea), workouts should be postponed. Do not exercise if you have flulike symptoms, such as fever, fatigue, nausea or widespread muscle aches.

If you do head out for that brisk walk, "listen" to your body and reduce the intensity and duration if necessary. If your symptoms worsen during your workout, take a break until they subside. A little extra rest is sometimes all that's needed to feel great again.

Cedric Bryant, PhD, chief science officer, American Council on Exercise, San Diego.

Extreme Exercise Hurts the Heart

In a recent finding, marathon runners who were followed over three decades had a 19% lower rate of death than nonrunners—but those who ran more than 20 to 25 miles each week ended up with the same risk as the couch potatoes in the study.

Self-defense: Exercise vigorously for no more than one hour a day.

James O'Keefe, MD, head of preventive cardiology at Mid America Heart Institute at Saint Luke's Health System, Kansas City, Missouri, quoted at Today.com.

5

Natural News

When the Best Medicine Is *Not* a Drug: 5 Supplements That Pack the Punch of Meds

Half of all Americans pop a multivitamin and/or a mineral supplement each day to try to stay healthy. But far fewer people turn to dietary supplements to replace over-the-counter (OTC) and prescription medications that are used for common conditions such as insomnia, allergies, high cholesterol and depression.

Why don't more people use supplements to treat such ailments?

One reason may be because these products are not manufactured by big pharmaceutical companies that heavily advertise their medications. But the supplements described in this article are in many cases just as effective as popular prescription medications—and, in general, the nondrug treatments have far fewer side effects.

Important: Be sure to consult your doctor before trying any of the supplements in this article or substituting any of them for a prescription drug you're taking. You may need to gradually reduce your medication dose, under a doctor's supervision, before transitioning to the supplement. Certain supplements may also interact with other drugs you're taking.

Best medication substitutes…

FOR ALLERGIES

• **Instead of allergy drugs.** Prescription and OTC medications, such as *fexofenadine*

Richard Firshein, DO, director and founder of the Firshein Center for Comprehensive Medicine in New York City, *www.FirsheinCenter.com*. Board-certified in family medicine and a licensed acupuncturist, he is an authority on preventive medicine and medical nutrition. Dr. Firshein is author of several books, including *Reversing Asthma* (Warner), *The Nutraceutical Revolution* (Riverhead) and *The Vitamin Prescription (for Life)* (Xlibris).

(Allegra), *loratadine* (Claritin) and *cetirizine* (Zyrtec), combat allergy symptoms, including a runny nose, itchy eyes and hives, by blocking the effects of histamine, a natural compound that the body releases in response to an allergen. But *quercetin*, a plant-derived flavonoid, goes a step further by *preventing* allergic reactions from happening in the first place.

Scientific evidence: Most studies showing quercetin's overall allergy-fighting effects have been performed in test tubes. However, a 2009 study published in *Allergology International* confirmed that quercetin prevented watery, itchy eyes among 24 human subjects allergic to a type of tree pollen more effectively than a placebo.

Why it's worth considering: People who have allergies may suffer from headaches and cough, and discontinuing the allergy drug can produce a "rebound effect" of worsening allergy symptoms. With quercetin, however, no such rebound effect occurs.

Also, quercetin does not cause the drowsiness that most antihistamines can cause. Side effects of quercetin are rare but may include headache and tingling in the arms and legs.

Typical dosage: Taking 300 milligrams (mg) daily of quercetin for several weeks or months before allergy season begins can help head off symptoms before they take hold.

HIGH CHOLESTEROL

• **Instead of statins.** *Atorvastatin* (Lipitor), *simvastatin* (Zocor) and other statin drugs help block an enzyme in the liver that produces cholesterol, lowering the amount that can seep into the bloodstream and clog arteries. The supplement *Cholestene* (made with high-quality cholesterol-lowering red yeast rice) also performs this function.

Scientific evidence: A 2009 study published in *Annals of Internal Medicine* showed that a red yeast rice supplement reduced cholesterol levels significantly more than a placebo among patients who couldn't tolerate side effects caused by statins. Some research has shown that red yeast rice decreases total cholesterol by as much as 19%.

Why it's worth considering: The severe muscle weakness and pain that can occur in some people who are prescribed a statin (sometimes within the first few months it's taken) is not likely to occur with Cholestene.

The side effects of Cholestene may include heartburn and/or mild dizziness. Any muscle weakness that may, in rare cases, develop with Cholestene tends to be mild. If this occurs, the supplement should be stopped.

Typical dosage: Two tablets twice daily.

FOR DEPRESSION

• **Instead of antidepressants.** The popular antidepressant *fluoxetine* (Prozac) and other *selective serotonin reuptake inhibitors* (SSRIs) …and, to a somewhat lesser extent, the tricyclic antidepressant *imipramine* (Tofranil) help prevent the breakdown of the key mood-boosting brain chemical *serotonin*.

But a naturally occurring amino acid known as *SAM-e* (short for *S-adenosyl methionine*) also helps keep serotonin levels high.

Scientific evidence: A 2002 study published in *The International Journal of Neuropsychopharmacology* showed that SAM-e was just as effective as imipramine at reducing symptoms of mild to moderate depression while producing far fewer side effects.

SAM-e has also been shown to boost the effect of Prozac and other SSRIs when taken in combination. However, be sure to talk to your doctor before using SAM-e in conjunction with any prescription antidepressant.

Why it's worth considering: In addition to its depression-fighting properties, SAM-e also has anti-inflammatory effects and can be used to help relieve arthritis symptoms. Side effects of SAM-e are generally mild but may include stomach upset.

Typical dosage: 400 mg daily.

FOR HEARTBURN

• **Instead of heartburn drugs.** OTC Mylanta, along with OTC or prescription antacids such as *ranitidine* (Zantac) and *famotidine* (Pepcid), neutralize acid that is produced by the stomach.

Aloe and *licorice* do the same thing, but they also coat and soothe the lining of the esophagus, which is susceptible to irritation.

While scant research has focused on these herbs, both have long histories of use in European and Asian medical traditions. I've also found the herbs to be highly effective in my practice.

Why they're worth considering: Prescription and OTC antacids come with a host of unpredictable side effects, including flulike illnesses, constipation, diarrhea, vomiting and skin rash. And prescription antacids, such as *esomeprazole* (Nexium), can raise the risk for fractures if taken for more than a year—they make it more difficult for the body to absorb calcium.

Aloe is mild and generally well tolerated but may cause diarrhea. If taking licorice, it's better to use a slightly processed form called *deglycyrrhizinated licorice* (DGL), which increases the production of protective mucus in the stomach without raising blood pressure and causing water retention as the unprocessed form can.

Typical dosage: Aloe juice, 1 ounce to 2 ounces daily…DGL, 300 mg to 400 mg in chewable form before each meal.

FOR INSOMNIA

• **Instead of sleeping pills.** The naturally occurring amino acid *5-hydroxytryptophan (5-HTP)* plays a key role in the production of serotonin, which not only helps regulate mood but also is a biochemical precursor to the sleep hormone *melatonin*. Some people prefer taking 5-HTP rather than a melatonin supplement because 5-HTP can also have an antidepressant effect.

Scientific evidence: Research published in *Experimental Brain Research* showed that 5-HTP promotes relaxation and deeper sleep.

Be sure to check with a doctor before using 5-HTP with any prescription medication you may be taking—5-HTP may interact with certain drugs.

Why it's worth considering: The sleep drug *zolpidem* (Ambien), while not addictive, can become habit-forming after being taken for prolonged periods. It can also induce amnesia or forgetfulness and trigger sleep-walking.

Side effects from 5-HTP are rare but may include excessive sleepiness and high blood pressure.

Typical dosage: 100 mg to 300 mg, as needed, 30 to 45 minutes before bedtime.

Healthy or Not? The Truth About 6 Popular Food Claims: Answers About Red Wine, Coffee, Bottled Water, More

Robert J. Davis, PhD, an adjunct professor at Emory University Rollins School of Public Health in Atlanta. An award-winning journalist, he is author of *Coffee Is Good for You: The Truth About Diet and Nutrition Claims* (Perigee), *www.CoffeeIsGoodforYouBook.com*, and the founder and editor-in-chief of Everwell.com, a provider of unbiased video content that helps people make informed choices about their health.

With nutritional research, it is often hard to know what you can believe. The latest study makes headlines, often when the research is far from definitive, then the opposite is asserted a few years later.

In general, claims that are supported by multiple high-quality studies—preferably, randomized trials involving thousands of participants—are more likely to be true than those derived from a single (and sometimes industry-funded) source.

What's believable and what's not…*

Claim #1: **Red wine is more healthful than other forms of alcohol.**

• **Limited evidence.** Twenty years ago, it was widely reported that red wine protected the saturated fat–loving French from heart disease. Red wine may have health benefits, but research as a whole suggests it's no better than white wine, beer or other alcoholic beverages.

*Conclusions regarding the nutritional claims in this article are based on a comprehensive review of the literature (including the quality of the actual studies) and what the preponderance of evidence has found.

You may have heard about *resveratrol*, an antioxidant that's present in red wine. It's possible that resveratrol helps prevent heart disease, but this hasn't been proven in long-term studies with humans. Researchers suspect that alcohol itself—not individual components in wine—is the protective factor.

All alcoholic beverages increase HDL, the protective ("good") form of cholesterol. Alcohol also reduces clotting, a cause of heart attacks. People who drink moderately (no more than two daily drinks for men or one for women) generally have less heart disease than nondrinkers.

Claim #2: **Coffee is good for you.**

•**Good evidence.** Despite what you have heard, coffee doesn't damage the heart or increase risk for cancer. In fact, moderate coffee drinkers are less likely to suffer from heart disease, diabetes, stroke and some cancers, such as colorectal and malignancies of the liver, than those who don't drink it. In general, decaffeinated coffee offers the same health benefits.

Caution: A cup of regular or decaf coffee without milk and/or sugar has only a few calories, but some of the "coffee beverages" at Starbucks and other restaurants can have 200 to 400 calories per serving. If you're watching your weight, you might want to drink your coffee black.

Claim #3: **Bottled water is safer than tap water.**

•**Limited evidence.** You might appreciate the taste and convenience of bottled water, but it's not necessarily more healthful than what comes from a tap in most areas of the US. In fact, there's a good chance that the bottled water you're drinking did come from a tap.

American tap water is regulated by the Environmental Protection Agency. It undergoes frequent testing to ensure that it does not contain harmful levels of chemicals, bacteria or other contaminants. Bottled water is regulated by the Food and Drug Administration, which has less stringent standards.

Surprisingly, bottled water is required to be tested only annually, while municipal tap water is sometimes tested several times a day. If you have old pipes in your home, you may want to ask your municipality to test the water for impurities.

Even though bottled-water companies often market their products with images of glaciers or mountain springs, it's usually just tap water that's been filtered to make the water taste or smell better. But, there are some bottled waters that actually come from natural springs.

Note: The chemical *Bisphenol A* (BPA) is not a potential health concern when drinking most brands of bottled water—most bottlers use safer plastics.

Claim #4: **Well-done meat increases cancer risk.**

•**Good evidence.** Meat (red, pork, poultry and, to a lesser extent, fish) that's well-done and/or is cooked at high temperatures—during grilling, panfrying and broiling, for example—produces *heterocyclic amines* (HCAs), chemical compounds that have been linked to a variety of cancers, including breast, prostate and stomach cancers.

The dangers are dose-related—the more well-done meat you eat, the higher your cancer risk. But even small servings of meat can increase the risk. One study, for example, found that men who averaged as little as one-third of an ounce of well-done meat daily had a 42% increased risk for prostate cancer. Lengthy cooking times and high-heat cooking methods produce the most HCAs.

Helpful: Marinate meat in a mixture (containing olive oil, for example) of antioxidant herbs, such as rosemary, thyme and garlic, before cooking to reduce levels of HCAs. Also, precooking meat in the microwave shortens cooking time.

Claim #5: **Olive oil is superior to other oils.**

•**Limited evidence.** Olive oil, used in the Mediterranean diet, is high in monounsaturated fat. For years, researchers have linked this type of fat to cardiovascular benefits.

However, one large study, which compiled data from other studies, found that participants who replaced saturated fat in their diets with polyunsaturated fat (as found in safflower and corn oil, for example) were less likely to suffer heart attacks, but that wasn't the case for those who consumed monounsaturated fat instead of saturated fat.

This does not mean that olive oil isn't a healthful choice. Both polyunsaturated and monounsaturated fats lower LDL cholesterol and raise protective HDL cholesterol. Both types of fats (and oils) are beneficial—and they're clearly superior to the saturated fat in meats and many processed foods.

Claim #6: **Sea salt is more healthful than other salts.**

• **Limited evidence.** Salt is salt. Both sea salt and table salt consist mainly of sodium and chloride. The only difference is that sea salt is produced by the evaporation of seawater, a process that leaves behind extra minerals, such as copper, magnesium and calcium.

Since the minerals are present only in trace amounts, there's little nutritional advantage to using sea salt. The minerals do add flavor, which means that you might use less salt—helpful for lowering blood pressure. Cutting back on table salt would have the same effect. Most table salt is iodized, but the typical American gets enough iodine from other food sources. So use sea salt if you prefer the taste, but it won't improve your health.

The Superfood You've Never Heard Of: Spirulina Slows Aging and Prevents Chronic Disease

Jennifer Adler, MS, CN, a certified nutritionist, natural foods chef and adjunct faculty member at Bastyr University, Seattle. She is the founder and owner of Passionate Nutrition, a nutrition practice with offices in eight locations in the Puget Sound area, and co-founder of the International Eating Disorders Institute. *www.PassionateNutrition.com*

When you think of a superfood, you probably think of salmon or blueberries—not the algae that floats on the surfaces of lakes, ponds and reservoirs.

But there's a type of blue-green algae that has been used for food and medicine in devel-oping countries for centuries…that NASA has recommended as an ideal food for long-term space missions…that is loaded with health-giving nutrients…and that might be a key component in a diet aimed at staying healthy, reversing chronic disease and slowing the aging process.

That algae is *spirulina*.

Spirulina grows mainly in subtropical and tropical countries, where there is year-round heat and sunlight. It is high in protein (up to 70%), rich in antioxidants and loaded with vitamins and minerals, particularly iron and vitamin B-12. And it has no *cellulose*—the cell wall of green plants—so its nutrients are easy for the body to digest and absorb.

GREEN MEDICINE

Dried into a powder, spirulina can be added to food or taken as a tablet or capsule. And ingested regularly, spirulina can do you a lot of good. *Scientific research shows there are many health problems that spirulina might help prevent or treat…*

• **Anemia.** Researchers from the University of California at Davis studied 40 people age 50 and older who had been diagnosed with *anemia* (iron deficiency), giving them a spirulina supplement every day for three months. The study participants had a steady rise in levels of *hemoglobin*, the iron-carrying component of red blood cells, along with several other factors that indicated increased levels of iron.

• **Weakened immunity.** In the UC Davis study mentioned above, most of the participants ages 61 to 70 also had increases in infection-fighting white blood cells and in an enzyme that is a marker for increased immune activity—in effect, reversing *immunosenescence,* the age-related weakening of the immune system. Immunosenescence is linked not only to a higher risk for infectious diseases such as the flu but also to chronic diseases with an inflammatory component, such as heart disease, Alzheimer's and cancer.

• **Allergies.** Spirulina offers anti-inflammatory properties and can prevent the release of *histamine* and other inflammatory factors that trigger and worsen allergic symptoms. Studies also show that spirulina can boost levels of

IgA, an antibody that defends against allergic reactions. In one study, people with allergies who took spirulina had less nasal discharge, sneezing, nasal congestion and itching.

●**Cataracts and age-related macular degeneration.** Using spirulina can double blood levels of *zeaxanthin*, an antioxidant linked to a reduced risk for cataracts and age-related macular degeneration, reported researchers in *British Medical Journal*.

●**Diabetes.** In several studies, researchers found that adding spirulina to the diets of people with type 2 diabetes significantly decreased blood sugar levels.

Caution: Spirulina has not been approved by the FDA for treating diabetes, so consult your doctor before taking.

●**Lack of endurance.** In a small study, men who took spirulina for one month were able to run more than 30% longer on a treadmill before having to stop because of fatigue, reported Greek researchers in *Medicine & Science in Sports & Exercise*.

●**Heart disease.** Nearly a dozen studies have looked at the effect of spirulina intake on risk factors for heart disease, both in healthy people and people with heart disease. Most of the studies found significant decreases in negative factors (such as LDL cholesterol, total cholesterol, triglycerides, *apolipoprotein B* and blood pressure) and increases in positive factors (such as HDL cholesterol and a*polipoprotein A1*).

IDEAL DOSE

A preventive daily dose of spirulina is one teaspoon. A therapeutic dose, to control or reverse disease, is about one tablespoon.

Spirulina has been on the market for more than a decade, and it's among the substances listed by the FDA as "Generally Recognized as Safe" (GRAS).

Caution: If you have an autoimmune disease, such as multiple sclerosis, rheumatoid arthritis or lupus, talk to your doctor. Spirulina could stimulate the immune system, making the condition worse.

BEST PRODUCTS

Like many products, the quality of spirulina varies. *What to look for…*

●**Clean taste.** Top-quality spirulina tastes fresh. If spirulina tastes fishy or "swampy" or has a lingering aftertaste, it's probably not a good product.

●**Bright color.** Spirulina should have a vibrant, bright blue-green appearance (more green than blue). If spirulina is olive-green, it's probably inferior.

●**Cost.** You get what you pay for—and good spirulina can be somewhat pricey.

Example: Spirulina Pacifica, from Nutrex Hawaii—grown on the Kona coast of Hawaii since 1984 and regarded by many health experts as one of the most nutritious and purest spirulina products on the market—costs $50 for a 16-ounce, 454-gram (g) jar of powder. Store it in the refrigerator.

●**Growing location.** The best spirulina is grown in clean water in a nonindustrialized setting, as far away as possible from an urban, polluted environment. If you can, find out the growing location of the product you're considering buying.

HOW TO ADD IT TO FOOD

There are many ways to include spirulina in your daily diet…

●**Put it in smoothies.** Add between one teaspoon and one tablespoon to any smoothie or shake.

●**Add to juice.** Add one teaspoon or tablespoon to an eight-ounce glass of juice or water, shake it up and drink it.

●**Sprinkle it on food.** Try spirulina popcorn, for instance—a great conversation starter at a potluck. To a bowl of popcorn, add one to two tablespoons of spirulina powder, three to four tablespoons of grated Parmesan cheese, two or three tablespoons of olive oil, one-half teaspoon of salt and one-eighth teaspoon of cayenne pepper.

●**Add it to condiments.** Put one-quarter teaspoon in a small jar of ketchup, barbecue sauce, mustard or salad dressing. This way you'll get a little each time you use these products.

The Vitamin That's Better Than Statins: The Natural Way to Fight Heart Disease

Steven Nissen, MD, chairman of the Robert and Suzanne Tomsich Department of Cardiovascular Medicine at the Cleveland Clinic main campus. He is editor of *Current Cardiology Reports* and senior consulting editor to the *Journal of the American College of Cardiology*. He is also coauthor, with Marc Gillinov, MD, of *Heart 411* (Three Rivers). *www.Heart411Book.com*

Niacin, a B vitamin, has been known as the best way to raise HDL "good" cholesterol, thus helping to reduce risk for heart attacks. But a recent study has called this into question—which has made many patients and doctors wonder just how effective niacin is. *What you need to know…*

NEW CONTROVERSY

A government study, reported in 2011 in *The New England Journal of Medicine*, involved 3,414 patients who were randomly assigned to receive either niacin or a placebo. All of the patients already were taking a cholesterol-lowering statin medication.

The study was stopped early when investigators concluded that patients getting niacin did not have fewer heart attacks or other cardiovascular events, even though they did have increases in HDL. The study, taken in isolation, suggests that increasing HDL with niacin isn't protective.

However, most authorities believe that the study, called AIM-HIGH, was seriously flawed. It involved a relatively small number of patients—the most authoritative cardiovascular studies typically include tens of thousands of patients. Also, patients in the control group were given small amounts of niacin to mimic the side effects of full-dose therapy. This prevented them from knowing they were taking a "placebo," but it could have skewed the results.

This study's findings were sufficiently different from previous research that they have to be viewed with caution. We'll need additional, larger studies to determine how much (if any) benefit patients will get from combining niacin with a statin.

Here's what we do know: Niacin alone is effective at raising HDL and, based upon older studies, probably reduces the risk for heart attack.

A PHARMACOLOGICAL VITAMIN

Most people with undesirable cholesterol are advised to take one of the statin medications, such as *atorvastatin* (Lipitor) or *simvastatin* (Zocor). These medications are very effective at lowering LDL "bad" cholesterol, but they have only a modest effect on HDL.

Niacin works both ways. It increases HDL by 15% to 35%. At the same time, it slightly lowers LDL (by about 10% to 12%) and triglycerides, blood fats that have been loosely linked to heart disease.

Like other B vitamins, niacin (vitamin B-3) is naturally present in foods, such as meats, leafy vegetables, legumes and whole grains. It also is contained in multivitamins and B-complex supplements.

WHEN TO USE IT

Some patients with low HDL who are at moderate risk for heart disease and who don't need statins to lower LDL may be advised to take niacin to reduce their risk. Men with an HDL level substantially below 40 milligrams per deciliter (mg/dL) and women with an HDL below 45 mg/dL might be candidates for treatment. For both men and women, an HDL of 60 mg/dL or higher is ideal.

Important: Niacin is recommended only when these patients have tried, without success, to significantly increase HDL with lifestyle changes.

Examples: Not smoking, regular exercise and eating a healthful diet. When combined, these factors can increase HDL by 10% to 15%. That's enough for some patients—but not for everyone.

Modest amounts of alcohol—no more than two alcoholic beverages a day for men or one alcoholic beverage for women—also have been shown to cause slight increases in HDL.

People who already are taking a statin to reduce LDL may be advised to take niacin to boost HDL. We usually wait for a few months after starting statin therapy before adding niacin because statins slightly increase HDL, which can affect the niacin dose.

Niacin is sometimes used as an alternative treatment for patients who can't tolerate statins (because of muscle pain, for example). Niacin doesn't reduce LDL anywhere near as much as statins, but it can help patients with slightly high LDL who also have low HDL and high triglycerides.

HOW TO USE IT

The standard dose of *nicotinic acid* (the form of niacin used to raise HDL) is 1 gram (g) to 3 g daily. Patients usually are advised to start with the lower dose, increasing it as needed to achieve the recommended HDL level.

In these doses, niacin almost always causes side effects. The main one is flushing, in which the skin (often on the face) reddens and feels hot. Flushing can last anywhere from a few minutes to several hours. It usually becomes less bothersome after patients have taken niacin for several weeks or months.

Other side effects may include an upset stomach, headache or, in rare cases, liver damage. Patients who take niacin or other medications for cholesterol usually are advised to get regular blood tests.

Over-the-counter (OTC) niacin supplements may be just as effective as prescription drugs. However, supplements are more loosely regulated than medications—it's difficult to know if the OTC product that you are taking has the amount of niacin listed on the label. But whether you get it OTC or by prescription, *don't take high-dose niacin without a doctor's supervision.*

TO REDUCE FLUSHING

To alleviate this common side effect, I recommend the following...

•**Use extended-release niacin, such as prescription Niaspan.** This is the only form of niacin I prefer because it causes somewhat less flushing than immediate-release niacin.

Warning: Do not take any product labeled "no flush niacin"—these products do not raise HDL at all.

•**Take it at bedtime.** You still will experience flushing, but you probably will sleep through it.

Also helpful: Don't drink alcohol within an hour of taking niacin. It increases the intensity of flushing.

•**Take one aspirin, wait an hour and then take niacin.** It's an effective way to reduce flushing.

Important: Take an 81-milligram (mg) to 325-mg regular aspirin. Be aware that enteric-coated forms will reduce the antiflushing benefit. Aspirin can cause bleeding and stomach ulcers, so always check with your doctor.

Grab a Handful of Pistachios for Better Heart Health

Pistachios are high in mono- and poly-unsaturated fats...low in saturated fats... and a good source of *phytosterols*, which help reduce LDL "bad" cholesterol and prevent plaque buildup in arteries.

Bonus: One ounce of pistachios provides 3 grams (g) of fiber and about as much protein as an egg. They also are a good source of *lutein* and *zeaxathin*, antioxidants that promote good vision.

Jill Nussinow, MS, RD, a dietitian in Santa Rosa, California, quoted in *Vegetarian Times. www.Vegetarian Times.com*

Peanuts Pack Protein

Peanuts (a legume) contain more protein than tree nuts, and just as much as fish, poultry and red meat, ounce for ounce.

Also: Peanuts contain healthy B vitamins, such as folate...cholesterol-lowering *phytosterols*...*phytochemicals*, such as *arginine*, that help relax blood vessels...and heart-healthy *resveratrol*.

Other key nutrients in peanuts: Vitamin E, magnesium, iron, copper and potassium.

University of California, Berkeley Wellness Letter. www.BerkeleyWellness.com

Good-for-Your-Heart Snack Food

Plain popcorn has twice as many *polyphenols* as fruit. Polyphenols are antioxidants found in plants that help counter the damaging effects of free radicals. They help guard against heart disease and other health problems.

Study on antioxidants in popcorn by researchers at University of Scranton, Pennsylvania, presented at the American Chemical Society's annual meeting, San Diego.

Berries Lower Heart Attack Risk

In a recent study of 93,600 women, those who consumed more than three servings of strawberries or blueberries per week had a 34% lower risk for heart attack compared with those who rarely ate these berries.

Theory: Berries are rich in antioxidant *anthocyanins*, which have been shown to help regulate blood pressure and improve blood vessel function.

For heart health: Eat a handful of fresh or frozen berries a few times a week.

Eric Rimm, ScD, associate professor of epidemiology and nutrition, Harvard School of Public Health, Boston.

Sesame Oil Blend Lowers Blood Pressure

In a study of 300 people (average age 57) with mild to moderately high blood pressure, those who added about one ounce of a blend of sesame oil and rice oil to their meals daily had average blood pressure drops of 14 points *systolic* (top number) and 11 points *diastolic* (bottom number). This was almost as much as blood pressure dropped in those taking the blood pressure drug *nifedipine* (Procardia).

Theory: The antioxidants and fatty acids contained in these oils may have a blood pressure–lowering effect.

The blend of oils used in the study is not commercially available, but you could make your own 50/50 mix.

Devarajan Sankar, MD, PhD, researcher, Fukuoka University Chikushi Hospital, Chikushino, Japan.

Butter vs. Margarine

Tub and spray margarines are healthier for you than butter.

But: Avoid stick margarines, which are high in partially hydrogenated vegetable oil (a trans fat). Trans fats raise LDL "bad" cholesterol and promote heart disease.

Nutrition Action Healthletter. www.CSPInet.org/NAH

Vitamin C Reduces Blood Pressure

In one recent study, about 500 milligrams (mg) of vitamin C taken daily for eight weeks reduced *systolic* pressure—the more important top number—by 3.84 millimeters of mercury (mm Hg)…and by 4.85 mm Hg in patients with hypertension. The dose is well below the daily limit of 2,000 mg.

Edgar Miller III, MD, PhD, associate professor of medicine and epidemiology at Johns Hopkins University School of Medicine, Baltimore, and senior author of an analysis of 29 studies, published in *American Journal of Clinical Nutrition*.

Lower Blood Pressure with Weight Training

In a recent study, middle-aged men with hypertension stopped their medication and lowered their *systolic*, *diastolic* and mean blood pressure by 16, 12 and 13 millimeters of mercury (mm Hg), respectively, through weight training three times a week for 12 weeks. Weight lifting directly improves nervous system function, and in this study, the men's blood pressure stayed low for four weeks after they stopped weight training.

Study by researchers at Federal University of São Paulo, Brazil, published in *The Journal of Strength and Conditioning Research*.

Quiet Mind = Healthy Heart

A recent study of patients with heart disease, funded by the National Institutes of Health, found that practicing *transcendental meditation* (TM) regularly decreased risk for heart attack and stroke by 48%. TM produces a state of restful awareness—a settled mind in a settled body. The technique must be taught—there is a standard seven-step course that takes about 10 hours over six days. Once learned, TM should be practiced for 20 minutes twice a day. To find a certified TM instructor, go to *www.TM.org*.

Joan-Ellen Macredis, ND, a naturopathic physician and licensed acupuncturist who is based in Stamford, Connecticut.

5 Surprising Foods to Help You Live Longer

Bonnie Taub-Dix, RD, a registered dietitian and owner of BTD Nutrition Consultants located in New York City. A nationally recognized nutrition expert and author of *Read It Before You Eat It* (Plume), she has advised patients on the best ways to control diabetes for more than three decades. *www.BonnieTaubDix.com*

Whether your blood sugar (glucose) levels are normal and you want to keep them that way…or you have diabetes and glucose control is your mantra… it is smart to eat a well-balanced diet to help keep your glucose readings healthy. In fact, maintaining healthy glucose levels may even help you live longer by avoiding diabetes—one of the leading causes of death in the US.

Most people already know that cinnamon is an excellent choice for blood sugar control. Consuming just one-half teaspoon to three teaspoons per day can reduce glucose levels by up to 24%. Cinnamon is great on cereals, vegetables, cottage cheese and snacks (think fresh apple slices sprinkled with cinnamon).

Other smart food choices…*

GLUCOSE-CONTROLLING FOOD #1: BLACK BEANS

Beans, in general, are the most underrated food in the supermarket.

Beans are high in protein as well as soluble and insoluble fiber. Soluble fiber helps you feel fuller longer, and insoluble fiber helps prevent constipation. Beans also break down slowly during digestion, which means more stable blood sugar levels.

Black beans, are particularly healthful because of their especially high fiber content. For example, one cup of cooked black beans contains 15 grams (g) of fiber, while a cup of pink beans has just 9 g.

Bonus: Beans protect the heart by lowering cholesterol and reducing damage from free radicals. For example, one study showed

*If you take diabetes medication, consult your doctor before making significant changes to your diet—drug dosages may need to be adjusted.

that you can lower your total and LDL ("bad") cholesterol by about 8% simply by eating one-half cup of cooked pinto beans every day.

Helpful: To shorten cooking times, use canned beans instead of dried beans. They are equally nutritious, and you can reduce the sodium in salted canned beans by about 40% by rinsing them.

Another healthful way to use beans: Hummus. In the Middle East, people eat this chickpea (garbanzo bean) spread as often as Americans eat bread. It is much healthier than bread because it contains both protein and olive oil—important for slowing the absorption of carbohydrate sugars and preventing blood sugar "spikes."

Hummus is a good weight-loss dish because it is high in fiber (about 15 g per cup) as well as protein (about 19 g). Ample amounts of protein and fiber allow you to satisfy your appetite with smaller portions of food.

Hummus is made with mashed chickpeas, tahini (a sesame seed paste), lemon juice, garlic, salt and a little olive oil. Stick to the serving size on the label, which is typically two to four tablespoons.

GLUCOSE-CONTROLLING FOOD #2:
COCOA

The flavanols in cocoa are potent antioxidants that not only fight heart disease but also help guard against diabetes. In recent studies, cocoa improved insulin sensitivity, the body's ability to transport sugar out of the bloodstream. It's wise for people with diabetes or high blood sugar to choose unsweetened cocoa and add a small amount of sugar or sugar substitute.

Cinnamon hot cocoa combines two glucose-controlling ingredients in one delicious recipe.

To prepare: Mix one-quarter cup of baking cocoa, one tablespoon of sugar (or Truvia to taste) and a pinch of salt. Gradually add one-quarter cup of boiling water and blend well. Add one cup of skim or 1% low-fat milk and a cinnamon stick. While stirring occasionally, heat on low for 10 minutes. Remove the cinnamon stick and enjoy!

GLUCOSE-CONTROLLING FOOD #3:
DATES

These little fruits are sweet enough to qualify as dessert but have more antioxidants per serving than oranges, grapes and even broccoli. The antioxidants can help prevent heart disease as well as neuropathy—nerve damage that frequently occurs in people who have diabetes.

A single serving (for example, seven deglet noor dates) has 4 g of fiber for better blood sugar management.

Be careful: Seven dates also have 140 calories and 32 g of sugar, so this must be added to your total daily carbohydrate intake, especially if you have diabetes. Dates, in general, have a low glycemic index, so they don't spike glucose levels. Medjool dates, however, are not an ideal choice. They have significantly more sugar and calories per serving than deglet noor dates.

GLUCOSE-CONTROLLING FOOD #4:
SARDINES

Many people know about the heart-healthy benefits of cold-water fish, such as salmon and mackerel. An analysis of studies involving hundreds of thousands of adults found that just one to two fish servings a week reduced the risk of dying from heart disease by more than one-third.

What is less well-known is that the high concentration of omega-3 fatty acids in cold-water fish also helps prevent a too-rapid rise in blood sugar. Besides being low on the glycemic index, fish contains protein, which blunts blood sugar levels.

Best for helping to prevent high blood sugar: In addition to salmon and mackerel, sardines are an excellent choice (when canned with bones, they also are a good source of calcium). Tuna, to a somewhat lesser extent, offers omega-3s (choose canned light—albacore white has higher levels of mercury). Also avoid large fish, such as king mackerel and swordfish, which have more mercury than smaller fish. Aim for a 3.5-ounce serving two or three times a week.

GLUCOSE-CONTROLLING FOOD #5:
ALMONDS

High in fiber, protein and beneficial fats, nuts can significantly lower glucose levels. In fact, women who ate a one-ounce serving of nuts at least five times a week were nearly 30% less likely to develop diabetes than women who rarely or never ate nuts, according to one study.

The poly- and monounsaturated fats in nuts improve the body's ability to use insulin. Nuts also help with cholesterol control—important because diabetes increases risk for heart disease.

All nuts are beneficial, but almonds contain more fiber, calcium and protein than most nuts (and are best for blood sugar control). Walnuts are highest in antioxidants and omega-3 fatty acids. Avoid salted nuts—they have too much sodium.

Excellent way to add nuts to your diet: Nut butters. Almost everyone likes peanut butter, and it is healthier than you might think. Like butters made from almonds, cashews or other nuts, the fats it contains are mostly monounsaturated, which are good for the heart. The fiber in nut butters (about 1 g to 2 g per tablespoon, depending on the nut) can help lower blood sugar.

Good choice for blood sugar control: One serving (one to two tablespoons) of almond butter (rich in potassium, vitamin E and calcium) several times a week. Look for nut butters that have a short list of ingredients—they are the most nutritious.

A SIMPLE BLOOD SUGAR BUSTER

Taking two tablespoons of apple-cider vinegar in eight ounces of water with meals or before bedtime can slow the absorption of sugar into the blood—vinegar helps to block the digestive enzymes that change carbs to sugar.

Harness the Power of Cocoa

Mark A. Stengler, NMD, a naturopathic medical doctor and leading authority on the practice of alternative and integrated medicine. Dr. Stengler is author of the *Health Revelations* newsletter, author of *The Natural Physician's Healing Therapies* (Bottom Line Books), founder and medical director of the Stengler Center for Integrative Medicine in Encinitas, California, and adjunct associate clinical professor at the National College of Natural Medicine in Portland, Oregon. *http://MarkStengler.com*

We see headlines all the time that tout the health benefits of chocolate. As a result, many people take that as a free pass to eat way more chocolate than is good for them.

What the headlines don't tell you: Chocolate, as most of us know it, is full of sugar and fat. It is chocolate's main ingredient—cocoa—that is good for you. So, put down those commercially made chocolate bars and learn how to get the real health benefits of this incredible ingredient, even if you are already a die-hard "chocoholic."

The first thing you need to know: The health claims are real. Research from the Karolinska Institute in Stockholm found that those who ate chocolate two or more times per week following a heart attack reduced their risk of dying from cardiovascular disease by 66%. And Spanish researchers recently found that consumption of chocolate reduced inflammation, a major component of many degenerative diseases.

THE BEST OF COCOA

Cocoa is made from the dried seed of the cacao tree, which is loaded with natural compounds called flavanols, plant nutrients with antioxidant properties. These flavanols can prevent fatlike substances in the bloodstream from clogging your arteries, have anti-inflammatory properties and can help the body produce nitric oxide, a chemical that dilates and relaxes arteries, improving circulation and reducing blood pressure.

Best: Whenever possible, use organic raw cocoa powder as an ingredient in your recipes.

It consists of 100% cocoa. Even though pure cocoa has a bitter taste, you need only use a small amount at a time to get the health benefits—and then the bitterness won't come through.

Examples: Add one to two tablespoons of cocoa powder to shakes and smoothies...or sprinkle it on fruit. Use it as a spice on vegetables and in salad dressings and soups. Of course, you can bake with it—and use it in a surprising variety of savory recipes, including chili, sauces and meat dishes.

Several companies make excellent organic raw cocoa powder products (raw cocoa and cocoa powder are the same thing).

Brands to try: Sunfood Chocolate Cacao Powder, 16 ounces for $18.95* (888-729-3663, *www.Sunfood.com*) and Navitas Naturals Raw Cacao Powder, eight ounces for $9.99 (888-645-4282, *www.NavitasNaturals.com*).

This type of cocoa is different from the type you buy in the baking section of the supermarket. Raw cocoa is cold-pressed (not cooked) to remove the fat. It provides more than three times as much antioxidant flavanols as cocoa that is produced from fermented and roasted beans.

Second best: Know how to choose the most healthful chocolate bar. Organic dark chocolate—with a minimum of chemicals, processing and added sugar—is better for you than milk chocolate or white chocolate (both have no cocoa at all). Look for bars that have 60% to 85% cocoa. Choose those with the fewest ingredients. (Many chocolate bars have a host of unpronounceable ingredients and preservatives.) Choose bars with cocoa solids or cocoa mass as the first ingredient, not sugar. Avoid those with milk, which negates the effects of the flavanols.

Brand to try: Scharffen Berger Extra Dark Chocolate or Bittersweet Chocolate, $4.95 for a three-ounce bar (866-972-6879, *www.Scharffenberger.com*), available at specialty grocery stores, such as Whole Foods. Savor a square or two of high-quality chocolate several times a week (no more)—and you will safely reap the benefits of cocoa.

*Prices subject to change.

IF YOU ARE A "CHOCOHOLIC"...

For some people, eating chocolate can trigger addiction-like behavior. If you are one of those people who can't stop at one or two squares, it might be best to avoid chocolate bars altogether and instead use cocoa powder. Or there are supplements with cocoa flavanols that offer the cardiovascular benefits of cocoa without the calories or the fat of a chocolate bar.

Example: ReserveAge Resveratrol Ultimate Antioxidant, which has 100 milligrams (mg) of a standardized cocoa extract per capsule (800-553-1896, *www.Reserveage.com*).

Good News for Beer Drinkers

The dried hops blossoms used in brewing beer have multiple health benefits. Hops contains two substances that can help regulate blood sugar, lower cholesterol, boost weight loss, relieve pain and fight inflammation. If you're not a beer drinker, talk to your doctor about taking a hops extract and the dosage that's right for you.

Chris Meletis, ND, executive director of Institute for Healthy Aging, Beaverton, Oregon. He is also author of *Enhancing Fertility: A Couple's Guide to Natural Approaches* (Read How You Want).

Simple Spice Prevents Diabetes

When given a curcumin extract (1.5 grams [g] daily) for nine months, study participants at risk for diabetes did not develop the disease. Among a similar group given a placebo, 16.4% developed the disease. Curcumin is the main compound in turmeric, a spice in curry powders and mustards.

Study of 240 people by researchers at Srinakharinwirot University, Bangkok, Thailand, published in *Tufts University Health & Nutrition Letter.*

The Power of Optimism

Each "unit increase" in optimism—the general expectation that more good than bad will happen in the future—decreased stroke risk by 9% over the next two years in a recent study. And each unit increase in sense of purpose reduced heart attack risk by 27% over the same period.

Possible reason: People with purpose and a positive outlook may take better care of themselves.

The late Christopher Peterson, PhD, professor of psychology, University of Michigan, Ann Arbor, and coauthor of two studies published in *Stroke*.

Lower Stroke Risk with a Cup of This—or This...

Coffee and green tea were both found in a new 13-year study of more than 83,000 adults (ages 45 to 74) to lower stroke risk.

Findings: People who drank at least one cup of coffee daily had about a 20% lower risk for stroke than those who seldom drank coffee. For green tea drinkers, a 14% reduction in stroke risk was found in those who consumed two to three cups daily versus those who rarely drank it.

A possible explanation: Coffee's glucose-lowering *chlorogenic acid* and green tea's antioxidant, anti-inflammatory *catechins* may provide the protective effect.

Yoshihiro Kokubo, MD, PhD, chief doctor, department of preventive cardiology, National Cerebral and Cardiovascular Center, Osaka, Japan.

Load Up on Citrus

Citrus fruit contains antioxidants called *flavanones*, which have anti-inflammatory and neuroprotective properties.

Recent finding: Women who ate the most citrus had 19% fewer *ischemic* strokes (the most common kind) than women who ate the least. The effect is likely to be similar in men.

Recommended: Two servings of citrus a day—preferably whole fruit. Juice also has flavanones but is high in calories and has little fiber.

Kathryn Rexrode, MD, MPH, associate professor of medicine at Harvard Medical School and associate physician at Brigham and Women's Hospital, both in Boston. She is senior author of a study of 69,622 women published in *Stroke*.

Tomato Sauce to the Rescue

People with the highest blood levels of the antioxidant *lycopene* had 55% lower risk for stroke than people with the lowest levels, according to a recent study. Lycopene is found in tomatoes, red peppers, carrots, papaya and watermelon. It is even more concentrated in cooked tomato products, such as tomato sauce.

Rafael Alexander Ortiz, MD, director of the Center for Stroke and Neuro-Endovascular Surgery, Lenox Hill Hospital, New York City.

More Protection from Coffee

In a recent finding, people who drank more than four cups of caffeinated coffee daily had about a 50% lower risk for death from cancer of the mouth or throat than people who never or only occasionally drank coffee. People who drank one cup every day had about a 25% reduced risk. Decaf coffee may also have some protective effect.

Janet Hildebrand, MPH, an epidemiologist with the American Cancer Society, Atlanta, and leader of a study of the coffee-drinking habits of nearly one million men and women, published in *American Journal of Epidemiology*.

Herb Relieves Cancer-Related Fatigue

In a recent study, cancer patients who took a 2,000-milligram (mg) supplement of *American ginseng* twice a day for eight weeks experienced a 20-point improvement on a 100-point fatigue scale. Those taking a placebo showed only a 10-point improvement.

Study of 340 patients with cancer-related fatigue from 40 community medical centers by researchers at Mayo Clinic, Rochester, Minnesota, presented at the American Society of Clinical Oncology's annual meeting.

Natural Cures for Arthritis: Research Shows They Really Work!

Steven Ehrlich, NMD, a naturopathic physician and founder of Solutions Acupuncture & Naturopathic Medicine in Phoenix. He has spent the last decade using natural medicine to treat chronic pain and illness. Dr. Ehrlich has also taught naturopathic techniques to both conventional and alternative medicine practitioners.

If you have arthritis, you may have shied away from natural medicine in the past because you didn't think that it would relieve your pain.

After all, there is no rigorous scientific evidence to back up these remedies, right?

Wrong.

Now: While it's true that many nondrug approaches for pain relief have been based primarily on their thousands of years of use by Asian, Indian and other traditional cultures, there is now an impressive body of scientific evidence that makes natural medicine a smarter choice than ever before for many arthritis sufferers. (These therapies have been studied most often for osteoarthritis but may also relieve pain due to rheumatoid arthritis. Check with your doctor.)

PAIN RELIEF WITH LESS RISK

Millions of Americans depend on high-dose pain relievers that cause side effects, including gastrointestinal upset or bleeding, in up to 60% of patients.

What you may not realize is that some natural therapies, which are far less likely to cause side effects, work just as well as the powerful pain-relieving drugs that are so commonly used for arthritis.

Many Americans take *glucosamine* (a dietary supplement that stimulates production of key components in cartilage) to help fight arthritis. However, arthritis pain symptoms improve only slightly or moderately in some patients—even when they take glucosamine sulfate, the most widely studied form of this supplement. (Research currently indicates that adding *chondroitin*, a supplement that's derived from shark or bovine cartilage or produced synthetically, isn't necessarily helpful for arthritis).

In my practice, I often recommend the following regimen (with or without glucosamine) to relieve arthritis pain—the typical arthritis patient might start with curcumin and fish oil (pain relief should begin within one week to a month). *Ginger can be added if more pain relief is needed…**

• **Curcumin.** A chemical compound in the spice turmeric, it helps inhibit inflammatory enzymes and reduces joint pain without the gastrointestinal side effects that often occur with aspirin and related drugs.

Scientific evidence: A study published in *The Journal of Alternative and Complementary Medicine* found that curcumin reduced arthritis pain and improved knee function about as well as *ibuprofen* (Motrin).

How to use curcumin: To obtain a concentrated dose of the active ingredient, try curcumin supplement capsules with a standardized *curcuminoid complex* (rather than kitchen turmeric, which would be difficult to consume in therapeutic amounts). Follow the label instructions—typically taking it three times daily during flare-ups. Between

*Consult with a doctor before trying these supplements—especially if you have a chronic condition or take medication. To find a physician near you with experience in prescribing botanical medicines, consult the American Association of Naturopathic Physicians at *www.Naturopathic.org*.

episodes of arthritis, you can take half this amount to prevent inflammation.

Caution: Curcumin can inhibit the ability of blood to clot. Use this supplement only under a doctor's supervision, particularly if you're also taking a blood-thinning medication such as *warfarin* (Coumadin) or aspirin.

• **Fish oil.** The omega-3 fatty acids in fish oil supplements increase the body's production of inhibitory *prostaglandins*, substances that prevent inflammation.

Scientific evidence: A study published in *Arthritis & Rheumatism* discovered that some arthritis patients who took fish oil improved so much that they were able to discontinue their use of conventional painkillers.

How to use fish oil: The amount of omega-3s found in dietary sources is insufficient for pain relief. Use a fish oil supplement—doses range from about 2,000 milligrams (mg) to 6,000 mg daily. Start with the lower dose, then gradually increase it until you notice improvement in pain and stiffness (the rate at which the dose is increased depends on the patient). If you take more than 2,000 mg of fish oil daily, you should be monitored by a physician—this supplement has a blood-thinning effect.

• **Ginger.** This spice has compounds that inhibit the effects of *cyclooxygenase*, an inflammatory enzyme.

Scientific evidence: A study that looked at 261 patients with knee arthritis discovered that those who took ginger supplements had less pain—and required fewer painkillers—than those taking placebos.

How to use ginger: Ginger spice will not provide enough of the active ingredient, so use a ginger supplement. The standard dose is 250 mg taken four times daily. Talk to your doctor before trying ginger—especially if it's used with a blood-thinning drug, curcumin and/or fish oil. Ginger can increase the risk for bleeding in some patients.

OTHER THERAPIES THAT HELP

The following approaches can accelerate and increase the pain-relieving effects offered by the supplements described earlier...

• **Balance Method acupuncture.** Acupuncture can be extremely effective because it increases the flow of blood and oxygen into painful areas while accelerating the removal of inflammatory chemicals.

Scientific evidence: A study that involved more than 3,500 patients with chronic hip and/or knee arthritis found that those given acupuncture (in addition to conventional care, including doctor visits and use of painkillers) had fewer symptoms and a better quality of life than those given only conventional treatments.

My advice: Consider trying Balance Method acupuncture. Rather than inserting needles above or near the painful areas (as occurs with standard acupuncture), the practitioner will use points on your arms or legs that "remotely" affect the joints. It seems to be more effective than standard acupuncture.

How acupuncture is used: Virtually all arthritis patients improve by the end of the third session—some after the first session. Most practitioners advise an initial series of 12 to 15 sessions, given once or twice a week, followed by monthly "tune-ups."

• **Meditation.** Meditation works in part by lowering levels of stress hormones. This decreases inflammation as well as the perception of pain. Patients who do meditation may still have pain, but it won't bother them as much as it did before.

Scientific evidence: In a study reported at an American College of Rheumatology meeting, arthritis patients who did meditation for 45 minutes each day, six days a week for six months had an 11% decrease in symptoms, a 46% reduction in *erythrocyte sedimentation rate* (a measure of inflammation) and a 33% reduction in psychological stress.

How meditation is used: Practice meditation for five to 10 minutes, once or twice a day—even during symptom-free periods.

Also helpful: "Tapping meditation," which incorporates elements of acupressure as the patient taps different areas of his/her body. It has been especially helpful for arthritis patients in my practice. Most health practitioners who recommend meditation can teach you how to perform tapping meditation.

•**Yoga.** Any form of exercise is helpful for arthritis as long as it doesn't put excessive pressure on the joints. Yoga is particularly beneficial because it gently stretches and strengthens the muscles. It also increases the movement of synovial (lubricating) fluid across bone surfaces.

Scientific evidence: Researchers recently found that patients with knee osteoarthritis who took a weekly yoga class had improvements in pain and mobility after just eight weeks.

How yoga is used: The yoga that's practiced in many health clubs and yoga studios may be too aggressive for patients who have arthritis. Start with a beginner's class, preferably one that's taught by an instructor who specializes in therapeutic yoga, which is designed to treat specific medical conditions. To find a yoga instructor who specializes in therapeutic yoga, consult the International Association of Yoga Therapists at *www.IAYT.org.*

Natural Help for Rheumatoid Arthritis

Harris H. McIlwain, MD, a board-certified rheumatologist, founder of the Tampa Medical Group and former chair of the Florida Osteoporosis Board. He is author, with Debra Fulghum Bruce, PhD, of *Diet for a Pain-Free Life* (Marlowe & Company).

The majority of rheumatoid arthritis (RA) sufferers eventually require prescription drugs, but everyone with the condition can benefit from natural approaches that reduce inflammation, pain and stiffness.

This blending of natural and conventional treatments often allows patients to reduce the frequency and doses of medications, which is important for curbing side effects, such as dizziness and increased risk for infection and, in rare cases, cancer.

Best natural treatments for RA…

•**Get regular low-impact exercise.** Any form of low-impact exercise, in particular walking and swimming, will increase joint lubrication and reduce inflammation, which helps people with RA perform daily tasks, such as dressing, without pain. Exercise will also increase *endorphins,* the body's natural painkillers.

•**Give up meat.** Studies have shown that RA sufferers who don't eat meat have less pain and greater mobility.

Reason: Beef (even organic, grass-fed beef) and other meats, such as lamb and pork, increase levels of arachidonic acid, a fatty acid that's transformed into inflammatory, pain-signaling compounds.

What we recommend for our RA patients: Avoid all meat (beef, lamb and pork), and replace it with other sources of protein—for example, from plants (such as legumes, including beans, and whole grains), poultry and fish. Fish is particularly good because the omega-3 fatty acids reduce inflammation. A fish oil supplement, which contains omega-3 fatty acids, also is sometimes advised. Consult your doctor for dosage.

•**Identify and manage food sensitivities.** The evidence isn't conclusive, but it appears that many people with RA are sensitive to one or more foods. For example, one of my patients has an immediate RA flare-up when he eats foods that contain corn syrup.

Helpful: An elimination diet to identify which food(s) you might be sensitive to.

How it works: Your doctor will advise you to stop eating certain foods, such as corn syrup, dairy, citrus, tomatoes, wheat and corn, for one to two weeks. Then, you reintroduce the foods, one at a time, over a period of weeks to see whether symptoms reappear.

•**Use anti-inflammatory spices,** such as ginger, turmeric, cumin, cinnamon, cardamom and garlic. They contain potent antioxidants that can reduce inflammation even in the amounts typically used in cooking.

DON'T NEGLECT CONVENTIONAL CARE

Natural approaches can help control RA, but unless you have an unusually mild case, you'll want to combine them with medication for the best results. That's because natural treatments help reduce pain and swelling but don't stop joint damage, which can become permanent if not promptly treated with medications.

Joint damage can be detected earliest with the use of imaging tests, such as an X-ray, MRI or ultrasound.

Important: Start medications right away if imaging tests show any degree of "destructive" arthritis. The natural approaches outlined earlier can be continued while you are undergoing drug therapy.

What's new: In March 2012, the American College of Rheumatology announced updated guidelines that call for the aggressive treatment of RA. In the past, doctors were more likely to use "mild" medications, such as *ibuprofen* (Motrin) and other *nonsteroidal anti-inflammatory drugs* (NSAIDs), before escalating to more potent drugs. The problem is, NSAIDs are usually good at relieving pain and stiffness, but they won't prevent joint damage. *Also needed…*

•**DMARDs.** Most people who experience severe and frequent RA symptoms should take one or more *disease-modifying anti-rheumatic drugs* (DMARDs), such as *methotrexate* (Rheumatrex), *hydroxychloroquine* (Plaquenil) or *sulfasalazine* (Azulfidine).

DMARDs, which suppress the immune system, reduce RA flare-ups and reduce risk for serious joint damage. If a DMARD is effective, it is usually continued indefinitely.

Important: DMARDs may make you more susceptible to infection. Other side effects may include nausea, abdominal pain or, rarely, liver damage. Be sure to get the appropriate vaccinations for flu, pneumonia, etc.

•**Biologics.** If you don't get adequate relief from one or more of the DMARDs, your doctor might switch you to a biologic drug. Medications in this class include *etanercept* (Enbrel), *adalimumab* (Humira) and others, and can actually delay or prevent joint damage.

These meds also increase the risk for infection, so ask your doctor about prevention strategies. In rare cases, these drugs can increase cancer risk as well.

4 Surprising Cures for Joint Pain

Jamison Starbuck, ND, a naturopathic physician in family practice and a guest lecturer at the University of Montana, both in Missoula. She is past president of the American Association of Naturopathic Physicians and a contributing editor to *The Alternative Advisor: The Complete Guide to Natural Therapies and Alternative Treatments* (Time Life). She is also a featured columnist in *Bottom Line/Health, www.BottomLinePublications.com.*

Exercise has so many health benefits that it's hard to understand why everyone isn't doing it on a regular basis. But what if it hurts to exercise? If you have joint pain, you may wonder whether exercise is good for you or even possible to do. In conventional medicine, joint pain is treated with synthetic medication, such as *naproxen* (Aleve) or *ibuprofen* (Motrin). These medicines usually are effective for short-term use, but they do not cure the problem, and they can harm your stomach.

For these reasons, I prefer to start with natural methods, which usually do a terrific job at reducing—and sometimes even eliminating—joint pain. *My favorite remedies for joint pain—roughly in order of importance…*

Remedy #1: **Get serious about stress reduction.** An increasing body of evidence now shows that stress reduction really does reduce pain. You may have noticed this through your own experiences—for example, perhaps pain lessens while you are on vacation or during a relaxed weekend. Three stress-reducing methods that I highly recommend are yoga, meditation and massage. I advise patients to engage in one or more of these practices on a regular basis. An ideal stress-reducing regimen might include daily meditation, yoga three times a week and/or massage once a week.

Remedy #2: **Investigate food allergies.** Consuming food to which you are allergic can significantly increase pain. Wheat, soy and peanuts are common food allergens. To start, eliminate suspected foods to see if your symptoms improve and then reappear when the foods are reintroduced. Or ask a naturopathic physician to test you for food allergies using a blood test for *IGG immunoglobulins* (antibodies reach high levels with food allergies). If food allergies don't seem to be contributing to your pain, you may want to consider giving up animal-based foods, including meat. Animal-based foods are generally inflammatory, which means that they contain a high percentage of arachidonic acids that can promote and aggravate pain. Keep in mind that you can often get more inflammation-fighting omega-3s from plant sources, such as flaxseed and walnuts, than from fish.

Remedy #3: **Try Boswellia serrata.** This herbal remedy contains nutrients that reduce inflammation and improve both acute and chronic joint pain.

Typical dose: 300 milligrams (mg) three times a day for four weeks, then 300 mg one to three times a day if needed for pain. It's generally safe, but check with your doctor before trying this remedy.

Remedy #4: **Get some mild exercise.** Many people mistakenly assume that exercise will damage joints and increase pain, but studies show that regular mild exercise, such as swimming, yoga or pilates, promotes circulation within joints and will reduce inflammation and pain. Work out up to the point of pain, then stop and repeat the exercise the next day—ideally, until you can do the activity for an hour a day, six days a week. If you have joint degeneration or severe pain, check with your doctor first.

Keep Your Body Limber with Vitamin D

People ages 70 to 79 with the highest levels of vitamin D were the least likely to have trouble walking and climbing stairs.

Reason: The vitamin repairs muscle, which helps maintain strength.

Denise Houston, PhD, RD, assistant professor, department of gerontology and geriatric medicine, Wake Forest School of Medicine, Winston-Salem, North Carolina, and author of a study of 2,099 people, published in *Journal of Gerontology: Medical Sciences.*

Say Good-Bye to Back Pain

Julie Silver, MD, a physiatrist and assistant professor in the department of physical medicine and rehabilitation at Harvard Medical School, Boston, where she is chief editor of books at Harvard Health Publications. She is author of *Say Goodbye to Back Pain! How to Handle Flare-Ups, Injuries and Everyday Back Health* (Chicken Soup for the Soul).

More than 80% of Americans will experience at least one episode of low-back pain during their lives. *Here's how to relieve the pain and prevent it from coming back…*

•**Act quickly.** Most back pain is caused by damage to muscle fibers.

Frequent causes: Overuse, repetitive motions (a type of overuse) or anxiety, tension or stress. The damage is accompanied by the release of substances that constrict blood vessels and reduce the oxygenation of tissues. Treating the pain can interrupt this chemical cascade. Take an over-the-counter anti-inflammatory medication such as ibuprofen. For mild pain, take 400 milligrams (mg)—you can treat more severe pain with 800 mg, but always talk to your doctor first.

Also helpful: Moist heat from a hot shower or bath. Or you can apply a cold pack to the area for about 20 minutes several times a day. Heat and cold both can be helpful. Use the one that seems to work best for you.

•**Keep moving even when it hurts.** Relaxing and contracting muscles with normal movements—walking, turning, climbing stairs, etc.—will increase blood flow and help the muscles relax.

Caution: I do not recommend exercise if you have severe pain…a flare-up of *sciatica* (nerve pain that typically travels down the leg)…or pain from a traumatic injury such as a sprained back. You'll want to relax and let things settle down before resuming normal activities. See your doctor if the pain persists for more than a few days or the pain is getting worse instead of better.

•**Treat depression.** The more that your pain limits your daily activities, the more likely you are to be depressed. Your doctor can refer you to a mental health professional. Studies show that patients who manage their emotions in a healthy way experience less pain.

•**Change position every 15 minutes.** People who spend hours in the same position are more likely to have back pain than those who move around. If you're in front of a computer all day, get up and walk every 15 minutes.

•**Lighten your load.** I see a lot of patients with "teacher bag syndrome," pain in the middle or lower back that's caused by carrying a heavy bag on one side of the body. You can lighten your load or increase your core strength (see below). Preferably, do both.

•**Strengthen your core.** Strong abdominal muscles are essential for treating and preventing back pain.

Self-test: Lie on your back with your arms folded across your chest. Try to sit up without using your arms. If you can't do it, you don't have enough core strength and should do curl-ups or other core-strengthening exercises.

To do a curl-up: Lie on your back with your knees bent and your hands under the small of your back. Slowly curl your head and shoulders a few inches off the floor. Pause for a moment, then lower back down. Repeat eight to 12 times.

•**Check your shoes.** If you wear the same pair of shoes often and they are more than six months old, the heels and soles are probably showing signs of wear. The uneven surfaces force your body to compensate, which puts unnecessary stress on your back. Get new shoes or have the bottoms replaced every six months or so.

Skip the Steroids for Disk Damage

Steroid injections were no more effective than a placebo for *umbosacral radiculopathy*, a common condition caused by damage to the disks between vertebrae. Steroids did provide short-term pain relief, but after one month, pain had decreased whether or not steroids were used. Exercise speeds recovery—ask your doctor what activities are best for you.

Study of 84 adults by researchers at Johns Hopkins University School of Medicine, Baltimore, published in *Annals of Internal Medicine.*

Foods That Fight Pain: Some Work Even Better Than Drugs

David Grotto, RD, founder and president of Nutrition Housecall, LLC, a consulting firm based in Chicago that provides nutrition communications, lecturing and consulting services as well as personalized, at-home dietary services. He is author of *The Best Things You Can Eat: For Everything from Aches to Zzzz* (Da Capo). www.DavidGrotto.com

Many of us turn to medications to relieve pain. But research has shown that you can help decrease specific types of pain—and avoid the side effects of drugs—just by choosing the right foods. Here, the common causes of pain and the foods that can help. *Unless otherwise noted, aim to eat the recommended foods daily...*

OSTEOARTHRITIS

Osteoarthritis causes pain and inflammation in the joints.

Best foods: Bing cherries, ginger, avocado oil and soybean oil.

A study in *The Journal of Nutrition* found that men and women who supplemented their diets with Bing cherries (about two cups of cherries throughout the day) had an 18% to 25% drop in *C-reactive protein,* a sign of inflammation. Bing cherries contain *flavonoids,* plant-based compounds with antioxidant properties that lower inflammation.

Ginger also offers potent anti-inflammatory agents that can reduce joint pain. A double-blind, placebo-controlled study reported that 63% of people who consumed ginger daily had less knee pain when walking or standing. I recommend one to two teaspoons of ground fresh ginger every day.

Avocado oil and soybean oil contain *avocado soybean unsaponifiables* (ASUs), which reduce inflammation and cartilage damage.

RHEUMATOID ARTHRITIS

This autoimmune disease causes *systemic* inflammation—your joints, your heart and even your lungs may be affected.

Best foods: Fish and vitamin C–rich foods.

The omega-3 fatty acids in fish increase the body's production of *inhibitory prostaglandins,* substances with anti-inflammatory effects. A recent study found that some patients who consumed fish oil supplements improved so much that they were able to discontinue aspirin, ibuprofen and similar medications.

Ideally, it's best to eat two to three servings of fish a week. Or take a daily fish oil supplement. The usual dose is 1,000 milligrams (mg) to 3,000 mg. Be sure to work with a qualified health professional to determine what supplement regimen is right for you.

Foods rich in vitamin C (citrus fruits, berries, red bell peppers) are effective analgesics because they help decrease joint inflammation. These foods also help protect and repair joint cartilage. A study in *American Journal of Nutrition* found that patients who ate the most vitamin C–rich fruits had 25% lower risk for inflammation.

GOUT

Gout is a form of arthritis that causes severe joint pain that can last for days—and that "flares" at unpredictable intervals.

Weight loss—and avoiding refined carbohydrates, such as white bread, commercially prepared baked goods and other processed foods—can help minimize flare-ups. You also should eat foods that reduce *uric acid*, a metabolic by-product that causes gout.

Best foods: Celery and cherries.

Celery contains the chemical compound *3-n-butylphthalide*, which reduces the body's production of uric acid. Celery also reduces inflammation.

Both sweet (Bing) and tart (Montmorency) pie cherries contain flavonoids, although the bulk of science supporting the anti-inflammatory and pain-relieving properties of cherries has been done using tart cherries. (An exception is the study that found that Bing cherries relieve osteoarthritis.) It is hard to find fresh tart cherries, so I recommend dried tart cherries or tart cherry juice.

MIGRAINES

These debilitating headaches are believed to be caused by the contraction and dilation of blood vessels in the brain.

Best foods: Oats, coffee and tea.

Oats are high in magnesium, a mineral that helps reduce painful muscle spasms—including those in the muscles that line the arteries. In one study, researchers found that people who took 600 mg of magnesium daily had a 41.6% reduction in the number of migraines over a 12-week period, compared with only a 15.8% reduction in those who took a placebo.

You can get plenty of magnesium by eating high-magnesium foods. A small bowl of cooked oat bran (about one cup), for example, provides more than 20% of the daily value. Other high-magnesium foods include oatmeal, almonds, broccoli and pumpkin seeds.

The caffeine in coffee and tea helps relieve migraine pain. The antioxidants in both beverages also are helpful.

Caution: Consuming *too much* caffeine—or abruptly giving it up if you are a regular coffee or tea drinker—can increase the frequency and severity of headaches. Limit yourself to a few cups daily.

MUSCLE PAIN

It usually is caused by tension, overuse or an actual injury (a strain or sprain). Because tendons and ligaments (the tissues that attach muscles to bones) have little circulation, muscle-related pain can be very slow to heal.

Best foods: Tart cherries and rose hip tea.

Eating as few as 20 dried tart cherries can help reduce pain. So can tart cherry juice.

Example: At the Sports and Exercise Science Research Centre at London South Bank University, researchers gave one-ounce servings of tart cherry juice twice daily to athletes who did intense workouts. These athletes regained more of their muscle function more quickly than those who didn't drink the juice. Studies also have shown that the juice can reduce muscle pain after exercise.

Rose hip tea is high in vitamin C, as well as anthcyanins and a substance called *galacto-lipid*—all of which have been shown to combat inflammation and may help ease muscle and joint pain. Have several cups daily.

NERVE PAIN

Inflammation or injury to a nerve can cause a burning, stabbing pain that is difficult to control with medications. Examples of conditions that cause nerve pain include *sciatica* (pain along the sciatic nerve from the lower spine down the back of the leg) and *neuropathy* (nerve damage), a painful complication of diabetes.

Best foods: Turmeric, figs and beans.

Turmeric, a yellow-orange spice that commonly is used in Indian and Asian cooking, is a very effective analgesic. Like ginger, it is an anti-inflammatory that has been shown to reduce pain about as well as ibuprofen—and with none of the side effects.

Both figs and beans—along with whole grains and green leafy vegetables—are rich in B-complex vitamins, which are essential for nerve health. One study, which looked at a form of vitamin B-1, found that patients who took as little as 25 mg four times daily had an improvement in neuropathy. Other B vitamins may have similar effects.

Medical Marijuana Works Better Than Pills for Certain Kinds of Pain

Gregory T. Carter, MD, a physiatrist, clinical professor at the University of Washington, Seattle, and medical director of the Muscular Dystrophy Association Regional Neuromuscular Center in Olympia, Washington. His research interests include the use of cannabis and other treatments for *amyotrophic lateral sclerosis* (ALS). He is senior associate editor for *Muscle & Nerve* and coauthor of *Medical Marijuana 101* (Quick American Archives).

The US government classifies marijuana as a Schedule 1 controlled substance—a dangerous drug with no medical value. Yet the Institute of Medicine, an elite group of scientists and physicians, has concluded that the chemical compounds in marijuana do have therapeutic properties.

The wrangling between scientists and policy makers won't stop anytime soon. Neither will the wrangling between the federal government and the states, 18 of which, along with the District of Columbia, allow the use of medical marijuana and two of which (Colorado and Washington) recently legalized marijuana for recreational use for people over age 21. But marijuana can be an effective medicine for some patients and can be very helpful in reducing pain.

Caution: Always use medical marijuana under a doctor's supervision.

•**Neuropathic pain.** Researchers from the University of California, Davis, reported in *The Journal of Pain* that patients with *neuropathy* (nerve pain) who used *cannabis* (the word scientists prefer to the slang "marijuana") were more likely to have significant relief than those taking a placebo. The chemical compounds in cannabis affect cell receptors in the brain, reducing pain and making it an alternative for patients who are unresponsive to standard drug therapies.

Neuropathy is common in diabetics, HIV patients and those with neuropathic disorders such as Guillain-Barré syndrome (in which the body's immune system attacks the nerves) and Charcot-Marie-Tooth disease (hereditary motor and sensory neuropathy). The prescription medications that currently are used aren't very effective. In my practice, about 90% of neuropathy patients who use cannabis have good results—often with fewer side effects than those who take drugs such as *gabapentin* (Neurontin).

•**Crohn's disease.** This is a potentially life-threatening inflammatory gastrointestinal (GI) disease that often causes severe abdominal pain, nausea and malnutrition, along with unpredictable bouts of diarrhea and/or constipation. Researchers at Tel Aviv University recently reported that 21 of 30 Crohn's patients who used cannabis had less pain and were able to reduce their use of other medications. They also were less likely to require surgery.

The chemical compounds in cannabis reduce not only pain but also inflammation that causes ongoing tissue damage in the intestinal tract. Currently, some Crohn's patients depend on narcotic medications for pain relief. Constipation is a common side effect of these drugs, which is dangerous for Crohn's patients. Cannabis is safer because it doesn't interfere with bowel movements.

● **Arthritis.** The anti-inflammatory and pain-relieving substances in cannabis appear to make it a good choice for different forms of arthritis, including rheumatoid arthritis and osteoarthritis.

● **Weight loss from cancer treatment.** Cancer patients who undergo chemotherapy and/or radiation treatments often suffer from severe weight loss and malnutrition. Cannabis stimulates appetite and can help patients get the calories they need to maintain a normal weight. Also, it's easier for patients with nausea to inhale a medication than to take—and keep down—a pill.

In the past, cannabis often was recommended for nausea, even in the absence of weight loss. It was clearly more effective than the early generation antinausea medication *dronabinol* (Marinol), which is synthesized from cannabis-based compounds. However, newer drugs for nausea, such as *ondansetron* (Zofran), are probably more effective than cannabis.

HOW TO USE IT

I don't recommend that my patients who use cannabis smoke it. Smoking can increase the risk for bronchitis or other respiratory problems. *Better methods…*

● **Vaporization.** When patients use a vaporizer, the active compounds in cannabis "boil" and turn into vapor—the plant material doesn't get hot enough to burn. This eliminates the harsh compounds in the smoke. It also causes less intoxication because the lower temperatures do not activate *tetrahydrocannabinol* (THC), the compound that causes most of the "high" associated with smoking marijuana.

● **Sublingual tincture.** With a prescription, you can buy this form of cannabis at some dispensaries. You also can make it at home by steeping about one ounce of cannabis flowers (available at dispensaries) in six ounces of glycerin for about a week. You put three or four drops under your tongue when you need a dose. It works almost as quickly as vaporized cannabis.

● **Juicing.** You can put a small amount of cannabis in a blender, add your choice of liquids such as milk or juice and drink it as a beverage. The intoxicating effects are reduced because the THC isn't heated.

Some people eat cannabis by adding it to brownies or other prepared foods. Don't do it. The intoxicating effects can be very strong. And because it can take an hour or longer to work, patients may think that they're not getting enough. They consume even more—and wind up getting too much.

HOW MUCH TO TAKE?

Some cannabis dispensaries (and growers) use devices known as *gas chromatographs* to measure the amounts of THC and other compounds in their products. This makes it easier to achieve batch-to-batch consistency. Typically, the cannabis sold by dispensaries has a THC concentration of about 15% to 20%.

Doctors who recommend cannabis usually rely on patient-titrated dosing. This simply means taking a small amount when you need a dose…waiting for about 20 to 30 minutes to see how you feel…and then increasing or decreasing subsequent doses, as needed. Effects typically last one to two hours.

WHAT AND WHERE TO BUY?

Different types of cannabis have markedly different effects. Cannabis that is rich in *cannabidol* (CBD) has fewer psychoactive effects than cannabis with a lot of THC. Patients who want to minimize the intoxicating effects can choose a strain with more CBD.

You can buy marijuana at dispensaries in the states where it is legal. Describe your symptoms to the clerk so that he/she can help you choose the right type of cannabis. If, for example, you have pain that mainly bothers you at night, you probably will want a cannabis that's high in CBD—it will help you fall asleep. Patients with certain conditions where fatigue is a symptom and who need a "lift" might do better with a higher-THC product.

SIDE EFFECTS

Recreational users of marijuana want to get high. For medical patients, this often is the main drawback. I recommend to my patients that they "start low, go slow." Take the lowest possible dose at first. Later, you can increase the dose if you need more relief. If you find that you're getting intoxicated, use less.

Obviously, you shouldn't drive, operate tools or machinery, or perform tasks that require a lot of concentration up to three hours after using cannabis, though residual effects have been reported up to 24 hours after using any medication that impairs mental functions.

Caution: If you have a serious psychiatric illness, such as bipolar disorder or schizophrenia, don't use cannabis without the supervision of a psychiatrist. I don't recommend cannabis for patients with a history of drug and/or alcohol abuse unless they've been referred by an addiction specialist.

Fun Way to Reduce Gallstone Risk *40%*!

A recent study found that regular exercise was associated with a 40% reduced risk for gallstones.

Also: Watch your weight, but do not drastically reduce calories. Both obesity and extreme diets put you at risk for gallstones.

Mayo Clinic Health Letter. www.HealthLetter.Mayo Clinic.com

Good News: Veggies Can Reduce Risk for ALS

In a recent finding, people who ate foods with the most *carotenoids* were 25% less likely to develop the muscle-paralyzing disease *amyotrophic lateral sclerosis* (ALS) than people who ate the least. The most beneficial carotenoids were *beta-carotene*, found

in carrots, squash and sweet potatoes...and *lutein*, in dark green vegetables, such as kale and spinach. Aim for nine servings daily.

Kathryn C. Fitzgerald, a doctoral student in the department of nutrition, Harvard School of Public Health, Boston, and leader of a study that was published online in *Annals of Neurology*.

Powerful Berries Prevent Parkinson's

People who eat blueberries and/or strawberries two or more times a week are nearly 25% less likely to develop Parkinson's disease than people who eat less than one serving a month.

Theory: These berries are rich in *anthocyanins*—antioxidants that reduce inflammation and may prevent brain cell damage. Other fruits high in anthocyanins include blackberries, plums, Concord grapes and raspberries.

Xiang Gao, MD, PhD, assistant professor of medicine at Harvard Medical School and associate epidemiologist at Brigham and Women's Hospital, both in Boston. He is lead author of a study published in *Neurology*.

7 Foods That Make You Smarter

Daniel G. Amen, MD, and Tana Amen, BSN. Dr. Amen is medical director of Amen Clinics, Inc. He is a clinical neuroscientist, psychiatrist, brain-imaging specialist and author of *Use Your Brain to Change Your Age* (Three Rivers). His wife, Tana Amen, is a nutritional expert and neurological intensive care nurse. *www.Amen Clinics.com*

We all know that we need to eat right to keep our minds sharp. But some foods really pack a punch when it comes to memory, learning and other cognitive abilities. *Here, one of America's top brain specialists reveals the seven super brain boosters...*

1. Coconut water. It's high in potassium, a mineral that is critical for brain health. Potassium causes nerve cells to "fire" at the right speed. People who don't get enough potassium tend to have a slower rate of brain activity and may experience confusion and slower reaction times.

Potassium is particularly important if you eat a lot of salt. The body needs to maintain a proper sodium-potassium balance. You should consume roughly twice as much potassium as sodium.

A medium-sized banana has more potassium (about 450 milligrams [mg]) than coconut water (about 250 mg per eight-ounce serving), but bananas also are higher on the glycemic index, a measure of how quickly the food is converted into glucose. The brain works more efficiently when sugars enter the bloodstream gradually rather than "spiking." Coconut water achieves this more readily than bananas.

Recommended: About one cup of coconut water daily. It has a light taste and is low in calories. If you want, you can add it to smoothies or mix it with milk and pour it over breakfast cereals.

2. Blueberries. Sure, blueberries are good for you, but you may not realize just how super rich in inflammation-fighting antioxidants they are. Their *oxygen radical absorbance capacity* (ORAC, a measure of a food's antioxidant ability) is 2,400, compared with 670 for cherries and 483 for pink grapefruit.

Studies at Tufts University showed that animals that had blueberries added to their diet performed better on cognitive tests than those given a standard diet. They also had increased cell growth in the hippocampus, the part of the brain associated with memory.

Recommended: One-half cup daily. If you don't like blueberries, opt for strawberries or acai berries (a purple, slightly tart berry available in many health-food stores).

Or try Concord grape juice. Researchers from the University of Cincinnati tested Concord grape juice versus a placebo beverage on 21 volunteers, average age 76, suffering from mild cognitive impairment. After 16 weeks, those in the grape-juice group scored better on tests of memory than those drinking the placebo. Also, MRI testing showed greater activation in key parts of the brain, suggesting increased blood flow.

3. Sardines. Salmon often is touted as a healthy fish that is high in omega-3 fatty acids, fats that protect the brain as well as the heart and arteries. Sardines are even better. They also contain generous amounts of omega-3s, but because of their small size, they accumulate lower levels of mercury and other toxins than larger fish.

The membranes that surround brain cells require omega-3s for the efficient transmission of signals. A Danish study that looked at the diets of more than 5,000 adults found that those who ate the most fish were more likely to maintain their memory than those who ate the least. Other research has shown that people who eat fish as little as once a week can lower their risk for dementia.

Recommended: At least two to three servings of fish a week. If you prefer salmon to sardines, be sure to buy wild salmon. It contains more omega-3s than farm-raised fish.

Also helpful: Avocados. They're among the best plant sources of omega-3s.

4. Walnuts. All nuts are good for the brain (as long as they are not roasted in oil and covered with salt). Like fish, nuts are rich in omega-3 fatty acids. They're also loaded with vitamin E, which, in some studies, has been shown to slow the progression of Alzheimer's disease. In addition, nuts reduce LDL "bad" cholesterol (important for preventing stroke). Walnuts are particularly good because they have very high levels of omega-3s. Macadamia nuts are another good choice.

Bonus: The Adventist Health Study, conducted by researchers at Loma Linda University, found that people who ate nuts five or more times a week were about half as likely to have a heart attack as those who rarely ate nuts.

Recommended: About one-quarter cup daily. Nuts are higher in calories than most plant foods, so you don't want to eat too many.

5. Sweet potatoes. They are another low-glycemic food that causes only small fluctuations in blood sugar. This can help you to maintain energy and concentration throughout the day. We routinely advise patients to eat sweet potatoes because they satisfy a craving for carbohydrates, and they're also high in beta-carotene and other important antioxidants that keep the brain sharp.

One sweet potato (when you eat the skin) provides more fiber than a bowl of oatmeal. Dietary fiber lowers cholesterol and improves brain circulation.

Recommended: Eat sweet potatoes two to three times a week. If you don't like sweet potatoes, eat yellow squash or spaghetti squash.

6. Green tea. It contains the potent antioxidant *epigallocatechin gallate* that protects brain cells from free radicals caused by air pollution, toxins, a high-fat diet, etc. Green tea also contains compounds that increase levels of *dopamine* in the brain. Dopamine is a neurotransmitter that stimulates the brain's reward and pleasure centers and makes you more motivated to make positive lifestyle choices.

Bonus: A double-blind study that looked at patients with mild cognitive impairment found that an amino acid in green tea, *L-theanine*, improved concentration and energy and reduced anxiety.

Recommended: Two cups daily.

7. Turmeric. The bright yellow color indicates high levels of antioxidants. People who use this spice several times a week have significant reductions in *C-reactive protein*, a substance that indicates inflammation in the brain and/or other tissues.

A study that looked at more than 1,000 elderly people discovered that those who ate curry—which includes generous amounts of turmeric—regularly scored better on mental-status evaluations than those who rarely or never ate it. All spices with bright, deep colors are high in neuroprotective antioxidants.

Examples: Both ginger and cinnamon appear to have brain-protective properties similar to those of turmeric. And sage improves memory.

Recommended: Add one-quarter teaspoon to one-half teaspoon of any of these spices to your food every day.

Olive Oil Boosts Memory

Saturated fat, such as that found in meat and cheese, contributes to declines in memory and cognition—but monounsaturated fat, like that in olive oil, seems to protect the brain.

Recent study: Women over age 65 who ate the most saturated fat were up to 65% more likely to experience cognitive decline over time than those who ate the least. Women who ate the most monounsaturated fat were 44% less likely to decline in verbal-memory scores and 48% less likely to decline in overall cognition.

Olivia I. Okereke, MD, an associate psychiatrist at Brigham and Women's Hospital in Boston, and leader of a study of 6,183 women, published in *Annals of Neurology*.

Get More from Your Salad

Salad dressings made using canola oil and/or olive oil—which contain healthy *monounsaturated fats*—aid in the absorption of a green salad's nutritious *carotenoids*, including *lutein, lycopene, beta-carotene* and *zeaxanthin*. Fat-free dressings have fewer calories, but they don't help with the absorption of essential vitamins and nutrients.

Study by researchers at Purdue University, West Lafayette, Indiana, published in *Molecular Nutrition & Food Research*.

6

Personal & Private

Dating the Second Time Around: Don't Let These Common Fears Hold You Back

If you were married for many years before losing a spouse to death or divorce, the prospect of dating again may seem intimidating. Yet with patience and persistence, you can find a wonderful partner—and enjoy the search in the meantime.

Common fears about dating and how to overcome them…

Fear: **"I'm too old/unattractive."**

Reality: **Age need not be a barrier to meeting someone new**—it even can be an advantage. At this stage in life, you likely have developed many sources of fulfillment aside from romance, such as an established career or hobbies that you are passionate about…as well as clarity about values and what matters most in life. Self-knowledge and the confidence it brings can make you radiant to the opposite sex.

As for attractiveness, you don't need classic good looks to appeal to the opposite sex. Health and vitality are powerful attractors. To project these qualities, get regular exercise. Walk with your spine long and your head high.

You also may want to consult an image consultant or department-store personal shopper to update your style. Whatever your body type, contemporary clothes that fit well will help you project a radiant image—and this goes for men as well as women.

Fear: **"I'll put a profile on a dating Web site, and no one will be interested."**

Sandy Weiner, dating coach, blogger and workshop leader who specializes in helping people over age 40. Based in Stamford, Connecticut, she is chief love officer at LastFirstDate.com, where she has posted many articles about dating in midlife. She hosts the online radio show *Courageous Conversations* at *www.Blog TalkRadio.com.*

Reality: **The 50+ segment is the fastest-growing group on dating Internet sites.** It should be a part of everyone's dating strategy. You can take simple steps to improve your on-line dating success and capture the attention of interesting people. *Keys to success online…*

• **Register with more than one site.** To increase your exposure to people who might be a good fit, start with two sites. One should cast a wide net, such as Match.com or eHarmony.com. The second should be more specialized, such as JDate.com (for Jewish singles), Catholic Mingle.com (for Catholics) or OurTime.com (for people over 50).

• **Show, don't tell.** Don't post a list of interests and adjectives about yourself—everyone does that. To stand out, tell brief stories about those qualities.

Example: Instead of vague phrases such as "love to travel," describe what inspired you about your most recent trip.

Ask friends what they see as your top five characteristics and for vignettes that illustrate them. Incorporate these examples into your profile.

• **Post current photos.** Choose four or five current photos that look like you and that show you at your best. The main profile photo should be a close-up of your face. The others should show you in a variety of poses doing things that you love. If you don't have recent photos, ask a friend to take some.

• **Don't wait to be discovered.** If someone's profile interests you, send him/her a message through the site. This applies to women as well as men—it is perfectly acceptable, and expected, for women to contact men on dating sites.

• **Make your message short, catchy and specific.** Mention one or two things in the profile that made the person stand out for you, such as a warm smile, a clever turn of phrase or a book title.

Don't be discouraged or take it personally if your message doesn't receive a reply—it happens to everyone. Keep viewing profiles and contacting new people who interest you.

Fear: **"I may put myself in danger."**

Reality: **You should take simple, sensible precautions to protect yourself…**

• **Protect your privacy.** Don't use your real name as your screen name—instead, use a hobby or personality trait, such as FilmFan or LoveSailing. Have a separate e-mail address that you use only for online dating messages. Don't give out your phone number until you have built up some rapport and trust via e-mail, and use your cell phone so that the number cannot be easily traced to your home address.

Whether you become acquainted online or through more traditional means such as a friend or a class, choose a public place for your first few dates. Tell others where you will be. Don't get picked up or dropped off at home until you have known the person for a while.

• **Do some checking.** As soon as you know a prospect's full name—which usually is early in the e-mail stage—do an online search to determine whether he has portrayed himself accurately. In addition to searching by name, you can copy his photo into a search engine such as Google Images and perform an image search. By using this technique, I learned early on that someone I had met online had disguised his identity, made up a sob story and asked a number of women for money.

Fear: **"First dates will be awkward."**

Reality: **First dates can be awkward, but they also can be interesting and fun.** Although meeting for coffee is a classic, low-key first date, consider more active options such as visiting a museum or taking a walk downtown. Standing or walking side by side is less awkward than sitting face to face, and your surroundings will provide conversation cues.

In addition to talking about mutual interests, ask lighthearted questions that delve beneath the surface.

Examples: What was your favorite toy when you were growing up? What would you love to do if there were no constraints? What's the best advice anyone ever gave you? If your house were on fire, what's the first thing you would grab to save?

Fear: **"There are a lot of losers out there."**

Reality: **More than any other factor, your attitude has the biggest impact on your satisfaction with dating and your ability to meet compatible people.** Television and other popular media reinforce negative stereotypes of the opposite sex by portraying single men as inept or self-centered and single women as confusing or impossible to please. But these are just caricatures.

The truth: Many men are capable and loving. Many women are straightforward and agreeable.

Assess a person's character by paying attention to the person's actions as well as words. Look for evidence of kindness, respect, integrity, emotional generosity and responsibility.

Examples: Does she show up when she agreed to or keep you waiting and make excuses for being late? How does he treat the staff at a café? Does she put her cell phone away during dates and give you her full attention? When the subject of past relationships comes up, does he dwell on his ex's negative traits?

Fear: **"He/she will want sex right away."**

Reality: **Plenty of people don't mind waiting,** and someone who is right for you will respect your boundaries.

If you are interested in someone but this person is getting more physical than you are comfortable with, express your feelings frankly in a positive, nonjudgmental way.

Examples: "I'm attracted to you, but I want to slow this down"…"I don't have sex with someone this soon, so for now why don't we just kiss and cuddle."

If and when you are ready to have sex, make sure that both of you have been tested for sexually transmitted diseases. Not only is this important for your health, it also is a good gauge of your relationship. If you don't trust each other enough to show each other your test results, you're not ready to have sex.

Bottom line: The biggest obstacle to finding love in midlife or later is staying home. So move those fears aside, and get out there and date.

Online Dating: Avoid These Typical Mistakes

Julie Spira, a dating coach who is publisher and editor in chief of Cyber-Dating Expert, an online dating advice Web site. She is author of *The Perils of Cyber-Dating: Confessions of a Hopeful Romantic Looking for Love Online* (Morgan James). *www.CyberDatingExpert.com*

Each year, online dating Web sites attract more than 40 million Americans, many of them in their 40s, 50s and 60s. In fact, the fastest-growing segment of online daters is people over age 50.

But there are many pitfalls that can get in the way of a successful online dating experience.

How to avoid the most common mistakes…

FLAWED PROFILES

The profile and photos that you post on a dating site will determine whether potential partners take an interest in you.

• **Don't focus on your life story.** Focus instead on what you're looking for in a partner and a relationship and what you enjoy doing. Be specific—for instance, don't just say that you enjoy travel and reading. Give interesting examples of where you like to go and what you like to read.

• **Don't write too much about yourself.** Daters tend to think longer profiles lead to better matches. But longer profiles often are not read at all. Save the nitty-gritty for e-mail correspondence and dates.

• **Don't rule out certain types of people in your profile.** Doing so will make you seem judgmental and negative. Say what you are looking for…and then, later, you can politely turn down (or not respond to) people who don't fit these criteria.

Example: One woman's profile instructed men not to e-mail her if their divorces weren't final or if they were experiencing financial problems. But these instructions sounded so judgmental that it turned off single, financially stable men, too.

• **Don't assume that mentioning your children or grandchildren is a turnoff.** It shows that you are family-oriented, something many potential partners in the over-50 age group find appealing.

•**Don't include suggestive photos.** Posting sexy, revealing photos might seem like a good way to attract a mate, but in my experience, it usually does more harm than good. Such photos are particularly likely to scare off people looking for a relationship, not just a fling. Select photos that make you seem warm, friendly and approachable, not hot and sultry.

Helpful: Include at least one photo that gives some indication of your overall body. Men in particular tend not to respond to potential mates if they cannot see a woman's general shape.

•**Don't include photos of yourself that also include members of the opposite sex.** These tend to significantly reduce responses. They make you seem like someone who isn't ready to settle down.

FAULTY FOLLOW-UP

What not to do when you make contact with potential partners…

•**Don't worry about "chemistry" too much when you exchange e-mails.** It's prudent to exchange a few e-mails with potential partners before meeting or chatting on the phone—just remember that some people don't express themselves well in text. Agree to chat on the phone if the match seems feasible even if you don't feel a spark from the e-mails. If the phone call is enjoyable, agree to meet in person even if that spark is still lacking—sometimes chemistry doesn't appear until couples meet in person.

Example: Jane, 52, thought Mark, 67, was too old for her as they exchanged e-mails and chatted on the phone. But when she met him in person, she found him warm and handsome and much more youthful than she had imagined.

•**Don't provide your home phone number and main e-mail.** You don't want to worry about angry calls or e-mails or, worse, stalking, if you decide not to pursue a relationship. Open an e-mail account and a Google Voice phone number (*www.Google.com/voice*) specifically for online dating.

•**Don't assume that you're in a relationship just because the e-mail exchange has gone well.** Online daters often cultivate several potential relationships to see which turns out best. You might be disappointed if you get your hopes up too soon.

•**Don't discuss prior marriages on a first date.** Prior marriages often come up when people in their 40s or beyond date. But if this comes up on a first date, say, "I wouldn't mind telling you about my marriage if we see each other again, but right now, I want to get to know you." Discussing prior marriages on a first date can be a downer.

•**Don't assume that online dating won't work for you because you don't express yourself well via e-mail.** One of the latest trends in online dating is "meet-ups," where dating-site members gather in person, typically in a bar. Match.com has been particularly active in arranging group events. It's a great option for people who struggle to express themselves in print…and those who prefer low-stress informal gatherings to digging through online profiles and asking people out.

Group events tend to be quite friendly, and the dating sites that sponsor them strive to make them gender balanced and age appropriate. Because the people who attend are looking for partners, the odds of finding a match are a lot better than they normally would be when approaching strangers.

Helpful: RSVP immediately if you get an invitation to a meet-up and wish to attend—they tend to fill up fast.

More from Julie Spira…

Dating Web Sites for Everyone

Dating sites can be divided into two categories—mainstream and niche.

MAINSTREAM SITES

These have the biggest memberships, providing more potential matches.

•**eHarmony** is more of a "matrimonial" dating site—most members are hoping to find a future spouse or long-term partner, not just a fling. New members complete a detailed questionnaire, which eHarmony's computers use to identify potential matches that it suggests to members. It has many members over age 40, making it a great choice for people in this demographic. ($59.95 per month*…$179.70 for six months.) *www.eHarmony.com*

Helpful: Be sure to answer the optional additional questions on eHarmony's questionnaire, not just those required.

•**Match.com** has some members looking to marry and others seeking more casual relationships. Members usually search Match.com's database on their own, although the company sends e-mails suggesting matches as well. ($39.95 per month…$119.94 for six months.) *www.Match.com*

•**Plenty of Fish** is the largest free dating site and is easy to use, but some people complain that the lack of membership fees results in too many ads and unappealing members. (Although a basic account is free, an "upgraded" account that features increased profile visibility and other advantages costs $35.40 for three months…$51 for six months.) *www.PoF.com*

NICHE SITES

These can be useful if you know the specific type of person you seek.

•**Alikewise** is for book lovers. Users can seek potential partners who share their reading preferences. (Free.) *www.Alikewise.com*

•**Christian Mingle,** whose slogan is "Find God's Match for You," includes questions on denomination and frequency of church attendance. It is the largest Christian dating site. ($29.99 per month…$83.94 for six months.) *www.ChristianMingle.com*

•**Date My Pet** is for animal lovers. ($14.95 per month…$39.95 for six months. Free "basic" membership also is available, but it does not allow you to initiate online exchanges, only respond to them.) *www.DateMyPet.com*

•**Fitness Singles** is for people who are in good shape. ($34.95 per month…$89.70 for six months.) *www.FitnessSingles.com*

•**JDate** is the largest of the Jewish dating sites, which also include SawYouatSinai.com—

*Prices subject to change.

a site that focuses on more observant Jews. (JDate is $39.99 per month…$119.94 for six months.) *www.JDate.com*

•**OurTime** is specifically for people over 50. ($19.99 per month…$71.94 for six months.) *www.OurTime.com*

•**VeggieDate** is for vegetarians. (Free two-week trial…$14.95 for six months.) *www.VeggieDate.org*

Have More Fun in Bed! All It Takes Is Some Sexual Intelligence…

Marty Klein, PhD, a licensed marriage and family therapist and certified sex therapist in Palo Alto, California. He is author of seven books, including most recently *Sexual Intelligence: What We Really Want from Sex and How to Get It* (HarperOne). *www.MartyKlein.com*

Are you sexually satisfied? For so many people, sex is more a source of anxiety than pleasure. Instead of bringing them closer to their partners, sex often makes them feel inadequate, perhaps due to concerns about their aging bodies. They look back nostalgically to a time when sex was satisfying and give a sigh, thinking that it's just something else you lose as the years pass.

But things could be very different. What really helps is a bit of intelligence—sexual intelligence. *Here's what that means…*

KEEPING UP WITH CHANGE

On TV and the Internet and in magazines and movies, we are surrounded by youthful, sexy people. Sex is portrayed as mind-blowing, athletic and amazing. We're conditioned to think that's the way all sex is supposed to be.

But as we grow older, our bodies—and our lives—change. Also, factors such as medication use, chronic pain, familiarity with your partner and accumulated resentments can reduce libido during this phase of life.

So it makes sense that sex will be different during middle age and beyond. It may be difficult to adjust expectations. But the way to change your sex life is to change your ideas about sex.

SEXUAL STATIC

It's a given that most people want pleasure and closeness from sex. *But many focus on other things altogether…*

• **How am I doing?** It is very easy to equate sex with performance. This can mean constant self-evaluation. Is my erection as firm as it should be? Will it last? Am I attractive or skillful enough?

• **Is this normal?** People may think, "I like this, but is it morally acceptable?" Unlike most activities they do for enjoyment, they may worry that their tastes in sex show them to be bad or wrong.

With all these anxieties, how much pleasure and closeness are people likely to experience when having sex?

AN INTELLIGENT SOLUTION

To have satisfying sexual experiences, you don't need to be a hotshot in bed. You need a combination of emotional skills and physical awareness, both of which are essential to sexual intelligence.

Partners must be patient and sensitive to each other's feelings and keep any disappointment in perspective.

Physical awareness includes understanding how your own body and your partner's body have changed over time. What are your bodies still capable of doing, and what can't they do anymore? It means knowing what makes you and your partner feel good—where you both like to be touched, how you both enjoy being kissed, what aids are preferred. Sexual intelligence means accommodating these preferences, whenever possible, with good humor.

Important: Remember that emotional skills and physical awareness typically are more central to good sex than sexual technique.

BE IN THE MOMENT

Many people get into the habit of having sex while thinking about something else entirely. This undermines pleasure and intimacy.

Much better: Focus on the physical sensations. What specifically are you feeling in your arms, legs, genitals, fingertips? What do you smell and taste?

Soak up the emotional experience, too. Feel the pleasure, relaxation, excitement and fun. Also feel the closeness to your partner. If you're anxious, worried or rushed, notice that, too, but don't judge or analyze the feeling then. Set it aside to think about or talk about later. Bringing your attention back to the moment is helpful when you start to worry about your performance or appearance or what your partner is thinking. More self-acceptance and less self-criticism often enhances libido.

DON'T BE SHY

For better communication, you must view the person you have sex with as a *partner* rather than as a critic or judge. Since this person is your partner, you shouldn't feel reluctant to ask for what you would like in bed.

Even better: Show your partner how you would like to be touched. And if something feels good, say so (and do it with a whisper—it's sexier).

Take time to discuss your sexual relationship. It may feel awkward at first, but talking about performance anxiety is the best way to get past it. Also, this is the time to discuss with your partner anything new that you would like to try. And, if there is anything that you definitely *don't* want to do again, make this clear. During this discussion, work out details, such as preferred time for sex (some people like the morning, others the night), place and even room temperature. Since initiating sex is a problem for many couples, discuss signals to use when one of you could be in the mood.

WHAT IS SEX, ANYWAY?

Most people consider "sex" to be intercourse. This thinking is unfortunate. There are drawbacks to intercourse that can make it inconvenient, ill-advised or even impossible. It requires an erect penis and lubricated vagina…it's difficult for people with various physical problems…chronic pain can make it uncomfortable…and it's not an effective way to have an orgasm for many women.

Speaking of orgasms—they probably get a good deal more attention than they merit. An orgasm is quite pleasant, but it lasts maybe five seconds during a sexual encounter that might be 20 minutes or more.

Consider that sex can be satisfying *without* intercourse and *without* orgasm. A broader range of physically and emotionally gratifying activities—oral sex, manual stimulation of body parts you may have ignored, watching each other masturbate, etc.—are all options.

SIMPLE QUESTIONS TO ASK

In fact, you can think of sex in the same way you would think of other things you do with your partner. Was it enjoyable? Did you feel close to each other? How can you make it even better next time? In this spirit, you're less likely to worry about success or failure and more likely to appreciate the rich range of experiences sex has to offer.

A couple should consider seeing a sex therapist if either or both have trouble discussing a sexual issue. To find a sex therapist, check with your doctor or consult the American Association of Sexuality Educators, Counselors and Therapists, *www.AASECT.org.*

Working Out Can Bring on the Big O

Debby Herbenick, PhD, MPH, codirector of the Center for Sexual Health Promotion and an associate research scientist in the department of applied health science, Kinsey Institute for Research in Sex, Gender and Reproduction, Indiana University, Bloomington. She also is the author of *Sex Made Easy: Your Awkward Questions Answered* (Running Press) and lead author of a study on exercise-induced orgasm published in *Sexual and Relationship Therapy.*

Most of us have our orgasms in bed… or maybe on the living room floor if we're feeling frisky. But would you have guessed that the gym is a Big-O hot spot? Well, it's surprisingly common! And it has nothing to do with the presence of muscle-bound male personal trainers. Rather, it's because certain types of exercise can trigger orgasms in some women, one recent study has found.

The online survey recruited participants via Web sites related to women's issues, fitness and sexual topics as well as via e-mail. Respondents included 530 women ages 18 to 64, most of whom were married or in a relationship. Exercise-induced orgasms were reported by 124 women (23% of survey respondents)… another 246 (46%) said they experienced exercise-induced sexual pleasure but not orgasm. Do those percentages sound high? The study wasn't designed to measure prevalence specifically, and researchers estimated that prevalence in the general adult female population is closer to 5% to 15%—but perhaps the phenomenon is more common than people realize because those who experience it keep quiet out of embarrassment. Indeed, the majority of orgasmic exercisers in the survey reported feeling self-conscious…though they also reported feeling happy about the experience.

Climax-producing moves: Among women reporting exercise-induced orgasms within the previous 90 days, 51% said the climaxes occurred while they were doing abdominal exercises. Other common triggers included Pilates (32%)…lifting weights (27%)…yoga (20%)…biking/spinning (16%)…running (13%)…and walking/hiking (10%).

What's up down there? Orgasm often is associated with fantasizing, but the orgasmic exercisers reported that they weren't thinking about sex while they were working out. One possible explanation for the phenomenon is that certain exercises work the muscles and stimulate the nerves of the pelvic floor, which in turn can enhance a woman's arousal. (Some men also climax while working out, a topic the researchers are studying currently.)

Intrigued? If you want, experiment with various abdominal exercises, such as crunches and sit-ups, which the survey showed were most commonly associated with exercise-induced orgasm. Participants also mentioned equipment called a captain's chair, which consists of a rack with back support and padded armrests that allow the legs to hang free. To use it, stand with your back pressed against the backrest, forearms on the armrests and hands gripping the handles…support your weight on your forearms as you bend both legs and raise your knees to your chest, keeping your legs together…then lower your feet to the floor...repeat 10 to 15 times. At the least, you'll wind up with fab abs—and maybe you'll get a secret bonus as well.

Spin Cycling Warning: It Can Hurt Your Sex Life!

Leaning too far forward in the bicycle seat puts pressure on genital tissues, possibly causing nerve damage and reduction of sexual sensation, a recent study has shown.

Self-defense: Set the seat so that when you stand next to the bike, the seat is at hip-bone height. And set handlebars at least two to three inches above the post where they attach to the bike. Sit close enough to the handlebars so that your hands rest comfortably on them without forcing your torso forward at more than a 45-degree angle. (This study focused only on women, but previous studies have shown similar effects for men.)

Ruth Zukerman, cofounder, Flywheel indoor cycling studios, New York City, quoted in *Prevention*.

Men, Take Note...

About 75% of men reach orgasm within just two minutes of beginning intercourse. Men who want to take longer should practice Kegel exercises daily for three months to strengthen the pelvic floor muscles.

To do the exercises: Clench the muscles you would use to stop urinating, release, then clench again for a total of 10 seconds.

Men's Journal. www.MensJournal.com

New ED Drug Works *Faster* Than Viagra

The latest erectile dysfunction (ED) drug, *avanafil* (sold as Stendra), is more quickly absorbed than Viagra, Cialis or Levitra, so it can work in as little as 15 minutes. Also, it may be better for men with heart problems who are taking *nitroglycerin*. Avanafil is less likely to cause a dramatic drop in blood pressure.

Peter N. Schlegel, MD, James J. Colt Professor and chairman, department of urology, Weill Medical College of Cornell University, and urologist-in-chief, New York-Presbyterian Hospital, both in New York City.

Trying to Conceive? Skip the Fat

In a recent finding, men whose diets included 37% or more calories from fat or 13% or more calories from saturated fat had 40% lower sperm production and concentration than men who consumed less fat. Further research is needed, but in light of other known dangers of high fat intake, such as cardiovascular disease, men concerned about fertility should moderate their dietary-fat intake.

Jill A. Attaman, MD, a reproductive endocrinologist at Dartmouth-Hitchcock Medical Center, Lebanon, New Hampshire, and leader of a study published online in *Human Reproduction*.

Walnuts Foster Fertility in Men

Eating about one-half cup of walnuts daily boosted sperm quality in healthy young men in a recent study.

Possible reason: Walnuts are the only nuts with significant levels of omega-3 fatty acids, which some studies have linked with better sperm quality.

Twelve-week study of 117 men, ages 21 to 35, by researchers at UCLA Fielding School of Public Health, funded in part by the California Walnut Commission, published online in *Biology of Reproduction*.

Big-Bellied Men Prone to Bedroom and Bathroom Problems

Steven A. Kaplan, MD, a professor of urology and chief of the Institute for Bladder and Prostate Health at Weill Cornell Medical College and director of the Iris Cantor Men's Health Center at NewYork-Presbyterian Hospital/Weill Cornell Medical Center, both in New York City. He is senior author of a study on male obesity and urological health published in *British Journal of Urology International*.

H as the sizzle gone out of your sex life because of your partner's performance problems? Check his belt. If he has been letting it out to make room for an expanding waistline, you may have found the culprit—particularly if he also has been making a lot of trips to the bathroom.

This surprising news comes from a recent study in which researchers set out to examine whether "central obesity" (meaning a large waist circumference) in men was linked to urinary problems. The study included 409 men ages 40 and up who had moderate or severe lower urinary tract symptoms, such as frequent daytime urination, waking during the night to use the bathroom, reduced flow and/or incontinence. The researchers divided the men into three groups based on girth—with the slimmest group having a waist of less than 35 inches...the middle group measuring 35 to 39 inches...and the biggest-bellied group measuring more than 39 inches around the waist.

Findings: The larger-waisted men were significantly more prone to a variety of urinary symptoms. But their problems did not stop there—because researchers discovered that a wide girth also was associated with a significantly increased likelihood of sexual problems. For instance, erectile dysfunction was reported by three-fourths of the men with the largest waists...about half of the men with medium-size waists...and only one-third of those with smaller waists. Ejaculation problems (such as having little or no semen leave the penis) also were most common among the biggest-bellied men and least common among the slimmest.

The connection: Obesity could cause blood flow changes to the pelvis and hormonal alterations that lead to male pelvic dysfunction, affecting both urinary and sexual health.

For the woman who wants to help: Share this encouraging news from the study researchers with your big-bellied man—trimming just 2.5 inches from his waistline may noticeably reduce the frequency of his trips to the bathroom...and significantly improve his success in the bedroom. And as a bonus, it will improve his heart health and metabolic health, too.

Real Relief for Prostate Pain

H. Ballentine Carter, MD, professor of urology and oncology and director of adult urology at Johns Hopkins University School of Medicine, Baltimore. He is an internationally recognized expert in the diagnosis and management of prostate cancer and other male urological disorders. He is coauthor, with Gerald Secor Couzens, of *The Whole Life Prostate Book: Everything That Every Man—at Every Age—Needs to Know About Maintaining Optimal Prostate Health* (Free Press).

A man who goes to his doctor with prostate-related pain will probably be told that he has prostatitis and that he needs an antibiotic for the infection that is assumed to be causing his discomfort.

In most cases, that diagnosis would be wrong. He probably doesn't have an infection, and antibiotics won't make a bit of difference.

Only 5% to 10% of men with prostate-related symptoms have a bacterial infection. Most have what's known as *chronic nonbacterial prostatitis/chronic pelvic pain syndrome* (CP/CPPS). It's a complicated condition that typically causes pain in the perineum (the area between the testicles and the anus) and/or in the penis, testicles and pelvic area.

The pain can be so great—and/or long lasting—that it can significantly interfere with a man's quality of life. *How to ease the pain...*

A COMMON PROBLEM

More than one-third of men 50 years old and older suffer from CP/CPPS, according to the National Institutes of Health. In this age group, it's the third most common urological diagnosis, after prostate cancer and lower urinary tract conditions.

CP/CPPS isn't a single disease with one specific treatment. The discomfort has different causes and can originate in different areas, including in the prostate gland, the ejaculatory ducts, the bladder or the muscles in the pelvic floor. It can affect one or all of these areas simultaneously.

If you have pelvic pain that has lasted three months or more, you could have CP/CPPS. The pain typically gets worse after ejaculation and tends to come and go. Some men will be pain-free for weeks or months, but the discomfort invariably comes back.

THE UPOINT EXAM

A man with CP/CPPS might not get an accurate diagnosis for a year or more. Many family doctors, internists and even urologists look only for a prostate infection. They don't realize that CP/CPPS can be caused by a constellation of different problems.

You may need to see a urologist who is affiliated with an academic medical center. He/she will be up-to-date on the latest diagnostic procedures and treatments for ongoing pelvic pain.

Recent approach: Researchers recently introduced the UPOINT (*urinary, psychosocial, organ specific, infection, neurologic/systemic and tenderness of skeletal muscles*) exam. It categorizes the different causes of CP/CPPS and helps doctors choose the best treatments.

Your doctor will perform a physical exam and take a detailed history. He will ask where the pain is, how often you have it and how severe it is. He also will ask if you've had recurrent urinary tract infections, sexually transmitted diseases, persistent muscle pain, etc.

Important: Arrive for your appointment with a full bladder. You might be asked to perform a two-glass urine test. You will urinate once into a container to test for bacteria/cells in the bladder. Then you will urinate a second time (following a prostate "massage") to test for bacteria/cells from the prostate gland.

NEXT STEPS

What your doctor looks for and what he may recommend…

• **Infection.** Even though it affects only a minority of men with pelvic pain, it's the first thing your doctor will check.

Consider yourself lucky if you have an infection: About 75% of men with bacterial prostatitis will improve when they take an antibiotic such as *ciprofloxacin* (Cipro).

The discomfort from an acute infection—pain, fever, chills—usually will disappear in about two or three days. You will keep taking antibiotics for several weeks to ensure that all of the bacteria are gone.

In rare cases, an infection will persist and become chronic. Men who experience symptoms after the initial antibiotic therapy will need to be retested. If the infection still is there, they will be retreated with antibiotics.

• **Urinary symptoms.** These include frequent urination, urinary urgency and residual urine that's due to an inability to completely empty the bladder. Your doctor might prescribe an alpha-blocker medication, such as *tamsulosin* (Flomax), to relax muscles in the prostate and make it easier to urinate.

Also helpful: Changes in lifestyle such as avoiding caffeine and limiting alcohol…not drinking anything before bedtime…and avoiding decongestants/antihistamines, which can interfere with urination.

• **Pelvic pain.** It is the most common symptom in men with CP/CPPS. It's usually caused by inflammation and/or tightness in the pelvic floor, a group of muscles that separates the pelvic area from the area near the anus and genitals. The pain can be limited to the pelvic area, or it can radiate to the lower back, thighs, hips, rectum or bladder. *Treatments…*

• Kegel exercises to ease muscle tension and pain. The next time you urinate, try to stop the flow in mid-stream—if you can do it, you're contracting the right muscles. To do a Kegel, squeeze those muscles hard for about five seconds…relax for five seconds…then squeeze again. Repeat the sequence five or 10 times—more often as the muscles get stronger. Do this five times a day.

• Mind-body approaches, including yoga and progressive relaxation exercises, can help reduce muscle spasms and pelvic pain.

• Anti-inflammatory drugs, such as ibuprofen or aspirin, as directed by your doctor. If you can't take these medications because of stomach upset or other side effects, ask your doctor about trying *quercetin* or *bee pollen* supplements. They appear to reduce inflammation in the prostate gland. Follow the dosing instructions on the label.

• Sitz bath (sitting in a few inches of warm water) can relieve perianal/genital pain during flare-ups. Soak for 15 to 30 minutes.

• **Depression, anxiety or stress.** Therapy and/or stress reduction are an important part of treatment because both approaches can reduce muscle tension. Also, patients who are emotionally healthy tend to experience less pain than those who are highly stressed.

Helpful: *Cognitive behavioral therapy* (CBT), which helps patients identify negative thought patterns and behaviors that increase pain and regular exercise, a natural mood-booster that helps reduce stress, anxiety and pain.

Circumcision May Lower Cancer Risk

In a recent study, men who were circumcised before the first time they had sexual intercourse had a 15% lower risk for prostate cancer than uncircumcised men.

Possible reason: Research shows that uncircumcised men are more likely to contract a sexually transmitted disease and that inflammation caused by the infection may be involved in the development of prostate cancer.

Study of 1,754 men with prostate cancer and 1,654 without the disease by researchers at University of Washington, Seattle, published in *Cancer.*

Common Drink Linked to Prostate Cancer

In a recent finding, men who drank more than seven cups of black tea a day were 50% more likely to develop prostate cancer than men who drank three or fewer cups a day. However, drinking black tea may have a positive health effect that trumps any correlation with prostate cancer. Previous research has suggested that tea drinking lowers the risk for cancer, heart disease and diabetes.

Forty-year study of 6,016 men between the ages of 21 and 75 by researchers at the Institute of Health and Wellbeing at University of Glasgow, published online in *Nutrition and Cancer.*

Prostate Cancer Surgery Can Lead to Eye Problems

Eye injuries in patients who had *robotic-assisted radical prostatectomy* increased tenfold when compared with patients who had nonrobotic surgery, a recent study found.

Possible reason: The surgery is done with the patient tilted head-down at a 45-degree angle, which changes blood flow in a way that tends to make eyes swell.

If you have eye pain, discomfort or burning after surgery, tell your doctor immediately.

Steven Roth, MD, professor of anesthesia and critical care at University of Chicago Medical Center and lead author of a review of prostate surgery presented at an American Society of Anesthesiologists meeting.

New Pap Smear Guidelines

Doctors and medical groups now recommend that women be given a Pap smear to screen for cervical cancer *every three years* instead of annually.

Reason: Studies have shown that lengthening the time between screenings leads to the same reduction in cancer deaths while reducing the number of false-positive results that lead to painful biopsies and reducing the risk for pregnancy complications.

Study by researchers at the US Preventative Services Task Force.

Good News for Women with Breast Cancer: 5 Recent Advances Are Dramatically Changing Treatment Approaches...

Jill Dietz, MD, director of the Hillcrest Breast Center, Cleveland Clinic Foundation. She is a fellow of the American College of Surgeons and member of several professional organizations, including the American Society of Breast Surgeons and Society of Surgical Oncology. A researcher and teacher, Dr. Dietz is also program director for the surgical breast fellowship at Cleveland Clinic.

Women who have breast cancer are now living longer than they did only five years ago—and not simply due to improved mammography techniques.

Reason: New scientific evidence is changing the way physicians can treat the disease—making these treatments much more selective and effective. *Key findings breast cancer patients need to know about...*

•**New thinking on double mastectomy.** Many women with breast cancer opt to surgically remove the breast with the malignancy *and* the healthy breast. Their decision to remove both breasts is driven by the fear that a new breast cancer will develop in the healthy breast. But new research suggests that double mastectomy for these women may be overused.

New scientific evidence: Researchers who followed up with 1,525 early-stage breast cancer patients four years after they had received mastectomy, double mastectomy or lumpectomy (a breast-conserving procedure that removes only the malignancy and surrounding tissue) found that women who had both breasts removed would have had a very low risk of developing cancer in the healthy breast.

Who should consider having a double mastectomy? According to the Society of Surgical Oncology, it may be warranted for a woman who is at increased risk for breast cancer because she has two or more immediate family members (a mother, sister or daughter) with breast or ovarian cancer...or has tested positive for mutations in the BRCA1 or BRCA2

gene. These criteria apply to women who have early-stage breast cancer as well as those who haven't developed the disease.

Self-defense: If you don't have a family history or genetic predisposition to develop breast cancer, carefully review your reasons for considering a double mastectomy.

•**Better results with tamoxifen.** Doctors have long told certain breast cancer patients to use an estrogen-blocking drug (*tamoxifen*) for about five years to stave off future breast malignancies.

New scientific evidence: For 15 years, researchers followed 6,846 breast cancer patients who took tamoxifen for an *additional* five years after five years of initial use while another group stopped the drug at five years.

Result: Those who used the medication for 10 years had a significantly reduced risk for breast cancer recurrence and death.

The benefits of longer-term tamoxifen use apply primarily to premenopausal women. That's because postmenopausal women have the option of taking another class of drugs called *aromatase inhibitors*, including *letrozole* (Femara), which are slightly more effective than tamoxifen at preventing future breast cancers but do not, for unknown reasons, offer the same benefit to premenopausal women. Research has not yet determined whether postmenopausal women would benefit from taking letrozole for 10 years rather than the standard five-year recommendation.

Self-defense: If you are a premenopausal woman with breast cancer (especially if the tumor was large and/or you had lymph nodes that tested positive for cancer), ask your doctor about the risks and benefits of taking tamoxifen for more than the standard five years. Using the drug increases risk for endometrial cancer and pulmonary embolism.

•**Less invasive treatment may improve survival for early-stage breast cancer.** Women with early-stage breast cancer perceive mastectomy to be more effective at eliminating their future risk for breast cancer, but research shows that this is probably not true.

New scientific evidence: In an analysis of more than 112,000 women with stage I or stage II breast cancer who were tracked for an average of 9.2 years, those who received lumpectomy plus radiation had odds of survival that were as good as or better than those who underwent mastectomy.

Self-defense: If you are diagnosed with stage I or stage II breast cancer, ask your doctor about lumpectomy plus radiation.

• **More women could benefit from reconstruction.** With breast reconstruction, a woman who has received a mastectomy (or, in some cases, a lumpectomy) can have her breast shape rebuilt with an implant and/or tissue from another part of her body (typically the abdomen, back or buttocks). When a patient opts for reconstruction, it is ideally performed with the initial breast cancer surgery for the best cosmetic result.

Breast reconstruction does not restore the breast's natural sensation or replace the nipple. However, a new "nipple-sparing" mastectomy, a technically difficult procedure in which the surgeon preserves the nipple and areola (the brownish or pink-colored tissue surrounding the nipple), is gaining popularity with women whose malignancy does not interfere with this type of surgery.

Recent scientific evidence: Even though breast reconstruction can offer both cosmetic and psychological advantages, not very many women choose to have it. In a study of more than 120,000 women who underwent mastectomy, fewer than one in four of the women with invasive breast cancer opted for reconstruction, while only about one in three of those with early-stage disease got it. Almost all women are candidates for reconstruction, which does not impact survival rates. In some cases, women require one or more subsequent surgeries to fine-tune the reconstruction.

Self-defense: Ask about reconstruction before your treatment begins. If you're a candidate, the breast surgeon can coordinate with a plastic surgeon. Breast reconstruction is often covered by insurance, but some insurers may require a co-pay.

• **Targeted therapies save lives.** Until 40 years ago, breast cancer was treated almost uniformly with radical mastectomy, radiation and some form of hormone therapy.

Recent scientific evidence: Using new genomic DNA–based tests, doctors are now able to customize treatment based on tumor biology, helping them better predict a patient's risk for recurrence and response to particular treatments. This may help thousands of women with breast cancer avoid chemotherapy, including *anthracyclines*, which are linked to heart damage and leukemia.

Self-defense: Ask your doctor whether you could benefit from genomic testing to help determine which breast cancer therapies would be most effective for you.

Superfoods That Lower Risk for Breast Cancer

Eating dark green or deep orange vegetables and fruits that are rich in *carotenoids* reduces the risk for *estrogen-receptor-negative* cancers by 13%. Eat spinach, broccoli, cantaloupe, carrots, apricots and other dark green or orange fruits and vegetables.

Review of data from 18 studies involving more than 1 million women by researchers at Harvard School of Public Health, Boston, published in *Nutrition Action Healthletter.*

Promising: Vitamin D May Protect Against Breast Cancer

In one recent study, women with the lowest blood levels of vitamin D in the three months before a diagnosis of premenopausal breast cancer had three times as high a risk for the disease as women with the highest vitamin D levels. Women should take at least 1,000 international units (IU) of vitamin D-3 daily.

Cedric F. Garland, DrPH, an adjunct professor in the department of family and preventive medicine at University of California, San Diego, and leader of a study of 1,200 women, published online in *Cancer Causes & Control.*

Bikini Wax Risk

Cherie A. LeFevre, MD, director of the Vulvar and Vaginal Disorders Specialty Center, St. Louis University School of Medicine.

Pubic hair protects the very delicate tissues in the vaginal area. It traps moisture and allows for its quick evaporation and keeps bacteria away from the skin and vaginal opening. After a Brazilian bikini wax (that removes all hair in the pubic area), most women will experience swelling, redness and slight irritation for a few days.

In addition, a Brazilian bikini wax as well as a standard wax (that removes hair only at the bikini line) can lead to microabrasions of the skin, which allow bacteria access to the body and can lead to *folliculitis* (infection around the hair follicles), ingrown hairs or *cellulitis* (bacterial infection of the skin). Cellulitis can be a serious infection that requires antibiotics to treat and can even lead to *sepsis* (a systemic blood infection) and hospitalization.

If you do get a bikini wax, make sure that the salon disinfects waxing tools and that the aesthetician wears gloves.

Women who are diabetic, have chronic kidney or liver disease or immune disorders have a greater risk for infection and should avoid waxing or shaving the pubic region.

Your Hormones May Be Out of Whack...Men, This Can Happen to You, Too

Alicia Stanton, MD, a physician who practices anti-aging and integrative medicine in the Hartford, Connecticut, area. A faculty member for the Institute for Functional Medicine, she is also coauthor, with Vera Tweed, of *Hormone Harmony* (Healthy Life Library). *www.DrAliciaStanton.com*

When it comes to hormonal changes, women get the most attention. But hormones have a profound effect on the health of women *and* men.

In fact, these important chemical messengers, which constantly send instructions from one part of the body to another, may be at the root of mysterious and frequently undiagnosed health problems such as fatigue, insomnia, memory loss, depression and weight gain.

Hormones always act together, much like instruments in an orchestra. That is why a hormonal *imbalance*—too much or too little of one or more hormones—can trip up your health in many ways. *Six important hormones that may be out of whack...**

CORTISOL (ADRENAL GLANDS)

The hormone cortisol tells the body to respond to stress—both external stresses (such as traffic jams and financial troubles) and internal stresses (such as inflammation and infections).

The danger: *Progesterone* (a hormone that is produced by the adrenal glands as well as the ovaries and, in smaller amounts, by the testes) acts as a chemical building block for cortisol as well as *estrogen* and *testosterone*. If you are constantly under stress, you generate high levels of cortisol, depleting progesterone and, in turn, reducing the production of estrogen and testosterone. That is why effective stress management is essential to *overall* hormonal balance in women and men.

Common signs of imbalance: High cortisol levels can cause excess belly fat, high blood pressure, insomnia, irritability, low libido and weakened immunity. Low cortisol levels—from exhausted adrenal glands that can no longer manufacture enough of the hormone—can cause such problems as allergies, apathy and chronic fatigue.

My advice: Make stress management a priority. *Simple techniques...*

• **Breathe deeply.** Simply breathe in for a count of four, hold for a count of six and breathe out for a count of six. Do this five times whenever you're feeling stressed.

• **Create boundaries.** Feeling helpless and out of control is extremely stressful. Identify your major source of stress—such as a difficult

*If you experience any of the signs or symptoms of a hormone imbalance, ask your doctor about getting your hormone levels tested.

relationship—and create boundaries to regain control. If a friend causes stress by always complaining, for example, tell her the topics you're willing to listen to—and those you're not.

• **Get enough sleep.** Sufficient sleep is crucial for balancing cortisol—and all other hormones. To improve sleep, keep your bedroom completely dark and a little cool…and don't watch TV at bedtime. End each day with a positive ritual, such as writing down things that you're grateful for or taking a warm bath.

INSULIN (PANCREAS)

Insulin regulates blood sugar (glucose), telling muscle cells to burn glucose for energy and fat cells to store it for future use.

Common signs of imbalance: Carbohydrate cravings, constipation, excess belly fat, poor memory, prediabetes and diabetes indicate high insulin levels, the most widespread insulin imbalance.

My advice: Balanced glucose levels lead to balanced insulin, and diet is the best way to balance glucose.

• **Eat six times per day.** Having healthful, smaller meals throughout the day balances glucose. Eat breakfast, a mid-morning snack, lunch, a mid-afternoon snack, dinner and a bedtime snack.

• **Include protein in snacks and at meals.** It helps keep glucose balanced.

Good protein sources: Nuts, cottage cheese, hummus and oily fish such as salmon and sardines.

• **Eat low-glycemic carbohydrates.** Slow-digesting carbohydrates that don't create spikes in glucose levels include nonstarchy vegetables, fruits, whole grains and beans.

THYROID HORMONE (THYROID GLAND)

This hormone regulates metabolism, including body temperature and heart rate.

Common signs of imbalance: Cold hands and feet, dry skin, fatigue, hair loss, slow heartbeat and/or weight gain could signal hypothyroidism, the most typical thyroid imbalance.

My advice: Reducing stress is key. *Also helpful…***

**Check with your doctor before taking any of these supplements—some may react with certain drugs.

• **Avoid gluten.** Research now links gluten intolerance to thyroid problems.

To determine if you are sensitive to gluten: Give up gluten-containing foods for two weeks and gradually reintroduce them. If symptoms (such as abdominal pain, bloating and diarrhea) return, you are probably gluten-sensitive.

• **Take zinc.** A daily 30-milligram (mg) dose of zinc helps restore normal thyroid levels. (Also take 2 mg of copper—zinc supplements can deplete copper.)

• **Take selenium.** A daily 100-microgram (mcg) dose of selenium, a potent antioxidant, helps to improve thyroid function.

• **Test for iodine.** If you have symptoms of thyroid imbalance, ask your doctor to test your iodine level. This mineral is crucial for production of thyroid hormone. If levels are low, eat more iodine-rich foods, such as sushi that contains seaweed.

ESTROGEN AND PROGESTERONE (OVARIES, ADRENAL GLANDS, TESTES)

These hormones work together to regulate functions in the brain, heart and every other organ.

Common signs of imbalance: For most premenopausal women, estrogen is too high and progesterone is too low. Symptoms include bloating, breast tenderness, heavy menstrual bleeding and moodiness. High estrogen also increases risk for breast cancer. For perimenopausal and menopausal women, estrogen is usually low, and symptoms can include hot flashes, urinary incontinence and vaginal pain and dryness. In men, low libido, increased belly fat and breast size, depression and erectile dysfunction may occur with imbalances of these hormones.

My advice: Controlling stress and following the eating habits described earlier in the insulin section are two of the best ways to balance estrogen and progesterone.

TESTOSTERONE (TESTES, OVARIES)

Testosterone affects sex drive and muscle mass in men and women.

What's often overlooked: In men, low testosterone levels are linked to higher rates of heart disease, type 2 diabetes, Alzheimer's disease, osteoporosis, prostate problems—and death from any cause.

Signs of imbalance: Fatigue, low libido, decrease in strength, erectile dysfunction, irritability, anxiety, depression, poor concentration, memory loss and weight gain.

My advice: To boost testosterone, do not smoke or drink alcohol excessively (for men, no more than two drinks a day). *Also helpful…*

• **Lose weight.** For men who are overweight, weight loss is one of the most effective ways to boost testosterone. Emphasize filling, low-calorie foods, such as vegetables, fruits, whole grains and beans.

• **Resistance training.** Lifting weights three times a week stimulates the production of testosterone.

• **Interval training.** This type of exercise also helps boost testosterone levels.

What to do: Exercise to maximum capacity for one minute…slow down until normal breathing is restored (usually about one minute)…then repeat the cycle for 20 minutes.

For women: Low testosterone can lead to weight gain and loss of sex drive. The self-care methods described above for men also work for most women. This includes no excessive drinking (for women, no more than one drink a day).

If you take a statin drug: Cholesterol is a building block of testosterone—and cholesterol-lowering statin therapy also can lower levels of the hormone.

If you're taking a statin and have signs of testosterone imbalance, ask your doctor to test your total testosterone. If levels are 400 nanograms per deciliter (ng/dL) or below in men, testosterone-replacement therapy should be considered. In women, a total testosterone level of 15 ng/dL or below is considered low.

Beware…Early Menopause Raises Cardiac Risks

Women who reach menopause at age 46 or younger—naturally or because of surgery—have twice the risk for stroke or heart disease as women who reach menopause later.

Self-defense: Use diet and exercise to maintain healthy blood pressure and cholesterol levels.

Study of 2,509 women by researchers at University of Alabama, Birmingham, published in *Menopause.*

For Hot Flashes, Try a Low-Fat Diet

In a recent finding, menopausal women on a low-fat diet were 14% less likely to have night sweats and hot flashes after a year than women on other diets.

Bonus: Women on the low-fat diet—which included eating more fruits, vegetables and whole grains—were three times more likely to lose weight than ones who continued with their usual foods.

Study of 17,473 menopausal women who were not on hormone therapy by researchers at Kaiser Permanente Northern California Division of Research, Oakland, published online in *Menopause.*

Do You Leak When You Laugh or Cough? Don't "Live with It" Anymore!

Leslie M. Rickey, MD, MPH, urologist and assistant professor in the departments of surgery and obstetrics/gynecology at the University of Maryland School of Medicine in Baltimore. She specializes in female pelvic medicine and reconstructive surgery and provides specialized care for patients with problems related to the lower urinary tract and pelvic floor.

Anyone can easily reduce the personal discomfort of urinary incontinence—and the risk for public embarrassment—by taking some simple steps. Unfortunately, many people simply choose to "live with it."

LIMITED CONTROL

Stress incontinence—when you leak urine while laughing, sneezing, coughing or exercising—is extremely common. But many people don't get help either because they're too embarrassed to talk about it or they think that nothing can be done about it.

Stress incontinence occurs when the *urinary sphincter*, a ring of muscle, isn't as strong as it should be. The muscle occasionally "slips" and allows urine to escape.

Women typically notice urine leakage for the first time during pregnancy or after vaginal childbirth, which can stretch and weaken the muscles that are needed for control. It also can start later in life, when muscles throughout the body naturally weaken. Men typically do not develop stress incontinence unless they have undergone prostate surgery.

EASY TO DIAGNOSE

Someone who leaks just a few drops of urine now and then might decide it's no big deal. But if it's happening every day, or you're leaking so much that you're going through multiple absorbent pads, you should see a doctor.

Your doctor first will look for underlying conditions—such as an infection or a neurological problem—that could be causing the problem. He/she also will want to confirm that you're suffering from this particular form of incontinence. Other kinds of urinary incontinence include *urge incontinence*, characterized by a sudden, intense need to urinate, and *overflow incontinence*, which is an inability to empty your bladder completely.

Most cases of uncomplicated stress incontinence can be diagnosed just from a description of your symptoms—when you leak, how often, what you're doing when it happens—as well as a stress test. Depending on your symptoms, medical history and prior treatments, your doctor may recommend more testing to confirm your diagnosis.

KEGELS FIRST

Pelvic-floor-muscle exercises, also known as *Kegels*, strengthen the muscles that give you bladder control. About 50% of people with mild-to-moderate problems can achieve nearly complete dryness with this approach alone. Pelvic-floor-muscle exercises frequently are recommended for men after undergoing prostatectomy.

Important: Even though the exercises are easy to do at home, I advise my patients to work with a specialist to learn them. A pelvic-floor physical therapist can help you identify the correct muscles so that you will know what they feel like when they contract and relax. Your doctor can refer you to a therapist. Typically, a physical therapy program consists of six to eight sessions, and then the patient's symptoms are reevaluated.

If you're doing the exercises without the help of a therapist...

• **Identify the muscles.** When you urinate, try to stop the flow in mid-stream. Those are the muscles you need to strengthen.

• **Squeeze and relax.** You can do this while sitting, standing or lying down. Squeeze the muscles as hard as you can for a few seconds, relax for a few seconds and then squeeze the muscles again. Each squeeze-relax cycle counts as one Kegel.

Do a series of Kegels two or three times a day. For each series, you'll squeeze and relax the muscles at least 10 times—more as you gain strength. You can work the exercises into your day—while watching a movie, in the car at a stoplight, etc. Also, cutting back on caffeine may help with incontinence.

THE NEXT STEP

While many women will have improved bladder control with pelvic-floor-muscle exercises, further treatment may be necessary if you continue to have frequent or heavy leakage.

At this point, some women will opt for a surgical procedure to achieve continence. Surgery for men is far less common, and the main options are an artificial urinary sphincter or a sling (see below).

• **Periurethral bulking.** This is the simplest procedure for stress incontinence—and it can be done in your doctor's office with a local anesthetic. A "bulking agent" is injected into the tissue that surrounds the urethra and urinary sphincter. Adding bulk to the area makes it more difficult for urine to leak out.

Advantages: There's little to no recovery time. It's a good choice for patients who might be too frail for surgery. Also, the injections can be repeated if you need more help.

Drawbacks: It's not as effective as surgery. One study found that only 30% to 40% of patients who had this procedure were "dry" one year later.

• **Sling surgery.** This is the procedure that most doctors recommend. Studies have shown that about 85% of patients who have it achieve total or near-total control.

During a sling surgery, a strip of polypropylene mesh or, alternatively, your own tissue taken from the thigh or abdominal wall is placed under the urethra, like a hammock. The extra support from the sling helps prevent leaks when patients cough, laugh, etc.

Drawbacks: It's tricky to adjust the tension on the sling so that it doesn't heal too tight. About 3% of patients will require a second procedure, known as "sling release," to loosen the sling and allow them to urinate normally.

About 10% to 15% of patients may experience new "overactive bladder" symptoms after sling surgery, resulting in increasing urinary urgency and frequency despite the original problem's being "fixed." However, doctors often are able to treat these new urinary symptoms if they persist, and overall satisfaction with sling surgeries remains high (85% to 90%).

Hypnotherapy Eases IBS

Scientists recently conducted research involving a total of 346 irritable bowel syndrome (IBS) patients to test the effectiveness of hypnotherapy as a treatment.

Result: Symptoms were satisfactorily reduced for 40% of patients who received one hour of hypnotherapy once a week for 12 weeks. The positive effect lasted for one to seven years.

Theory: IBS patients can learn to control their symptoms through deep relaxation and hypnotic suggestion.

Magnus Simren, MD, professor of gastroenterology, The Sahlgrenska Academy of the University of Gothenburg, Sweden.

"White Food" Warning

A diet high in white bread, white rice, white potatoes, sugar and other low-nutrition carbohydrates can increase colorectal cancer risk by 25% or more, according to a recent meta-analysis in *The American Journal of Clinical Nutrition*.

Theory: Consuming refined carbohydrates increases production of insulin—which feeds the growth of cancerous cells.

Joel Fuhrman, MD, a family physician specializing in natural and nutritional medicine, Flemington, New Jersey. He is author of seven books, including *Super Immunity* (HarperOne). *www.DrFuhrman.com*

Breakthrough: "Super" Aspirin

Aspirin has been shown to reduce colon cancer risk by 50%, on average, in regular users.

What's new: An experimental, chemically enhanced form of aspirin is up to 250,000 times more potent—and is less likely to cause gastric bleeding than regular aspirin.

ACS Medicinal Chemistry Letters.

Alcohol Alert for Seniors

Older Americans are more likely to binge drink. Binge drinking is defined as having between four and nine alcoholic beverages within a two-to-three-hour period. Binge drinkers over age 65 binge drink nearly six times a month—compared with an average of four times a month for younger binge drinkers—and the actual rate of binge drinking among seniors may even be higher because people tend to underreport their drinking.

Survey of 457,677 adults conducted by the Centers for Disease Control and Prevention, Atlanta, reported in *Mind, Mood & Memory*.

7

Money Manager

How America's 1st Family of Finance Resolves Its Own Fights About Money

Couples who frequently argue about financial matters often end up divorced. A 2009 study from Utah State University found that repeated money squabbles were likely to lead to breakups—more so than arguments on other topics.

Ken and Daria Dolan have a unique perspective on money fights. They have spent more than two decades helping people sort out financial problems on radio and television call-in shows and in columns. They also have had to overcome their own money squabbles. It turns out that having a pair of money pros under the same roof doesn't prevent money arguments. If anything, it makes those arguments more intense because both Ken and Daria possess strong, well-informed opinions on money-related matters—opinions that more than occasionally are at odds.

Four of the biggest financial arguments that the Dolans have had in their 41 years of marriage and what we all can learn from them...

THE SURPRISE-SPENDING FIGHT

Daria: Two days before Ken and I wed, I learned that Ken had a $3,000 credit card balance that he couldn't afford to pay off. I talked my father into cosigning on a loan so that we wouldn't begin our lives together burdened with credit card debt. A few months later—with that loan not yet repaid—bills started arriving at our home for purchases Ken had made

---

Ken and Daria Dolan, personal finance experts who hosted radio and television money call-in programs, including shows on CNN and CNBC, for more than 20 years. Based in Florida, they were named to *Vanity Fair* magazine's Radio Hall of Fame and are authors of financial advice books including *Don't Mess with My Money* (Doubleday Business).

123

without my knowledge. Those bills triggered the first big money fight of our marriage.

Resolution: We agreed that henceforth we would discuss any purchase greater than a few hundred dollars before making it. More than four decades later, we still hold ourselves to that rule, even though our financial resources are much greater now than they were back then.

Lesson: A married person has the right to spend some money without consulting a spouse—but marriages run more smoothly when spouses yield that right. Even if a purchase is unquestionably reasonable, consulting with one's spouse ensures that both partners feel included and respected. Besides, that partner might know about a competing product that offers better quality...or a different retailer that offers a lower price. And discussing purchases together before making them increases the odds that couples will really think through intended purchases, which then can cut down on the household's wasteful spending.

THE AGGRESSIVE-INVESTMENT FIGHT

Ken: I'm a more aggressive investor than Daria. Usually our divergent risk tolerances work in our favor—Daria's safe investments and my aggressive ones add up to a well-balanced portfolio.

But in the late 1990s, our different investment philosophies caused a fight. I bought shares of computer-networking company Cisco Systems and several other tech stocks at the height of the dot.com bubble. Daria hated those investments—she thought the companies lacked sufficient earnings to justify their sky-high share prices. We fought about it a lot.

Resolution: Daria eventually gave up arguing with me about those tech stocks, but she never stopped providing me with the information I needed to change my own mind about them. Every morning over coffee, she would read me my stocks' ever-higher share prices and their low earnings—some had no earnings at all—then ask me if stocks with such astronomical price-to-earnings ratios still seemed like the most promising investments available for our portfolio. In late 1999, I finally

conceded that the downside of Cisco and my other high-flying high-tech stocks outweighed their upside and sold. Cisco stock soon lost more than two-thirds of its value and has never fully recovered.

Lesson: When strong-willed spouses have argued repeatedly and emotionally about a money matter without coming any closer to a resolution, further arguments on the topic are unlikely to help—in fact, they probably will just lead to increased animosity. Instead, stop arguing and start calmly, patiently and dispassionately providing information that supports your position. Our spouses are more likely to recognize the reality of the situation when emotions are replaced by cold facts.

THE CAREER-CHANGE FIGHT

Daria: When Ken was in his early 40s, he was in charge of the Florida office of a successful brokerage firm. He hosted a call-in money show on a local AM radio station, too, but only to help promote the brokerage firm. Then Ken was asked to fill in for the injured host of a New York City money radio show. The fill-in assignment went so well that he was offered his own show on WOR, then America's top-rated talk-radio station.

It was an incredibly fast climb up the radio ladder for someone who had no media background, and Ken, who had fallen in love with broadcasting, was anxious to accept. I wasn't. The job was in New York City, and we had only recently moved to Florida—I didn't want to relocate the family again or see Ken only on weekends. And taking the radio job meant taking a 70% pay cut from Ken's brokerage salary—I wasn't sure we could manage on so much less. It was the biggest strain in our 41 years of marriage.

Resolution: Ken took the job but agreed that if his media career did not quickly flourish, he would return to the brokerage sector after his contract expired. I decided to find a job, too, to supplement Ken's lower salary—I had left the workplace years before to raise our daughter.

Lesson: We can ask a lot of our spouses, but we cannot ask them to surrender a chance to follow their dreams—assuming that those dreams have a plausible chance of coming true, which Ken's did after he was offered a show on WOR. If that means other family members must make some adjustments, then they must do so. But that doesn't mean that our spouses are free to pursue their dreams forever. Married people have an obligation to balance their dreams against a clear-headed understanding of the reality of a situation. If Ken's radio career had stalled, Daria had every right to expect him to return to a more promising career path.

THE BAILOUT FIGHT

Daria: Our daughter, Meredith, ran up $10,000 in credit card bills shortly after graduating from college. When Ken found out, he wanted to pay the debt for her. I feared that if we paid off that debt, Meredith would not learn from her mistake and would expect us to bail her out again.

Resolution: We advised Meredith to cash out a $10,000 Treasury bill that she had purchased with money inherited from her great-grandfather—which she did. That way, she would not be saddled with credit card debt, but neither would she escape her overspending without consequences—all of her savings were gone. If she hadn't had that Treasury bill, we could have loaned her the money—but we would have insisted that she repay us. Meredith never overspent on credit cards again.

Lesson: Sometimes the best money gift you can give your children is to not give them money. The sooner young people learn to live within their means—and feel the pain of failing to do so—the less likely they are to make the same mistake again. It's better to learn this lesson early, before higher credit limits make it possible to dig a hole so deep that you can't easily climb out.

My Favorite Money Apps: Get the Best Deals…Track Your Investments…Find a Cash Machine Anywhere

Jeff Rose, CFP, CEO of Alliance Wealth Management, a financial-planning firm based in Carbondale, Illinois. He writes a personal finance blog at *www.GoodFinancialCents.com*.

Y ou may know about some basic smartphone financial apps such as those that help you with your taxes or your bank and brokerage accounts. But there are many more that can help you keep on top of your personal finances in a variety of ways.

Here, my favorite apps for various financial goals. All of the apps have versions for iPhones and Android-based devices. They also work with handheld devices that are not connected to cellular networks, such as the iPod Touch and Samsung Galaxy Player, as long as you have wireless Internet access (Wi-Fi).

MANAGING YOUR MONEY

•**Spending tracker.** *Easy Envelope Budget Aid* is a digital version of the old "envelope" method of budgeting. It helps you stick to weekly or monthly budget limits without the hassle of keeping the actual cash separated. You set up virtual envelopes on your smartphone in categories such as groceries, rent, transportation and entertainment, and you specify how much cash goes in each. When you conduct a transaction, you manually input it on the Easy Envelope Budget Aid app and that amount automatically is subtracted from the appropriate envelope. Inputting is easy because your GPS location is used to suggest payees such as a grocery store or gas station that you have frequented in the past.

The app also allows the data that you input to sync with the smartphones of your spouse, other family members or a roommate. The free version, which includes 10 weekly virtual envelopes and 10 annual ones, allows for two smartphone users. Other versions, which provide additional envelopes and support more smartphones, start at $3 per month.* *www.EE BACanHelp.com*

●**Account coordinator.** *Mint*, which has more than 10 million users, provides a snapshot of where you stand financially right on your smartphone. You input password and account-number information from all your credit cards, mortgages, bill payments, investment brokerage and bank accounts and more. Mint automatically compiles and updates all the information. You also can search through past transactions. Free. *www.Mint.com*

●**Digital expense reports.** If you are not careful about keeping business lunch receipts or dislike hunting through crumpled scraps of paper to document your tax deductions or travel and entertainment expenses for work, *Shoeboxed Receipt Tracker* is for you.

How it works: You snap a picture of your receipts with the Shoeboxed app and Shoeboxed enters the information, including dates, total amounts, the form of payment used and scans of the original documents, and stores it all in a searchable digital account for you. You can categorize the digitalized receipts and generate expense reports, then e-mail them or export them to personal finance, accounting or tax-preparation software. Free 30-day trial…$9.95/month after that. *www.Shoeboxed.com*

ACCESSING YOUR MONEY

●**Money finder.** *ATM Hunter* helps you find cash machines close to your location anywhere in the world. Your phone's GPS identifies where you are and provides a list of ATMs in the MasterCard, Maestro and Cirrus networks, along with directions and maps. Tailor your search based on features such as operating hours…the ability to make a deposit…ATMs that are surcharge-free…and ATMs in particular banks. Free. *www.MasterCard.us/mobile/atm-hunter.html*

●**Payment processor.** The mobile version of the leading online payment processor, *PayPal*, allows you to send money for personal or business use from the road, withdraw funds from your PayPal account or transfer money to other PayPal accounts or to your own bank account. It also helps you locate merchants in the area who accept PayPal. Free. *www.PayPal.com*

*Prices subject to change.

SPENDING YOUR MONEY

●**Converter.** *Currency* is a foreign currency conversion calculator with exchange rates updated daily for more than 180 countries. Free. *www.CurrencyApp.com*

●**Loyalty card keeper.** *Key Ring* scans and saves the bar-coded information from plastic loyalty and rewards cards that you get from supermarkets, pharmacies and the like so that you don't need to clutter your key ring or wallet with physical versions. You just call up the reward card bar code on your smartphone at the checkout counter and let the clerk scan it. You also can receive digital updates on special offers from the stores. Free. *www.KeyRing App.com*

●**Price comparer.** *RedLaser* bar-code scanner allows you to scan any item in a store, then automatically access the Internet and search Google, Amazon and other online shopping guides to get price comparisons from online and offline retailers, including stores close to your location.

Example: A camera for $748.99 at Best Buy was found online for $549—almost $200 saved. Free. *http://RedLaser.com*

Bank Fees You May Not Know About

An *early account closure fee of $25* may be charged for accounts closed within 180 days of being opened…a *check-cash fee of $5* could be applied if you are not a bank's customer…an *empty-envelope fee of $35* can be assessed if someone puts an empty envelope into an ATM as a "deposit" and then withdraws the deposit amount for quick cash even if he/she meant to enclose a check…a *return-mail fee of up to $15* might be levied if you relocate and the bank's mail is returned to it…and an *inactivity fee of up to $15* could be assessed for accounts that are dormant for six to 12 months.

MarketWatch.com

Sneaky Credit Card Fees: The Government Stopped Some, but These Slipped Through...

Kathleen Day, spokesperson for the Center for Responsible Lending in Washington, DC, a nonprofit research and policy organization focused on consumer lending. She previously worked for 22 years as a financial services reporter for *The Washington Post*. *www.ResponsibleLending.org*

The federal government has taken steps to protect consumers from the credit card industry's worst abuses. But several common practices still vex credit cardholders.

Example: Capital One recently was ordered to refund $150 million to 2 million customers and pay $60 million in penalties because of its "deceptive marketing tactics" used to convince consumers to buy payment-protection plans. Discover Financial Services recently said that it might face similar actions by the newly created Consumer Financial Protection Bureau.

How to protect yourself from tricks used by the credit card industry...

FEE TRAPS

•**Don't fall for claims that you need a payment-protection plan.** Payment-protection plans, also known as payment insurance, are supposed to pay or suspend cardholders' minimum payments should those cardholders become disabled or unemployed.

The trap: Payment-protection plans are overpriced and so riddled with loopholes that they usually provide little or no assistance, even when cardholders do become disabled or unemployed.

The marketing tactics that are used to sell these plans sometimes are quite questionable, as evidenced by the action against Capital One. Consumers have been told that signing up will help their credit scores...that the program is required...or that it is free—none of which is true. Some issuers, including Bank of America, have stopped offering payment-protection plans—but others still are pushing them.

What to do: Never purchase payment protection. Take the money you would have spent for it each month, and use that money to pay down your credit card balances instead.

•**Don't assume that a weekend gives you an extra day to make a payment.** Before the *Credit Card Act of 2009*, consumers who delayed their payments until the last minute often were charged late-payment penalties when their payment due dates fell on weekends or holidays. That's because banks weren't open to accept payments on those deadline days. Now, thanks to the *Credit Card Act*, if the card issuer is closed on the payment due date, cardholders can pay without penalty on the next open day.

The trap: Some card issuers have responded by keeping an office open to process payments on weekends and holidays. Cardholders might erroneously assume that their banks are closed, incurring an avoidable penalty.

What to do: If you realize that your payment is due immediately, pay on that day online or by phone if possible, even if it's a weekend or holiday. Better yet, pay credit card bills well in advance of their due dates.

•**Don't assume that fees on subprime cards must be reasonable.** Credit cards available to consumers with low credit scores often have steep annual fees and low credit limits. That's understandable, but the *Credit Card Act* attempted to put a reasonable cciling on these charges, capping total annual fees at 25% of a card's available credit line in the first year that the account is open.

The trap: First Premier Bank successfully argued that the 25% cap applies only to annual fees charged during the first year after an account is up and running—not to setup fees imposed before the account officially is opened. Thus card issuers still can charge huge fees simply by charging many of them at the outset.

What to do: If you have poor credit, do not assume that the *Credit Card Act* protects you from excessive credit card fees. You still must carefully compare the rates and fees of credit cards available to you—including initial setup fees—before signing up.

INTEREST RATE TRAPS

• **Don't miss warnings of rate increases.** According to the *Credit Card Act*, issuers must notify cardholders at least 45 days in advance of any interest rate increases, unless you have a variable interest rate linked to an index or an introductory rate.

The trap: Few consumers read all the paperwork that comes with their credit card statements, and fewer still read paperwork sent separately—this often is mistaken for advertising.

What to do: Open all mailings from your credit card issuers to make sure that they are not alerting you to rate increases. If your rate is increased to a level that you consider unacceptable, contact the issuer to check whether you can get the new rate reduced. If you cannot and want to avoid the higher rate, call to cancel the card or just stop using it. To be safe, take the card out of your wallet so that you don't use it accidentally. Also, transfer any automatic payments made with this card to other cards. Using the card again constitutes acceptance of the higher rate.

• **Realize that "0% interest on balance transfers" does not mean "zero cost."** Offers of 0% interest on transfers abound in the wake of the *Credit Card Act*.

The trap: Expect to be charged a steep fee for the right to make these "no-interest" balance transfers. Balance transfer fees of 3% to 5% of the amount transferred are nothing new, but in years past, they tended to be capped at less than $100. These days, there usually is no cap on this fee at all, a subtle but expensive difference.

What's more, these 0% offers rarely last long. Fail to pay off your debt before this introductory rate expires and your interest rate might leap to a fairly steep rate. Keep in mind that issuers have ways of tempting cardholders not to pay off their balances in time.

Example: Many 0% balance transfer cards now feature attractive rewards programs to encourage cardholders to use these cards for new purchases, too. That way their balances go up, not down, during the 0% window.

Also, people who apply for 0% balance transfers actually might be approved for less appealing terms—something they might not realize until after the balance has been transferred if they fail to read approval notices carefully.

What to do: Add up the fees before you jump at a 0% balance-transfer offer. Make a realistic assessment of your ability to pay off the debt before the 0% interest period expires, and consider the interest rate that will apply once the 0% period ends. Avoid using this card for new purchases if doing so will inhibit your ability to pay off the debt before the 0% period ends.

• **Don't lose finance-charge rebates or rewards points by paying late.** Before the *Credit Card Act*, issuers often dramatically increased interest rates if cardholders were even a single day late with a payment. The *Card Act* now prevents them from increasing rates on existing balances unless cardholders are at least 60 days late with payments. But a case can be made that Citibank has found a loophole to this rule—one that other banks might copy. Citibank offers special interest rate reductions to cardholders who make on-time payments on their Citi Forward or Citi Forward for College Students cards.

The trap: The *Credit Card Act*'s rule about rate increases triggered by late payments does not apply to these special rate reductions. They could be revoked if you're a single day late with a payment, effectively increasing your rate.

What to do: Be very cautious about running a balance on a card that provides finance-charge rebates. Your effective rates could be upped at your first misstep.

• **Don't accidentally pay just the minimum required.** Paying credit card bills online can be very convenient, but if you don't pay close attention, you could make a costly mistake.

The trap: Some card issuer Web sites automatically fill in the minimum required amount in the payment box of the online form rather than the full balance. Cardholders who intend to pay the full balance might not notice this and end up paying interest on an unpaid balance unintentionally.

What to do: Double-check that you are paying the amount that you intend to pay.

More from Kathleen Day...

Beware of Payday Loans

Beware of payday loans from big banks. These short-term loans now offered by major banks typically allow cash-strapped consumers to borrow up to a few hundred dollars for periods of a week to a month.

Problem: The loans have astronomical fees and borrowers who can't pay them off renew them over and over. Big banks such as Wells Fargo and US Bancorp are marketing payday loans under names such as "Direct Deposit Advance" and "Checking Account Advance."

A Prepaid Card May Be Right for You...If You Select the Right One

Bill Hardekopf, CEO of LowCards.com, which helps consumers compare credit cards. He is coauthor of *The Credit Card Guidebook* (Lulu).

Prepaid cards are promoted as simple, easy-to-obtain alternatives to conventional credit and debit cards and even checking accounts. You just preload money and use the card to pay for things or withdraw cash. And unlike checking accounts, there are no overdraft fees or minimum balance requirements. Unfortunately, most prepaid cards are not covered by recent legislation intended to protect consumers, so many remain laden with steep fees. A recent study found that a prepaid card costs a minimum of $3 to $10.50 per month. Also, most lack crucial safeguards.

Example: Prepaid card issuers are not legally required to refund your losses if a thief drains your account.

Recently a small number of prepaid cards with more reasonable fees and safeguards have become available. *They could be appropriate if...*

● **You have children going to college.** Parents can load money onto a prepaid card repeatedly so that their kids can make necessary purchases but not accumulate big debts.

● **You have trouble controlling spending.** Prepaid cards let you spend only up to the amount that you have deposited.

● **You don't have a checking account.** It can be cheaper and easier to have paychecks directly deposited into a prepaid card account than to use a check-cashing store.

● **Your credit score is too low for a mainstream credit card.** Prepaid cards do not require a credit check.

THE BEST CARDS

Here are some prepaid cards that have reasonable fees. *They provide extensive protection against unauthorized transactions as long as those transactions are reported promptly...*

● **American Express Prepaid Card** has no annual or monthly free, activation fee or overdraft fee and no reload fee when adding money through a bank account or direct-deposit. American Express does not charge a fee for the first ATM withdrawal each month, but the ATM provider might. Amex charges $2 for each subsequent ATM withdrawal.

A new variation: Amex and Walmart recently rolled out a new prepaid card called Bluebird with features similar to the American Express Prepaid Card. The new one is free if obtained online or $5 at Walmart stores.* Cardholders can add cash to the cards for free at Walmart stores and, if they enroll in paycheck direct-deposit, can access MoneyPass network ATMs for free. Otherwise, ATM transactions are $2. Checks can be deposited with the use of a smartphone.

● **Chase Liquid** charges a monthly fee of $4.95, but it could be a good choice if you live or work near a Chase branch or Chase ATM. There is no activation charge, overdraft/shortage fee or fee for loading money in any Chase branch, at Chase ATMs that don't require deposit envelopes or via direct-deposit or smartphone. There also is no fee for withdrawing cash from a Chase ATM or branch, but there is a $2 fee for using a non-Chase

*Prices subject to change.

ATM in addition to any fee imposed by the ATM provider.

More from Bill Hardekopf...

The High Cost of Convenience Checks

Offers from card issuers to use these checks, which are linked to credit card accounts and can be used to get cash or make purchases, have proliferated.

Little noticed: There is a fee, usually 3% to 4% of the check amount...typically you will be charged the interest rate for a cash advance, often above 20%, once any low-rate introductory offer passes...purchases using these checks normally do not earn rewards and don't include purchase protections...exceeding your credit limit will hurt your credit score and could cause the check to bounce.

Best: Shred the checks, and ask the card issuer to stop sending them.

How to Teach Your Teen About Credit

If you want your teen to have a credit card and learn to use it responsibly, give him/her one linked to yours so that you can see how much he is spending. Review spending monthly when the bill arrives, and explain the importance of building and keeping good credit. Use a payoff calculator to show how long it will take to pay off a credit card debt by making only the minimum monthly payment. And avoid bailing out a teen who overspends. Finally, be sure to teach about the dangers of credit card fraud and identity theft—and how to avoid them.

Example: Make sure your teenager never lends out a card or gives out the number to a questionable caller.

Recommendations from the National Foundation for Credit Counseling. *www.NFCC.org*

New Factors That May Affect Your Credit Score

Rental history is now included in credit reports...payday loans and debt settlements are also now taken into account...and a fix became effective in 2013 to prevent people who have recently retired, gone through a divorce or been widowed from getting rejected for credit because of insufficient income in their own names. To get more information from the Consumer Financial Protection Bureau, go to *www.ConsumerFinance.gov.*

Lynnette Khalfani-Cox, personal finance expert writing at AARP.org.

How to Fix an Error on Your Credit Report and Raise Your Credit Score

John Ulzheimer, president of consumer education for SmartCredit.com, a credit information Web site. He formerly worked with credit-rating organizations Fair Isaac (FICO) and Equifax and has taught courses on credit reporting and credit scoring at Emory University. He is author of *You're Nothing But a Number: Why Achieving Great Credit Scores Should Be on Your List of Wealth Building Strategies* (Credit.com Educational Services).

The credit reports of more than one out of every five Americans include errors, according to a study by the Federal Trade Commission. In millions of cases, such errors can lower credit scores and make it more difficult, or even impossible, to obtain a mortgage and other loans at attractive rates...qualify for appealing credit card deals...or even land a job or rent an apartment.

The errors, which lead to about eight million disputes filed by consumers each year, are frustratingly difficult to correct. That is because the three leading credit-reporting agencies automatically take the word of creditors or collection agencies over the word of consumers, a fact that some critics consider to be a violation of the agencies' obligations under federal law.

The usual advice when you find a mistake in a credit report is to file a dispute with the credit-reporting agency—Equifax, Experian or TransUnion. But consumers who do this often have their complaints rejected, even when they have strong evidence on their side.

Here is a four-step plan that gives you better odds of getting an error on your credit report corrected...*

Step #1: Call the creditor that reported the erroneous information to the credit-reporting agency. The customer service phone number might be listed in the credit report. If it's not, it probably can be found by doing a Web search.

Explain that you wish to dispute something that the company has reported, and ask to speak with the appropriate person. When you are transferred to that person, briefly and calmly explain why you disagree with the credit report listing. (If you have evidence that supports your position—for example, bank or credit card statements that show you paid the bill in question—gather these before placing the call.)

Examples of what to say: "The credit report listing says that I was late with a payment, but my bank account statement shows I always paid on time." "It's true that I was behind on the loan, but I'm now current on it and my credit report should be updated to reflect this."

Take notes during the call, including the name of the person you speak with and anything he/she says that seems to support your position.

Businesses that supply information to credit-reporting agencies are required by federal law to investigate consumer complaints such as these. If they discover mistakes, they are required to report them to all three credit-reporting agencies within 30 days.

*You can obtain a free copy of your credit report from each of the three credit-reporting agencies once every 12 months through AnnualCreditReport.com.

Alternative: If the company that furnished the erroneous information is a collection agency, call this agency and demand that it contact the original creditor to "verify the debt." If the collection agency later tells you that the creditor has confirmed that the debt is correct, then that creditor—not the collection agency—likely is responsible for the mistake. If so, contact that creditor as described above. Ask the collection agency to verify the debt again after the creditor has agreed that it made an error to make sure that it has been corrected.

Why dispute an error on your credit report with the creditor rather than the credit-reporting agency? Because the agencies are just middlemen that parrot information provided to them by creditors. If you take your dispute to one of the agencies—as most people do when they discover errors—the agency will simply contact the creditor and ask whether the disputed information is accurate. If you haven't already explained to this creditor why the information is wrong and/or given the creditor proof, there's a good chance that it will simply confirm the erroneous information and the reporting agency will reject your dispute.

Any evidence or well-reasoned arguments that you present to the reporting agency likely will do you no good. The agencies are supposed to pass the details of consumers' disputes along to creditors, but a study by the Consumer Financial Protection Bureau found that they just reduce the information to a one- or two-digit numeric code and possibly—in just one in four cases—a bare-bones written summary of the dispute, which gives the creditor little to go on.

Exception: If the error stems from a mistake in the public record—for example, a nonexistent bankruptcy filing or missing release of a lien—that mistake isn't being supplied by a creditor. It is being collected directly by the credit-reporting agency. In these situations, you should dispute the information directly with the credit-reporting agency—skip ahead to step 4 for details. If the problem involves documents that are missing from the public record, attach copies of these documents when you mail your complaint to the reporting agency.

Step #2: Follow up your phone call with a certified letter, return receipt requested, to the creditor. This letter should reiterate that you are disputing a specific piece of information and briefly explain why it is incorrect. (Ask the person you speak with on the phone for the proper mailing address.) Keep this letter short and simple—it will be skimmed quickly by a low-level employee or a computer program. Attach photocopies of any evidence you have to defend your position.

Step #3: Call the creditor again—and again and again if necessary until you reach someone willing to help—if your initial complaint is rejected. Do your best to stay calm and patient when you call. Getting angry reduces the odds that someone will want to help you. Ask for a manager if you're forced to make repeated calls because he may have more authority to help you.

Step #4: Send the credit-reporting agency (or agencies) a certified letter, return receipt requested, disputing the erroneous information, too. This letter should be short and simple, like the one you sent to the creditor. Wait until after the creditor has responded to your complaint before mailing this letter.

Exception: Send letters to both the creditor and credit-reporting agency as soon as possible if you're in a big rush to fix your credit score.

Why send a letter to the reporting agency when you already have raised the matter with the creditor? First, if the creditor agrees with your complaint and changes its records, this letter ensures that the agency will learn of the change. Creditors are supposed to inform the agencies when they discover mistakes, but that doesn't always happen. And second, only by informing the agency of your complaint do you obtain the right to later sue it under the Fair Credit Reporting Act if the error is not corrected (see below).

Warning: The agencies offer the option of disputing credit report information online, but

sending a letter allows you to supply details and/or evidence. True, the reporting agencies probably won't pay much attention to the details and evidence, as discussed above. But if you eventually must sue, the fact that the agency ignored your evidence and well-reasoned arguments could strengthen your case.

Keep copies of all your correspondence and enclosures and detailed notes of your phone conversations—including names of the people you speak with.

More from John Ulzheimer…

When to Sue Over Your Credit Report

If incorrect information remains in your credit report despite your repeated attempts to get it removed, you could sue the credit-reporting agency and/or creditor in state, federal or small-claims court.

If you want to sue in state or federal court, click the "Find an Attorney" link on the Web site of the National Association of Consumer Advocates (*www.NACA.net*) to find lawyers who have the right qualifications and experience. If you have a strong case, you should be able to find an attorney willing to take it on contingency—that is, in exchange for 30% to 40% of the amount you win rather than an hourly or flat rate. If so, the matter may be settled quickly—creditors and credit-reporting agencies take your argument more seriously when confronted by lawyers.

Do not expect to receive much of a settlement—typically $2,500 to $5,000, minus your lawyer's cut—but at least the error will be removed from your credit report. Sometimes cases that don't end in settlement result in much bigger awards after a trial verdict.

Do not pursue the matter with a lawyer if you can't find one willing to take your case on contingency. That could be a sign that your case isn't strong enough to settle quickly. The legal fees from an extended battle likely would be prohibitively steep.

Be Extra-Vigilant About Credit Card Debt

Although credit card debt recently reached a multiyear low, that was mostly because banks tightened standards and would not extend credit to many people.

Also: Most of the recent decline in mortgage debt is attributable to foreclosures—not to people thriftily paying down their mortgages.

What to do: Retain a cautious attitude toward credit, even as your income improves and banks loosen lending requirements—to avoid going deeply into debt and having serious financial trouble in the event of another recession.

Greg McBride, CFA, a senior financial analyst at Bankrate.com.

Before You Buy a Brand-New Home, Read This...

Robert Irwin, who has more than 40 years of experience as a real estate broker and investor, Westlake Village, California. He is author of several books about real estate, including *Tips & Traps When Buying a Home* (McGraw-Hill). *www.RobertIrwin.com*

Home builders once again are building new homes. New-home construction has surged in recent months to levels not seen in more than four years, according to the Commerce Department, and sales are the highest in more than two years.

For home buyers, the appeal of a newly built home is obvious—everything is fresh and new...little maintenance is required... and buyers can have input on things such as paint colors, flooring and fixture choices, assuming that they buy before construction is completed. And most new homes come with warranties. New homes tend to cost a bit more than existing ones per square foot, but much of that premium is soon recouped in reduced maintenance and heating and cooling bills for an energy-efficient new home.

However, buying a new home has various challenges and potential problems. *What would-be buyers need to know...*

TODAY'S MARKET

•**The days of desperation sales are over in most areas.** Wonderful deals were available on new homes in many areas for much of the past five years as builders tried to unload unsold homes in a slow housing market. But the backlog is now gone in most areas, and today few builders will even start construction on a home until they've lined up a buyer.

What to do: If your goal is to find a bargain, call builders operating in the area that you are interested in and ask if they have any homes for sale that are completed or nearly completed. This isn't common, but even in this era of cautious home builders, it's possible that a deal fell through after construction was under way. If so, negotiate hard on price—you might be able to obtain a discount of perhaps 5% to 10% below the usual sale price, depending on the local market and the builder's financial situation.

•**It's almost impossible to time the sale of your current home perfectly.** Builders usually expect buyers to sign contracts before construction begins, and they offer few guarantees about when it will be completed. Prior to the housing-market meltdown, the conventional wisdom was that buyers should wait until their homes were virtually completed before listing their current homes for sale. That's risky in today's less predictable real estate market—if your existing home doesn't sell quickly, you could be stuck paying two mortgages.

What to do: Sell your current home before signing the contract to build the new home. Put most of your possessions in storage, and rent until the new home is ready.

•**Most new homes are being built in outlying areas.** Home buyers increasingly prefer homes located near downtowns, public transportation, shopping centers and other municipal infrastructure—but in most cases today, home builders are building farther from the action, where land is cheap. That could detract from the home's selling price later.

What to do: Lean toward new homes close to downtowns, major employers and/or public transit when possible. Or search for new homes in areas where there are plans for shopping centers, office buildings, municipal infrastructure and public transit options.

YOUR CHOICES

•**New-home upgrades usually are overpriced.** Some home builders offer a wide range of appliance, cabinetry and flooring alternatives, among other options. But select anything above the base option, and you are probably paying above market price—upgrades are a major source of profit for many, though not all, home builders.

What to do: Negotiate for lower prices on the upgrades that you want. Builders usually are willing to negotiate on upgrade prices because their profit margins on them are so steep. In some cases, you actually may do better financially by taking a builder's base-level option and then upgrading on your own.

•**Certain components that typically come with existing homes often aren't included with new homes.** Your new home might not come with landscaping, a deck and/or patio, fencing and/or window coverings.

What to do: Confirm that these are not included, and factor in the cost of adding them when making your home-buying decisions.

THE NEIGHBORHOOD

•**Expect noise.** Buying a home in a new subdivision might mean putting up with construction noise for months or years as additional houses are erected.

What to do: If noise is a major issue for you, lean toward new homes that are not in new subdivisions or toward subdivisions where most of the lots are already developed.

•**Expect to take a loss if you try to resell your new home quickly.** If you try to sell while part of the subdivision still is under construction, you will have to compete with the builder for buyers—and unlike the builder, you can't offer financing, customization or a brand-new home. Your landscaping also might not yet be

mature, which could cost your home curb appeal compared with existing properties.

What to do: Don't buy a home in a large new development unless you're likely to live in it for at least four to five years.

CONTRACTS AND FINANCING

•**Your contract might be lacking key contingencies.** Contracts that home builders ask buyers to sign often do not include clauses that make the purchase contingent on the property passing a home inspector's inspection…or on the buyer's ability to obtain outside financing.

What to do: Insist that these clauses be inserted before you sign. (The financing contingency is not necessary if you are paying cash.) Definitely hire a home inspector—new homes can have problems, too.

•**Contracts generally contain arbitration clauses.** That means you can't sue the builder even if there are major problems with the home that the builder won't fix. Your only recourse will be an arbitration process—which might be stacked in the builder's favor.

What to do: Ask to have the arbitration clause removed from your contract before signing. Most builders won't agree to this, but it's worth a try. Before signing a contract with a builder, check the builder's reputation for doing quality work and dealing fairly with buyers. Ask your real estate agent and real estate attorney for their opinions of the builder. Ask for off-the-record opinions from staffers in the town's building department, too (either in the town where you're buying or other towns where the builder has operated). Even knock on a few doors in developments that the builder has recently built to solicit home owners' opinions.

•**New home warranties vary greatly in quality.** Some provide limited or no coverage for certain home components or include exclusions for major issues such as mold. Others impose unreasonable maintenance requirements on home owners so that claims can be denied when home owners fail to comply. Lengthy 10-year warranties might cover only very specific elements of the home for a full decade, with many other components covered for as little as a year or two.

What to do: Ask your real estate agent and/or your attorney to examine the warranty to determine if it seems adequate before signing anything.

More from Robert Irwin...

What Real Estate Web Sites Don't Want You to Know

Nowadays, many home buyers and sellers depend on Web sites such as Trulia.com, Zillow.com and Realtor.com for real estate listings...information about prices and local market conditions...and real estate trends. But much of the information may be inaccurate and/or out of date.

Ways these sites may mislead you...

1. Their home-value estimates can be way off. Zillow and Trulia estimate the values of most homes across the country—but those estimates are less accurate than people imagine. Placing too much faith in them could lead sellers to set their asking prices too high or too low...or encourage buyers to offer too much or too little.

The sites don't send out home appraisers. They just gather data about the property and nearby properties and run this through a formula to come up with an educated guess.

Example: If the home next door to yours is about the same size as yours and sold for $250,000 last year, these sites probably will guess that yours is worth around $250,000, too. They won't know and so won't factor in that your home was recently renovated while the one next door is decades out of date.

The value estimates tend to be particularly questionable in states where home sale prices are not in the public record—Alaska, Idaho, Indiana, Kansas, Louisiana, Maine, Mississippi, Missouri, Montana, New Mexico, North Dakota, Texas, Utah and Wyoming.

To fix false information about your home: If you are selling your home or expect to do so soon, check the "Zillow Zestimate" and "Trulia Estimate" for the home to make sure that the information is accurate. Review the sales price history, tax assessment history and home description, then report any missing or inaccurate details to the Web site—though various home owners have complained that these Web sites can be slow to respond to complaints, sometimes even taking months. There are varying options to try to address a discrepancy. On Zillow, click "Report problem with listing" under the "More" button or "Claim this home." On Trulia, click "Edit home facts" or "Flag." Or ask your broker to try to fix the problem.

Home buyers, in particular, also should check how accurate the Web site claims its estimates are for the area in question. Only if you dig deep into these Web sites will you discover that even they admit that their estimates can be fairly inaccurate in some parts of the country. Knowing what level of accuracy they claim for the area at least provides a clue as to how reliable the data might be.

On Zillow, click the "About Zestimates" tab near the bottom of the home page, then click "States/Counties" in the "Data Coverage and Zestimate Accuracy Table." On Trulia, select "Trulia Estimates" from the "Explore Trulia" menu near the bottom of the home page, then click "Coverage and Accuracy."

2. Many of their listings are no longer on the market. According to a 2012 study conducted by consulting firm WAV Group, more than 35% of the homes listed for sale on Zillow and Trulia at any given time already have been sold or pulled from the market. Outdated listings linger in part because it isn't in the Web sites' interest to pull them—the more listings a real estate site has, the bigger and more useful it appears.

3. Their asking prices can be outdated. Third-party real estate sites such as Trulia and Zillow sometimes fail to promptly update listings to reflect asking price reductions. That means that buyers who use the search tools on these sites to view only properties in their price range might never see the listings of properties that weren't originally in their price range but now are because of price cuts.

What to do: Expand your search parameters to include homes 10% above the high end of your price range when you are searching for properties on Zillow or Trulia. Their current prices might now be in your price range. Even those that aren't may be close enough that the sellers might accept offers in your price range. Also search the listings on Realtor.com, where asking prices tend to be more up to date.

4. Their "days on the market" figures could be way off the mark. Homes new to the market often attract interest from multiple buyers, while those that have sat for 90 days or more tend to be ignored. Buyers often are wise to be aggressive with their offers on new listings, while low-ball offers might be accepted on older listings.

But the days-on-the-market data provided by real estate Web sites can be misleading. The figure could reflect the number of days since the property was added to the Web site, which might not have occurred until weeks after it actually went on the market with third-party sites such as Zillow and Trulia. And listing agents sometimes reset the days-on-the-market clock by taking the property off the market briefly, then relisting it.

What to do: Buyers should dig deeper to see if a listing's "days on the market" is telling the whole story before making an offer. Zillow and Trulia include a "price history" section that lists other recent times the home was on the market. Also, ask your buyer's agent—the real estate agent representing the home buyer—for details about the property's recent sales history. A buyer's agent can tell you if a home was pulled from the market and then quickly returned.

5. Some of the most desirable properties don't appear on sites until after they've sold. It can take a week for a new listing to appear on Realtor.com and longer still to appear on third-party Web sites such as Trulia and Zillow—and that's if the seller's agent submits the listing promptly to the Multiple Listing Service. Agents have been known to keep a few choice listings to themselves for a week or two when they think they can find a buyer on their own, in hopes of earning the full commission rather than splitting it with a buyer's agent.

Buyers who wait for listings to appear on Trulia and Zillow could miss out, particularly

if they're in the market for a rare and desirable property, such as a waterfront home or a home located in the area's most prestigious neighborhood.

What to do: If your local real estate market has heated up and your goal is to buy a property that's likely to be in great demand, choose one of the area's busiest, best-known agents as your buyer's agent. That increases the odds that you'll be one of the lucky few who gets to see desirable properties before they reach the sites. Also, visit open houses to meet other area agents, and let them know what you're looking for.

6. Listings on "for-sale-by-owner" sites often have inflated or inaccurate property descriptions. The property descriptions provided in home listings inevitably are written to put the property in the best possible light. In most cases, those descriptions are at least written by real estate agents who understand the difference between portraying a property in a good light and fabricating information. On for-sale-by-owner sites, however, the property descriptions usually are written by home owners themselves, who are more likely to distort descriptions.

You Can Win the Refinancing Game: Strategies to Get the Lowest Mortgage Rate

Keith Gumbinger, vice president of HSH Associates, publisher of mortgage and consumer loan information based in Pompton Plains, New Jersey. *www.HSH.com*

With mortgage rates near record lows, this seems like the perfect time to refinance—except for the fact that many home owners are having a tough time qualifying.

Lending standards have tightened greatly, making refinancing a challenge for home owners who have less-than-stellar credit ratings or high debt-to-income ratios. And reduced home values have left many home owners with insufficient home equity to qualify for refinancing.

But don't give up on today's amazingly good home mortgage deals—because there are solutions. *To clear major refinancing hurdles…*

LOW APPRAISAL VALUE

• **In order to qualify for refinancing, your home's value typically must be appraised,** and often nowadays the appraised value is so low that you end up with dramatically less equity in your home than you thought you had. The home's value even may be lower than the balance on your existing mortgage, leaving you "underwater." Lenders typically won't issue a refinance loan unless you have at least a 10% equity stake—meaning that you don't owe more than 90% of the home's value. A 20% equity stake typically is required to avoid paying *private mortgage insurance* (PMI).

What to do: There are four potential solutions if an appraisal suggests that refinancing (or refinancing without PMI) is impossible…

• **Get a second appraisal.** Ask the lender for a copy of the appraiser's report. It might be worth challenging the appraisal by paying for a second appraisal with the same lender if the lender is willing. Or you could shift to a different lender and get a new appraisal.

Using a second appraiser might be especially worthwhile if the first appraiser fell just short of the required value and if he/she failed to account for substantial improvements that you made to your home…or if he based the appraisal value largely on the sales prices of foreclosed or distressed homes or on homes in neighborhoods significantly less appealing than yours. This is not a step to take lightly, however—you'll typically have to pay $250 to $500 for a second appraisal.*

Helpful: If you believe that the original appraisal was flawed because it failed to properly account for the desirability of your neighborhood, ask your lender to select an appraiser based closer to where you live. This appraiser might better understand what the homes in your area are worth.

• **Do a "cash-in refinance."** Home owners who have sufficient cash can pay down their mortgages to reach the required equity levels.

*Prices and rates subject to change.

Warning: If you have a second mortgage, you might have no choice but to pay this off to refinance.

• **Refinance through the Home Affordable Refinance Program (HARP).** If your mortgage is owned or guaranteed by Fannie Mae or Freddie Mac, the most recent version of the government's HARP program might allow you to refinance even if you are underwater or you have a limited equity position. The Web site MakingHomeAffordable.gov can help you determine if your mortgage qualifies (select "Does Fannie or Freddie Own Your Loan?" from the "Tools" menu). If so, contact your mortgage servicer and ask if it is taking part in the HARP program. If your servicer is not taking part, you are allowed to refinance through a participating lender.

• **Refinance through the National Mortgage Settlement.** If your underwater mortgage is owned and serviced by Ally Financial, Bank of America, Citigroup, JPMorgan Chase or Wells Fargo, you might qualify for refinancing through a settlement that those mortgage issuers made in 2012 with government regulators to make up for questionable foreclosure practices. To be eligible, you must have a current interest rate of at least 5.25% and no late payments within the past 12 months…the property must be owner-occupied and underwater…and the new loan must slash at least $100 per month or be at least one-quarter of a percentage point lower than the borrower's existing rate, among other requirements. Contact your loan servicer for details if you think you might be eligible.

LOW CREDIT SCORE

It's possible to refinance with a FICO credit score as low as 620—but don't expect to be offered attractive refinancing terms these days unless your credit score is 740 or above.

What to do: Purchase a copy of your FICO credit score through MyFICO.com for $19.95, which includes a score and credit report based on information on file with one of the three main credit-reporting bureaus.

If your score is about 740 or lower, obtain copies of your credit reports from the three reporting bureaus—Equifax (*www.Equifax.com*),

Experian (*www.Experian.com*) and Trans Union (*www.TransUnion.com*). Then contact those bureaus to correct any inaccurate information on the reports. Avoid running up big credit card balances, making payments late or applying for new credit in the months before applying to refinance a mortgage. Pay down credit card balances and other debts if possible.

If you cannot increase your credit score to 740, a Federal Housing Administration (FHA) mortgage might be the only way to refinance at an attractive rate. FHA-refinanced mortgages officially are available to those with credit scores as low as 580, but in practice, lenders make them difficult or expensive to obtain for home owners whose credit scores are below 620. Contact local mortgage lenders that deal with FHA loans for the details (select "Lender Locator" from the "Resources" menu at *www. HUD.gov*).

HIGH DEBT VS. INCOME

Five or six years ago, mortgage lenders considered a person's total debt-to-income ratio of 55% or even 60% sufficient to refinance—and many lenders often didn't even bother to confirm borrowers' income. These days, a ratio no higher than 38% is likely to be required—a small percentage of lenders will go as high as 41%—and every element of the borrower's financial situation will be scrutinized.

What to do: First, determine the ratio of your monthly debt payments to your monthly income, either using an online calculator (type "debt-to-income ratio calculator" into a search engine) or by asking a lender for help. If you've been paying down your mortgage for many years without borrowing against the value of the home, your debt-to-income ratio might not be as high as you fear. If you are slightly above the 38% mark, it might make sense to use liquid assets to pay down your debts enough to qualify for refinancing.

Lenders' recent emphasis on income verification can make refinancing particularly difficult for the self-employed. For these home owners, the best option often is refinancing through a credit union or community bank with which they have a long-standing relationship.

More from Keith Gumbinger...

Who Should Refinance?

Among those who should attempt to refinance a mortgage...

•**Home owners currently paying 6% or higher.** Fixed rates recently averaged about 4.5% for a 30-year mortgage.* If your mortgage rate is 6% or higher, you will almost certainly save money by refinancing—unless you sell the home in the next year or two. If you're paying between 4.5% and 5%, refinancing might be worthwhile, particularly if you expect to remain in your home for at least five years. A refinancing calculator such as the one that's on HSH's Web site (*www.HSH.com/refinance-calculator*) can help you run the numbers.

•**Those who need improved cash flow today.** Refinancing to a new 30-year mortgage can lower your interest rate and stretch your payments out over a new 30-year period. That could reduce your monthly mortgage bill by hundreds of dollars.

•**Those who want to build equity and pay down their mortgages fast.** You don't have to opt for a new 30-year mortgage when you refinance—you could choose a 20- or 15-year mortgage instead. Rates on these shorter mortgages are even lower than those available for mortgages of 30 years—recently averaging just 3.5% for a 15-year fixed mortgage—which means home owners might be able to pay off their mortgages quickly without greatly increasing their monthly mortgage bills.

Alternative: Refinancing to a hybrid adjustable-rate mortgage (ARM), such as a 5/1 ARM, where the rate is fixed for five years and then adjustable for one-year periods, is appropriate for those who want the lowest possible interest rates for the next five years or so and who are confident that they will sell the home before the fixed introductory-rate period ends. Rates on 5/1 ARMs recently averaged about 3.4%.

•**Those with ARMs.** If you're currently in an ARM and don't plan to sell your house anytime soon, definitely consider refinancing to

*Rates as of mid-August 2013.

lock in today's extremely low fixed rates. This may be prudent even if refinancing would result in a rate increase.

For a Great Mortgage Rate...Avoid These Common Mistakes If You're Refinancing or Buying

Dale Robyn Siegel, Esq., owner of Circle Mortgage Group, a mortgage brokerage company based in Harrison, New York. She is an adjunct professor at New York University and Baruch College, both in New York City, and author of *The New Rules for Mortgages* (Alpha). *www.DaleSiegel.com*

Mortgage rates are near record lows—borrowers could find 30-year fixed-rate mortgages around 4.5% recently.* But very low interest rates are not enough to guarantee that borrowers will get great mortgage deals when they buy homes or refinance. *They also must steer clear of these mortgage mistakes…*

Mistake: **Ignoring the age of your old loan when refinancing.** If you're 10 years into a 30-year mortgage when you refinance to a new 30-year loan, you will have to make 10 additional years of payments to pay it off—and when it comes to loan payments, time is money.

Example: You might think that you are saving a fortune if you refinance a 6% 30-year fixed mortgage with 20 years remaining into a new 3.75% 30-year mortgage. And assuming an original loan amount of $150,000, your monthly payment would indeed drop from $904 all the way to $619. But because you're adding 10 additional years of interest payments, you're actually costing yourself money over the life of the loan. With the old mortgage, the remaining payments would have come to around $217,000—but with the new one, you'll pay around $223,000, plus perhaps

*Rates as of mid-August 2013.

$3,000 in closing costs. That's a net loss of around $9,000.

Better: Unless your primary goal is to free up cash in your current budget, strongly consider opting for a mortgage shorter than 30 years when you refinance. In the example above, you could refinance that 6% 30-year mortgage to a new 20-year mortgage at 3.5%. That would reduce your monthly payments to $775 without extending your loan payments. You would make a total of around $186,000 in loan payments to pay off the loan—and even with $3,000 in closing costs, you would save around $28,000 in the long run.

Mistake: **Buying a car or changing jobs before you close on your mortgage.** The loan-approval process does not actually end when your mortgage is approved. Your lender is likely to reconfirm your employment and financials in the week before your loan closes—Fannie Mae's recently implemented Loan Quality Initiative now requires lenders to track changes in borrower circumstances between the application date and closing, for example. Your lender might back away from a previously approved loan or alter the loan's terms if it discovers that you have changed jobs or taken out a car loan—potentially even if you've acquired a new credit card.

Better: Delay doing anything that could significantly alter your credit score or employment history until after the mortgage closes.

Mistake: **Assuming that the lowest advertised mortgage rate must be the best deal.** You really cannot compare mortgage offers simply by comparing interest rates—a lender could quote a low rate by jacking up the loan's closing costs.

Better: When you contact lenders, do not ask, "What's your rate?" Instead ask, "What's your 30-year fixed rate with zero points if I lock it in for 60 days?" Even if that isn't exactly the mortgage you end up choosing, phrasing the question this precisely increases the odds that you're comparing apples to apples when you get quotes.

Mistake: **Letting a lender charge you hidden points.** Just because a lender tells you that a mortgage has low or no points doesn't guarantee that it has low or no fees. Points are a type of fee charged as a percentage of the loan amount. Some lenders instead charge steep flat fees—rather than fees calculated as a percentage—so they can tell borrowers that their loans have low or no points without technically lying.

Better: When the lender quotes you loan terms, first ask if there's a "discount fee," an "origination fee" or a "broker fee." These are the labels lenders typically use when they try to hide points in the form of flat fees. Also, immediately request a written good-faith estimate of the mortgage's terms. Lenders are required to provide good-faith estimates within three days of receiving a loan application, but borrowers can and should request these estimates as early as their initial contact with the lender. Read the estimates to confirm that there are no steep undisclosed fees.

Mistake: **Allowing rates to float too long rather than locking them in.** Borrowers typically either lock in a mortgage rate with a lender when their loan is approved or allow the rate to "float"—remain unfixed until closing. Because rates have been trending generally downward for years, many borrowers opt to let their rate float—that is, to remain unfixed until closing—in hopes that rates will continue to decline between approval and closing. That's a poor gamble in today's ultralow-rate environment. Rates indeed might fall slightly, but they already are so low that they couldn't possibly fall far. On the other hand, there's at least a small chance that rates could rebound significantly, perhaps if the economy suddenly showed strong signs of life.

Caution: Although you don't want to gamble that rates will not rise by the time you close, you also don't want to lock in a rate too early in the process because then your lock-in window could expire before your mortgage closes. If that happens, you might have to pay a significant penalty to extend the lock-in…or it may not be possible to extend the lock-in, leaving you stuck with whatever rate is available on your closing date.

Better: Before locking in a rate, ask the lender what your options will be if you overrun the lock-up period. Also ask if it's pos-

sible to initially allow the rate to float, then later lock it in, perhaps a few weeks down the road.

True, there's some risk that interest rates could increase before you lock in, but odds are good that they won't climb very far if you postpone only a few weeks. The odds of a significant increase are much greater if you overrun a 30- or 60-day lock-in, because significantly more time will have passed. (Lenders might offer longer lock-in windows as well—perhaps 90 days—but only at significantly higher interest rates.)

Mistake: **Choosing an adjustable-rate mortgage (ARM) because you expect to sell the home before the interest rate resets.** Rates quoted on ARMs are inevitably lower than those of fixed mortgages. Lately, borrowers could find 5/1 ARMs (ARMs that offer fixed rates for the first five years, followed by annual rate adjustments thereafter) at around 3.4%, compared with 4.5% for 30-year fixed mortgages. There is no downside to choosing that 5/1 ARM if you sell the home before the rate resets in five years. Trouble is, people are not very good at predicting how long they will stay in their homes.

Better: Chose a fixed-rate mortgage, and lock in today's very low rates even if you do expect to move before an ARM's rate resets. Interest rates are likely to climb substantially from today's historically low levels over the course of the coming decade, making ARMs not worth the risk if there's any significant chance that you still will own the home after the loan's rate resets.

Mortgage Savings from a Warehouse Club

Costco has teamed up with 10 banks to process, approve and complete low-cost mortgages for club members, though Costco itself doesn't actually offer the mortgages. Costco Executive members pay discounted lending fees of $600 or less, and GoldStar members pay $750 or less—potentially big savings over the usual charge of 1% or more of the loan amount. Closing costs (such as appraisal, title and credit report fees) are extra.

Information: http://CostcoFinance.com.

What to do: Comparison-shop for mortgages using the Costco offers as well as ones from lenders.

Kiplinger's Personal Finance. www.Kiplinger.com

More Help from Banks for Borrowers Struggling with Mortgage Payments

The Consumer Financial Protection Bureau (CFPB) says mortgage-loan servicers must consider troubled borrowers for all loan-assistance options that are allowed by mortgage investors, such as Fannie Mae and Freddie Mac. The lending industry will be required to help borrowers consider all possible ways to retain their homes when the CFPB rules take effect in 2014.

If you are having trouble meeting mortgage payments: Contact your lender, and ask for help exploring all available ways of staying in your home. Some lenders have already adopted at least some CFPB standards.

The Wall Street Journal. www.WSJ.com

Shop Around for a Title Insurer

You may save hundreds of dollars by finding your own title insurer when buying a home. Insurers who are recommended by real estate agents often pay the agents a referral fee, which makes the title service more expensive.

What to do: Ask for quotes from direct-to-consumer title insurance companies such as Entitle Direct (*www.EntitleDirect.com*) and TitleInsurance.com (*www.TitleInsurance.com*). Compare costs at a local title insurer that is not affiliated with a lender or real estate broker.

To save on closing costs: Get a loan-origination fee estimate from several lenders. You may be able to negotiate certain fees. For example, try to get your agent to strike any administrative brokerage commission (ABC) fee from your listing agreement. This fee typically costs the buyer and the seller $100 to $300 each.*

Kiplinger's Personal Finance. www.Kiplinger.com
*Rates subject to change.

The Secret to Getting Top Dollar for Your Home—Find the Right Real Estate Agent

Kathy Mayer Braddock, a founding partner of Braddock + Purcell, a real estate advocacy group that helps New York area home buyers and sellers select agents. She previously was executive managing director and general sales manager for Douglas Elliman, greater New York City's largest residential real estate company, where she was in charge of more than 1,100 agents. She also is cofounder of Rutenberg Realty, New York City. *www.BandP.com*

Some people put less thought into selecting a real estate agent to sell their home than they do into picking a restaurant for dinner. They hire an agent they know socially or the one who has the biggest ad in the Yellow Pages—then wonder why their home doesn't sell quickly or for as much as their neighbor's home.

Property values finally are stabilizing across much of the country, but the days when every listing received competitive offers aren't coming back anytime soon. In this market, an agent's ability to properly price and market a home can make a substantial difference in the amount of attention it receives and its eventual sales price.

Here's a five-step plan for selecting the right real estate agent for you...

1. Ask for the "relocation coordinator" when you initially contact agencies. Sellers who call agencies typically are routed to whichever agent happens to be up in the rotation that day—it's like spinning a roulette wheel to decide who sells your most valuable asset.

In contrast, relocation coordinators can be objective because they don't sell homes themselves—their job is to assist executives who are moving to the area. The relocation coordinator often is willing to provide an insider's opinion about which of the agents at the agency is most appropriate for a particular listing, given the home's location and approximate value.

If you're not certain which agencies to call, lean toward those that seem to have lots of homes for sale in your neighborhood, based on yard signs or listings on Web sites such as *www.Zillow.com* or *www.Trulia.com*. These are likely to be active, respected agencies that have a strong knowledge of your specific area. Real estate is extremely local—an agency that sells lots of home in your neighborhood likely understands the nuances of home values in the neighborhood.

Helpful: Small agencies often do not have relocation coordinators. If this is the case, ask to be represented by the broker/owner or at least obtain the broker/owner's guidance in selecting the agent most appropriate for you.

2. Research agents before you meet with them. Experienced agents should have Web pages detailing their background and recent sales, typically on their agencies' Web sites—be wary of those who don't. Use this Web page to confirm that the agent has extensive experience selling homes in your price range and area—familiarity with homes much like yours is crucial. Also confirm that this is a full-time real estate agent—you don't want to trust your home to a part-timer.

Do a Google search of the agent's name and agency, too. Choose a different agent if this turns up numerous complaints from previous clients.

3. Interview at least three agents from different agencies—ideally four or five—before settling on one. Interviewing three or more agents lets sellers weed out those whose opinions on the listing price and needed improvements diverge significantly from the consensus. Why avoid these outliers? If your agent's views differ greatly from those of most other agents, your home is likely to seem mispriced or flawed to the agents who represent potential buyers, too.

Example: Two of the three agents you speak with say your home should be listed for $450,000 and that the dingy carpet in the living room should be replaced. A third says that it should be listed for $500,000 as is. There's a good chance that the third is either misreading the market or telling you what he/she thinks you want to hear to win the listing.

4. During interviews, ask agents about their marketing strategies, pricing recommendations and background. Agents should be able to lay out fairly detailed marketing plans that may include open houses, brochures, advertising and online marketing—and be able to explain their reasoning for each element of this plan. Often it's the explanation of why the strategy has been selected that's most telling.

Example: Perhaps the agent has learned from earlier sales that placing ads in a specific publication that caters primarily to vacationers visiting the area is a great way to find potential buyers for area lake homes.

Steer clear of real estate agents who recommend a listing price immediately upon viewing your home. An agent might reasonably discuss a general pricing strategy or a price range when asked about recommendations for a listing price during this initial interview, but a responsible agent should take some time back at the office to review recent comparable sales before citing a specific listing price. Don't work with an agent who asks you what you want to ask for the home. Agents who solicit clients' opinions about listing price often set listing prices based on clients' desires rather than on reality.

Helpful: When agents call back later with their proposed listing prices, ask how they arrived at the figures. It should be based mainly on the closing prices of homes such as yours that recently have sold or that are in the process of closing. It should not primarily be based on the prices being asked for homes still on the market. Savvy agents understand that what matters most is what buyers are paying, not what sellers are asking.

Eliminate agents whose guidance deviates significantly from the consensus, then chose the one who most impressed you throughout the process. If your initial interviews produce no clear consensus about your home's listing price or needs, continue interviewing agents until a consensus emerges. If you don't have time for that, lean toward an agent whose opinion is in the middle of the pack.

A more experienced real estate agent usually is preferable to a less experienced one—particularly if that experience includes many homes sold in your home's price range and neighborhood. An agent with limited experience might be acceptable if he is working in conjunction with a more experienced colleague, however.

5. Ask for contact information for the agent's five most recent sales. Contact at least a few of these sellers to confirm that they had a positive experience with the agent.

Helpful: If the agent lists recent sales on his Web page, use these to confirm that you really have been given the five most recent sales. If not, ask about the missing seller—the agent might be hiding a less-than-satisfied client from you.

Trying to Sell Your Home? Spruce Up Your Bathroom

There are several easy, low-cost things you can do to make your bath more appealing without spending a lot. First, regrout the tiles around the tub, and recaulk where the tub meets the tiles and where it meets the floor. Revitalize a wooden vanity with a coat of dark semigloss paint. Replace a worn toilet seat and install new light fixtures, faucets and cabinet pulls. Also, add a new shower curtain, bath mat and fluffy towels. Finally, make sure that the bathroom is sparkling clean and that all toiletries have been put away.

Donna Dazzo, president of the home staging company Designed to Appeal, with locations in New York City and the Hamptons, New York, quoted in *The New York Times.*

Get More Money for College: Avoid These 6 Traps

Kalman A. Chany, founder and president of Campus Consultants, a New York City–located company founded in 1984 that has helped thousands of families maximize their financial aid. He is author of *Paying for College Without Going Broke* (Princeton Review). www.CampusConsultants.com

To get the most financial aid possible for college, you and your child need to understand how the complicated eligibility formulas work. This applies whether the assistance is in the form of need-based scholarships or grants that don't need to be paid back or federally subsidized loans.

This is especially important in light of the increased competition for financial aid in recent years.

Traps to avoid…

Trap #1: **Waiting until your child's senior year of high school to think about financial aid.** During that year, you can submit the *Free Application for Federal Student Aid* (FAFSA), starting January 1, and possibly other forms, which may be required earlier. But the financial criteria that determine your financial-aid package are based in part on your family's income for the entire calendar year before your child enrolls in college.

In other words, the year that really counts is the calendar year that begins January 1 during your child's junior year of high school and runs through December 31 in his/her senior year. This is known as the first "base income year," and it's critical because financial-aid officers use it as a basis for the first year's financial-aid package.

For many people, it's important to act in advance of the first base income year to aggressively lower the income that you will report on the aid forms for that base income year (as well as the remaining base income years that follow during college because financial-aid forms must be submitted for each year and your eligibility is reassessed each time).

For aid purposes, your income includes your Adjusted Gross Income (AGI) if you file taxes plus various types of untaxed income. For most families, income plays the biggest role in determining the amount of college costs that your family is expected to be able to pay—known as the "expected family contribution," or EFC—under various aid formulas.

Ways to reduce income…

• **Accelerate sales of any stocks or property that you are ready to sell and that will have capital gains.** You should do this prior to any base income year. In addition, try to offset capital gains with capital losses during any base income year.

• **Avoid overpaying state and local taxes in the year prior to the base income year if you are going to itemize your deductions.** Reason: If you overpay these taxes in the year before the base income year, you'll receive refunds for the overpayment during the base year—and these refunds will be considered part of your AGI.

Helpful: It also makes sense to reduce your assets before you file your aid forms because assets are another important factor in determining financial aid. Although you don't want to go on a shopping spree to reduce the amount of cash you have in your bank accounts, consider paying off credit card and car-loan debt or spending money on a major purchase or project that you were planning anyway, such as buying a new car or fixing the roof on your house.

Trap #2: **Not filing a FAFSA because you believe that your income is too high for you to qualify for aid.** There are many other factors that determine aid eligibility, including the cost of the school. In some cases, families with incomes above $100,000 or even $200,000 qualify for assistance—especially if there will be more than one child in college

during the same academic year or a child is attending a private college.

Trap #3: **Putting money in your child's name.** If you are otherwise eligible for financial aid—especially need-based scholarships and grants—avoid custodial accounts (UTMAs or UGMAs) and trust funds.

Reason: The federal government and colleges figure that a student should be required to spend a far greater percentage of his own money for college than his parents' money, so student assets have a far greater impact on lowering your family's eligibility for financial assistance.

In determining eligibility for aid, up to just 5.65% of parental assets are counted in the aid formulas, compared with 20% to 25% of a student's assets. (Retirement accounts generally are excluded in the aid formulas for both parents and students.)

What to do: Think twice before putting assets in a child's name.

Trap #4: **Encouraging your child to earn large amounts of money during college years.** Some parents push their children to work so much to help pay for college that it cuts into their study time. They may not realize that under the FAFSA formula, once the child's income exceeds a certain amount in the base income year ($6,130 for the 2013–2014 school year), he may lose 50 cents of financial aid for every dollar above that. For some schools, the trigger number is as low as $4,147.

Exception: Earnings from a federal work-study program are excluded from income in the aid formulas. (For more on federal work-study jobs, go to *http://StudentAid.ed.gov.* Under "Types of Aid," click "Work-Study Jobs.")

Trap #5: **Letting grandparents chip in too directly.** Generous grandparents can be an enormous help in funding a college education, but they also can hurt a student's financial-aid eligibility if their contributions are not handled correctly.

For instance, some grandparents write a check directly to the school to cover a portion of the child's educational expenses. That's not a good idea because such payments can reduce financial aid on a dollar-for-dollar basis.

Other grandparents establish 529 college savings plans in their own names with their grandchildren as the beneficiaries. Unlike 529s owned by parents or students, the money in a grandparent-owned 529 doesn't need to be reported on the FAFSA at all.

Problem: Distributions from grandparent 529s are considered part of the student's base year income, whereas distributions from parent- or student-owned 529s are not counted as income in the financial-aid calculations.

My advice: If your goal is to maximize your financial aid, the grandparents could simply hold off on contributing to the grandchild's education finances at all until the student graduates, then help him pay off his student loans. Alternatively, if a grandparent already has established a 529 college savings plan, he might wait until after the final financial-aid application for the student's college years is filed before making a distribution—that typically means after January 1 of the grandchild's junior year of college.

Trap #6: **Not cooperating with the student's other parent if you are divorced or separated.** Only the "custodial" parent is required to list his income or assets on a FAFSA. That's the parent with whom the student has lived the majority of time in the 12 months preceding the day the application is filed, regardless of who has legal custody or who claims the child as a dependent on his/her tax returns. The finances of the noncustodial parent are not considered at all by most colleges when awarding aid.

So if you are looking for the biggest aid package at one of those colleges, you may decide to have the child live primarily with the parent who can demonstrate the most need for financial assistance.

However, some colleges—primarily some very selective private colleges and some state universities—do require financial information from the noncustodial parent and his/her spouse when awarding the school's own financial aid. (That is not the case with federal aid.)

Keep in mind that if the custodial parent has remarried, the stepparent's income and assets must be included on the FAFSA and possibly other aid applications.

More from Kalman A. Chany...

Student Loan Rules Are Changing

Rules for Stafford loans—government loans made directly to students—are about to change in ways not beneficial to students.

If your college student didn't max out his/her available subsidized Stafford loans this current school year, it's probably wise to do so. (With subsidized Stafford loans, the government pays the interest while the student is in school...with unsubsidized Stafford loans, the government does not.)

• **The interest rate (currently 3.86% fixed for subsidized undergraduate loans for the 2013–2014 school year) will probably rise for new applicants in future years** (though borrowers who have the current rate can keep it for the life of the loan).

• **Students will be charged interest during the "grace period"**—the six months after the student leaves college but before repayment begins. This applies to loans dispersed after July 1, 2012.

• **A loan origination fee rebate of 0.5% is no longer offered.**

• **Loans to graduate/professional school students are unsubsidized.** Interest will accrue while grad students still are in school.

These changes affect only Stafford loans. Other federal loan programs—Perkins loans for undergraduate and graduate students, PLUS loans for parents of undergraduate students and GradPlus loans for graduate and professional school students—are not expected to change in the near future.

Colleges Sometimes Waive Application Fees

The average college application fee is nearly $40 and students apply to an average of eight schools.

To avoid the application fee: Go to college fairs—some schools offer fee waivers to promising students. If you visit a college in person, ask the admissions office for a fee waiver or reduction. Some colleges waive the fee for online applications. And if you have family alumni or apply early, be sure to ask about a fee waiver. Finally, if you are in a lower-income bracket or are suffering financial hardship, talk to a guidance counselor or contact the National Association for College Admission Counseling (*www. NACACNet.org*) to request a waiver.

The Wall Street Journal. www.WSJ.com

How America Is Cutting College Costs

Families are cutting college costs by choosing less expensive schools and by finding less costly ways for students to attend. More students are taking advantage of grants and scholarships and friends and relatives are helping to pay costs. In addition, attendance at two-year public colleges is up and more students are living at home.

"How America Pays for College 2012," survey by student-loan company Sallie Mae.

College Tuitions Can Vary by Major

More than 140 public universities are currently charging more for majors in math, science and business—areas that cost more to teach and can lead to higher-paying jobs for graduates. Tuition for these majors can be $50 more per credit.

Some schools that currently charge tuition based on majors: Iowa State University, Rutgers University, South Dakota State University, University of Illinois, University of Nebraska-Lincoln, University of Tennessee-Knoxville.

Some that are considering differential tuition: University of Florida, Florida State University, University of Maryland-College Park, University of Minnesota, University of Buffalo, Stony Brook University, Binghamton University, University at Albany, University of California-Berkeley, University of California-Los Angeles.

Study by Cornell Higher Education Research Institute, reported in *USA Today*.

8

Insurance Insights

Hidden Traps and Loopholes in the Health-Care Law: This Article Could Save You $10,000!

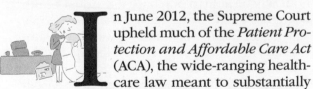

In June 2012, the Supreme Court upheld much of the *Patient Protection and Affordable Care Act* (ACA), the wide-ranging health-care law meant to substantially alter America's health insurance system.

You've probably seen hundreds of headlines about the best-known parts of the ACA—the fact that it will require most Americans to have health insurance or pay a "penalty"…will require insurance companies to offer policies to all who apply (even those who are sick)… and will raise the Medicare tax on people who earn more than $200,000 ($250,000 for married couples filing jointly).

But some important elements of the ACA have not made headlines or are commonly misunderstood. Depending on your situation, it may be very important that you know about these elements. *Among the ACA's lesser-known consequences and hidden loopholes are the following…*

•**Your retirement could cost your adult child his/her health insurance.** One of the much-ballyhooed aspects of the ACA is that it allows adult children to remain on their parents' health insurance coverage through age 26. But there's an important exception to this rule that hasn't received much attention—it usually does not apply to retiree health plans.

Vital: If your adult child is on your health insurance coverage and you expect to retire soon, confirm that your retiree plan will cover the child. If it won't, the adult child should

Maura Carley, MPH, CIC, CEO of Healthcare Navigation, LLC, a patient advocacy and consulting company based in Shelton, Connecticut. She previously held senior management positions with Yale-New Haven Hospital, Stamford Hospital and Kaiser Permanente. She is author of *Health Insurance: Navigating Traps & Gaps* (Ampersand, Inc.). *www.HealthCareNavigation.com*

start researching alternative coverage options well before your retirement date. Alternatives might include individual coverage…COBRA coverage from the parent's former employer's plan…or Medicaid coverage if the adult child has very limited income and assets.

•**Preventive care sometimes isn't 100% covered despite news reports to the contrary.** One well-publicized aspect of the ACA is that insurers now are required to provide many forms of preventive care—things such as routine checkups, mammograms and colonoscopies—without the patient paying a penny out-of-pocket.

What's rarely mentioned is that this preventive-care provision is so loaded with confusing caveats that patients who seek "free" preventive treatments might end up with unexpected medical bills. For example, if your insurer has not made major changes to your plan since the ACA passed in 2010, the plan might be "grandfathered" and not obliged to fully cover preventive services. Preventive care also might not be fully covered if you seek treatment from an out-of-network provider…you have a limited-benefit plan that has obtained a government waiver freeing it from the preventive-care mandate…or the specific preventive treatment that you receive is not one covered by the ACA.

Self-defense: To avoid surprises, contact your plan provider or your employer's benefits department to confirm the coverage level before you schedule any preventive services.

•**The ACA's attempt to close the Medicare Part D "donut hole" has made selecting the right Part D plan more important—and more difficult.** Medicare recipients face a gap in their prescription drug coverage—the so-called Part D "donut hole." If you incur significant pharmaceutical bills during a year, you might have to pay thousands of dollars of drug costs out-of-pocket before your Part D benefits resume.

The ACA will slowly close that Part D donut hole over the coming years. It will force drug manufacturers to offer steep discounts to buyers who reach the donut hole and will require Part D plans to pay most of the remaining costs. Trouble is, drug manufacturers and the private companies that sell Part D plans inevitably will pass the cost of that expanded coverage along to Part D plan participants—and some will do so in subtle ways that might not be noticeable at first.

Example: An insurer might remove many brand-name drugs from its *formulary*—its list of covered drugs. You probably won't notice until you refill a prescription or receive a first-time prescription for one of these drugs.

As different insurance companies adopt ways to pass along the cost of closing the donut hole in the coming years, the differences among Part D plans will increase, making it more important than ever for patients to carefully examine available Part D options during the open-enrollment period. Do this every year even if you are pleased with your current Part D plan—your current plan might change substantially from year to year as insurers adjust to the ACA's rules. This is happening already—I have a client who would have faced $10,000 more in out-of-pocket costs this year with one Part D plan than with another.

Useful resource: The Medicare Web site, *www.MyMedicare.gov*, can help you analyze Part D options.

•**If you have any health condition that makes obtaining insurance on the individual market difficult or impossible, you may have to wait until next year to find affordable coverage.** People with preexisting conditions will be able to purchase individual health insurance at the same rates as healthy people starting in 2014. Until then, government-subsidized high-risk pools were supposed to be available to help these people get insurance. But President Obama suspended new enrollments in the program in early 2013 because of a lack of funding.

These high-risk pools had attracted little attention and relatively few participants, in part because of their strict eligibility requirements—only people who have been without health insurance for at least six months can join, among other restrictions. But these pools were a tremendous deal for those who got in before enrollment closed. Some states are running their own high-risk pools, while others offer pools run by the Department of Health and Human Services (DHHS). Rates vary, but in general, they are even lower than the rates likely to be available starting in 2014.

Example: A 50-year-old who has serious health problems that make him otherwise uninsurable could obtain coverage for between $214 and $559 per month* through a DHHS-administered pool, depending on his state of residence and other factors—less than many perfectly healthy people his age pay. Rates tend to be much steeper in high-risk pool programs that were created by states before the ACA. Those programs vary, too, but are not federally subsidized. Those that are not federally subsidized may be accepting new enrollments.

What to do: If you have a preexisting condition and have been without health insurance for at least six months, visit the government's high-risk pool Web site, *www.PCIP.gov.*

*Rates subject to change.

How to Find Health Insurance on Your Own

To find the best health insurance if you are unemployed, self-employed or if your company doesn't offer medical coverage, first contact the Foundation for Health Coverage Education (*www.CoverageforAll.org*) to determine your best options. If you recently left a job that offered health insurance, you can continue your coverage under COBRA.

Information on individual insurance plans is available at *www.HealthCare.gov.* You can find a licensed health insurance agent through the National Association of Health Underwriters (*www.NAHU.org*), or check with your auto or homeowner's insurance broker to see if the company offers medical coverage as well.

If you have a preexisting condition, can't get private coverage and have been without coverage for at least six months, you may qualify under a federal plan.

More information: Visit *www.PCIP.gov.*
Los Angeles Times. www.LATimes.com

Fewer Workers Are Buying Company Health Insurance

Because of the weak economy, more employees are declining insurance from their employers. About 90% of workers who did not take the insurance said it was too expensive. Many employers have gradually been raising premiums, deductibles and co-payments to control insurance rates.

What to do: Make budgeting for health insurance a priority. Be aware that company plans usually are much less expensive than anything a person can buy as an individual.

Paul Fronstin, PhD, director, health research and education program, Employee Benefit Research Institute, Washington, DC, quoted online at *www.MSNBC. MSN.com.*

Before Making an Appointment with a New Doctor...

Prior to seeing new doctors, double-check whether they are in-network or out-of-network. Insurers' directories often are out-of-date—check directly with your insurer. Be aware that some specialists, such as anesthesiologists and emergency physicians, rarely accept any insurance plans. Find out what your insurer will pay—some now pay only Medicare rates for out-of-network care, which can leave you with a bigger bill than you expect. And many insurers now cover only 70% of out-of-network costs, not 80% as in the past.

What to do: If checking into a hospital, request in writing to be seen only by in-network providers. If you must go out of network, call the hospital's or doctor's billing office directly and try to negotiate a lower fee—aim for about a one-third reduction.

Money. www.Money.CNN.com

Don't Assume Anesthesia Is Covered by Insurance

Anesthesia may not be covered by health insurance.

Example: A colonoscopy can be done either with conscious sedation or full anesthesia. If the procedure is done with full anesthesia that is not deemed medically necessary, the anesthesia may not be covered unless the doctor makes a case for it.

Self-defense: You might not be able to meet the anesthesiologist in advance, so make it clear to your doctor—in writing, if there is any question—that anesthesia must be administered only if necessary and only by a participating provider in your plan.

Charles B. Inlander, a health-care consultant and consumer advocate based in Fogelsville, Pennsylvania, and the founding president of the People's Medical Society.

Can You Afford Long-Term Care? Big Insurers Are Bailing Out...What to Do Now

Robert Carlson, JD, CPA, managing member of Carlson Wealth Advisors, LLC. Based in Fairfax, Virginia, he is editor of the monthly newsletter *Retirement Watch*. *www.RetirementWatch.com*

Buying long-term-care (LTC) coverage is supposed to ease your financial anxieties about retirement by guaranteeing that you can afford extended nursing care if needed. But lately the LTC insurance sector has been in such a state of upheaval that buying and owning a policy have been anything but reassuring.

Half of the 20 largest LTC providers have stopped issuing policies, including giants such as Unum and MetLife. Many of the insurers that remain have been dramatically increasing premiums for new and existing policyholders.

150

The average annual premium now is around $3,500 per year.

Helpful: Existing policyholders can remain with insurers that stop issuing new policies. Even if the issuer increases premiums, switching likely would be even more expensive because you would be signing up at a higher age.

Providers have been tightening underwriting rules, too, making it difficult for someone who has a significant health issue to obtain coverage except perhaps through very expensive "high-risk" pools. But despite the drawbacks, for many people the right kind of LTC insurance could make sense if they shop carefully. *Here's what you need to know...*

WHO SHOULD BUY IT

If you have less than $300,000 in assets when you reach your 50s or 60s, you're probably better off skipping the LTC insurance and spending down your assets to qualify for Medicaid if you later require long-term care. If you have more than $2 million in assets, you probably can skip the coverage and just pay for any care that's needed out of pocket unless you have a family history that suggests that a long nursing home stay is likely. But if your savings fall between $300,000 and $2 million, an LTC policy likely makes sense. If so, it's best to obtain coverage while still in your mid-to-late 50s because insurers are dramatically tightening their underwriting standards. The older you are when you attempt to obtain coverage, the greater the odds that you will have a health problem that disqualifies you from the best rates—or from obtaining coverage at all. Buying at a younger age also means that you'll pay a lower annual premium.

WHAT TO BUY

Today's high premiums make it even more important to buy only coverage that you really need. *Among the options...*

• **The daily benefit.** The average daily rate for a private room in a nursing home reached $248 in 2012. But that's a national average that hides the extreme regional differences in nursing home costs. Daily rates are several times higher in some places than others.

Strategy: Use the survey of regional LTC costs available at Genworth Financial's Web site (*www.Genworth.com*) to determine nursing home daily rates in the region where you would most likely receive care. Your insurance need not cover 100% of this daily amount if you would have enough assets to pay the difference out of pocket, but it should cover more than 50%—and significantly more, if possible. If you can't afford insurance that pays at least that portion, it probably isn't worth buying coverage at all. An extended nursing home stay would likely eat up all of your savings anyway, at which point you would qualify for Medicaid.

• **Maximum length of coverage.** Lifetime coverage has become rare and prohibitively expensive when it is offered.

Strategy: Two to five years of coverage usually is sufficient. Two-thirds of those who enter a nursing home stay less than one year. Only 10% stay five years or longer. If you do outlive your coverage, you will have to spend down your assets and rely on Medicaid—but if you purchase a "partnership policy" (see below), you might not have to spend down your assets.

• **Inflation protection.** Inflation has been minimal in recent years, and even nursing home bills and other LTC costs have been increasing at "only" a 4% annual rate, down from 7% previously. But don't be fooled. If your policy does not include strong inflation protection, even 4% annual price increases could render it almost worthless decades from now when you need it.

Strategy: Opt for the best inflation protection you can afford. An inflation rider offering a compound—not simple—5% rate of inflation protection is ideal. Compound 3% inflation protection is the least you should accept.

• **Elimination period** is the number of days of care that the policyholder must pay out of pocket before benefits begin.

Strategy: Opt for a 90-day elimination period. Insurers now charge prohibitively steep prices for policies with shorter elimination periods, and longer periods mean huge amounts

must be paid out of pocket before benefits kick in.

• **Joint coverage.** This allows married couples to purchase one policy for both partners to share—typically for much less than the cost of separate policies.

Strategy: Joint coverage usually is the best option for married people. There is some danger that couples might exhaust the policy's coverage if both spouses require lengthy nursing home stays, but this is very unlikely.

• **Partnership policies.** Those who exceed their policy time limits typically must pay for care out of pocket until their assets are almost completely depleted and they qualify for Medicaid LTC benefits. But if your policy is written under the public/private "partnership" program, which now is available in about 40 states, you can keep much more of your savings and still qualify for Medicaid. Your assets will be protected up to the total amount of coverage you received from your policy before you exceeded the coverage limits, which is likely to be hundreds of thousands of dollars.

Strategy: Check whether your state participates in this program. If so, strongly lean toward choosing a policy that qualifies. It's an extra measure of asset protection at no added cost.

• **Hybrid option.** Some insurers now offer "hybrid" policies that combine elements of LTC insurance and either life insurance or an annuity. Trouble is, the LTC insurance element of these hybrids tends to be fairly limited, and the life insurance or annuity portion can be expensive.

Strategy: Hybrid policies typically make sense only if you intended to purchase life insurance or an annuity similar to what's included anyway…and/or you cannot pass the medical underwriting standards of a typical LTC insurance policy—hybrid policies often feature more lax underwriting.

COMPARING OFFERS

Obtain quotes from at least three LTC insurance agents or brokers. Rather than just one quote from each insurance company, request a matrix of quotes at different daily benefit levels, lengths of coverage and inflation protection percentages.

Don't just purchase the policy that offers the lowest premiums for a given level of coverage. Historically, the LTC insurers that offer the lowest premiums tend to later impose the steepest rate increases and/or decline the highest percentage of claims. Instead, ask the agents for the premium increase history and claim-approval history of every LTC insurer from which you receive quotes. Your state insurance department also should be able to provide these figures.

Little-Known Medicaid Benefit

Medicaid recipients in some states may be allowed to hire and pay family members to provide in-home care. However, eligibility requirements are strict. For more information, contact your local Medicare office.

AARP The Magazine. www.AARP.org/magazine

Check for Unclaimed Life Insurance Benefits

A billion dollars has gone unclaimed in life insurance benefits—almost always because beneficiaries do not know a policy exists. Some of the money is at insurers. Some has been moved to state abandoned-property departments.

What to do: If you think you may be entitled to a payout, contact the insurer or your state's insurance department—some have search services for identifying policies. In New York, the average payout has been $7,465.

Alternative: Visit the National Association of Unclaimed Property Administrators Web site (*www.Unclaimed.org)*, and follow instructions to do a search.

Or: Check with the MIB Group (*www.MIB Group.com*), which charges $75* to do a search

*Price subject to change.

152

to find out whether a deceased person applied for life insurance and where the application was made.

The Wall Street Journal. www.WSJ.com

What Insurance Really Covers When a Storm Damages Your Home...

Robert D'Amore, who has spent more than 40 years in the insurance industry as an adjuster, supervisor and claims manager. Over the past 22 years, he has been an independent adjuster licensed by New York and Connecticut to represent policyholders against insurance companies. Based in Mohegan Lake, New York, he is president of the New York Public Adjusters Association. *www.DAmoreAdjusters.com*

When bad weather causes costly damage to homes, home owners often are confused about what is covered by insurance—and what is not covered. *Here are the answers to common questions...*

WINTER STORMS

• **Will insurance pay for repairs if a winter storm knocks out my power for days, shutting down my furnace and making my pipes freeze and crack?**

Frozen-pipe damage typically is covered (minus the deductible) if you have done your best to avoid having your pipes freeze.

What constitutes doing your best is subject to interpretation by the insurance company and depends on whether you could reasonably predict that the power would be out long enough to freeze the pipes—which tends to be two to three days. If it is clear that this is the case, then you might be expected to take steps to prevent a freeze-up—for example, quickly winterizing the home's pipes by shutting off the water supply, draining the pipes and appliances, and putting a nontoxic antifreeze in all drains—either on your own if you are handy or by hiring a plumber. But if it is not clear that the power will be out that long, you might not be expected to take such measures.

• **Will homeowner's insurance cover water damage stemming from an ice dam on my roof?**

Homeowner's insurance will cover any damage to the structure of the home due to ice damming but not necessarily to the contents of the home. In the standard homeowner's policy, water damage to the contents of a home is covered (minus the deductible) only in specific, named circumstances, and an ice dam, which can occur when water gets backed up and freezes on the roof, is not one of the circumstances that policies typically name.

What to do if you want coverage: Buy an "all risk" policy, also known as a "super deluxe" policy, available from just a few insurers, including Chubb and Fireman's Fund. These policies tend to be extremely expensive, however.

HURRICANES AND FLOODS

• **Does it really matter whether a storm is officially declared a hurricane?**

It might. Some policies have special hurricane deductibles that take effect when sustained hurricane-force winds of 74 miles per hour (mph) or above are recorded at the nearest weather station. These deductibles are higher than standard policy deductibles—typically they are 2% to 5% of the total coverage amount. If a home is insured for $500,000 and has a 5% hurricane deductible, for example, the home owner pays $25,000 out of pocket.

Other policies have "named storm" deductibles. The higher deductible applies if any named storm enters the state, even if that named storm creates winds below hurricane speed. Worse still are policies that have "wind storm" deductibles, where higher deductibles apply to damage caused by any wind.

Sandy, the superstorm that struck the Northeast in late October 2012, no longer had hurricane-force winds when it reached shore, so the governors of New Jersey, New York, Connecticut and Maryland informed insurance companies that they could not apply hurricane deductibles—but named-storm deductibles and wind-storm deductibles still would apply.

• **How does flood insurance coverage differ from homeowner's insurance coverage?**

Flood insurance, issued by the federal government's National Flood Insurance Program (*www.FloodSmart.gov*) and sold through insurance agents, is more restrictive than homeowner's insurance. Coverage for the home is capped at $250,000, not enough to replace a large home. Coverage for the home's contents is capped at $100,000. Flood insurance does not cover things that are on the property but not part of the home, such as swimming pools, fences and walkways.

Coverage for flood damage to basements is very limited. Structural elements and essential equipment such as furnaces, water heaters and circuit-breaker boxes are covered, but basement furnishings, possessions and improvements such as flooring are not.

The way flood insurance defines basements can be confusing. If a level of the home is even slightly sunken below ground level, it's officially a basement, even if it's part of the living area of the home…but if the house is built into a hill and any part of the basement floor is even with or above ground level, it's not officially considered a basement, even if it's unfinished.

• **Is there any way to get help for repairing flood damage if I do not have flood insurance?**

Grants and/or loans might be available to you via the Federal Emergency Management Agency (FEMA) if the government declares your area a federal disaster area. Go to *www.DisasterAssistance.gov* for details.

• **Homeowner's insurance covers water damage when high winds rip off a roof, allowing rain to enter. But what if heavy rains cause my home to flood?**

This would be covered only by flood insurance. Homeowner's insurance covers rain damage only when the damage is from rain falling from the sky. Once rainwater is on or under the ground, it's considered floodwater, even if it was rain just moments earlier. That's why it's a good idea to buy flood insurance if your home is at the base of a hill or in a valley, even if you don't live near a body of water prone to flooding. Flood insurance is priced by zone and often is very affordable for those who don't live near flood-prone bodies of water.

Flood insurance won't cover basement improvements and possessions kept in the basement, but it will cover damage to heating systems, water heaters and electrical boxes in the basement.

• **Does homeowner's insurance typically cover basement flooding caused by sump pump failure?**

A standard homeowner's policy doesn't, but most insurers allow policyholders to add a sump pump endorsement for as little as $50 per year* for $10,000 in coverage. It's money well-spent if you have a sump pump.

If your sump pump stops working during a flood because of a power failure, this endorsement should provide at least some coverage—though in a major flood, the insurer might contend that the sump pump couldn't have prevented the flood damage even if it continued to operate.

TREES

• **Does homeowner's insurance pay for tree removal when trees are downed by storms?**

If a tree falls on your home—or some other covered property, such as your garage, shed, swimming pool or fence—the policy will pay the cost of taking the tree off the home or covered property and repairing the damage (minus your deductible). But the policy will not necessarily pay the full cost of chopping up the tree and hauling it away. Most policies limit coverage for this to $500 per storm, though I have seen limits as high as $1,500.

That assumes that the tree came down on your home or some other covered property. If it landed only on your yard or driveway, insurance probably won't cover removal costs at all. (It is worth reading the policy or calling your agent, however—some policies do allow that $500 to $1,500 limited tree-removal coverage to be used in this situation.)

• **If a tree in my yard falls onto my neighbor's home, whose insurance pays?**

Your neighbor's—unless the tree was obviously rotten or dead before it fell. If the tree

*Prices subject to change.

154

was in such bad shape that you should have noticed the problem and had it removed, a court could find you liable for failing to do so, shifting the cost of repairing the damage and removing the tree to you and your insurer. This becomes more likely if the neighbor had alerted you to the danger in advance.

More from Robert D'Amore...

Does Insurance Cover Spoiled Food?

Homeowner's insurance does generally cover the cost of food that spoils during an extended power failure. And the deductible often is lower than the policy's standard deductible—sometimes just $100,* but in some policies, there's no deductible at all. However, food spoilage coverage typically is capped at $500.

Don't be reluctant to make food spoilage claims. Insurers almost never discontinue coverage or raise premiums because of spoilage claims. Take digital photos of the contents of the fridge and freezer before throwing spoiled food away in case you're asked for evidence of your losses.

*Prices subject to change.

Slash the Cost of Homeowner's Insurance by 40%!

If you update your alarm system or add a fire sprinkler system, it could lower home insurance costs by 15%, or $132 off the typical bill. Redoing electrical, plumbing, and heating and cooling systems in a way that would help protect against costly water claims and fire damage could lead to a discount of 40% or more. Be sure to let your insurer know whenever you make a significant change to your home's systems.

CNNMoney.com

Are You Covered If You Forgot to Turn on the Alarm?

In most cases, you probably will be covered for a theft loss if you just forgot to turn on your home alarm one time. However, each insurance company has its own rules regarding home alarm use and property loss. Be sure to carefully read the "protective safeguard endorsement" that typically is added to your insurance policy when you get a reduced premium for having an alarm system. That should explain what is required of you regarding the alarm system.

J.D. Howard, executive director, Insurance Consumer Advocate Network, Springfield, Missouri. *www.ICAN2000.com*

Self-Defense Insurance for Gun Owners

The standard homeowner's and auto policies specifically exclude injuries or damage caused intentionally—for instance, by firing a gun. A few policies do contain a self-defense exception (when gun owners fire to protect themselves or their homes) to that exclusion, but most do not.

What to do: Look into National Rifle Association coverage, underwritten by Lloyd's of London and starting at $165 per year*...and Self-Defense Shield from the US Concealed Carry Association through Savers Property & Casualty, which starts at $127 per year.

Bankrate.com

*Prices subject to change.

Is Fido a Legal Liability? Don't Let Your Dog Take a Bite Out of Your Assets

Kenneth M. Phillips, JD, an attorney whose law practice has been devoted to dog-bite cases since 1990. Based in Beverly Hills, he is author of *Dog Bite Law* and *What to Do If Your Dog Is Injured or Killed* (both available through his Web site). *www.DogBiteLaw.com*

If you own a dog, your assets might be at risk. There are more than 4.7 million reported dog-bite injuries in the US every year. And the average dog-bite liability case is settled for more than $29,000, with costs climbing much higher when extensive plastic surgery is required. You can be liable even if your dog has never bitten anyone before—and you can be liable, even if you don't own the dog but are simply taking care of it.

Helpful: Cat owners can be liable when their pets bite or scratch, but such cases are rare and usually less costly.

Dog owners tend to assume that their homeowner's insurance will cover the costs if they are sued because of a dog bite, but that insurance might not provide as much protection as they think. It's becoming increasingly common for insurance providers to quietly limit or eliminate the dog-bite coverage in their homeowner's policies. *What dog owners need to know...*

DOG-BITE INSURANCE

If you own a dog, take a close look at your homeowner's or renter's insurance policy to make sure that it does not exclude dog-bite coverage. Read the "Exclusions" paragraph in the "Coverage" section to make sure that it does not mention dogs or animals in general. The wording of this exclusion can vary, but it might exclude "any animal-inflicted injury"..."any canine-inflicted injury"...or "any injury by a dog of certain breeds," followed by a list of breeds.

If your insurance excludes coverage for specific breeds, it's likely that pit bulls and rottweilers will be on the list. Other breeds sometimes excluded are Akitas, Alaskan mal-amutes, Chow chows, Doberman pinschers, German shepherds, Great Danes, Presa Canarios, Siberian huskies and Staffordshire bull terriers.

Helpful: The list of excluded dog breeds typically applies only to pure-bred dogs. If your dog is a mixed breed, it likely is not af-fected, even if its heritage includes one or more of the breeds listed. Still, read the word-ing of this dog-breed exclusion carefully to confirm that it is not worded in a way that includes mixed breeds, too.

Also, read any "endorsements" mailed to you by your insurance provider. Endorsements are amendments to your insurance policy and could include changes to the policy's dog-bite coverage. If you have not read endorsements mailed to you by your insurer carefully in the past, contact the insurer and request a copy of your policy and all effective endorsements.

Next, check the "Declarations" section of your homeowner's policy to make sure that your insurer hasn't set your dog-bite liability limits lower than your overall liability limits.

Example: A wealthy Hollywood execu-tive was sued when her dog bit another wom-an. The executive had a homeowner's policy with $500,000 in liability coverage, so she assumed that she was protected. She didn't realize that her policy provided only $50,000 in dog-bite liability coverage, not enough to cover the victim's plastic surgery bills.

If your policy does not provide adequate coverage for dog bites, consider purchasing an umbrella policy to supplement it. For a very reasonable amount—often less than $100 per year—an umbrella policy can increase your li-ability protection to $1 million. Ask insurance agents for quotes. If your homeowner's policy specifically excludes coverage for dog bites or for your breed of dog, confirm that the um-brella policy will cover your pet before sign-ing up.

If you cannot find an umbrella policy that will cover your dog, either shop around for a different homeowner's or renter's policy or purchase a canine-liability policy to supple-ment your insurance. A canine-liability policy could cost anywhere from $150 to $1,000 or more per year depending on the breed and size of your dog, its history of aggression and other factors. Insurance brokers offering these policies include Einhorn Insurance Agency (619-313-4643 or *www.EinhornInsurance.com*) …Evolution Insurance Brokers (877-678-7342 or *www.EIBDirect.com*)…and Lester Kalmanson Agency (407-645-5000 or *www.LKalmanson. com*).

DOG-BITE LAW

In approximately two-thirds of the states, pet owners can be held liable for dog bites even when those dogs have never previously shown any sign of aggression. In the remain-ing states (Alaska, Arkansas, Hawaii, Idaho, Kansas, Maryland, Mississippi, Nevada, New Mexico, North Carolina, North Dakota, Ore-gon, South Dakota, Texas, Vermont, Virginia and Wyoming), the so-called "one bite" rule applies. In these states, the dog owner gen-erally is legally responsible for damages only if the dog has previously bitten, attempted to bite or exhibited other signs of aggressive be-havior toward humans.

Exception: A dog owner in a one-bite state could be liable for his dog's first bite, even if the dog has never previously shown signs of aggression, if the bite occurs while the dog owner is engaged in outrageous or reckless behavior…is negligent in controlling the dog… or is in violation of a local animal-control law. Dog owners might accidentally increase their risk of liability if they don't know their local animal-control laws. Google the name of your city or town and the words "municipal code" to find animal-control laws in your area, then repeat the process with the name of your county and the word "ordinance." Local laws might dictate a maximum leash length of six feet, for example, or limit the number of dogs that can be walked at one time to two—rules that even responsible dog owners could un-knowingly violate.

People who work with dogs as part of their professions, such as veterinarians and profes-sional dog walkers, generally cannot sue for damages if they're bitten by a dog while per-forming their professional duties, provided that you previously warned them if your dog is aggressive. However, the laws vary widely from state to state on this issue.

In some cases, the dog owner is not the only one potentially liable when a dog bites. *Depending on your state's laws, you might be liable as...*

• **The harborer of a dog.** Feed or provide water to a dog that you don't own, and you could be liable if it bites.

• **The keeper of a dog.** Agree to look after someone else's dog, and you might be liable for its actions—if you know that the dog has a history of biting.

Example: A man asked a group of women he met in a bar in Venice Beach, California, to look after his dog briefly. The dog bit two people while in the women's care. The women were liable for the second bite because after the first one, they should have realized that the dog was dangerous.

Dog owners can be liable if their dogs bite other dogs, too. Given the high cost of veterinary surgery, this liability can be substantial.

Exception: It's a legal gray area whether you are liable if your dog bites another dog—or another person—in a dog park. A case could be made that the bite victim assumed the risk of being bitten when he/she entered the dog park.

More from Kenneth M. Phillips, JD...

To Prevent Dog Bites...

Six ways dog owners can reduce the odds that they will be sued for dog bites...

• **Keep your dog away from children.** Children are particularly likely to be dog-bite victims—and dog owners often are held liable even when the child was being aggressive and the dog bit only out of fear. Steer your dog away from young children when you're out in public, and politely turn down kids' requests to pet your dog.

• **Instruct dog sitters and friends who look after your dog to keep it away from strangers.** Dogs tend to be particularly aggressive when they are separated from their owners.

• **Be extremely cautious in the first 60 days after you adopt a dog.** A dog is most likely to bite soon after it joins a household, perhaps because it is not yet completely comfortable around its new family.

• **Do not tie up your dog.** "Tethering" tends to make dogs panicky, greatly increasing the odds of bites. It's even been outlawed in some states.

• **Post a "Beware of Dog" sign.** Not only will this deter people from entering your property where they could get bitten, it can reduce the odds that you will be liable if they are bitten. As long as the sign was clearly visible, the bite victim essentially agreed to take the risk of being bitten when he/she entered.

• **Be cautious about adopting dogs from rescue organizations.** Many dog rescue organizations are wonderful, but some care more about protecting animals than protecting people. Such organizations have been known to place dogs that have bitten before without revealing those dogs' troubled histories. Buying from a reputable breeder could be the safer choice.

Time to Get Pet Health-Care Insurance?

One emergency veterinary visit can now run $500 or more.

Best strategy: Consider a basic pet health insurance plan that covers the costs of treating illnesses and injuries but not annual checkups or vaccinations. Monthly premiums start at $20 to $30 for younger pets* and $45 to $50 for older ones.

Emily Pointer, DMV, medical coordinator, ASPCA-Bergh Memorial Animal Hospital, New York City. *www. ASPCA.org*

*Prices subject to change.

Your Zip Code Affects Your Auto Insurance Rates *Dramatically*

The same vehicle driven the same number of miles annually can cost as little as $730/year* to insure or as much as $4,214/year, depending on the area. Of the 10 least expensive cities in which to insure a car, six are in Maine and four are in Arizona.

To find out where your city ranks: Go to *www.CarInsurance.com* for a rate-comparison tool.

When it is time for you to buy insurance: Shop around. Even though you cannot change your zip code, insurers treat a given area differently—the same location may cost less with one company than with another.

CBSMoneyWatch.com

*Prices subject to change.

Pay-as-You-Drive Insurance

Pay-as-you-drive insurance modifies policy premiums based on driving habits. Several automobile insurers, including Allstate, The Hartford, Progressive and State Farm, offer a version of it in at least some states. Insurers require drivers to give up some privacy to get the lower rates—you must allow installation of a monitoring device or give the insurer access to onboard equipment that collects data. Pay-as-you-drive is most likely to save you money if you drive 10,000 or fewer miles per year... never drive faster than 80 miles an hour...take corners and curves slowly...and drive a 1996 or newer vehicle.

What to do: If you meet these criteria and are not concerned about giving up some privacy, ask your insurer if it offers discounts in return for being allowed to monitor your driving habits.

Consensus of auto insurers offering pay-as-you-drive plans, reported in *The Wall Street Journal*.

Save on Auto Insurance for Teens

To save on car insurance for your new teen driver, add him/her to your existing policy instead of taking out a new policy—that way, your discounts pass through to him. Also, be sure to tell your insurer if your teen goes to college more than 100 miles away and does not take a car—your premiums will go down, but he still will be covered when home. Insist that your teen take a defensive-driving course, both for safety and to lower insurance rates. And, if you are buying your teen a car, get one with as many safety features as possible—and avoid sports cars and SUVs, which cost more to insure. Finally, shop around for insurance—costs for teens vary widely. When a teen turns 18, he may get a better deal by buying his own insurance policy.

CBSNews.com

9

Tax Talk

Taxpayer Victories: How Ordinary Citizens Beat the IRS

You may think that you do not stand a chance in fighting the IRS, but you would be so wrong. Taxpayers can be successful. Here are some recent disputes that resulted in taxpayer victories that can help you in your future handling of similar tax matters and reduce your taxes…

AN UNBUILT HOME CAN PROVIDE A TAX BREAK

Mortgage interest on a personal residence can be claimed while a home is under construction, but what if it is never built? One recent Tax Court case focused on Thomas and Cheryl Rose, who bought beachfront property in Fort Myers Beach, Florida, for $1,575,000 in 2006 with the intention of building their dream vacation home. The 2006 sale required the seller to demolish the existing home before closing, which the seller did. The couple borrowed $1.26 million to swing the purchase. To obtain a construction permit, they had to perform numerous activities, which included conducting surveys and core drilling. The permit was granted on February 11, 2008, almost two years after the purchase date.

The owners needed to secure additional financing for the construction but were unable to do this because of plunging home values amid the real estate market collapse. They ultimately sold the property at a loss for $750,000 in June 2009 and never saw their dream come true. However, for 2006 and 2007, they deducted home mortgage interest of $87,016 and $82,201, respectively, on the grounds that the home was "under construction."

Barbara Weltman, Esq., an attorney in Millwood, New York, author of *J.K. Lasser's 1001 Deductions and Tax Breaks* (Wiley) and publisher of *Big Ideas for Small Business,* a free monthly e-newsletter. *www.Barbara Weltman.com*

IRS Position: The couple cannot deduct the interest because construction of the home never actually started.

Tax Court Ruling: Construction includes work done in applying for permits, doing preparatory measurements, surveying, drawing plans, demolishing an existing home and clearing the site. The court rejected the IRS argument that "under construction" includes only physical construction activity such as pouring the foundation.

Lesson: In trying to write off interest before physical construction begins, a home owner should keep a log of activities "in furtherance of construction."

Thomas G. Rose and Cheryl G. Rose, TC Summary Opinion 2011-117

A TAX BREAK WITHOUT RECEIPTS

A gain on the sale of a personal residence is determined by comparing the sale price with the cost basis, which includes the original price that the owner paid for the home and the costs of capital improvements made over the years. However, many home owners fail to keep records and receipts proving the amount spent on these improvements. Can they be estimated?

In April 2002, Louis Greenwald bought a home in Santa Barbara, California. He made various improvements to the home but retained only some of the invoices. He sold the home in 2005 for $2,650,000. He reported a capital gain of $638,802. His cost basis reflected improvements totaling $387,735.

IRS Position: The gain was $356,515 more than he claimed because he could not substantiate most of the improvements.

Tax Court: The court applied the Cohan doctrine, under which a court can allow a claimed expense even if the taxpayer cannot fully substantiate it. But this requires what the court called an "evidentiary basis" for claiming the expense. The Cohan doctrine typically is used for unsubstantiated travel and entertainment expenses, but the court said that it could and would apply the doctrine to improvements to a residence. It allowed all but $950 of Greenwald's claimed improvements

because he was able to list what they were and to estimate how much each cost.

What to do: Even though receipts were not necessary in this case, it's best to keep them, and you should maintain an ongoing record of capital improvements to your home to minimize the gain on an eventual sale. Find a list of improvements to track in IRS Publication 523, Selling Your Home, at *www.IRS.gov.*

Louis Greenwald, TC Memo 2011-239

VOLUNTEERS MUST PROVE EXPENSES TO CLAIM DEDUCTIONS

Volunteers can claim a tax deduction for out-of-pocket costs—these costs are considered a charitable contribution—but the costs must be substantiated.

In a recent case, Jan Elizabeth Van Dusen of Oakland, California, cared for a total of 70 to 80 feral cats under a foster-cat program. She paid for their food, veterinary bills (for tests, treatment, vaccines and surgery) and other pet supplies totaling $12,068. She had receipts, credit card bills and other documentary proof of her outlays. In 2004, she claimed those costs for a tax deduction.

In another case, Tawana Bradley of Louisville, Kentucky, acting as a volunteer coach for a football cheerleading squad, paid for pizza, party favors and other supplies for a squad celebration totaling $162.27. She had receipts. In 2006, she claimed this expense for a tax deduction.

IRS Position: Volunteer expenses are subject to the same substantiation rule as cash contributions—they must be proven by canceled checks or bank statements, which these two taxpayers did not have.

Amounts of $250 or more also must be substantiated by a written acknowledgment from the charity.

Tax Court Ruling: Volunteer expenses up to $249 can be substantiated by receipts, credit card slips and other documentary proof—they are acceptable substitutes for canceled checks. Although Van Dusen was able to declare only a small portion of her expenses, the ruling set a precedent for other cases, such as Bradley's.

Caution: If the amount to be deducted is $250 or more, you do need a written acknowledgment from the charity, just as if you had made a cash donation.

Lesson: Learn all the substantiation rules for charitable donations (go to IRS Publication 526, *Charitable Contributions,* at *www.IRS.gov*) to claim the full extent of your out-of-pocket costs.

For example, track vehicle mileage incurred on behalf of charitable activities so that you can deduct mileage at the rate of 14¢ per mile.

Jan Elizabeth Van Dusen, 136 TC No. 25 (2011); Tawana Bradley, TC Summary Opinion 2011-120

PROVING THAT A BUSINESS IS NOT A HOBBY FOR TAX PURPOSES

An activity that loses money may be treated as a hobby by the IRS—meaning that expenses in excess of the business's income are not deductible—unless the taxpayer can demonstrate that there is a "profit motive."

In one recent case, Peter Morton, co-founder of the Hard Rock Cafe, owned or controlled several businesses related to his Hard Rock brand. One was an *S corporation* (a corporation that does not pay federal income tax) that owned a Gulfstream jet. This S corporation never made money.

IRS Position: Losses from the S corporation that owns the plane are nondeductible because the S corporation represented a hobby activity.

Federal Claims Court: The determination of whether a taxpayer has a profit motive (and therefore is not engaged in a hobby activity) can be based on the "aggregation" of business activities—treating them as related activities—rather than considering the businesses as entirely separate. In this case, Morton's various corporations were interrelated in terms of their activities—and all furthered the Hard Rock brand. As detailed by flight logs, he used the plane for personal and business travel, including the promotion of the Hard Rock brand and activities related to the Hard Rock Hotel and Casino in Las Vegas. Since his use was in furtherance of his corporate "brand," it sup-

ported his overall profit motive and so was not a hobby activity.

Lesson: You don't have to be a mogul (or own a jet) for this ruling to help you. What it means is that you can maintain separate but related companies—even small companies—while aggregating them only for the tax purpose of demonstrating a profit motive.

Morton v. United States, No. 08-804C (Fed. Cl 2011)

New Hurdles for Medical Deductions: How to Qualify Anyway

Starting in 2013, most people can deduct medical expenses on federal income taxes only to the extent that the expenses exceed 10% of their adjusted gross income, up from a threshold of 7.5% in prior years. But there are rules that may help you qualify.

If either you or your spouse will be 65 or older as of December 31, 2013, the higher threshold will not affect you until 2017. If not, you can try to shift some medical expenses—such as new eyeglasses and dental work—to maximize the total amount in a given year while minimizing it in the next year. (That way you are maximizing the amount that exceeds the 10% threshold.)

Also, if you pay medical expenses for a parent who is your dependent (meaning that you pay more than half of his/her support for the year), you can add those medical expenses to your own for itemized deduction purposes. And don't overlook the fact that medical premiums you pay for long-term care (subject to limits) count as medical costs.

MarketWatch.com

Coming Soon: Easier Home-Office Deductions

Starting with this year's taxes—to be filed in 2014—taxpayers will have the option of claiming a flat $5 per square foot for a home office, up to 300 square feet. The form for claiming the deduction—which is capped at $1,500 per year—will be "significantly simplified," the IRS says. Under the old rules, claiming the deduction requires filling out a 43-line form, which often involves calculating the percentage of the home used solely for business and the percentage of expenses that apply to the office—a complex process that often triggers an audit. Those rules will continue to be available to taxpayers who choose to use them. Under the new rules, home owners can't depreciate the portion of the home used for a trade or business, but they can claim allowable mortgage interest, real estate taxes and casualty losses as itemized deductions.

If you currently claim a deduction of more than $1,500: Decide whether the more complex rules will be better for you when you file your 2013 taxes.

The New York Times. www.NYTimes.com

Winnings Are Taxable

Even modest winnings from sweepstakes, instant-win games and contests are taxable. Winners of $600 or more will receive IRS Form 1099, though winnings in any amount must be reported. Prizes cannot be claimed as "gifts."

Internal Revenue Service. www.IRS.gov

Free Tax Prep

The *AARP Tax-Aide Program* is the largest free tax-preparation and assistance service in the US. It is offered by AARP together with the IRS. Volunteers work on returns for low- and middle-income taxpayers and file about 90% of returns electronically. Tax aides are trained to help people file Form 1040 and basic schedules.

To find out more or to volunteer: Apply for the program by going to *www.AARP.org/taxaide.*

Julie Jason, JD, principal, Jackson, Grant Investment Advisers in Stamford, Connecticut, and author of *The AARP Retirement Survival Guide* (Sterling), writing in *The Stamford Advocate.*

The New Inheritance Rules Are Tricky: Important Steps to Take *Now*

Martin M. Shenkman, CPA, JD, an estate- and tax-planning attorney with the law firm Martin M. Shenkman, PC, with offices in New York City and Paramus, New Jersey. He is also author of many books, including *Inherit More* (Wiley) and *Estate Planning for People with a Chronic Condition or Disability* (Demos Health). *www.LawEasy.com*

For most people, the federal estate tax became a thing of the past at the beginning of this year. But that doesn't mean you can entirely shove aside the task of estate planning—not if you care about who inherits your assets…how much of those assets your heirs get to keep after taxes…and who will make decisions for you if you are unable to make them yourself.

WHAT CHANGED

Congress made permanent a high estate tax exemption—$5.25 million for people who die in 2013, with inflation adjustments in future years—rather than allowing it to automatically revert to $1 million in 2013 with the expiration of Bush-era tax cuts. Under a provision called portability, that exemption can double when a surviving spouse assumes a deceased spouse's exemption—and unlike in the past, you do not need a so-called bypass trust to make this happen. Any estate assets below the exemption amount won't be hit with federal estate tax.

That means any estate planning that you require now will likely be simpler and cheaper because of the new rules—but you still need to consider the following issues...

• **You might need to undo (or repurpose) existing trusts or family partnerships.** Under the new rules, those existing estate plans actually might work against your heirs.

Example: A man stipulated in his will that a bypass trust be set up upon his death to preserve the estate tax exemption for his wife. Because the couple's assets are well below the federal exemption, leaving that trust in place now could force the couple's heirs to later pay higher capital gains taxes than they would without the bypass trust in place. That's because assets placed in a bypass trust do not receive a "step-up in basis" upon the death of the second spouse—that is, heirs can't minimize capital gains taxes because they can't use the fair value of the assets at the time of the second spouse's death as their new cost basis when they calculate capital gains taxes in the future.

Consider meeting with an estate-planning attorney to discuss the pros and cons of dismantling no-longer-needed trusts or family partnerships. Ask whether these estate-planning tools could be repurposed rather than dismantled entirely, since you have already paid to set them up.

Example: A family partnership originally set up to minimize estate taxes could instead be used to shift assets to low-tax-bracket family members to minimize income taxes.

• **Federal estate taxes aren't the only estate taxes to worry about.** Some states have estate tax exemptions much lower than $5.25 million (see the next article).

If you live in one of these states, estate taxes could be a concern even if your estate is well below the federal exemption, but that doesn't always mean it's wise to set up a bypass trust as you might have in years past to avoid federal estate tax. While a bypass trust could help shield assets from state estate taxes, those tax rates are a small fraction of the federal estate tax rate. The trust may not save you enough in state estate taxes to make up for the additional capital gains taxes and Medicare taxes that your heirs might have to pay because of the loss of a step-up in basis, as discussed previously.

Two potential strategies worth discussing with an estate-planning attorney if state estate taxes are a concern...

• Give money to trusts that name your spouse and other heirs as beneficiaries. This counts as a gift, but only one state—Connecticut—imposes a state gift tax.

• Use a bypass trust, but fund it only with assets that are unlikely to appreciate significantly, such as money market funds or certificates of deposit (CDs). The lost step-up in basis isn't a major concern if there isn't much appreciation.

• **Trusts provide asset protection.** Placing assets in trusts can shield them from legal judgments against you. That's particularly useful for doctors, contractors and people in other professions where lawsuits are common. Trusts also can protect assets from wasteful spending by young heirs who might not yet be ready to handle a windfall inheritance. It's worth speaking with an estate-planning attorney to address such concerns.

• **Portability means relying on the decisions of your spouse.** The now-permanent portability rule means that a married person can preserve his/her full estate tax exemption by leaving his assets to a spouse—rather than to a bypass trust.

But when you leave your assets largely or entirely to your spouse rather than to a trust, you depend on that spouse to later leave remaining assets to your intended heirs. Your hard-earned assets could end up wasted or in the hands of someone else entirely if your spouse has a falling out with your intended heirs...overspends...remarries...becomes enamored with a charity...or makes poor investments due to the onset of a degenerative mental condition.

Instead of leaving the assets to your spouse outright, consider putting them in a marital trust that allows your spouse reasonable access but protects your other heirs from the above risks. A marital trust might be funded with assets unlikely to see great appreciation to minimize the effect of the lost step-up in basis, as discussed above.

• **Reevaluate your life insurance.** Life insurance was a popular estate-planning tool in years past. A policy's death benefits could pass to an insured person's heirs outside the taxable estate or benefits could be used to pay estate taxes.

Policies purchased for these purposes might no longer be needed now that the estate tax exemption is so high, but don't just let these policies lapse. They still could be valuable for the income tax–free benefits that life insurance can provide to heirs. Review your life insurance policies with an insurance expert before making any decisions.

WHAT HASN'T CHANGED

You still should designate who will make your health-care and financial decisions if you are incapacitated…and who will inherit your assets when you die. That means drafting and keeping up-to-date documents such as financial and health-care powers of attorney. It's still also important to have a will to spell out how you wish to divide your assets after your death.

And be sure to name beneficiaries on your financial accounts, including brokerage, mutual fund and bank accounts, so that those assets end up where you want them.

You Still May Be Walloped by Your State's Estate Tax

Mary Randolph, JD, editor in chief of Nolo, publisher of legal-information books and consumer-oriented legal Web sites. Based in Berkeley, California, she is author of *The Executor's Guide* (Nolo). *www.Nolo.com*

While most people no longer have to worry about federal estate taxes, many people don't realize that they still could be hit by state estate and/or inheritance taxes. That's because 13 states and Washington, DC, have *much lower exemptions* than the federal tax does.

A recent federal law set the 2013 federal estate tax exemption at $5.25 million per person or double that for a married couple. Estate assets above those amounts will be taxed at 40%. Inflation adjustments will be made in future years.

State estate tax exemptions, however, are as low as $675,000, the threshold in New Jersey, where assets above that amount are taxed at between 11% and 16%.

2013 exemption levels for the various states (and Washington, DC) that have their own estate taxes and that have exemptions much lower than the federal levels…

Connecticut ($2 million)…District of Columbia ($1 million)…Illinois ($4 million)…Maine ($2 million)…Maryland ($1 million)…Massachusetts ($1 million)…Minnesota ($1 million) …New Jersey ($675,000)…New York ($1 million)…Oregon ($1 million)…Rhode Island ($910,725)…Tennessee ($1.25 million)…Vermont ($2.75 million)…Washington State ($2 million). Hawaii has a state estate tax exemption level similar to the federal level.

Taxpayers who live in states where their assets may exceed the state estate tax exemption should consider consulting with a tax adviser for ways to soften the blow. These include reducing assets by making annual gifts (only Connecticut has a state tax on gifts, and the federal government's annual gift tax exclusion is $14,000 per recipient for 2013, to be adjusted for inflation in the future.) Keep in mind that rules on which assets are included in taxable estates and which are not vary somewhat by state.

Also, six states impose an inheritance tax, which is paid by people who inherit the assets rather than by the estate. States that impose an inheritance tax are Iowa, Kentucky, Maryland, Nebraska, New Jersey and Pennsylvania.

For details on any of the above types of taxes, go to *www.Nolo.com* and enter the type of tax in the search box.

Your Digital Estate: Make Sure Your Heirs Inherit Your Online Photos, Bank Accounts, Web Sites, More

Naomi R. Cahn, Esq., the Harold H. Greene Professor of Law at The George Washington University Law School, Washington, DC. She is author of a paper published in *Probate & Property* entitled "Postmortem Life On-Line."

Our real-world possessions might not be all that we want to leave to our heirs when we die. Nowadays most people have assets in the cyberworld to pass on as well.

These could include online financial accounts such as PayPal balances, bank accounts and brokerage accounts accessed only through the Internet...Web sites or blogs that we own and operate...our digital photo albums, e-mail accounts and social media accounts...collections of ebooks...and downloaded digital music and movies.

These digital assets could have significant value for our heirs—sentimental value in the case of digital photos, for instance, or financial value in the case of a PayPal account or a money-generating Web site.

But when we die, such virtual possessions might be overlooked by heirs who don't know they exist...be inaccessible to heirs who don't have the passwords...or be the subject of disputes among heirs and possibly even curious or litigious outsiders.

Don't expect existing laws to provide a great deal of help in sorting out digital estate issues for your heirs. Most states do not yet have laws on this topic, leaving heirs at the mercy of the policies of online service providers.

Example: Yahoo refused to grant the family of a Marine killed in Iraq access to the man's e-mails until the family got a probate judge to grant them access. Although many people might want to hide their digital secrets from prying eyes, this soldier had intended to use his e-mails to compile a scrapbook of his wartime experiences, and his family wished to do the same as a memorial to him.

Here's how to improve the odds that your digital estate will be handled according to your wishes when you die or if you become incapacitated...

FINANCIAL ACCOUNTS

Online financial accounts may be difficult for heirs to access even with estate-planning documents in hand.

Example: A Chicago woman had a power of attorney that allowed her to manage her husband's financial accounts after his degenerative mental condition made it impossible for him to do so. Unfortunately, her husband's bank told her that it did not recognize power of attorney for online banking, making it very difficult for her to oversee the account.

What to do: If you have money in an online account that does not mail you printed statements, make sure this account is clearly listed in your estate documents to ensure that it's not overlooked by heirs. And confirm with the financial institution that your power of attorney will be sufficient to allow your spouse or heir to access the account if necessary. If not, consider switching to a different financial institution.

You could add a spouse or heir as joint owner of your online account so that this person can seamlessly take over its management if needed. But be aware that this would put your assets at risk—the joint owner might be able to withdraw money without your permission, and the assets would be vulnerable if the joint owner were sued or divorced.

Also: If you have recurring bills that you pay online, provide a list of these to your spouse or heir and any user names and passwords required to access these accounts. That way, important online bill payments won't be overlooked. Provide a list of online services and recurring online bills that will no longer be needed after your death, too, and ask this person to cancel them for you so that your estate does not go on paying them needlessly.

WEB SITES AND BLOGS

If you have a popular and/or revenue-generating blog or Web site, include it in your estate plan so that this asset doesn't go to waste. Either leave it to an heir who is interested in taking it over or provide instructions for how it should be sold. Make sure that at least one trusted friend or relative has the passwords needed to run the blog or Web site or knows where to find them. Better yet, add a chosen heir as a joint blogger or site administrator while you still are alive to smooth the transition.

Warning: With a blog, check the provider's terms of service for any specific rules about transferring blog ownership.

List any domain names you own but do not use among your assets in your estate plan as well. Some domain names have resale value.

E-MAIL, SOCIAL MEDIA, PHOTOS

Do you want your heirs to have access to your e-mail and/or social media accounts after you're gone, or do you want them deleted? What about the digital photos and videos that you have stored on a photo-sharing Web site such as Shutterfly?

If you fail to think these issues through, these digital documentations of your life easily could be lost to your heirs forever. Or, conversely, a highly personal e-mail or photo could be brought to light against your wishes. Or many Facebook and LinkedIn visitors may never catch on that you're gone.

Most states do not yet have laws governing rights to access the digital accounts of deceased loved ones. (The exceptions are Connecticut, Idaho, Indiana, Oklahoma and Rhode Island, which have laws governing rights to e-mail and, in some cases, social media accounts. The details of these laws vary.)

With few laws in place, legal rights to access these accounts usually depend on the policies of the company that provides the account. Those companies tend to err on the side of protecting the privacy of the deceased.

Example: The parents of a college student who committed suicide hoped that the young man's Facebook and e-mail accounts would provide some answers about why he had taken his life, but they were denied access by the providers.

What to do: Ask a trustworthy, tech-savvy friend or relative to deal with your accounts after you're gone. Give this person a list of your account user IDs and passwords, or keep this list somewhere safe and tell this friend where to find it. Update the list whenever you open a new account or change a password.

Provide the friend with written instructions about how you would like each account handled. *Should it be…*

- **Closed?**
- **Expunged of certain private information** but allowed to continue?
- **Maintained but with a posting or automated response** added to explain that you have passed away?
- **Printed out and given to a family member** interested in family history?

Facebook also offers the option of "memorializing" a deceased person's page. The account's wall remains open for confirmed friends to continue to post messages in remembrance, but most of the account can no longer be accessed or altered.

Warning: Do not list your accounts and their passwords in your will. Not only would it be difficult to update your will every time you change a password, but also your will becomes public record soon after your death.

E-BOOKS, MUSIC AND MOVIES

You may want to leave downloaded collections of books, music and movies to your heirs. But you might not have a legal right to do this even if you have the account IDs and passwords.

Read the small print the next time you purchase one of these digital products. With many sellers, you'll discover that you're not technically purchasing the book, song or movie at all, only a nontransferable license to use it, such as with iTunes.

What to do: If you have spent hundreds or thousands of dollars on digital content, consider speaking with an estate-planning attorney about placing it into a trust. In theory, the trust's beneficiaries would then have a legal right to access the content after you're gone—though this theory has not yet been tested in court.

Digital Estate-Planning Services

If you need help passing on your cyberworld assets, consider using a service that makes it easier to handle such transitions.

These Internet-based services can store and protect your crucial information during your life, then share it with designated people after your death. They will store your important digital documents, such as copies of your wills, trusts, contracts and confidential projects…save messages to be sent to your loved ones after your death…and provide a place to keep your passwords during your life in case you forget them. *Two of the best…*

•**Legacy Locker.** $29.99/year* or $299.99 for a lifetime subscription. *http://LegacyLocker.com*

•**SecureSafe.** Prices range from free to $12.90 per month depending on options selected. *www.SecureSafe.com*

Evan Carroll, cofounder of TheDigitalBeyond.com and coauthor of *Your Digital Afterlife* (New Riders).

*Prices subject to change.

Loving Gifts to Give Your Heirs (Long Before You Die)

Robert Carlson, JD, CPA, managing member of Carlson Wealth Advisors, LLC, and chairman of the board of trustees of the Fairfax County (Virginia) Employees' Retirement System. He is editor and publisher of the newsletter *Retirement Watch. www.RetirementWatch.com*

You don't have to wait until you pass away to bestow financial benefits upon your eventual heirs. And there are some creative and money-saving ways to do this other than splitting up your estate in a will.

In fact, those of us in or approaching retirement might be able to help our heirs right now, even if we don't have a lot of money to spare. Some gifts that are very valuable to our heirs end up costing us relatively little or even nothing at all. Better yet, there are forms of financial assistance we can provide during our lives that will be rewarding for us as well as our heirs—and that could strengthen family ties. *Among the options…*

THE GIFT OF VACATION

If you own a vacation home or recreational vehicle, your relatives may have thought about inquiring whether they could use it but were too shy to ask. You could offer to let them use it when you're not using it yourself. This costs you virtually nothing but saves them the hundreds or even thousands of dollars.

If you don't own a vacation property, you could offer to pay most or all of the cost of a group vacation for yourself, your offspring and their families…and/or other relatives you would include in your will.

That does require money out of your pocket, but you probably can find a significantly lower rate on one large vacation home rental than the combined amounts that family members would pay for lodging if they vacationed separately. Renting one large home rather than many hotel rooms also fosters family togetherness—and it means that the family can pool child-care and food-preparation duties, making the vacation less work for everyone.

Tax loophole: There is an additional benefit if your estate will likely top $5.25 million—paying for family vacations removes money from your estate without depleting your lifetime gift-tax exemption or annual gift-tax exclusion. The IRS has never attempted to treat family vacations as taxable gifts.

THE GIFT OF FINANCIAL PLANNING

If you have financial advisers you trust, consider paying for your future heirs to become their clients, too. This gift will pay for itself many times over if it puts your adult children or grandchildren on the path to prudent money management. It also can provide you with some peace of mind that any inheritance your heirs later receive from you will not be squandered.

If family members' financial interests overlap, as they often do, hiring the same financial adviser to work with multiple family members will make it easier to integrate everyone's financial plans as well.

Example: You intend to give several of your heirs joint ownership of a piece of property. Transferring and coordinating property ownership will be much easier if all of the family members use the same adviser.

And paying one adviser to work with multiple family members offers an opportunity for savings. If the adviser bills based on a percentage of assets under management, there likely is a sliding scale—clients with more assets pay a lower percentage than those with fewer assets. Advisers typically agree to bill extended families based on the entire family's asset pool, resulting in a lower billing rate. An adviser who charges by the hour also might be willing to offer a discount in exchange for bringing in heirs as clients.

Helpful: If some of your heirs live far away, they can meet with this adviser when they visit you—it is an added incentive for these distant heirs to make annual visits. They can communicate with the adviser via phone or e-mail during the rest of the year.

LOW-INTEREST FAMILY LOANS

Today's low interest rates make this a wonderful time to lend money to family members. IRS rules require that interest be charged on loans—if it isn't, the IRS considers those loans to be gifts and taxes them accordingly. But the minimum interest rate that must be charged to avoid this drawback varies based on Treasury bill and bond yields. And those yields currently are so low that it's possible to charge family members nearly no interest without tax consequences.

Helpful: Precisely how much interest must be charged depends on the length of the loan, among other factors. Check the most recent "Applicable Federal Rates" table for details—Google the terms "IRS" and "applicable federal rates" to locate this. These interest payments can later be forgiven, if you like, though forgiven payments will count toward your lifetime or annual gift tax exclusion.

Intrafamily loans will be particularly welcome to heirs who cannot otherwise qualify for attractive interest rates because of less-than-perfect credit histories.

If you provide a mortgage loan to a family member, the borrower even can deduct his mortgage interest payments, just as he could deduct those made to a conventional lender. The mortgage must be secured against the property to qualify for this deduction, and certain other conditions must be met as well. See IRS Publication 936, *Home Mortgage Interest Deduction,* for details.

Or make low-rate loans to heirs so that they have money to invest. Your heirs might need long-term investment growth more than you do at this point in your life.

If you do make a family loan, draft and sign a formal loan agreement, complete with payment schedule, in case you later need to provide the IRS with proof that this really was a loan and not a gift.

Inform your estate-planning attorney of any family loans of significant size so that they can be noted in your estate plan. Otherwise, if you pass away before the loan is repaid, your assets might not be divided among your heirs as you had intended.

How to Fight for Your Inheritance When a Will Seems Unfair

Martin M. Shenkman, CPA, JD, an estate- and tax-planning attorney with the law firm Martin M. Shenkman, PC, with offices in New York City and Paramus, New Jersey. He is also author of many books, including *Inherit More* (Wiley) and *Estate Planning for People with a Chronic Condition or Disability* (Demos Health). *www.LawEasy.com*

A woman expects to inherit her widowed mother's estate…but the bulk of it passes to her mother's boyfriend instead. A man is left 25% of his parent's estate… and his sister gets 75%.

People blindsided by uneven, unfair or unexpectedly small inheritances from a loved one's estate often wonder whether they should challenge the will in court. The lost assets likely aren't the only reason they're upset— distress over the deceased loved one's choices about how to divide the assets can become intertwined with the hurt and anger they feel at being treated unfairly.

HOW TO CHALLENGE

You can't challenge a will simply because you think that you deserve more or you didn't receive an asset that you had been told you'd get. *Wills can be challenged for only certain reasons that often are very difficult to prove...*

•**Someone exerted undue influence over the deceased,** affecting the distribution of assets. Not all influence constitutes undue influence. Typically, there must be a coercive element. *Example:* A home health aide refuses to provide an infirm client with food or medicine until the aide is named a beneficiary in the client's will.

Your odds of proving undue influence may be improved if the deceased had infirmities that made him/her dependent on a beneficiary who received a surprisingly large inheritance...if this beneficiary attempted to prevent other potential heirs from seeing the deceased prior to death...and/or if there are any prior wills naming others as heirs before this beneficiary gained control.

•**The deceased was not competent at the time the will was signed.** This might be difficult to prove. Even if there's no question that the deceased was in a state of mental decline, the will may have been signed years earlier when his mental state was less clear-cut. Odds of success are much better if there are medical records and other evidence from the time period when the will was signed establishing the deceased's lack of competency.

•**The will was not executed according to the laws of the state.** Each state has detailed laws governing how a will must be signed and witnessed. *Example:* A man's will was successfully challenged and declared invalid because one of his witnesses was not in the room at the moment that the will was signed, as required.

State laws also dictate the minimum share of the estate that a surviving spouse should receive. Generally, states require that one-third go to the spouse if the deceased has children and one-half if there are no children.

•**The will is a fraud or forgery.** A will can be challenged on the grounds that it is not actually the deceased's will, it was not actually signed by the deceased or that it was signed by the deceased under false pretenses—for example, if the deceased was told that he was signing something other than a will.

Three scenarios that could improve the odds that a challenge to a will succeeds (or, more commonly, that the executor's attorney offers a settlement before the case reaches court)...

•**The will was changed shortly before the deceased passed away from a prolonged health problem.** People suffering from debilitating illnesses, especially illnesses with cognitive impact, may be particularly vulnerable. They often are dependent on care providers. That opens the door to challenges based both on incompetence and/or undue influence.

•**The will is inconsistent with the deceased's beneficiary designations in a way that favors one particular heir.** *Example:* The deceased had two IRAs, three insurance policies and a deed to a home that all listed his two sons as equal beneficiaries for many years—yet his recent will lists just one son as the sole heir. The disinherited son quite reasonably questioned whether his brother had exerted undue influence over his father to alter the will.

•**The will seems to disinherit a descendant accidentally.** *Example:* A will divides the estate evenly among a man's children but is never updated to include a child born after the will is drafted. While the language in most wills is broad enough to address this, sometimes it is not.

WHO CAN CHALLENGE

There also are strict rules about who can challenge a will in court. Generally, you can challenge only if you are a named beneficiary in the will...or if you would inherit according to your state's *intestate succession laws* (the laws spelling out inheritance rules when there is no valid will)—which occasionally means that even distant relatives can challenge if there are no direct descendants or a surviving spouse.

Additionally, you might be able to challenge if you were a beneficiary in a prior version of the will that would once again be valid if the current will were ruled invalid by the court. However, copies of the prior version often are destroyed to avoid challenges such as these.

DRAWBACKS OF CHALLENGING A WILL

Challenging a will in court is very expensive. Expect attorney fees to start at $10,000 to $25,000 and potentially much more. Thus it may not make financial sense to challenge if the estate is small. And that's only half the story—the executor or trustees of the will that you challenge will pay their legal bills out of the estate, reducing the amount.

Will challenges also can force families to take sides. Family members often end up aligned against the individual who brought the challenge because challenges deplete the size of the estate and delay its distribution.

YOUR ALTERNATIVES

Contact the executor before you challenge a will in court, and calmly say, "I'm not clear about [some element of the estate]. Could you help me understand it?" Even if the answer is not what you're hoping for, it could reassure you that you're not being cheated and eliminate the desire to go to court.

Consider paying an attorney on a per-hour basis before you call the executor. This attorney can help you determine if you're being treated fairly…lay out your legal options…review letters and e-mails you send to family members or executors about the estate…and assist you so that you don't miss deadlines if you decide to challenge the will in court.

Downplay the fact that you have hired a lawyer—if other family members learn this, it could ratchet up the tension or encourage them to hire lawyers, too, increasing the odds of a court battle. You may wish to choose an attorney who is very familiar with wills but who does not litigate, so he has little incentive to steer you into an expensive legal battle if you're not likely to win. A probate attorney often is a good choice.

Alternatively, if your family has used the same accountant or financial adviser for years, consider bringing your concerns to him/her

Can You Inherit Frequent-Flier Miles?

Inheriting frequent-flier miles is permitted by several airlines despite formal policies against it at some. American AAdvantage miles can be transferred to a beneficiary's account after the surviving spouse, the sole heir or the executor of the estate signs an affidavit and provides a death certificate. US Airways Dividend Miles can be transferred within a year of the member's death after a copy of the will and death certificate are provided. United has a transfer form available from customer service and charges a $75 fee,* even though it has a rule against transfers. Southwest has a policy against the transfer of Rapid-Rewards points, but family members who know the deceased member's account number and password may be able to book tickets using the frequent-flier miles if the points have not expired.

The New York Times. www.NYTimes.com

*Price subject to change.

What to Do with an Unwanted Inheritance

Karen Larson, editor, *Bottom Line/Personal*, 281 Tresser Blvd., Stamford, Connecticut 06901. *www.BottomLine Publications.com*

My friend's brother recently died and left my friend his beloved pickup truck. The problem is, my friend doesn't need or want a truck. Heirs are bequeathed pets that they don't want, unsightly family heirlooms and partial ownership of property that's more trouble than it's worth.

If you have something you want to pass along that carries costs or responsibilities, it's only fair to discuss it with the intended heir, says Crystal Thorpe, MSW, coauthor of *Mom Always Liked You Best: A Guide for Resolving*

Family Feuds, Inheritance Battles & Eldercare Crises and a partner with Elder Decisions in Norwood, Massachusetts. If you sense any resistance, consider selecting a different heir.

If you're an heir, you can decline without hurting the giver's feelings by framing the rejection as an attempt to ensure that the giver's goals are met. For example, my friend could have said, "I want you to feel confident that the truck will be in the hands of someone who truly appreciates it, but I don't think I'm the best person for it." If possible, name a potential heir who would be better. It's too late for my friend to do that, but he could ask his brother's closest friends and relatives for suggestions about how the truck could be better used.

Another option would be to sell the truck, but my friend wondered if he would owe taxes on the sale. Probably not, says Martin M. Shenkman, CPA, JD, an estate-planning attorney with offices in New York and Paramus, New Jersey. You usually owe capital gains taxes when you sell a possession for a profit. Even though your friend didn't pay anything for the truck, he would generally be allowed to treat its value on the day of his brother's death as the cost basis. Used vehicles almost always decline in value over time, so the selling price would likely be less than the cost basis and no capital gains taxes would likely be owed.

To determine whether the inherited truck is being sold for more or less than its cost basis, your friend should ask the executor of the estate if a federal or state tax return was filed for the estate. If so, this return should list the truck's value at the time of death. If a return was not filed, the *Kelley Blue Book* value published closest to the date of death may provide an acceptable estimate of the truck's value at the time. As long as the sale price does not exceed this amount, there should be no capital gains taxes owed. Capital gains taxes are more likely to be an issue when inherited art, jewelry or collectibles are sold, as these sometimes do appreciate in value.

Note: If a state imposes fees and/or vehicle transfer taxes upon the sale of a vehicle, these would likely be owed regardless of how the vehicle was acquired.

Caring for Your Pet After You Die

Rachel Hirschfeld, Esq., a New York City–based attorney specializing in animal law. She is author of *Petriarch: The Complete Guide to Financial and Legal Planning for a Pet's Continued Care* (American Institute of Certified Public Accountants) and created the Pet Protection Agreement and the Hirschfeld Pet Trust. *www.PetTrust Lawyer.com*

Without proper planning, there is a very real chance that a beloved pet will be euthanized shortly after your death. From the perspective of the court, pets are treated as property, not loving companions. *What you need to know…*

PUTTING PETS IN WILLS POSES PROBLEMS

In recent decades, many states have enacted "pet trust statutes." These pet trusts relate only to animal provisions in wills. In theory, these trusts provide assets for the pet's continued care, but they have some potentially dangerous drawbacks. *Pet trusts written into wills…*

• **Are not enforced until the probate process is complete,** which can take months or years. Pets might be euthanized before then.

• **Often are legally unenforceable.** *Example:* You could leave your pet and the money to pay for its care to an heir in your will, but nothing in the law prevents that heir from pocketing the money and sending your pet to the pound.

• **Do nothing to ensure the care of pets when their owners are alive but in a coma** or otherwise unable to look after their animals.

• **Are not honored in every state.** Even if you live in a state where they are honored, the trust could be thrown out if you happen to die while in a state where they are not.

• **Can be overruled.** Courts sometimes step in and overrule pet-care provisions in wills.

BETTER OPTIONS

• **A freestanding pet trust**—that is, a pet trust not included in your will—avoids all of the problems described above if properly constructed. These trusts are not cheap, however. An attorney is likely to charge $1,500* or so to draft the trust, and assets must be set aside to fund the trust.

*Prices subject to change.

Helpful: It can be difficult to find an attorney who has experience with these trusts. Ask your state bar association to recommend attorneys who specialize in animal law, then call these attorneys and confirm that they have experience drafting pet trusts.

• **Pet Protection Agreement (PPA),** which I created, is a legally enforceable document signed by both the pet owner and a pet guardian (someone who agrees to care for the pet if the owner cannot) that ensures continuing care for your pet. PPAs can be completed without the assistance—and expense—of an attorney, using a form available from LegalZoom for $39. (Go to LegalZoom.com, then select "Pet Protection Agreement" from the "Wills & Trusts" section. Some proceeds from the sale of this form go to charity.) PPAs need not provide assets to the pet guardian for the pet's care, though they can do so. The signed PPA should be notarized.

KEY POINTS

Whether you opt for a freestanding pet trust or a PPA, take the following steps to help ensure your pet's safety…

• **Clarify who owns the pet.** Your whole family might love and care for the animal, but for the purposes of estate planning, one family member should be the pet's legal owner.

Helpful: If any adults living in the pet's household are not named in the pet trust or PPA in any capacity, ask them to sign the trust or PPA document, too. Their signatures help confirm that they are aware of the document and that they agree that another family member is the pet's legal owner.

If you adopted your pet, confirm with the organization from which you adopted it that you are the animal's legal owner. Some breed-rescue organizations officially continue to own the animals that they place with families.

Example: Ellen DeGeneres felt that she had to give up her dog, Iggy, because it did not get along with her cats. DeGeneres's hairdresser's family wanted to adopt him—but the breed-rescue organization from which DeGeneres had adopted the dog swept in, took Iggy away and gave him to a different family.

• **Include as many successor pet guardians as possible.** By the time you are no longer able to care for your pet, the person who agreed to care for it in your place might have passed away…moved into a condo that doesn't allow pets…or entered a relationship with someone who is allergic to your pet. Secure agreements from additional friends and relatives stating that they will take in the pet if your primary pet guardian cannot. List these successor pet guardians in the PPA or trust. Successor pet guardians do not need to sign the agreement, but I prefer that they do.

Include multiple ways of contacting each potential pet guardian—landline and cell-phone numbers, e-mail and mailing addresses—in case some contact information changes.

Helpful: Consider naming an appropriate animal organization to serve as a successor pet guardian should your pet guardian and successor pet guardians be unable to take in the animal. Confirm with the organization that it is willing to serve in this capacity.

• **Make sure that the pet trust or PPA includes all of your pets**—even those you acquire after the document is completed. List and describe each of your animals in the document but also include the phrases "all my pets" and "this includes any other animals I have at the time this trust/pet protection arrangement is enacted."

• **Have the trust/PPA take effect when you "are unable or unwilling to provide for the pet's care."** These documents often are written to take effect when the pet owner is "incapacitated," but that term is best avoided—it can open the door for a court to step in and arrange a pet guardian. The wording "unable or unwilling" keeps this decision in your hands.

• **Get copies of your pet trust or PPA into many hands.** Give copies to all trustees, pet guardians and pet successor guardians listed in the document. Also give copies to your pet's veterinarian, your neighbors, your family members, your dogwalker and anyone else who might be present and willing to act on your pet's behalf when you cannot. Ask all of these people to check in if they hear that you've been hospitalized (or have died) to make sure that the pet is OK.

10

Investment Insider

The Safer Portfolio: Aims for Steady Gains Even in a Difficult Market

Many nervous investors have been telling top financial adviser Louis P. Stanasolovich that they're now more confused than at any time since the 2008–2009 recession. They are worried about the dysfunctional Congress...an economy stuck in low gear...a stock market that looks to them to be wildly overvalued...and bonds with the lowest yields in decades whose value could plunge when interest rates start to rise.

They want to ratchet down their risk—even if that means forgoing potentially bigger returns in some years. Stanasolovich has designed a low-volatility portfolio of funds meant to preserve assets even in bad markets and register modest but steady gains even in tough times.

LESS VOLATILITY

Volatility will be a major problem in the coming years, with not much reward for investors who take big risks. My team expects stocks to return an average of about 5% annually over the next decade and US Treasury bonds just 2%, and both could suffer double-digit losses in any given year. There are no guarantees, but for especially cautious investors, a safer portfolio could seek to average between 3% and 4% annually, with little chance of more than a mid-single-digit percentage loss in any year. The key is putting together a diversified mix of between 12 and 20 mutual and exchange-traded funds (ETFs). I look for fund managers who don't just analyze

Louis P. Stanasolovich, CFP, president of Legend Financial Advisors, a fee-only financial advisory with $320 million under management, Pittsburgh. He was selected 12 times by *Worth* magazine as one of the "Top 100 Wealth Advisors" in America. *www.Legend-Financial.com*

individual stocks and bonds. They also make big-picture decisions regarding where interest rates are headed and what mix of asset classes will achieve the best total returns under current conditions—and they have great flexibility to adjust their portfolios.

My portfolio includes…

•**70% in fixed-income funds.** This ultra-conservative portfolio is heavily invested in fixed-income funds because we believe that they will be relatively stable this year and will help offset potential stock market declines. The fund managers have great flexibility to shift among bonds with different ranges of maturities and credit ratings.

Important: If economic growth strengthens considerably and we do get fast-rising interest rates and inflation—and that could happen in 2014 or beyond, but we don't expect it this year—these funds are agile enough to minimize losses and even produce gains. However, in such an environment, we would also decrease overall bond exposure markedly and increase investments that do better in such times, such as stocks and gold.

•**27% in alternative-stock funds.** Stocks could be especially volatile this year because of so much uncertainty in Congress about how to deal with our many economic problems. Many of the stock funds in this portfolio will capture a large portion of the upside if stocks soar. And if stocks plunge, these funds can keep risk at bay by switching into alternative investments, such as foreign currencies and commodities, as well as shorting (betting against) stocks and hedging current holdings with futures contracts that allow them to buy or sell investments at a specified price.

•**3% in gold-bullion funds.** Although gold's prices can be volatile, it is an excellent diversifier to help balance the overall portfolio, and it has little correlation to either stock or bond returns.

Even if you already have an extensive portfolio, adding or transitioning to some of the funds below can reduce your concerns about big losses.

FIXED-INCOME FUNDS

•**DoubleLine Total Return Bond Fund (DLTNX).** Jeffrey Gundlach, who manages this fund launched in 2010, has become a superstar investor over the years by mastering a lesser-known part of the bond world—high-quality government agency mortgage-backed securities. Fully backed by the US government, they can exhibit low volatility in both good times and bad.

Recent yield: 5.04%.* *www.DoubleLineFunds. com*

•**Eaton Vance Floating Rate Fund (EABLX)** invests in loans made by banks to companies with lower-quality credit ratings. Since default rates among these firms are quite low right now, it offers an attractive yield without much risk. And yields on bank loans are not fixed like those on corporate bonds—they adjust every 30 to 90 days.

Recent yield: 3.58%. *www.EatonVance.com*

•**Osterweis Strategic Income Fund (OSTIX).** This multisector fund buys a wide range of lower-quality corporate bonds for their higher yields but tempers volatility by keeping the average maturity at three and a half years.

Recent yield: 5.42%. *www.Osterweis.com*

•**Pimco Total Return Fund (PTRRX).** Run by famed fixed-income manager Bill Gross, this intermediate-term bond fund is a core holding for low-volatility investors.

Recent yield: 3.17%. *www.Pimco.com*

•**RS Low Duration Bond Fund (RSDYX).** This short-term bond fund looks for undervalued government and corporate bonds with an average maturity of a little more than two years.

Recent yield: 1.92%. *www.RSInvestments.com*

•**Templeton Global Bond Fund (FGBRX)** invests in government bonds and currencies in fast-growing emerging-market countries in Asia and Latin America.

Recent yield: 5.12%. *www.FranklinTempleton. com*

STOCK FUNDS

•**Caldwell & Orkin Market Opportunity Fund (COAGX)** typically keeps a portion of

*Yields as of August 16, 2013.

its portfolio in stocks that it buys "long," betting that their prices will rise, but unlike most stock funds, it also offers substantial protection in declines by "shorting" stocks, betting that their prices will fall.

Performance: 3.81%.** *www.CaldwellOrkin. com*

• **Ironclad Managed Risk Fund (IRONX),** launched in 2010, uses a strategy involving stock options contracts that sharply reduces losses in market declines and limits gains in rising markets.

One-year performance: 3.72%, compared with 19.6% for the S&P 500. *www.Ironclad Funds.com*

• **Invesco Balanced-Risk Allocation Fund (ABRYX),** launched in 2009, is a global fund that divides its portfolio among bonds, commodities and stocks.

Performance: 9.03%. *www.Invesco.com*

• **Leuthold Asset Allocation Fund (LAALX)** is a global fund that uses computer models to analyze economic factors and trends, then invests in a wide range of stocks and bonds.

Performance: 7.04%. *www.LeutholdFunds. com*

• **Pimco All Asset All Authority Fund (PAUDX).** Highly respected fund manager Robert Arnott uses computers to figure out what combination of asset classes will produce optimal returns with low volatility. The fund typically invests in about 40 individual Pimco mutual funds.

Performance: 4.06%. *www.Pimco.com*

GOLD

• **SPDR Gold Shares ETF (GLD)** is an ETF that offers the convenience of owning gold without taking physical possession.

Performance: 3.46%. *www.SPDRGoldShares. com*

**Performance figures based on three-year annualized returns through August 16, 2013.

A Master Stockpicker's 5 Big Stocks for the Next 10 Years

Donald Yacktman, president of Yacktman Asset Management, Austin, Texas, and comanager of the Yacktman Fund (YACKX) and the Yacktman Focused Fund (YAFFX), both of which had annualized returns of more than 10% over the past decade, putting them among the top 10 of all US stock funds. *www.Yacktman.com*

Based on the weak and volatile stock market returns of the past decade, many investors believe that the traditional strategy of buying and holding a stock for many years is dead. But some top mutual fund managers say that if you pick the right stocks, that strategy could still deliver strong returns. To determine how to pick the best stocks to hold for at least the next 10 years, we spoke with a master of buy-and-hold investing—Donald Yacktman, whose Yacktman Focused Fund delivered the best returns of any diversified US large-cap stock fund over the past 10 years.

FOCUS ON MEGA-CAPS

I focus on great businesses whose products are staples of today's global society. That affords these businesses long-term predictability and consistency even in an environment where there is a high degree of uncertainty. A company must have brand-name products and services that dominate their markets and are tapping into sustainable trends...operations on a scale big and efficient enough to reap cost savings...and the ability to raise prices easily if inflation becomes an issue. Now I am finding the most compelling long-term buys among jumbo-sized companies—so-called mega-cap stocks—many of which are undervalued. *Some of my favorites, starting with the most attractive...*

• **Procter & Gamble (PG).** This consumer-goods giant has more household brands that top $1 billion in annual revenue—such as Bounty and Crest—than any global competitor. Its predictability, market-share dominance and attractive prices make it the Yacktman Focused Fund's top holding. Some investors worry about PG's sluggish growth in developed markets, but it is ramping up marketing in developing countries and divesting noncore businesses such as Pringles. Even modest annual growth of 2% to 4% in its mature markets, which is a very attainable goal, will yield attractive stock returns.

Recent share price: $79.90.*

● **Twenty-First Century Fox (FOXA).** Despite the enormous scandal surrounding CEO Rupert Murdoch, the global media giant has become a model of how to successfully transition from old media (newspapers and book publishing) to the realities of the 24-hour news cycle. The company's earnings come exclusively from its cable network business, including Fox News, Fox Sports, FX and a variety of international channels throughout Asia, now that its newspaper and publishing properties have spun off into a separate company, which kept the firm's old name, News Corp. (NWSA).

The recent phone hacking scandal at News Corp.'s British newspaper *News of the World* and a British parliamentary committee's scolding of Murdoch as "not a fit person" to run an international company were tremendously embarrassing but, from an investment point of view, rather negligible in the long run. Moreover, the 82-year-old Murdoch has positioned Fox to maintain its position as a global powerhouse even after he steps down.

Recent share price: $31.97.

● **PepsiCo (PEP).** Investors who are focused on the fact that Pepsi plays second fiddle to Coca-Cola are missing the point. It really is the world's most dominant snack food company, deriving less than half its revenues from cola and the rest from snack foods under the Frito-Lay division and other beverages including Tropicana juices and Gatorade. Consumers tend to accept snack food price hikes without switching brands.

Recent share price: $80.18.

● **Microsoft (MSFT).** Another favorite investment theme is "Old Tech"—mature technology companies that still dominate their

*Prices and rates as of August 16, 2013.

markets but have settled into slower rates of sales and earnings growth. They are better investments than most hot young tech firms for the next decade because their stocks will do well with much lower risk. Microsoft's products may not generate feverish excitement, but it has nearly $76 billion in cash, an ultra-cheap stock price and expectations so low that it needs only to deliver stable results for me to earn double-digit returns in the years ahead. I expect Microsoft will do much better than that, thanks to new product releases such as the Windows 8 operating system and Office 15 software package.

Recent share price: $31.80.

● **Sysco Corporation (SYY)** provides more than 400,000 food and equipment products needed to run eating establishments ranging from The Four Seasons restaurant in New York City to your local Applebee's. Although food service is a low-margin business that can suffer during economic slowdowns, Sysco has increased sales and dividends (recently yielding 3.5%) every single year since it went public in 1970.

Recent share price: $32.45.

How to Invest in Stocks and Still Sleep at Night

Tom Lydon, president of Global Trends Investments, Irvine, California, which manages more than $80 million of assets in all-ETF portfolios. He is also founder of ETFTrends.com and coauthor of *iMoney: Profitable ETF Strategies for Every Investor* (FT Press).

After the investment world's wild ride of the past several years, many investors are aching for more tranquility. Wall Street is addressing that yearning with a range of new exchange-traded funds (ETFs)* that are designed to smooth out the wild swings.

*ETFs are funds that typically track a particular investment index but can be bought and sold on an exchange like individual stocks. They tend to have lower annual expenses than comparable mutual funds.

More than a dozen of these low-volatility ETFs now are available.

And lower volatility doesn't mean that you have to settle for lower returns. Over the past five years, the Standard & Poor's 500 Low Volatility Index returned 9.9% annualized versus 7.4% for the S&P 500 stock index.

Here's how low-volatility ETFs can be right for you…

HOW THEY WORK

By investing in low-volatility stocks, these ETFs can reduce the impact of the market's jolts.

Example: When the S&P 500 moves up or down by 1%, a low-volatility version of the index tends to move 0.9% in the same direction.

Major investment companies that offer low-volatility ETFs, such as Blackrock, Russell and Invesco, focus on several factors to choose the low-volatility stocks that make up the ETFs. *These factors include…*

• **How much the stocks swing up and down relative to their average long-term price.**

• **How much the stocks move relative to the larger index that they track.**

• **How correlated or uncorrelated they are to one other.**

In response to these considerations, low-volatility ETFs often load up on stocks that are in stable sectors, such as household goods and utilities that consumers don't eliminate even during difficult economic times. But even when various low-volatility ETFs seem similar, they are not simply clones of one another. They cover slightly different indexes…reevaluate their holdings at different intervals…and sometimes impose restrictions on how much they allocate to particular countries or sectors.

Important: Despite their appeal as safer investments with possibly better returns, low-volatility ETFs are all-stock offerings, which means that they still will be significantly riskier than funds that include bonds or a mix of bonds and stocks in their portfolios. Also, you are better off holding these ETFs in tax-deferred accounts, since most adjust their portfolios several times a year, which is likely to lead to higher turnover and more tax implications than many index funds.

Finally, if you invest in a low-volatility ETF, you probably will need to adjust your expectations downward in bull markets. While these ETFs can provide some protection and returns in down times, they are unlikely to keep pace with the overall market when stocks are rising sharply.

HOW TO USE THEM

Low-volatility ETFs can be very useful tools to help you accomplish the following…

• **Reduce overall risk without getting out of stocks completely.** During rough times, investing in low-volatility ETFs is a less drastic alternative than trying to time the market by shifting assets to cash or bonds.

• **Gain exposure to riskier asset classes that can boost your long-term returns.** For example, if you are a retiree invested mostly in bonds but still need substantial growth in your portfolio, you may feel more comfortable adding a low-volatility foreign stock fund than a standard one.

Here are a variety of low-volatility ETFs for you to consider. *They all are from reputable money-management firms that use a disciplined selection process…*

LARGE-CAP

• **PowerShares S&P 500 Low Volatility Portfolio (SPLV).** The largest of the low-volatility ETFs, it has attracted nearly $4.7 billion in assets. It consists of the 100 stocks from the S&P 500 with the lowest volatility over the past 12 months. Every three months, the portfolio is reevaluated and stocks are replaced if necessary.

Recent share price: $31.21.**

• **Russell 1000 Low Volatility ETF (LGLV)** picks from the 1,000 largest US companies and can hold up to 200 stocks. It uses more complex criteria than the PowerShares ETF to choose stocks and keeps a tighter rein on volatility in both up and down markets. To ensure it remains focused on low-volatility stocks, the portfolio is reconstituted every month.

Recent share price: $63.45.

**Prices as of August 16, 2013.

SMALL-CAP

•**SPDR Russell 2000 Low Volatility ETF (SMLV)** currently is the only small-cap ETF devoted to low-volatility stocks. It holds up to 400 of the least volatile stocks in the Russell 2000. The ETF has about 39% of its portfolio in real estate and utilities, and it is reconstituted every month.

Recent share price: $62.25.

FOREIGN

•**iShares MSCI EAFE Minimum Volatility Index (EFAV)** tracks the MSCI EAFE Minimum Volatility Index, which attempts to create the least volatile portfolio of up to 200 stocks from the MSCI EAFE Index. That index includes developed nations in Europe, the Australia region and the Far East. The ETF reevaluates and reconstitutes its portfolio only twice a year. In attempting to reduce the ETF's volatility, it imposes certain constraints that its competitors don't, such as limiting the percentage of assets that can go into any one sector or country. The ETF also has one of the lowest annual expense ratios of any low-volatility ETF, just 0.2%.

Recent share price: $59.44.

•**PowerShares S&P International Developed Low Volatility Portfolio (IDLV).** This ETF tracks the 200 stocks in the S&P Developed Ex.-US-Korea LargeMidCap Index that have had the lowest volatility over the past 12 months, with 16% of its portfolio currently devoted to Canadian firms. (South Korea sometimes is regarded as a developed country, but is not included in this index because of the high volatility of its stock market.) The ETF is rebalanced and reconstituted quarterly and is a more conservative offering than the iShares MSCI EAFE Minimum Volatility Index ETF.

Recent share price: $30.02.

More from Tom Lydon...

Tricky ETFs

Don't be fooled by ETFs with misleading names.

Examples: SPDR S&P Emerging Middle East & Africa ETF essentially is a single-country fund with 91% of its assets in South African stocks...Vanguard Dividend Appreciation ETF implies a heavy emphasis on dividends, but its recent 2% annual yield was about the same as that of the S&P 500 stock index...and SPDR S&P Homebuilders ETF has only one-quarter of its assets in home-builder stocks.

Betting on #2: Why the Stocks of Second-Place Companies Come in *First*

Thomas H. Forester, CFA, president of Forester Capital Management in Lake Forest, Illinois. His flagship fund is Forester Value (FVALX). *www.ForesterValue.com*

Nothing intrigues leading stock picker Thomas Forester more than a company that is second-best at what it does.

That approach goes against conventional wisdom, which says you should favor the top dog in an industry, the one with the largest market share. The dominance and stability of these leaders make them hard to beat, and sometimes even Forester owns shares in them. But just because number one has greater revenue doesn't mean that it's the better stock investment, Forester says.

It often is smarter to bet on the number-two company, even if it has no chance of ever taking the lead. A second banana might produce superior long-term returns—if its stock price makes it a bigger bargain...it offers more attractive dividends...it is more innovative... and/or it has greater prospects for growth.

Forester's favorite second-place companies for investors...

FOR A BARGAIN PRICE

•**Chevron (CVX) is one of my favorite bargain-priced stocks.** Its $231 billion in revenue in 2012 puts it in second place behind industry leader ExxonMobil's $482 billion among US-based oil and natural gas companies (although foreign-based giants BP and Royal Dutch Shell have higher annual revenues than Chevron). But Chevron stock's annualized return over the past five years was 9.8% versus 4.8% for ExxonMobil.*

Recent share price: $125.11.

Why it's a better investment: Although ExxonMobil and Chevron both will benefit from rising global demand for energy in the coming decades, Chevron receives the edge because its shares are significantly cheaper. ExxonMobil—for many years the most highly valued publicly traded company in the US before falling behind Apple this year—has been such a popular investment with large financial institutions that its stock typically is priced at a premium and rarely drops to bargain levels. Chevron's accomplishments and potential are less noticed or revered by Wall Street investors. Its forward *price-to-earnings ratio* (P/E), a measure of how expensive a stock is based on estimates of future earnings, is just 9.5 versus 10.3 for ExxonMobil.

Chevron has several other advantages. It has the most cash of any publicly traded energy company, more than $22 billion. In addition, Chevron relies much less on natural gas as a percentage of total revenue than ExxonMobil does. ExxonMobil continues to be hurt by a glut in natural gas that has sent prices to their lowest levels in two years.

FOR INNOVATION

• **CVS Caremark (CVS)** is my favorite company for innovation among second-place giants. The retail pharmacy chain, with more than 7,300 pharmacies in 41 states, had $73 billion in revenue last year from its pharmacy division. It trails Walgreens, which has nearly 8,000 outlets (operating under the Walgreens and Duane Reade names) in all 50 states and 2012 revenue of $71 billion. CVS stock has averaged a 9.6% annualized return over the past five years, compared with 7.2% for Walgreens.

Recent share price: $58.57.

Why it's a better investment: Second-place companies typically are forced to be more innovative and take more chances as they attempt

*Rates and prices as of August 16, 2013.

to differentiate themselves from the industry leader and play catch-up. CVS is a great example of this.

CVS created in-house, low-cost Minute Clinics, staffed by nurse practitioners and physician assistants, and expects to operate 1,000 of them by 2016. CVS also spent $27 billion in 2007 to purchase Caremark, one of the country's leading pharmacy benefits managers (PBMs). PBMs work as middlemen managing drug-benefit programs for health plans and employers. As a result, CVS has become the biggest dispenser of drugs in the US, handling pharmacy benefits for more than 50 million customers, including those gained from a recent $3 billion Federal Employee Program contract. Meanwhile, Walgreens spent much of the past year in an ugly dispute over payment issues with another PBM, Express Scripts, many of whose customers went to CVS/Caremark to get their prescriptions filled, costing Walgreens some $4 billion in revenue.

FOR FASTER GROWTH

• **Target (TGT) is my favorite company for growth potential among second-place firms.** The discount general-merchandise retailer now has nearly 1,800 stores in the US and had 2012 revenue of $73 billion, compared with industry leader Walmart's more than 10,000 stores worldwide that generated $470 billion in revenue.

Recent share price: $68.58.

Why it's a better investment: Even though Walmart continues to be a formidable merchandiser, it is tough for first-place giants to grow year after year as they get staggeringly large. If Walmart were a country, based on its annual revenue it would rank 25th in the world in gross domestic product (GDP).

Target's relatively small size will enable it to grow at a faster rate and achieve better returns for investors. There are several catalysts for Target's growth. The company has taken a page out of Walmart's playbook by stocking more groceries and perishable foods such as dairy, frozen foods, baked goods and deli foods in order to increase traffic in its stores. Helped by an acquisition in Canada last year, Target is planning a major expansion into that country with 150 store openings by 2014. It has been able to differentiate itself from Wal-mart with more chic and upscale merchandise. That will benefit Target because an improving economy causes consumers to shift away from deep-discount retailers and upgrade the types of items that they purchase.

More Companies Sell Stocks Direct

Dozens of publicly traded firms now allow you to buy stock shares *directly*, rather than through a brokerage firm, often without a fee or with a fee of $6 or less for up to 100 shares.* Some direct-purchase plans offer a 3% to 5% discount on the stock price at the time of purchase.

Companies worth considering now: Consumer goods giant Church & Dwight (CHD)... asset manager Franklin Resources (BEN)... and global miner Freeport-McMoran Copper & Gold (FCX).

Charles B. Carlson, CFA, editor of the *DRIP Investor* newsletter, which tracks more than 1,100 companies offering dividend-reinvestment and direct-share purchase plans. *www.DripInvestor.com*

*Price subject to change.

How to Invest in Health Care *Now* (Hint: Don't Buy Hospital Stocks)

Kris Jenner, MD, PhD, portfolio manager of the T. Rowe Price Health Sciences Fund (PRHSX). For the past 15 years through August 16, 2013, the fund has produced an annualized return of 13.4%, which ranks in the top 1% of its category. *www.TRowePrice.com*

For investors, the Supreme Court's ruling to uphold most of President Obama's health-care reform legislation has lifted some of the uncertainty that has held back many health-care stocks.

But that doesn't make things as simple as it might seem for investors.

Reason: Although the *Patient Protection and Affordable Care Act* (ACA) will add more than 30 million new customers for health insurance companies and provide an enormous tailwind for the industry, things still are changing rapidly—in fact, you could say that we now have just moved past the *beginning* of health-care reform. In the coming months and years, the new challenge in Washington, DC, and across the country will be how to contain health care's soaring costs and get higher-quality care for the money spent. Only those companies that can continue to grow revenue and remain highly profitable in this phase will see their stocks keep rising.

For example, hospital stocks received a boost from the new law because the mandate that nearly all Americans be insured means that hospitals will no longer need to worry about the huge cost of providing care to the uninsured. Nevertheless, I am avoiding these stocks because hospitals will continue to see their profits whittled away by lower payments from insurers and the federal government.

How to position your portfolio now...

CLEAREST WINNERS

•**Health information-technology firms.** The health-care law seeks to increase the accuracy and lower the cost of medical records by getting all hospitals, doctors and pharmacies to convert to electronic record-keeping. *My favorite now...*

McKesson Inc. (MCK), one of the country's largest providers of health-care information technology, with more than $122.5 billion in annual revenue. Its software and hardware technology is installed in more than 70% of the nation's hospitals that have more than 200 beds.

Recent share price: $121.86.*

•**Pharmacy benefit managers.** These companies process prescriptions and administer drug benefits for employers and managed-care organizations, as well as negotiate discounts

*Prices as of August 16, 2013.

with pharmacies and drug distributors. *My favorite now...*

Catamaran Corp (CTRX). After a recent merger, this mid-sized company now manages benefits for 25 million insured individuals—with plenty of potential for additional growth.

Recent share price: $55.10.

• **Biotechnology firms.** Under the ACA, biotech companies get longer patent protections and new research-and-development tax credits. Plus, many are not required to pay additional taxes and fees that large pharmaceutical companies face. *My favorite now...*

Gilead Sciences (GILD). This biotech firm focuses on high-margin antiviral therapies.

Recent share price: $56.91.

TOUGHER CALLS

• **Medical device manufacturers.** These companies face a 2.3% annual excise tax on their total revenues starting in 2013. At the same time, they are less likely to benefit from a large influx of new customers because many of the newly insured individuals will be young and won't (for a while) need devices such as pacemakers and artificial knees. *A stock that I still like...*

Edwards Lifesciences Corp (EW), which makes cutting-edge and cost-saving heart-related devices, such as a minimally invasive heart valve that can be installed through a catheter.

Recent share price: $70.01.

• **Health insurers.** Here's the big irony—for insurers, the huge increase in new customers resulting from the ACA likely will be undercut by the law's many profit-restraining regulations (hence, "Affordable" care).

Nevertheless, I do believe certain insurance companies—including those that are well-run and well-positioned in fast-expanding areas of coverage such as Medicare and Medicaid—will overcome these challenges and be very profitable. *A stock that I still like...*

UnitedHealth Group (UNH). This health insurer uses its national infrastructure and massive size (it has 75 million members) to keep down costs and negotiate large discounts with health-care providers.

Recent share price: $71.43.

Investment Opportunity: Natural Gas Vehicles

Vehicles that run on natural gas are poised to gain market share. Huge natural gas discoveries have driven down prices to about half of gasoline prices. Chrysler, Ford and GM have launched production of natural gas–powered pickup trucks. And about 20% of transit buses in the US run on natural gas.

Stocks likely to benefit: Clean Energy Fuels (CLNE)...Fuel Systems Solutions (FSYS)...and Westport Innovations (WPRT).

Graham Mattison, an analyst in Boston specializing in energy infrastructure and auto parts stocks at Lazard Capital Markets. *www.LazardCap.com*

Sector to Watch: Latin American Airlines

Latin America is the fastest-growing airline market in the world, growing more than twice as fast as North America, because there is poor train and road infrastructure in many of these countries...and a burgeoning middle class in Brazil and Chile that now is affluent enough to fly.

Most likely to benefit: Panama-based Copa Holdings (CPA)...and Chile's Lan Airlines (LFL).

Neal Dihora, CFA, an equity analyst who covers the airline industry at Morningstar, Inc., which tracks 385,000 investment offerings, Chicago. *www.Morningstar.com*

Attractive Stock: Cell Phone Towers

Cell phone–tower stocks will benefit from the spread of LTE wireless technology. Soaring sales of smartphones from Apple and Samsung that use the faster, more efficient transmission technology—Long-Term Evolution (LTE) or 4G (fourth generation)—are creating a surge in demand from wireless carriers for bandwidth space on the giant antennas used to transmit voice and data signals.

Favorite cell phone–tower stocks: American Tower (AMT)...Crown Castle International (CCI)...and SBA Communications (SBAC).

Imari Love, an analyst specializing in telecommunications stocks for Morningstar, Inc., Chicago, which tracks more than 385,000 investment offerings. *www.Morningstar.com*

Time to Invest in Smartphone Finance

Companies that enable financial transactions via smartphones are a good stock opportunity. These transactions—including paying for purchases by waving a smartphone over a payment terminal—are expected to reach $1 trillion worldwide by 2015.

Attractive: ARM Holdings (ARMH), based in the UK, whose chip designs are in more than 90% of smartphones...and NXP Semiconductors N.V. (NXPI), based in the Netherlands, whose technology enables secure transactions.

Anil Doradla, an analyst specializing in wireless-communications companies, William Blair & Company, Chicago. *www.WilliamBlair.com*

Stock Opportunity: Housing Recovery

Furniture and home-appliance sellers will benefit from the strengthening housing recovery. Stock prices for this sector are very attractive relative to home-builder stocks, which rose by more than 75% in 2012.

Favorites: Conn's (CONN), a fast-growing home-appliance chain...La-Z-Boy (LZB)...and Pier 1 Imports (PIR).

Bradley B. Thomas, CFA, a director and equity research analyst with KeyBanc Capital Markets, New York City. He specializes in the hard goods retailing industry.

The Best Emerging-Market Fund for YOU: Whether You're a Cautious Investor or an Aggressive One

Todd Rosenbluth, a senior director for S&P Capital IQ, an equity research firm that provides investment research and analytical tools to more than 4,000 investment banks, private-equity firms and financial-services clients, New York City. He oversees analysis and rankings of mutual funds. *www.SPCapitalIQ.com*

For many investors, there no longer is a question of whether to invest some of their money in funds that focus on the world's emerging markets—the question now is *which funds*?

Since the first emerging-market fund was introduced to US investors 25 years ago, hundreds have been launched covering a wide range of approaches. There are funds for the most aggressive investors and funds for more cautious ones...some that specialize in bonds rather than stocks...funds that concentrate on particular parts of the world...and even funds that invest in single countries.

Many emerging-market nations have healthier balance sheets and better outlooks for fast economic growth than developed nations, especially when much of Europe is struggling with recession and the US economy is only creeping upward. Emerging-market companies offer opportunities for attractive returns, in part because some benefit not just from exports to developed nations but also from booming local and regional economies.

Emerging markets have rewarded patient long-term investors with 10.7% annualized returns over the past 10 years, more than the 7.3% gain of the Standard & Poor's 500 stock index.

We asked international fund specialist Todd Rosenbluth to describe the outlook for emerging markets and sort out which funds are best for various types of investors...

WHAT TO EXPECT

Research at my firm points to a moderately good performance in 2013 for emerging-market stock funds—which averaged overall gains of 3.1% for the year ending August 16, 2013—and significantly higher returns in the long run.

That forecast is based, in part, on my belief that there won't be the kind of financial meltdown in the eurozone that could trigger a global recession...and that China, the world's second-largest economy, will generate economic growth around 8%. That's less than the 10%-plus annual growth it had become used to but still strong enough to help lift other Asian countries. Overall, emerging-market economies will likely grow by 5.7% in 2014, compared with the 2% or so growth that's likely in the US.

Of course, there are near-term risks that investors need to be aware of. Volatility will remain very high...and some big emerging markets such as India continue to suffer from persistent inflation and a business environment plagued by corruption and government red tape.

Given the risks and opportunities, a typical investor's portfolio of 60% stocks and 40% bonds should have about 5% of the overall assets in emerging markets. This can improve your overall returns in the next decade without raising your risk level too much.

BEST FUNDS

•**A fund that provides a simple low-cost way to get exposure to a wide range of stocks in emerging markets**—Vanguard MSCI Emerging Markets ETF (VWO). With nearly 900 stocks spread across 21 countries, this fund is a good core holding, with an annual expense ratio of just 0.18%. Top stocks include telecommunication giants China Mobile and América Móvil based in Mexico, as well as the Russian oil-and-gas company Gazprom.

Performance: 1.8%.* *www.Vanguard.com*

•**A fund that provides substantial income as well as growth from emerging-market**

*Performance figures based on five-year annualized returns through August 16, 2013.

stocks—WisdomTree Emerging Markets Equity Income Fund (DEM). In addition to income, dividends can provide evidence of a foreign company's strong cash flow and management's commitment to shareholders. This fund owns shares in about 250 of the highest-dividend-yielding stocks in 17 emerging markets, with heavy emphasis on Brazil, China and Russia. Top holdings include China Construction Bank Corp. and the Brazilian mining company Vale.

Recent yield: 4.2%.

Performance: 4.5%. *www.WisdomTree.com*

•**A fund that has lower risk than most emerging-market funds but still produces good returns**—Laudus Mondrian Emerging Markets Fund (LEMIX) looks for big undervalued companies with strong balance sheets. It keeps one-quarter of its assets in financial-services firms that dominate their local markets. The fund has done much better than its peers in avoiding big drops in down markets.

Performance: 1.7%. *www.LaudusFunds.com*

•**A fund that takes bigger risks and reaps bigger rewards**—Oppenheimer Developing Markets Fund (ODVYX) practices a theme-based approach—for instance, investing in large retailers in developing nations to take advantage of the spending habits of the growing middle classes. Top holdings among the fund's more than 100 stocks include FEMSA, which operates Mexico's largest convenience store chain, and Chinese Web services firm, Baidu.

Performance: 7.3%. *www.OppenheimerFunds.com*

•**A very aggressive fund that focuses on some of the fastest-growing countries in the world**—Matthews Asia Growth Fund (MPACX). Asia will be a sweet spot in the next few years. Countries such as Indonesia, the Philippines, Thailand and Vietnam all are experiencing annual economic growth rates of 5% to 6%. China's new generation of leaders took their posts in early 2013 and started instituting policies that will encourage stronger domestic growth. But betting on a single Asian country is too risky for most investors. This fund spreads its bets among about a dozen Asian countries, focusing on companies with sustainable growth selling at reasonable prices. These include Sinopharm Group, China's largest health-care products distributor, and NagaCorp, a Cambodian gambling and hotel operator. The fund also lowers volatility by investing in developed nations in the region that profit from Asia's growth, such as Australia.

Performance: 11.4%. *www.MatthewsAsia. com*

•**A fund that provides high yields**—Fidelity New Markets Income Fund (FNMIX). This fund keeps about two-thirds of its assets in emerging-market government bonds (denominated in US dollars to avoid making bets on foreign exchange rates) and one-third in emerging-market investment-grade corporate bonds. This mix has produced a recent yield of 5.4% versus 2.5% for a comparable portfolio of US bonds. Fidelity has proved adept at identifying undervalued bonds in smaller developing markets such as Croatia, Poland and Venezuela. This fund is best for aggressive, long-term bond investors because it can be more volatile than comparable US bond funds.

Performance: 9.3%. *www.Fidelity.com*

More from Todd Rosenbluth…

Eurogeddon: How to Protect Your Portfolio Now

Is Europe a treasure trove of bargain-priced stocks now…or the most dangerous place on the planet for investors? Is the US a safe haven…or will it fall back into recession? And will a wrenching slowdown in China's economic growth cast a shadow over the entire world?

If you're not comfortable coming up with answers to these questions on your own, consider investing in one of the global mutual funds whose managers shift their investment choices back and forth around the world to try to boost returns, depending on where they

see the greatest opportunities and the least frightening risks.

We spoke with fund expert Todd Rosenbluth to find out which of the 800 "global" funds are best able to cushion your portfolio from global upheaval…

WHY YOU NEED THEM

Global funds have the freedom to roam as the varying outlooks for companies headquartered in different parts of the world shift. They also take great advantage of the fact that many companies generate much of their revenue and profits in various parts of the world, no matter where they are headquartered.

Over the past five years, global funds have returned, on average, 5.1% annually, beating the major foreign stock index, the MSCI EAFE (-0.42%).

In deciding on a mix of stocks, most global fund managers first look at a key benchmark index—the MSCI All Country World Index, which targets US stocks as 45% of the mix… foreign stocks as 45%…and emerging-market stocks as 10%. Many of the global managers then adjust those allocations to varying degrees, sometimes dramatically, according to changing conditions.

AS A CORE HOLDING

The most cautious investors can use conservative global funds that tend to perform well in down markets as a core holding, replacing many of their US and foreign stock funds. *My recommendations for core no-load global funds…*

•**Tweedy, Browne Value Fund (TWEBX).** This is the low-volatility way to play global stocks. The portfolio of about 50 large-cap, blue-chip value stocks focuses on consumer companies that have dominant brand names in many countries and whose shares trade for at least 30% below what the managers believe they are worth. Given the intense uncertainty in the world now, the fund currently has about 14% of its assets in cash, with the rest split evenly between US and foreign stocks. This includes some big winners over the past year, such as the UK-based company Diageo, the world's leading producer of branded premium spirits, and Swiss drugmaker Roche Holding.

(Of course, some investors may want to steer clear of a fund that takes heavy positions in companies that benefit from liquor and cigarette consumption.)

Through the financial crisis of 2008, the fund beat the S&P 500 by 12 percentage points and the MSCI EAFE index by 19 points.

Performance: 8.9%.* *www.Tweedy.com*

Note: Investors seeking more fixed income can opt for the Tweedy, Browne Worldwide High Dividend Yield Value Fund (TBHDX).

•**USAA World Growth Fund (USAWX).** This 20-year-old fund, run by the global asset-management firm MFS Investments, is one of the oldest and largest in the world stock category. It is for relatively conservative investors who want to take a bit more risk than the Tweedy, Browne Value Fund takes, owning growth stocks with strong balance sheets and, in the managers' estimation, the potential to increase earnings by at least 8% a year. The fund limits its holdings to about 100 blue-chip, large-cap names, recently including Walt Disney and France-based LVMH Moët Hennessy Louis Vuitton S.A. The fund holds almost no stocks of companies headquartered in emerging markets.

Performance: 8.5%. *www.USAA.com*

AS A SUPPORT PLAYER

If you feel fairly comfortable with your core mutual funds but want to add a global fund for a portion of your assets, consider putting 10% or more of your portfolio into funds that often delve into small- and mid-cap companies and faster-growing, more volatile sectors such as technology. *My recommendations for no-load global funds to use in a support role…*

•**Artisan Global Value Fund (ARTGX).** This tiny fund, launched in 2007, is for relatively aggressive investors. It is run by the same team that manages Artisan International Value—they were chosen as Morningstar International Stock Fund Managers of the Year for 2008. The managers use a similar strategy here, hunting for undervalued businesses of any size that have a sustainable competitive advantage and strong free cash flow. The managers take a more daring approach than most global funds, willing to hold as few as 30 stocks in their portfolio, with as much as half the assets in small- and mid-cap companies and as much as 30% of the portfolio in emerging markets if conditions are right.

Many of the fund's holdings are under-the-radar stocks that small investors may not own or buy on their own, such as Aon Corp., a global insurance broker and human resources consulting firm that recently changed its headquarters from the US to the UK to get better tax treatment. The fund recently had 46% of its portfolio in US stocks, including companies with a global focus as well as those with a domestic focus.

Performance: 11%. *www.ArtisanFunds.com*

•**Janus Global Research Fund (JWGRX).** This fund has about 150 undervalued growth stocks. One-fifth of the stocks are small- or mid-caps. The fund is up by 9.6% through August 16, 2013, with 52% of assets in US stocks and 43% in foreign stocks, including 4.3% in emerging markets, reflecting caution on the global outlook.

Performance: 5.5%. *www.Janus.com*

How to Make Europe's Pain Your Gain

Elliott Gue, founder and chief analyst, Capitalist Times and Energy & Income Advisor, Alexandria, Virginia. *www.EnergyandIncomeAdvisor.com*

Y ou may want to keep individual stocks in your portfolio rather than depend entirely on global mutual fund managers to steer you through the world's economic upheavals. If so, you might want to shift to "defensive" stocks that are well-suited to today's environment.

---

*Performance figures based on five-year annualized returns through August 16, 2013.

It's especially important to pick stocks that are resistant to the possible effects of Europe's massive debt crisis spinning out of control. The financial turmoil already has cut into profits for many companies around the world and could lead to worsening recessions across Europe...trillions of dollars in loan defaults... waves of bank failures...and the collapse of the euro.

And it's not enough to just avoid investing in the most vulnerable European stocks. The economic shock waves could spread across the globe, reaching China, the US and other countries that serve as global economic engines.

We spoke with leading financial strategist Elliott Gue about the kind of stocks that can provide a relatively safe haven amid all the uncertainty...

THE OLD DEFENSIVE STOCKS

Many savvy investors are shifting to defensive stocks, typically those from giant US corporations that make products that people will continue to buy even in a global recession. Owning these stocks can mute losses in your portfolio if the global situation continues to deteriorate but still allow you to participate in market rallies if Europe pulls back from the brink—something it has done several times in the past three years. Unfortunately, many classic defensive stocks that investors relied on in past recessions and crises—such as HJ Heinz and McDonald's—may not hold up this time around. These companies and many others depend on Europe for a large portion of their revenues. And because the US dollar is so strong now relative to the euro, the euros that these companies do earn are worth less once they are converted back to dollars for financial-reporting purposes.

THE NEW DEFENSE

For defensive stocks that still are attractive, look for the following...

•**Modest exposure to Europe.** The company should get most of its revenue from the US and emerging markets. Yes, those economies have slowed, too, but they still are relatively strong compared with most other nations.

•**Modest valuations.** The company doesn't have to be a bargain, but it should trade at a reasonable price. Many defensive stocks have become prohibitively expensive. In fact, seven of the 30 stocks in the Dow Jones Industrial Average reached record highs last year. Risk-averse investors also have bid up the prices of other safe-haven favorites such as utilities.

Solid balance sheet and a consistent dividend. I like companies that have increased their dividend in at least eight of the last 10 years.

•**Downside resistance.** Make sure that the stock price has held up during the last US recession and in bear markets. It should have lost substantially less than the S&P 500 stock index lost in 2008.

•**Low beta.** Beta is a measure of how volatile a stock is compared with the S&P 500. A beta of 1.0 means that the stock moves essentially in line with the index. A low beta means less volatility. For instance, a beta of 0.5 indicates that the stock is half as volatile as the S&P 500. (You can find the beta for a stock at *http://Finance.Yahoo.com*.)

FAVORITES

•**Bristol-Myers Squibb Company (BMY).** Pharmaceutical companies tend to hold up well through bad times because consumers don't cut way back on prescription medicines. Bristol-Myers Squibb has the lowest exposure to Europe of the major US pharmaceutical giants and unusually low stock volatility. Its beta is just 0.09%,* and the stock price dropped a mere 6.5% in the last bear market back in 2008, bolstered by a dividend that recently yielded 3.3%. Moreover, the company has taken several smart steps that will help insulate it from the expiration of drug patents and economic downturns in the future. These include selling off businesses unrelated to its core strategy of developing high-margin prescription drugs, especially cancer drugs, and creating cost-saving partnerships with other pharmaceutical firms to lower development costs and diversify the risks of the Food and Drug Administration approval process.

*Rates and prices as of August 16, 2013.

Recent share price: $41.68.

• **Hillshire Brands Co. (HSH).** This is a very attractive stock for the current environment. In June 2012, the iconic American business Sara Lee spun off the riskier international parts of the company, retained its North American brands (including Jimmy Dean sausages, Ball Park hot dogs and Sara Lee baked goods) and renamed itself Hillshire Brands. It is now a safer, more focused version of the old Sara Lee, with a hefty dividend recently yielding 2.1%.

Recent share price: $32.79.

• **Johnson & Johnson (JNJ).** If I had to pick one company to hang on to through a European Armageddon, it would be the world's largest and most diverse health-care company, which has dozens of leading consumer brands, such as Band-Aid, Sudafed and Tylenol. J&J has raised its annual dividend, recently yielding 3%, for the past 50 consecutive years. It's only one of four corporations on the planet that still has a AAA credit rating, and its stock lost just 7.6% in the 2008 bear market. The biggest driver of earnings—the company's prescription drug division—has a strong pipeline of new drugs and less exposure to patent losses in the next few years than any other major pharmaceutical firm.

Recent share price: $89.37.

• **Kimberly-Clark Corp. (KMB).** Like food and health-care companies, manufacturers of consumer-staple products have been in excellent positions to hide out in bear markets. Kimberly-Clark is a leader in the global health and hygiene category, with dominant brands that include Kleenex tissues, Scott paper towels, Cottonelle toilet paper and Huggies diapers, as well as infection-prevention products. Rising income and birth rates in emerging markets will help the company grow earnings by about 8% annually over the next five years. Add in a dividend recently yielding 3.4%, annual free cash flow of more than $2 billion and a beta of just -0.05%, and the stock should be able to greatly outperform the broad market in troubled times.

Recent share price: $94.94.

• **Nestlé SA ADR (NSRGY).** A company headquartered in the heart of Europe seems like an unlikely defensive stock in case the European economy crumbles. But Nestlé, the largest packaged-good company in the world, with a wide variety of brands such as Nestlé hot chocolate, Gerber baby food and Purina Cat Chow, is misunderstood by many investors. It happens to be based in Switzerland, but it derives less revenue from Europe than many of its US competitors. That misunderstanding has kept the stock's valuations reasonable. In the 2008 bear market, Nestlé's returns beat the S&P 500 stock index by 25 percentage points. The company has increased its annual dividend payment every year over the past decade by an average of 12.5% per year.

Recent share price: $66.90.

The King of Balance: How This Small-Town Fund Manager Gets Big Returns in Any Market

Frank James, PhD, founder and chairman of James Investment Research, Alpha, Ohio. He oversees $3.5 billion in assets, including the James Balanced: Golden Rainbow Fund (GLRBX), which had 8% annualized returns over the past 10 years as of August 16, 2013, putting it in the top 1% of its Morningstar category. *www.JamesFunds.com*

Y ou might call Frank James "The King of Balance." Over the past 20 years, the fund manager has shown an uncanny ability to get strong returns while avoiding big drops. His insights are especially valuable at a time when investors are trying to balance the potential for stock market gains with a heavy dose of caution.

We spoke with James, who is based far from Wall Street in rural Alpha, Ohio (population less than 500), to find out how you can benefit from his simple strategy…

THE SECRETS TO BALANCE

I got my start investing mutual fund assets for the trust department of a tiny thrift bank, so my style always has been to protect against big losses but figure out a way to get high, single-digit returns most years. I don't go in for fancy alternative investments or complex hedging strategies. Instead, I start with a balance of about 50% stocks and 50% bonds. Then, every few months, I adjust my allocations slightly up or down depending on more than 100 risk indicators and my forecast for the economy and stock market. In January 2008, I told clients that an extended recession was likely. As the 2008 market crash approached, I positioned my portfolio with approximately 25% stocks and 75% bonds, keeping my losses to just 5.5% that year, compared with a 37% loss for the Standard & Poor's 500 stock index.

I take as little risk as possible with the bond portion of my portfolio, holding mostly US Treasuries. I don't worry about yield because I use bonds mostly as shock absorbers against volatility.

That allows me to take an added element of risk with stocks. Unlike many balanced-fund managers, I normally tend to keep more than half of my equity allocation in micro-, small- and mid-cap companies that are growing as fast as their peers but are unloved or overlooked by Wall Street analysts, so they sell at much steeper discounts. It's like buying an insurance policy. When the market turns downward, these smaller-cap, undervalued stocks fall less than stocks that have had bigger run-ups.

A CAUTIOUS OUTLOOK NOW

I have grown quite cautious because of re-emerging troubles in Europe. It's not so much the possibility of countries such as Greece or even Spain and Italy defaulting on their debt but something less dramatic and far more plausible—Europe falling into a long, severe recession that could upset our own fragile recovery. A European recession will exacerbate China's slowdown in economic growth, drag down global growth and hurt our markets, especially stocks of large multinational companies that depend on global exports for the bulk of their revenues.

Moves to make now...

• **Raise bond allocations.** About 46% of my portfolio now is in bonds. About two-thirds of that is in US Treasuries. Despite the amazing performance of Treasuries during 2011, I think that they will continue to appreciate as long as the European crisis persists and the world treats Treasuries as a refuge from investment uncertainty. However, I am using new cash and capital that I get from selling stocks to buy government agency bonds (Ginnie Maes)... very high-quality corporate bonds...and even municipal bonds. Like Treasuries, munis appreciate when the rest of the world looks for safety, and they offer better valuations than Treasuries after last year's run-up.

• **Reduce bond maturities.** The prices of longer-term bonds are severely hurt by rising interest rates, so I am gradually shortening maturities of the bonds that I buy to lower my average to five to six years.

• **Reduce stock allocations.** I am holding only about 40% of my portfolio in stocks and avoiding companies that derive significant revenue from selling overseas because I think slower global growth and a strong dollar will hurt their export businesses. In this environment, companies will have a hard time passing along cost increases, which will hurt their profit margins.

Include large-cap dividend stocks—but be sure that they are bargains. Although I continue to hold small- and mid-cap stocks, it is time also to invest in large-caps with strong balance sheets and cash flow and hefty annual dividends. They offer the best overall value now. They also will hold up better than the overall market if the US economy takes a downturn. For most investors, I would recommend placing about half the assets in a stock portfolio in large-caps and about half in mid- and small-caps.

FAVORITE LARGE-CAPS

• **BCE (BCE)** is the largest communications company in Canada. The stock is cheap because investors dismiss BCE as a boring utility and worry that its landline phone business of roughly nine million customers will continue to suffer attrition year after year. But the company, whose dividend recently yielded 4.9%

and has grown steadily, offers considerable strengths, including the largest satellite-TV business in Canada...the country's number-one television network...and thriving cell phone and high-speed Internet services.

Recent share price: $41.05.*

Focus on importers and companies with high domestic sales. I look for firms closely tied to positive trends in the US economy rather than dependence on the global economy...retailers that can import cheap inventory because of the strong dollar...and discount retailers that appeal to price-conscious consumers still worried about the recovery. *My favorites now...*

•**Big Lots (BIG).** The nation's largest close-out retailer operates more than 1,450 stores in 48 states. The fast-growing company purchases brand-name items in bulk, then resells them at steeply discounted prices.

Recent share price: $33.77.

•**Dillards (DDS).** Wall Street has written off many brick-and-mortar retailers due to online competition. But Dillards, a well-managed company with more than 300 department stores that sells moderately priced goods in small shopping centers, is experiencing a resurgence.

Recent share price: $81.24.

•**Hi-Tech Pharmacal Co. (HITK)** manufactures more than 100 generic and branded medicines sold over-the-counter and through prescriptions. With the bulk of its sales in the US, it has found a lucrative niche in liquid and spray products such as its generic version of Flonase.

Recent share price: $35.15.

•**Sturm, Ruger & Co (RGR).** One of the largest makers of firearms, this company is benefiting from strong sales due to political factors. Changing state laws make it easier to get handgun permits, and some gun owners are buying additional weapons now out of fear that an Obama reelection could lead to restrictions on firearms.

Recent share price: $52.12.

*Prices as of August 16, 2013.

Avoid ETFs with a High Risk of Closing

Issuers have recently been closing dozens of exchange-traded funds that track narrow segments of the market and that have not attracted large numbers of investors. Issuers wind down the assets of the weak funds in an orderly way, but until they do, money that could be better placed in stronger funds stays in the soon-to-close funds. Those doomed funds may be selling at an especially low price, partly because of poor liquidity.

What to do: Be sure any ETF that you choose has at least $100 million in assets—most of the funds that have closed had less than $25 million. Generally, the bigger an ETF, the less expensive it is to run.

Consumer Reports Money Adviser. www.Consumer Reports.org/bookstore

Break the Rules! Says Sheldon Jacobs... and See Your Mutual Funds Take Off

Sheldon Jacobs, widely regarded as the dean of no-load mutual fund advisers. He was a founding adviser to Charles Schwabs Financial Advisory Service Board. The newsletter he founded, *The No-Load Fund Investor*, was the top-performing newsletter over a 15-year period during his tenure there, which ended in 2006. He still is a contributing editor to the newsletter and is author of *Investing Without Wall Street: The Five Essentials of Financial Freedom* (Wiley).

For years, Sheldon Jacobs built up a treasure trove of investment rules to help small investors beat Wall Street professionals. These rules proved so valuable that the newsletter he founded, *The No-Load Fund Investor*, won a first-place ranking over a 15-year period for risk-adjusted performance.

In the past decade, the rules have changed dramatically because of the wrenching transformation of stock markets and the global economy. *Here's how Jacobs has adjusted his rules for today's investment climate…*

A LONG-TERM BEAR MARKET

First you have to realize that no matter how giddy investors get from time to time, we're currently in a long-term bear market that is stifling the overall performance of stocks. This bear market may include cycles of bull markets, but they are followed, and then dominated, by larger bear markets. This easily could last another decade as we slowly work off the excesses of a 20-year bull market that ended in 2000 and a staggering housing bubble that peaked in 2007.

For the next decade, I expect plenty of extreme volatility and annual returns that average perhaps 6% for US stocks. You can smooth out the ride and beat those returns if you follow my new rules.

FORGET 10-YEAR RECORDS

The old rule: Look at long-term returns, such as 10-year periods or longer, to judge actively managed funds (those that rely on a manager's decisions rather than tracking an index).

My new strategy: Focus on shorter-term performance periods—three months, six months and one-, three- and five years.

Why it's necessary: You want to find funds that have excelled in comparison to their peers under the challenging conditions of the past few years. That's because these types of conditions are likely to continue for some time. They have included the market collapse of 2008…the bullish rallies of 2009 and 2010…and the grinding, volatile markets of 2011 and 2012.

It's largely irrelevant to look at longer time periods, such as 10 years. In many cases, the current manager was not there for the entire period…or the fund has grown from millions of dollars in assets a decade ago to less manageable billions of dollars now…or one terrific year early on has covered up many years of mediocrity.

AVOID TARGET-DATE FUNDS

The standard rule: Rely on target-date mutual funds, which have been around since the early 1990s, to automatically shift your asset mix to a more conservative stance as you approach and live through your retirement years. These funds have grown tremendously popular in recent years, especially in retirement accounts such as 401(k)s and IRAs.

My new strategy: There are better alternatives that allow you to adjust to changing conditions.

Why it's necessary: Target-date funds, which theoretically decrease risk by lowering the proportion of stocks in your portfolio and increasing the proportion of bonds and other conservative investments as you grow older, have inherent weaknesses in this extended bear market. First, many fund companies, striving to maintain high returns so they can beat the competition, keep as much as two-thirds of the typical target-date portfolio in stocks even as investors are just a few years from retirement. That's too aggressive if the market has a big down year. Second, the funds ignore current market conditions when deciding on allocations.

Better: "Asset-allocation" funds own both stocks and bonds but have more flexibility to vary allocations depending on market conditions. For example, many of these funds are positioned heavily in stocks now because the managers consider this a better environment for stocks than bonds. But the funds can make changes if the outlook shifts—for instance, if the managers sense that the market is likely to tank soon. This makes a lot more sense to me and exposes you to less risk over the long run.

Important: Asset-allocation funds are best suited for tax-deferred or tax-exempt retirement accounts rather than taxable accounts because they tend to generate large amounts of taxable income.

Attractive asset-allocation funds now…

•**Fidelity Four-In-One Index (FFNOX).** This fund shifts allocations among four Fidelity index funds that give you broad exposure to large- and small-cap US stocks, foreign stocks and bonds. Its recent allocations lean

190

heavily toward US stocks and keep just about 15% of the portfolio in bonds and cash.

Performance: 6.5%.* *www.Fidelity.com*

• **T. Rowe Price Balanced (RPBAX)** invests in a mix of stocks as well as actively managed in-house funds such as T. Rowe Price Real Assets and T. Rowe Price High Yield. The fund has about one-third of its portfolio in bonds and cash and the rest in US and foreign stocks.

Performance: 7.0%. *www.TRowePrice.com*

FOCUS ON EMERGING MARKETS

The old rule: Use foreign stock funds to diversify your portfolio and reduce your overall risk. The idea was that domestic and foreign funds moved independently of each other.

My new strategy: Continue to use foreign funds—especially those focusing on emerging markets—as potential growth engines in your portfolio, but don't expect to get as much diversification benefit as before or to reduce your overall portfolio risk.

Why it's necessary: As the world continues to grow more economically interconnected, returns in the US and overseas tend to move in the same direction. But annualized returns of emerging-market stocks, although more volatile, have been double those of developed-market stocks over the past 10 years, on average, and will continue to do better. I keep about 10% of my overall portfolio in developed-market foreign stocks and 5% in emerging-market stocks.

Attractive now…

• **iShares MSCI EAFE ETF (EFA)** invests in nearly 1,000 stocks from 22 developed markets outside Canada and the US.

Performance: 2.8%. *www.iShares.com*

• **Vanguard Emerging Markets Stock Index Fund (VEIEX)** tracks more than 800 stocks.

Performance: 1.9%. *www.Vanguard.com*

IMPROVE YOUR INDEXING

The old rule: Use traditional index funds as the core of your portfolio because of their unbeatable low costs.

My new strategy: If you want to use index funds, switch 50% of the assets that you hold in them to "fundamental" index funds.

Why it's necessary: These new index funds perform better in bear markets because they are relatively light on high-flying stocks that can easily plummet. If you own a traditional fund that tracks a well-known major index such as the Standard & Poor's 500 stock index, it is "capitalization-weighted," which means that companies whose overall stock market values are greatest and rising quickly tend to dominate the index. That's great in bull markets because the more that a stock price goes up, the bigger its presence in the index. But it can be risky in bear markets or when a particular stock that dominates the index goes sour. Apple, for instance, whose stock price has soared, takes up a hefty 7.5% of the entire S&P 500 stock index.

Capitalization-weighted indexing can get swept up in manias, bubbles and overreaction to good news. Fundamental indexes, on the other hand, weigh stock holdings by measures of a company's value that include dividends, cash flow, sales, book value and price-to-earnings ratio. The index weightings don't change dramatically just because a company's stock price rises rapidly.

Attractive now…

• **PowerShares FTSE RAFI US 1000 ETF (PRF)** is a large-cap index fund that currently is dominated by stocks such as AT&T and Exxon Mobil and allocates just 0.9% to Apple.

Performance: 10.9%. *www.InvescoPowerShares.com*

• **PowerShares FTSE RAFI US 1500 Small-Mid Portfolio ETF (PRFZ).**

Performance: 12.7%. *www.InvescoPowerShares.com*

• **Schwab Fundamental International Large Company Index (SFNNX).**

Performance: 3.2%. *www.Schwab.com*

• **Schwab Fundamental Emerging Markets Index (SFENX).**

Performance: 1.6%. *www.Schwab.com*

*Performance figures based on five-year annualized returns through August 16, 2013.

A Mutual Fund Question

Christine Benz, director of personal finance, Morningstar, Inc., Chicago. She is coauthor of *Morningstar Guide to Mutual Funds: 5-Star Strategies for Success* (Wiley). www.Morningstar.com

Not long ago, a customer posed the following question to me…"Recently, I wanted to buy a top-performing mutual fund but was told by my brokerage firm that the fund was closed to new investors. I checked directly with the mutual fund, which said it is open to new investors. Can a fund be closed at one place and open at another?"

My answer: The growth of multiple distribution and sales channels—including fund "supermarkets"—has made the process of closing funds more complex. For example, in 2012 the T. Rowe Price Health Sciences Fund instituted a limited or "soft" close meant to slow down the flow of new investment money into the fund but not cut it off. That means investors can no longer open new accounts through third-party financial intermediaries such as Fidelity or Schwab. But new investors still can gain access by opening an account directly with T. Rowe Price, though it's less convenient.

Fund companies nowadays can restrict access in other ways, too, such as providing access only to employee retirement plans…to an IRA rollover from a retirement plan that offers shares of the fund…or to investors who have $1 million or more invested at a fund company.

New Bond Funds Guard Against a Crash

Matthew Tuttle, CFP, CEO of Tuttle Wealth Management, a wealth advisory firm overseeing $110 million in assets, Stamford, Connecticut. He is author of *How Harvard and Yale Beat the Market: What Individual Investors Can Learn from University Endowments to Help Them Prosper in an Uncertain Market* (Wiley). www.TuttleWealth.com

For decades, you could put some of your money into mainstream bond funds for a fairly safe cushion against the volatility of the stock market. Not anymore.

Interest rates are so low and the likelihood that they will rise over the next several years is so high that typical bond funds could end up suffering significant losses, as some funds did early this year when rates rose. (Bond prices move inversely to interest rates.)

But in recent years, various money-management firms have come up with a new kind of fund—the "unconstrained" bond fund. These funds, free of the typical restrictions and guidelines and able to use elaborate defensive strategies, can make big bets and dramatic and sudden shifts in their portfolios to avoid risks as they search the globe for opportunities. *What you need to know…*

HOW THEY WORK

Unconstrained bond funds give managers plenty of freedom to choose fixed-income investments, regardless of the length of maturity, credit quality, type of issuer or country. They're even able to bet that bond prices will drop, and they buy exotic instruments such as credit default swaps, which act like insurance in case of bond defaults.

HOW TO USE THEM

I wouldn't completely replace an investor's core bond funds with unconstrained funds just yet. They have to prove themselves in a prolonged period of rising interest rates. Instead, I recommend that investors use these to replace the riskiest portions of their fixed-income portfolios. These include funds holding bonds with average durations greater than 10 years. (Duration is a measure of how much a bond's price is likely to rise or fall as a result of interest rate changes.) The longer-duration funds are likely to suffer double-digit losses if rates rise significantly.

Three no-load, unconstrained bond funds to consider…

•**Pimco Unconstrained Bond Fund (PU-BRX).** With $29 billion in assets, this four-year-old fund is one of the oldest and, by far, the largest in the category. It also is one of the most conservative, spreading its bets across more than 1,500 bonds, with a recent average duration of less than half a year. Fund manager Chris Dialynas works with legendary Pimco manager Bill Gross to shape a portfolio with low volatility. Because of the fund's cautious approach, its returns, which totaled 8.3% in 2012 and -2.72% as of August 16, 2013, are likely to trail more aggressive offerings over the long term.

Expenses: 1.55%. *www.Pimco.com*

• **Metropolitan West Unconstrained Bond Fund (MWCRX)** is more aggressive than the Pimco fund, with better returns since its debut in September 2011 and lower expenses. Forays into high-yield and emerging-market debt and mortgage-backed securities boosted returns in 2012, which totaled 15.8%, and 0.57% as of August 16, 2013.

Average duration: 1.4 years.

Expenses: 0.99%. *www.MWAMLLC.com*

• **Scout Unconstrained Bond Fund (SUB-YX)** is one of the boldest, with a portfolio of nearly 40 bond holdings. Since the fund's September 2011 launch, manager Mark Egan has produced some of the best returns in the category, thanks to a successful gamble on asset-backed securities, which are pools of credit card debt, leases and other loans packaged like bonds. The fund had returns of 22.8% in 2012 and 1.35% through August 16, 2013.

Expenses: 0.8%. *www.ScoutFunds.com*

Dollar-Cost Averaging Alert

Dollar-cost averaging is likely to hurt more investors than it helps. A recent finding by mutual fund giant Vanguard Group goes against the common wisdom that if you have a big chunk of money to invest, it's best to average it into the market, committing a little at a time on a regular schedule. Vanguard ran hundreds of computer simulations to test what would happen if investors stretched out their investments of a set amount of money over periods ranging from six months to three years, compared with investing it all at once.

Results: Two-thirds of the time, investors who spread out their investments over a year underperformed those who invested the entire amount all at once. Longer stretch-outs produced similar results. Vanguard based its findings on past market returns for rolling 10-year periods starting in February 1926.

MarketWatch.com

What to Do If You're Not Happy with Your Financial Adviser

Sheryl Garrett, CFP, founder of The Garrett Planning Network, Inc., Shawnee Mission, Kansas, an international network of fee-only planners. She is author of *Personal Finance Workbook for Dummies* (Wiley) and was recognized by Investment Advisor five times as "One of the Top 25 Most Influential People in Financial Planning." *www.GarrettPlanningNetwork.com*

Financial advisers can provide valuable help, but problems often arise that could prevent you from getting the most value for the money that you are paying a financial planner, estate planner or other adviser. *Common problems and how to get what you pay for…*

Problem: Your portfolio is consistently losing money or significantly underperforming the overall market.

What to do: Make sure that you are using the appropriate benchmarks when you judge your portfolio's performance depending on your mix of investments.

Example: If 60% of your portfolio under the adviser's supervision is supposed to be large-cap stocks and 40% small-caps, compare its performance to that of a portfolio that is 60% the Standard & Poor's 500 Index and 40% the Russell 2000 Index. If your portfolio is trailing the benchmark for the past five years, ask the adviser what value hc/she is adding. Realize that even if you are lagging the overall market, your adviser could be giving you exactly what you asked for. Your portfolio might be designed to experience less volatility but lower gains than the overall market, especially over short periods.

Problem: Lack of personal attention. Three or four days go by before your adviser returns your phone call, or he contacts you only when he has a new product to sell.

What to do: Say, "I'm concerned that you are getting too busy and that I'm not an important enough client for you." Most investors can expect a written quarterly update on portfolio performance if the adviser is providing money-management services. Also expect a sit-down meeting twice a year to discuss tweaks to the plan and phone calls returned within 24 hours.

Problem: You want to change your adviser. Over the years, a client and planner can grow apart. For example, you may be entering a phase of your life, such as the end of your career, when you need someone who has more experience with retirees.

What to do: Find a replacement before you leave your old adviser. Your new financial representative can take care of all the paperwork surrounding the transfer of your portfolio and assets. That relieves you of the burden of communicating with your old adviser if you choose not to. You can find a financial planner near you through the National Association of Personal Financial Advisors (NAPFA) at *www. NAPFA.org*.

When Your Financial Adviser Leaves the Firm...

If your financial adviser goes to a new firm, find out why. Contact the person at your current firm who informed you, and ask some key questions—such as whether there has been a lot of turnover or if issues facing the firm could have caused your adviser to leave.

If you get empty assurances that everything will be fine, that could be a red flag about the credibility or future of the firm. You want specific information—for instance, that your adviser left to start his/her own firm.

What to do: Decide whether the firm or the adviser matters more to you. Consider whether a new adviser at the same firm will meet your needs or whether you want to follow your previous one.

If you might want to move your account, you may have to reach out and contact your former adviser—firms often forbid advisers who leave from actively soliciting former clients.

The Wall Street Journal. www.WSJ.com

Perks from Your Financial Planner

Perks that some financial planners are offering to help distinguish themselves from competing advisers—assisting clients who are moving with house-hunting, finding moving companies and remodeling...and helping to make decisions about college financial-aid packages...negotiating big-ticket purchases, ranging from cars and boats to retirement homes and weddings...and helping out with some tasks of everyday life, such as arranging medical appointments and even acting as travel companions.

Reason: One-fifth of households with at least $100,000 to invest say that they are considering switching financial advisers in the next year, so advisers are seeking ways to keep business and attract new clients.

What to do: Shop around. Judge an adviser based primarily on investment criteria and cost, not on any added perks that may be offered.

Consensus of investment advisers and clients, reported in *The Wall Street Journal.*

11

Consumer Confidential

From the Ultimate Cheapskate: 3 Little Ways to Save BIG!

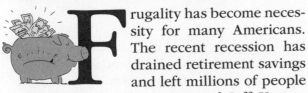

Frugality has become necessity for many Americans. The recent recession has drained retirement savings and left millions of people without work. That prompted Jeff Yeager, dubbed the "Ultimate Cheapskate," to write *How to Retire the Cheapskate Way.*

Below are three of his ideas for anyone who wants to spend less. *You may be surprised by how much you can save…*

SAVE ON DRIVING

• **Rent a car for high-mileage-driving days rather than driving your own.**

Savings: $50 a day.

The auto-rental industry has become very competitive in the past decade. It's possible now to rent a car for $19 to $29 per day,* sometimes even with unlimited mileage. That could be less than the cost of using your own vehicle on days when you do a lot of driving.

Example: If you pay $25 to rent an economy vehicle that delivers 30 miles per gallon (mpg), then use it to drive 300 miles that you otherwise would have put on your own 20-mpg vehicle, you'll save around $17.50 in gas (at $3.50 a gallon) and perhaps $60 in vehicle depreciation, for a net savings of more than $50. (The typical new car costs around $30,000 and provides perhaps 150,000 miles of service before the repair and maintenance bills start to add up, suggesting that cars depreciate at a rate of roughly 20 cents a mile, though this, of course, varies.)

*Prices and rates are subject to change

Jeff Yeager, author of *How to Retire the Cheapskate Way* (Three Rivers). Located in Accokeek, Maryland, he is the official Savings Expert of AARP and founder of the Ultimate Cheapskate Web site at *www.Ultimate Cheapskate.com.*

195

Driving a rental brings peace of mind, too. If your rental car breaks down, the rental company will bring you a replacement. If your own car breaks down on a distant road, you will have to trust a mechanic you don't know and arrange lodging and/or transport until the repairs are complete.

Shop around—rental rates vary dramatically among rental companies. Make sure that the rental comes with unlimited miles—or at least enough miles for your journey. Also make sure that your auto insurance or credit card provides rental-car coverage so that you can skip the rental company's expensive coverage.

SAVE ON YOUR CELL PHONE BILL

•**See if cellular discounts are available through your employer or a nonprofit with which you volunteer.**

Savings: $150 a year.

The cellular provider that supplies cell phone service to your employer might offer discounted rates to the company's employees as well. Similar discounts sometimes are available to those who volunteer with nonprofits—they're particularly common through volunteer fire departments. These discounts can be as much as 20% off standard rates. The typical individual's annual cell phone bill is now more than $850, so a 20% discount could easily save you in excess of $150 per year. Typically, any size company can qualify. Ask your employer's benefits department for details, or check its cellular provider's Web site.

INSURANCE SAVINGS

•**Cancel no-longer-needed insurance.**

Savings: $3,000 a year.

When you no longer have dependents and/or earned income, you might no longer require life insurance or disability insurance. Eliminating these can save thousands of dollars a year.

Example: A 60-year-old man might be paying more than $3,000 a year for a $300,000 term-life insurance policy and a similar amount for a disability policy.

But talk with a financial adviser you trust to confirm that you no longer need insurance.

When you retire and no longer have a commute, you also might be able to save 10% or so on your auto insurance by informing your insurer that you now drive significantly fewer miles per year.

Personalized Presents: Special Gifts That Won't Break Your Budget

Lindsay Roberts, founder of The Gift Insider, a Web site featuring gift ideas. She also shares her gift expertise regularly on Chicago's WGN-TV News. Roberts previously worked in the sales and marketing departments of *Good Housekeeping* and *Esquire* magazines. *www.TheGiftInsider.com*

Looking for just the perfect gift? There are merchants and artisans who produce wonderful customized products relatively quickly, then sell them at reasonable prices over the Internet. *Among my favorites…*

•**China from Hull's Happiest Days Designs.** You can have fine china plates and mugs imprinted with customized messages—perhaps a favorite saying, an inside joke or a date and location that have special meaning. Allow at least three weeks for your china to be made and delivered.

Prices: As little as $17.50 for a single mug,* latte cup or dessert plate…and up to $120 for a set of four mugs and dessert plates. *www. HappiestDaysDesigns.com*

•**Poker set from The Stationery Suite.** This set includes 300 high-quality clay chips, professional-grade playing cards and an attractive case that can be customized with the recipient's name and your choice of more than 30 designs. Delivery can take up to a month.

Prices: $99. *www.TheStationerySuite.com*

•**Purses from Laudi Vidni.** Use this Chicago boutique's online purse design tool to create your own high-fashion handbags. You choose the purse's shape—as well as the type and color of leather, fabric and hardware. Orders can take up to four weeks to arrive.

*Prices subject to change.

Prices: As little as $95 for a small wristlet up to more than $600 for a large leather bag. 773-697-7847, *www.LaudiVidni.com*

• **Bowling balls from OnTheBallBowling. com.** Upload a digital photo and a short message to this company's Web site, and it can print them on a regulation 8.5-inch bowling ball. This is a real bowling ball that even can be drilled and used if so desired. Allow at least four weeks for your order to arrive.

Price: $189.99. 866-682-2695, *www.OnThe BallBowling.com*

• **Soaps from Valsey and Me.** These all-natural guest room soaps, each individually wrapped up in a personalized label, are a very thoughtful gift.

Example: The personalized label might read, "Welcome to the Roberts' Lake House." Orders take about two weeks to arrive.

Prices: $30 for a mini box containing 14 soaps (each soap is two inches by one inch by one-eighth-inch thick). *www.ValseyandMe. com*

• **Sterling silver guitar picks from River Valley Designs.** This Ohio jewelry maker will stamp a musician's or a band's name or a short personalized message into an attractive metal guitar pick. Allow six weeks for orders to arrive.

Price: $32 for sterling silver...or $21 for aluminum, copper or brass. *www.RiverValley Jewelry.Etsy.com*

• **Romance novels from YourNovel.com.** You and your partner can be the main characters in a romance novel. Simply fill out a short questionnaire about you and your partner on the YourNovel.com Web site...select a setting and framework for the story...specify how steamy you want the love scenes to be... and upload a romantic photo of you and your partner for the cover (optional). Books usually arrive within one week. E-books are delivered within hours electronically.

Prices: From $39.95 to $119.95. *www.Your Novel.com*

• **Etched and hand-painted wine bottles from Etching Expressions.** Upload a photo to this California company's Web site, and it uses glass etching and hand painting to re-create it on a bottle of wine—your choice of Merlot, Chardonnay, Cabernet Sauvignon, champagne or other options. The process typically takes less than two weeks, including shipping.

Price: $65. 866-944-3824, *www.Etching Expressions.com*

• **Fake magazine covers from YourCover.** Design a fake magazine cover featuring the recipient. Simply upload a photo of the recipient to the Web site, select an appropriate fake magazine to put it on and personalize the headlines.

Price: $12.95 for a cover that you print out at home, or $19.95 to have the cover printed and mailed to you. 877-972-6837, *www.Your Cover.com*

Save Your Money! 5 Quick Tips

Here are five simple ways to save some money now...

• **Before paying for a simple repair or task such as installing software,** type a question or paste an error message into a search engine to find out how to handle the issue yourself.

• **Skip PC tune-ups.** They are overpriced and do little to speed up your computer.

• **Friend finders are not worth the money either**—you can look up phone numbers and addresses for free or find people through Facebook.

• **Cut down on app purchases**—often you enjoy them once, then forget about them.

• **Rent-to-own is the most expensive way to buy anything**—financing on your credit card costs less if you cannot pay all at once.

Money.MSN.com

Lease Solar Power and Save $$$ on Your Electric Bill

Jason Szumlanski, vice president and general manager for Fafco Solar Energy, based in Cape Coral, Florida, which has been installing solar-powered products since 1974 and deals with every major solar manufacturer. Szumlanski has worked in the solar industry since 1999, previously installing solar systems in the Caribbean.

Despite falling prices and various tax credits, the cost of solar energy systems that power your whole home can be fairly high. But for many home owners, solar still can be an environmentally friendly way to save lots of money, especially if you take advantage of attractive leasing arrangements or use solar just to power a water heater or an attic fan.

Here's what you need to know about home solar systems and whether one could save you money...

THE LEASING ALTERNATIVE

Some suppliers now are offering the option of leasing *photovoltaic systems* (also known as solar electric systems). Under these lease agreements, the supplier owns the equipment and collects all solar power tax incentives. The home owner makes a fixed monthly lease payment but, compared with buying the equipment, enjoys a greatly reduced up-front payment. In some cases, there is no up-front payment at all.

Leasing solar to provide your home's electricity could be a smart move for you if...

•**You pay less each month to lease the system** than you would pay for the electricity that the system replaces.

•**You don't want to spend $25,000 to $35,000 or much more** up front to buy and install equipment.

Lease terms can vary greatly, so shop extensively before signing a contract. Solar leases often last 15 to 20 years and might contain substantial penalties for early termination, so read contracts very carefully. Make sure that the provider pays maintenance and repair expenses and that you can arrange to remove or relocate the system or transfer the lease if you sell the home.

Helpful: On rooftops in the US, southern exposure is the best position for the solar panels that are used to supply electricity to the home. A solar system is unlikely to be cost effective if tall trees or buildings block your home's southern exposure.

Among the large solar companies offering leases are SolarCity (888-765-2489, *www.Solar City.com*)...SunPower (800-786-7693, *http://us. SunPowerCorp.com*)...Sunrun (855-478-6786, *www.SunrunHome.com*)...and Sungevity (866-786-4255, *www.Sungevity.com*).

SOLAR WATER HEATERS

Unlike whole-house photovoltaic systems, solar water heaters are economically viable across much of the US now. They can cost $4,000 to $10,000 installed,* but they qualify for the 30% federal tax credit. State incentives might be available as well—visit the US Department of Energy's Database of State Incentives for Renewables and Efficiency (*www. DSIREusa.org*) for details. Payback can come in as little as three to five years for households in Sunbelt states that have high electricity rates and use lots of hot water...or five to 10 years elsewhere.

Solar water heaters typically use rooftop solar collectors to heat an antifreeze solution, which is pumped to a heat exchanger where it warms water. Depending on your solar package, this warmed water can feed into a conventional water heater, which also can provide backup. Because the water entering the water heater is already quite warm, the heater doesn't consume as much electricity, gas or oil to heat the water to the desired temperature. The typical household can reduce water-heating costs by 50% to 80% without any loss of comfort.

SOLAR ATTIC FANS

Standard attic fans reduce your air-conditioning bills by blowing hot air out of the attic in warm weather, reducing the temperature differential between the attic and the living space below.

*Prices subject to change.

Problem: An electric attic fan can generate annual electricity bills of between $150 and $250.

In contrast, solar-powered attic fans are money savers. They often cost just $500 to $750, plus $150 to $300 for installation. Installation is simple, so many home owners do it themselves—solar attic fans don't even have to be wired into the home's electrical system.

The fans qualify for the 30% federal tax credit and occasionally for state incentives, too. They tend to pay for themselves in two or three years in the Sunbelt and in three to six years elsewhere.

Leading makers include SunRise Solar Inc. (219-558-2211, *www.SunRiseSolar.net*) and Natural Light Energy Systems (800-363-9865, *www. SolarAtticFan.com*).

Trick to Reduce Your Phone Bill

Karen Larson, editor, *Bottom Line/Personal*, 281 Tresser Blvd., Stamford, Connecticut 06901. *www.BottomLine Publications.com*

My colleague recently called his local phone company to cancel one of his two residential phone lines. The customer service rep said that dropping one line would reduce his $87 monthly bill—but only to $60.

My colleague had already visited the phone company's Web site and determined that residential lines with unlimited local and long distance were offered at $42 a month. When my colleague noted this, the rep discovered that not only was this lower rate available but that a special rebate could reduce the price to $34 per month for the first year—almost half the $60 initially quoted.

Phone representatives sometimes overlook low-cost options…or are encouraged to push high-cost choices says Allan Keiter, former president of the shopping comparison Web site MyRatePlan.com.

Keiter says my colleague's strategy—searching for the best rates offered on a company's Web site before calling—is wise. Also, check the company's newspaper ads and mail solicitations for lower rates before dialing.

If the phone rep says that the low rate you found is available only to Internet customers, you always can hang up and sign up online. If the rep says that the low rate is only for new customers, ask if it could be given to you as a reward for your continued loyalty. If the rep says no, say that you're thinking about canceling your service and ask to speak to the customer-retention department. If there is no retention department, ask for a manager.

If you're not offered an appealing rate, say that you will think it over, then call back and repeat the process with a different phone rep. It can be worth it—my colleague saved himself more than $300.

Save on Phone Costs Abroad

To save on voice and data costs on foreign trips—rent a local cell phone from a company such as TravelCell (*www.TravelCell.com*) if you will be in one country for an extended time…use Skype for free video, but be sure that you are not incurring cellular-data charges…turn off apps, data roaming, fetch data and automatic synching on your phone—constant checks will quickly run up your bill… and ask your cell carrier about global roaming plans—some may be priced reasonably. Finally, arrange for people to call you instead of you calling them, if possible—cellular plans often have lower rates for incoming calls than for outgoing ones.

The Wall Street Journal. www.WSJ.com

Get the Signal: Finally, Better Cell Phone Reception at Home

Roger Entner, founder of Recon Analytics, a wireless consulting firm in Dedham, Massachusetts. Entner was previously a senior vice president and head of telecom research for The Nielsen Company. His Web site is *www.ReconAnalytics.com*.

Nearly 70% of cell phone users report spotty coverage in their homes because wireless signals from a cell tower often are blocked or degraded by landscaping and a home's walls. There are various amplifying devices that can be effective, but not all types work well in all homes.

Ways to get better reception in your home…

• **Boosters or "signal repeaters" capture a weak cell phone signal from a cell tower,** amplify it and rebroadcast it at four- or five-bar signal strength. They work with most US phone carriers. These are best for people who want a portable device that they can use not just in the house but in a car or office, too, and who only need to rebroadcast the cell phone signal over a small area—within 20 feet.

Disadvantages: You need to install a little antenna near a window or on the roof of your car, and there must be at least two bars of signal strength from a cell tower to amplify.

Popular: Wilson Electronics Sleek is a compact amplifier that boosts voice call signals and 3G data speed on all US networks except Nextel's. $85 at online retailers such as Amazon.com.*

• **Femtocells are miniature cell phone towers that you plug into your Internet router.** They work by acquiring a cell phone signal through your Internet connection and then redistributing the signal inside your home. These are best for rural areas where there may not be any cell phone signals to amplify or in dense urban areas where the signals can be too weak to boost. They typically give you five-bar coverage across an area of up to 100 feet away. Make sure to buy a femtocell that supports your particular cell phone network.

Typical cost: $200 to $300 at online retailers such as Amazon.com. You also may be able to purchase one directly from your cellphone service provider. You may have to pay a monthly $5 to $20 fee in addition to your monthly cell phone bill.

Easy Ways to Lower Household Bills

Five simple ways you can save around the house…

• **Unplug your cell phone and other electronics as soon as they are charged.**

• **If you are an older adult, you may be entitled to discounted trash pickup**—call the company and ask.

• **Go to a local sawmill, and buy scrap wood to use as firewood** instead of buying wood for $150 (or more) a cord.

• **Retune your HDTV**—most are shipped set for showroom-level brightness and contrast, which uses more energy and is not needed at home. Go to the setup menu, and look for "home" mode or similar wording.

• **When boiling water for tea, use only the amount you need** to avoid wasting energy by heating water you will not use.

AARP.org

Green Ways to Save

Karen Larson, editor, *Bottom Line/Personal*, 281 Tresser Blvd., Stamford, Connecticut 06901. *www.BottomLine Publications.com*

How would you like to save money… do something good for the planet… and get a free e-book? The Massachusetts-based green marketing consultant Shel Horowitz, author of *Guerrilla*

*Prices subject to change.

Marketing Goes Green (Wiley), has made it his mission to promote simple strategies that are good for the environment. Some even can save us money. He has compiled these strategies in an e-booklet called *Painless Green*. (Log on to *www.PainlessGreenBook.com/earthday*, then enter the code word "Earthday," to get your free download.) *Among Horowitz's tips…*

•**Skip the dishwasher dry cycle.** Most dishwashers use a lot of electricity to evaporate water off dishes. Instead, open the dishwasher door and let dishes air-dry.

•**Switch from bottled water to filtered tap water.**

•**Cook multiple meals at once.** When you cook a meal, also precook something that will keep in the fridge and reheat easily in the microwave, such as a casserole or baked potatoes.

•**If you steam or boil vegetables, freeze the cooking water to use as soup stock later.**

•**Put a plastic bottle in your toilet tank.** To reduce the amount of water a toilet uses per flush, fill a plastic quart container with water and place it in the toilet's tank. Don't use a brick—it can slowly erode in the tank and clog your plumbing.

•**Make your next computer laser printer one that prints on both sides of the page.** These don't cost much more than other laser printers, and they can trim your paper use—and paper costs—by around 40%.

Tricks to Save on Dry Cleaning

Mary Marlowe Leverette, who has taught fabric care at Clemson University. Based in Columbia, South Carolina, she has a degree in home economics with a specialty in textiles and is the Guide to Laundry expert for the Web site About.com. *http://Laundry.about.com*

Having a garment dry-cleaned can cost anywhere from a few dollars to $20 or more, depending on the garment and your region. *Here's how to greatly reduce dry-cleaning costs…*

IS IT REALLY "DRY CLEAN ONLY"?
Dry cleaning is truly required only if…

•**The garment is "structured,"** meaning that it's designed to hold its shape. This includes most suits, jackets and some heavily tailored blouses.

•**The garment is made from acetate, rayon, leather or suede,** fabrics that can be damaged by washing in water. Dry cleaning also is prudent with silk and wool garments that have "dry clean only" tags. But nonstructured wool garments with "dry clean only" tags usually can be gently hand-washed using a delicate detergent designed for wool, such as Woolite.

•**The garment isn't colorfast.** Place a few drops of water on an interior seam, and rub it with a cotton swab. If color comes off on the swab, the garment should be dry-cleaned.

If a garment does not fall into any of the above categories, it probably can be safely washed using a gentle, natural soap that contains no enzymes, such as Castile soap. Hand-wash if you have the time. If not, set your washer to cold water and gentle cycle. Hang to dry, or lay the garment flat on a towel or a mesh rack.

DO-IT-YOURSELF DRY CLEANING
If clothes do require dry cleaning…

•**Use home dry-cleaning kits.** These kits are effective at removing odors, light wrinkles and minor stains, but they are not for major stains, oil-based stains or heavy creases.

Basically, you treat the stains using the solution in the kit…put the garments into a sealable dryer bag with a towelette moistened with dry-cleaning solvent…then put the bag in the dryer for 30 minutes. Remove, and hang garments (or lay them flat) immediately after the dryer cycle ends.

Example: Dryel home dry-cleaning kits do an excellent job (*www.Dryel.com*).

•**Keep a stain stick or stain removal wipes handy.** These prevent many types of stains from setting. They're safe for most "dry clean only" fabrics, but not silk or wool.

Example: Goddard's Dry Clean Spot Remover is the best I've found ($6.30, six-ounce can,* *www.Amazon.com*).

• **Buy a laundry steamer.** These can remove light wrinkles and freshen up "dry clean only" clothes.

Example: Steamfast SF-407 ($59.99, *www.Steamfast.com*).

• **Let "dry clean only" garments air out for at least several hours after wearing.** Wrinkles sometimes fall away when fabrics are allowed to hang freely.

Smart idea: Keep a 12-inch section of hanger space open in your closet for the clothes you wore the prior day.

• **Search for coupons on cleaners' Web sites and in local papers.** Also some cleaners offer discounts when garments are brought in midweek.

*Prices subject to change.

For a Better-Fitting Suit...

A man's suit should hug his shoulders, not swallow them. The jacket should be contoured to the body. Opt for a two-button suit jacket, which flatters most body sizes and shapes. Sleeves should end just above the wrists—one-quarter to one-half inch of the shirt's cuff should show. And the lapel should be about two inches at the widest point. Select slim-cut, flat-front pants that have very little break at the ankle to achieve a long, clean look.

GQ.com

Weddings Cost Less on This Day

Facilities often charge less on Fridays than on weekends, and some couples prefer Fridays because guests get an extra day to recover from indulging at the reception before returning to work.

To save more: Book a wedding on Friday the 13th—wedding bookings usually are 10% lower on that date than other Fridays.

Consumerist.com

Renting an Apartment? What You Must Know Now

Joseph R. Costello, partner at the Brooklyn, New York–based law firm Costello & Costello, PC, founded in 1959. He specializes in landlord-tenant disputes.

In recent years, rental apartments have soared in popularity. But along with the popularity have come rising rents and unwelcome surprises for renters who fail to ask the right questions or to get important details written into their leases.

Even with a detailed lease, there's no guarantee that the other party will follow the agreement, but here are strategies to help renters avoid disputes with landlords...

• **Mention all parties who will be living in the apartment.** Misrepresentation or omission of tenants can be grounds for a landlord to terminate your lease.

Example: A couple signs a lease and fails to mention an adult son who will be living with them. For an apartment whose rent is limited by law, including him in the lease also may give the adult son succession rights, meaning that he might be able to take over the apartment when the parents pass on.

• **If your landlord says you can have pets and/or bring your own major appliances, such as a washer and dryer, make sure it is written into the lease.** Also specify how many pets—say, two dogs or one cat and one canary...and/or which appliances you are adding so that you are not forced to get rid of them later.

• **Do research on the possible legal problems.** Instead of taking the landlord's word that there are no liens or foreclosures on the property, check that yourself. It is important because if the property is in foreclosure, the bank could evict the tenant and the tenant would not be able to recoup the rent paid even if he/she has a lease.

You might be able to look up property records on your municipality's or county's Web site to see whether the property is the subject of litigation, which could mean it is in foreclosure proceedings. If you find that the property is the subject of litigation, go to the county office and pull the "notice of pendency" for details.

However, a lien (foreclosure or otherwise) may not be listed on the Internet, so you may have to check the court system, your county's register of deeds or the appropriate governmental agency. In lieu of doing this, you can ask any title company to run a limited search for any type of lien, which can cost $200 to $300.*

• **Check the certificate of occupancy if you are renting a basement apartment.** Illegal basement units are common in some municipalities. The certificate of occupancy tells you the number of families that can legally occupy the building.

The landlord might say that the house is a legal three-family home when it really is a two-family home with an illegal basement apartment. If the municipality sends out an inspector who finds the apartment to be illegal, a notice could be sent to the owner requiring that you be evicted.

• **Find out who pays for utilities.** Your lease should state which utilities are your responsibility and which utilities are your landlord's responsibility.

Example: Water and sewage typically are paid by the landlord of a multifamily building. However, if the water bill increases with a new tenant, landlords sometimes try to pass on that extra cost to the tenant. If your lease states that water is covered by the landlord, you are protected against this.

*Prices subject to change.

To Keep Moving Costs as Low as Possible...

Planning a move? *Here are some ways to keep costs down...*

• **Move on a weekday in the middle of the month**—weekend rates are higher, as are rates when leases turn over at the start or end of a month.

• **Have a yard sale or give away items before moving.**

• **Long-distance moves are priced by weight and volume**...local moves, by volume and time. Either way, moving less costs less.

• **Shop around**—get at least three written estimates based on in-home inspections. Do as much of your own packing as possible.

• **Check the daily-deal Web sites**—movers sometimes offer discounts.

• **Review insurance coverage carefully**—your renter's or homeowner's policy may cover items in transit or you can buy coverage from the moving company. You might also consider moving valuable items yourself.

SmartMoney.com

Make Money on Items You Don't Use Often

Web sites such as SnapGoods.com and Rentalic.com arrange for owners to rent items—from tools to automobiles—to local residents. You set the fee, and borrowers pick up the item. The sites usually keep 5% to 10% of what you charge.

AARP The Magazine. www.AARP.org/magazine

How to Make a Sale on Craigslist!

Tips for writing a selling ad on Craigslist—write a short headline with one clear descriptive adjective…avoid all caps in headlines and rows of exclamation points…upload a full-length picture of the item and several close-ups from various angles…bullet your list of descriptive points in the ad, rather than write one long paragraph…place ads on Thursday between 6:00 pm and 7:00 pm to reach weekend bargain shoppers…if an item has not sold by Friday, delete the listing and repost on Saturday…and avoid saying a price is firm—if you are determined to get a certain amount, set the price higher and try to negotiate the price you want.

Roundup of advice from financial and personal Web sites, reported at ReadersDigest.com.

How I Saved $30,000 on My Wife's Hospital Bill

Charles B. Inlander, a consumer advocate and health-care consultant based in Fogelsville, Pennsylvania. He was the founding president of the nonprofit People's Medical Society, a consumer advocacy organization that is credited with key improvements in the quality of US health care in the 1980s and 1990s, and is author or coauthor of more than 20 consumer-health books. He is also a featured columnist in *BottomLine/Health, www. BottomLinePublications.com.*

Last fall, my wife had a medical procedure performed at her doctor's office. During the process, the doctor inadvertently nicked a blood vessel, which meant that my wife had to be taken to a nearby hospital so that the doctor could perform a 15-minute procedure to cauterize and close the injury. We entered the hospital at 10 pm and left three hours later when my wife had recovered from the anesthesia.

Two weeks later, we received a bill from the hospital for $34,000! I called the hospital and found out that the insurer had refused to pay because it had never approved an overnight admission. I let the insurer know that my wife was never admitted—she was at the hospital for only three hours. I refused to pay a penny of the bill. Our doctor backed us up by writing to the insurer and confirming that she had not been admitted. In the end, the bill was reduced to a still unbelievable $4,000, but the total amount was covered by our insurance.

These days, outrageous hospital bills are not uncommon. A recent media investigation found sky-high hospital charges such as $8 for one Tylenol caplet, $28 for a pair of latex gloves and $17 for an ice pack. *And these hospital costs can be directly passed on to you if you get caught in one of the worst traps snaring an increasing number of people…*

ADMISSION VS. OBSERVATION

For many patients, the difference between being formally admitted to a hospital versus simply being held for observation can be thousands of dollars. There is really no difference between being "admitted" versus being "observed," except in the way a hospital can bill Medicare or some other insurer. If you are admitted, most charges are covered. If you are being observed, far less of the costs are covered.

Fearing that they might get audited by Medicare or private insurers for an improper admission, hospitals may try to protect themselves by keeping you for observation. And if you are held for observation, Medicare and other insurers will not pay for medicines (among other costs), such as diabetes or blood pressure drugs, that you may normally take outside the hospital while you are simply being observed. This is true even if you are being "observed" for up to 48 hours or even longer. As a result, hospitals may bill you whatever they want for those medications—often well above retail price.

And, because of the hospitals' fear of audits for improper admissions, the number of observation patients has *more than tripled* recently. Patients often are shocked by a huge bill that insurance doesn't cover.

My advice: If you are being kept at a hospital for more than a few hours (time in an emergency department does not count) or being kept overnight, insist that you be formally admitted. The doctor treating you can make the decision, and the hospital usually must comply. Because it's not always clear whether you or a family member is being observed or admitted, it's a good idea to ask the doctor, nurse or case-worker what the patient's status is.

Reduce Health-Care Costs

The cost of health care continues to sky-rocket. *Here are some ways to save…*

• **Try a free week of yoga classes** during National Yoga Month (September)—participating studios are at *www.YogaMonth.org/yoga_month*. Also, take advantage of introductory offers at gyms or check the Internet for free classes.

• **Get prescriptions filled at Costco or Sam's Club**—you do not have to be a member.

• **If you need health insurance,** go to *http://FindaHealthCenter.HRSA.gov* for a list of federally funded centers with sliding-scale fees based on your ability to pay.

• **You may qualify for a free medical eye exam and a free year of care** if you are age 65 or older—go to *www.EyeCareAmerica.org*.

• **For free or low-cost dental care,** contact a local dental school or get information at *www.NIDCR.nih.gov*.

AARP.org

Generics Not Always Cheapest

Generic drugs will not always save you money if you have health insurance. In fact, certain brand-name drugs actually are cheaper than their generic versions because drugmakers negotiate deals with insurance providers to offer medicines at a discount. To see which is cheapest, use your insurer's prescription drug calculator.

Douglas Kamerow, chief scientist, RTI International, an independent research institute based in Research Triangle Park, North Carolina, quoted in *Men's Health Magazine*.

Safer Online Pharmacies

Ninety-seven percent of online pharmacies violate state and/or federal laws by selling fake, expired or contaminated products or products not approved by the FDA. A safe online pharmacy requires a doctor's prescription…provides a physical address and phone number in the US…has a pharmacist available to answer questions…and is licensed with your state's board of pharmacy.

Study of 10,065 online pharmacies by the National Association of Boards of Pharmacy. *www.NABP.net*

Better Vitamin Buying

Earl Mindell, RPh, PhD, nutritionist in Beverly Hills, California, and author of *New Vitamin Bible* (Hachette) and *Prescription Alternatives* (McGraw-Hill).

The best place to buy vitamins is in a natural-foods store or other place that focuses on dietary supplements. Their products, unlike those at chain pharmacies, are most likely to contain the most potent forms—and no artificial colors or preservatives. *What to look for…*

• **Vitamin E.** The *gamma tocopherol* form is natural and more potent than *dl-alpha tocopherol*, the synthetic form.

• **Vitamin C.** The best forms come from rose hips, tapioca or other natural sources. In addition to ascorbic acid, they contain powerful bioflavonoids.

• **Vitamin B.** Supplements should contain equal amounts of B-1 (*thiamine*), B-2 (*riboflavin*) and B-6 (*pyridoxine*). The best ones are made from rice, yeast or other natural products.

Also important…

• **If possible, buy vitamins in dark-colored or opaque containers.** They will last longer.

• **Don't purchase more than a two-month supply at a time.** And make sure that products are not past their expiration dates.

• **Always keep vitamins away from moisture.** When you open the container, remove any cotton balls, which absorb moisture and can cause vitamins to disintegrate. Don't store vitamins in the bathroom or refrigerator unless the label tells you to.

Who Needs Cash or Credit Cards? Turn Your Smartphone into a Virtual Wallet

Jessica Dolcourt, a senior editor with CNET, a leading technology review Web site that's now owned by CBS Interactive. Based in San Francisco, she specializes in smartphones and other cell phones and writes CNET's monthly "Smartphones Unlocked" column. *www.CNET.com*

Your smartphone might not just replace your home phone—it also could replace your ATM and even your wallet before long. A range of new smartphone apps for "mobile payments"—some fairly well-known and others less so—enable consumers to use their phones to manage their bank accounts…transfer money to friends…and even scan credit cards, allowing a small business or even someone holding a yard sale to accept payment in plastic. And some stores are starting to accept payments via smartphone, although various kinks remain to be worked out before that practice becomes widespread.

BANKING VIA SMARTPHONE

Online banking has become mainstream. Now an increasing number of banks allow customers to perform many transactions right from their smartphones. That's handy for people who spend a lot of time on the road or who often need to transfer money between bank accounts, pay recurring bills or check balances on short notice.

Some banks and credit unions even let account holders deposit checks though their smartphones. Just use the smartphone's camera to photograph both sides of the endorsed check, then submit it through the bank's app.

Examples: Large banks that offer mobile check deposit include Bank of America, Chase, Citibank, PNC and US Bank. Credit unions include Alliant and Patelco.

Is it safe?: Mobile banking transactions are encrypted, and accounts are password-protected, so a thief who steals your phone should not be able to access your bank accounts. Still, digital accounts can be hacked.

What to do: Confirm that your bank does not hold you liable, or at least limits liability, for mobile fraud losses. Avoid making banking transactions over public Wi-Fi connections. Monitor accounts, and report unusual activity to the bank immediately to limit your potential liability.

PROCESS CARD PAYMENTS

Several companies now offer low-cost ways to turn smartphones into credit card–processing devices. That means smartphone owners can accept credit card payments at their yard sales, community fund-raisers and part-time businesses.

Examples: Square, a company launched by one of the cofounders of Twitter, offers tiny credit card readers that attach to the headphone jacks of iPhones, iPads and Android smartphones. The card reader and accompanying app are free, but Square takes 2.75% of each swiped credit card payment.* The rest of the payment is deposited in the user's bank account (*www.SquareUp.com*). PayAnywhere is very similar, but it works with BlackBerry smartphones, as well as Apple and Android devices, and charges 2.69% per swiped credit card transaction (*www.PayAnywhere.com*).

Is it safe?: For the seller, risks should be minimal. Buyers might have some qualms about handing over their credit cards to strangers to scan through their smartphones—though this really isn't much riskier than handing a credit card to a waiter in a restaurant.

Buyers should use a credit card rather than a debit card for smartphone transactions to limit their liability if the account information does fall into the wrong hands—fraud losses for credit card users typically are capped at

*Rates subject to change.

$50, assuming that the problem is reported promptly.

PAY FRIENDS

Maybe you dined out with a friend only to discover that the restaurant doesn't take credit cards and you don't have enough cash to pay your share…or perhaps you lost a bet on the golf course but don't have sufficient funds on hand to make good. If you don't like to have debts hanging over your head—or you're afraid that the debt might slip your mind— you could use your smartphone to transfer the money immediately.

Example: With the *PayPal Mobile* smartphone app, you can send money from your BlackBerry, Apple or Android smartphone to anyone else—even someone who does not yet have a PayPal account (though he/she will have to open one to retrieve your payment). All you need is the recipient's e-mail address or mobile phone number. PayPal will send a message explaining how to claim the money or saying that the money has been deposited in the person's account if the phone number or e-mail address already has been linked to a PayPal account.

There's no fee for transferring money this way within the US if your PayPal account is linked to a bank account or PayPal balance. If it's linked to a debit or credit card, there's a fee of 2.9% plus 30 cents per transaction. (On *www.PayPal.com*, search for "Fees" near the bottom of the page.)

Is it safe?: Using PayPal Mobile on a smartphone essentially should be as safe as using the well-established PayPal on a computer. Each PayPal Mobile money transfer requires confirmation with your personal identification number (PIN), so a crook who steals your smartphone shouldn't be able to make unauthorized transfers. PayPal promises 100% protection for unauthorized transfers, assuming that PayPal is notified within 60 days and certain other conditions are met.

What to do: A high-tech crook who manages to load a virus onto your smartphone might be able to obtain your PIN and make unauthorized transfers. PayPal's $0 liability guarantee should protect customers if this occurs, but consider linking the account to a credit card rather than a bank account to obtain the additional consumer protections that credit cards provide.

MAKE PURCHASES

We are slowly gaining the ability to pay for purchases simply by waving our smartphone in front of a scanner at the register or typing a PIN into an app on the phone. The credit card, debit card or PayPal account information that we have previously stored in a "mobile wallet" app in the phone is then transmitted to the merchant.

Smartphone payments such as these already are possible at a few retailers, including Foot Locker, The Home Depot, Macy's and Starbucks. Trouble is, even if you patronize a retailer that accepts mobile payments and you have a mobile wallet app on your smartphone, you won't necessarily be able to pay this way.

There currently are several competing mobile payment technologies and apps, including *Google Wallet*…*Isis Mobile Wallet*…and *PayPal Mobile*. Even retailers who accept mobile payments are unlikely to accept them all.

Example: Starbucks has perhaps the most widely used mobile payments program—but it accepts only its own Starbucks app.

Many analysts expected Google Wallet to dominate the sector—Google dominates most of the sectors it enters—but thus far, it has found limited acceptance. Google Wallet requires smartphones with "near field communications" (NFC) technology. Sprint, Virgin Mobile and US Cellular support the Google Wallet platform for a variety of phones. And Microsoft's Windows Phone 8 operating system supports NFC technology.

Mobile payments might become more widely accepted in the near future as an increasing number of phones equipped with NFC technology reach the market.

But for most consumers, there's little reason to worry about any of this, at least not until the technology sorts itself out in the coming years. The advantages of paying by phone are not great, at least for now. It might save you a few seconds—particularly if you're someone who has your smartphone in your hand much of the time anyway—but paying by credit card or cash is pretty fast, too.

Is it safe?: Proponents of mobile payments say that loading credit card data into a smartphone is safer than carrying around the card itself—because both the smartphone and the app can be password-protected and because a victim is likely to quickly notice if a smartphone is stolen.

But until mobile payments achieve widespread acceptance, we will have to carry our credit cards around, too, negating those advantages. Meanwhile, security experts have shown that mobile wallet apps such as Google Wallet can be hacked if the phone is stolen.

What to do: If you do use a mobile wallet app, set passwords for both your smartphone overall and the mobile wallet application.

Load credit card—not debit card—account information into the app to take advantage of stronger credit card consumer protections, and monitor that credit card account closely. If your smartphone supports a "remote wipe" feature, install this and know how to use it so that you can clear the phone's memory quickly if it is stolen.

Smarter Shopping with Your Smartphone

These free apps can help you save money and stay on budget…

•**Mint** (iPhone and Android) links with all your checking accounts, credit cards and other financial accounts. The app shows you live balances on linked accounts and features budgeting tools.

•**Redlaser** (iPhone, Android and Windows phone) is a bar code and QR code scanner. It displays the price of the item you scan at online and off-line locations.

•**Dealnews** (Apple and Android) gives you daily shopping deals and coupon codes.

USA Today. www.USAToday.com

Better Online Shopping

When shopping online, leave items in your shopping cart for a few days—you may get a discount. Some merchants e-mail coupons or discount codes to customers who load up a shopping cart and then quit without buying. Levi's, ThinkGeek, Coastal and some smaller stores may send coupons…larger merchants, such as Amazon and Newegg, will notify you when items in your cart drop in price.

Caution: Prices also could rise.

To find coupons before ordering anything: Go to *www.RetailMeNot.com*.

LifeHacker.com

The Rebate Runaround

Karen Larson, editor, *Bottom Line/Personal*, 281 Tresser Blvd., Stamford, Connecticut 06901. *www.BottomLine Publications.com*

My coworker's daughter recently made a costly mistake—she threw away the packaging that came with her new smartphone. Without the UPC code from the box, she couldn't apply for the manufacturer's sizable mail-in rebate.

Is there anything my friend's daughter can do to get her rebate without that UPC code? Maybe, says David Bakke, consumer advocacy expert with personal finance Web site MoneyCrashers.com. But her best bet is to bypass the rebate-processing company and instead contact the customer service department of the manufacturer or retailer offering the rebate via phone or social media. She should explain her problem and ask if they can do anything to help. Even if they won't allow the rebate, they might give her some perk just to keep a customer happy.

The odds are somewhat better for consumers who lose the other paperwork required by rebate offers. A replacement rebate form might be available through the retailer or manufacturer's Web site or in the store. Some retailers will reprint lost register receipts.

Follow rebate instructions to the letter, adds Bakke—rebate-processing companies can be sticklers for rules. For example, if the instructions tell you to circle the purchase price on your receipt, do not underline it. Bakke also suggests taping the UPC code to a sheet of paper rather than leaving it loose in the envelope to reduce the chance that it will be lost by the processing company.

Make copies of the receipt, UPC code and completed rebate form prior to submitting them. These will strengthen your case if your rebate never arrives.

Stores with Excellent Return Policies

CVS accepts returns of store-brand items and beauty products anytime—with a receipt. *Kohl's* lets you return anything, anytime, even without a receipt. *Lands' End* takes products back anytime, for any reason with a return form, which is available online. *Nordstrom* takes things back anytime and pays shipping for online returns with a return form that is available online. *REI* allows returns of anything, anytime, even without the receipt—including worn items if you wash them. Some additional restrictions may apply.

Consumer Reports Money Adviser. www.Consumer Reports.org/bookstore

Calling Customer Service? Tips to Get Heard

Adam Goldkamp, chief operating officer of Boston-based GetHuman.com, a free Web site that supplies consumers with toll-free customer service phone numbers and phone-tree tips for nearly 10,000 companies.

Three new tricks worth trying when you must phone a customer service call center…

•**Get angry at the voice-recognition system** (but not at the human phone rep, which will only make him/her less likely to help you). Some companies are adding voice-recognition analysis technology that monitors callers' speech and transfers them to a person faster if they exhibit signs of anger or frustration—the companies hope to prevent that anger from growing worse.

•**Get specific with the voice-recognition system.** If your customer service call is answered by a computer, say the name of the product or service you need help with—even if this has not been listed among your options. With some systems, this will route you directly to the person you need to speak with, skipping the tedious phone tree. (If the system realizes that you have spoken but doesn't understand what you said, try saying something more general such as "agent" or "representative.")

•**Get a US-based rep if you have difficulty understanding accents.** An increasing percentage of large US companies are once again maintaining domestic call centers—but usually only as a small part of an international customer service network. If you don't get a US agent when you call and you have difficulty communicating, request to be transferred to one. Some companies allow this.

Get Rewarded for Your Opinions

Many survey companies are willing to pay for your opinion with cash, rewards points that you can use for gift cards or sweepstakes entries. The compensation generally is the equivalent of a few dollars per survey, but that can add up.

Example: One man averages approximately $2,000 a year by completing up to 20 surveys a week.

Also, consumers enjoy being able to potentially influence or preview products before they come to market.

Before working with a survey company, search for the company and the word "scam" on the Web to see if there are any complaints. And remember that legitimate survey companies will never ask you to pay to take a survey or ask you for your bank account information or Social Security number. (You will have to provide demographic information such as your address, birth date, etc.) A good place to start is GetPaidSurveys.com or SurveyPolice.com.

Consumer Reports Money Advisor. www.Consumer Reports.org/bookstore

How Big Companies Use "Plain English" to Rob You Blind

David Cay Johnston, a Pulitzer Prize–winning reporter formerly with *The New York Times*. Based in Rochester, New York, he is author of *The Fine Print: How Big Companies Use "Plain English" to Rob You Blind* (Portfolio). *www.DavidCayJohnston.com*

You typically cannot buy a car, open a bank account or obtain Internet service without signing a contract. Those contracts inevitably are drafted by the company offering the product or service. That's a perfectly sensible system—it wouldn't make sense to hire a lawyer to hammer out a contract every time you wanted to obtain phone service or a credit card.

Problem: The contracts that companies are asking us to sign have become increasingly one-sided in the companies' favor in recent decades. Hidden in their small print are unexpected and unfair fees, rules and restrictions.

Among the dangers in small print…

ARBITRATION CLAUSES

Contracts from financial institutions, car-rental companies and other corporations often force consumers to forgo their right to sue—even if the consumer clearly has been wronged. Consumers who sign these contracts must instead settle any conflicts through binding arbitration. That may sound reasonable, but the arbitration process usually is strongly slanted against the consumer. Arbitrators have an economic incentive to side with the companies rather than the consumers—if they don't, they won't get work from those companies in the future.

Many contractual arbitration clauses also grant the company tremendous power in the selection of the arbitrators. They let the company choose where the arbitration will take place, which can lead to prohibitive travel expenses for consumers. They require consumers to pay half or more of the arbitrators' fees, which can be $400 an hour.* And they might even include rules that limit the consumer's ability to present evidence.

What to do: When you're handed a contract containing an arbitration clause, write "I disavow this section of the contract" next to this clause and then initial the modification. (Make a copy.) There's no guarantee that the company will accept this—or that the disavowal will hold up in court—but there's little harm in trying, and in some cases the tactic could increase the odds that the company will be willing to agree to an out-of-court settlement rather than risk the possibility that you could force a court case.

If you are asked to sign a contract containing an arbitration clause and a very large sum of money is involved—for instance, the contract may be with the investment company that you intend to entrust with your retirement savings—it's worth paying a lawyer to review the contract before signing.

If you become entangled in a serious dispute with a company with which you have signed a contract containing an arbitration clause, a jury trial still might be possible—but you will need an attorney who has a very specific background to achieve this. Google the words "arbitration," "clause," "case" and the name of your state to find attorneys who have handled and won such cases, or contact your state bar association.

ESCAPE HATCHES

Companies sometimes insert language into the small print of their contracts that allows them to escape promises they have made to

*Price subject to change.

their customers—even promises they made in writing—without being legally liable for the consequences.

Example: A condominium buyer secures a promise from the real estate developer that it will repair his/her unit's leaking windows. The developer then fails to do the repairs, and water damage ruins the condo—yet depending on the wording of the contract, the buyer might have no legal recourse.

Companies do this in two ways…

• **They insert language in contracts that grants them the right to unilaterally change the terms of the agreement after it is made.** Consumers later are mailed notices of contractual changes, but the language tends to be dense, difficult-to-interpret legalese.

• **They write contracts in a way that takes advantage of the legal distinction between a promise and the duty to live up to that promise.** In the eyes of the law, these are distinct things. A company that exploits this distinction might be shielded from charges of fraud unless consumers can prove that the company had an intention to deceive when the promise was made—and intent is extremely difficult to prove.

What to do: When lots of money is at stake, pay an attorney specializing in contracts to confirm that the contract really does require the company to do what it has promised to do.

If you get a notice of updated contract terms from a financial institution—or any other company with whom you have signed a contract—wade through the legalese of the notice to determine what, specifically, has changed. If these new terms are not acceptable to you, it might be time to take your business elsewhere.

There is some good news—you might escape a contract without penalty if a company changes the terms of its agreement with you in a way that works against your interests. For example, contractual changes sometimes offer a way out of multiyear cellular-service contracts without incurring early termination fees.

PHONE AND INTERNET TRAPS

Phone and Internet provider contracts have become riddled with small print—and the bills so laden with incomprehensible fees—that consumers often aren't sure what they're being charged for or what they're receiving. *Two examples…*

• **Phone bills have increased by more than twice the rate of inflation in the past 20 years** despite technological advances that should have dramatically reduced the price of calls. Much of this price increase has been quietly slipped onto bills in the form of new fees. Typically these added fees are fairly low, so consumers don't bother to complain about them, but there are so many of them that they quickly add up. Some of these fees even are designed to look like taxes—that "FCC subscriber line charge" that appears on many phone bills isn't really imposed by the Federal Communications Commission. It's simply a fee that the phone company charges to let the customer have access to the long-distance network.

What to do: The only way to reduce phone fees is to reduce the number of phone lines you pay for, perhaps by canceling your landline and using only a cell phone or Internet-based phone.

• **Internet speed usually is not as fast as what customers think they have been promised.** Take a close look at the small print in high-speed Internet service contracts. Whatever speed customers order, they are promised only "up to" that speed. Usually they receive much slower service, particularly at peak usage hours.

What to do: If you have multiple Internet providers in your area, it is possible that one offers noticeably faster connections in practice even if all advertise similar speeds, something you can determine by asking your neighbors which providers they use and how fast their connection speeds have been.

You Can Get Out of a Contract!

If you lease a car and then want to get out of the lease, SwapaLease.com can match you with someone who is looking to assume a lease. *If you refinance the mortgage on your primary home with a new lender and change your mind*, the *Truth in Lending Act* gives you three days after midnight of the day you sign the papers to exercise your right of rescission in writing…or three years if your lender never notified you of your rescission rights. *If you buy a time-share property*, you generally have between three and 21 days (depending on state law) to pull out of the deal.

Lynnette Khalfani-Cox, personal finance expert, writing at AARP.org.

---

5 Things Your Lawyer Might Say…but Shouldn't

John F. Phillips, Esq., an attorney in Fort Lauderdale, Florida, with 30 years of experience primarily in civil litigation. He is coauthor of *How & When to Sue Your Lawyer* (Square One).

S ome lawyers stretch the truth with clients and prospective clients. If your lawyer or a lawyer you're considering hiring tells you any of the following, it's reasonable to wonder whether he/she is being totally honest and whether you should recheck his background or even go elsewhere…

• **"This case is a winner. I** guarantee it." An experienced lawyer might be able to tell you that you have a strong case, but an attorney who guarantees a win is being dishonest. The human element of our legal system makes it impossible to guarantee results…juries and judges sometimes produce unexpected outcomes…and crucial witnesses sometimes fail to show up in court or say what's expected.

• **"This is my specialty."** Many lawyers do have specialties, but sometimes a lawyer in need of clients will claim to specialize in the legal services that you need even if he/she doesn't.

What to do: Before you hire an attorney, look him up on the Martindale-Hubble Web site (*www.Martindale.com*) or the state bar association's site. These should list his actual areas of practice, background and training.

• **"You can call me anytime."** You can call, but he often won't pick up. A busy attorney doesn't answer the phone every time a client calls and may not even get back to you within a day. And you need to be careful not to call or even e-mail too much. The time it takes for an attorney to respond—even if it's by e-mail—may run up your bill.

What to do: Get the attorney's direct e-mail address, but don't contact him unnecessarily. While attorneys are notoriously bad at taking clients' calls, most do respond fairly promptly to e-mails. Communicating with your attorney via e-mail also creates a virtual paper trail, which could come in handy if the attorney botches your case and you pursue a malpractice suit against him.

• **"I already filed the papers."** Although many lawyers do file important paperwork promptly, some will say that they have even when they haven't because they are disorganized or put a low priority on your case. The attorney's foot dragging could delay the proceedings or, worse, lead to missed deadlines that result in the forfeiture of your case.

What to do: If your attorney has moved slowly throughout your case, ask him to e-mail you a copy of the documents that he says he has filed. If he hesitates, it could mean that he hasn't really completed the paperwork yet. Contact the court clerk's office to confirm that the documents are on the docket sheet. Some state and county courts now make it possible to check docket sheets online.

• **"Don't worry about the estate.** I'll take care of everything." Probate attorneys often say comforting things such as this to grieving relatives. But some of them are just trying to build trust so that no one bothers to ask how much they intend to charge.

What to do: The executor of the estate should ask an attorney how much he charges for probate services and try to negotiate before hiring him.

12

Retirement Report

Social Security Traps: One False Move and Married Couples Could Lose Thousands

Every day, more Americans discover the Social Security safety net they rely on is filled with complex traps that can reduce their potential benefits by tens of thousands of dollars.

One of the complications: For married couples, Social Security rules and strategies can be very different from what they are for people who are single, widowed or divorced.

Below we explain ways to avoid some of the most common, confusing and potentially costly traps for married couples and explore a quandary that affects all kinds of retirees— when to start collecting benefits.

Trap #1: **Many men think that they should start receiving benefits as soon as they are**

eligible because men have shorter life spans, on average, than women. Monthly benefit checks increase in size for every month that you delay retirement from age 62 to 70. But many men assume that it's sensible to start benefits as soon as they retire because longevity tables (and in some cases, family history and/or their own health) indicate that they're unlikely to live far into their 80s. And Social Security calculators often suggest that delaying benefits is a money loser if you die before age 80.

While that logic can be sound for single men, it tends to be a mistake for husbands— particularly husbands who significantly outearned their wives during their careers and are older than their wives and/or have healthy wives from long-lived families.

William Meyer, founder and managing principal of Social Security Solutions, Inc., which provides personalized Social Security benefits optimization strategies, Leawood, Kansas. He previously served in executive roles at H&R Block and Charles Schwab & Co. *www.Social SecuritySolutions.com*

213

Better strategy: Generally, higher-earning husbands should base decisions about whether to take benefits early on the longer of the two spouses' projected life spans, which usually is the wife's. That's because after a man in this situation dies, his widow is entitled to a survivor benefit equal to the benefit that the husband had been receiving. (However, this survivor benefit would be reduced if the widow began receiving it prior to her so-called "standard" or "full" retirement age. That age varies according to what year you were born and may be slightly different for widows/widowers—see Trap 2 below.)

Once this survivor benefit is taken into account, many households would be better off if the husband delays starting his benefits as long as possible up to age 70—even if that means he doesn't receive much from Social Security before he dies. (This also could apply to wives who significantly outearned younger husbands, but because women tend to have longer life spans, benefit calculators are less likely to suggest that women should claim their benefits early.)

Example: Mr. Jones, who is 66 (his standard retirement age) starts collecting $2,000 per month. If he lives 16 more years—a typical life span for a 66-year-old man—he will have received a total of $384,000* from Social Security. Waiting until age 70 to start benefits might reduce the total benefits he receives—his monthly checks would increase to $2,640, but the loss of four years' worth of checks means that his take would be just over $380,000, which is nearly $4,000 less than if he had started collecting at age 66.

But if Mr. Jones is married, for instance to a healthy woman four years his junior, then delaying benefits until age 70 might pay off better. In that case, after Mr. Jones dies, Mrs. Jones continues to receive $2,640 per month in survivor benefits, rather than the $2,000 she would have received had Mr. Jones started his benefits at age 66. If she lives a typical woman's life span—in this case, staying alive for seven years after her husband's death—she would receive $53,760 extra from Social

Security, offsetting her husband's $4,000 loss many times over.

Trap #2: **Many people don't realize that they might earn nothing extra by postponing spousal benefits past their standard retirement age.** After reaching standard retirement age, Social Security allows married people to choose between filing for their own retirement benefits (based on their own earnings history) and spousal benefits (based on their spouse's earnings history). You even can switch from one of these alternatives to the other along the way to allow the size of monthly checks under the postponed option to grow until you switch to that option. Using this strategy, you can maximize your lifetime benefits.

For instance, a woman might file for her own retirement benefits and then eventually switch to higher spousal benefits. But postponing the switch to spousal benefits beyond her standard retirement age will not continue to increase her spousal benefits.

This surprises many people because it is different from the rule that applies to Social Security benefits based on your own earnings history. Postponing the start of your own retirement benefits beyond your standard retirement age will increase your benefit checks by 7% to 8% per year until age 70.

(For a widow/widower, survivor benefits do *not* increase after she/he reaches standard retirement age.)

Trap #3: **If one spouse—for instance the husband—files for benefits...and later the wife files before reaching her standard retirement age, the wife could lose the ability to eventually switch to the highest possible benefits.** That's because the wife runs into a complication called the "deemed filing rule." In this circumstance, when the wife tries to claim her own retirement benefits before reaching standard retirement age, she is deemed to be filing for her husband's benefits as well—even though that isn't what she meant to do. That means neither her own benefits nor the spousal benefits will grow—thwarting her plan to get the highest possible benefits by switching at a later date.

*Estimates of future Social Security income provided in this article do not include future inflation adjustments.

Example: Mr. Smith files for his own benefits at age 66—his standard retirement age—and starts collecting $2,100 per month. Mrs. Smith, 63, plans to apply for her own retirement benefits at the same time, collecting $720 a month. She figures that she will switch to spousal benefits of $1,050 per month (half of her husband's $2,100 benefit) when she reaches her standard retirement age of 66, thus allowing the eventual monthly spousal benefit to be bigger than if she had filed for spousal benefits when she was 63. But, in reality, she triggered the deemed filing rule at age 63. At that point, she became eligible for $833 a month—the equivalent of spousal benefits, which in this case are higher than her own benefits—but the amount will not grow in subsequent years.

A better strategy: Assuming that she has many years left to live, Mrs. Smith would be better off waiting until her standard retirement age…starting to collect spousal benefits of $1,050 a month at that point…and then at age 70, switching to her own benefits, which will have grown to $1,188.

(Similarly, the deemed filing rule kicks in if one spouse—say, the husband—files for his own benefits and the wife then files for spousal benefits before reaching standard retirement age. As a result, when the wife switches to her own benefits at a later date, those benefits will not have grown.)

More from William Meyer…

Social Security Traps for Singles

Some of the traps that ensnare current and future Social Security recipients apply especially to people who are single or widowed…

TRAPS FOR SINGLES

Trap #1: **Bad timing.** If you're single, there are certain ages when it is most advantageous to wait a little longer to start receiving benefits. That's because your monthly benefit amount increases in size for every month that you delay starting Social Security from age 62

to 70—but it doesn't increase at a consistent pace throughout those years.*

For instance, if you start your benefits at age 66, or whatever your so-called "standard" or "full" retirement age is, you probably are doing so exactly at the moment when continuing to postpone the start offers the greatest rewards—even though it's the age that the Social Security Administration (SSA) considers the "normal" time to retire.

When you crunch the numbers, it turns out that there actually are two windows during which it is especially inopportune for most single people to claim benefits if they wish to maximize the total amount they receive. One window runs from age 62 and one month through age 63 and 11 months…while the other is centered around your standard retirement age—age 65 and five months through age 66 and seven months if your standard retirement age is 66.

If your standard retirement age is higher than 66, the windows during which it's best not to start benefits are within eight months before or after your standard retirement age and within approximately 12 months before or after the date that is three years prior to your standard retirement age.

Example: If your standard retirement age is 67, the windows to avoid are between 66 and four months and 67 and eight months…and between approximately age 63 and age 65.

All this is true for married people, too, but married people have additional benefits options, such as spousal benefits and switching strategies that mean starting benefits at standard retirement age sometimes makes sense.

Trap #2: **Neglecting to *file* for benefits at your standard retirement age.** You should file even if you don't plan to start collecting until later. But when you file, immediately suspend your benefits.

*To calculate the amounts you could get at each age, go to *www.SSA.gov/oact/quickcalc/index.html*. Decisions about when to start Social Security also depend on life expectancy (visit *www.SSA.gov/oact/population/longevity. html* for a guide to life-expectancy calculations) and on whether you still are earning substantial employment income, which could mean much of your Social Security benefits would be lost to taxes.

This "file-and-suspend" technique is a more common tactic and more obvious advantage for married couples. In general, the higher-earning spouse files and suspends so that the lower-earning spouse is eligible to claim spousal benefits while the higher-earner's eventual benefits continue to grow in size.

But file-and-suspend offers advantages for singles, too. When you suspend your benefits, you remain entitled to the benefits held in suspension. That means you have the option to collect those past benefits as a lump sum at any point until you lift the suspension and begin receiving your monthly benefit checks.

This lump-sum option could come in handy if you suddenly find yourself in need of money. And it could allow you to get as much as possible out of the Social Security system if, while the suspension is in place, you learn that you don't have long to live.

If you request the lump sum, your future monthly benefit checks will be calculated as if you had started your benefits when you originally filed and suspended—meaning that they will be on the low side. If you don't take the lump sum, they will be calculated as though you had started them on the day you lifted the suspension—that is, as though you had never filed and suspended at all.

Example: A man who is eligible for $2,000 per month at his full retirement age of 66 files and suspends at that point. Three years later, he learns that he has terminal cancer. He requests a lump sum and receives the three years of benefits that were suspended—$72,000.** He receives two additional monthly checks before passing away, bringing his total benefits to $76,000. Had this man simply delayed filing until he received his bad news, he would have received just two payments totaling $4,000.

TRAPS FOR WIDOWS AND WIDOWERS

Trap #3: **Permanently choosing between survivor benefits and your own retirement benefits.** The best option usually isn't one or the other—it's one and *then* the other. Many

**Estimates of future Social Security income provided in this article do not include future inflation adjustments.

widows and widowers depend on their Social Security checks to pay the bills. Yet most receive less from the Social Security system than they should because of this simple trap.

When widows and widowers explore their benefit options, they typically are told that they must choose between claiming a benefit based on their own earnings and claiming survivor benefits based on their departed spouse's earnings—not both. The vast majority select whichever of these is larger and then receive that amount each month for the rest of their lives. These checks often are relatively small because survivors tend to start their benefits as soon as they're eligible—some don't have any other way to pay the bills.

Widows and widowers are allowed to start their survivor benefits as early as age 60, but the sooner they claim them, the lower their monthly checks will be. Start benefits at age 60, and you will receive just 71.5% of the amount you would receive if you start benefits at your standard retirement age (assuming that is age 66).

What most widows and widowers don't realize is that while they can't receive both their retirement benefit and their survivor benefit at the same time, they can—and, in most cases, should—eventually switch from one to the other. This switching strategy can produce tens of thousands of dollars in additional benefits, particularly when both spouses had significant earnings during their working lives.

Example: A woman is widowed at age 62. She has a standard retirement benefit of $1,657 and a standard survivor benefit of $2,245. In this situation, most widows simply would take the survivor benefit and receive $1,862 per month for life (that's the $2,245 survivor benefit minus a reduction for starting benefits at 62, four years prior to standard retirement age). If this woman lives to age 85, she will receive a total of $506,464 from the Social Security system.

Much better: If this woman instead claimed her own retirement benefit at age 62, she would receive $1,277 per month ($1,657 minus the reduction for starting four years before standard retirement age) until age 66...at which point she could switch to her standard

$2,245 survivor benefit. This strategy would produce additional benefits of more than $62,000 if she lives past age 85.

***Trap #4:* Your standard retirement age for survivor benefits might be different from your standard retirement age for retiree benefits.** The SSA is slowly phasing in a higher standard retirement age. If you were born in 1937 or earlier, you can retire at age 65 and receive your standard retirement benefit. But if you were born after 1937, your standard retirement age falls somewhere between age 65 and two months and age 67, depending on the year of your birth.

What most people don't realize: The SSA is using a slightly different schedule to increase the standard retirement age for survivor benefits. This could cause widows and widowers to accidentally delay the start of survivor benefits beyond their survivor benefits standard retirement age, costing them some monthly checks without increasing the size of future checks. (Those born between 1945 and 1956 are not affected—for them, both standard retirement ages are 66.)

To find your survivor standard retirement age: Go to *www.SSA.gov/survivorplan/survivorchartred.htm.*

Example: If you were born in 1956, your standard retirement age for retiree benefits is 66 and four months—but your standard retirement age for survivor benefits is exactly 66.

How to Find Your Lost Pension Money

Jim Miller, an advocate for older Americans, writes "Savvy Senior," a weekly information column syndicated in more than 400 newspapers nationwide. Based in Norman, Oklahoma, Miller also offers a free senior news service at *www.SavvySenior.org.*

It's not unusual for a worker to lose track of a pension benefit. Perhaps you left an employer long ago and forgot that you left behind a pension. Or maybe you worked for a company that changed owners or went belly up many years ago, and you figured the pen-

sion went with it...but you might have been wrong.

Today, millions of dollars in benefits are sitting in pension plans across the US or with the Pension Benefit Guaranty Corporation (PBGC), a federal government agency, waiting to be claimed by their rightful owners. The average unclaimed benefit with PBGC is $6,550.

To help you look for a pension, here are some steps to take and some free resources that can help you search if your previous employer has gone out of business, relocated, changed owners or merged with another firm...

CONTACT THE EMPLOYER

If you think you have a pension and the company you worked for still is in business, your first step is to call the human resources department and ask how to contact the pension plan administrator. Ask the administrator whether you have a pension, how much it is worth and how to claim it. Depending on how complete the administrator's records are, you may need to show proof that you once worked for the company and that you are pension eligible.

If you haven't saved your old tax returns from these years, you can get a copy of your earnings record from the Social Security Administration, which will show how much you were paid each calendar year by each employer. Call 800-772-1213, and ask for Form SSA-7050, *Request for Social Security Earnings Information*, or you can download it at *www.SSA.gov/online/ssa-7050.pdf.* You will pay a small fee for the report, depending on the number of years of data you request.

Some other old forms that can help you prove pension eligibility are summary plan descriptions that you should have received from your employer when you worked there...and any individual benefit statements that you received during your employment.

SEARCH PBGC

If your former employer went out of business or if the company still is in business but terminated its pension plan, check with the PBGC, which guarantees pension payouts to private-sector workers if their pension plans fail, up to annual limits. Most people receive the full benefit they earned before the plan was terminated. The PBGC offers an online pension-search directory tool at *http://search. PBGC.gov/mp/mp.aspx*, or call 800-400-7242.

GET HELP

If you need help tracking down your former company because it may have moved, changed owners or merged with another firm, contact the Pension Rights Center, a nonprofit consumer organization that offers seven free Pension Counseling and Information Projects around the US that serve 30 states. For more information, visit *www.PensionRights.org* or call 888-420-6550. If you, your company or your pension plan happens to be outside the 30-state area served by the projects, or if you're trying to locate a federal or military pension, use Pension Help America at *www.Pension Help.org*. This resource can connect you with government agencies and private organizations that provide free information and assistance to help your search.

Also, the PBGC has a free publication called *Finding a Lost Pension*. Go to *www.PBGC.gov/ res* (scroll down to "Additional Resources") to see it online, or call 800-400-7242 and ask for a copy to be mailed to you.

New Way to Create Tax-Free Growth

Peter Philipp, CFA, CFP, a financial adviser who manages the San Francisco office of Newport Advisory, LLC. He specializes in employee benefits and investment management for businesses and individuals. He also is an instructor in wealth management at University of California-Berkeley. *www.NewportAdvisory SF.com*

A little-noticed feature of the fiscal cliff tax deal could benefit many employees who have traditional 401(k) retirement plans. The provision in the new law allows employees to convert pretax assets in those 401(k)s to Roth 401(k) assets, which could mean years of permanently tax-free growth of those assets. The new rule also applies to 403(b) and 457(b) plans.

About half of employers that offer traditional 401(k)s—which require you to pay taxes once you withdraw the money but not when you first contribute it—also offer Roth 401(k)s. Because of the new rule change, it's likely that most of them will amend their plan rules within a few months to permit conversions to Roth 401(k)s, which require you to pay taxes when you contribute the money but then allow it to grow without facing taxes ever again, even when you withdraw it.

Prior to the new law, conversions to a Roth 401(k) were allowed only when the assets were "distributable," which generally meant when you changed jobs, retired or reached age 59½. The new rules don't have such restrictions.

The amount that is converted from a traditional 401(k) to a Roth 401(k) is taxed as ordinary income for the year in which it is converted.

WHO SHOULD CONVERT

Roth conversions generally make the most sense for people who expect to be taxed at a higher rate when they eventually withdraw money from a retirement account. This might be the case if your income is unusually low during the conversion year…if your career is just getting started and so your income and tax rate will likely grow for many years…or if you believe the government is likely to increase your tax rate in the future.

Conversions tend not to be worthwhile for those who will retire and start withdrawing assets from the account within five years or so, though there's an exception to this—a Roth 401(k) conversion can be a useful estate-planning tool for high-net-worth individuals even if retirement is looming or already under way. Your heirs can receive tax-free dollars when they inherit your Roth.

For most people, it is prudent to keep significant assets in traditional 401(k)s and/or IRAs but convert a portion to a Roth if you don't have sizable Roth 401(k) and/or Roth IRA savings already. That way you will have pools of both tax-deferred and tax-free savings to draw from during retirement.

How much to convert depends, in part, on the following…

●**How much you can afford to pay** in extra income tax during the conversion year without tapping tax-advantaged accounts to help pay those extra taxes.

●**How much you can convert** before a portion of the extra "income" that the converted amount represents would be taxed at a higher rate because it puts you in a higher tax bracket.

IRA VS. 401(K) CONVERSIONS

A conversion to a Roth 401(k) has a significant drawback in comparison to the conversion of a traditional IRA to a Roth IRA. When you convert an IRA to a Roth, you have the option of "recharacterizing" the conversion, essentially undoing it, by October 15 of the year following the year of the conversion. Recharacterization currently is not an option with Roth 401(k) conversions.

Example: If the IRA assets you convert decline sharply in value soon after the conversion, you could recharacterize them back to a traditional IRA, wait out an IRS-imposed waiting period, then convert the assets to a Roth again—this time paying taxes only on the now much-lower asset value.

More from Peter Philipp, CFA, CFP...

Leaving a Job? How to Decide If Your 401(K) Should Go, Too

Americans change jobs more than 10 times, on average, staying in each job just 4.4 years, according to the Bureau of Labor Statistics. And each job change typically comes with an important decision—whether to leave a 401(k) retirement account in place or roll it over into an IRA.

New wrinkles have emerged in the decision-making process, as 401(k) plan providers are under pressure to lower expenses and reveal more details about those expenses and as some employers expand and/or improve the investment options—all of which could make 401(k)s more attractive.

But brokerage firms, eager for the assets, urge savers not to leave their 401(k)s behind, and several of them, including Fidelity, Schwab and TD Ameritrade, have offered bonuses as high as $2,500 if you bring your workplace retirement account to them and convert it to an IRA.

Warning: There's a third choice as well—you could cash out your 401(k) when you leave a job. But this usually is the worst option unless the money is desperately needed. Better to let the assets continue to grow tax-deferred for as long as possible in either a 401(k) or an IRA. *How to decide what to do...*

WHEN IT'S BEST TO KEEP THE 401(K) IN PLACE

In the following situations, lean toward keeping the 401(k) where it is.

●**You separate from an employer in your late 50s and might need to tap the account soon.** If you separate from an employer in or after the year in which you reach age 55, you may be able to make withdrawals directly from that employer's 401(k) without penalty. If you rolled that money over to an IRA, you would face a 10% early-withdrawal penalty on withdrawals made from the IRA before age 59½. Public safety employees, including police officers, firefighters and medics who worked for state or local governments, can qualify for penalty-free 401(k) and 403(b) withdrawals as early as age 50 if they separate from service at or after this age.

It's best not to withdraw money from tax-deferred accounts when you're in your 50s—it's better to let this money grow. But withdrawals might become necessary if you have limited savings outside of tax-deferred accounts and have trouble finding a new job.

●**Your 401(k) offers great investment options with low fees and expenses.** Some 401(k) plans charge modest fees and offer a wide range of desirable investment options. These might include access to low-expense institutional shares of mutual funds not otherwise available to individual investors...or "brokerage windows"—side doors that allow 401(k) plan participants to escape the limited investment options available through their 401(k) plans and opt for other mutual funds, stocks and securities instead.

Unfortunately, many 401(k) plans feature low-quality or limited investment options and impose relatively steep fees and expenses.

What to do: Evaluate the quality and costs of the investments available through your 401(k) before deciding whether to roll over to an IRA. All 401(k) providers now are required to supply fee disclosures to the participants, which should help in this evaluation. Check the 401(k)'s administrative fees—anything significantly above $50 per year is on the high side. Next, use an independent resource such as research firm Morningstar to compare the rankings, returns and expense ratios of the mutual funds available through your 401(k) to those of comparable funds offered by low-cost IRA providers such as Vanguard and Fidelity.

If you don't feel qualified to evaluate your former employer's 401(k) plan on your own, pay a fee-only financial planner to help. But confirm that you're working with a fee-only planner—someone who gets paid only an hourly fee. A financial adviser who earns commissions on investment sales may have a financial incentive to encourage you to roll the money into an IRA.

Rule of thumb: If an employer has fewer than 100 employees, there's a good chance that its 401(k) has relatively high costs. If it has more than 1,000 employees, there's a good chance that it imposes lower costs than those available through an IRA. There are plenty of exceptions to this, however.

●**You might require protection from creditors.** Federal law provides 401(k) assets with relatively strong protection from creditors, even in bankruptcy. In contrast, federal law provides only limited protection for IRAs when you file a bankruptcy claim, and outside of bankruptcy, IRA protections vary from state to state.

If you suspect that you might have to declare bankruptcy in the future…or you might be targeted in a lawsuit—perhaps because you're a doctor, contractor or in some other profession where lawsuits are common—ask an attorney how well your state shields IRAs from creditors. If the protection is weak, it could be worth leaving assets in the 401(k).

WHEN IT'S BEST TO MAKE A SHIFT

As indicated above, it may make sense to roll over a 401(k) to an IRA if the 401(k) has poor investment options and/or high fees and expenses. You can choose better investments from a low-cost IRA provider such as Vanguard or Fidelity.

Also, in the following situations, lean toward shifting your assets…

●**If you join a new employer that has a 401(k) plan offering excellent investment options and low costs,** you might be allowed to roll your existing 401(k) into the new employer's 401(k) plan. Ask the new employer's benefits department for details.

●**You want to maintain as much control as possible over your money.** When you leave your money in a former employer's 401(k), that money is at the mercy of the employer's decisions.

Example: If a former employer changes from one 401(k) provider to another, your money can be moved into investments that you have not selected unless you promptly choose from among the new investment options. Your money also will be unavailable to you in a "blackout" period during this transition between 401(k) providers.

One option is to leave your money in the former employer's 401(k) for now, then roll it over if the 401(k)'s investment options later change for the worse. But most people fail to carefully track changes in their former employers' 401(k) plans. Some don't read the notices that the plan sends them, while others stop receiving notices entirely because they failed to inform the plan's administrators of an address change.

Also: In rare cases, 401(k) plans are disqualified because employers fail to follow IRS rules. Employees and former employees who have assets in these disqualified plans might have those assets distributed to them, costing them their chance for continued tax-deferred growth. Rolling 401(k) assets into an IRA avoids this danger.

●**You have many 401(k)s and want to keep your financial life as simple as possible.** The more 401(k)s you have with prior employers, the greater the odds that you will lose track of some of them…and the more difficult it becomes to monitor the overall asset allocations of your savings. Consolidating multiple 401(k)s into a single IRA simplifies your financial life and reduces the odds that you'll lose track of any savings.

• **You have a significant amount of highly appreciated company stock in your 401(k),** and you're age 55 or older. The tax code offers a little-known opportunity for those who have company stock in their 401(k)s. If you roll this 401(k) into an IRA, you have the option of distributing the company stock into a taxable account rather than the IRA.

Shifting assets from a 401(k) to a taxable account generally means paying income tax on the full market value of those assets. But with company stock, you're required to pay income taxes only on the "cost basis" of the shares—the amount you originally paid for them. You will have to pay long-term capital gains tax on the stock's "net unrealized appreciation"—the difference between that cost basis and the eventual sales price—when you later sell the shares.

For most people, long-term capital gains tax rates are substantially lower than income tax rates, so you should come out well ahead.

It is worth speaking with a financial adviser or tax professional before attempting this— the rules are complicated.

Warning: If you separate from your job prior to the year in which you turn 55, rolling company stock into a taxable account in this way will result in a 10% early-withdrawal penalty.

• **You have less than $5,000 in the 401(k).** If your 401(k) balance is below $5,000, your employer can require you to either roll it over or cash it out when you leave.

Possible 401(K) Mistake

Contributing a large amount to your 401(k) all at once can be a mistake if your company matches contributions. You may be better off contributing smaller amounts over the course of the year.

Example: If a company caps contribution matches at 3% of each paycheck, contributing a large amount may result in only a small fraction of that contribution being matched.

Helpful: Find out if your company has a *true-up plan provision*. That means the plan calculates the potential maximum match you would receive based on the total amount contributed—and that is how much the company provides. If your firm does not have this provision, spread your contributions throughout the year.

Morningstar.com

Retire Richer! Use Your Health Savings Account to Boost Your Nest Egg

Roy Ramthun, president of HSA Consulting Services, LLC, a health-care consulting practice specializing in HSAs and consumer-driven health-care issues, Silver Spring, Maryland. Formerly, he was senior adviser to the Secretary of the US Treasury and senior health policy adviser to President George W. Bush regarding health-care issues, such as HSAs, Medicare and Medicaid. *www.HSAConsultingServices.com*

More than 13.5 million people now use *Health Savings Accounts* (HSAs) to set aside pretax dollars for their medical expenses. But because you don't have to use the money in an HSA by any particular deadline, HSAs also can serve as powerful savings tools to supplement your retirement accounts or to provide some emergency cash.

As a former senior adviser to the Secretary of the US Treasury for health initiatives, I helped implement HSAs nationwide a decade ago. Their features make them far more useful, flexible and valuable than most people realize.

One of the greatest advantages is that, unlike the more popular *Flexible Spending Account* (FSA) that requires employees to predict their medical spending for the year in advance and contribute a defined amount, the IRS allows you to fund your HSA with pretax dollars after a medical expense* has occurred, then immediately reimburse yourself. In fact, you have until April 15, 2014, to fund your HSA for 2013 expenses.

Smart strategies for using HSAs...

•**Pay insurance premiums.** You might know that if you change jobs or lose your job, you still keep your HSA and have access to all the money you have contributed. That means that even if you aren't eligible to make contributions because you are no longer enrolled in a high-deductible health insurance plan, the money still can be withdrawn tax-free and penalty-free to cover medical expenses.

But you might not know that if you get fired, laid off or quit your job, the IRS allows you to use HSA money to pay premiums for temporary COBRA health insurance coverage. Moreover, if you are receiving federal or state unemployment benefits, you can tap your HSA to pay the premiums for any health-insurance coverage.

Once you turn 65, HSA flexibility increases even further. At that point, the IRS allows you to withdraw your HSA money tax-free and penalty-free to cover your premiums for Medicare and long-term-care insurance.

•**Supplement your nest egg.** You might know that the money in your HSA account can be invested and can grow tax-deferred just like your IRA assets in investments such as certificates of deposit, stocks, bonds and mutual funds, depending on which kinds of investments your HSA provider offers.

But you may not know that once you turn 65, HSA money can be used—without paying a penalty—for any reason, medical or otherwise, although if you use it for purposes other than qualified medical costs or insurance premiums, you have to pay income tax on the withdrawn amount.

*HSA money can be used tax-free for only "qualified" medical expenses, which include most ordinary procedures, treatments and prescribed medications but not over-the-counter medications, vitamins or cosmetic surgery. HSA contributions are deductible for federal income tax and for state income tax in all states except Alabama, California and New Jersey. If you withdraw HSA funds for unqualified medical expenses before age 65, you are subject to a 20% penalty plus income tax on the amount withdrawn.

That makes the HSA so attractive that I often recommend that while someone is employed, he/she should fund it to the maximum allowable amount year after year—even before fully funding IRAs and even if he doesn't expect to spend nearly that amount in the same year he makes the contribution.

I also recommend that if someone can afford to, he should consider paying for all or a portion of medical expenses with non-HSA money in years when he is contributing to his HSA. That way, HSA investments can grow tax-free, as they would in an IRA, for many years.

•**Leave your HSA to your spouse.** When you die, your HSA can be transferred to your spouse tax-free, and it becomes his/her HSA. The surviving spouse can continue to make contributions if otherwise eligible to do so and can use the HSA money to pay for qualified medical expenses or for other purposes outlined above. But, if your HSA is left to another beneficiary, it converts to a regular bank account and loses any tax advantages.

More from Roy Ramthun...

HSA Rules

To qualify for an HSA, you need to be enrolled in a high-deductible health insurance plan, which means that insurance does not pick up your health-care costs until you meet your annual deductible, which must be at least $1,250 for singles and $2,500 for families in 2013 and 2014. After that, your insurance will cover additional expenses. Your maximum annual out-of-pocket expenses under the plan (including all of the deductibles, co-pays and coinsurance) cannot exceed $6,250 in 2013 ($6,350 in 2014) for an individual with self-only coverage or $12,500 in 2013 ($12,700 in 2014) for an individual with family coverage.

To contribute: You can put up to $3,250 for individuals and $6,450 for families in your HSA in 2013 ($3,300 for individuals, $6,550 for families in 2014). Figures include money your employer may contribute to your HSA. If you are over age 55, the IRS allows you to add an additional $1,000 annually over your HSA contribution limits.

How Much to Save for Retirement

Save eight times your final salary to be able to meet basic income needs in retirement. To be on track to replace 85% of preretirement income, the average worker should have saved about one year of salary by age 35...three times annual salary by age 45...five times salary by age 55...and six times by age 60.

Beth McHugh, vice president of thought leadership at Fidelity Investments, Boston, which developed new guidelines for retirement savings.

Don't Dip into Retirement Savings!

Using retirement funds to pay current expenses is becoming more common—and undermining workers' future security. More than one-fourth of American employees with 401(k) and other retirement accounts use them to pay expenses. Among people in their 40s, one-third turn to retirement accounts for non-retirement costs.

The Washington Post. www.WashingtonPost.com

The 10 Most Tax-Friendly States for Retirees

Kiplinger's Personal Finance. www.Kiplinger.com

The following 10 states impose some of the lowest taxes on retirees in the US. All of these exempt Social Security benefits from taxation (and some impose no state income tax at all). Many of them exclude government and military pensions from income taxes, and some exempt private pensions, too. A few offer blanket exclusions up to a specific dollar amount of retirement income from a wide variety of sources. Property taxes were also a factor in the equation. *Here, the 10 most tax-friendly states, starting with the most friendly...*

1. Alaska	6. Alabama
2. Nevada	7. South Carolina
3. Wyoming	8. Louisiana
4. Mississippi	9. Delaware
5. Georgia	10. Pennsylvania

States stingy with tax breaks...

1. Connecticut	6. Nebraska
2. Vermont	7. Oregon
3. Rhode Island	8. California
4. Montana	9. New Jersey
5. Minnesota	10. New York

For more information on your state, go to *www.Kiplinger.com/tools/retiree_map.*

How to Stay Out of a Nursing Home

Charles B. Inlander, consumer advocate and health-care consultant based in Fogelsville, Pennsylvania. He was the founding president of the nonprofit People's Medical Society, a consumer advocacy organization that is credited with key improvements in the quality of US health care in the 1980s and 1990s, and is author or co-author of more than 20 consumer-health books. He is also a featured columnist in *Bottom Line/Health, www. BottomLinePublications.com.*

Most people I know are adamant that they want to stay in their homes as long as possible as they grow older. The good news is that there are now many affordable—and sometimes surprising—alternatives to nursing homes. *Best approaches...*

• **Use new technology to stay at home.** For example, you can now buy home medication-dispensing devices that store all your pills, unlock when it's time to take them and alert you with a signal at pill time. These devices are even wired to a remote command center that will call you or a relative if you miss just one dose! In addition, home-care agencies can set up devices (with sensors worn by the patient) for daily monitoring of blood pressure and body temperature.

Recent development: Medicare has just agreed to cover many such home services for people who otherwise would be placed in a more costly nursing home.

• **Try a "granny apartment."** That's what today's so-called accessory dwelling units (ADUs) were called years ago. An ADU (fully equipped with bathroom and kitchen) is a one-room, freestanding house or a small addition to a relative's home.

Latest development: Years ago, zoning laws in most communities put major restrictions on these units, but that has now changed in many areas. A friend of mine built an addition onto her house (for $65,000—less than the cost of a year in a nursing home) for her mother who had Alzheimer's disease. Her mother lived there until her death eight years later with the costs mostly covered by her Social Security payments, her small savings and Medicare (with a Medigap supplemental policy).

My friend also used community services, including adult day care and occasional in-home caregiving aides. To learn more about such community services, consult the Administration on Aging's resources Web site, *www. ElderCare.gov*, or call 800-677-1116.

• **Consider "campus" living.** It may not be quite as much fun as a college campus, but assisted-living facilities do offer their own activities (such as bridge, yoga classes and book clubs) and can be ideal for people who can't stay in a traditional home or live with relatives. With assisted living, you have your own apartment and receive three meals a day, medical monitoring and medication assistance (by a nurse or an aide). *Cost:* $1,000 to $5,000 per person per month.*

Recent development: Growing numbers of so-called continuing-care communities. They offer independent (often freestanding homes) and assisted-living programs in addition to skilled nursing home services all on the same campus. These communities can be expensive, often requiring a front-end, onetime payment of $100,000 or more, plus monthly fees for meals and other services.

*Prices subject to change.

224

Good to know: Many continuing-care communities now have a variety of payment options to make them more affordable. Go to the AARP Web site, *www.AARP.org*, and search "Caregiving," to research different payment methods.

Safer Senior Living at Home: Amazing New Gadgets and Services

Jim Miller, an advocate for older Americans, writes "Savvy Senior," a weekly information column syndicated in more than 400 newspapers nationwide. Based in Norman, Oklahoma, Miller also offers a free senior news service at *www.SavvySenior.org*.

Helping an aging parent or other loved one to remain independent and living in his/her own home has become much easier in recent years, thanks to a host of new or improved products and services. Some of the best…

IN-HOME ALERT DEVICES

One of the most common concerns is that an elderly loved one may fall and need help when no one is around. For this danger, a medical-alert device—also known as a *personal emergency response system* (PERS)—has long been the tool of choice. New versions of these devices overcome past shortcomings.

The devices, which rent for around $1 per day,* provide a wearable "SOS" button—typically in the form of a necklace pendant or bracelet—and a base station that connects to the home phone line. At the press of a button, your loved one could call and talk to a trained operator through the system's base station receiver, which works like a powerful speakerphone. (Two base stations often are used in large or two-story homes.) The operator will find out what's wrong and notify family members, a neighbor, friend or emergency services, as needed.

Concerns about the old versions of these devices include seniors falling and becoming disoriented and forgetting to activate the

*Prices subject to change.

device. Older devices also have range limitations and will work only if the senior is in or around the house.

To overcome some of these challenges, Philips, maker of the Lifeline, the most widely used home medical-alert service in the US, offers an Auto Alert option that has sensors built into the SOS button to detect falls. When triggered by these sensors, the device automatically can summon help without your loved one having to press a button. The Lifeline with Auto Alert generally costs $48 a month, and the standard medical alert service without Auto Alert runs $35 per month. (800-380-3111, *www.LifeLineSys.com*)

HOME MONITORS

A more sophisticated technology for keeping tabs on an elderly loved one at home is a monitoring system. These systems will let you know whether your loved one is waking up and going to bed on time, eating properly, showering and taking his/her medicine.

They work through small wireless sensors (not cameras) placed in key locations throughout the home. The sensors track movements and learn the person's daily activity patterns and routines. The system will notify you or other family members via text message, e-mail or phone if something out of the ordinary is happening.

For instance, if your loved one does not open the medicine cabinet at the usual time, it could mean that he/she forgot to take his medication...or if he went to the bathroom and didn't leave it, that could indicate a fall or other emergency.

You also can check up on your loved one's patterns anytime you want through the system's password-protected Web site. And for additional protection, most services offer SOS call buttons that can be worn or placed around the house.

One reliable company that offers these services is BeClose (866-574-1784, *www.BeClose. com*), whose system costs from $400 for three sensors to $500 for six, plus a service fee that ranges from $70 to $100 per month.

GrandCare Systems (262-338-6147, *www. GrandCare.com*) adds a social connectivity component to go along with the activity moni-

toring. It does this through a touch-screen computer that provides your loved one with easy access to Skype for video calls and to e-mail, photos, caller ID, games and brain exercises, as well as a calendar to keep up with appointments and events.

If your loved one does not want to use a computer, GrandCare can set up a dedicated channel on his television set so that he can see pictures, e-mails, calendar events, news, weather and more. The contents of the channel can be changed remotely by a caregiver through a Web site.

GrandCare Systems typically run between $950 and $1,500 for a one-bedroom apartment, with a monthly subscription fee of $30 to $50. Leasing options also are available.

OUTSIDE THE HOME

To deal with falls or health emergencies outside the home, there are a number of new mobile-alert products available that work anywhere. These pendant-style devices, which fit in the palm of your hand, work like cell phones with GPS tracking capabilities and can be carried in a purse, worn on a belt or attached to a key chain.

To call for help, your loved one pushes one button and an operator from the device's emergency-monitoring service is on the line to assist him. The devices allow your loved one to speak and listen to the operator through the pendant, and because of the GPS technology, the operator knows the exact location, which is critical in emergency situations. These alerts, however, do not have fall-detection sensors.

Top products in this category include the 5Star Urgent Response from GreatCall (800-733-6632, *www.GreatCall.com*) for $50 plus a $35 activation fee and a $15 monthly service charge...and MobileHelp (800-800-1710, *www. MobileHelpNow.com*), which offers a duo system that includes a mobile device, an indoor base station and pendant buttons for home use—$37 per month if paid a year in advance with no activation fee to $42 per month with a $100 activation fee.

MEDICATION MANAGEMENT

To help loved ones keep up with medication regimens, there's a wide variety of pillboxes, medication organizers, vibrating watches and beeping dispensers. To find these types of products, visit *www.EPill.com* (800-549-0095), where there are dozens to choose from. One popular option is the Cadex 12 Alarm Medication Reminder Watch for $100. It provides up to 12 daily alarms and displays a message of what medication to take at scheduled times throughout the day. And there is the monthly MedCenter System ($80), which comes with 31 color-coded pillboxes, each with four compartments for different times of the day and a four-alarm clock for reminders.

There also are a number of Web-based services that can notify your loved one when it's time to take a medication.

Examples: MyMedSchedule (908-234-1701, *www.MyMedSchedule.com*) and RememberIt-Now (925-388-6030, *www.RememberItNow.com*) offer free text-message and e-mail reminders. OnTimeRX (866-944-8966, *www.OnTimeRX.com*) provides phone call reminders in addition to text messages and e-mails for all types of scheduled activities, including daily medications, monthly refills, doctor appointments, wake-up calls and other events. These charge between $10 and $30 per month depending on how many reminders you need.

Another option is CARE Call Reassurance (602-265-5968, extension 7, *www.Call-Reassurance.com*), which provides automated call reminders to your loved one's phone. If he fails to answer or acknowledge a call, the service will contact a family member or a designated caregiver via phone, e-mail or text message. The cost is $15 per month if paid in advance for a year.

If your loved one needs a more comprehensive medication-management system, consider the MedMinder Automated Pill Dispenser (888-633-6463, *www.MedMinder.com*). This is a computerized pillbox that flashes when it's time for your loved one to take his medication and beeps or calls his phone with an automated reminder if he forgets. It will even alert him if he takes the wrong pill.

This device also can be set up to call, e-mail or text a family member and caregiver if the loved one misses a dose, takes the wrong

medication or doesn't refill the dispenser. The MedMinder rents for $40 per month.

Another good medication dispensing system is the Philips Medication Dispensing Service (888-632-3261, *www.ManageMyPills.com*), a countertop appliance that dispenses medicine on schedule, provides verbal reminders and notifies caregivers if the pills aren't taken. Monthly rental and monitoring fees for the Philips service run $75 with an $85 installation fee.

Smart Way to Save for Retirement Medical Costs

The medical expenses for 65-year-olds retiring in 2012 were about $240,000 even without nursing-home care. Health-care cost estimates have been rising by an average of 6% a year since 2002 for people relying on traditional Medicare. Health care is likely to be among most people's biggest expenses in retirement—and people who rely on Social Security for their retirement will find almost 61% of their monthly checks going to health care by 2027.

What to do: If you haven't yet retired, look into a "high-deductible" health insurance policy with a *Health Savings Account* (HSA)—this may allow you to save up pretax money now to use for health expenses in retirement.

Fidelity Investments' annual calculation of retiree health-care costs, reported online at *www.Fidelity.com*.

Planning End-of-Life Care

Choose a decision-maker for your end-of-life care, such as a spouse, child or best friend. Decide what matters most to you—living as long as possible…being comfortable at the end of life…being able to communicate with others…or something else. Discuss whether the decision-maker should have flexibility or should follow your instructions no matter what. Tell others of your wishes, including family members, doctors and friends.

Recommendations from the Prepare program, designed to help people prepare for medical decision-making. *www.PrepareforYourCare.org*

Sell Your Home and See the World!

The Martins—Lynne, age 72, and Tim, 67—a retired couple who, for the past two years, have traveled the world without a fixed home. They run the Web site HomeFreeAdventures.com. Lynne's book about full-time travel in retirement is due out from Source Books in spring 2014.

How would you like to make the world your retirement home? Lynne and Tim Martin did just that. Two years ago, they sold their home in California, and they have been traveling the world ever since.

The Martins' advice…

MAKING THE MONEY WORK

Our financial manager sends us $6,000 per month generated by our investments, but we also have Social Security and a small pension. People certainly could live on less than we do. Accommodations are a good place to cut back—the cost of rentals overseas varies considerably with size, season, location and amenities.

●**Housing.** Most tourists stay in pricey hotels and visit areas for only a week or two. We rent furnished apartments and stay a minimum of one month in each location, usually longer. That greatly lowers our housing and travel costs and lets us get a far better feel for the area before we move on.

In California, our total housing expenses added up to around $3,600 a month, including the mortgage, home-maintenance bills, utility bills, homeowner's insurance, taxes and so forth. On the road, our rentals typically cost $1,500 to $2,500 per month and include utilities and Internet service. Those rental prices are modest in part because we usually rent one- or two-bedroom apartments, not large homes. With just the two of us and few personal possessions, that's sufficient space.

Renting tips: We've had success using the rental-listing sites VRBO.com and HomeAway.com. These sites seem to do a good job vetting their property owners. *Also…*

●We arrange rentals at least several months in advance—even longer for popular travel destinations such as Paris. The best deals are long gone by the time the rental date approaches.

●We favor properties whose owners live nearby. That makes it much easier to solve any problems that arise.

●We avoid properties with negative feedback on the rental Web site from prior renters.

●We use the Internet—and conversations with other travelers we meet—to vet neighborhoods before renting there. Google Maps can supply a look at the neighborhood, and Googling the name of the neighborhood can provide a sense of what others think about it.

●**Destinations.** We try not to spend too much time in pricey cities such as London and Paris. When we do visit an expensive location, we balance our budget by staying some place much more affordable next, such as Portugal, Mexico or Turkey. We often can keep our spending to $5,000 a month in such places.

●**Dining.** We try not to eat more than three or four meals per week in restaurants. Furnished rental apartments include kitchens, cookware, dishes and utensils, so we easily can cook for ourselves. One of the first things we do when we arrive in a new rental is find a nearby grocery store—the sooner we get groceries into the apartment, the lower our temptation to eat out. We also look for local farmers' markets—great for fresh and affordable ingredients and fun to visit, too.

●**Transportation within a country.** We usually choose properties near a public transit system. Monthly public transit passes are quite affordable in most cities, and there often is a senior discount. In many months, our transportation expenses are comparable to, or even below, the $700 we previously paid each month to own and insure two cars in California.

●**Transportation to and from countries.** We take planes and trains and, when it's practical, rent cars. We buy almost everything with a credit card to rack up mileage points.

We also use repositioning cruises. These are voyages that cruise lines schedule primarily to move a ship from one part of the world to another. They can be an economical and enjoyable way to travel between continents. You can find repositioning cruises listed on RepositioningCruises.com or on the cruise lines' own Web sites.

Example: We recently paid $2,500 for a nice cabin on an 18-day cruise from Miami, Florida, to Venice, Italy. That is a great deal considering that in addition to passage for two to Europe, we got all of our food, housing and entertainment for more than half a month.

LIVING WITH LESS STUFF

When we decided to travel full-time, we put some of our possessions in storage, gave some to our kids and got rid of the rest. One of our daughters receives the mail, which has dwindled to almost nothing.

We each have a 30-inch rolling duffel bag and a carry-on bag. We initially worried that living with limited possessions would be a challenge. In fact, it has been liberating and wonderful. Our lives have become less about our stuff and more about the things we do, the places we visit and—above all—the people we meet. Traveling light does mean that we have to wash and rewear relatively few garments over and over again, but that's not a great inconvenience.

One thing we do travel with in abundance is electronics. *We each have…*

•**A laptop computer.** These allow us to pay our bills online, though we have few bills since we eliminated home ownership. We also use our computers to stay in touch with friends and family via e-mail and Skype. And we can watch movies and TV shows over the Internet when we wish to spend an evening in.

Helpful: We travel with an HDMI cable so that we can connect our laptops to TVs to watch movies and shows on full-sized screens. We also travel with a portable speaker so that we have decent sound quality when our only option is to watch shows or movies on our laptop screens.

•**A smartphone.** These serve as our phones only when we're in the US. Overseas we use them to run apps, but it can be difficult and expensive to make a US cell phone work abroad. It's usually cheaper and easier to purchase inexpensive local cell phones when we arrive in a region and load minutes onto them.

•**An E-reader.** E-readers allow us to travel with an entire library of books without carrying much weight.

FRIENDS AND FAMILY

Skype and e-mail aren't our only options for keeping in contact with friends and family. When we want to reconnect with our old life, we simply rent a furnished apartment back in our former hometown. We recently spent two months there.

And once your friends and family realize how much fun you're having traveling the world, don't be surprised if they want to join you on occasion. One of our daughters visited us in Italy last year, and another is meeting up with us later this year in Paris. She's even bringing along one of our grandkids.

HEALTH MATTERS

Health care can be a concern for full-time travelers. Living on the road means that you can't see your regular doctor when you're sick …and Medicare doesn't cover medical care obtained outside the US.

We pay around $400 a month for a high-deductible international insurance policy that provides coverage for foreign medical emergencies and will evacuate us back to the US for medical care if necessary. Companies offering policies such as these include Seven Corners (*www.SevenCorners.com*) and Allianz (*www.AllianzWorldwideCare.com*), among others.

We're fortunate to be very healthy. We take few medications, and all the prescriptions we do use, we take along with us. We schedule checkups with our regular doctors and dentists when we return to California. If we become ill in another part of the world, we ask the owner of the property we're renting for a doctor recommendation or we ask other expats or locals we've met in the area.

In our experience, very good medical care is available around much of the world, and it often costs substantially less than in the US.

13

Travel Time

Going It Alone…and *Loving It*: Wonderful Tours for Solo Travelers

Today more and more people are traveling by themselves. Either they do not have a partner…or their partner has different interests—and friends and family aren't available to go along. Fortunately, there are so many wonderful opportunities for single travel. You can have a great time in a group or on your own. *Here's how…*

BIKING, WALKING AND MORE

Many travel companies offer trips focused on an activity such as cycling and walking. In general, these are not created as "singles" trips—though some are (see below)—but activity trips tend to attract single people because they provide a focus and typically lots of structure, so you're rarely alone. Also, the groups usually are small, so everyone winds up feeling like "family" quite quickly. There often is a single supplement for solo travelers (a slightly higher price for not sharing a room), but some companies can pair individuals up as roommates. Before making a reservation, ask about this. The tour company also may be able to give you an idea of how many singles are signed up at that time.

The prices quoted below include any single supplement and are subject to change. (*Note*: These prices do not include transportation to and from the destinations—visit Web sites for details on other costs covered.)

Examples…

•**Cycling trips.** The biking tour company Backroads offers Singles + Solos Trips (no

Susan Farewell, a travel journalist and founder of Farewell Travels LLC, a travel concierge that provides ideas, recommendations and referrals for worldwide travel. Based in Westport, Connecticut, she advises singles, couples and families on which travel experiences are right for them. *www.FarewellTravels.com*

couples allowed) in the US, Canada, Europe, Latin America, Asia and the Pacific. One tempting itinerary takes you through France's Loire Valley, where you will see fabulous châteaux and visit landmarks such as Clos Lucé, Leonardo da Vinci's last residence. Cost for the six-day trip for single occupancy is about $3,848 ($3,298 for double occupancy). *www. Backroads.com/award-winning-tours/solo-singles*

Some companies combine cycling with culinary explorations of the regions. Chef-owned and run ItaliaOutdoors Food and Wine organizes trips to Italy for groups of eight that include cycling (all fitness levels), wine tastings, cooking classes and group dinners, so singles aren't left on their own. At dinner, the meals include wine, so individual travelers do not have to purchase their own bottles, which can be expensive as well as wasteful. A seven-day bike-and-wine holiday in northeast Italy explores the alpine landscape of Trentino-Alto Adige and the history-rich Veneto region. Cost for single travelers is about $4,495 ($3,895 double occupancy). *www.Italia OutdoorsFood andWine.com*

• **Walking vacations.** One of the best ways to see a country is on foot. UK-based Wayfarers offers walking tours in a variety of countries and regions including the British Isles, Germany, Croatia, South Africa and Patagonia. In the UK alone, you can walk from one tiny and tidy stone village to the next in The Cotswolds…explore the mountains, valleys and beach of Snowdonia in Wales…or walk coast to coast, from the Lake District through Yorkshire to Whitby on the North Sea, taking in hills, dales, lakes and moorlands. These trips typically attract singles. *Sample cost:* The Cotswolds and Oxford, six nights for singles, $4,530 (or $3,995 for double occupancy)—the company will try to pair travelers up in rooms, but it's not guaranteed. *www.TheWayfarers.com*

• **Travel photography tours.** Having a common focus is what Photo Quest Adventures is all about. This company tends to attract mostly individual travelers who want to visit fabulous foreign destinations and have something to show for it. Three trips planned

in 2014 include Venice Carnival, China Sister Meal Festival and Falkland Islands. The prices for single travelers range from $6,450 ($4,800 double occupancy) to $10,050 ($8,400 double occupancy). *www.PhotoQuestAdventures.com*

SPECIAL INTERESTS

Some companies organize individual visits that enable solo travelers to become a part of a local community. Prices for the following vary depending on specific arrangements made. Examples…

• **For music lovers.** Insider's View of Tuscany, which is owned and operated by the owners of the Daniel Ferro Vocal Program (where young artists work on their craft in Tuscany), designs visits that invite travelers to join the music community in the Chianti region of Tuscany in July and August. For example, a seven-night trip (including lodging, breakfast daily, five lunches, VIP seating at weekly concerts and receptions, assistance with sightseeing, master class observation and Italian language studies) starts at $1,999 for single travelers. *www.InsidersViewofTuscany.com*

• **Living with families in India.** One of the most authentic experiences to have in India is to stay with a local family. You can get true insider tips on the city's best markets, restaurants and things to do from those who live there. Indian HomeStays can arrange for such visits in much of India. A home stay in a good safe locality in Delhi costs about $60 a night, including a full breakfast. The family often will accommodate additional meal requests for $6.00 per person and arrange for airport or railroad pick-up/drop-off for around $20. *www.IndianHomeStays.org*

• **Exploring Morocco solo.** Travel Exploration Morocco customizes individual visits as well as group tours. It can design a trip for a solo traveler wanting to see the country on his/her own that includes cooking workshops, pottery making, yoga, hiking and ziplining in the Atlas Mountains. Contact the company for prices. *www.Travel-Exploration.com*

SOLO SAVINGS

Increasingly, travel companies are waiving single supplement fees (or reducing them).

Examples…

• **Abercrombie & Kent waives the single supplement**—or reduces it by as much as 75%—on its Solo Savings departures, which include popular destinations such as Egypt, Turkey, Kenya and Tanzania. *www.Abercrombie Kent.com/discover/solo-travel*

• **Tauck** has dropped the single supplement for certain cabins on its 2013 and 2014 European river cruises. *www.Tauck.com*

WOMEN-ONLY TRIPS

• **WanderTours offers a variety of trips for women only.** Some examples include a 12-day Culture and Festival Tour of Bhutan, at the eastern end of the Himalayas, starting at about $4,295 per person…and an 18-day itinerary in Vietnam and Cambodia, starting at $4,718 per person. *www.WanderTours.com*

The Best Outdoor Markets in Europe: Shop Like the Locals and Soak Up the Culture

Marjorie R. Williams, coauthor and photographer of the new second edition of *Markets of Paris* (The Little Bookroom). *www.MarjorieRWilliams.com*

Andrew Kershman, managing director of London's Metro Publications Ltd. He is author of *The London Market Guide* (Metro Publications). *www.MetroPublications.com*

Europe's outdoor markets are not just places to shop for antiques, art, souvenirs and great food at reasonable prices. For American visitors to Europe, they also are a memorable way to explore a foreign country's culture.

Among the markets that offer the best products and atmosphere…

PARIS
Marjorie R. Williams,
coauthor, *Markets of Paris*

Best for food: Le Marché Raspail is a standard farmers' market on Tuesday and Friday, but on Sunday, it becomes Le Marché Biologique Raspail, one of the city's best organic food markets. On that day, you'll find wonderful artisan cheeses, distinctive breads, delicious pastries and organically produced meats and produce, as well as freshly prepared foods. Try the wonderful potato-onion pancakes from Les Gallatins…paella from Interface 3000…and baked goods from the Valérie Debiais-Healey's stand. Or just sip hot chocolate or tea from Buvette du Marché.

Details: On boulevard Raspail, between rue du Cherche-Midi and rue de Rennes in the sixth arrondissement. Tuesday and Friday 7 to 2:30, Sunday 7 to 3.

Best for atmosphere: Rue Mouffetard offers delicious breads, cheeses, fruits and more, but it truly stands out as the perfect place to soak up Parisian ambiance. The market dates back to 1350, and the street's cobblestones and centuries-old buildings give it a decidedly medieval character. Try the rotisserie chicken from Boucherie Saint-Médard for your picnic lunch, or linger over a glass of wine at Cave la Bourgogne.

Details: On rue Mouffetard, between rue Calvin and rue Edouard Quénu in the Latin Quarter. Tuesday to Saturday 10 to 6, Sunday 10 to 12.

Best flea market: Le Marché aux Puces de la Porte de Vanves. There are treasures buried among the bric-a-brac—Parisian antiques dealers buy merchandise here. Even if you don't find a masterpiece, vintage French items can make distinctive and affordable souvenirs and home décor pieces.

Details: On avenue Marc Sangnier and avenue Georges-Lafenestre in the 14th arrondissement. Saturday and Sunday 7 to 6.

Best for antiques: Le Marché aux Puces de Saint-Ouen, often called Les Puces Clignancourt, officially is a flea market, but it has evolved into a sprawling series of upscale antiques markets. It is a great place to find distinctive home décor such as vintage lithographs and antique armchairs that you could ship home. There are hundreds of vendors—too many to see in one day.

Details: Clignancourt sprawls across several blocks, but many of the best markets are off the rue des Rosiers. Monday 11 to 5, Saturday 9 to 6, Sunday 10 to 6.

Best for art: **Le Marché de la Création Edgar Quinet** offers works from more than 100 undiscovered artists. Quality is uneven, but you will find plenty of beautiful works here, many for less than $100. I bought some very nice watercolors of Parisian scenes for less than $50 apiece. I also got to chat with the artist.

Details: Boulevard Edgar Quinet, between rue Huyghens and rue du Départ. Sunday 10 to 7.

LONDON
Andrew Kershman,
author, *The London Market Guide*

Best for food: **Borough Market** gives you the chance to sample exceptional British and international produce, baked goods, cheese, wine and more. It also is a great place to talk food—many stalls are manned by the skilled food producers themselves. There are plenty of delicious foods to eat on the go as well, such as the chorizo sandwich from the stall outside Tapas Brindisa...or the pork belly sandwich from Roast restaurant.

Details: This market spans several blocks near Cathedral Street and Middle Row in Borough. Thursday 11 to 5, Friday 12 to 6, Saturday 8 to 5. *www.BoroughMarket.org.uk*

Also: At Covent Garden Market's Real Food Market, there are delicious artisanal cheeses, meats and breads for a picnic or pastries and cakes for dessert.

Details: Located in the East Piazza of Covent Garden, close to the Royal Opera House. Thursday 11 to 7.

Best for antiques: **Portobello Market** actually is several street markets rolled into one along a three-mile stretch of road—and tourists unfamiliar with Portobello Market sometimes give up before they reach the world-class antiques market at the southern end, which is open only on Saturday, 8:30 to 5. The northern end is a somewhat scruffy flea market. Farther south is a vintage clothing market, fol-

lowed by a food market. Arrive before 10 am to avoid the crowds.

Details: The antiques section of the market is on Portobello Road, between Chepstow Villas and Elgin Crescent in Notting Hill. *www. PortobelloRoad.co.uk*

Best for exploring London's ethnic cultures: **Brixton Market** offers samples of authentic African and Caribbean foods as well as products for purchase.

Details: Electric Avenue, Pope's Road and Brixton Station Road, Brixton. Monday, Tuesday, Thursday, Friday and Saturday 8 to 6. Wednesday 8 to 3. *http://BrixtonMarket.net*

Also: Ridley Road Market provides a wide range of interesting Indian, African, Caribbean and Mediterranean foods, and plenty of general merchandise, too. It has a wonderfully energetic atmosphere.

Details: Ridley Road in Dalston. Monday through Thursday 6 to 6, Friday and Saturday 6 to 7.

More Great European Markets from Amsterdam to Rome

Patricia Schultz, a New York City–based travel journalist with more than 25 years of experience. She is author of the new second edition of *1,000 Places to See Before You Die* (Workman). *www.1000Places.com*

There are great outdoor markets throughout Europe excelling in items ranging from herring to Soviet-era memorabilia.

Amsterdam: **Albert Cuyp Market** is the city's oldest, largest and most diverse. You can find everything from umbrellas to underwear here, though it's best-known for food vendors. When the local herring is in season from mid-May to mid-July, this is the perfect place to taste it prepared in countless ways.

Details: On Albert Cuypstraat, between Ferdinand Bolstraat and Van Woustraat in the

De Pijp area of the Oud-Zuid district. Monday through Saturday 9 to 5.

Berlin: **Flohmarkt am Mauerpark,** a flea market, is a great place to search for distinctive Soviet-era memorabilia and vintage fashion items, in addition to the usual knick-knacks and housewares. The food stalls are quite good, too—have a sausage for lunch, then a waffle covered in applesauce or jelly for dessert. You can see the remnants of the Berlin Wall in the adjoining park.

Details: At Bernauer Strasse 63-64, Berlin Mitte. Sunday 8 to 6.

Madrid: **El Rastro** is perhaps the largest flea market in Europe, with more than 3,000 vendors. Many sell made-in-China junk, but there are plenty of interesting items, too. On Calle San Cayetano, you'll find lots of art…and Plaza de Cascorro specializes in clothing. If you get hungry, try the spicy stewed snails at El Rastro's Los Caracoles bar or one of the many excellent tapas bars in nearby Plaza de la Cabada and the surrounding streets.

Details: El Rastro sprawls across a large area surrounding Plaza de Cascorro and Ribera de Cutidores in central Madrid. Sundays and public holidays 7 to 3. *www.ElRastro.org*

Munich: **Viktualienmarkt** is the city's most beloved food market, with more than 140 stalls and vendors. The aroma of grilled sausages fills the air of the nearly 200-year-old market. Fresh pretzels, artisanal cheeses and fresh produce abound as well. Don't miss the chestnut-tree-shaded beer garden.

Details: At Viktualienmarkt 6, adjacent to the Marienplatz. Monday through Friday 10 to 6, Saturday 10 to 3.

Rome: **Campo de' Fiori** is the best and oldest of Rome's outdoor markets. Find fresh produce and meats, or take in the language and character of Rome as merchants and buyers haggle over prices. Interesting shops and restaurants line the square—try the white sauceless pizza (pizza bianca) at Antico Forno.

Details: Located in the Piazza di Campo de' Fiori in Old Rome. Monday through Saturday 7 to 1.

3 Ways to Save on… Spring Break for Grown-Ups

Pauline Frommer, a nationally syndicated newspaper columnist and radio talk show host. She is a member of the Frommer guidebook family and a two-time winner of the North American Travel Journalists Association's Guidebook of the Year award. *www.Frommers.com/pauline*

Does any vacation period have a more salacious reputation than spring break? *But you don't have to "go wild" to enjoy a great—and affordable—getaway…*

1. Avoid the students. March is one of the most popular times for schools to schedule their spring breaks.

If you're not tied to a school's schedule, you will want to travel either in February (except over President's Day weekend, when prices are sky-high) or in April. If you are tied to a school schedule, avoid Cancun (Mexico), Panama City (Florida), Punta Cana (Dominican Republic), South Padre Island (Texas), Nassau (Bahamas) and Las Vegas.

2. Time your airfare purchase. A study by the Airlines Reporting Corporation (the organization that acts as middleman between travel agents and airlines) found that people who purchase airline tickets six weeks before their trips generally pay the least amount of money. Booking on a Tuesday or Wednesday also is a good strategy, as fare sales tend to be announced late in the day on Mondays and matched by the other carriers on Tuesdays.

3. Consider Europe or Central America. Airfares to Europe stay at their winter lows through March, as do hotel prices. Airfares to Central America are decent year-round, and the rate of exchange generally favors the dollar.

More from Pauline Frommer...

3 Ways to Save on... Cruises

With nightly rates dropping to as little as $60 per person,* booking an economical cruise would seem to be as simple as stuffing yourself at the onboard dinner buffet. But many cruisers, initially pulled in by low fares, end up spending far more than expected on "extras." *The following three tips can keep your cruising budget afloat...*

1. Compare sellers. Though the base price for cruising won't change that much, those travel agencies that sell a number of cruises are rewarded by the cruise lines with extra perks for their customers. Shop around and see which sellers will be willing to "gift" you with free cabin upgrades, onboard ship credits (of $100 to $200), a waiving of gratuities and more. Start with large companies such as CruisesOnly.com...VacationsToGo.com...and Cruises.com.

2. Cruise on the fringe. Choose the sailings that occur on the fringes of the regular season, say, Alaska or the Mediterranean in May or September...or the Caribbean during hurricane season. That last suggestion isn't as crazy as it sounds—the chances of being in the Caribbean during a storm are quite low.

3. Book your own excursions. On average, vacationers spend an additional 25% of the cost of the cruise once on board the ship and up to 75% more if they frequent the spa or casino! So set a budget, and stick to it. Shore excursions are the priciest onboard purchases, so book your own in advance through such companies as CruisingExcursions.com or Viator.com.

*Prices subject to change.

Also from Pauline Frommer...

3 Ways to Save on... Last-Minute Travel

Sometimes it pays to procrastinate. You can get some great last-minute travel deals...

1. Follow the deals. Never considered Iceland, but the price is superb? Why not! Three days in Vegas for a song? Doesn't matter that you don't gamble, really! For cruises leaving within 90 days, try *www.VacationsToGo.com.* Air/hotel packages at the last minute can be found through all the major companies (Priceline, Expedia, etc.), as well as specialists such as LastMinute.com.

2. Get Tweet bargains. Twitter has become the best source for last-minute airfares. Instead of losing a hefty commission fee to third-party Web sites (such as Orbitz or Travelocity), the airlines post "flash sales" on Twitter to move unsold seats through their own Web sites. The most prominent tweeter is @JetBlueCheeps, which posts sales for the coming weekend. @VirginAmerica and @AllegiantAir also are excellent sources, though even biggies such as American Airlines and Delta will tweet flash sales occasionally.

3. Go for this app. One hotel app (available for smartphones and tablets) tends to beat the pants off the competition. Called Hotel Tonight, it can be used only starting at noon on the day of travel and for 55 American cities (plus a handful in Canada, the UK, Holland and Ireland). It finds the cheapest rates three out of four times (at some very cushy properties), prices that are as much as 70% off the lowest rate.

Example: A $249 room at a Houston hotel recently went for $99, for a savings of $150.

How to Fly for Free

Airlines typically give passengers bumped from flights vouchers for $200 to $800, so it may pay to be bumped.

If your schedule is flexible and you want to increase your odds of being bumped: Travel at peak times...book as many connections as possible to raise the chance of being bumped somewhere along the line...check the seat map before booking so you can choose a flight that is almost full...arrive at the gate early and tell the person at the check in counter that you are available to be bumped…and take only a carry-on bag so your luggage does not have to be pulled from the plane.

Helpful: Voucher amounts often can be negotiated.

Scott Ford, a traveler who used vouchers to visit 400 cities in one year after being laid off and unable to find a job, quoted online at DailyFinance.com.

Airline Miles Can Be Easily Stolen

Thieves send faxes or e-mails using legitimate airline logos, saying people have won round-trip tickets that they can claim by clicking through to a Web site. The site asks personal questions, which the scammers use to commit identity theft, steal the airline miles and sometimes download malware to a victim's computer. One couple found that 175,000 miles in their United Airlines account had been stripped down to 12,000.

What to do: If in doubt about a supposed offer, call the airline or go to its Web site. Type in the Web address—do not click on one contained in an e-mail.

MarketWatch.com

Cash for Frequent-Flier Miles

Instead of using miles for flights or to buy items at airline "shopping malls," you can convert miles from some airlines into "virtual cash" that will be deposited into your PayPal account for purchases at online retailers. You also can move the cash into a PayPal-linked bank account. So far, American Airlines, US Airways and Aeroplan offer the service, using mileage manager Points.com to convert the miles. United Continental is expected to launch a program soon.

Caution: Converted miles may be worth less in virtual cash than when you use the miles to book flights.

SmartMoney.com

Few Airlines Now Offer Bereavement Fares

Airlines that still provide these special fares for those who need to travel, often at the last minute, because of a death in the family, may base them on seat availability, length of stay, destination and other factors. The fares may not be the cheapest available despite the discounts. Requirements for the airfares vary widely.

Airlines that offer some type of bereavement fare: Air Canada, Air France, American, Delta, Lufthansa and United.

These fares are not available on AirTran, Alaskan, Allegiant, El Al, Frontier, Hawaiian, JetBlue, KLM, Southwest, Spirit, US Airways and Virgin Atlantic.

What to do: Call each airline for details and to book bereavement tickets—they usually cannot be purchased online.

Bankrate.com

For Families Flying with Small Children…

United no longer permits families with small children to board early. American recommends that families pay $10 for "Group 1" boarding* but says that it will allow people with small children to board after first-class passengers. US Airways lets families board only after its "Zone 2," and Southwest allows family boarding after its "A group." Consider Alaska, Delta and JetBlue—all still allow families with small children to board early.

DailyFinance.com

*Price subject to change.

If You're a Large-Sized Passenger...

United passengers must show that they can put down the armrests and have them stay down—if this is not possible, the passenger must buy a second seat. Delta has no specific policy but may ask a larger passenger to change seats or wait for a later flight with available seats. Southwest asks passengers who do not fit in the 17 inches between armrests to buy a second seat prior to travel or risk having to wait for a later flight. Passengers who book the second seat on a flight that is not full can get a refund. American asks larger passengers to handle seating needs when booking their flight—booking two adjacent seats in advance will get the passenger the same rate for each seat. US Airways says it will offer extra space to passengers who require it, although they may be asked to wait for a flight with available seats.

AirfareWatchdog.com

Protect Your Checked Luggage

Photograph the contents of your luggage, and keep an itemized list in a safe place. Also, put an itinerary with contact information and your e-mail address in a visible place inside the bag. And remove tags from previous trips as well as straps or lock wheels that could cause the bag to get stuck on a conveyor belt. Finally, open your luggage shortly after landing to be sure that everything is there. If anything is missing, submit a claim as soon as possible with the airline and your insurance company.

Condé Nast Traveler. www.CNTraveler.com

Airport Security Less Rigid for Some Travelers

The Transportation Security Administration (TSA) has launched *PreCheck*—a trusted traveler pilot program. PreCheck allows travelers registered with the US Customs and Border Protection Agency's Trusted Traveler program and specially selected Delta, United, US Airways, American, Virgin America, Hawaiian Airlines and Alaska Airlines frequent-fliers* to pass through security checkpoints at 40 airports possibly without having to take off their shoes, belt and light outerwear. PreCheck also may allow these travelers to leave their laptops inside their carry-ons.

Note: Starting in 2015, the TSA plans to allow travelers to keep their shoes on, but you will have to step onto a shoe-scanning mat.

Travel + Leisure. www.TravelandLeisure.com

*As of mid-August 2013.

Flying Makes Food Taste Bland

The combination of dry cabin air and the change in air pressure at cruising altitude numbs one-third of a traveler's taste buds and reduces the sensitivity of his/her nose—smell is a big component of taste. To try to counteract these physical changes, the airlines salt and spice food heavily and serve full-bodied wines instead of delicate ones, which would taste like juice. Major carriers now are working with well-known chefs to try to develop more appetizing in-flight meals.

The New York Times. www.NYTimes.com

Afraid of Flying? Natural Help

There are alternatives to drugs to reduce anxiety about flying.

Try one-half teaspoon of baking soda in six ounces of warm water. This helps regulate pH levels and, for many people, quickly reduces anxiety.

Also helpful: Supplements that contain a mixture of *valerian* and *hops*, which can be found at health-food stores.

If these do not work, go to a naturopathic doctor (ND) and ask him/her to create a personalized tincture containing multiple extracts plus appropriate homeopathics.

Andrew L. Rubman, ND, founder and director of the Southbury Clinic for Traditional Medicine, Southbury, Connecticut. *www.SouthburyClinic.com*

Don't Get on That Plane! Warning from a Former Inspector General

Mary F. Schiavo, who was inspector general of the US Department of Transportation from 1990 to 1996. She is a licensed pilot, former McConnell Aviation Chair of the department of aviation at The Ohio State University and currently heads the aviation litigation team for Motley Rice, a law firm based in Mount Pleasant, South Carolina.

It may take a while before it makes sense for you to fly on one of the new Boeing 787 Dreamliners, says Mary F. Schiavo, former inspector general of the US Transportation Department.

In January 2013, the Federal Aviation Administration (FAA) told United to ground its six new 787s after a lithium-ion battery on a parked Japan Airlines 787 caught fire and a battery problem set off a smoke alarm on an All Nippon Airways 787, which then made an emergency landing.

The technologically innovative 787 is the first commercial passenger jet to be powered in part by lithium-ion batteries—a type of battery prone to overheating when overcharged or rapidly discharged. These type of batteries can burn at very high temperatures, emit flammable gases or explode. Notably, Cessna once attempted to use lithium-ion batteries on a private jet, and it, too, experienced a fire in late 2011.

The Dreamliners were allowed to return to service in April 2013 after Boeing engineered a solution that satisfied the US aviation authorities. But a fire and a "technical issue" aboard two Dreamliners in July 2013 raised new safety concerns.

There are two reasons why it's best to avoid Dreamliners for a while…

•**Safety.** Getting to the root of these problems might be tricky.

In addition to issues with lithium-ion batteries, there have been unrelated issues involving fuel leaks and a cracked windshield, and the list of problems will only grow. New jets go through a shakeout period, and the 787 is so cutting-edge new in many ways (including a body largely composed of carbon-fiber reinforced plastic, which does not show cracks or fatigue as readily as traditional metal) that the odds of additional problems are particularly high.

•**Scheduling.** These inevitable glitches and issues will cause delays, cancellations and perhaps even emergency landings—all of which will create major headaches for travelers.

Still, based on Boeing's history with new aircraft introductions, it's probable that in late 2014 or 2015 travelers will be able to fly on the 787 without major safety or scheduling concerns. The 787 likely isn't a bad plane, just a new and highly complex one going through unavoidable growing pains. Boeing experienced similar problems when it introduced its 777 in the mid-1990s but worked out the bugs in about 18 to 24 months.

It's worth noting that the FAA did not withdraw the 787's Airworthiness Certificate when it grounded the jet…it merely issued a directive stating that the plane should not be used for commercial flights until this battery issue was fixed to the FAA's satisfaction.

In the meantime, airline passengers should be aware that they have no legal right to decline to fly on a particular type of jet. If you buy a ticket on a 777 but the airline later substitutes a 787, you can't insist on switching planes.

Right now, United is the only US airline with 787s. Foreign airlines include Air India, Qatar Airways, Ethiopian Airlines, Chile's LAN Airlines and LOT Polish Airlines in addition to the Japanese airlines.

Turbulence Won't Cause Your Plane to Crash!

John A. Greaves, a licensed pilot with more than 40 years of flying experience and a former captain of commercial jet planes. He now is a litigation attorney representing airline accident victims at the law firm Baum, Hedlund, Aristei & Goldman, PC, in Los Angeles. *www.BaumHedlundLaw.com*

You are 30,000 feet up in the air inside a plane that starts shaking violently. Your first thought—could it break in half? Rest assured, turbulence will not pull the plane apart or cause it to plunge. Each year, pilots report about 70,000 cases of turbulence over the US. These incidents usually are caused when a plane passes through shifting air currents that are strong enough to push the craft up or down just a few feet or as much as 100 feet.

During episodes of strong turbulence, you could experience minor bumps that spill your drink or powerful jolts and lurches or even feelings of being in free fall. Among US flights, about 60 midair injuries a year are caused by turbulence, two-thirds of them involving flight attendants.

But the plane itself can handle the turbulence. The wings and tail of a typical commercial aircraft are designed to withstand load forces of up to about 3.5 Gs, about 1.5 times the maximum load they likely will ever face in flight. As a result, the only way that turbulence in midair could cause catastrophic structural damage on a passenger jet is through gross pilot error.

Example: A pilot trying to fight the turbulence and overcompensating.

This possibly could happen during a thunderstorm (where turbulence typically is most severe) or when flying over a mountainous region (where it is most unpredictable because of the air passing over and around varying terrains). However, pilots are trained to handle these situations and to maintain lower speeds at these times because it's easier to lose control and sustain damage if the plane is going very fast.

The only other time a crash occurs due to turbulence is during takeoff or landing when one plane follows another too closely and gets caught up in its airflow—but this, too, is very rare.

Self-defense: If you're a nervous flier, try to schedule your flight in the morning when thunderstorms are less likely…and don't sit in the back of the plane, where turbulence often is roughest.

Is It Safe to Fly After a Heart Attack?

There are no general guidelines about flying after a stroke or heart attack, but keep in mind that modern jet aircraft are pressurized to the equivalent of 8,000 feet—an altitude at which even normally healthy individuals have reduced blood oxygen levels and increased heart rate. Talk to your doctor about whether this may be a factor for you—it could be for some patients, especially on long flights.

Also: Consider where you plan to go. If advanced health-care services are not available at your destination, you may have difficulty obtaining care if it becomes necessary.

Steven E. Nissen, MD, chairman, department of cardiovascular medicine, Cleveland Clinic Foundation, and professor of medicine, Cleveland Clinic Lerner School of Medicine, Case Western Reserve University.

Blood-Clot Risk Is No Higher in Economy Class

Travelers' blood clots have been called *economy-class syndrome* because of the belief that they are related to tight seating—but the real risk comes from not getting up and moving during long flights. Flights lasting more than six hours produce the greatest risk for blood clots called *deep vein thrombosis*, and people in window seats have somewhat higher risk because they are less likely to move around the cabin. Most people who develop the clots have risk factors such as obesity, older age or recent surgery.

The American College of Chest Physicians' *Antithrombotic Therapy and Prevention of Thrombosis Guidelines*.

Air Travel May Cause IBD Flare-Ups

Air travel may cause *inflammatory bowel disease* (IBD) symptoms to flare. Airline cabins are pressurized to 8,000 feet—which means that plane passengers get about 25% less oxygen than people at sea level. The lower oxygen level can cause the body to produce higher levels of molecules that activate inflammatory pathways, resulting in a recurrence of IBD symptoms.

Study of 103 patients by researchers at Triemli Hospital, Zurich, Switzerland, reported at a recent Digestive Disease Week conference.

Rental Car Traps

Rental car firms often charge for "loss of use" of a damaged vehicle. Although personal auto insurance and/or credit card insurance may cover accidents, they may not cover loss of use—the rental firm's lost income while the car is being repaired. Avis, Budget and Hertz charge for loss of use, which can run hundreds of dollars unless you opt for the rental firm's insurance.

Eight states require insurers to cover loss of use: Alaska, Connecticut, Louisiana, Minnesota, New York, North Dakota, Rhode Island and Texas.

Jeremy Acevedo, an analyst at Edmunds.com, Los Angeles, a Web site that provides a variety of auto industry information.

Pitfalls of Car Rental Insurance in Europe

Credit card coverage typically is good for 30 to 45 consecutive days, depending on the card that is used. However, many cards do not insure certain classes of vehicles, such as pickups and cars valued at more than $50,000. And many cards do not insure rentals in Ireland. In Italy, renters are required to buy a collision damage waiver and theft protection from the rental agency.

Alternative to renting: Short-term leasing. It typically includes no-deductible collision and theft insurance.

Information: On the Web at *www.Best-Car-Rental-Tips.com*.

Paula Lyons, who runs the Web site Best-Car-Rental-Tips.com, quoted in *Travel + Leisure*.

Save Big on Hotels by Mastering Priceline.com

Marc Peyser, editor of *Budget Travel* magazine, New York City. *www.BudgetTravel.com*

The "bidding" feature on Priceline.com has become one of the most popular tools for travelers to slash prices on hotels. *But to get the lowest price, know the best strategies…*

HOW BIDDING WORKS

Using the "Name Your Own Price" option, hotel room bidders select an area (such as a city or a neighborhood)…a quality level based on a star system…and the amount they're willing to pay. If a hotel accepts the bid, the bidder's credit card is charged—he/she cannot reject the hotel or cancel the booking later. Discounts often are 50% off standard rates or even much greater.

Caution: Be wary of bidding for airline tickets. You might get a flight with a long layover or a predawn departure.

BEFORE BIDDING

Visit BiddingTraveler.com, which tracks successful Priceline bids. Enter your destination and travel dates (weekend rates can differ significantly from weekday rates), then take note of the average and lowest winning bids for hotels of the quality that you want (click the link below the hotel).

Helpful: If you're willing to invest some more time, also check BiddingForTravel.com and BetterBidding.com, online forums where Priceline.com users share information about bids. Check the posted rates offered by discount travel Web sites such as Hotwire.com, Kayak.com and Orbitz.com.

HOW TO BID

Set your initial Priceline bid near the low end of the range of accepted or stated offers you found, or if you want to simplify your task, set your initial bid near the average winning bid amount.

If your bid is too low and so is not accepted, the official policy is that you cannot try a different bid for 24 hours unless you adjust one of your bidding parameters other than price. But there's a way to get around this restriction. Simply add an additional nearby geographic area to your hotel search—but choose an area that doesn't contain any hotels of the quality you requested. With no appropriate additional hotels added to your parameters, you're effectively bidding on the original area again. To find areas that lack hotels of a given quality, select from the areas listed one by one. If the star level you want is listed in gray and can't

be selected, the area does not have hotels of that quality.

Helpful: Priceline will occasionally make "counteroffers." Reject these offers. They usually mean that you're coming close to a price that will be accepted. Bid slightly more than your last bid but less than the counteroffer.

ALTERNATIVE STRATEGIES

Try starting your search several days early so you can rebid every 24 hours without changing your parameters.

For a second chance to bid right away at a different price, your spouse or other traveling companion can try the second time under his/her name.

If you want to stay at a particular hotel, call it directly (not the chain's 800-number) after checking BiddingTraveler.com for a bid typically accepted for that hotel, and ask to speak with someone in guest relations or the manager. Tell this person that you know the hotel often accepts Priceline bids of that amount, and ask if you can have that rate if you book directly. Hotels sometimes agree to this because it saves them Priceline's fee.

Best Budget Hotel Chains in the US and Europe

Pauline Frommer, a nationally syndicated newspaper columnist and radio talk show host. She is a member of the Frommer guidebook family and a two-time winner of the North American Travel Journalists Association's Guidebook of the Year award. *www.Frommers.com/pauline*

The trouble with truly budget hotel chains is that travelers don't always know what they're getting. Hotels in low-cost chains tend to be individually owned franchises that might not even have been initially constructed to be part of the chain. Thus hotel quality, upkeep, amenities and service can vary dramatically. *But a few hotel chains can be counted on to provide a nice room at a reasonable price…*

MICROTEL INNS & SUITES

Microtel has ranked number one in guest satisfaction among economy and budget hotel chains for 10 consecutive years, according to surveys by J.D. Power and Associates. All Microtel locations are built specifically for this chain, so they are very consistent from one to the next. It's a relatively new chain, too—most locations are less than 15 years old—so the Microtels almost never seem rundown and dingy, a very common complaint in the budget-hotel category. Rooms run as low as $49 a night* (and are of average size, despite the hotel name).

Microtel hotels also offer perks not common in the budget-hotel category, such as free continental breakfast, free wireless Internet, free local phone calls and even free long-distance calls inside the continental US. (800-337-0050, *www.MicrotelInn.com*)

FOUR POINTS BY SHERATON

This budget line of Sheraton hotels offers a level of service and style usually associated with considerably more expensive hotels. This is not a bargain-priced chain like Microtel, but it is quite affordable—the basic "rack rate" tends to start at just $115 or so, though rates vary considerably depending on location and time of year.

Four Points' staff is friendly and well-trained, and the décor is attractive. Most Four Points hotels have been recently renovated, and many feature fitness centers. All provide free Internet and bottled water. (800-368-7764, *www.StarwoodHotels.com/fourpoints*)

TRAVELODGE (UK)

Travelodge (UK) is a wonderful lodging bargain for those visiting Britain, Ireland or Spain. (Europe's Travelodge has no affiliation with the American chain of the same name.)

Deals available through Travelodge's Web site can cut the cost of rooms to as little as 19 pounds (about $30) a night if you book at least three weeks ahead. That's less than one-third of what you would otherwise pay for rooms of this quality.

A good percentage of Travelodge rooms include pullout couches, allowing families of four

*Prices subject to change.

to stay for the price of a double room. That's an unusual perk in Europe, where quad rooms usually go for significantly more money.

Frequent travelers should sign up online to receive special e-mail offers. (Log on to *www. Travelodge.co.uk*, click "Deals.")

Travelodge does cut a few corners to keep prices low—expect fewer towels and toiletries, for example. A few of the chain's London locations seem a bit older and worn, too, though these are the exception. Overall, it's hard to find a better lodging bargain in Europe. (*www.Travelodge.co.uk*)

LANDING THE LOWEST PRICES

These days the lowest hotel room rates often are offered through hotel chains' own Web sites. *But it's worth checking a few rate-search travel Web sites…*

•**HotelsCombined.com** and Trivago.com search a wide range of other travel Web sites to find the best deals.

•**Hipmunk.com** not only searches other Internet sites for low hotel rates, it searches AirBnB.com for houses, apartments and rooms in private homes that are available as short-term rentals.

•**Tingo.com** will refund the difference on certain rooms if the offered rate drops after you book your stay.

More from Pauline Frommer…

3 Ways to Save on… Hotel Rates

Hotel prices can change by the day, even by the hour. But you can game the system somewhat by using the right Web sites…

1. Air-hotel package Web sites. "Bundling" airfare and hotel can offer significant savings. That's because travel sellers can "hide" the hotel price within a package so that it's not so obvious how deeply the room rate has been slashed. For Europe, try Gate1Travel.com…GoToday.com…and BMIT.com. Within the US, look at SouthwestVacations.com and the big sites such as Expedia, Travelocity and Orbitz. Expedia also is good for tropical destinations such as Hawaii and the Caribbean. Compare its offerings with those from VacMart.com… BookIt.com…and PleasantHolidays.com.

2. GetaRoom.com. The thinking here is that some prices are too good to be shown on the Internet. So this company encourages users to call its 800 number (800-468-3578) to get the most deeply slashed rates. Sometimes it works, sometimes not, but it doesn't cost anything to try.

3. Tingo.com. If you book a "Money Back" hotel room through Tingo, it promises to keep checking the rate for price changes. If the rate drops, it automatically refunds you the difference.

Example: One user was recently refunded $153 on a Paris hotel. It works very well on pricey properties, but on midrange and budget hotels, Tingo often doesn't have the lowest rates to begin with. You might do better at a more budget-oriented site, such as Hipmunk. com or Booking.com.

How to Get Your Hotel Room Upgraded for Free

Look up a specific high-end room prior to checking in, and then ask to be upgraded to that room by name, such as the honeymoon suite. Make the front desk clerk's job easier by being specific about the type of room you want, such as one with a pool view, instead of just asking for a better room. If there are problems with your room, ask to be upgraded because of the inconvenience. If it's a special occasion such as a birthday or anniversary, be sure to tell the front desk clerk.

Men's Health. www.MensHealth.com

Use Your Smartphone as a TV Remote in a Hotel Room

To use your smartphone as a TV remote, download the free LodgeNet mobile app

from iTunes or the Android Market, and you can change channels, adjust the volume and order movies in more than 600,000 US hotels.

Nancy Dunnan, editor, *TravelSmart* newsletter. *www. TravelSmartNewsletter.com*

More from Nancy Dunnan…

Pet Hotels at Airports

Pet hotels are open round the clock at some airports. Travelers can drop off their pets on the day of departure instead of a day in advance. Fees, parking and shuttle services vary.

Some airports offering pet hotels: Atlanta, Charlotte, Chicago, Houston, New Orleans and Tallahassee.

For information: Pet Paradise, 877-738-7752, *www.PetParadiseResort.com*…and Paradise 4 Paws, 847-678-1200, *www.Paradise4Paws.com.*

When Trip Insurance Makes Sense…

Anne Banas, executive editor of SmarterTravel.com, an independent online travel information Internet site based in Boston.

Should you bet that your expensive trip will come off without a hitch? Unforeseen events sometimes cause costly trips to be canceled or interrupted. Trip-cancellation insurance could cover your financial losses when they do. Expect to pay a premium equal to 4% to 10% of the trip's nonrefundable travel costs for this coverage. Older travelers generally pay more than younger ones. *How to decide if trip insurance is right for you…*

WHAT'S COVERED?

Covered reasons generally include health problems for the traveler(s)…health problems for a nontraveling member of the family that require the traveler to provide care (the policy will specify which relations qualify)…the death of the traveler or a family member…weather-related events and related natural disasters… airplane mechanical problems…airline strikes …and terrorist events that result in mandatory evacuation. (Terrorist events typically must be within 30 days of travel and in a stop on your itinerary.)

Some policies offer as an option the right to cancel the trip "for any reason." This typically adds 40% to 50% to the cost of the policy, however, so it's worthwhile only if you're concerned about a particular cancellation cause that otherwise wouldn't be covered.

Examples: Your daughter is due to give birth not long after your cruise, and you want to be able to cancel if the baby arrives early. Or your best client sometimes has emergencies that require your attention on short notice.

Caution: You typically can't buy insurance for just a portion of a trip. For instance, if you are flying to Europe and staying in a hotel, you can't buy insurance to cover the hotel stay but not the flight (unless you are paying for the flight with frequent-flier miles, which are not insurable). And if you can cancel your hotel reservation penalty-free before the trip starts, you may not need insurance.

Insurers often bundle trip-cancellation coverage together with lost-luggage coverage, foreign medical coverage and medical evacuation coverage—US medical insurance and Medicare rarely extend beyond the border. The terms of this additional coverage can vary greatly. Compare coverage limits and deductibles before settling on a policy.

WHEN TO BUY

Buy the insurance within 14 days of making your first trip-related payment. Policies purchased after this 14-day window closes often don't cover losses stemming from preexisting medical conditions. (Some companies extend this window to 21 or 30 days.) Buying coverage well in advance of the intended departure date also reduces the odds that losses will not be covered because they stem from "foreseen circumstances"—risks that were known at the time the policy was issued.

Example: Trip insurance does not cover losses caused by tropical storms or hurricanes already named when the policy was issued.

LEADING PROVIDERS

Leading trip-cancellation insurance providers include Travel Guard (800-826-4919, *www.TravelGuard.com*) and Allianz Global Assistance (800-284-8300, *www.AllianzTravel Insurance.com*). Alternatively, SquareMouth (800-240-0369, *www.Squaremouth.com*) and InsureMyTrip (800-487-4722, *www.InsureMy Trip.com*) provide quotes from multiple travel insurance providers.

How Much to Tip When Traveling

When traveling, give the bell staffer who brings bags to your room, $2 per bag… tip the cab driver, 15% to 20%…concierge, $10 to $20 for arranging hard-to-get reservations… doorman, $1 for hailing a cab…hotel housekeeper, $2 to $5 per night…restaurant server, 18% to 20%…and skycap, $2 per bag.

Steve Dublanica, author of *Keep the Change* (Ecco), quoted in *USA Today*.

Eating Etiquette Around the World

Helpful tips on table manners when traveling abroad…

Middle East, India and parts of Africa: Do not eat or touch the plate with your left hand—that hand is associated with bodily functions.

Mexico: Do not eat tacos with a fork and knife—it is considered snobbish.

Italy: Drink cappuccino only before noon— espresso is acceptable later in the day.

France: Eat bread with food or with the cheese course at the end of the meal—not as a premeal appetizer.

China: Do not flip over a whole fish after finishing one side—it is considered bad luck. Instead, pull out the bones to get to the lower portion.

Korea: Lift your glass with both hands when an older person offers you a drink.

This is an important sign of respect. You also should never start eating before the oldest male has started.

Travel.Yahoo.com

Emergency Abroad? Travel-Assistance Companies to the Rescue

Firms such as International SOS (*www.InternationalSOS.com*), Control Risks (*www.ControlRisks.com*) and FrontierMEDEX (*www.FrontierMEDEX.com*) monitor current events that could put travelers at risk…provide assistance during emergency situations…and help coordinate evacuations. Rates vary depending on the number of travel destinations and travelers.

Example: International SOS will usually charge an individual traveler $84* for safety information, evacuation coverage, help with lost baggage and passports and other benefits.

USA Today. www.USAToday.com

*Price subject to change.

Beware of These Diseases Abroad

Fran Lessans, RN, president, founder and CEO of Passport Health, a national network of travel health clinics based in the US. *www.PassportHealthUSA.com*

Among the potentially serious diseases that international travelers may be exposed to…

• **H1N1 (swine) flu.** Ordinary flu shots protect against this virus. Booster shots are recommended for people who are traveling in foreign countries during the flu season.

• **Dengue.** Outbreaks of this mosquito-borne viral disease have been reported recently in the Caribbean, Southeast Asia and Central and South America. No vaccines or other preventive treatments are available. To protect yourself when going outdoors, use controlled-release insect repellent containing 20% to 30% DEET. Permethrin repellent can be sprayed on clothing, bedding and mosquito nets.

• **Malaria.** This is another mosquito-borne disease—but one for which prophylactic drugs are available.

Among the travelers at risk: People on African safaris…visitors to parts of South America and southern Asia. Antimalarial drugs are not 100% effective, so you still must protect yourself against mosquitoes.

• **Hepatitis A.** This viral disease is transmitted from person to person and through contaminated food or drink. Most travel-related cases are associated with Mexico and Central and South America. Vaccines are available.

Self-defense: Four to six weeks before an international trip is the optimal time to visit a travel clinic or other health-care provider to start any necessary immunizations or other preventive treatments. But if you must leave sooner, immunizations still are recommended.

What to Do If You Lose Your Passport When Abroad…

If you lose your passport in a foreign country, go to the nearest US consulate or embassy to report the loss and have the passport invalidated—to prevent identity theft. You'll need to fill out two forms, DS-11 and DS-64, available at *www.Travel.State.gov*, plus submit a copy of your outbound itinerary. Getting a new passport will cost $135.* In some countries, you will be issued a temporary passport that expires after three months.

Travel + Leisure. www.TravelandLeisure.com

*Price subject to change.

14

Focus on Fun

The 5 Best Bets in the Casino…and the 5 Worst

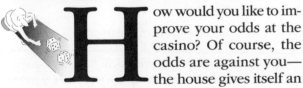

How would you like to improve your odds at the casino? Of course, the odds are against you—the house gives itself an advantage so that it can turn a profit.

But how greatly the odds are stacked against you depends on which games you play and which bets you place.

If you play blackjack or poker extremely well, those games offer attractive odds—but they are poor choices if you haven't mastered them.

Among the casino bets with the smallest house edge* that don't require a great deal of gambling skill…

*House edge (advantage) is the ratio of average loss to the entire bet.

BACCARAT BANKER BET: 1.06% HOUSE EDGE

Baccarat offers fair odds and is very easy to play. Gamblers simply decide whether to bet on the banker, the player or a tie before each hand. The banker bet offers the lowest house edge.

Once the bets are down, both the player and the banker receive either two or three cards. (The rules for when a third card is dealt can be confusing, but you don't need to understand this to play.) Aces are worth one… face cards and 10s are worth zero…and other cards are worth their face value. The totals are added up, and the score with the higher final digit wins.

Example: A hand containing a three and a five beats one containing an eight and a nine because three and five make eight, while eight

Thomas Gallagher, a former Las Vegas casino pit boss who now serves as a gambling coach and instructor. He is author of numerous gambling guidebooks, including *Craps Made Simple* (Thomas Company). *www. Poker911.net* and nine add up to seventeen—which is a score of seven because only the last digit counts.

CRAPS PASS LINE BET:
1.41% HOUSE EDGE

The craps table features some of the best bets in the casino. Put your chips on the pass line, and you will win if a seven or an 11 is rolled and lose if a two, three or 12 is rolled. If any other number is rolled, you will win if that number is rolled again before a seven is rolled but lose if it isn't.

Helpful: The "don't pass" line actually offers slightly better odds than the pass line. But the advantage is extremely slim—just two cents for every $100 bet—and gamblers who bet "don't pass" are betting against their fellow players. The tiny advantage isn't worth the nasty looks.

CRAPS ODDS BET:
0% HOUSE EDGE

This is a rare example of a bet where the house has no advantage. It's such an attractive bet that casinos don't promote it—craps tables don't specify where odds bets should be placed, and dealers don't mention these bets as an option. One catch—you can place an odds bet only if you already have placed a pass line bet.

It works like this—if you make a pass line bet and a four, five, six, eight, nine or 10 is rolled, you place additional chips on the open green felt behind your original pass line bet. If the point is made—that is, if the number rolled on the initial "come out" roll is rolled again before a seven—this additional bet pays off two-to-one if the point was four or 10… three-to-two if it was five or nine…or six-to-five if it was six or eight.

Casinos limit the size of odds bets. These limits vary depending on house rules, the amount initially bet and the point to be made. There should be a sign listing these limits on the table.

Example: If the sign says "3-4-5X," you can bet up to three times the amount of your pass line bet if the point is four or 10…four times if it's five or nine…or five times if it's six or eight.

If you're not certain of the size of the odds bet that you're allowed to make, ask the dealer for clarification. Dealers sometimes even will provide these limits on a hand-by-hand basis—particularly for gamblers who tip.

CRAPS 6/8 BET:
1.52% HOUSE EDGE

If you get bored making pass line and odds bets at the craps table, consider making a place bet on six or eight. You'll win if the number you selected is rolled before a seven but lose if it isn't. The bet remains until one of these numbers appears, even if it takes many rolls. A winning six or eight place bet pays $7 for every $6 bet—always make this bet in multiples of $6. (You can make place bets on numbers other than six and eight, but the odds are less attractive.)

To make a place bet, wait until the stickman controls the dice and you have the dealer's attention, then say, "Place the six, please," or "Place the eight, please," and push the chips you wish to bet toward the dealer. Do not attempt to put your chips in the six or eight box yourself. If you win, the dealer will give you your winnings but leave the original bet in place. If you don't wish to continue betting this number, say, "Take down the six" or "Take down the eight."

Warning: Don't put your chips in the "Big six and Big eight" box just inside the pass line—this offers worse odds.

PAI GOW POKER:
2.3% HOUSE EDGE

Pai Gow requires some skill, but it's easy to learn and fun to play and the odds aren't stacked too badly against players. The pace of play is relatively slow—perhaps three to four minutes per hand—further limiting potential losses.

Players are dealt seven cards facedown, which they divide up into two hands—one a traditional five-card poker hand…the other a two-card hand where only pairs and high cards matter, not flushes or straights. Each player's five-card hand must beat his two-card hand, a rule novices sometimes forget.

Casino gamblers play Pai Gow poker against the house (or a player acting as the banker), not against the other players. Beat the dealer with both the five-card and two-card hand, and it pays even money, minus a 5% commission. If the dealer and the player have the same hands—called a copy—the tie goes to the dealer. If the player wins one hand and loses the other hand, it is a push—you keep your bet but win nothing. Pushes are fairly common, so competent players can play a lot of cards without losing a lot of money. If the dealer wins both hands, the player loses the entire wager.

Google the terms "Pai Gow" and "strategy" to learn the basics before you play in a casino. It takes only a few minutes to learn enough to get by.

Warning: The Pai Gow poker deck includes a joker, but at most casinos, this joker is not completely wild—it can be used only as an ace or to complete a straight, flush or straight flush.

More from Thomas Gallagher...

Worst Bets

Casinos claim much more than their fair share from unwary gamblers on certain bets. *Among the bets to avoid...*

• **Baccarat Tie Bet.** 14.36% house edge. This is the one truly bad bet at the baccarat table.

• **Blackjack insurance bet.** 7.47% house edge (assuming an eight-deck game). When the house shows an ace, players can buy "insurance" against the chance that it has a 10 or face card in the hole (underneath). Decline this offer—insurance costs a lot more than it saves in the long run.

• **Craps prop bets.** 5% to 17% house edge. All of the bets in the middle of the craps table offer very poor odds.

Examples: "Hardways" and "One Roll" bets.

• **Keno.** 25% house edge. This game is designed to appeal to lottery players—and the odds are nearly as bad.

• **Slot machines.** 5% to 17% house edge. Not only does the house have a big edge with slots, the game moves very quickly, accelerating gamblers' losses.

Go to the Head of the Line

To avoid long lines at casino buffets, ask any floor person for a line pass. (Floor people supervise the dealers—you can find them standing behind blackjack or craps areas.) You will pay for your meal but can go in through the VIP entrance and be seated immediately.

Acting for Fun and Profit: How to Get Parts in Commercials, TV Shows and Movies

Kathy Wickline, CSA, founder of Kathy Wickline Casting in Philadelphia. She has cast thousands of projects, including commercials for BlueCross, NBC and Comcast. She also cast the Academy Award–winning feature films *Witness* and *Philadelphia*. Her CD *So You Want to Be an Actor* is available at *www.WicklineCasting.com* (click on "Actors").

Wouldn't it be fun to be in the movies? You don't have to move to Hollywood or New York City, and you do not need to have movie-star good looks. *Here's what you need to know...*

WHAT DIRECTORS WANT

One myth about acting is that it is a young person's profession. While it's true that movies and TV shows feature people in their 20s, older actors have an easier time landing roles in markets outside Los Angeles. There are so many young people trying to make it as actors that the competition for young parts is extremely stiff. Besides, outside Hollywood and New York City, most professional acting jobs are parts in local commercials and corporate training films. Directors want actors who look like the company's actual customers and employees—in other words, like ordinary people.

247

Extras can earn $75 to $150 per day,* while principal work can pay $600 or more per day.

WHERE TO FIND WORK

Three resources for aspiring actors in search of roles…

• **The Web sites of state and city film offices often list opportunities to appear in films being produced in the area.** Type "film office" and the name of your city or state into Google to find local film offices, then monitor the announcements or job listings for appropriate opportunities. These jobs are posted by independent filmmakers as well as by casting directors.

• **Casting directors represent production companies and ad agencies that hire actors and models.** Google the term "casting director" and the name of your state or the nearest sizable city to find casting directors in your area. Visit these casting directors' Web sites to find out if they have "open calls"—auditions open to anyone interested in trying out. Most casting directors have these once a month. Casting directors who like your look and acting abilities will keep you in mind for future projects.

• **Talent agencies represent actors and models, typically in exchange for 10% to 20% of their future acting and modeling earnings.** Many might charge an up-front fee of $150 to a few hundred dollars as well. This covers uploading information and head shots into their databases. Legitimate talent agencies have working relationships with casting directors that greatly increase their clients' odds of getting auditions. Most agencies also have print departments, which help actors and models find work posing for print ads, magazines and annual reports.

Helpful: If you're a novice actor, take some acting classes prior to approaching a talent agency. Agents won't recommend you to casting directors over their existing clients unless they are confident that you know what you're doing.

Before visiting casting directors or talent agencies, rehearse a short monologue. Books of monologues suitable for auditions are avail-

*Rates and prices subject to change.

able at libraries and bookstores or online. Choose a monologue appropriate for someone of your age and looks.

Important: Be persistent. The actors and actresses who find success tend to be the ones who audition as frequently as possible and continually monitor their regional film offices' Web sites for opportunities.

DON'T GET SCAMMED

Confirm that you're dealing with a legitimate casting director or talent agency. Some companies charge thousands in up-front fees in exchange for vague promises about launching aspiring actors' careers. Legitimate casting directors do not charge any up-front fees, and legitimate talent agencies charge no more than a few hundred dollars, plus a percentage of future earnings. *Also…*

• **Check casting directors' Web sites for a list of credits.** Legitimate, experienced casting directors will have a long list of projects that they have worked on in the past.

• **Make sure talent agencies are licensed by the state.** Licensing requirements vary by state.

Helpful: The Web site of the Screen Actors Guild is one place you can find legitimate talent agencies. (On *www.SAGAFTRA.org*, select "Agency Relations" from the "Union Info" menu, then select "SAG Franchised Agents," and choose your state or region from the list near the bottom of the page.)

**OBTAINING EXPERIENCE
AND TRAINING**

There is work available to actors who have little experience and training. This typically includes nonspeaking roles and small roles in independent film productions (independent films often pay actors little or nothing, however).

But to land more and better roles, you probably will need some acting experience and/or training. Taking roles in local amateur theatrical productions is one way to gain this experience. Taking acting classes can be an even better way to improve your acting skills and employability. A local talent agent should be able to recommend classes, or you can conduct an Internet search for the phrase "acting classes," along with the name of nearby cities or large towns. A four-to-six-week class is likely to cost a few hundred dollars.

Examples: A class focused on on-camera acting for commercials and corporate-training films will be particularly useful if your goal is to launch a part-time acting career and you don't live near Hollywood or New York City. If you're more interested in becoming a stage actor, ask local theater companies if they offer acting classes.

Helpful: Local casting directors and talent agencies sometimes offer personal consultations with prospective actors about how to get started in the business and/or seminars about the business side of acting. These can be very helpful. Prices vary, depending on the reputation of the casting director or talent agent involved, but shouldn't be more than a few hundred dollars for an hour-long private consultation and less for a seminar.

AUDITION LIKE A PRO

When you audition, dress for the role you hope to land. Appropriate wardrobe can help the filmmakers see you in the part. *Also…*

• **Arrive at least 15 minutes before your audition time.** The script often is not provided until you arrive.

Warning: Don't attempt to memorize the script unless it's only a few sentences. Quickly memorizing scripts can lead to constrained, expressionless performances.

• **Bring a résumé detailing your acting experience (if any) to the audition.** Type the words "actor's résumé" into a search engine to find examples of how these should be structured. If you haven't yet landed many— or any—professional roles, it's fine to include amateur acting experience, even local theater productions from decades ago.

• **Bring a professional head shot to auditions as well.** A talent agent should be able to recommend an area photographer. Expect the photographer to charge $175 to $400 (most include the cost of a makeup artist).

To Save on Movie Tickets…

To get low-cost movie tickets, join AAA—it offers $8.25 tickets* to Regal, United Artists and Edwards theaters, but you must go to an AAA office to buy them. Or buy movie packs from warehouse clubs. *Example:* A four-pack of tickets from AMC, Cinemark or Regal costs $34.99 at Costco.com. You could also wait until movies come to second-run theaters, which charge $3 to $6 for admission. And afternoon matinees save you 30% to 50%. Do not forget to ask about discounts for seniors. Some AMC theaters offer them for anyone over age 60—Cinemark has a Seniors Day on Mondays for people 62 and older. Bring an ID to prove your age.

Andrea Woroch, consumer advocate, Windsor, Colorado. *www.AndreaWoroch.com*

*Prices subject to change.

Secrets of the Golf Pros: Surefire Tips to Improve Your Game

Joel Zuckerman, an avid golfer and author of seven books on golf, including *Pete Dye Golf Courses: 50 Years of Visionary Design* (Abrams), honored as the 2009 Book of the Year by the International Network of Golf. This article is taken from his latest book, *Pro's Pros—Extraordinary Club Professionals Making Golf Great* (Saron). *www.VagabondGolfer.com*

How would you like to shave a few strokes off your handicap? Here, some of the most accomplished PGA professionals at some of America's most renowned golf clubs offer tips on how to get the most out of your game.

USE ENOUGH CLUB
Ron Branca
Salt Lake Country Club, Salt Lake City

Most amateurs don't use enough club for the required shot. In other words, they try to force an 8-iron when a 7-iron is the better choice. They might try to muscle a 5-iron when the

4-iron will get the job done with less effort. The more club you use, the less swing you need. The shorter the swing, the fewer things there are to go wrong. Good balance usually is the first benefit of using more club with less swing. Better balance leads to more consistent shots.

KEEP YOUR HEAD UP
John Dahl
Oxbow Country Club, Oxbow, North Dakota

The more a player's head drops down during his setup, the higher the handicap. When you watch a very good golfer from a front-on view, you will see a good portion of his face. On the flip side, when you watch a higher-handicap player from the same position, the top of his head is visible while the face can't be seen. If your head is buried into your chest in the setup, it is almost impossible to move behind the ball as needed during your backswing. The next time you get in position to make a swing, try glancing down but keep your face up. Don't stare down at the ball.

SWING THE WEIGHT
Mike Harmon
Secession Golf Club, Beaufort, South Carolina

I have swung a weighted club (it has extra weight in the clubhead) daily for almost 40 years in order to develop and maintain my golf swing. If you do this —even if you seldom play and rarely hit practice balls—your golf muscles will remain toned. You can purchase a weighted club at a sporting-goods store or look for one online. Then swing it in slow motion 20 times daily, using the same technique and motions that you use when playing. It takes only two to three minutes, but if you do it religiously each day, you soon will feel flexibility returning to your swing motion and a muscle memory that helps immensely when you are on the course.

RELAX GRIP PRESSURE
J.D. Turner
Turner Golf Group, Inc., Savannah

Most players hold the club too tightly. By squeezing the grip, you lose rhythm, speed and balance. An effective exercise to learn proper grip pressure is to play catch underhanded with a golf ball. Toss the ball back and forth with a friend or up and down by

yourself. You will toss it the perfect distance, height and speed every time. This is because you automatically hold the ball softly in your fingers. If you hold the club as you hold the ball, your accuracy and power will increase.

MAKE THOSE SHORT PUTTS
Bill Safrin
Myopia Hunt Club, South Hamilton, Massachusetts

As someone who has struggled to sink short putts, I found a solution to this problem. *Follow these steps, and your percentages will increase substantially...*

• **Take the putter slowly away from the ball.**

• **Make your backswing short.**

• **Make sure your follow-through is twice as long as the distance you pull the club back.**

• **Listen for the ball to go in with your head down so as not to prematurely look up** and possibly make a jerky stroke.

Photo Tricks from the Pros

Susan Farewell, a travel journalist and founder of Farewell Travels LLC, a travel concierge that provides ideas, recommendations and referrals for worldwide travel. Based in Westport, Connecticut, she has taken a number of travel photo workshops and advises private clients about which ones are best for them. *www. FarewellTravels.com*

The difference between a ho-hum shot and a "let's enter this in a contest" photo isn't usually about the locale—it's about how you take the shot, such as which angle you shoot from. *Here, what the professionals recommend...*

BEFORE YOU GO

• **Choose your camera carefully.** While a point-and-shoot camera is less expensive, smaller and lighter, you have limited control over aperture, shutter speed and focus. With a *Digital SLR* (DSLR), you have full manual control. For learning purposes, many of the organized travel photography trips and workshops expect participants to use a DSLR. However, there may be some exceptions. Each company has an equipment packing list.

• **Select lenses carefully.** To keep it simple, carry a zoom lens that will go from wide angle to telephoto. That way, you don't have to worry about changing the lens to capture the image you want.

• **Travel with several high-capacity cards.** With today's high-capacity digital storage media, no one should have to delete images on a trip to make room for new ones. All too often this can lead to mistakes (such as deleting a special picture).

Solution: Take twice the number of cards that you expect to need.

• **Pack a back-up device.** A small netbook, external hard drive or other storage device can hold all the photos you take on your trip. Get in the habit of backing up every night. You don't want to learn the hard way that once images are gone, they're forever lost. You could lose a camera, drop it into water or inadvertently delete images.

• **Take a power strip.** This way you can charge your cell phone, camera battery and other family members' electronics at the same time. Be sure to also take along the right plug adapter for the country you'll be visiting.

ON THE ROAD

• **Shoot in raw.** If you're planning to use *Photoshop* or any other editing software, by shooting in "raw" photo format (which is available in the settings of most DSLRs), you'll have greater flexibility when editing the images.

• **Ask permission to take photographs of locals.** This simple courtesy can turn a frown into a smile very quickly. Take one shot, show it to the person on your camera and offer to e-mail it to him/her.

• **Go hunting for photos.** Don't just wait for something to happen in your path. Go off exploring—wander down little streets or climb over sand dunes.

• **Shoot toward the sun.** This is a classic photography no-no, but the fact is that you can sometimes get great silhouettes and other special effects by pointing your lens in the direction of the sun.

• **When shooting wildlife, get down and dirty if you have to.** Lay in the mud, hide in the tall grass—the best wildlife photographs often require going that extra mile. But always keep a safe distance.

• **Avoid the temptation to capture people and an entire building or landmark in a photo.** If you're photographing a person in front of a pyramid, don't expect to get the whole person and the whole pyramid. Instead zoom in close to the person, and show just the edge of the pyramid.

BACK HOME

• **Tell stories with your photos.** While you might be tempted to post all 276 photographs of the elephants crossing the river on your Africa trip,· take the time to edit them down to just a handful of shots. Put them together so that they tell a story. And if you're sharing on social-media networks (such as Facebook), take a moment to identify where the pictures were taken and who or what is in them.

To Manage Digital Photos...

Once a month, download pictures to your computer from your camera or phone. Put them in a photo-management program such as Picasa or iPhoto. Review and edit them, deleting low-quality pictures. Make folders to organize them—perhaps, chronologically or by theme. Rename each photo. Back up immediately to an external drive or online, or make prints.

Jody Al-Saigh, founder, Picture Perfect Organizing, Arlington, Virginia, quoted in *Better Homes & Gardens*.

Stock Your e-Reader for Free!

To stock your e-reader for free, visit your local library—more than two-thirds offer access to e-books, although only one person can have a copy at a time. You can also read works whose copyrights have expired.

Find them at sites such as *www.Gutenberg. org...http://OpenLibrary.org...*and *http://Many Books.net.* Another helpful source is online bookstores—search for free e-books at *www. BN.com...www.Amazon.com...*or iTunes. Or borrow from other readers through sharing Web sites such as *www.BookLending.com* and *www.eBookFling.com.* Works by new writers are available from *www.Free-eBooks.net.*

Money. www.Money.CNN.com

How to Get Your Orchid to Rebloom

William Cullina, executive director of Coastal Maine Botanical Gardens, Boothbay, Maine. He is the 2012 winner of the Scott Medal, awarded by the Scott Arboretum of Swarthmore College for outstanding contributions to the science and art of gardening. Cullina is author of *Understanding Orchids: An Uncomplicated Guide to Growing the World's Most Exotic Plants* (Houghton Mifflin Harcourt). *www.MaineGardens.org*

Orchids were once an expensive rarity, but within the past decade or two, they've become widely available at supermarkets for just $10 to $15 apiece. *They will bloom for months and rebloom indefinitely—if they're handled properly...*

• **Opt for a moth orchid.** Orchids are the largest family of flowers, with around 35,000 species and perhaps twice as many hybrids. I strongly recommend that novices opt for a moth orchid (*Phalaenopsis*). It's the most widely available and affordable of orchids. It also is quite easy to grow, attractive and long-blooming.

Helpful: The following guidance is specifically intended for moth orchids. Other orchid species might have different preferences and characteristics. Consult a garden shop or an orchid-growing guide for details.

• **Give orchids the proper amount of sun.** Orchids that don't receive sufficient sunlight often fail to rebloom. A spot near a sunny east-facing window tends to be ideal. A south-facing window can be a good choice as well, though this might provide too much sunlight, particularly in the southern US or during the summer.

Helpful: A moth orchid's leaves should be medium-green in color. Dark green leaves might indicate insufficient light...while light green leaves, leaves that have a red tint or leaves with patches that look dried or burned might indicate excessive light.

• **Water like a passing downpour.** Once every five to seven days take your orchid to the kitchen sink and use the faucet (use the sink sprayer if you have one) to drench its potting mix until it's truly soaked. Wait 30 seconds, then drench again. Make sure that the water drains out. In the wild, most orchids do not grow in soil—they attach themselves to tree limbs, so their roots are not designed to sit for extended periods in wet soil or water.

• **Fertilize lightly.** Orchids benefit from fertilizer, but do not overdo it—high concentrations of fertilizer can do an orchid more harm than good. Because orchid roots don't normally grow in soil, they're not designed to take in large quantities of nutrients.

• **Feed your orchid liquid fertilizer every week or two when you see new leaves or roots growing,** but use only half the amount recommended on the fertilizer's label. (If you don't see new leaves or roots, don't fertilize.) There is no need to pay extra for specialty orchid fertilizer—a standard liquid houseplant fertilizer is fine.

• **Prune judiciously.** Do not immediately prune off a moth orchid's flower spike after the last of its flowers stops blooming. Unlike most orchids, moth orchids can rebloom off the same spike, below earlier flowers. Check the spike for small, fleshy green nodes. If you find them, use a sterile blade (use rubbing alcohol or a lighter to sterilize the blade) to trim the spike an inch or so above the second or third node.

Go ahead and prune off the entire spike if the nodes on the flower spike seem dried out or if you trim the spike as described above, but it turns brown before reblooming.

• **Repot every year or two because the potting mix breaks down.** Buy a potting mix specifically designed for orchids. You can put the orchid back in the original pot but thoroughly scrub it first to remove salt buildup.

15

Auto Adviser

Lost a High-Tech Car Key? How to Replace It for Hundreds Less

Hardware stores used to copy car keys for just one dollar or two. But now most car keys are high-tech devices that can cost hundreds of dollars to replace. Fortunately, there can be ways to save. *What you need to know...*

TYPES OF KEYS

Different cars use a variety of key technologies with varying replacement costs. For all the key types, dealerships charge an extra $40 to $150 for 30 to 60 minutes of labor* to program them for your car. Labor costs might be higher if you don't have any remaining copies of the key because programming might be more difficult—all the locks might need to be

*Prices subject to change.

recoded. You probably will have to have the vehicle towed to a dealership, too.

• **Transponder keys** have computer chips hidden inside their plastic heads. When the ignition is turned on, the vehicle sends a signal to the key as a theft deterrent. The car won't start unless the chip in the key sends back the proper response. Dealerships charge $40 to $200 for replacement transponder keys. Valet keys vary in functionality but generally are less expensive to replace.

• **Electronic key fobs** attach to key rings and feature buttons that remotely open doors or perform other functions. Dealerships typically charge $50 to $100 for replacement fobs.

• **Smart keys** are electronic devices similar to fobs, only they wirelessly transmit security codes that allow cars to be started with-

Ron Montoya, consumer-advice editor, Edmunds.com, a leading provider of automotive information. Based in Santa Monica, California, the company has been providing information on new and used cars since 1966. *www.Edmunds.com*

253

out mechanical keys, although some include a manual key for emergencies. Dealerships often charge $200 to $400 for smart keys.

• **Laser-cut keys**—also called "sidewinder" keys—have thicker shanks and fewer grooves than conventional keys. Dealerships will often charge $150 to $250 for replacements.

NONDEALER OPTIONS

Some locksmiths, hardware stores and auto-parts stores can replace laser-cut keys and can replace and program certain transponder keys. Prices usually are well below dealership rates, but they can vary significantly, so call around for quotes.

Helpful: Locksmiths who belong to Associated Locksmiths of America are likely to have the equipment and the know-how. *www.Find aLocksmith.com*

Replacement transponder keys, fobs and smart keys are available on eBay and elsewhere online for well below dealership or locksmith prices—but people who purchase these sometimes discover that the keys don't work with their vehicles or don't work at all. I would steer clear unless the device is guaranteed to come from the original manufacturer… you locate confirmation in a car-owner chat group that reprogramming eBay-purchased keys has worked for others with your specific vehicle…the seller receives excellent feedback from other eBay buyers…and the price of the eBay part is far enough below dealership and locksmith prices that it is worth the gamble.

ADDITIONAL MONEY SAVERS

Five more potential money savers…

• **Labor charges might be avoidable even when the dealership is the only option.** Some dealerships act as if programming a transponder key is a difficult job—and with some models and in some cases, it does indeed require a pro. But assuming that you still have at least one of your keys, programming a replacement key could be simply a matter of inserting and turning keys in a particular sequence.

Example: With some models, you just put the working key in the ignition, turn it to on, turn it back to off, then quickly insert the new key and again turn the ignition to on. If the

procedure is not detailed in your owner's manual, Google your make and model along with the words "program" and "key" (or "fob").

If it is possible to program your car's keys and fobs without dealership assistance, another owner likely has posted the instructions in a vehicle chat group. Web sites that sell replacement transponder keys also might provide online directions.

• **Investigate the process for programming your vehicle's keys before you lose a key.** Occasionally this procedure requires both of the keys issued with the car. If so, it might be worth buying and programming a spare key before either of the originals is lost, particularly if you're someone who loses things frequently.

• **Call several dealerships for price quotes** if you must replace a key or fob through a dealership. Rates can vary significantly. Make sure that quotes include both parts and labor.

• **Turn down lost-key insurance if a salesman offers it to you.** It's overpriced. If you're very concerned about losing your keys, use your money to purchase and program a spare key instead.

• **Buy a key-locator device if you lose your keys often.** These gadgets are available on Amazon.com and elsewhere for less than $50. Their range tends to be limited, however—these devices can help you locate your keys when you lose them in your home or workplace but probably not when you lose them around town. Taping your e-mail address and possibly a "reward if found" message to the key ring might help.

"Yo-Yo Financing" Scams

You trade in your old car or put down a deposit and sign an attractive financing contract for a new car. A few days later, the dealer claims that the financing has fallen through, then pressures you to agree to a new loan. Those who agree to a new contract pay an average interest rate five percentage points higher than what someone with the same creditworthiness would normally pay.

Self-defense: Do not take the car until financing is finalized.

Delvin Davis, senior researcher, Center for Responsible Lending, Durham, North Carolina. *www.Responsible Lending.org*

Secret to Lower Lease Payments

Get lower car lease payments by negotiating the purchase price of the car—what leasing agents call the *capitalized cost.* The lower this cost, the lower the monthly payments will be.

What to do: Visit Web sites that list the typical price that others have paid for the car you want to lease—Edmunds.com, TrueCar.com and KBB.com. Aim for a capitalized cost close to the car's true market value.

Richard Arca, senior pricing manager, Edmunds.com, quoted at CNNMoney.com.

Few Hybrid Owners Buy One Again

Only 35% of hybrid owners purchased another hybrid the next time they were in the market for a car. The rate falls to less than 25% if Toyota Prius owners are excluded. Repeat hybrid buyers generally prefer cars from the same company that made their first hybrid—60% of Toyota hybrid owners bought another Toyota…and 52% of Honda hybrid owners purchased another Honda. Sales of hybrid vehicles have not maintained their momentum partly because of the higher cost of hybrid cars, as well as the fact that compact and midsized cars are becoming more fuel-efficient.

Study of purchase behavior from 2008 to 2011 by Polk, an auto-industry data provider and research company. *www.Polk.com*

Are MPG Estimates Accurate?

Karen Larson, editor, *Bottom Line/Personal,* 281 Tresser Blvd., Stamford, Connecticut 06901. *www.BottomLine Publications.com*

Fuel efficiency is a major selling point for vehicles now that gas is so expensive. It's certainly something I considered before buying my Honda. But can we trust those EPA efficiency figures?

The EPA announced late in 2012 that 13 Hyundai and Kia models from the 2011–2013 model years fell short of their rated efficiency. Hyundai (which makes both brands) subsequently agreed to reimburse affected car buyers for certain fuel costs. Now some car owners and reviewers are saying that two models from Ford—C-Max and Fusion hybrids—fall well short of their rated mileage as well. Official EPA fuel-economy estimates claim that these vehicles provide 47 miles per gallon (mpg), but independent testers have come up with results of just 33 to 39 mpg.

How could the EPA numbers be so wrong? The fact is, EPA fuel-efficiency figures aren't calculated by the EPA at all—they're calculated by the automakers themselves. Automakers must follow specific EPA guidelines, but they could mistakenly or purposely test outside these guidelines, says John O'Dell, senior editor for fuel economy and green cars at Edmunds.com. He adds that the EPA does do spot checks of about 190 models a year.

Another flaw is the test itself—it doesn't really replicate how we drive. Most of us drive more aggressively than the test calls for. The typical driver will fall around 20% short of a vehicle's EPA fuel efficiency, according to O'Dell—around 30% if you drive a hybrid.

Does Ethanol-Free Gas Improve Mileage?

John O'Dell, senior editor of car information site Edmunds.com and a member of the National Research Council to Advise Congress on Alternative Fuels and Cars. *www.Edmunds.com*

The fuel at most US gas stations is 10% ethanol. Federal law requires that gasoline be oxygenated because it helps the fuel burn off more completely and cuts down on pollution. And 30 years of federal tax credits for ethanol (which expired in 2011) have helped make ethanol the most popular oxygenator.

Ethanol-free gasoline can be found at several thousand gas stations, but availability varies greatly by state. For instance, a directory lists 638 stations with ethanol-free gas in Wisconsin—the most of any state—but just six in California and none in New Jersey.

Ethanol-free gas does deliver better mileage than standard 10% ethanol fuel, which is called E10, but the difference is not large—typically about 3%, according to the EPA. And ethanol-free gas costs more, anywhere from 10 to 40 cents more per gallon. With that price differential, any savings is diminished or disappears.

Web sites that list stations selling ethanol-free gas include *www.Pure-Gas.org*, which lists more than 6,700 stations, and *www.BuyReal Gas.com*.

Fuel Facts and Myths

Most cars don't need premium fuel. Usually, only sports and luxury vehicles with higher-performing engines need premium gas. If the owner's manual says it is "recommended," you probably can use regular fuel—but if the manual says premium is "required," use it. Another way to save on gas is to go to an independent station. The gas will be cheaper but usually comes from brand-name companies and is just as good.

Contrary to popular opinion: It does not matter what time of day you fill up—most stations store fuel underground, so its temperature and density change very little during the day. Any extra gas you get by filling up when the air is cooler will be minimal.

And: It is not necessary to warm up a car before driving—engines work best at regular operating temperature, which is reached most quickly by starting to drive right after startup.

Consumer Reports. www.ConsumerReports.com

What Magicians Can Teach Us About Car Crashes

Karen Larson, editor, *Bottom Line/Personal*, 281 Tresser Blvd., Stamford, Connecticut 06901. *www.BottomLine Publications.com*

I had always thought that magicians trick us by misdirecting our gaze. More often, they actually misdirect our attention, says Alex Stone, a journalist and an amateur magician who wrote *Fooling Houdini: Magicians, Mentalists, Math Geeks & the Hidden Powers of the Mind* (Harper).

What's the difference? Our attention can be diverted even if our eyes never look away. For example, magicians often ask their audiences questions during their magic acts. Those questions might sound like they're just part of the usual showman's patter, but they have a hidden purpose. Answering questions—or just considering potential answers—is so distracting to our minds that even if we keep our eyes glued to the magician's hands, we tend to fail to notice what those hands are doing.

Psychologists call this "inattentional blindness," and it isn't just a magician's trick—it can be a potentially deadly road hazard.

Many drivers think that hands-free devices make it safe to talk on cell phones while behind the wheel. But talking on a cell phone while driving isn't dangerous primarily because it ties up our hands or even because we might glance away from the road momentarily to dial. It's dangerous because, like answering a magician's questions, speaking on a phone can distract our minds so much that we fail to register things that occur right before our eyes.

There is some good news—it's relatively safe to chat with passengers who are in the vehicle as we drive. A passenger typically pays a degree of attention to the road, too, providing a second set of eyes—and a second mind—that can help compensate for driver distraction. It isn't ideal—but talking on the phone is much worse.

Watch Out for That Truck!

Karen Larson, editor, *Bottom Line/Personal*, 281 Tresser Blvd., Stamford, Connecticut 06901. *www.BottomLine Publications.com*

I am always a little unnerved when I am driving beside a big truck. I worry that the driver won't see me and will veer into my lane.

That's a real possibility, said Allen Boyd, a truck driver for Walmart Transportation who has more than 30 years of experience. He is a member of America's Road Team, an outreach group of the American Trucking Associations that educates drivers about highway safety. "If you're driving next to a truck, glance at the driver's side-view mirror—if you can't see his face, then he probably can't see your car."

If you're driving behind a truck, make sure that you can see both of the truck's side-view mirrors. If you can't, slow down and leave a greater gap between your car and the truck.

Passing a truck is another challenge. You might be hanging next to it for an uncomfortably long time (given how long a truck is). "You'll probably be eager to dive back into the lane, in front of the truck, as soon as possible," said Boyd. But make sure that you have moved far enough ahead in the passing lane to see the truck's entire cab (the front part of the truck, where the driver sits) in your rear-view mirror. When possible, it's best to pass the truck on the left—the blind spot on the right side is much larger.

If a truck is trying to pass you but seems to be hugging your left side for a long time, it's not because the driver wants to stay there. "For safety reasons, 67% of trucks are programmed so that drivers can't exceed the speed limit," said Boyd. You may have to slow down temporarily so that the driver can pass you more easily.

Hybrid Danger?

Karen Larson, editor, *Bottom Line/Personal*, 281 Tresser Blvd., Stamford, Connecticut 06901. *www.BottomLine Publications.com*

Hybrid and electric vehicle batteries are many times more powerful than typical car batteries—powerful enough to kill. In fact, a task force formed by SAE International (formerly the Society of Automotive Engineers) recently recommended that hybrid and electric vehicles be more clearly labeled, in part so that firefighters don't accidentally electrocute themselves while trying to extract passengers from crashes.

Fortunately, hybrid and electric vehicles do not pose significant electrocution dangers for drivers in a crash, according to John Frala, professor of Alternative Fuels Technology at Rio Hondo College and a member of the SAE task force. These vehicles have multiple safety switches that automatically shut off the flow of current when they sense an impact. (The risk is slightly greater for rescue personnel, who could possibly cut into something that's still charged.)

There's no need to worry about dangerous chemicals spilling from a hybrid or electric vehicle's batteries, either. The electrolyte in these advanced batteries can't spill, says Frala, because it's not in liquid form.

In fact, these vehicles actually might be safer. They generally have a small gas tank or no tank, so there's less fuel to catch fire. And their heavy batteries add weight low in the vehicle, improving stability. A recent study found that the odds of being injured in a crash are 25% lower for people in hybrids.

Do the Latest Auto-Safety Devices Prevent Car Crashes?—Some Do… Some Don't

Dan Edmunds, director of vehicle testing for automotive information provider Edmunds, Inc. He previously worked as a vehicle evaluation engineer for Toyota and Hyundai/Kia. Located in Santa Monica, California, the company has been providing information on new and used cars since 1966. Its Web site gets about 18 million visitors a month. *www.Edmunds.com*

The latest automotive-safety technologies don't just help us survive car crashes— they actually can prevent crashes. The devices include systems that can automatically nudge a vehicle back into its lane when it drifts…or hit the brakes for us when a collision is imminent.

But are they truly worth their cost? Some of the latest, greatest devices tend to be offered only on high-end models or in option packages that can add thousands of dollars to the price of a vehicle.

Here's how to decide which of the latest safety technologies are truly worth the cost…

•**Adaptive cruise control** doesn't just lock in your speed. When engaged, it uses radar or lasers to track the vehicle ahead of you in traffic, then maintains a safe following distance. If the car ahead slows, your car will slow, too, as you approach an unsafe distance.

Examples: Most of the major automakers are in the process of developing and rolling out adaptive cruise control for more mainstream vehicles. In many cases, it still is limited to the high-end cars in their fleets, but that is rapidly changing. Mainstream vehicles offering the technology include some more expensive versions of the Subaru Legacy and Outback and Ford Edge, Explorer, Flex, Fusion and Taurus.

Verdict: Adaptive cruise control can be very useful if you do a lot of highway driving—but not if that highway driving is done in heavy traffic. These systems require a fairly long following distance. In heavy traffic, other drivers will continually pull into the space that is left in front of you—and each time they do, your adaptive cruise control will slow your vehicle, which can make for annoying and fuel-inefficient travel.

•**Adaptive headlights** turn slightly when the steering wheel is turned or when a turn signal is engaged, helping drivers better see the road ahead at night. It's not a new idea, but it is only now coming into widespread use. Adaptive headlights often are combined with high-intensity bulbs and leveling systems that keep headlights aimed at the road—not into the eyes of oncoming drivers—even when weight in the trunk tilts your car upward.

Examples: Adaptive headlights are available on a wide range of high-end luxury and performance vehicles plus quite a few more affordable ones, such as the Mazda 3 and CX-5.

Verdict: These headlights can be worth the money for drivers who do lots of nighttime driving on curvy roads that are not well lit by streetlights.

•**Lane-departure warning/lane-assist systems** use cameras to sense when your vehicle is drifting out of its lane. Lane-departure warning systems then sound an alarm or give some other signal to call your attention to the problem…while lane-assist systems apply brakes on one side to nudge the car back into the lane.

Examples: Lane-departure warning systems are fairly widely available. Lane assist is most common with luxury cars including Audi, Lexus and Mercedes, but it now is available in some mainstream vehicles, too, including the Ford Fusion and Explorer.

Verdict: Lane-assist and lane-departure systems could save your life if you drive when you are drowsy or distracted (though the better solution is to not drive while drowsy and to avoid distractions). These systems tend to work best on multilane highways and are less effective on country roads that lack painted outer lines. Some drivers find it annoying that when these systems are engaged, drivers must use their blinkers before changing lanes, even if they are the only ones on the road—if the blinker isn't used, the system interprets the lane change as drifting.

Related: Mercedes Attention Assist monitors drivers for signs of fatigue and suggests stopping for a rest when prudent. It's standard on many Mercedes models and useful for people who do lots of night driving. A new Cadillac system on the ATS and XTS sedans and SRX crossover is a variation on this. It vibrates the seat cushion when you drift out of the lane to startle you back into paying attention—but the jury still is out on this method.

● **Blind-spot detection** provides a warning noise or light when there's a vehicle in your blind spots—the areas slightly behind and to the side of your car that cannot easily be seen in your mirrors. Some blind-spot detection systems gently apply the brakes on one side to avoid a collision with a vehicle in your blind spot.

Example: Infiniti's Blind Spot Intervention System will pull your vehicle away from a vehicle in your blind spot if it senses that you're about to collide with that vehicle.

Verdict: Blind-spot warning systems have some value, but only if you often drive on multilane roads in moderate or light traffic. When traffic is heavy, these systems sound warnings so often that they're more of an annoyance than a safety feature. These systems should not be considered a substitute for turning one's head to check blind spots. And it's not clear that these systems are that much more effective than simply aiming a vehicle's mirrors properly—you should barely be able to see the sides of your own vehicle in your side mirrors—and adding an inexpensive aftermarket stick-on blind-spot convex mirror, available in any auto-parts store.

● **Forward collision warnings/brake support systems** sound warnings when they sense that you're about to hit something. They also might precharge the brakes to make them extra responsive in an emergency stop.

Some even feature self-braking systems that apply the brakes on their own if the driver fails to do so. These self-braking systems generally are capable of avoiding collisions only when traveling below 20 to 25 miles per hour (mph), but they can reduce the vehicle's speed at impact, tighten seat belts and take other steps to increase safety during higher-speed crashes.

Examples: The Volvo City Safety system …Mercedes-Benz Distronic Plus with Pre-Safe Brake system…and Acura Collision Mitigation Braking System are available on select models.

Verdict: It works. Research by the Highway Loss Data Institute found that vehicles equipped with forward collision avoidance systems are 14% less likely to get into accidents. Edmunds tested the Volvo City Safety system extensively and also concluded that it legitimately helps prevent rear-end collisions.

● **Night vision** uses an infrared camera to display a real-time image of the road ahead onto a screen on the dash or center console. This infrared camera can detect dangers that are very difficult to spot in the dark or fog.

Examples: BMW Night Vision…Mercedes Night View Assist.

Verdict: The infrared images look cool, but this feature is not tremendously useful. Drivers generally are better off keeping their eyes on the road, not a display screen. Night vision could be useful for people who drive on roads where deer often dart unexpectedly out of the darkness, however.

● **Seat belt airbags** inflate in accidents, distributing the impact of the belt across the torso.

Example: Ford now offers inflatable rear-seat seat belts as an option in certain models.

Verdict: These do provide some safety advantages in crashes, but they are noticeably thicker and less comfortable than standard seat belts. That could create a dramatic reduction in safety if it discourages passengers from wearing their seat belts at all. Test inflatable belts for comfort before buying.

When It's Time to Give Up Driving...

Red flags that you may need to give up driving—you are having trouble seeing cars or pedestrians at night, as well as trouble braking quickly when needed...reacting slowly to sirens or flashing emergency lights...receiving frequent traffic tickets...getting honked at by other drivers...or you have been involved in any crash or near-misses during the last two years.

Additionally: If you have health conditions such as angina, severe arthritis, cataracts or cognitive problems, ask your doctor to assess whether or not your condition is affecting your ability to drive.

University of California, Berkeley Wellness Letter. www.BerkeleyWellness.com

Beware of Flood-Damaged Cars

Flood-damaged vehicles can be shipped anywhere for resale and often remain in the marketplace for as long as a year after a major flood.

Before buying a used car: Get a *Carfax Vehicle History Report*, which may show if the vehicle was in a flood, fire or major accident. Smell the interior to see if there are any damp or musty odors. If the carpet has been replaced or shampooed, pull it back in different areas to look for mud, dirt or water stains on the floor. Also, look for signs of mud and dirt on the underside of the dashboard—an area that is difficult to clean. And check for corrosion under the vehicle. Open all doors and the hood and trunk to search for corrosion, mud, dirt or discoloration.

Important: Before you buy any used vehicle, always have it inspected by a trusted, high-quality repair shop.

AAA, Heathrow, Florida. www.AAA.com

Cars Most Likely to Be Stolen

Cars that were most likely to be stolen in 2012, in descending order—Nissan Maxima, Nissan Altima, Acura Integra, Dodge pickup (full size), Dodge Caravan, Toyota Camry, Chevrolet pickup (full size), Ford pickup (full size), Honda Civic and Honda Accord.

Statistics from the National Insurance Crime Bureau.

Replace Tires Before Selling a Car?

It almost never makes sense to replace the tires on a car you're selling or trading in. If you are selling it to a dealer or trading it in, the dealer can buy new tires much more cheaply than you can. If you are selling to an individual, the buyer will probably underestimate how much you paid for the tires and you won't get your money out of it. You might offer to cut $200 from the price of the car if the potential buyer complains that the tires are very worn.

Jack Nerad, executive editorial director and market analyst for Kelley Blue Book and KBB.com. He hosts the radio show America on the Road and is author of several books, including The Complete Idiot's Guide to Buying or Leasing a Car (Alpha Books). www.KBB. com

16

Happy Home

How to Stay Together *Forever*

If you want your marriage to succeed, it pays to know why other marriages fail. I have tracked 373 married couples for the past 26 years as part of a study funded by the National Institutes of Health. The goal was to investigate how marriages really work over the long term—but many marriages don't work, at least not forever. Of those 373 couples, 46% have divorced, roughly in line with national averages.

What went wrong in those failed marriages? And what would those divorced people do differently if they could start over again? When I put those questions to my study participants, key trends emerged. Surprising: Sex was not a major issue when it came to what divorced people said they would "change" if they could start over again. And it wasn't a key predictor of divorce over time in my study.

EXPAND CONVERSATIONS

Divorced people typically report that a lack of communication wasn't the problem in their relationships—they spoke with their spouses often during their marriages. But when these divorced people considered the *content* of their conversations, many admitted that the vast majority were about the business of the household—what chores needed to get done, what time they would be returning home from work, whether they were running low on peanut butter. Such conversations are necessary in a marriage, but they do little to make couples feel close.

What to do: Discuss your goals and dreams regularly with your partner, and encourage your partner to do the same with you. Do this even if you've been married for years and

Terri L. Orbuch, PhD, a psychologist and research professor at the University of Michigan Institute for Social Research, Ann Arbor. She is author of *Finding Love Again: 6 Simple Steps to a New and Happy Relationship* (Sourcebooks Casablanca). *www.DrTerritheLoveDoctor.com*

already know quite well what your spouse wants out of life. Even if very little new information is supplied, having these conversations increases the odds that you and your spouse will continue to see each other as partners in your pursuit of your goals and dreams.

On days when you don't chat about big things such as goals and dreams, at least have conversations about subjects you both enjoy talking about. These might include books, movies or current events—anything you both appreciate that's unrelated to your responsibilities and your marriage.

EXPRESS YOUR LOVE DAILY

Many of the divorced people in my study admitted that their partners often got pushed to the back burner when life became busy. Their spouses wound up feeling taken for granted—a feeling that can lead to divorce when it is allowed to persist.

What to do: Make a gesture that shows your love and makes your spouse feel special every day. These gestures can be quite simple. Take your spouse's hand and say, "I love you," or "Thank you for being a great husband/wife." Provide a kiss or hug at an unexpected moment. Or do a little thing that makes your spouse's life easier without being asked, such as bringing in the newspaper or starting the coffee in the morning. It isn't the size of the gestures that prevents spouses from feeling taken for granted. It is the consistency with which these gestures are made—once a day at a minimum.

Warning: Some people believe that wives care more about receiving gestures of love than husbands. In fact, divorce is particularly likely when husbands fail to receive these gestures. This probably is because married women tend to receive gestures of love from their friends and relations in addition to their husbands. Husbands typically receive them only from their wives, so they miss them even more when their wives don't provide them.

TALK MORE ABOUT MONEY

Many married couples don't talk about money any more than necessary. Finances are the number-one source of conflict in marriage, so avoiding this topic can seem like a good way to avoid stirring up trouble. But my research shows that talking less about money actually increases the odds of divorce. True, talks about money can trigger spats—but couples who avoid money talks increase the risk that their money issues will remain unresolved and escalate until they endanger the marriage.

Example: If a relationship's lines of communication about finances are closed, one partner might spend freely, not realizing that the other is becoming angrier and angrier about the couple's inability to save for retirement.

What to do: First, consider what money means to you. Does it represent security? Status? Love? Success as a provider? Think about how your parents handled finances, too, and whether that might be affecting your financial beliefs and behavior. Also, reflect upon your financial goals and priorities.

Next, have a few chats with your spouse about noninflammatory money-related topics, such as money you've managed to save or upcoming expenses that you both agree upon. Mixing in some low-stress money talks can prevent anxiety levels from skyrocketing every time money is mentioned.

After you have had a few painless money conversations, share your financial goals and priorities with your spouse, as well as any thoughts you have about what money means to you. Ask your partner to do the same, then try to find common ground with your spouse about family spending rules and limits.

Example: Agree to consult with each other on all purchases over a certain dollar amount.

BLAME "US" FOR PROBLEMS

When one or both spouses chronically blame the other for the marriage's problems, the result tends to be escalating anger. When one or both spouses chronically blame himself or herself for the marriage's problems, the result tends to be feelings of guilt or depression. In either case, the odds of divorce increase.

What to do: When you have a fight, try to blame the relationship or circumstances, not your spouse or yourself. Say things such as, "We were both tired when we said those things"…or "We just weren't communicating well."

Also, people who already have divorced should take care to not blame their former spouses or themselves for the failure of that marriage. Use phrases that absolve you both such as, "We married too young"…or "We just weren't compatible." People who persist in blaming their exes or themselves are more likely to struggle in future relationships as well.

DON'T LET BOREDOM LINGER

All long-term relationships go through ruts when nothing new happens. If those ruts are allowed to persist for years, the result can be boredom, which increases the odds of divorce.

What to do: Inject passion and excitement into your marriage. *Ways to do that…*

• **Add a new shared activity.** Take a new class together or travel together to an unfamiliar location. Doing new things together mimics the feelings of adventure and passion that you experienced back in the exciting early days of the relationship.

• **Add mystery and surprise.** Leave a love note for your spouse in an unexpected place or plan a getaway for the two of you without telling your partner where you're going.

• **Add adrenaline.** Ride a roller coaster together…see a scary movie together…or exercise together. Anything that gets your heart racing and adrenaline pumping will release chemicals into your brain similar to those experienced by people who are passionately in love. Do such things together with your spouse a few times, and these chemicals could help rekindle your passion, excitement and sexual arousal for each other.

Improve Your Marriage in Just 7 Minutes

Rebecca Shannonhouse, editor, *Bottom Line/Health*, 281 Tresser Blvd., Stamford, Connecticut 06901. *www. BottomLinePublications.com*

Count yourself lucky if you have a good marriage. More than half of people who are "very happy" in their marriages are very happy in general. They're also healthier.

One study found that happily married heart patients were 3.2 times more likely to live 15 years or more after surgery than those with less satisfactory marriages. Sadly, however, marriage quality often declines over time.

Main reason: A cycle of negativity ("It's not my fault, it's your fault").

Good news: You can improve the quality of your marriage with a simple exercise called third-party perspective-taking. It takes only about seven minutes and helps curb fault-finding, says psychologist Eli J. Finkel, PhD, of Northwestern University. *Each spouse writes brief responses to these questions…*

1. What would an observer notice about the arguments you have with your spouse—and how might these observations help?

Example: "The observer would say that we've been fighting about housework for a long time and that we should finally resolve the problem."

2. Why is it difficult to view conflicts from a third-party perspective? You or your spouse might write, "I have trouble thinking that way because I'm too busy trying to keep track of my own feelings."

3. How can you use a third-party perspective in the future?

Example: "I'd have to ask my spouse more questions instead of just talking about myself."

Do the exercise once every four months. A new study of 120 couples whose marriages were suffering found that the exercise virtually eliminated the decline in marital satisfaction over a one-year period.

For Better Communication… Say It in Person

When long-distance couples express feelings over the phone, they are less likely to fully appreciate one another, which could lead to unhappiness. When the words are accompanied by body language, the full meaning is better received.

If you must share your emotions over the phone: Accompany them with physical descriptions, too, such as, "I wish I could hug you now."

Study by researchers at Purdue University, West Lafayette, Indiana, reported in *Men's Health*.

Children in the House? Turn Off the TV!

Children who play in rooms where a TV is on and tuned to an adult show spend less time with individual toys and switch their attention more quickly from one activity to another—compared with their behavior when the television is off. And kids pay less attention to what a parent says when a TV is on in the background.

Troubling: Children younger than age eight spend nearly four hours a day near unattended televisions—and those from eight months to two years old have a TV on, in the background, for an average of nearly six hours a day.

Study of more than 1,500 households with at least one child between eight months and eight years old by researchers from the University of North Carolina Wilmington, University of Iowa, Iowa City, and University of Amsterdam, the Netherlands, published in *Pediatrics*.

Good Parenting Really Does Make a Difference

Harmful parenting behaviors can create constant stress for a child, which may lead to emotional problems in adulthood.

Recent finding: Adults who recall being punished as a child by being pushed, slapped or hit are at higher risk for depression, anxiety

and/or personality disorders. (The study did not include anyone who reported more severe forms of abuse.)

Study of census data from 2004 and 2005 of approximately 35,000 adults by researchers at University of Manitoba, Winnipeg, Canada, published in *Pediatrics*.

Teach Children to Be Quiet

Teach children how to whisper before taking them to places where they need to be quiet. Show them the difference between a loud "outside" voice and a quiet "inside" voice. Try recording their voices and playing them back so that the kids can hear themselves. Serve dinner by candlelight—this seems to lower voices. And create signals to correct table manners. For example, say "30" instead of "talk more quietly." This makes correcting children less obvious.

Vicki Lansky, author in Deephaven, Minnesota, of more than 30 books, including *Practical Parenting Tips: New Edition* (Book Peddlers).

More from Vicki Lansky...

Easier Ways to Give Children Medicine

If it's difficult to give your child medicine, ask your doctor for more concentrated medication—if the medicine is twice as strong, the child has to swallow only half as much. Taste the medication yourself—and tell the child if it tastes bad so that he/she can get ready. Try chilling liquid medicine to improve the taste. You can also rub an ice cube over a child's taste buds to numb them and reduce a bad taste.

Be a Role Model When Teaching Teens to Drive

Parents are often distracted when teaching their teenagers to drive. Fifty-three percent of parents admitted to being distracted by electronic devices, including cell phones, when helping their teenage children learn to drive...and 61% of teens said their parents were distracted.

Troubling: Teens may adopt their parents' behavior and endanger themselves and others on the road.

Chris Mullen, director of technology and research, State Farm, Bedford, New Hampshire. *www.StateFarm. com*

Parents Are Clueless About Teen Drinking and Drugging

Matthew M. Davis, MD, the director of the University of Michigan C.S. Mott Children's Hospital National Poll on Children's Health, an associate professor of pediatrics and internal medicine at the University of Michigan Health System, and an associate professor of public policy at the University of Michigan Gerald R. Ford School of Public Policy, all in Ann Arbor.

Y ou would think that today's parents, having been teenagers themselves in the "let it all hang out" era, would be savvy about what kids really get up to. Yet a recent poll about teens' use of booze and pot shows that parents have their heads in the sand.

Details: In a large-scale survey of adolescents nationwide, 52% of tenth graders reported drinking alcohol in the previous year...28% reported using marijuana in the previous year. But when 667 parents of teens ages 13 to 17 were polled, only 10% believed that their own teens had drunk alcohol and only 5% believed that their own teens had smoked pot in the previous year. Curiously, though, when it came to other people's kids, many of these same parents overestimated teens' substance use.

Parents: Acknowledging the possibility—in fact, the likelihood—that your own teen has experimented with alcohol and/or drugs can open the door to honest communication. Visit the Web site of the National Institute on Drug Abuse at *www.DrugAbuse.gov* for more

information, including warning signs to watch for...then talk with your kids, their friends and their friends' parents about the dangers of substance use and strategies for resisting peer pressure.

Scared-to-Death Parents

Karen Larson, editor, *Bottom Line/Personal*, 281 Tresser Blvd., Stamford, Connecticut 06901. *www.BottomLine Publications.com*

W hen my daughter was a freshman in college, she decided to take skydiving lessons. Luckily for me, I didn't find out about it until the lessons were over. I didn't have to spend nights worrying. My friends haven't been so lucky. One friend's daughter backpacked alone through China and Vietnam. And another friend's son biked through seven countries after being treated for cancer.

We may not be able to control our kids, but there are a few things we can do to control our anxieties, even if nothing is going to eliminate those anxieties entirely, says Jane Adams, PhD, a social psychologist specializing in parent/adult child relationships and author of *I'm Still Your Mother* (iUniverse).

Start by asking your child questions about a few of the things that you fear could go wrong. The answers might reassure you that your child has grown into a sensible adult who has put thought into this plan. Dr. Adams says my friend could have asked her backpacking daughter, "What will you do if you get sick?"... "How will you know the dangerous areas to avoid?" If the child's answers suggest a lack of sufficient planning, be aware that simply posing "what could go wrong?" questions subtly encourages kids to think things through in greater depth.

Parents also can think back to their own young adulthoods. Most of us did things that our parents considered to be dangerous, yet we survived.

Finally, try to focus on the fact that having a child who is willing to take risks is better than having one who is afraid to live life. The risk takers of the world tend to be those who achieve greatness.

Legal Steps When Your Child Turns 18

When your child is 18-years-old, have him/her sign a durable power of attorney and health proxy for emergencies. If he has any trusts, review them and see if they have an age-based payout triggered at age 18. If he drives a family car, consider transferring the car title to him if there is adequate auto and liability insurance. If he has a job, encourage him to start an IRA and get a credit card to build credit records in his own name.

What else to do: Show him how to get a free credit report at *www.AnnualCreditReport. com.*

Martin M. Shenkman, CPA, JD, estate-planning attorney, Martin M. Shenkman, PC, Paramus, New Jersey, and New York City, and publisher of the monthly newsletter *Practical Planner. www.LawEasy.com*

Better Tattoo Removal

Laser treatments for tattoo removal previously took months or even years because the skin had to heal in between sessions. Now with the new treatment *R20*, patients have to wait just 20 minutes between laser treatments—this allows doctors to do as many as four treatments in one day without increasing risk for scarring or other complications.

Caution: The doctor should be board-certified and have experience using at least three types of lasers that work on various colors.

Mitchell Chasin, MD, medical director, Reflections Center for Skin and Body, Livingston, New Jersey, quoted in *Shape.*

Is Your Loved One's Hearing Loss Driving You Nuts? Secrets to Making a Hearing Aid Much More Appealing

Richard E. Carmen, AuD, an audiologist who practiced in Los Angeles for 20 years and in Sedona, Arizona, for 16 years. He has held several national board posts and counseled thousands of patients on the ways hearing loss affects relationships. He is editor, coauthor or author of several books, including editor of *The Consumer Handbook on Hearing Loss & Hearing Aids*, and author of *How Hearing Loss Impacts Relationships: Motivating Your Loved One* (both from Auricle Ink).

About 36 million Americans suffer from hearing loss—but only one in five people who would benefit from a hearing aid actually wears one.

How does untreated hearing loss affect the sufferer's loved ones? Over time, it can seriously strain—or even destroy—a marriage or parent-child relationship due, for example, to misunderstandings and frayed nerves in the person who must constantly repeat himself/ herself. *Fortunately, you can motivate your loved one to take action…*

MORE THAN JUST HEARING LOSS

Understanding the full extent to which hearing loss impacts your loved one will strengthen your resolve to motivate him to get treatment. The psychological effects are huge. People with untreated hearing loss tend to become withdrawn and are significantly more prone to depression and anxiety than those with adequate hearing. Anger, confusion, discouragement, loss of self-esteem and shame often occur as well.

Important recent discovery: Researchers at Johns Hopkins University and the National Institute on Aging found that even mild hearing loss was associated with twice the risk for dementia, while people with severe hearing loss were five times more likely to develop the condition—a link that gives sufferers yet another reason to consider getting hearing aids.

BREAKING THROUGH DENIAL

More than two-thirds of people who refuse hearing aids do so because they think "my hearing isn't bad enough," according to research conducted by the National Council on Aging. It is also easy for the person with hearing loss to blame other people ("you're just mumbling").

The most direct way to respond to this situation is to use "tough love." This means that you must *stop being your loved one's ears*. Take sensible steps to optimize communication—for example, speak clearly and face to face, not from another room. However, do not repeat yourself every time your loved one asks what you said and don't shout yourself hoarse just so he can hear. If you stop filling in the information that your loved one isn't hearing, he will be more likely to get treated.

Helpful: Tell your loved one that you're going to begin this practice out of love and concern and to make both your lives better. It is not a step that you're taking out of anger or vindictiveness.

If it feels too extreme to stop helping your loved one when he doesn't hear something, try this: Keep repeating yourself and/or conveying what others are saying, but preface it each time with the phrase "*hearing help.*" This reminds your loved one of the hearing problem without cutting off communication.

Important: If you can't bear to try one of these approaches with your loved one, take an honest look at your own feelings about the situation. Is it possible that you find some degree of satisfaction in being your spouse's or parent's link to the world and having that person depend on you so much? Wanting to help is a wonderful human trait, but when you need to help your loved one, it locks you both into a pattern of *codependence*. If you suspect that you're caught in such a cycle, seeing a therapist can help—even in just a session or two.

KNOWLEDGE IS POWER

If your loved one recognizes his hearing problem but still won't get treated, here are some possible reasons why—and how you can respond...

• **Vanity.** Research shows that 20% of those who refuse to have their hearing corrected said the following about using a hearing aid: "It makes me feel old"…"I'm too embarrassed to wear one"…or "I don't like what others will think of me."

What to do: Tell your loved one that the inability to hear is far more noticeable than a hearing aid and may well be interpreted as a cognitive problem or other illness. Then ask your loved one if he is familiar with modern hearing devices, which are much smaller and far less intrusive than those used years ago.

• **Expense.** Even many people who can well afford the cost of a hearing aid use price as an excuse to avoid treatment.

What to do: Ask if your loved one knows exactly how much hearing aids cost. Mention that many different devices are available and that costs vary widely.

Then remind your loved one how hearing loss impacts his life, yours and other family members'—and ask, "What's it worth for you to keep these relationships intact?"

• **Inferior equipment.** Many people say, "I've been told that hearing aids don't work so well."

What to do: Ask for the source of your loved one's information to determine how reliable it is. Then ask whether he's willing to take a 30-day trial to test the effectiveness of hearing aids. Most state laws mandate a trial period. Check local laws by contacting your state's Department of Consumer Affairs. If your state does not require a 30-day trial, ask that it be written into any hearing-aid sales agreement—reputable sellers will agree to this.

If a loved one says, "I tried hearing aids and they didn't work," find out when and where the devices were purchased and suggest that he go to another audiologist. To find one near you, check with the American Academy of Audiology, *www.Audiology.org*.

STRONG MEDICINE

If you try these approaches and your loved one still won't address his hearing loss, even stronger actions may be necessary. Be sure to consider your loved one's personality—can he deal with more direct confrontation, even if done in a gentle, loving way? *If so, you might try…*

• **Videotape.** Make a videotape of your loved one in a situation where he struggles to hear, such as a family get-together. Then sit down and view the tape with him privately to prevent embarrassment.

• **Intervention.** Without prior warning to the loved one, family members meet with him for 10 to 15 minutes to talk about how the problem has affected them. The overall message of the meeting should be how much the family members care…and want a higher quality of life for the person with hearing loss (and for themselves).

How to Keep Your Cool with Aging Parents

Judy Kuriansky, PhD, a clinical psychologist and sex therapist on the adjunct faculty of Teachers College, Columbia University in New York City. She is author of five books, including *The Complete Idiot's Guide to a Healthy Relationship* (Alpha). *www.DrJudy.com*

Your once sharp-minded mother has begun to make mistakes when paying her bills…your once strong-as-a-bull father has started to struggle with bags of groceries. Of course, your heart aches to see your aging parents in decline, and you want to be supportive. But let's be frank—sometimes it is really, really hard not to be irritable and impatient or even to explode in anger. Doing so, however, only makes everyone feel worse. *To be patient and compassionate…*

• **Remind yourself that role reversal is inevitable.** Even though you've been an adult for decades, it is hard to adjust emotionally to the fact that your parents no longer take care of you and instead you must take care of them. It's normal to feel disappointed and distressed about this transition. But realize that your parents, like you, also are making difficult adjustments necessitated by their loss of abilities and independence. As their world shrinks and their dependence on you grows, they become increasingly embarrassed about

their decline, desperate for attention and anxious about not being in control of their lives.

Remember how when your children were small, fear and frustration made them act clingy or throw tantrums? For the same reasons, your aging parents' emotional tumult may lead them to complain that you don't love them (for example, if they think that you don't call often enough) or to lash out at you even when you're being helpful (accusing you of being critical or controlling when you insist on taking over their bill-paying). Understanding these facts can help you accept the new reality.

• **Acknowledge your fears for your own future.** When you lose your temper with your parents, don't berate yourself for being a bad daughter. True, you probably would find it easier to be patient with an elderly stranger than with your own parents. But this doesn't stem from lack of love—it happens because your parents' failings hit closer to home, triggering fears of your own inevitable deterioration. Whenever irritation with Mom or Dad mounts, take a deep breath and say to yourself, "I'm upset because I'm worried about getting old myself, but that is the future, not the present." This reminder makes it easier to deal patiently with your parents in the here-and-now.

• **Be respectful.** Pointing out your parents' failures only adds to their distress, so make a conscious effort to be as positive as possible. Acknowledge what they do well, voicing your approval ("I'm impressed that you always keep the house so clean") and appreciation ("Thank you for remembering your granddaughter's birthday"). This helps them feel empowered and competent. When challenges arise, unless there truly is a time crunch, express acceptance ("There's no rush, you can take your time figuring out what you'd like for dinner")…and offer encouragement ("Let's try again, I think we can find that book you're looking for").

• **Vent to a third party, not to your parents.** When your emotions threaten to overwhelm you, find an understanding friend or another family member to whom you can voice your complaints…or join a support group for children of aging parents. Do not express your anger directly to your parents—this only makes them feel defensive or insecure and causes them to become argumentative or to withdraw into a shell. If you do lose your cool, apologize and be reassuring of your love, saying, "I am so sorry that I got upset. Changes are tough for all of us, but I love you now as much as ever—and always will."

Real Help for Alzheimer's Patients and Their Families

The best online sites include Alzheimer's Association (at *www.alz.org*), which lists warning signs, disease stages, treatments, care options and financial-planning advice. It has message boards for patients and caregivers. Alzheimer's Disease Education and Referral Center (*www.NIHSeniorHealth.gov*), from the National Institute on Aging, has information on the latest studies about the disease's causes and possible cures. And PBS offers a 90-minute documentary on Alzheimer's patients and their families (see *www.PBS.org/theforgetting*). Finally, This Caring Home (*www.ThisCaring Home.org*), from Weill Cornell Medical College, gives room-by-room safety recommendations and solutions to problems.

Kiplinger's Retirement Report. www.Kiplinger.com

How to Offer Comfort to Someone Who Is Dying

Maggie Callanan, RN, who has specialized in the care of the dying for more than 30 years. She is author of *Final Journeys: A Practical Guide for Bringing Care and Comfort at the End of Life* and coauthor, with Patricia Kelley, of *Final Gifts: Understanding the Special Awareness, Needs, and Communications of the Dying* (both from Bantam).

It's one of the most dreaded pieces of news we can receive—a friend or loved one is dying. How you respond to the situation can affect not only the person's death, but also your own eventual grieving process.

But few of us have much experience in being with someone who is dying. What should we say—and not say? What if the prospect of a visit seems overwhelming? *Here's what helps most…*

PLANNING THE VISIT

Anxiety about visiting a dying friend or relative is very normal. Death can arouse uneasiness and worry about how the person will have changed—particularly if you have not seen him/her for some time.

But if you can, go ahead and visit. The fact that you care enough to overcome your discomfort will mean a great deal to your friend or relative. And the fact that you got to visit or say good-bye to your loved one before he died may help you avoid any regrets.

During visits, one of the most important messages we can convey to a dying person is a sense of what has not changed—that deep down inside, your loved one is still the same wonderful friend, beloved brother or cousin.

To maintain that sense of connection, remember that dying doesn't change your fundamental relationship. Be who you are—don't act differently or phony. If humor has been a big part of your relationship, don't stop now. If you and the ill person typically talked about sports, then it's fine to mention a recent game.

If you used to get together once a month, resist the temptation to visit every other day—others may have the same idea, putting a burden on the dying person and caregivers.

To maximize your time with the person: A good rule of thumb is to increase the frequency of your get-togethers by half—for example, every two weeks instead of every three.

Ask caregivers about the frequency of visits. They will know what other visits are planned and can gauge the dying person's condition and mood. Always call, text or e-mail the caregiver (depending on the method of contact he prefers) before you come.

If you are living with a dying person, recognize that he may become quiet and introspective and may not want a lot of conversation with you. Pay attention to signals.

269

WHAT TO SAY

At the end of life, it's common for the dying person to focus less on physical infirmities (assuming pain is controlled) and increasingly on emotional and spiritual concerns and worries about those being left behind.

What helps: Rather than asking, "How are you feeling?" a gentle query such as "How are things?" is often a more appropriate opening. Also, you may want to ask, "Is there anything you'd like to talk about?" If the person doesn't wish to talk, don't persist. If you don't know what to say, you can praise the person, if it seems appropriate. "I really admire how you're handling your illness. I don't think I could deal with it with such dignity."

Also helpful: If words fail you at the moment, don't be afraid of silence. If it's appropriate to your relationship, put your hand on the other person's. Touch can speak volumes.

Important: If the dying person is in a phase of denial about his impending death, be compassionate and do not try to break through with the truth. For example, if your brother talks about joining you at the family beach house, there's no need to tell him that he won't be going. Instead, validate the feeling behind his wish. "What a delightful place! We've always had so much fun there, haven't we?" You can then reminisce about the happy times you shared there.

SHOW HOW YOU FEEL

You may think that you need to put on a brave face. But the fact is, you're sad about the impending death, so you won't fool anyone by acting otherwise. Even worse, it could leave the impression that you don't care.

What helps: Let yourself cry. Don't worry that if you cry the dying person will start crying, too. Perhaps he will, but there's nothing wrong with crying together.

Important: Avoid the temptation to shelter children from these painful emotions. How else can they learn to grieve and cope with such situations later in their lives?

You can take children to visit a dying person. If excluded, they often imagine something far worse than reality.

Exception: Avoid taking children to the intensive care unit (ICU). Many hospitals do not allow anyone under age 12 in an ICU, and children tend to get frightened of the medical equipment and machines.

CAN YOU FACE IT?

If you just can't face the prospect of being with someone who is dying, stay home. Uncontrolled sobbing won't help anyone.

If you're not able to visit: Send cards, letters and e-mails showing that you care. Think of practical ways that you can ease the burden on the dying and the caregivers—for example, shop for food or cut the lawn. Leave a pot of tulips on the person's doorstep with a card. Or drop off a CD of music.

YOUR GIFTS TO THE DYING

As most people prepare to leave the world, they look back and need to know—has my life made a difference? Whether you're a son or daughter or friend, let the person know how he has enriched your life.

What helps: You can say: "You've taught me so much," "Remember all the great times we had?" You can also put together an album of photos recalling your life together.

Contrary to a myth, it's fine to recognize that life will go on after the person is gone. You can tell him that his loved ones will take care of one another and that their shared memories will be a continuing source of strength.

Also: Most people have a final need—to convey the wisdom they've acquired during a lifetime. Listen. You also might want to write down or tape-record these remarks.

Cats Can Get Alzheimer's

To determine if a cat is experiencing cognitive decline, look for disorientation…altered social interactions…sleep disturbances, including nighttime howling…house soiling…and altered activity level. If a cat shows more than one of these symptoms over a period of a few months, see your veterinarian.

Nicholas H. Dodman, BVMS, veterinarian and program director of the animal behavior department of clinical sciences, Tufts' Cummings School of Veterinary Medicine, Medford, Massachusetts, quoted in *Catnip*.

Surprising Cures for Dogs and Cats

Robert L. Ridgway, DVM, a veterinarian at Orange County Animal Services in Orlando, Florida. He previously served in the US Army Veterinary Corps, where he headed the Department of Defense Military Dog Veterinary Service at Lackland Air Force Base. He is author of *How to Treat Your Dogs and Cats with Over-the-Counter Drugs* (iUniverse).

Visits to the veterinarian can cost pet owners a pretty penny, but there are situations when pet owners can safely avoid vet bills by treating their pets themselves or by taking action to prevent dog or cat health problems. *Among them…*

MOTION SICKNESS

Over-the-counter (OTC) allergy medication *diphenhydramine* (Benadryl) is a safe and effective motion sickness treatment for dogs and cats that become nauseated on trips, just as it is for humans. Benadryl also causes drowsiness, calming pets made anxious by travel.

The challenge is getting the dosage right—most pets are significantly smaller than people, and they require lower doses. One milligram of Benadryl per pound of body weight is a reasonable rule of thumb, but start with a much smaller dose—perhaps one-quarter of a milligram per pound—when you give a pet Benadryl for the first time. This medication makes most pets and people drowsy, but causes the opposite reaction in a small percentage of users. Stop use if the animal becomes hyperactive.

Helpful: To get dogs and cats to take medications, you can put soft cheese, bread or peanut butter around a pill or add liquid medicine to canned pet food or other food that your pet enjoys.

EAR INFECTIONS

Signs of ear infections in pets include redness and swelling around the ear, loss of balance, red or yellow discharge from the ear or persistent ear scratching and head shaking. Once a pet develops an ear infection, a trip to the vet is required. But pet owners can help prevent ear infections by cleaning pets' ears when needed. Look for accumulations of black-looking material or other matter.

Lie the dog or cat on its side. Ask a family member to help hold the pet down if it is large or feisty. Fill its ear with mineral oil, massage the area, then fill the ear with warm water to rinse out the oil. Ideally this process should be repeated three times with each ear, letting the pet shake its head to clear out the liquid after each filling of mineral oil or warm water.

Do this ear cleaning in the bathroom or outside. Otherwise the mineral oil and earwax could stain furniture or carpets.

"PRICKERS" IN THE SKIN

A widespread weed, known as foxtail or grass awns, has aggressive seeds (awns) that stick to pets' fur and burrow into skin, causing infections or abscesses.

In some cases, grass awns work their way into an animal's chest or abdominal cavity, causing serious lifelong health problems or even death. Both dogs and cats can be affected, though problems are less common with cats, which often can remove grass awns while grooming. The best solution is prevention—regularly mow lawns where pets spend time and keep pets out of tall, weedy grass.

When a pet does get into tall grass, examine the animal very carefully and remove any seedpods and stickers. A trip to the veterinarian is required once a grass awn gets into the pet's skin.

CANINE KENNEL COUGH

If a dog exhibits a dry and hacking cough that becomes worse when temperatures drop in the evening, the cause probably is kennel cough, which typically lasts two to three weeks. Kennel cough is spread like the common cold, so any contact with an infected dog potentially can transmit the disease. There's little point to taking a dog with kennel cough to the vet right away—as with the common cold, there is no cure.

To help relieve the cough so that you and the dog can get some sleep, try Robitussin DM, the same OTC medicine that you might use yourself. This won't cure the underlying problem, but it can at least calm the cough for a while so that the pet—and everyone else in the house—can relax and sleep through the night. One teaspoon is a reasonable dose for a large dog…one-half teaspoon for a small dog. If the cough persists, it's probably worth a trip to the vet.

CAT HAIR BALL INTESTINAL BLOCKAGES

Cats use their tongues to groom their fur, and some fur inevitably is ingested. While most ingested fur simply passes through the cat, some of it can remain in the stomach, becoming a hair ball.

If you have good reason to believe that your cat has developed an intestinal blockage—an empty litter box suggesting constipation, for example, or repeated retching without producing a hair ball—put undiluted Carnation concentrated canned milk in its dish and let it drink. Soon after, the cat will have loose stools, cleaning out the intestines. If symptoms persist, see a veterinarian.

DOGS WITH RED, INFLAMED LIPS AND NOSE

Plastic food and water bowls often are to blame when dogs develop these symptoms— some dogs are allergic to chemicals found in plastics. If so, switching to a stainless steel or ceramic bowl should solve the problem.

See a vet if the dog has not been eating from plastic bowls or if you make the switch and don't see any improvement within two weeks or so. Plastic bowls don't seem to cause these problems for cats.

More from Dr. Robert L. Ridgway…

Choking Danger for Dogs

Dogs that enjoy retrieving balls and carrying them around in their mouths sometimes get those balls lodged in their throats. When that happens, there isn't time to get to a veterinarian's office—the dog is unlikely to survive more than three to five minutes if its airway is not cleared.

The best solution is prevention—select toy balls large enough that they can't fit in the dog's throat, yet small enough that the dog can carry them in its mouth. Tennis balls often are too small for large breeds.

If your dog does get a ball lodged in its throat, first try to open the dog's mouth and reach a finger behind the ball to pull it free.

Do not attempt to grip the ball from the top if you cannot get a finger behind it—that's more likely to push the ball farther down the throat than pull it out.

If that fails, pick the dog up if it's small enough to lift, turn it mouth-end down and give a few shakes. If the dog is too large to pick up, lift up its back legs, tilting the dog forward.

If that too fails, try the *Heimlich maneuver*. While standing behind or over the dog, reach under its belly with both hands and find the last rib with your thumb. Position your hands just past the end of the rib cage, make a fist with one hand, wrap your other hand around this fist, then give a quick jerk inward and upward, into the abdomen. Use enough force to lift the back end of the dog up off the ground. Repeat several times if necessary.

Save on Pet Meds

To keep pet medication costs down, check drugstore prices before having your vet fill the prescription—you might save as much as $10 on a prescription. Also, ask for the generic drug when one is available—that may save you more than $200/month for long-term daily medications. And become a member of AAA—you save an average of 24% on prescription drugs for pets and humans. To find participating pharmacies, go to *www.AAA.com/ prescriptions*.

Woman's Day. www.WomansDay.com

Road Trip with Your Pet? Don't Forget This…

When taking pets across state lines, a Certificate of Veterinary Inspection from your vet is required, confirming that the animal has no signs of contagious diseases. Pet owners are rarely stopped for not having a certificate, but if you are, the fine can be as much as $1,000.

Woman's Day. www.WomansDay.com

17

Household Hints

Wow! This Is My House? Simple Renovations That Can Transform Any Home

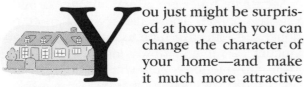

You just might be surprised at how much you can change the character of your home—and make it much more attractive to potential buyers—without going broke doing it.

If you make changes that are popular with today's buyers, your renovation won't just provide you with a nicer home to live in—it will make the home easier to sell.

Here are eight renovations and modifications that you can enjoy now and that can help you sell your home in what remains very much a buyer's market…

• **Add a full glass wall.** Glass exterior walls provide three benefits that today's buyers love—they bring in massive amounts of natu-ral light…make the home feel more connected to the outdoors…and make a small room feel bigger.

Replacing a 12-to-14-foot wall with floor-to-ceiling windows that slide open will cost around $15,000. Adding nice curtains or blinds sufficient to cover this window wall could add several hundred or more to the price, depend-ing on the materials selected.

Yes, that's a lot of money, but it really will turn the room into a distinctive selling point for the home.

Consider adding a patio and deck furniture right outside the sliding glass wall to create some outdoor living space. That's like adding a room to your home without the relatively high costs of an addition.

Jonathan and Drew Scott, hosts of *Property Brothers*, an HGTV program about renovating fixer-uppers, Wednesdays at 9:00 pm EST. Jonathan is a licensed contractor…his twin brother, Drew, a real estate agent. Together they own Scott Real Estate Inc., which has offices in Las Vegas and Vancouver and Calgary, Canada. *www.HGTV.com*

273

• **Remove interior walls in the main living space.** Today's home buyers like open floor plans with good sight lines. Ripping out some of the walls that separate the kitchen, dining area and living room could make an old, cramped home seem significantly more modern and spacious.

Costs will vary greatly depending mainly on whether the walls removed are load-bearing walls. Pulling down nonload-bearing walls and patching and repainting the resulting gaps in the drywall, ceiling and floor could cost as little as $500 to $1,000.*

Removing a load-bearing wall could cost well into the thousands—perhaps as much as $10,000—depending on the size of the wall and the amount of structural work required.

Warning: Consult a contractor or residential structural engineer before removing any walls unless you have access to the blueprints and are absolutely certain that the wall is not load-bearing.

• **Combine two bedrooms of modest size into a master bedroom suite.** An impressive master bedroom suite featuring a big bedroom, spacious closets and a roomy master bath helps sell a home these days—more so than a large number of bedrooms. Perhaps that's because couples are marrying later and having fewer children.

It typically costs just a few thousand dollars to convert two small adjacent bedrooms into one big one. However, prices could climb into the low five figures if the project includes adding a new bathroom or completely remodeling an existing bathroom and/or if a load-bearing wall is removed.

• **Turn a dining room into an office.** Today's home buyers don't see much value in having multiple eating areas. If a home's kitchen is large enough for a full-sized table, consider alternative uses for the dining room.

It could become part of an open floor plan, as discussed earlier, but another option is to convert the dining room into an office. This might be as simple as framing a door into an open dining room entryway, which should cost well under $1,000.

*Prices subject to change.

Warning: Some people turn their dining room into an extra bedroom, but having a bedroom right next to the kitchen usually is an awkward configuration. An office is more appropriate in this location. Buyers with big families still can use the office as a bedroom if they like.

• **Add built-in storage.** Many Americans consider extensive built-in storage a big plus. Woodworkers might charge tens of thousands of dollars to build custom cabinets, but there are more cost-effective options.

For example, Ikea's wardrobe systems are well-designed, stylish and affordable. On the Ikea Web site (*www.Ikea.com*), select "Bedroom," then "Bedroom storage" and finally "Wardrobes" to see the styles that are available. For a few thousand dollars, you can line an entire wall with these, then hire a drywall contractor for about $500 to add wallboard above and at the ends of the wardrobes so that they appear to be built-in components.

• **Add windows, skylights or solar light tubes** to bring more natural light into dark rooms. Older homes often have less sunlight than today's buyers like. Adding windows or skylights could be an option, depending on the layout of the home, but each one that you add could cost upward of $1,000, between the cost of the unit itself and the cost of professional installation.

Solar light tubes are a more affordable and versatile option. These use a small rooftop dome and reflective tube to pull a surprising amount of sunlight down into the house—even into interior rooms where adding windows and skylights is not feasible. From inside the room, these just look like overhead lights on the ceiling.

One light tube should be enough for a small room, though two or more might be needed in a large space. They can make a dark room sunny and bright for perhaps $500 or $600 apiece installed. Solatube is the nation's leading provider (888-765-2882, *www.Solatube.com*).

• **Replace your kitchen countertop.** Countertops are the single kitchen element most likely to influence a buyer's opinion of the room. Granite and quartz countertops convey a sense of high-end quality—even though they have come down significantly in price in recent years.

Shop carefully, and you now can find these for as little as $3,500, including installation, assuming that your kitchen is of average size.

Adding impressive new countertops above old, worn kitchen cabinets won't fool anyone, however. If your cabinets are showing some age but they still are in reasonable shape, you could paint them white and add attractive new hardware—big-box stores such as Walmart, Lowe's and The Home Depot sometimes sell bags of attractive brushed nickel cabinet hardware for as little as $1 per piece.

If your kitchen cabinets are beyond basic rehab, new prefab cabinets of reasonable quality can be found at big-box stores for as little as $3,000 to $4,000.

• **Replace old bathroom vanities.** The single most cost-effective way to make a bathroom seem more upscale is to install a vanity that has a granite or quartz top and dark-wood cabinets.

I've come across these for as little as $800 at Costco (*www.Costco.com*). Grab one if you see such a deal and the item seems right for your bathroom—that's less than you would normally pay for the granite top alone.

Renovating? Tricks to Contain the Dust

Jeffery C. May, principal scientist with May Indoor Air Investigations LLC, an air-quality assessment company in Tyngsborough, Massachusetts. He is author of *Jeff May's Healthy Home Tips: A Workbook for Detecting, Diagnosing, and Eliminating Pesky Pests, Stinky Stenches, Musty Mold, and Other Aggravating Home Problems* (The Johns Hopkins University Press). *www. MayIndoorAir.com*

Home fix-ups can release renovation dust into a home's air. The dust can spread throughout your home, making cleanup difficult. And the dust even can cause respiratory distress. *What to do to protect your home and family...*

• **Isolate the work area.** Hang fire-resistant, clear six-mil-thick polyethylene sheeting to separate the area under renovation from the rest of the home, or ask contractors to do so. Expect to pay about $100 for a 20-foot-by-100-foot roll at a home center.*

"Zipper tape"—a zipper designed to adhere to plastic sheeting—is an effective way to seal the entrance to the work area. It typically costs $10 to $20 in home centers.

Helpful: The extending pole system Zip-Pole allows plastic sheeting to be hung without stapling or taping to walls and ceilings (800-718-2255, *www.ZipWall.com*, $126.85 for a four-pole system on Amazon.com).

Use plastic sheeting to create an enclosed walkway from the work area to the nearest exit, too. If that's impractical, at least place an adhesive doormat by the work-area exit to collect dust from shoes. Products include Pro Tect Floor Protection Surface Mats (800-545-0826 *www.Pro-Tect.com*, $58 for two 30-sheet mats) and 3M Dirt Catcher Super Sticky Mat (one 15-sheet mat for less than $30 on Amazon.com).

• **Create negative air pressure.** Place an exhaust fan in a work-area window. Aim it outward so that it pulls air from the work area to the outdoors. This prevents airflow from circulating work-area dust to the rest of the home—the airflow will move in the other direction.

• **Cover carpets.** If there's carpeting in the renovation area, cover it with Pro Tect's Carpet Protection Film (800-545-0826, *www.Pro-Tect. com*, $44 for a 2-foot-by-200-foot roll). Otherwise, dust from the renovation will settle in the carpet, where it becomes a long-term problem. All vacuuming during renovation and cleanup should be done with a high-efficiency particulate air (HEPA) vacuum.

Warning: Basic plastic sheeting does not adequately protect carpets during renovations—workers' feet are likely to pull it out of place.

• **Protect your home's heating, ventilation and air-conditioning (HVAC) system.** Do not operate your home's HVAC system during a renovation unless the registers and grilles—the openings where air is released from or returned to the duct system—in the

*Prices subject to change.

work area have been completely covered by plastic sheeting or aluminum foil that is securely taped in place with removable tape. Otherwise, dust from the renovation will get into the ducts, where it could cause long-term air-quality issues. Renovation dust such as sawdust could encourage the growth of mold inside the HVAC system.

Also, radiators and baseboard convectors in the work area should be covered with plastic during renovations. After renovations, vacuum the radiators (use a crevice tool if needed) and the baseboard convectors. For dusty "fin" tubing in the baseboards, use compressed air or a steam vapor machine to clear away any dust that got past the sheeting.

Helpful: If heating or cooling is needed in the work area, rent portable heaters or a window air-conditioning unit.

Home Repair Guide: Little Problems You Must Fix *Now* and Those You Can Let Slide

Danny Lipford, who has worked as a contractor for more than 30 years. Based in Mobile, Alabama, he hosts the nationally syndicated TV program *Today's Homeowner with Danny Lipford*, airing on more than 200 stations nationwide. *www.DannyLipford.com*

Houses sometimes develop problems in bunches, and there is not always enough money or time to tackle all the needed repairs at once. *Here's how to decide which projects must take priority…*

Priority #1: **Leaky roof.** If water is dripping into your home, it must be stopped immediately. Delay would almost certainly lead to mold, mildew, rotted wood and/or water-damaged ceilings. A small roof leak might drip into an attic for months before it shows through the ceiling of the living space below. Take a bright flashlight into your attic during heavy rainstorms a few times each year to scan for leaks. Pay special attention to the areas around chimneys and roof vents.

Related: Dripping pipes and plumbing fixtures also should be treated as a top priority if the water is dripping into the home, not into a drain. If you can't stop the drip, turn off the water main—or at least position a bucket to catch the drip—and call a plumber immediately.

Priority #2: **Electrical issues.** If your circuit breakers often trip…or turning on power-hungry electrical devices causes your lights to dim…or some of your home's switches or outlets work sporadically or become hot to the touch, call an electrician to evaluate your system very soon. Your home might have serious electrical issues that could cause a fire. The $100 to $300* or so that an electrician will charge to evaluate your home and perhaps replace a breaker or an outlet is worth it for the peace of mind alone. If the electrician finds serious shortcomings in your electrical system, it might cost $2,000 to $3,000 to upgrade your electrical service or $4,000 to $8,000 or more to rewire the home.

Priority #3: **Slip-and-fall risks.** A slippery step might seem like a mild annoyance—until someone has a serious fall. Do not wait until that happens. Eliminating household slip-and-fall risks usually is an inexpensive do-it-yourself project. *Common danger spots…*

•**Slick concrete porches.** Paint these with a textured antislip paint to reduce the risk. Expect to pay around $30 per gallon, which covers 300 square feet.

•**Slick or steep stairs.** Apply antiskid tape to the steps, especially near the front edge of each step.

Example: A two-inch-by-five-yard roll of 3M Safety Walk Indoor/Outdoor Tread costs less than $15. Or install carpeting.

•**Loose or weak handrails.** A handrail that isn't strong enough to support someone leaning on it is a fall waiting to happen. If the loose rail is attached to wood, remove the screws and reattach the rail using wood screws that are at least one inch longer than the existing screws. Screw these into studs or floor joists, not just drywall or flooring. If the

*Prices subject to change.

handrail is attached to concrete, sink lead anchors into the concrete, then screw stainless or coated steel bolts into these. If the concrete is cracked or crumbling where the handrail attaches, use a concrete repair product, such as concrete repair epoxy, to hold the lead anchor in place.

Priority #4: **Foundation cracks.** The longer a foundation crack is left unrepaired, the larger that crack is likely to grow—and the more expensive it will likely be to correct. Meanwhile, it will serve as a path for water and insects to enter the home, and it could cause shifting, settling and cracking in the house.

Helpful: Hairline cracks usually are not big problems, but horizontal cracks and wide cracks often are.

For $150 or so, a structural engineer or home inspector should be able to take a quick look and tell you how serious the problem is. You might be able to patch a minor crack yourself with a tube of mortar repair caulk, available for less than $10. This caulk should at least stop more water from entering, preventing the problem from becoming worse. If major foundation repairs are needed, they could cost anywhere from $1,500 to $10,000 or more.

Priority #5: **Loose or damaged shingles or roof flashing…**or tree limbs that rub against the roof during storms. These problems might not be causing water leaks through your roof yet, but they eventually will if permitted to linger. Use binoculars to scan for shingle or flashing problems if you are not comfortable climbing onto your roof. A roofer should be able to fix minor shingle or flashing issues for $200 to $400. Hiring a professional tree trimmer to cut back branches rubbing against the roof could cost $250 to $500 or more.

Priority #6: **Peeling exterior paint.** This isn't just an aesthetic issue. It lets water penetrate your wood siding or trim, leading to rot. If your paint is peeling in only a few spots that are accessible, you could sand, prime and paint these areas yourself. This won't look perfect, but it should prevent further water damage to the siding. If the peeling is widespread, a new paint job is needed relatively soon. A quality job is likely to cost $8,000 to $12,000.

Priority #7: **Aged heating and air-conditioning components.** If your furnace or boiler, air conditioner and water heater still are working, you can safely put off replacing them. Still, updating old heating, ventilation and air-conditioning (HVAC) systems and water-heating components should be somewhere on your to-do list—today's high energy costs make it expensive to operate inefficient equipment. Once these heating and cooling components pass their twelfth birthday, it is wise to replace them rather than repair them when they break down.

Low-Cost Appliance Repairs Anyone Can Do

Vernon Schmidt, who has more than 35 years of experience in appliance repair. He is service operations manager for Clark Appliance in Indianapolis and answers appliance questions through his RefrigDoc.com Web site. Schmidt is author of *Appliance Handbook for Women: Simple Enough Even Men Can Understand* (AuthorHouse), available from Amazon.com and *www. RefrigDoc.com.*

Appliance repair people often charge $80 to $150 just to walk in your front door…and the average bill for repairs is well into the hundreds.

Sometimes this can't be helped—appliances have become extremely complex, which puts many repairs outside the abilities of even handy home owners. But there are exceptions.

Four appliance problems that many home owners can tackle themselves, saving hundreds of dollars in the process…

FRIDGE NOT COOL ENOUGH

If your refrigerator is no longer as cold inside as it should be, a broken or jammed condenser fan could be to blame.

Step #1: **Make sure that the temperature control is not turned up too high by mistake.** Then if you have a stand-alone (not built-in) refrigerator, pull it away from the wall to gain access to the back and remove the cover at the bottom rear. (With a built-in fridge, the condenser fan often is on top rather than at the lower rear part of the fridge—but built-in refrigerators are so pricey and difficult to access that it is probably not a job for a do-it-yourselfer.)

Step #2: **One of the components that you'll find inside is the condenser fan.** If you don't see or hear the condenser fan working, put your hand on the compressor—that's the cylindrical tank, usually black in color. If the compressor is warm to the touch and vibrating slightly, that means the compressor is running—and when the compressor is running, the fan motor should be, too. If the fan motor isn't operating, a jammed or broken fan motor very likely is the problem.

Wait a half hour, and recheck to rule out the possibility that the fan isn't operating simply because the fridge is in automatic defrost mode.

Step #3: **Unplug the fridge, and try to spin the blades to see whether the fan spins freely.** If it doesn't, try to remove any obstructions. Then check whether the wires to the fan motor have come loose or have been nibbled by mice—mice occasionally are attracted by the warmth of the motor. If the wires are loose, try to tighten the wires. If mice have chewed the wires or if neither of these is the problem, replace the fan motor. It is simple to install and usually costs less than $50,* though some cost more.

Step #4: **The easiest way to install a condenser fan motor is to first remove the entire fan assembly**—including the motor, fan blades and bracket—from the refrigerator. That typically means unscrewing three or four screws that hold the bracket in place and disconnecting two wires. You typically can remove the fan blade from the old motor simply by loosening a nut.

When you reinstall the assembly with the new motor attached, make sure that the spinning fan blades cannot contact the wires. Tape or strap the wires into a safe position if necessary.

WASHER LEAVES CLOTHES TOO WET

If your front-load washer is not spinning clothes sufficiently dry, the problem might

be a clogged drain line. Most, though not all, front-load washers have a trap in the drain line between the washing basin and the pump.

This trap can become clogged over time with lint or small items, making it difficult for water to drain from the basin. Front-load washers will not spin at full speed when water still is inside, so clothes do not get as dry as they should.

Step #1: **If your front-load washer does have a drain-line trap, solving this problem is simple.** Remove the cover from the trap—it likely looks like a small door on the lower front of your washer, but consult your manual for details.

Step #2: **Open the trap, then remove anything you find inside.** (Be ready with a towel and a bowl—some water typically comes out when this trap is opened.) This process should be explained in the owner's manual—yet repairmen still get calls for this all the time.

Alternative: Out-of-balance loads of laundry are another potential cause of insufficient spin drying in a front-load washer. This can be solved by not over- or underloading the washer and by washing similar types of fabrics together—a single heavy, water-saturated towel or pair of denim jeans can throw a load of lightweight fabrics out of balance.

DRYER TAKES TOO LONG TO DRY CLOTHES

If your dryer consistently takes more than one cycle to dry clothes, you probably have an airflow problem. If you have already cleared out your dryer's lint filter and the ductwork leading from the back of your dryer to the outside of your home, this air blockage could be underneath the lint filter.

Step #1: **Pull out the filter, and use a flashlight to scan the area underneath it for lint or other obstructions.** A small dryer vent brush (sometimes called a lint trap brush) can help you clean out anything you find—this area often is difficult to reach by hand. Dryer vent brushes are available for a few dollars in home centers and online.

Step #2: **Check whether the lint filter is torn.** If so, purchase a replacement filter through one of the online parts sellers mentioned on the next page. Prices range from

*Prices subject to change.

less than $10 to more than $50, depending on the dryer model.

OVEN LACKS HEAT

If your electric oven is not heating well (or not heating at all)…

Step #1: **Turn the oven off and unplug it,** then open the oven door and look for the bake element—that's the dark, tubular piece of metal located near the bottom of the oven's interior. (If you cannot easily unplug the oven, turn off the circuit breaker, then check that the oven is truly no longer powered—the bulb inside should not come on, for example—to be certain that you flipped the correct breaker.)

Step #2: **Not all electric ovens have exposed bake elements,** but if yours does, examine it closely. It should appear smooth. If yours is bubbling in places or cracked—or you noticed sparking from the bake element before you turned off the oven—it's likely that replacing this element will fix your problem.

Step #3: **Even when the bake element looks good, it still can be bad.** You can test the element with an ohm meter or take it to an appliance-parts dealer to test it for you.

Step #4: **Removing an exposed bake element is simple.** There typically are two screws that must be removed and two wires that must be disconnected. Then simply pull the element out through the front of the oven. Replacements usually cost $30 to $75.

If your oven does not have an exposed bake element, accessing the bake element can be difficult even for a professional and likely not a task for the average do-it-yourselfer.

WHERE TO FIND PARTS

Web sites, including AppliancePartsPros.com, RepairClinic.com and Sears.com (*http://parts.Sears.com*), sell many of the appliance parts mentioned in this article at reasonable prices.

The Queen of Clean's Amazing Stain-Removing Tricks for Counters, Carpets, Furniture, More

Linda Cobb, known as the "Queen of Clean," author of *Talking Dirty with the Queen of Clean* (Pocket) and six other books on cleaning. Based in Phoenix, Arizona, she has appeared as a cleaning expert on local and national radio and television talk shows and offers her tips at guest speaking engagements. *www.Queen ofClean.com*

No matter what household miracles a cleanser promises, certain stains appear destined to become permanent fixtures in our décor. These unsightly spots resist our best efforts to scrub or spray them away, whether we're using a popular product or great-grandma's homegrown concoction. Before throwing in the paper towel, you might do well to try these effective ways to remove seemingly immovable spots on counters, carpets, furniture, walls and appliances.*

THE KITCHEN

•**Countertops.** On porous granite or marble countertops, tough spills, such as wine and tomato-based stains, require quick action for the best results. Immediately blot up and spray water on the spot, then cover the area with a paste of baking soda and water that is the consistency of thick pancake batter. Cover this poultice with plastic wrap for 24 hours, then remove and wash with mild dish soap and water. Reapply if the stain isn't gone.

For especially difficult stains that are resistant to the baking soda poultice, especially stains that you have not dealt with immediately, try 3% hydrogen peroxide, first testing a small, discreet area for possible discoloration of the stone. Fold a piece of cotton gauze so that it is roughly the size of the stain, and saturate it with the hydrogen peroxide. Place the pad on the stain, then cover with plastic wrap and secure the edges with painter's tape.

*With any cleaning method that you are trying on a particular surface for the first time, always test an inconspicuous area to make sure there are no adverse effects that outweigh the benefits.

Leave a plate or other heavy object on top for 24 hours. Reapply if necessary. Wash off well when done.

On laminate countertops, which are especially prone to coffee, tea and wine stains, try a mixture of cream of tartar and lemon juice as thick as pancake batter. Rub gently in a circular motion, letting the mixture sit for an hour if necessary. Again, test in an inconspicuous spot first. For especially tough stains, nail polish remover or paint thinner may work, but if either one touches the counter seams, it can damage the glue. To avoid scratches, never use steel wool or abrasives on the counter.

On a wood counter, for a heat mark (a white mark where a hot object drew moisture from wood), massage petroleum jelly into the mark with your fingers, let it sit overnight and then wipe it off in the morning. If the mark is lighter but not gone, repeat the treatment. If this doesn't work, consider the following, but use extreme care.

Lay a folded towel over the spot, and press with an iron on the medium-hot setting for about a minute. If the mark isn't disappearing, turn to the steam setting on your iron and go over the towel again, alternating between steam and no steam.

Caution: Keep the iron moving, and keep it on the towel.

• **Stainless steel appliances** might look impressive, but they can pose a huge cleaning problem—their finishes easily becoming smeared. Trying to clean them with soap and water can build up residue. After much trial and error, I found two methods that work.

CLR Stainless Steel Cleaner, a quick spray-and-wipe product, leaves a streak-free shine and removes fingerprints. *www.Jelmar.com*

For mix-it-yourselfers, wring out a microfiber cloth in a solution of 50% warm water and 50% white vinegar. Wipe down the stainless steel surface, and quickly buff with a clean, dry microfiber cloth.

THE BATHROOM

• **Shower.** Soap scum on glass shower doors can pose a tough problem. To clean, rub on some undiluted liquid fabric softener, let it sit for about an hour, apply more softener, then rub with a gentle scrubbing sponge. Wash with liquid dish soap and water, then rinse and buff.

To remove soap scum, mold and mildew from plastic shower curtains and liners, put them in the washing machine with regular detergent and two cups of white vinegar. Add several old towels, and run them through the regular wash cycle. When the wash is done, gather the curtain in a towel to avoid dripping water and rehang in the bathroom, stretching it fully to dry.

• **Toilet.** Waterline ring can be a stubborn, nasty eyesore. To clean, shut off the water at the toilet tank and flush. Then spray on white vinegar, and sprinkle on borax. Rub the line with a piece of very fine drywall sandpaper. Turn the water back on, and flush.

• **Tile and grout.** Try one cup of borax, two cups of baking soda and one-to-two cups of hot water. Mix to pancake-batter consistency, then scrub on tiles and grout with a brush, and rinse well when done. Make sure that the brush is soft enough to avoid scratching the tile.

CARPETS AND BEDS

Rugs and wall-to-wall carpeting attract all manner of stains.

• **Pet urine** is probably the number-one carpet stain problem, and I have found a particularly helpful product.

Pee Whiz, a lightly scented, natural product, breaks up the protein in pet and human urine, which is necessary to remove the stain. (*Disclosure:* I sometimes am paid to appear at events to speak about Pee Whiz, but I began using it many years before I started doing the endorsements.)

First, blot up as much urine as possible, then spray on a heavy dose of the Pee Whiz. Wait a few hours, blot, then lightly spray again. For old, deep urine stains, apply the product heavily. After a few hours, extract the product with a carpet-cleaning machine.

Note: Pee Whiz also works on food, vomit and feces stains, and can be used on beds.

• **Food.** For food on carpets, keep a bottle of club soda handy. When you have a liquid spill, pour on club soda and blot with a paper towel or cloth. The carbonation will lift the spill to the surface, and the salts will reduce staining. Keep applying and blotting until you see only clear water on your towel. Place a large pad of paper towels on the spot, and stand on it until the area is mostly dry, then gently brush the carpet.

●**Red wine.** White wine not only pairs well with fish, it also works on red-wine carpet spills. Pour white wine on the spill to neutralize the red wine and blot well. Follow by pouring on club soda and, again, blotting thoroughly.

For any sort of set-in carpet stain, try one cup of 3% hydrogen peroxide and one teaspoon of ammonia. Saturate the stain, let it sit for a few hours, then blot. If the solution releases some of the stain, continue to treat until the spot is gone.

Caution: Never mix ammonia and chlorine bleach.

WALLS AND FURNITURE

●**Walls.** Young children often leave their creative marks in unexpected places. For felt-tip marker on hard surfaces such as furniture and plastic, rub firmly with a clean dollar bill. This often will remove the spot entirely.

Using washable crayons can prevent problems. For regular crayon on walls, spray a paper towel with WD-40 lubricant and wipe off the marks. Wash with warm water and liquid dish soap, then rinse.

To remove kids' stickers from walls or other hard surfaces, heat the sticker with a blow dryer, pointing it at an angle to the sticker. Use a dull edge—a credit card or putty knife—to gently peel up the sticker.

If you have soot on the wall near a fireplace, don't touch it with water. Instead, use a dry dirt-and-soot-removal sponge to erase the soot. You can find these at most hardware stores.

●**Furniture.** Have water rings on wood furniture? Add a little salt to a glob of regular mayonnaise, work it into the ring in a circular motion for a few minutes and leave overnight. Wipe it off in the morning. If there's improvement, keep at it until the mark is gone.

To Get Rid of Difficult Stains...

To remove a red wine stain from clothing, make a paste of baking soda and water and apply to the stain. Flush the stain generously with water. Remove rust stains with lemon juice or vinegar applied directly from the bottle. Get rid of an ink stain with rubbing alcohol. Remove fresh blood with salt water. Always try to treat stains before they dry.

Research done by the Chemical Heritage Foundation, an organization that promotes the understanding of chemistry's impact on society, Philadelphia. *www. ChemHeritage.org*

Cheaper Ways to Keep Clean

To save money, stick with regular soap—antibacterial soap costs about three times as much as regular soap, and studies have shown it to be no more effective at killing germs. Use less laundry detergent, and add a half cup of baking soda to each load to soften fabrics and remove stains and odors. Remove tarnish from silver with nongel toothpaste—just apply it, then rub with a damp cloth and buff dry. Clean brass with lemon juice or Worcestershire sauce—use a little on a cloth and rub the brass, then rinse with warm, soapy water and thoroughly dry. To clean toilet bowls, pour one-quarter cup of baking soda and one cup of white distilled vinegar into the toilet, and let it sit for a few minutes. Then scrub and flush.

AARP.org

Little-Known Uses for Nail Polish Remover

Nail polish remover does more than remove nail polish. It eliminates ink stains from skin...takes paint off windows...removes stains from china...removes melted plastic from heating appliances...and dissolves Super Glue.

Reader's Digest. www.RD.com

Ways to Make Clothes Last Longer...

Try using baking soda and hot water to brighten whites instead of bleach, which can break down cloth fibers. Fasten zippers and Velcro fasteners before laundering to avoid damage. Keep shoes dry—do not wear the same pair of shoes two days in a row so that they have time to dry out completely. Stuff shoes with newspaper to help get rid of moisture.

Jeff Yeager, author of *The Ultimate Cheapskate's Road Map to True Riches* (Broadway) and *Don't Throw That Away!* (Three Rivers).

Itchy Sweater? Try This...

To make wool sweaters less itchy, wash them with distilled white vinegar. Set your washer for a small-size load, and add two cups of vinegar during the rinse cycle. Repeat until the itchiness is gone.

Alternative: Hand-wash with *glycerin*. Fill a sink with lukewarm or cool water, and add two to three tablespoons of glycerin. Stir thoroughly. Let the garment soak, then hand-wash it as you normally would.

For both processes, reshape and lay the sweater flat to dry.

eHow.com

Keep Groceries Fresh Longer

Refrigerate whole-grain bread or freeze it (in its own bag) if you're not going to use

it within a few days. Keep berries in the fridge, and don't wash them until you are ready to use them. Remove damaged berries to prevent spoilage. To ripen tomatoes, store them in a paper bag in a cool spot (not the fridge) for up to five days. Store already ripe tomatoes at room temperature and out of direct sunlight. Slice the stems of tender-leaf herbs, such as parsley, basil, cilantro, dill and tarragon, on the bias (as you would some flowers), and stand them in a container of cool water. Place a plastic bag loosely over the herbs and store in the fridge. Basil will stay fresh three to five days, but most herbs last up to 10 days.

Health. www.Health.com

Should You Throw That Food Out?

If you lose electricity for more than four hours, throw out perishable food in the refrigerator, including meat, dairy products, leftovers and cut fruits and vegetables. Uncut produce and condiments should be all right. A fully stocked stand-alone freezer keeps its temperature for two days...a half-full freezer for one day. The freezer part of a refrigerator does not stay cold as long. Frozen foods are safe to eat if they are hard or icy, but meat and fish may lose texture. Throw away ice cream if it has melted. If you are unsure about any food, don't taste it—throw it out.

Good Housekeeping. www.GoodHousekeeping.com

Toxic Sofas and Beds

Karen Larson, editor, *Bottom Line/Personal*, 281 Tresser Blvd., Stamford Connecticut 09601. *www.BottomLine Publications.com*

A new study by researchers at Duke and North Carolina State universities found that Firemaster 550—a flame-retardant chemical mixture added to the polyurethane foam used in many mattresses, sofas and other products—causes cardiovascular problems, extreme weight gain and developmental issues in lab rats. These health problems were observed even when rats were given very small doses comparable to the amounts that humans who have furniture containing *Firemaster 550* might ingest in the form of household dust. That made me wonder if I owned anything containing Firemaster 550. Unfortunately, that's hard to tell, says Heather Patisaul, PhD, assistant professor of biology at North Carolina State University and lead author of the paper describing the study. Firemaster 550 typically isn't disclosed on labels or on makers' Web sites.

As a rule, however, if you have any furniture made in the past decade or two that contains foam, it's likely that it contains some sort of chemical fire retardant—and Firemaster 550 is far from the first of these to be suspected of causing health problems. *One clue*: If foam furniture has a label or tag reading "Compliant with California Technical Bulletin 117," it almost certainly contains a flame retardant.

There's not enough evidence yet to get rid of foam furniture. But if you are shopping for anything that could have foam padding, lean toward products with polyester-fill padding—which tend not to include fire-retardant chemicals—instead of polyurethane foam products, which usually do.

Dangerous Dishwashers!

Dishwashers can be breeding grounds for dangerous fungi. In one recent finding, of 189 dishwashers tested, 62% tested positive for fungi...and 56% had a fungal species known as *Exophiala*, which looks like black slime and can cause fatal infections. The fungi is highly resistant to heat and detergents. You can wipe away the slime, but researchers are working on methods for permanently removing the fungi from dishwashers.

Nina Gunde-Cimerman, PhD, chair of molecular genetics and microbiology, University of Ljubljana, Slovenia, and leader of a study of 189 dishwashers from 18 countries, published in *Fungal Biology*.

Hidden Toxins in Your Home: Poisonous Chemicals and Dangerous Fungi May Be Lurking Right Under Your Nose

Mitchell Gaynor, MD, assistant clinical professor of medicine at Weill Medical College of Cornell University in New York City. He is the founder and president of Gaynor Integrative Oncology and is board-certified in oncology, hematology and internal medicine. He has written several books, including one about environmental dangers.

If you don't think that toxins are lurking, undetected and invisible in your home, this fact will make you sit up and take notice. The air inside our homes may be anywhere from two to 100 times more polluted than the air just beyond our front doors, according to the Environmental Protection Agency. How could this be? It turns out that the air we breathe in our homes may contain contaminants, fungi or chemical by-products that can harm our health.

It is easy to feel overwhelmed when reading about all of these dangers, but the good news is that by taking simple steps you can stay ahead of the game in terms of protecting yourself and your family...

THE THREAT: MOLD

This may come as no surprise to you: It is estimated that about half of all US homes are contaminated with mold. Mold (and its cousin, mildew) are fungi, and their spores are everywhere, both indoors and out. But mold needs moisture to grow, which is why it thrives wherever there is moisture in your home—in large areas, such as damp basements, or even in small piles of damp clothing.

If you are exposed long enough—mainly through inhaling mold spores—you may become allergic, experiencing a chronic runny nose, red eyes, itchy skin rashes, sneezing and asthma. Some types of mold produce secondary compounds called *mycotoxins* that can even cause pneumonia or trigger autoimmune illness such as arthritis.

What you may not know: Moisture control must begin promptly—you have about 24 to 48 hours to completely dry out wet areas or dampness before mold starts to grow. This time frame can help you cope with small areas of moisture and reduce your exposure to mold.

Examples: It's important to quickly dry wet clothes left in a gym bag or in a washer or dryer…damp windowsills…and spills in the refrigerator. You can reduce or eliminate mildew in your bathroom by running the exhaust fan for a half-hour after showering—and leaving a window open if possible. When cleaning pillows and duvets, make sure to wash and dry them according to manufacturers' instructions—otherwise the filler may retain moisture, encouraging mold growth.

To remove small areas of mold (it can be black, brown, green, yellow or white and may have an acrid smell), scrub them with a mixture of one-eighth cup of laundry detergent, a cup of bleach and a gallon of water.

Mold on a wall often is a sign that mold is also within the wall, so you'll need to consult a professional about removal, especially if the area is larger than 10 square feet.

THE THREAT: WATER

Up to 700 chemicals have been found in tap water, many of which have been linked with cancer, hypothyroidism and immune system damage. Chemicals such as *cadmium* (a highly toxic metal that is used in batteries)…*perfluorochemicals* (utilized in making Teflon-coated pans)…and *polychlorinated biphenyls* or PCBs (the coating on electrical transformers used in fluorescent lighting), among others, make their way into our tap water when they are dumped into soil, contaminating groundwater.

You can find out details about the water in your area by going to *www.EWG.org/tap-water* and entering your Zip code. At this site, you will find out about some of the contaminants in your tap water, such as lead and barium. You also will find out which ones might exceed health guidelines. In high amounts, these contaminants may cause brain damage, cancer and liver and kidney damage.

What you may not know: Contaminants in tap water, when heated, can become inhalable gasses in the shower. When inhaled while showering, chloramines and chlorine, which often are used to treat drinking water, vaporize and can raise risk for bladder cancer, hypertension, allergies and lung damage.

To prevent exposure to inhalable gasses and chlorine, buy a showerhead filter. It should remove chloramines, chlorine, lead, mercury and barium.

Good brand: Santé (*www.SanteforHealth. com*, various models are available for under $200*).

THE THREAT: RADON

Radon is an invisible, odorless toxin created naturally during the breakdown of uranium in soil, rock and water. This radioactive gas can sneak into your home via cracks in the foundation. It is the number-one cause of lung cancer among nonsmokers—and smokers are even more susceptible.

Most people know about testing for radon when they sell or buy a home. The EPA recommends in-home testing for anyone who lives in a basement or on the ground, first or second floors. You can purchase an affordable short-term test kit. (One brand to try is Kidde Radon Detection Kit, under $20).

Long-term radon testing kits take into account weather variations and humidity levels that can throw off short-term results. If a short-term kit reveals elevated levels, then you need to do long-term testing.

What you may not know: The EPA sets an acceptable level of radon at anything below 4 picocuries per liter (pCi/L). However, in 2009 the World Health Organization determined that a dangerous level of radon was 2.7 pCi/L or higher.

My advice: Do periodic testing and keep 2.7 in mind for acceptable radon levels.

*Prices subject to change.

18

Life Lessons

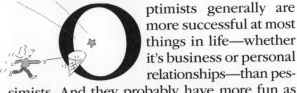

Even You Can Become an Optimist! Start Now for Better Health and a Longer Life

Optimists generally are more successful at most things in life—whether it's business or personal relationships—than pessimists. And they probably have more fun as well. But even more importantly, there's now scientific evidence that optimists are *healthier* and *live longer*.

Recent study: A 2012 Harvard School of Public Health study found that optimistic individuals had up to 50% less risk of having a first heart attack, stroke or other cardiovascular event than their less optimistic peers.

BORN THAT WAY?

Many people believe that outlook or disposition, be it gloomy or sunny, is something you're just born with. To some extent, that's true—a person's brain tends to be wired either toward optimism or pessimism. But both of these tendencies are reinforced by mental habits.

The latest research: By changing how you think, live and act, it is actually possible to *change your disposition*.

RETRAIN YOUR BRAIN

Here's how you can train yourself to be more optimistic using positive emotions and experiences…

•**What makes you feel good?** Research shows that people exhibit flourishing mental health when positive emotions, such as hope, joy and wonder, exceed negative emotions, such as anger, disgust, fear, sadness and shame, by a ratio of three to one. While you

Elaine Fox, PhD, director of the Affective Neuroscience Laboratory in the department of psychology at the University of Essex, Colchester, UK. She is also author of *Rainy Brain, Sunny Brain: How to Retrain Your Brain to Overcome Pessimism and Achieve a More Positive Outlook* (Basic). *www.RainyBrainSunnyBrain.com*

can't eliminate all problems and negativity in life, you can offset them with an ample supply of things that make you feel good.

Think about simple things that make you feel positive. Maybe it's petting a dog, listening to music, working out or meeting a friend for coffee. Make an effort to include some of these things in your *daily* routine—and jot down your positive experiences in a notebook to reinforce them.

•**Live in the present.** Increasing evidence shows that *mindfulness meditation*—a practice in which you become more aware of your own sensations, thoughts and emotions without judgment—not only relaxes and calms your mind, but also boosts your ability to curb negativity.

What to do: Take a 10- to 15-minute break for mindfulness meditation several times a day. Turn off the phone and close your door, or take a walk in the park. Devote this time to tune in to the thoughts and feelings that pass through your mind and body. If upsetting thoughts enter your mind, don't dwell on them—let them simply drift away.

After adding mindfulness meditation to their routines, most people find they're able to deal more effectively with problems and worries.

•*Act* **like an optimist.** Research has shown that activating the muscles used for smiling—by holding a pencil between your front teeth, for example—can boost your mood. In the same way, adopting the *behavior patterns of optimism,* even if they are not natural to you, will go a long way toward cultivating a sunnier nature. *Try the following…*

•Give it a go. Optimists are not afraid to take risks or try things out. Unsuccessful results tend to be viewed as learning experiences rather than failures. And optimists are game to try again. *Example:* Go ahead and apply for your dream job. If you don't get it, you will be disappointed but will learn from the process so you can try again.

•Be more flexible. Do something new—even if it's as minor as taking a different route on your morning run or chatting with a neighbor you usually pass by with a nod. Each positive alteration in your routine, no matter how small,

helps to retrain your brain and builds the flexibility and creativity that characterize optimism.

•Take command. Optimists tend to feel a sense of control over their lives, which has been shown to reduce stress and provide other health benefits. *Best:* Increase your sense of control in small steps. For example, if you'd like to have fewer interruptions at work, you might start by curbing the number of times you check your e-mail—set aside specific times to review it, and don't look at it any other time.

Important: Recognize each small advance so you'll gain confidence to make other changes that will help you feel more in control.

OPTIMISM 101
Optimists tend to be…

•**Proactive.** They take action and get things done.

•**Persistent.** They pursue their goals and try again after failure.

•**Creative.** If one approach fails, they find another one.

•**Confident.** They expect things to work out in the long run.

Crucial: Optimists tend to notice and focus on the positive things in their lives, such as rewarding experiences and possibilities, rather than the negative.

What Do You Talk About?

In a recent finding, the happiest people had *twice* as many substantive conversations or discussions that covered meaningful information (such as philosophy and current affairs) and one-third as much small talk (discussions about trivial information, such as the weather) as the unhappiest people. Also, happy people spend less time alone and more time talking to others than unhappy people.

Matthias R. Mehl, PhD, assistant professor of psychology, University of Arizona, Tucson, and Simine Vazire, PhD, assistant professor of psychology, Washington University, St. Louis. They are the coauthors of a study published in *Psychological Science.*

Forget Self-Esteem! Self-Compassion Is the Key to a Happier, Healthier Life...

Kristin Neff, PhD, associate professor of human development and culture at The University of Texas at Austin. She is author of *Self-Compassion: Stop Beating Yourself Up and Leave Insecurity Behind* (William Morrow). *www.Self-Compassion.org*

For years, self-esteem has been touted as the key to happiness and fulfillment. But there's increasing evidence that another quality is even more important to a successful life—*self-compassion*.

New research: A 2012 analysis of 14 studies found that people high in self-compassion were less vulnerable to depression, anxiety and stress. Other research has shown that with self-compassion comes higher motivation to exercise, greater likelihood to have regular doctor checkups, less susceptibility to eating disorders and better ability to cope with chronic pain.

THE PROBLEM WITH SELF-ESTEEM

Our highly competitive culture tells us we need to be special or at least above average to feel good about ourselves. But this can lead to constant, debilitating self-criticism. And in individuals who do have high self-esteem, it can contribute to a sense of superiority or entitlement, which can feed into prejudice and bullying.

What's more, self-esteem can be very fragile. It lasts only as long as you see yourself as successful, smart or attractive...and evaporates when you stumble or don't like what you see in the mirror.

Conversely, self-compassion is stable and constructive. When you see yourself clearly—both positive and negative traits—you can more easily cope with the setbacks and mistakes that are inevitable in life and make the changes needed to reach your full potential.

TREASURE YOURSELF

Self-compassion means treating yourself in the same way you would treat a treasured friend.

The biggest reason most people don't do this is that they think they need self-criticism to motivate themselves. They're afraid that if they permit self-compassion, they will keep making the same mistakes and never improve themselves.

But growing research confirms that self-criticism is a poor success strategy. Rather than motivating, it makes people feel anxious, incompetent and depressed.

BUILDING SELF-COMPASSION

Gestures of caring—a kind word or warm embrace—trigger the release of *oxytocin*, a brain chemical that promotes feelings of trust, calm and safety. *To do this for yourself...*

• **Say soothing words to yourself when you're upset.** Use the same kind of language you would use to comfort a friend in need. You might say to yourself, "I know you're feeling bad right now, and I want you to be happy. I'm here to support you in any way I can."

• **Listen in on your self-talk.** If you hear harsh tones of self-judgment, quiet your inner critic. You could tell yourself, "I know you're trying to make me a better person, but your angry words aren't helping. Please don't be so critical." But if there's a character flaw you would like to address, you might say, "This behavior is causing problems, and I don't want you to suffer. Can you try harder to change? I believe in you." These words can help put you in the calm and safe state required to do your best and make needed changes.

• **Find an inconspicuous self-caress that soothes you.** Physical gestures of kindness and warmth are the most direct way to calm anyone, including yourself. For some people, gently placing a hand on the heart or belly turns self-blame into self-compassion. You also can try cradling your face in your hand or wrapping your arms around your body for a brief embrace.

MORE SELF-COMFORT

To have self-compassion, you must accept certain painful feelings without denying or fighting against them. Notice where in your body you experience emotions like sadness and anger—maybe it's a feeling of constriction in your throat or tight muscles in your chest.

Helpful: Lie down in a quiet place and do a *body scan*. Start with the soles of your feet and slowly move upward. Consciously offer comfort to areas where unpleasant feelings arise—by putting a warm hand on the spot… relaxing tightness in the area by tensing then releasing the muscle…or by saying some comforting words.

WRITE YOURSELF A LETTER

In one study, people who wrote themselves one-paragraph self-compassionate letters (daily for one week) reported feeling happier and less depressed three months later.

You can do this for yourself. In your daily letter, focus on whatever troubles you. Write your letter from the perspective of a truly compassionate friend or wise grandmother who unconditionally loves you. Express the kind of understanding and gentle encouragement you would offer someone you care deeply about.

Take the quiz: To find out how self-compassionate you are, go to the site *www.SelfCompassion.org.*

The Power of Introverts

Susan Cain, founder of The Negotiation Company, a consultancy that teaches negotiation skills, New York City. She is a former attorney whose clients have included JP Morgan and General Electric. A self-described introvert, she is author of *Quiet: The Power of Introverts in a World That Can't Stop Talking* (Crown). *www.ThePowerofIntroverts.com*

O ur culture extols extroverts. Outgoing, personable people are praised, while introverts are often derided as antisocial. But introversion is not what people tend to think it is. Introverts have skills that often are overlooked—and the challenges of introversion usually can be overcome.

Examples: Warren Buffett, Albert Einstein, Steven Spielberg, Eleanor Roosevelt and Mahatma Gandhi are among the introverts who have achieved incredible success.

Here's what introverts and those around them need to know…

WHAT IT REALLY MEANS TO BE AN INTROVERT

At least one-third of us are introverts. Being introverted is not the same as being shy, although the two do overlap. While shy people live in fear of social disapproval or humiliation, introverts simply feel overwhelmed when faced with competing demands for their attention. They prefer quiet and solitude to interacting with people—not because they're antisocial but because their brains have trouble handling all the information that bombards them when they're in a group. Introverts can have just as much trouble coping with competing demands for their attention that have nothing to do with other people.

Example: If loud music is playing, introverts typically have trouble reading.

But recent research suggests that introverts have crucial areas of strength…

• **Introverts are better than extroverts at absorbing knowledge.** A study of college students found that introverts knew more than extroverts in 19 of 20 subjects tested. Introverts also win a disproportionate share of National Merit Scholarships and Phi Beta Kappa keys. Introverts aren't smarter than extroverts—the IQs of these groups are roughly equal—but they have stronger powers of concentration and less temptation to choose social activities over work and study responsibilities.

• **Introverts are disproportionately represented in the ranks of the spectacularly creative.** Extroverts' social nature makes them prone to creativity-killing "group think." Introverts are more likely to work—and think—independently.

• **Introverts are better than extroverts at leading creative employees.** We tend to assume that extroverts make the best leaders—their charisma fits our mental image of what a leader should be. But creative employees actually produce superior results under introverted managers, according to research by Wharton management professor Adam Grant, PhD. Introverted managers are significantly more likely to listen to what innovative employees have to say. Extroverted leaders often are interested in pursuing only their own ideas.

• **Introverts take fewer foolish risks than extroverts.** Introverts tend to think more before acting. The risks they do take usually are calculated and thoughtful. As a result, introverts' marriages are less likely to be damaged by affairs…their careers and businesses are less likely to be derailed by impulsive missteps…and they endure fewer life-threatening accidents.

Example: A study by a psychologist from Newcastle University in the UK found that extroverts are significantly more likely than introverts to be hospitalized as a result of injury.

SUCCEEDING IN AN EXTROVERTED WORLD

Introverts are most likely to prosper when they find workplaces and living arrangements that offer plenty of time for quiet thought. But we all must deal with crowds and interpersonal interactions from time to time. *Strategies that can help introverts through these situations…*

• **Learn confident body language.** Take careful note of your body position and facial expression the next time you feel calm and confident. When you later find yourself in an uncomfortable social situation, adopt the same pose. The mind takes cues from the body, so striking a confident pose can make you feel more comfortable.

• **Seek out "restorative niches."** Spending extended time surrounded by crowds or cacophonous noise can be draining for an introvert. Excuse yourself occasionally and spend five minutes alone in a bathroom stall…or use your lunch break to walk through a nearby park. Even a few minutes of solitude and quiet can be healing.

Example: Robert Rubin, an introvert who served as Secretary of the Treasury, always selected a seat slightly off to the side during Cabinet meetings. He found that being just a few feet removed from the group helped to create a sense of separation that made him more comfortable.

• **View large gatherings as a series of one-on-one conversations.** Introverts tend to be better at coping with one-on-one interactions than big crowds. When you can't escape a crowd, find one person standing alone with whom you can chat for a while, ignoring everyone else. When you must give a speech, tell yourself that the audience is a single unit, not a large number of individuals. Many introverts report that they actually enjoy public speaking once they master this trick.

• **Have deep conversations.** Introverts might not be great at making small talk, but they tend to be better than extroverts at having one-on-one chats about serious topics. Discussing weighty subjects tends to forge deeper connections than small talk anyway.

• **Remind yourself that you're not under attack when you argue with an extrovert.** Extroverts often debate issues in a way that appears confrontational to introverts. Meanwhile, an introvert's tendency to become quiet during conflicts often gives extroverts the impression that they have won the point. Don't be afraid to take your time. Do your best to be assertive when you confront an extrovert. If you do fall silent, explain that you're not yielding—you just need time to respond properly.

• **Find ways to contribute during meetings that don't require you to voice ideas on the spur of the moment.** Introverts generally like to take time to mull things over. That can make them seem uninvolved during fast-paced meetings. If you can't keep up, find another way to speak up. Raise thoughtful questions… or volunteer to serve as the meeting's moderator, a role many introverts don't mind.

• **Make friends online.** Social networking Web sites offer a great opportunity for introverts to meet new people without feeling uncomfortable. When you chat online, you filter out most of the information that introverts find so overwhelming when they meet people

Are You an Introvert?

Take this quiz to find out if you're an introvert. Answer each question True or False, choosing the answer that applies to you more often than not.

1. I prefer one-on-one conversations to group activities. ☐ True ☐ False
2. I often prefer to express myself in writing. ☐ True ☐ False
3. I enjoy solitude. ☐ True ☐ False
4. I seem to care about wealth, fame and status less than my peers. ☐ True ☐ False
5. People tell me that I'm a good listener. ☐ True ☐ False
6. I'm not a big risk-taker. ☐ True ☐ False
7. I enjoy work that allows me to "dive in" with few interruptions. ☐ True ☐ False
8. I like to celebrate birthdays on a small scale, with only one or two close friends or family members. ☐ True ☐ False
9. People describe me as "soft-spoken" or "mellow." ☐ True ☐ False
10. I prefer not to show or discuss my work with others until it's finished. ☐ True ☐ False
11. I tend to think before I speak. ☐ True ☐ False
12. I often let calls go through to voice mail. ☐ True ☐ False

The more often you answered True, the more introverted you are.

Note: This is an informal quiz, excerpted from *Quiet* (Crown) by Susan Cain, not a scientifically validated personality test. The questions were formulated based on characteristics of introversion often accepted by contemporary researchers.

for the first time. You can focus on what's being said without distraction.

GETTING ALONG WITH AN INTROVERT

Introverts and extroverts often are drawn to each other—in friendship, business and especially romance. These pairs can enjoy great excitement and mutual admiration, a sense that each completes the other. But it also can cause problems.

Probably the most common and damaging misunderstanding is that there's "something wrong" with introverts, which, of course, is not the case. What psychologists deem "the need for intimacy" is present in introverts and extroverts alike. It's just that introverts are more likely to think quality over quantity. Extroverts need to respect their loved ones' need for solitude and not take it personally.

Are You a Low Talker? Easy Ways to Be Heard

Susan Berkley, president of The Great Voice Company, Englewood Cliffs, New Jersey, and author of *Speak to Influence: How to Unlock the Hidden Power of Your Voice* (Campbell Hall). She is the voice-over artist who says, "Thank you for using AT&T." *www.GreatVoice.com*

D o people often ask you to speak up? *Use these simple techniques to make sure that you're heard...*

• **Add resonance.** The voice originates in the larynx, where the sound is very weak, then resonates through the sinuses, throat, mouth, nose and chest, where the volume gets pumped up. To be most powerful, your voice should come from every part of the facial mask, the inverted triangular area that stretches between the two sinuses and the throat. Practice engaging this area by humming as you count to 10, blending the hum with the numbers in a smooth flow—mmm/one, mmm/two, mmm/three, etc. (Your lips and nose should tingle.) Do this daily.

●**Work the phone.** When you're on a call, imagine that the other person is several feet away from you. This will help you project your voice. Never cradle the handset between your ear and shoulder—that makes you sound as if you are calling for ransom money.

●**Strengthen your vocal cords.** Susan Miller, PhD, director of the Center for the Voice at Georgetown University Hospital, recommends a way to build up the vocal cords by vibrating the lips. You can stick out your tongue and make a raspberry sound or trill the "r" sound. The vibration should be powered by your lungs, not your lips.

●**Polish your vowels and consonants.** If people say you mumble, it could be that your diction needs a little help. Say the following sequence of phrases slowly several times each day to improve your clarity—Green tea ice cream is a treat to eat…Mean men may cause harm…Go with the flow to stay in the know…Ed said get into bed…She lost her poise after hearing the noise…I knew the crew in a blue canoe.

●**Believe that you deserve to be heard.** Insecure people often speak softly. Remind yourself that your ideas are as important as anyone else's.

●**See a doctor if you have hoarseness, laryngitis and/or pain while speaking.** These could be signs of a medical problem.

Why What You Say Isn't Always What They Hear

Frank I. Luntz, PhD, chairman and CEO of Luntz Global, LLC, a message-creation and image-management company for commercial and political clients in Alexandria, Virginia. He is author of *Words That Work: It's Not What You Say, It's What People Hear* (Hyperion). *www.LuntzGlobal.com*

Did you know that it's not *what you say* that matters? It's what people *hear you say* that really counts.

As a pollster and consultant for Fortune 500 companies, I've met scores of politicians and corporate executives who are surprised that the messages they think they are delivering are not at all what the public is receiving.

Over the years, I've developed guidelines to make sure that listeners really hear what my clients are saying—guidelines that break through preconceptions and prejudices…

●**Point out the positives.** Tell your listener how he/she will benefit from your point of view. If you want your spouse to eat right and exercise, don't say, "If you don't take care of yourself, you'll get sick." Instead tell him the benefits of healthy living. Say, "If you take care of yourself, you'll have the energy to enjoy all the fun things we can do together." That way you tap into his idealized self-image and he's more likely to listen to you. You also are letting him know that you have faith in him and confidence in his ability to rise to the occasion.

●**Focus on the future.** In general, it's better to concentrate on what's ahead instead of what's happened in the past. For example, if you plan to ask for a raise, keep in mind that most bosses view a raise as an investment in future work, not a reward for past performance. What's most likely going on in his/her mind is, What's this person going to do for me tomorrow? Remind your boss that the company is making a major pitch to a client next month and that you can write that pitch better than anyone.

●**Ask questions.** If you're having a disagreement with your spouse, ask, "What did I do wrong?" When you offer an explanation, end with the question, "Does that make sense to you?" Asking questions gives the other person the chance to be heard, which opens him up to listening to what you have to say.

How to Handle a Constant Interrupter

When starting to speak, explain that you need to finish—you might say that there are numerous aspects to your explanation and you need time to present them all. Lower your voice slightly, keep an even pace and simply keep talking—do not stop to give the interrupter an opening. Ask for input from others, saying that the interrupter has already spoken and that it is time for additional views.

Talk to the group about improving communication without pointing the finger at the interrupter. You may also want to speak with the person privately to say that there is a chronic problem. Listen to his/her response…and if the person has a legitimate answer, change your own behavior as necessary.

CBSNews.com

Put an *End* to a Disagreement

To help end the back-and-forth when talking with someone whose viewpoint differs from yours, broaden the discussion by saying that you respect his/her opinion and then ask a wide-ranging question on a different topic. Decline to keep the discussion going by saying that your answer is your answer. Keep repeating your position until the other person acknowledges it and moves on to a different subject.

If all else fails, take a break—tell the other person that you need time to think further about the subject and will get back to him at a later time.

Barbara Pachter, president, Pachter & Associates, a business etiquette and communications firm, Cherry Hill, New Jersey, and author of *Greet! Eat! Tweet! 52 Business Etiquette Postings to Avoid Pitfalls & Boost Your Career* (CreateSpace). *www.Pachter.com*

How the CIA Spots Lies and You Can, Too

Michael Floyd, JD, a former officer with the Central Intelligence Agency, the National Security Agency and the US Army Military Police. He is a founder of QVerity, a behavioral analysis and screening provider for corporations, and Advanced Polygraph Services. Based in Napa, California, he is coauthor, along with two other former CIA officers, of *Spy the Lie: Former CIA Officers Teach You How to Detect Deception* (St. Martin's). *www. QVerity.com*

Everybody lies to some degree. Sometimes they are mild fibs, but other times they can be harmful deceptions. The trick for the listener is to figure out when someone is lying. This can be helpful when you are interviewing a potential new employee or asking your boss for a raise…confronting a spouse over suspected infidelity or a child over possible drug use…negotiating with a car dealer…or consulting with a financial adviser.

Folk wisdom says that poor eye contact suggests dishonesty. Some psychologists recommend watching for "microexpressions"—very brief changes in facial expression. But studies suggest that these and many other commonly cited indicators are either incorrect, unreliable or extremely difficult to spot.

The CIA has developed a more reliable system for spotting lies. It involves monitoring people's words and actions for more than two dozen different possible signs of deception. When a cluster of two or more of these signs appears in a single response, it may suggest a lie. You can ask follow-up questions on the topic and see if they, too, elicit clusters of deceptive behaviors (see the following article).

The CIA may not have detected that its own director, David Petraeus, was concealing an affair that led to his resignation, but in general, it is very successful at ferreting out the truth.

Possible signs of deception…

VERBAL SIGNS

• **"Convincing" statements.** These do not directly answer the question posed but instead attempt to influence the questioner's perception of the person being questioned.

Example: An employee who is asked about an inflated expense report responds, "I'm an honest person," or "I would never jeopardize my job by doing something like that."

•**Unusually long pauses.** It takes more time to think up a plausible lie than to tell the truth. Consider a pause to be a sign of deception if it is especially long for the nature of the question.

•**Relying on religion.** When people use God to establish their honesty, it sometimes means that they're lying.

Examples: "I swear on a stack of Bibles…" or "As God is my witness…"

•**Nondenial denials.** This can suggest dishonesty when people assert, "I would never do such a thing" (or words to that effect), yet they fail to deny the *specific allegation*…or when they bury denials deep in long-winded responses…or they offer responses that sound like denials but upon close consideration are not.

Example: A Senator was asked if he had used a profanity on the Senate floor. Rather than say "No," he said, "That's not the kind of language I ordinarily use."

•**Repeating the question or commenting on it before answering.** Dishonest people sometimes do this to stall for time while they think through a lie.

Example: "I'm glad you asked me that."

•**Attack mode.** This could involve questioning the questioner's competence or fairness.

Example: "Who are you to question me?"

•**Inconsistent statements.** Liars who have trouble keeping track of their lies might provide contradictory answers.

•**Unnecessarily detailed answers.** The speaker might be trying to hide a lie among a flood of truths…or narrow the scope of the response so that it's deceptive but not technically dishonest.

Example: A CEO who was asked about quarterly sales responded with, "Our domestic sales are up higher than we expected." He specified domestic sales—a level of detail not requested—to avoid saying that overall sales were way down.

•**Sudden onset of politeness.** Note when the level of politeness increases in response to a particular question.

Example: An employee answers various questions without saying "sir" and then responds, "No, sir," to "Did you take money from the register?"

•**Inappropriate level of concern.** When people downplay the importance of serious misdeeds, it may be because they're the ones who committed them.

•**Making complaints about the interviewing process.**

Example: "How long are these questions going to take?"

•**Appearing to misunderstand straightforward questions.** People sometimes do this intentionally because they don't want to answer the question.

•**Referring back to earlier responses.** Liars may stress that they have already answered similar questions in a similar fashion.

Example: "As I told you yesterday…"

•**Using qualifiers.** Qualifiers include words intended to stress the speaker's credibility, such as "frankly," or "truthfully"…and words that suggest that the answer provided might not be 100% complete, such as "basically" or "for the most part."

NONVERBAL SIGNS

People's faces and bodies can provide hints that they're lying…

•**Hiding the mouth or eyes behind a hand and/or closing the eyes for an extended period during the response.** The speaker might be trying to cover a lie or avoid seeing the response that a lie triggers.

•**Hand-to-face activity.** Lying can trigger the brain's fight-or-flight response. Blood rushes out of the face when this occurs, leaving it feeling itchy or cold.

Examples: Repeated rubbing or scratching of the face…licking the lips…pulling the ears.

•**Nervous movements.** Watch for movement in the hands, feet and legs in reaction to a question.

• **Clearing the throat or swallowing.** These can signal anxiety about a lie—but only if they occur before the verbal response, not after.

• **Grooming.** Liars sometimes dissipate anxiety by straightening their clothing, hair or items in their vicinity.

Examples: Adjusting a tie...smoothing a skirt...aligning pens on a desk.

INTERPRETING THE EVIDENCE

Watch and listen for the signs of deception listed above within the first five seconds after asking a question. If one appears, continue monitoring for additional signs during the remainder of the response. Remember, it takes a cluster of two or more to suggest dishonesty—even honest people exhibit one or another of these signs from time to time.

Note: A cluster consists of two or more different signs of deception. If the same sign is repeated several times during a response, it does not count as a cluster on its own. The exception is "convincing" statements, which are such powerful deception indicators that two of them alone constitute a cluster.

It's difficult to listen and look for dozens of different signs of deception at the same time. Practice by watching people respond to difficult questions on TV investigative news programs.

More from Michael Floyd, JD...

Questions That Uncover Lies

To uncover lies, ask short, straightforward questions. Even honest people can seem to send signs of deception when they struggle to answer complex questions. Remain friendly and calm even if you think you're being lied to. Becoming angry will only raise the liar's defenses, making it more difficult to spot additional signs of deception.

Types of questions to ask...

• **Presumptive questions.** These contain assumptions you cannot yet prove.

Example: You want to know if your teenager was at a raucous party the previous night. Rather than ask, "Were you there?" ask, "What

happened at the party last night?"—which presumes that the teen was there and catches him/her off guard.

• **Bait questions.** These present hypothetical situations and often begin, "Is there any reason that..."

Example: Jewelry went missing from your bedroom while workmen were working elsewhere in your home. Rather than ask each workman if he did it, ask each, "Is there any reason someone might have seen you going into the master bedroom this morning?" If you previously asked this person where he was at the time of the theft, he might now change his story and supply a reason why he could have been seen near your bedroom.

• **Questions preceded by prologue traps.** Preface key questions with mini-monologues that offer responders a way to minimize, rationalize or pass the blame for misdeeds. These prologues sometimes convince them that it's safe to admit to "minor" transgressions.

Examples: Cash is missing from your purse. Before asking a family member if he/she took it, say, "I realize the mistake might have been mine. I never explained that you should ask first when you need to borrow money from me."

• **"What else?"** When someone admits to a misdeed or lie, keep asking, "What else?" until it seems no more details are being withheld.

How to Break Bad News (and When to Hold Your Tongue)

Judy Kuriansky, PhD, a clinical psychologist and sex therapist on the adjunct faculty of Teachers College, Columbia University in New York City. She is the author of five books, including *The Complete Idiot's Guide to a Healthy Relationship* (Alpha). *www.DrJudy.com*

You spotted a friend's husband dining by candlelight with another woman. The letter you opened by mistake said that your son didn't get into his first-choice college. Your elderly neighbor weeps for hours on end and you're afraid that her daughter doesn't have a clue.

When you're privy to sensitive information concerning someone else, it can be tough to know how—or even whether—to break the bad news. Following the guidelines below can make a difficult situation less traumatic for all involved.

Stay silent if…

•**The individual on the receiving end couldn't handle the news.** Someone who is physically frail or emotionally unstable should not be unnecessarily burdened with troubling information. If it is essential that the news be shared, recruit an appropriate professional—such as the person's doctor, lawyer or spiritual leader—to handle the matter.

•**You have an inappropriate agenda.** If you're in emotional turmoil yourself, stress could be muddying your motives. *Ask yourself:* Are you mad at the person to whom you're tempted to tell the bad news and thus subconsciously want to see her squirm? Do you feel inferior and want to blab to prove that you're "in the know"? Are you facing a similar trauma (such as a cheating husband) and misery loves company? If you suspect that your motives for speaking out are less than 100% supportive, hold your tongue.

If you do decide to break the bad news…

•**Choose the right moment.** The best time to start the conversation is when the other person is relaxed (for instance, sitting restfully after a satisfying meal) or after discussing something that made her or him feel good (such as your friend's positive job performance review or your son's game-winning touchdown).

•**Avoid melodrama.** There's no need to open the conversation with an alarmist line such as, "You'd better be sitting down…" or "I know that your life will never be the same after you find out." *Better:* "I'm sorry to be the bearer of bad news, but there's something I think you should know."

•**Be prepared for a negative reaction.** Hearing unwanted news can unleash strong emotions. If the other person misdirects her anger at you, remind yourself that "shooting the messenger" is a common knee-jerk response and try not to get defensive. If she is in denial about the situation, simply state the facts as you understand them without exaggerating their seriousness, acknowledge that it may take time for her to process the information, then back off. If an overly sensitive person gets hysterical at the news, remain calm yourself as you try to help her stop catastrophizing and focus on solutions.

•**Soften the blow.** Unleashing the whole story in one fell swoop could be emotionally devastating, so go slowly and use the other person's reaction to judge how much she wants to hear. Provide what support you can—for instance, offering your neighbor's daughter an article you found on depression in the elderly…or sharing with your son a story about a setback of your own that ultimately opened up a golden opportunity.

•**Be clear about how far you are prepared to go to help.** In the days to come, follow through by making good on whatever you promised to do to help the other person get through this difficult time.

Take Charge of Your Anger to Protect Your Health: It Can Contribute to Stroke, Stomach Problems, More

W. Robert Nay, PhD, clinical psychologist and clinical associate professor of psychiatry at Georgetown University School of Medicine in Washington, DC. The author of *Taking Charge of Anger* (Guilford), he is in private practice in McLean, Virginia, and Annapolis, Maryland, and trains professionals in anger management. *www.WRobertNay.com*

All you have to do is pick up a newspaper or go online to read a story about the many ways that poorly managed anger ruins lives—in schools, offices, relationships and more. Every week, I treat patients who simply "can't" control their anger. These are usually good, caring people, but their inability to handle their intense feelings of anger hurts their relationships, their ability to work effectively—and their health.

What anger does to your body and effective ways to defuse it...

YOUR BODY ON ANGER

In small doses, anger can be a helpful emotion—it signals to you and others that important needs are not being met. Perhaps you've been lied to by a loved one or feel overburdened by demands from the family.

If you can learn to manage your irate feelings, you can use them as energy to solve problems. For instance, if you see a neighbor illegally burning leaves, instead of starting an argument, you can remain calm and educate him/her about safer ways to dispose of his trash.

However, if you're not able to effectively manage anger, it can blaze out of control. When this happens, you feel threatened, and the primitive *fight-or-flight response* kicks in to prepare your body mentally and physically for survival. Without conscious thought, adrenaline is released, shoulders tense, the heart beats faster and blood rushes to the face, all of which can have a negative impact on your health.

Anger can contribute to...

•**Heart attack and stroke.** Anger increases your heart rate and blood pressure, raising the risk of developing coronary heart disease (or suffering further complications if you already have it). Because of the fight-or-flight response, your red blood cells become more "sticky" (to increase clotting ability in case you are injured), while your liver releases more fats into your blood (for muscles to burn)—both of which increase odds of a cardiac event.

•**Stomach problems.** When you are fuming, blood from your stomach and gastrointestinal (GI) system is diverted to your brain and muscles, which can contribute to stomach upset, acid reflux, nausea, changes in bowel and urination frequency and irritable bowel syndrome (IBS).

•**Muscle tension.** Your muscles tighten in a state of anger—they become poised to help you "fight" or "flee" from the situation. The shoulders, neck, forehead and jaw are all typical hot spots. As anger continues, soreness or musculoskeletal pain may occur.

•**Breathing issues.** When you're feeling outraged, respiration speeds up in an effort to deliver blood to the brain and muscles, resulting in shallow breathing and sensations of chest heaviness and throat constriction.

Also, blood vessels in the face, hands and elsewhere constrict during anger. Your face and neck might feel flushed or warm ("hot under the collar") or may even look bright red.

ANGER MANAGEMENT

If you experience any of these effects, anger is likely impacting your health in a negative way. Besides the symptoms mentioned above, you may notice that you are constantly on edge and have trouble relaxing. You also could have little energy, and the simplest activity might seem overwhelming.

But, if you're aware of your anger being triggered, you can effectively manage it to help prevent these harmful automatic responses from happening and harming your health.

The following techniques will build your self-awareness and help you better manage your anger by promoting deep relaxation. Do them when you first notice signs of anger in your body. The first step for each technique is to sit down, lean back and let the chair support your back.

•**Deep breathing.** Relax your abdomen muscles and breathe in through your nose, allowing your lungs to completely fill with air and expand into the abdominal area. Exhale very slowly through your pursed lips, as if you were letting air out of a small valve. As you exhale, silently count backward from 10 to one, which helps distract you from thoughts of anger. Doing this can help you feel calm and secure. Many people are so used to shallow chest breathing that this may feel odd at first. It becomes more natural with practice. About 15 minutes before bedtime, practice deep breathing for three to five minutes, so you can use it as needed. It also helps promote deep sleep.

• **Progressive muscle relaxation.*** Starting with your fists, begin tensing specific muscle groups (in the forearms, shoulders and legs, for example) for 10 to 15 seconds each. Tense each group until it's quivering. Take a small breath toward the end of the tensing period, then release your breath and the tension. Repeat, then move on to the next muscle group.

Muscle relaxation helps make you aware of when your muscles are tensing and gives you a simple way to relax them. Do this exercise for at least 15 minutes once each day for the first two weeks. Then use it whenever you feel the need.

3 QUICK WAYS TO DEFUSE ANGER...

• **Sit down!** Your brain interprets a seated or reclining position as safe and relaxing, interrupting the flow of anger-enhancing adrenaline. The next time you're in an argument, get yourself (and the other person) to sit down. Say something like, "Let's sit and discuss this." If you're already sitting down when angered, try leaning back and relaxing your muscles.

• **Never go to bed angry.** Research proves that the old saying is right! A recent study found that hitting the sack after having negative emotions appears to reinforce them. Try to resolve disagreements before saying good night.

• **Become an observer.** The next time your blood boils, step back and view the situation from a distance. Evaluate how angry you are on a scale of 0 to 100. Then project what may happen if you don't lower that figure by using some of the techniques here. This will help you remain calm.

TIME TO GET HELP?

If you have extreme fight-or-flight symptoms, are getting angry more often or if others are complaining about your temper, seek professional help. Visit the American Psychological Association at *http://locator.APA.org* to find an anger-management expert.

*If you have a muscle disorder or chronic pain, check with your doctor before starting this technique as it could worsen these conditions.

How to Break a Bad Habit for Good (Hint: Willpower Won't Work)

Charles Duhigg, an investigative journalist for *The New York Times,* New York City. He is author of the best-seller *The Power of Habit: Why We Do What We Do in Life and Business* (Random House). *www.CharlesDuhigg.com*

Almost all of us have bad habits that we have tried to break but cannot. That's because we have relied on willpower. Willpower can be effective, but it's like a muscle that grows fatigued after a while, and we tend to slip back into old patterns.

I spent the past few years uncovering new scientific research on the neurology and psychology of habits. *The findings indicate a much more effective way to break bad habits...*

THE HABIT LOOP

Habits are neurological shortcuts that we use to save mental effort and get through life more efficiently. But the dependence on automatic routines—MIT researchers say more than 40% of our daily actions are habits—has a downside. Our brains go on autopilot, and we reach for a cigarette, bite our nails or turn on the TV without thinking.

Habits like these may seem complicated, but they all can be broken down into three components...

• **Cue,** which triggers an urge or a craving that we need to satisfy and causes a habitual behavior to unfold (for example, you feel sluggish and want to perk up).

• **Routine** or actual behavior you want to change (you reach for a can of cola).

• **Reward,** the deep-seated desire satisfied by your behavior (the soda's sugar, caffeine and fizziness energize you).

Over time, these three components become so intertwined and encoded in the structures of our brains that they form an intense loop of craving and anticipation of the associated reward.

STEP 1: ANALYZE THE LOOP

Awareness of the mechanisms of your own particular habit can make it easier to change...

• **Identify the routine.** It's the most obvious and visible part of the loop.

Example: Every day, I would get up from my desk at *The New York Times* building, wander to the cafeteria and eat a cookie while I chatted with whomever was there. I am a disciplined person, so it was frustrating and embarrassing that this daily habit had caused me to gain several pounds over the course of a year despite my efforts to resist. I would even put notes on my computer that read "No More Cookies." But most days, I gave in.

• **Isolate the cue.** Scientists have determined that almost all habitual cues fit into one of five categories. Ask yourself the following questions when you feel an urge that sets off a behavior pattern—*What time is it?…Where am I?…Who else is around?…What was I just doing?…What emotion am I feeling?* One or more of the answers is your cue. It took me several days of self-observation to discover the trigger for my cookie binge. It would happen every day between 3 pm and 4 pm. I wasn't hungry or stressed out at the time, but I did feel isolated after working alone in my office for many hours.

• **Figure out the actual reward.** Because I wasn't eating cookies to stem my hunger, some other powerful craving was being satisfied. You can pinpoint the craving with some experimentation using alternate rewards.

Example: One day when I felt the urge to go to the cafeteria and get a cookie, I walked briskly around the block without eating anything. The next day, I brought a cookie from home and ate it at my desk. The day after, I had an apple and a cup of coffee with people at the cafeteria. After each experiment, I waited 15 minutes. If I still felt the urge to go to the cafeteria for a cookie, I assumed that the habit wasn't motivated by that particular reward. I soon realized what I was craving was the distraction and relief that came from socializing. Only after gossiping with colleagues in the cafeteria was I able to get back to work without further urges.

STEP 2: ADJUST THE ROUTINE

Trying to ignore my craving and suppress my behavior took what seemed like bottom-

less reserves of willpower. Studies suggested that I would have much more success if I tinkered with the *routine,* simply modifying it to be less destructive. That's the secret to gaining leverage—cues and rewards are primal needs that are difficult to deny, but routines are quite malleable and often can be replaced. Every afternoon when I felt the urge to have a cookie, I would visit the office of a friend and chat with him for at least 10 minutes.

STEP 3: GIVE IT TIME

My new behavior pattern, which I tracked on paper each day, still required effort and willpower. I often felt like slipping back into the old routine, and in fact, I did have setbacks, especially when I was under a lot of stress or out of my usual environment. But resisting the cookie was more manageable than applying blind discipline and writing notes to myself. Habits are an accretive process—each time you perform a modified loop, there is a thickening of neural pathways in the brain and the new behavior gets marginally easier. After about a month, I suddenly realized that I had a powerful craving to chat with a friend in the afternoon—but I no longer felt the urge to eat cookies. *Other helpful findings…*

• **Begin with minor, easy-to-change habits.** A series of small wins makes you believe that you can cope with deeply entrenched cravings in a different way.

• **Get involved with others trying to break the same habit.** Becoming part of a like-minded social group provides more than just inspiration and a measure of accountability. Their experience is helpful in analyzing your cues and rewards and in suggesting alternative routines and behaviors.

CREATING GOOD HABITS

Trying to start a positive, new habit, such as exercising more or eating better, presents a different kind of challenge. Instead of analyzing and altering an existing loop, you have to establish one from scratch. *What works…*

• **Focus on "keystone" habits.** There are certain good habits that seem to echo through one's life and make it easier to change other habits. For instance, people who exercise regularly start eating better, stop using their credit cards quite so much, procrastinate less and have more patience with colleagues and family. Other keystone habits include a healthful, consistent sleep routine…maintaining good track of your finances…and keeping your living space organized.

• **Use a concrete and consistent cue.** Studies show that if you are hungry when you get home at the end of the day and there is nothing readily available to eat for dinner, you are much more likely to eat poorly. Just a simple cue like leaving vegetables out on the counter—even if you do not eat them—results in healthier eating.

• **Make sure that the reward you choose is something you really crave.** For instance, you want to get in better shape. When you first start jogging or going to the gym, the rewards (such as losing weight or gaining more energy) may not happen quickly enough to keep you motivated or to turn the behavior into an automatic habit. You may need to trick your brain the first few weeks by rewarding yourself with something more lavish and immediate after you exercise, such as a piece of chocolate or a soak in a hot tub.

Cure for Cell Phone Addiction

Karen Larson, editor, *Bottom Line/Personal,* 281 Tresser Blvd., Stamford, Connecticut 06901. *www.BottomLine Publications.com*

A friend of mine seems to be addicted to her iPhone. She checks it every few minutes for messages and e-mails. And she's far from alone. About one in every five baby boomers—and one in every three teenagers—checks his/her cell phone at least once every 15 minutes.

Technically, my friend doesn't have an "addiction" to her phone. She has a "compulsion," says Larry Rosen, PhD, past chair of psychology at California State University, Dominguez Hills, and author of *iDisorder: Understanding Our Obsession with Technology and Overcom-*

ing Its Hold on Us (Palgrave Macmillan). Addicts do things because it triggers the release of *dopamine* in their brains, which feels pleasurable. Compulsives do things because it relieves anxiety—and anxiety is precisely what people who endlessly recheck their phones are feeling. They're worried that someone might be trying to reach them, that there could be breaking news or that they might have lost their phones.

Cell phone compulsion can be a serious problem. It makes us seem distant and detracts significantly from our focus, which can damage our relationships and job performance. It prevents our brains from truly relaxing. Just keeping a cell phone within arm's reach at night reduces the quality of our sleep—even if the phone doesn't ring.

Dr. Rosen suggests that my friend turn her phone's ringer to silent and place the phone upside down or out of sight so that she can't see incoming messages. Then she should set a timer or a wristwatch alarm to buzz every 15 minutes, when she can quickly check her phone. She should gradually push the 15-minute interval up to 20 or beyond. Knowing that she'll soon be able to check her phone should be enough to allow her to calmly focus on other matters between buzzes.

Sleep Deprivation Can Lead to Lying?!

In a recent finding, people who lied about their scores on a test had slept an average of 22.39 minutes less the night before than people who were honest about their scores.

Possible reason: Glucose levels in certain regions of the brain may be limited when people are low on sleep, resulting in a diminished ability to make good decisions.

Christopher M. Barnes, PhD, assistant professor, department of management, Pamplin School of Business, Virginia Tech, Blacksburg, and leader of a study published in *Organizational Behavior and Human Decision Processes.*

How a Chronic Procrastinator Gets Things Done...Even When He Really, Really Doesn't Want To

John Perry, PhD, Henry Waldgrave Stuart Professor of Philosophy Emeritus at Stanford University, where he has taught for nearly four decades, and Distinguished Professor of Philosophy at University of California at Riverside. He is a member of the American Academy of Arts and Sciences and a recipient of the top honors in philosophy including the Nicod and Humboldt prizes. He is author of *The Art of Procrastination* (Workman). Dr. Perry lives in Palo Alto, California. *www.Structured Procrastination.com*

Stanford University professor John Perry, PhD, has risen to the top of the academic world and built a reputation for being highly productive. He has written 10 books and more than 100 articles...cohosts a national radio talk show...won numerous awards...and has become one of the most popular lecturers on campus. But all along, he has harbored a deep secret—he is a chronic procrastinator.

Procrastination arises from a complex mix of fear, anxiety, boredom and rebellion. Even the most accomplished and efficient people procrastinate sometimes. That's because ignoring a dreaded task brings an immediate sense of relief...and even positive feelings, because you have good intentions of doing it tomorrow. Or you rationalize how much better you can work if you just surf the Internet or fiddle with your smartphone first. But these types of mental games eventually leave you feeling like a failure and sap your motivation, which only perpetuates the desire to delay.

Dr. Perry realized that he had to think out of the box and devise creative strategies to refine and accommodate his instincts to procrastinate, rather than simply trying to overpower them...

START AT THE BOTTOM

I recently wrote a book about procrastination because completing it was a way to avoid the many higher-priority tasks that I had as a professor, such as reading student dissertations, filling out textbook orders and evaluating grant applications. I always have had the energy and time for every other task except top priorities. This observation has led me to a practice I use regularly and call "structured procrastination."

How it works: Create a list of tasks ranked by hierarchy of importance. Make sure that you have plenty of worthwhile tasks to perform that appear lower on your list. Doing those lesser (but important) tasks allows procrastinators to give in to the intense urge to delay but still be productive.

Of course, one eventually does have to confront the tasks at the very top of the list. In these cases, I find that facing a deadline does wonders for my focus. Or I am able to get into enough of a flow performing lower-priority tasks to make the priority ones seem less daunting—and so I do them.

TAME TECHNOLOGY

An enemy for procrastinators such as myself is wasting time on frivolous, nonproductive activities. Unfortunately, technology has made this much more convenient and prevalent. A study conducted by AOL and Microsoft found that the average worker wastes 40% of his/her entire workweek surfing the Internet and 23% socializing. When I feel an urge to procrastinate this way, I establish safeguards that prevent me from losing too much time. For instance, I don't start surfing the Internet unless I know I have a class to teach in 20 minutes or when my laptop has only 10 minutes of battery power left.

LOWER THE BAR

One of the most common reasons I procrastinate is that when I take on a new task, I fantasize about doing it perfectly.

Example: A dean wanted me to write a memo about whether we should teach philosophy courses in summer school. I felt that the memo needed to be full of groundbreaking ideas. I set the bar so high that I began to feel fear and pressure and put off doing it. Finally, with the deadline for the memo just an hour away, I sat down and did a respectable but less-than-perfect job.

Procrastinating gave me permission to lower the bar...which I should have done in the first place. In fact, the great majority of tasks that people procrastinate over require just an adequate job.

DELEGATE AND DELAY

Sometimes there's a good reason why I stall over a particular task. Perhaps I lack the skills to complete it or it bores me. If this happens regularly over the same task, I do everything I can to delegate it. My life is far more productive when I play to my strengths and passions and sidestep my weaknesses.

I also find that delay can be effective in getting a sense of how important a task is. Many tasks disappear if you wait. For example, my e-mail in-box is flooded every day with messages that have been flagged as "urgent" by the senders. Rather than confront the drudgery of promptly answering this deluge, I decide what truly is urgent and then take a long time getting around to the others. If a person really needs to reach me, he will send another urgent e-mail.

TAKE SMALL "KAIZEN" STEPS

Kaizen is the popular Japanese philosophy of continuous improvement through small, implementable steps.

I break big projects into subtasks, which makes them less intimidating and motivates me by offering options. If I'm resistant to starting some of the subtasks, I usually find others that I'm enthusiastic enough about to take action. When I am feeling particularly prone to dragging my feet, I get even more Kaizen and break down everyday tasks just so that I can check off lots of them and feel a small rush of accomplishment.

Example from a recent to-do list: 1. Pour cup of coffee...2. Sit down at the desk...3. Do not Google "Meg Ryan"...4. Start Microsoft Word...5. Select document called "National Science Foundation Proposal." It may sound comical, but it works.

Include "Do Nots" in your list if you are concerned about specific temptations. (In the above list, I had watched a Meg Ryan movie the night before.) Resisting "Do Nots" and crossing them off my list give me a psychological lift and a sense of momentum.

TEAM UP

Much of my productivity has come from seeking out collaborators who are type-A go-getters.

Example: Years ago, I had an idea for a radio talk show that would mix issues in popular culture with larger, philosophical perspectives. The idea gave me great pleasure, but I did nothing to make it a reality. Then I enlisted help from my superproductive friend Professor Ken Taylor at Stanford. Before I knew it, we had raised money for a pilot, gotten students to provide us with ideas and guests, and pitched our show at radio program conventions. *Philosophy Talk* now broadcasts each Sunday morning in almost 30 states.

What to Do If You Think a Loved One Is Depressed...

Richard O'Connor, PhD, a psychotherapist in private practice who has offices in Canaan, Connecticut, and New York City. He is former executive director of the Northwest Center for Family Service and Mental Health and author of *Undoing Depression: What Therapy Doesn't Teach You and Medication Can't Give You* (Berkley Trade). *www.UndoingDepression.com*

It's difficult for healthy people to fully understand what depression feels like. It's more than feeling "down." People with depression don't experience normal emotions. They blame themselves for things that aren't their fault...or get angry for trivial reasons... or misinterpret disagreement as rejection and withdraw from normal interactions.

Important: Don't expect someone with depression to "snap out of it." It is a disease. You can't solve depressed people's problems, but you can help them get the help they need. *What to do...*

●**Don't take it personally.** It's easy for your feelings to be hurt when you're dealing with someone who is depressed. His/her communication skills may be impaired, and he will find it difficult to give the expressions of support that are normal in healthy relationships. Remind yourself that it's not about you. When you are helping someone who is depressed, try to be objective and keep your emotions out of it.

●**Point out recent changes.** Denial is one of the main defense mechanisms of depressed people. They often don't recognize—or choose not to recognize—that they're depressed. Without being judgmental, explain what you've noticed. Stick to the facts. Maybe he sleeps all the time or is less active than he used to be. He might have given up activities that he used to enjoy. He probably spends more time alone— watching TV, using the Internet, etc. He might be overly sensitive or get angry easily.

You can suggest (but not insist) that the changes might be due to depression. Encourage him to get professional help.

Important: Don't expect that one conversation will change things. You might have to bring it up repeatedly. Also, men and women tend to react differently when people bring up their depression. Men are more likely to get angry and defensive…while women tend to feel hurt.

●**Explain why he needs help.** A depressed person is highly vulnerable to criticism. Try not to give the impression that you're blaming or judging. Do help him understand that his behavior is affecting his loved ones.

Example: You might point out that some behaviors, such as a hair-trigger temper, are frightening. Saying, "You're different than you used to be," might prompt him to get help.

●**Encourage exercise.** Studies have shown that people with mild-to-moderate depression who exercise three or more times a week for about 30 minutes each time improve about as much as those taking antidepressants. Those who continue to exercise are less likely to have future episodes of depression than those who rely on medications alone.

Any form of exercise is likely to be helpful, but aerobic exercise—swimming, biking, fast walking—is probably superior to other types of workouts. It increases brain levels of *endorphins*, the so-called "happy hormones." It also boosts confidence.

●**Join him in social activities.** Social isolation is one of the hallmarks of depression. But people with depression want human contact even when they're too insecure or withdrawn to seek it out.

You can help him overcome his reluctance by introducing him to safe social settings without a lot of pressure. You could, for example, accept a dinner invitation from close friends, those with whom your loved one won't feel as though he has to perform. Or you could go to an art opening or other social event where you will be around other people but your loved one won't have to engage unless he wants to.

●**Keep at it.** Start conversations. Ask about his day. Make plans to meet for lunch or dinner. You'll probably get a lot of rejection, but keep trying.

Important: Being around someone with depression is draining. Allow yourself to back away when you feel that you can't cope with it anymore. Take a break. Then, when you're feeling strong, reach out again.

●**Ask about suicide.** It's an uncomfortable topic, but it is essential to talk about. Up to 15% of those with serious depression will end their lives by suicide.

If you've talked to your loved one about depression and he admits that it's a problem, follow up by asking something such as, "Are you having thoughts of hurting yourself? Have you thought about suicide?"

Few people will admit to having these thoughts unless they're asked—the majority of suicides come as a complete surprise to loved ones. People who are depressed are ashamed of having these thoughts, and they don't want to put a burden on their loved ones. Bringing up the subject gives him permission to talk about it. If he is having suicidal thoughts, you will know that the depression is serious and that it is urgent that he get immediate help.

19

Business Bulletin

Start a Business That People Hate...and Other Success Secrets

Despite the still sluggish economy, right now is a wonderful time to start a new business. Social-media services including Twitter, Facebook and Google Plus currently make it possible to conduct effective marketing campaigns for free. High unemployment rates mean skilled workers are available even to employers who cannot offer fat paychecks. And prices of commercial real estate have plunged to bargain levels in many areas. *Here are the secrets to getting a project off the ground and headed in the right direction...*

• **Put away the spreadsheets, skip the market research and get right to work on a prototype.** Would-be entrepreneurs often think that they need reams of financial pro-

jections and market analysis before they actually start doing anything—but that up-front research and analysis typically turn out to be a waste of time. It's extremely difficult to project how an idea will translate to the real world, so these projections tend to be little more than fantasy—time-consuming, inertia-inducing fantasy. The more innovative the business idea, the less accurate the projections are likely to be. Constructing a prototype—or conducting trial runs of the service that the business intends to provide—is a much more useful way to learn the real challenges that the prospective business will face.

Yes, you'll have to put together financial projections and market analysis eventually—investors and lenders like to see these things—

Guy Kawasaki, former chief evangelist of Apple Computer. He is cofounder of Alltop.com, an index of online articles sorted by categories, and founding partner of Garage Technology Ventures, a venture capital fund in Palo Alto, California. Kawasaki is author of numerous books, including *The Art of the Start: The Time-Tested, Battle-Hardened Guide for Anyone Starting Anything* (Portfolio/Penguin). *www.GuyKawasaki.com*

but delay doing so as long as possible. The further along the project is, the more accurate the projections will be. In the meantime, a working version of the products and/or services you intend to sell will help you win over investors and lenders more than any spreadsheet ever could.

Skip the business plan, too. A study by Babson College researchers published in 2007 found that small companies that lacked business plans were, on average, at least as likely to succeed as those that wrote them. Once business plans are in place, young companies tend to stick to them as if they were scripture—even when adjustments are warranted. Write up a business plan only when you begin to make inroads with potential investors.

●**Be polarizing.** If you set out to create something that no one hates, you're likely to end up with something that no one truly loves either— or something just like what your competitors already produce. Better to come up with something that some potential customers love and others hate, but everyone talks about.

Example: Two of the fairly recent success stories in the auto industry are the Mini and the Scion. Both succeeded by producing unconventional-looking cars.

Yes, you will alienate some prospective clients, but you also will spark discussion and earn passionate fans.

●**Target a small niche.** Almost all great companies started by focusing on just one small niche and expanding from that beachhead only after their initial project was a success.

Example: 3M today is one of the most diversified and innovative companies in the world, but in its early years, it focused on sandpaper.

Best: Choose a single niche for your business that's large enough to be profitable but small enough that more established, better-financed companies are not heavily focused on it.

●**Innovate with your product and marketing—not your business model.** While it often is a boon to a business to have an innovative product or service, it's best to just copy the business model—the details of how you

expect to attract revenue and who your target customers will be—of a successful company that does something comparable to what you hope to do. Over the centuries, people have already dreamed up plenty of ways to get paid for providing a product or service—and there's no reason for you to dream up a new one.

●**Don't trust your gut on hiring.** The job applicants who feel right to a new business owner tend to be the applicants who are most like the owner—but the best employees for a young company are those whose skills and viewpoints are substantially different from those of the company founder. Such people fill in the gaps in the owner's abilities rather than duplicating skills and viewpoints that the company already has.

Also, avoid the temptation to hire the most experienced applicants or the applicants who have the most prestigious titles and/or degrees on their résumés. Instead, hire smart but somewhat inexperienced people with "improper" backgrounds—just make sure that they legitimately love what your company does. It's easier to teach people skills than to teach them passion. These hires won't just work hard for you and remain loyal to you…they will spread their passion for your endeavor to coworkers and customers.

Exceptions: The employees who keep your company's books and oversee its computer systems should have sufficient experience in those fields—those are not areas where you want people learning on the fly.

Three ways to confirm that an applicant truly is in love with your project and is not just saying so to get the job…

1. If possible, ask the candidate to demonstrate your product or service to you. He/she should be able to demonstrate it in a way that makes it seem great.

2. Track the amount of time the candidate spends talking about your company during the interview process and the amount of time spent talking about his potential compensation. The higher the ratio of company talk to pay talk, the more promising the candidate.

3. Pay attention to the questions the candidate asks. Does he have an intuitive grasp of what you are trying to accomplish…who your customer is…and who your competition is?

• **Scale up as slowly as possible.** Entrepreneurs want to be able to deliver as soon as demand takes off.

Trouble is, demand rarely takes off as quickly as entrepreneurs expect, even for companies that do go on to be successful. Delays and missteps are the norm. Companies that scaled up quickly tend to burn through their capital and fail, while those that remained as lean as possible are far more likely to survive.

• **Forgo the mission statement and just craft a mantra.** Corporate mission statements tend to be so long and jargony that no one ever remembers them, much less believes in them. A well-crafted *mantra*—a two-to-four-word phrase—is far more likely to be remembered and can keep everyone who is involved in the project on the same page.

Examples of powerful mantras: Disney's "Fun family entertainment"…Starbucks' "Rewarding everyday moments"…and Nike's "Authentic athletic performance."

The $100 Start-Up: How to Launch a Business for $100 or Less

Chris Guillebeau, author of *The $100 Startup: Reinvent the Way You Make a Living, Do What You Love, and Create a New Future* (Crown). Based in Portland, Oregon, he is the founder of The Art of Non-Conformity, a blog about changing the world by achieving personal goals. *www.ChrisGuillebeau.com*

The old adage "It takes money to make money" isn't always on the money! You can start a successful business without a lot of start-up capital.

I identified 1,500 people who earn $50,000 or more each year from businesses they founded with an initial investment of $100 or less. *Their secrets…*

SELL INFORMATION

Most successful $100 start-ups sell information. Unlike most businesses, information providers typically don't require expensive inventory, equipment, employees or leases.

What information should you sell? If you're an expert in some aspect of your profession, that's likely to be your best bet. *If not, ask yourself…*

• **What's a task that many people consider inscrutable and aggravating that I understand and enjoy?** People are happy to pay those who can help to alleviate their major annoyances.

Example: Most people consider redeeming airline frequent-flier miles to be extremely frustrating. Gary Leff, the CFO of a Virginia University research center, enjoyed the challenge of mastering his frequent-flier miles. He began charging other travelers $150 per trip to help them get the most from their miles. Last year, this second job earned him $75,000 in his spare time. *www.BookYourAward.com*

• **What knowledge have I obtained by pursuing my interests that others might pay for?** The knowledge you've acquired might be salable.

Example: Ireland native Benny Lewis became adept at learning foreign languages while traveling. He created a successful Web site and guidebook sharing his strategy for achieving fluency quickly. *www.Fluentin3 Months.com*

• **When do I feel I lack the information that I need to make wise decisions?** If others feel the same way, they might be willing to pay you to provide the facts they lack.

Example: Those who use travel-bidding Web sites such as Priceline.com typically must blindly guess at what bids might be accepted. The Web sites BiddingforTravel.com and BetterBidding.com were created to help people gather the information they need to place more informed bids.

• **What do people ask for my help with?** If friends and family solicit your guidance on a topic, people you don't know might be willing to pay for it.

Example: A California man named Brett Kelly realized that people were asking for his help with *Evernote* (a note-taking software program that he used) in part because there was no English-language guide to the program. He wrote *Evernote Essentials*, an eBook that has generated more than $100,000 in sales so far. *www.NerdGap.com*

●**What information could I provide that would be useful to those participating in a new fad?** If something is new and popular, there might not yet be many resources available for those interested in it.

Example: The trendy Paleo diet (which mimics the diet of our hunter-gatherer ancestors) can be difficult to follow. Jason Glaspey of Portland, Oregon, launched PaleoPlan.com, a Web site that offers meal plans, grocery lists and other helpful resources.

HOW TO MAKE MONEY

Decide how you will make money from the information you provide. *Low-cost alternatives include…*

●**Serving as a consultant or instructor.**

●**Writing and selling an eBook**—Amazon. com's Kindle Direct Publishing charges no up-front costs to publish eBooks (*http://KDP. Amazon.com*).

●**Launching a Web site or blog,** then selling ads on it or providing links to Internet retailer Web sites that provide commissions—Amazon.com's Associates program pays up to 10% (*http://Affiliate-Program.Amazon.com*).

TEST THE MARKET

Test the market for your idea before devoting much time to it. *Two low-cost ways to make sure that there's as much demand for your idea as you think…*

●**Contact people you consider potential customers.** Ask if they would be interested in what you intend to provide…if there's any other related information or service that they would consider to be even more helpful…and what their biggest challenges and questions are in regard to this area. To locate these potential customers, brainstorm about where such people would be likely to gather, either in your region or online. If your intended customers are other businesses, simply call some of them.

●**Do a Google search of the keywords someone might enter** if he/she were looking for a business such as the one you intend

to create. The results might give you a sense of how many people would be interested in your idea and whether there already are businesses that adequately serve their needs.

Example: If the Google search leads to a lot of questions related to the topic on sites such as Answers.google.com but few Web sites are providing adequate answers, you might be on the right track for a new business.

DON'T WAIT

If there does seem to be a market for your business, don't waste time with endless planning and don't try to achieve perfection before you start to sell. Get your idea into development and then onto the market as quickly as possible. The sooner you start making sales, the sooner you'll start receiving useful feedback from customers about how to refine and improve your offerings.

Example: Map designers Jen Adrion and Omar Noory responded to feedback from their early customers by expanding the range of maps they sold. *www.TheseAreThings.com*

If you go above and beyond for your initial customers, they might even become evangelists for your brand, spreading the word to their acquaintances about how great you are. That word of mouth is one of the most cost-effective ways to grow a young business.

THINK FREE

Many effective marketing options involve providing things for free…

●**Give freebies to tastemakers.** Send samples of your work to those who have the power to influence others.

Example: Megan Hunt, an Omaha-based dress designer, custom makes dresses for two or three fashion bloggers every year. Those bloggers inevitably are grateful for the freebies and write complimentary posts about her dresses.

●**Write free guest posts on popular Web sites visited by your prospective customers.** Many Web sites are happy to run well-thought-out content from people willing to provide it for free. Those who read your articles are likely to consider you an expert on the topic.

●**Offer free consulting.** Charge nothing (or very little) for information or services that usually come at a price, and you will attract prospective customers who later might hire you for paying jobs.

Example: An unemployed Seattle architect named John Morefield set up a booth in a farmers' market offering "Architecture 5¢." His advice impressed so many prospective clients that he soon had a flourishing freelance practice.

• **Use contests to provide free stuff on your blog.** It's amazing how attracted Internet users are to the possibility of free merchandise. Hold a drawing for something as simple as a free T-shirt with your company logo and dozens or hundreds of people might submit their e-mail addresses in hopes of winning. Those e-mails are prospective future customers.

Example: I recently received more than 1,000 entries in a drawing for a free copy of my book.

Get Money to Fund Your Business

Crowdfunding is a way entrepreneurs can use the Web to raise money from investors for a product or business. Before jumping in, there are several things to consider. First, explore how much interest there may be in investing in your product or service through sites such as Kickstarter.com or IndieGogo.com. In this way, you also are testing how much interest there may be in buying your product or service—a very useful form of market research. If backers are willing to give you money, that means you may well have a marketable product. If not, you may have to go back to the drawing board.

Second, try multiple sites—there are dozens of crowdfunding sites, each with its own requirements, fees and processes. Try to find a site that seems like it would be a good match for your product. Third, understand that crowdfunding is a form of social media—expect to get feedback, deal with potential investors' ideas and criticisms, and handle considerable back-and-forth discussion before finding out whether your concept will be funded.

Consensus of attorneys and observers of crowdfunding, reported online at DailyFinance.com.

3 Steps to Naming a Business

First figure out what you want your business name to do, such as convey an emotion or show your competitive advantage. Next, study competitors' names and other trademarks by searching for businesses with similar names at the US Patent and Trademark Office Web site, *www.USPTO.gov/ebc/tess*. Then look for creative ways to use language, such as combining two words to make a new one (Zipcar, HubSpot, Facebook) or modifying an existing word to create something new that suggests value (Expedia, Acura). Aim for a name with three or fewer syllables—these are easiest to remember and use in search engines.

John Bradberry, author of 6 Secrets to Startup Success (AMACOM) and CEO of Ready Founder Services, Charlotte, North Carolina. www.ReadyFounder.com

You Did What?! The Biggest Business Mistakes and What We All Can Learn

Laurence G. Weinzimmer, PhD, Caterpillar Inc. Professor of Management at Bradley University, Peoria, Illinois, and an adviser to numerous Fortune 500 companies, including General Motors, Goodyear, 3M and Caterpillar. He is also coauthor of The Wisdom of Failure: How to Learn the Tough Leadership Lessons Without Paying the Price (Jossey-Bass). www.TheWisdomofFailure.com

Stories of business failure and mistakes frequently are swept under the rug. Colleagues and bosses generally don't like to tell one another about their missteps, and when business leaders give interviews or write books, they focus much more on their victories than their failures.

That's a shame. The lessons learned from business bungles have tremendous value to all kinds of managers—particularly in difficult economies such as this one, when the risk for failure is greatest. My coauthor and I spent seven years interviewing nearly 1,000 managers across 21 industries to identify the most common and costly business mistakes—mistakes with the potential to ruin careers and companies but also to teach us important lessons.

Lessons we can learn from the worst business mistakes…

1. Don't try to be all things to all customers. Managers tend to say yes when customers offer them business—even if the job isn't in line with the company's chosen direction. As Jeff Hoffman, a founder of Priceline.com, puts it, "It's hard to say no to money."

But companies that lack the discipline to say no can lose their focus.

Example: L.A. Gear was a very successful maker of women's designer athletic footwear in the 1980s. In the 1990s, the company jumped at the chance to make men's performance athletic footwear, then to get its products into Walmart. Both of those opportunities were at odds with L.A. Gear's up-market, fashion-oriented direction and diluted its brand. The company filed for bankruptcy by decade's end.

There are several steps you need to take to gain focus…

• Define your business or department based on the needs it serves and value it provides, then say no to opportunities that don't fit.

• Relentlessly pursue business opportunities that do fit. The more opportunities you see, the less likely you will be to jump at bad-fit opportunities just because they happen to present themselves.

• If an important client asks you to do something outside your chosen direction, you don't have to do it to keep the customer satisfied—you could partner with a company that specializes in the service.

2. Don't "think outside the box" on strategic direction. While think-outside-the-box brainstorming sessions are fine for marketing

or design decisions, they can be disastrous when it comes to charting the direction of a business or department. Focus and discipline could be replaced with creativity for creativity's sake. The end result often is dabbling—doing a little business here, a little there without any true direction.

Example: Allstate Insurance noticed that it was sending large numbers of out-of-state business travelers—Allstate employees and employees of companies that were working with Allstate—to hotels near the company's Illinois headquarters. Their outside-the-box idea was to open an Allstate hotel to serve those travelers. The hotel was booked to capacity but still failed because Allstate knew nothing about running hotels.

What to do: Before pursuing any outside-the-box strategic direction, stop and consider whether the idea has synergy with your existing business.

3. Don't be a bully or allow bullying. According to a survey by CareerBuilder.com, 27% of employees believe that they have been bullied in the workplace, usually by a boss. This workplace bullying can lead to lower morale, lower productivity and increased absenteeism and turnover.

Bully bosses usually don't consider themselves bullies, and most don't do anything as overt as yelling at employees. Instead they use sarcasm, ridicule, unfair workloads or threats of unemployment to intimidate.

What to do: Encourage feedback from people who work or previously worked for you about whether you bully employees. If you are repeatedly told that you do, accept that you are viewed this way even if you don't consider yourself a bully—the line between being tough but fair and being a bully can be difficult to determine. Make an effort to alter the specific behaviors that others see as bullying. Also, ask whether anyone who works under you is a bully, and make it clear to these people that their bullying behavior needs to change.

4. Don't encourage false workplace harmony. Some bosses believe that it's important for everyone in the company or department to be like a family, with themselves at the head.

In reality, it's rare for everyone in a large group to get along. Requiring them to do so can create a toxic atmosphere where people gripe about one another behind closed doors because they can't air differences in the open. Emphasizing workplace harmony also can stifle creative debate and cause frustration—employees who receive only positive feedback might feel cheated when they don't receive promotions and/or their ideas are not implemented. Besides, employees who never receive criticism might never improve.

Example: A Portland law firm gave only positive performance reviews to its support staff, even though this staff didn't work very hard—the firm's managing partner wanted his company to be a big happy family. The firm's best associates became frustrated with the resulting lack of help from the support staff and left.

What to do: Encourage debate and open communication, not consensus. Strive to be respected by employees, not liked. Don't hide bad news from employees—in the long run, it will make them feel lied to, not protected.

5. Don't hoard power. Rise far enough in the corporate hierarchy, and eventually it's no longer feasible to handle every detail and decision yourself—you'll have to delegate. Fail to do this, and your department or company will grind to a halt as everyone waits for your decisions...you'll be so distracted by endless details that you won't pay sufficient attention to the big picture...and your employees won't develop their own skills and confidence.

Example: Jill Barad was a great product manager at toy company Mattel because of her attention to detail. But that strength became a weakness when she was named CEO and insisted on personally overseeing every detail about virtually every product Mattel produced. She was forced to resign after just three years.

What to do: If you have trouble handing off responsibility to employees, try viewing yourself as less of a boss and more of a coach. Coaches rarely set foot on the field. Instead they take pride in formulating a smart game plan and preparing their players as well as they can.

6. Don't be self-absorbed. It's easy to become self-centered when you're running a company or large department. Some leaders start to think that they can do no wrong. Others revel a bit too much in being the center of attention or fail to share credit for successes. In fact, our interviews suggest that this is the single most common misstep bosses make.

What to do: Find a "truth teller" within your company whose opinion you respect. Give this person your permission to tell you what you need to hear—for example, when one of your decisions needs to be rethought or when the image you're projecting is not as positive as you believe.

5 Surprising Ways LinkedIn Can Grow Your Business

Kevin Knebl, founder of Knebl Communications, LLC, a Colorado-based company that trains and advises businesses about social media, online and offline networking, LinkedIn and related topics. He is coauthor of *The Social Media Sales Revolution: The New Rules for Finding Customers, Building Relationships, and Closing More Sales Through Online Networking* (McGraw-Hill). *www.KevinKnebl.com*

Many business owners and professionals have signed up for LinkedIn.com, but very few take *full advantage* of the networking site's ability to help them grow their businesses and succeed professionally.

The following are five underutilized ways that LinkedIn can make you more successful, whether you're self-employed or have numerous employees...

• **Use LinkedIn's Advanced People Search function to find customers and clients**—and find a way to get introduced to them. LinkedIn isn't just a database of more than 175 million professionals...it also is a powerful search engine that you can use to sort through all those people. Click the "Advanced" button to the right of LinkedIn's search box to access

"Advanced People Search." Use this tool to search for potential clients and customers who have particular reasons to meet with you and buy from you.

Examples: Enter the college you attended in Advanced People Search's "School" box, select the industries that your business sells to and generate a list of fellow alums who work in the field you wish to reach. Or skip your school, and instead enter the name of a fraternal organization you belong to or a charity you volunteer with as keywords.

LinkedIn Advanced People Search doesn't just generate a list of names. With each profile that appears, you also will see who you know who knows this person, to help you arrange an introduction.

Helpful: After you conduct an Advanced People Search, click "Save Search" in the upper-right-hand corner so that you can refer back to this list later. With a standard account, you can save up to three searches.

• **Ensure that your LinkedIn profile is one of the first ones that people see when they search for people like you.** Your LinkedIn profile can be a powerful advertisement for your business—but only if you know how to get it noticed.

People increasingly are using LinkedIn to locate businesses and professionals that provide the services they require, not just to network. But hundreds of profiles might pop up when someone searches for professionals in your field. For your LinkedIn profile to be effective advertising for your business, it must be among the very first on these lists. The secret to achieving that? Mention the services you provide multiple times in your profile. LinkedIn's search tool prioritizes profiles that include the search terms the most times.

Example: A man who owns a landscaping company might include the words "landscaping," "mowing," "grass" and "tree removal" in his description of his current business… then again in his description of each of his previous jobs in the landscaping sector…and again anywhere else he can include these keywords in his profile without it seeming awkward.

Helpful: Your profile also should include your up-to-date contact information, a headshot (one in which you're smiling) and a clear explanation of your current and previous skills, positions and responsibilities.

• **Give your company its own LinkedIn page.** Business people aren't the only ones who should set up LinkedIn profiles—businesses now can have profiles of their own. Click "Companies" on LinkedIn, then click the yellow "Add a Company" button to create a separate page for your business.

Having a profile for both yourself and your business increases the odds that someone in need of the services you provide will find you. Your business's profile should explain what your business does and provide its mission statement, but don't stop there. You can upload videos, documents and spreadsheets that show what your company does, too.

Also, ask satisfied customers to write brief testimonials about their positive experiences working with your company. Customer testimonials are particularly powerful on LinkedIn because they come from other LinkedIn users. Potential customers can visit these customers' LinkedIn pages to confirm that the customers really exist—in contrast, phony testimonials from made-up clients are common elsewhere on the Internet.

• **Use LinkedIn to pose questions and facilitate professional discussions.** You can ask the LinkedIn community questions through the Help Forum or LinkedIn Polls. Or search for answers at the Help Center. Start a discussion with LinkedIn Groups.

• **Use LinkedIn to find great potential employees when you hire.** The trouble with posting job openings on job-hunt Web sites such as Monster.com is that you hear back only from people who are actively looking for work.

Instead, enter the skills and experience you are looking for into LinkedIn's Advanced People Search as keywords to produce a list of candidates, then contact the most appealing of these candidates to see if they're interested in working for you. This way, you will reach candidates who are willing to consider changing jobs but who have not yet started searching the job listings.

Contacting top performers in your sector is time well-spent, even if they are not interested in the job. These people might contact you when they do enter the job market down the road, or they might know other top performers who could be interested in your job opening.

Best Way to Get Feedback from Customers

Call and ask for just seven minutes of your customers' time—they will usually feel that they can spare that amount of time. Then ask five to seven open-ended questions regarding your products and services. Ask follow-up questions about any concern customers mention or area of your business that they focus on. Finally, ask if you can use their feedback for a testimonial.

Kathleen M. McEntee, founder and president of McEntee and Associates, Ltd., business management and marketing communications firm, Chicago and La Quinta, California.

Employees You Can Do Without

Some types of employees may deserve to be terminated so that your company can innovate and grow. Those who can be described as *Victims* see problems as evidence of persecution, not challenges to overcome. *Nonbelievers* think change will never happen and are reluctant to innovate. *Know-It-Alls* put a premium on knowledge that they already have, not on new things to be learned, and quickly attack new ideas to explain why they will not work.

What to do: Challenge and attempt to retrain employees who do not accept a culture

of innovation and change. But be prepared to let them go if their negative reactions are so deeply entrenched that they remain obstacles to new ways of thinking.

G. Michael Maddock and Raphael Louis Vitón, chief executive and president, respectively, Maddock Douglas, innovation consultants in Chicago. www.Maddock Douglas.com

Protect Your Small Business from Spammers

To make it easy for customers to contact you but hard for automated bots to bombard you with spam, give your address without the "@" sign or the period on your company Web site—for example, *company at companydomain dot com*. Or insert an image of your address on the page instead of using text—bots don't interpret images well. Consider a contact form instead of giving out your e-mail at all—the form will send you a message through your site without revealing the address.

CBSNews.com

Small Businesses Vulnerable to Cybercriminals

Small business bank accounts are especially vulnerable to unauthorized withdrawals by cybercriminals. And most banks don't provide the same protection for business accounts as they do for personal accounts. More than 10% of small businesses have had funds stolen from bank accounts—a total of more than $2 billion.

Self-defense: Forbid social-media use at work because it can allow entry of malicious software, and train workers to avoid unusual links and e-mails. Keep firewalls up-to-date. Limit the number of employees with access to business accounts. Consider dedicating a single computer to online banking, and make sure that employees do not send e-mail or browse the Internet on it. Also consider getting fraud insurance.

The New York Times. www.NYTimes.com

Tax Benefits of Hiring Your Spouse

If you hire your spouse to work at your small business, your company can deduct contributions made to a qualified retirement plan that benefits your spouse. Annual limits depend on whether you have a defined-contribution or 401(k) plan. And if you run a firm organized as a C corporation and it is in a higher tax bracket than your personal bracket, you may save on taxes if your spouse draws a salary.

Other benefits: If your spouse goes with you on a business trip, his/her travel expenses are deductible. Plus, your company generally can deduct 100% of your spouse's health insurance costs. Your spouse is entitled to the same group-term life insurance coverage as other employees.

What to do: Consult your tax adviser—there are limits and requirements for all these benefits.

Small Business Tax Strategies. www.SmallBizTax.net

5 Things Never to Say When You Lose a Job

Sheryl Spanier, a career consultant and executive coach in New York City and coauthor of *Leave Happy: Making the Elegant Executive Transition* (CreateSpace). *www.SherylSpanier.com*

People can sometimes say the stupidest things when they lose a job—and they end up regretting it. Words said in frustration can burn bridges with employers and/or colleagues you may need later on.

Among the things not to say on your way out the door…

• **"This place is going under anyway."** Voicing doubt about the firm's future is a bad idea even if it's true. This will only cause pain and worry for those who hear the gloomy prediction—particularly if there's a chance that you're right—and inflicting that will make you seem like a jerk. Also, former coworkers can be contacts for you if you leave on positive terms.

• **"I should have left years ago."** Saying this makes people wonder why you stayed as long as you did. It creates the impression that you have been a disgruntled employee who probably didn't give his/her all and casts a shadow over your accomplishments.

• **"Expect to hear from my lawyer."** This is a foolish thing to say if you don't intend to call a lawyer because it will create an adversarial relationship between you and the former employer, virtually ensuring that you won't receive a positive reference or any consideration for future openings.

While it may be advisable to seek legal advice, especially if you are asked to sign any releases, keep these plans to yourself. If you believe that you were wrongfully terminated and truly intend to call a lawyer, it still is foolish to threaten legal action because it will inspire your boss to immediately call the company's lawyers, giving them additional time to prepare a defense.

• **"I quit before they could fire me."** People like to say that they quit rather than admit that they were fired because quitting makes them seem less like helpless victims. But when you tell prospective employers that you quit, they wonder, Why? Unless you are taking a better job, saying that you quit could make you seem impulsive, not in control—particularly in this weak job market.

Rather than say you were fired, consider saying, "I got caught up in the changes going on at the company, and now I'm looking for another opportunity." And rather than saying, "I quit," consider saying, "I had been trying to both do my job and search for the next

312

opportunity, but there was no way to give both the attention they required."

• **"Let me give you some advice."** Some well-meaning people try to offer constructive criticism to former coworkers as they leave a company. Trouble is, anything you say, helpful or not, is likely to be discounted by the person you're speaking with—after all, if you knew so much about working successfully for this company, why are you leaving? Besides, many people take constructive criticism poorly, so offering it risks damaging a relationship that might be a useful contact. Instead, pick the thing that this person does best, and tell him/her how much you admire him for it.

Don't Let Your Employer Ruin Your Career: How to Defeat a Noncompete Agreement

Alan L. Sklover, an attorney specializing in employment law, executive compensation and severance agreement negotiation. He is the founding partner of Sklover & Donath, LLC, New York City. *www.SkloverWorking Wisdom.com*

Can your previous employer stop you from getting a new job? Possibly, if you signed a noncompete agreement.

Noncompete agreements—legal documents that bar employees from working for competing businesses for months or years after leaving an employer—have become increasingly common in this weak economy. Companies that cannot afford raises and bonuses are using noncompete agreements to prevent employees from jumping ship. New hires are told that they must sign these agreements if they want jobs…and existing employees are told that they must sign to keep their jobs or qualify for benefits.

But signing a noncompete could significantly inhibit your career, preventing you from landing appealing positions in this challenging job market. *Here's how to prevent a noncompete from damaging your career…*

GROUNDS FOR CHALLENGE

Eight strategies that can be effective in noncompete agreement challenges, either in negotiations with former employers or in court…

• **Show that the new position would not violate the precise terms of your noncompete agreement.** Give the agreement a very close read—the human resources department should be able to supply a copy if you don't have one. The terms might not be as limiting as you expect.

Example: A man wished to take a job with his current employer's competitor despite a noncompete agreement. He discovered that his noncompete barred him from working only for an employer that used "the same or similar technology." The competitor used a significantly different technology.

• **Show that your employer engaged in illegal or dishonest behavior toward its clients.** Employers don't want former employees discussing corporate misbehavior in court, so they will usually agree to waive noncompete agreements when former employees tactfully raise these matters.

Example: A saleswoman left her employer because it was intentionally overcharging clients and she did not wish to participate. The employer agreed to her request to free her from her noncompete agreement.

• **Show that your former employer lacks a "legitimate business interest" for enforcing the noncompete.** Noncompete agreements are supposed to protect companies' trade secrets and business relationships. If your role with the company did not give you access to trade secrets or clients, you should be allowed to take a job with whomever you like.

• **Show that the noncompete agreement is unreasonably broad in terms of time, geography or activities.** If your current employer does business in only one state, your noncompete should not prevent you from taking a job with a company that does not do business in that state. If your former employer is in just one market niche, your noncompete should not bar you from working in the entire sector. If your insider knowledge of the company's plans extends only to the end of the current fiscal year, your noncompete should not ban you from working in the industry for five years.

Example: A New York judge ruled that the online business world changes so fast that Internet-sector insider knowledge usually is out-of-date within one month. By that standard, almost any noncompete is unreasonably long for Internet-sector workers.

• **Show that the employer breached the terms of your employment contract.** If your employer did not live up to the terms of its contract with you, you likely cannot be forced to live up to your noncompete agreement with it.

Example: A struggling Los Angeles lingerie company could not afford to pay an executive the lump-sum severance package promised in her contract and instead paid the severance in several installments. The courts ruled that this breach of contract was sufficient to void her noncompete agreement.

• **Show that the employer tricked you into signing the noncompete by making promises that it did not live up to.**

Example: An employer verbally promises an employee that a noncompete will not be enforced unless he tries to join one particular competitor—then enforces it when he tries to work for a different company.

Helpful: If any verbal promises were made to you regarding limits to the enforcement of your noncompete and/or the benefits that you receive for signing it, send an e-mail requesting clarification. Save the e-mailed response— this could be important evidence if you later need to challenge the noncompete.

• **Show that you were terminated without cause.** The courts are inconsistent on this point, but in some cases, they have ruled that employers cannot enforce noncompetes when employees are let go without doing anything wrong, as in mass layoffs.

• **Show that the noncompete agreement was never signed.** Don't assume that your former employer has a valid noncompete agreement. If you don't recall signing, ask to see a copy.

Example: Employers will occasionally assume that they have noncompete agreements in place because they required all employees to sign them. But employees sometimes ask to consult with their lawyers before signing, then never get around to turning in the agreement.

MAKING YOUR CASE

If possible, approach your former employer to challenge your noncompete agreement before you start applying for new jobs. You might not even need to hire a lawyer. Begin by sending an e-mail to a decision maker at your former employer using one or more of the reasons listed above to explain why you think your noncompete agreement is not valid…or why you think it does not preclude you from taking a specific job or type of job you have in mind.

If this decision maker promises that the noncompete will not be enforced, save this message to show any potential employers who ask about prior noncompete agreements.

If your former employer insists on holding you to the noncompete agreement, hire an attorney who specializes in employment law to write a letter to the former employer. This should take only an hour or two of an attorney's time. If the employer still does not back down, you might have to go to court to challenge the noncompete. This could lead to thousands of dollars in legal fees, but it usually is not necessary. Employers generally prefer to negotiate before these cases get to court.

To Find a Job, Break the Rules!

Marty Nemko, PhD, a career coach based in Oakland, California, who was named "The Bay Area's Best Career Coach" by the *San Francisco Bay Guardian* and called "Career Coach Extraordinaire" by US News & World Report. He is author of numerous books, including *How to Do Life: What They Didn't Teach You in School* (CreateSpace). *www.MartyNemko.com*

In this tough job market, you can't play by the old "rules." As a career coach who has helped thousands of clients, I have found that contrarian job-search advice often is more effective. *Here's what to keep in mind…*

Old advice: **Foster long-term relationships.**

New advice: **Develop instant deep ones.**

Conventional wisdom says that you need long-term relationships to get significant career help. Alas, by the time you've developed a long-term relationship, you may have given up on finding a job.

Good news: It's possible to create a deep enough connection with someone that you've just met to land a job lead.

The key: In the first few minutes, unearth a person's core hot button, something that he/she cares deeply about. Usually it's related to money, success, family, looks or health.

Let's say that you meet someone at a professional conference and have the following conversation…

You: (*In line for snacks or drinks*) Sure is a big crowd.

She: Sure is.

You: I'm Joe Jobseeker. I'm an accountant. Well, I was until last week. They laid us all off and sent the jobs to India. (*It's important to be quickly revealing without appearing desperate. That sets the stage for developing a quick connection.*) You?

She: Sally Smith. I'm a marketing manager. (*This is said in a flat tone.*)

You: (*Using a light tone.*) You sound thrilled with it.

She: No, it's OK. It's just that with three kids, my plate's pretty full. (*Aha! Her children could be her hot button—you'll know this if she becomes more animated while talking about her kids.*)

You: I can understand. How old are your kids? (*She talks, you listen, sharing parallel experiences and showing empathy. When you sense that she's feeling somewhat connected to you, make what I call "The Ask."*)

You: As I mentioned, I'm looking for my next accounting job. Might you know someone I could speak with?"

If she knows someone, she may tell you… even though you just met.

Old advice: **Rely on LinkedIn.com.**

New advice: **Use Twitter also.**

Twitter, used wisely, can be a surprisingly helpful job-search tool. "Follow" a dozen employers you would like to work for. Occasionally, retweet their tweets and make a smart or kind comment when possible. After a while, send a message to one or more of them—"I have an idea I'd love to share with you. May I e-mail it to you?" With little effort, you've upped your chances of landing a job.

Old advice: **Don't e-mail a cover letter.**

New advice: **Cover letters do matter.**

Sure, large employers screen applications by computer, but eventually someone decides whom to interview. The cover letter increases your chances of being selected. Start the letter with something such as, "I was pleased to see this job opening because I'm a good fit." Then list the first major requirement just as it is written in the ad. Below that, explain how you meet that requirement. Repeat that for each major requirement. Then say something along the lines of, "Of course, there is more to me than that. People say I'm (*insert one of your desirable qualities*), so I'm hoping that you'll interview me."

Old advice: **In résumés, it's numbers that count.**

New advice: **Tell stories.**

The standard advice is, "Quantify all your accomplishments." But desperate job seekers have so jumped on that bandwagon that if you totaled up all the dollars job candidates claimed to have produced for companies, it would transcend the gross domestic product. Most employers now are wise to this, so it's important to supplement those numbers with two or three "PAR" stories—a thorny *Problem* you faced…the smart way you *Approached* it…and its positive *Resolution.*

Example: "Our pizza shop was struggling, so I asked local bakeries if they wanted to rent our ovens after midnight so that they would have more fresh-baked goods for the morning. One said yes, which yielded us $8,000 a year without our lifting a finger or investing a dime."

Old advice: **Send a thank-you note.**

New advice: **Send an influencing packet.**

A thank-you note alone won't help you rise above your competitors. *Instead, along with the note, send one or more of these…*

• A short paper, even a one-pager, that you've written that would impress that employer. For example, if you're applying for a software marketing position, "Four Things Every Software Marketer Must Know in 2013."

• A humbly offered proposal for what you or the company might do. For example, a step-by-step proposal for a pilot test on replacing outsourcing with in-sourcing to improve quality and save money.

• New information that would entice the employer. For example, a client who was interviewed for a job selling toxic-waste services sent the interviewer a list of 10 federal decision makers he would contact if hired. He added, "I have 40 more. Hire me, and I'll use them." He was hired.

Finding a Work-at-Home Job: Most Are Scams, but These 7 Are for Real

Michael Haaren, CEO of Staffcentrix, a training and development company that has offices in Annandale, Virginia, and in Woodstock, Connecticut. Staffcentrix's clients have included the US Department of State, US Air Force and US Army. Haaren is also coauthor of *Work at Home Now: The No-Nonsense Guide to Finding Your Perfect Home-Based Job, Avoiding Scams, and Making a Great Living* (Career Press). *www.RatRaceRebellion.com*

A growing number of employers are willing to use home-based employees, assuming those employees have access to a phone, computer and high-speed Internet connection. That's good news for people with disabilities or who are caring for children or an elderly relative or who live in an area where jobs are scarce. It's also good news for people who could find work outside the home but prefer to spend more time with their families and less time sitting in traffic.

The bad news is that there are roughly 60 "work from home" job scams on the Internet

for each legitimate opportunity, according to our research.

Here's how to avoid the scams and land a good work-at-home position…

LANDING WORK-AT-HOME JOBS

Tweak your résumé before you start applying for work-at-home jobs. Stress any work experience that shows that you can work productively without direct supervision or handle projects outside the workplace. Be sure to mention any experience you have with communications technology, such as videoconferencing tools and tablet computers.

If your work history is light on projects outside the workplace, consider taking a virtual volunteer position and listing this on your résumé.

Example: The United Nations Volunteers program offers plenty of volunteer-from-home opportunities and looks impressive on a résumé (*www.OnlineVolunteering.org*).

Interviews for online positions often are conducted via phone or Skype video call. If you are not naturally comfortable speaking on the phone or you lack experience with Skype video calls, practice with friends before the interview.

Helpful: If the interview is a Skype video call, make sure that the backdrop behind you is uncluttered and looks professional.

HOME-BASED CAREERS HIRING NOW

Among the career opportunities open to the home-based…

1. Customer service agents field calls from their employers' customers and prospective customers—they do not place telemarketing calls. Major employers of home-based workers in this field include LiveOps (*http://join.LiveOps.com*)…Alpine Access (*www.AlpineAccess.com*)…and Arise (*http://Partner.Arise.com*).

Other well-known companies that frequently hire home-based customer service agents include American Express (on *http://careers.AmericanExpress.com*, click on "Search Jobs" and enter "Work at Home" in the keyword search box)…Amazon.com (on *www.Amazon.com*, select "Careers" from the "Get to Know Us" menu near the bottom of the page, then enter "Work at Home" in the keyword box)… and the Home Shopping Network (on *www. HSN.com*, select "Careers at HSN" from the "About HSN" menu near the bottom of the page, then select "Work at Home" from the "Why HSN" menu). To find other companies hiring in this field, select the "Call Center & Cust. Service" listing on the left of the home page of my company's Web site, *www.RatRace Rebellion.com*.

Pay typically is $9 to $12 an hour,* though it can reach $20 an hour or more.

2. Internet ad assessors conduct Internet searches and make sure that search results are appropriate for the search terms used. Extensive tech skills are not needed—just basic Internet skills. Companies hiring home-based workers in this area include Google (on *www.Google.com/about/jobs*, search for the job "Ad Rater")…Lionbridge (on *www.Lion bridge.com*, select "Careers," then "Work-at-Home Opportunities") and Leapforce (*www. LeapforceatHome.com*). The pay is about $10 to $15 per hour.

3. Web site testers visit Web sites and record their impressions of those sites. It is like being part of a focus group except that you can do it from home. Employers offering home-based employment in the field include Userlytics (on *www.Userlytics.com*, select "Join Our Tester Panel" near the bottom of the page) and UserTesting.com (on *www.UserTest ing.com*, select "Be a Tester" near the top of the page).

Reviews typically take around 10 to 20 minutes apiece and pay perhaps $10 per review. But don't expect to make a lot of money or make this a full-time career—testers typically get occasional assignments, not regular work.

4. Online moderators oversee Web site communities, Facebook groups and interactive online games, stepping in to remove offensive comments or to ban troublemakers. Employers that hire home-based moderators include LiveWorld.com (*www.LiveWorld.com/ about/jobs/moderator*) and Zynga.com (go to *http://company.Zynga.com/about/jobs*, click on "Careers," select "Careers by Location"). The

*Rates subject to change.

job requires tact, interpersonal skills and experience with social media. The pay for this work tends to be toward the lower end of the scale—often $10 an hour.

5. Virtual task freelancers perform chores posted on Web sites such as TaskRabbit.com. Some of the chores require travel and thus are not appropriate for the exclusively home-based—picking up a client's dry cleaning or assembling new IKEA furniture, for example. But others can be performed from home, such as conducting online research or doing data entry.

Job seekers typically bid on tasks. If their bid is accepted, they are paid directly by the individual or company that needs the work done.

Comparable Web sites include Amazon's Mechanical Turk (*www.MTurk.com*) and Click-worker (*www.Clickworker.com*). Also, the site Fiverr (*www.Fiverr.com*) lets people post tasks that they're willing to perform for $5.

6. Transcriptionists type verbatim accounts of board meetings, presentations, conference calls, etc., from audio recordings. Some of the companies that hire home-based transcriptionists include Tigerfish (go to *www.Tigerfish.com/ employment.html*)…Ubiqus (*www.Ubiqus.com,* choose "Working for Us")…and Cambridge Transcriptions (*www.CTran.com/employment*).

The pay for transcriptionists can vary with typing speed but generally is around $10 per hour.

7. Freelance posters are paid to post content to blogs. Topics vary widely, depending on the theme of the blog. Pay can range from just a few dollars per post to $50 and above, and usually is made directly to the poster by the owner of the blog. Short posts on generic themes such as lifestyle and fashion generally pay less, while specialized posts requiring more research (on economic issues, for example) pay more. These are listed on such Web sites as Problogger.net (click on "Jobs") and BloggingPro.com (click on "Job Board")…Postloop (on *www.Postloop.com*, click "Join")…and Wired Flame (on *www.WiredFlame.com*, select "Writers").

More from Michael Haaren...

Work-at-Home Scam Alert

Some work-from-home scams are easy to spot—they promise big paydays without much effort, feature photos of people clutching wads of cash or require applicants to pay up-front "membership" fees or similar fees—but other work-at-home scams are more subtle.

The best way to avoid these scams is to search for work-at-home jobs only on Web sites that make some effort to weed out scammers. These include Indeed.com (click on "Advanced Job Search," type "Work from Home" without quotes into the "exact phrase" field, and leave the location field blank) and the Work from Home section of About.com (on *http://JobSearch.about.com*, select "Find a Job," then "Work from Home Jobs"). We've also posted more than 18,000 screened job leads on my company's Web site, *www.RatRaceRebellion.com*.

Warning: Con artists are constantly fine-tuning their scams, and occasionally a bogus offer will slip through at Indeed.com and similar "job aggregator" Web sites. Job seekers should always proceed with caution. Use a search engine to research the potential employer to make sure it appears legitimate before applying. Also visit work-at-home forums such as WAHM.com and WorkPlaceLikeHome.com to learn what other home-based employees and job seekers have to say about the employer.

Your Résumé and More

Depending on what sort of position you are applying for, you may want to include *QR codes* that can be scanned by smartphones to direct employers to a video résumé, online portfolio or other relevant information. But stay focused on *content*, not presentation—many employers spend less than one minute on each résumé and will be distracted or turned off by elements that they consider gimmicky. A well-crafted cover letter and a résumé showing career progression may work best.

318

Also: Spend more time actively networking and less on preparation and submission of your résumé.

MarketWatch.com

Looking for Work? Turn Negative Traits Around

Traits that can cost you a job even if you are well-qualified—and what to do about them... *Lack of energy*—you must be enthusiastic about the job and company, and show it in the interview. *Poor use of free time*—employers look for candidates with interesting hobbies or a second job that shows you use free time to expand skills and areas of interest. *Procrastination*—give examples of times you have seen a big project through to completion. *Being unprepared*—demonstrate a working knowledge of the company and its clients at the interview. *Job hopping*—this can indicate that you are hard to work with or unsure of what you want to do. If you have changed jobs often, explain why.

Also: Have a solid online presence—a professional Twitter account or blog, for example. More than one-third of hiring managers check candidates' social-media sites.

AOL Jobs. http://Jobs.AOL.com

Job Interview Dos and Don'ts

•**Do practice your handshake before an interview**—it should be firm but not overly strong, and your hand should be dry. Wipe off any perspiration before meeting with the interviewer.

•**Don't touch your face**—many people interpret it as a sign of dishonesty.

•**Don't cross your arms**—it indicates defensiveness and passive aggression.

- **Do put your hands on the table during the interview**—that will keep you aware of them and they will not cause you any trouble.
- **Don't stare**—maintain eye contact only in moderation.
- **Avoid too frequent or too enthusiastic nodding.** Nod only when it is appropriate to do so.

CBSNews.com

Great Questions to Ask a Job Interviewer

Ask an interviewer how success will be measured. And, if the interviewer would be your manager, ask him/her to describe his own management style. Find out what the company's biggest current problem is—this shows that you are already thinking like an employee, especially if you follow up with more questions or suggestions on what to do. Also ask why the position is open—whether the company is expanding, creating a new job or replacing someone who left.

What else to do: Ask what comes next— find out where the hiring process stands and when and how you should follow up.

CBSNews.com

Hiring Decisions Based on Credit Scores

Hiring decisions based on credit scores have become increasingly common—but now they are restricted in California, Connecticut, Hawaii, Illinois, Maryland, Oregon, Vermont and Washington state. Lawmakers in those states say that some people have bad credit through no fault of their own and should not be rejected for jobs because of that. Exceptions usually are made for positions responsible for handling large sums of cash. Business groups contend that small firms need every available tool to make good hiring decisions and that credit reports provide valuable objective information about an applicant's past.

Heather Morton, program principal, National Conference of State Legislatures, Denver, quoted in *USA Today.*

Good Answers to Illegal Job Interview Questions

In general, an interviewer is not allowed to ask about age, race, national origin, marital or parental status or disabilities, but common questions include... *Do you have kids?* Assume the interviewer is trying to find out if you can put in extra hours, and say, "My personal life will not prevent me from working any hours required." *Do you play any sports?* The interviewer may want to know if you are physically able to handle the job, so say, "Looking at all the job functions, I would be able to perform all of them." *You have an accent—where are you from?* The interviewer may wonder if you can work legally in the US. Say, "I have been working legally in the country for a long time and will be glad to share my documentation with Human Resources." *You're my age, right?* Refocus the question onto your experience— "I would like to use my knowledge and background to help you and the company."

Also: Keep answers light and friendly—interviewers don't always know that they are asking illegal questions.

Employment experts quoted at Bankrate.com.

Expect a Background Check When You Apply for a Job

To prepare for a possible background check when applying for a job, get your credit reports from the three major agencies—Equifax, Experian and TransUnion—and correct any errors. In addition, search for yourself online, and if you find unflattering information on Web sites, contact the operators of those sites and request that the information be removed. Get rid of anything on social-networking sites that you would not want an employer to see. Also ask your previous employer to show you the contents of your personnel file. And remember to tell friends and associates that they may be contacted by the company to which you have applied.

What else to do: Consider paying for your own background check to see what turns up—get a referral from a corporate executive to a company that does background checks.

Los Angeles Times. www.LATimes.com

How to Beat Age Bias When Job Hunting

If a job interviewer makes age-related assumptions—for instance, that older workers do not get along with younger ones—address the subject directly by saying, "I like to learn from people of all ages." Expect tough questions and have answers ready.

Example: If the interviewer asks why you are applying for a lower-level job than you had in the past, say you enjoyed management but would prefer more hands-on involvement in projects at this point in your career. Tailor your résumé to what employers want—describe your experience in terms of the specific skills desired by the company you are targeting.

Andrea Kay, career consultant and author of *This Is How to Get Your Next Job* (Amacom), quoted online at MarketWatch.com.

More Workers Suing Over These Violations

Lawsuits related to wage-and-hour violations have increased by 400% in the last decade.

Biggest complaints from workers: They were required to work more than 40 hours a week without receiving overtime pay…their jobs were misclassified as exempt from over-

time requirements…and their personal time was intruded upon by smartphones and other technology.

USA Today. www.USAToday.com

New on the Job? 10 Ways to Make Them *Really* Glad They Hired You

Alan L. Sklover, an attorney specializing in employment law, executive compensation and severance agreement negotiation. He is the founding partner of Sklover & Donath, LLC, New York City. *www.SkloverWorking Wisdom.com*

We don't just have to learn a new set of responsibilities when we start a new job…we also must learn to interact with a new set of colleagues and bosses. These people will form lasting opinions of us during our first few months on the job. If those opinions are unfavorable, it could affect our ability to earn promotions or even hold on to the job. *Ten things we can do during our first three months in a new workplace to foster a positive image…*

1. Listen 10 times as much as you speak. It's dangerous to talk a lot before you know the lay of the land in a new workplace. You might say something that reveals your lack of experience with the company, its products or its customers…or you might propose a plan that already has been tried unsuccessfully.

Listening is less dangerous and more useful. After three months of dedicated listening, you should know the company, your colleagues and your bosses well enough so that you can open your mouth without substantial risk of putting your foot in it. Until then, contribute to discussions mainly by asking intelligent questions.

2. Don't challenge authority—even limited authority. It's probably obvious to new employees that they shouldn't question their boss's or the CEO's authority. But new employees often do question the authority of those who are not above them in the corporate hierarchy—for example, the office manager who denies them the office supplies they want or the security guard who says they must sign in until a permanent ID is issued.

Resist the urge to argue with such coworkers during your first three months. People who have very little power often jealously guard the power they do have. Questioning their authority could create an enemy who could be more dangerous than you realize—for example, if it turns out this low-level employee has the ear of a top executive.

3. Ignore offensive remarks. If someone says or does something you consider offensive during your early months in a new workplace, just let it go. If you make waves, others in the organization might conclude that you're someone who imagines or overreacts to slights.

Exceptions: Speak up if the offensive comments or actions recur...or if the offensive comment suggests that the speaker might try to hinder your career.

4. Don't say you need something unless you absolutely do. Employers can become frustrated with a new employee who acts as if the company is there to serve his/her needs rather than the other way around. Each time you tell your new employer that you need something—even something minor such as a better desk chair, a particular brand of pen or an afternoon off—the more likely the employer is to conclude that you put yourself ahead of the company.

If there's something that you absolutely require to be productive, it's OK to request it—but don't make more than one or two of these requests in your first three months, and be sure to phrase these as requests, not "needs."

5. Don't suggest or implement changes right off the bat. Long-standing employees sometimes resent newcomers who think they know better from the moment they walk through the door. Besides, the changes new employees suggest often are flawed because new employees don't yet fully understand why things are done the way they are.

Example: A man hired to run a government agency tasked with distributing money to other agencies decided to stop sending money to recipient agencies that filed their paperwork improperly. He thought this would spur those agencies into filing correctly. He didn't understand that cutting off these funds meant Americans who relied on government aid would not be able to pay their rent or buy food. He was fired.

6. Steer clear of complainer colleagues. In many workplaces, there are employees who moan and complain continually. Avoid these people as if they have the plague, especially during your first three months in a new job. If you spend time with them, you might be considered one of them.

Make polite excuses for why you can't lunch or socialize with complainers. If your boss is a complainer, you might listen as a courtesy, but don't join in.

7. Observe colleagues carefully to learn the unwritten rules and behavioral norms of your new workplace. Run afoul of an unwritten rule, and you might be viewed as someone who doesn't fit in.

Example: Early in my career, I worked in an office where employees often loosened their neckties, so I did, too. I failed to note that they tightened up their ties before meetings with senior partners. When I did not tighten my tie before such a meeting, a senior partner grabbed it and angrily tightened it for me.

8. Put in longer hours than your boss. Arrive early, take a short lunch and stay late. If your boss and other colleagues see you at your post when they arrive and leave, you will develop a reputation as a committed employee. If you're not present just a few times when your boss seeks you out during your first three months, you could develop a reputation as a slacker.

Working long hours even can earn you face time with the company's top executives, who often work long hours themselves. My daughter Jamie rode the elevator with the CEO when she arrived at 7:00 am on one of her first days at a new job. From then on, the most powerful person in the company recognized her and associated her with early arrival.

If you're a worker who is paid by the hour and limited to a certain number of hours, find a way to devote additional efforts to your job without requesting additional payment.

9. Don't discuss lofty career goals with colleagues. Your plans for fast advancement might make you seem like a threat to colleagues or even bosses who have their eyes on the same promotions. Besides, talking about promotions when you haven't yet shown you can excel in your current position could make you seem cocky or unrealistic.

10. Treat every colleague as a potential future best friend. Be polite, gracious and friendly with everyone you meet in your new workplace. Introduce yourself to those you don't know. Act very pleased to see every colleague whose path you cross. Smile.

If people in your new organization decide that they like you personally, they will be more inclined to agree with your opinions and see you as a productive employee.

3 Words Never to Say When You're Eating Out with a Client or the Boss

Barbara Pachter, president, Pachter & Associates, a business communications and etiquette firm, based in Cherry Hill, New Jersey. She is author of *New Rules @ Work: 79 Etiquette Tips, Tools, and Techniques to Get Ahead and Stay Ahead* (Prentice Hall). *www.Pachter. com*

The impression we make at the dining table can affect the way others see us. It even can affect our career if we're treating a client to dinner, having a lunch interview with a potential employer or sharing a bite to eat with the boss.

The table manners your mother might have drilled into you as a child—such as elbows off the table and don't talk with your mouth full—are just a start. *More mistakes...*

WHAT *NOT* TO ORDER

• **Ordering food that's challenging to eat.** Order spaghetti in tomato sauce, and a single splatter could make you look like a slob. Order crab legs, and your attention might be focused on cracking them open, rather than on the person you hope to impress. Order a simple, easy-

to-eat meal that you have eaten before and that always agrees with your stomach.

• **Failing to mirror your guest's order.** If your dining companion orders an appetizer, you should order an appetizer. If he/she orders dessert, you should order dessert. Otherwise, there will be an awkward time when one of you is eating and the other is not. You don't have to eat all of the food.

• **Placing a complex order.** Ordering off the menu or saying things such as "hold this" or "put that on the side" can make you seem difficult to please, not the sort of person whom others want to deal with.

HOW *NOT* TO EAT

Tucking your napkin into your shirt isn't the only faux pas when the food arrives...

• **Eating much faster or slower than your dining companions.** Matching your tablemates' eating pace will make them feel more comfortable and in tune with you.

• **Eating someone else's bread.** Some people accidentally take their neighbor's bread or water when seated around a round table. Just recall automaker BMW to keep it straight—your Bread is to your left, your Meal in the middle, your Water to your right.

• **Saying, "Take this back."** When the meeting is more important than the meal itself, you're better off eating poorly prepared food than saying, "Take this back." Sending food back means that your guest will have food while you don't, which throws off the timing of the meal. It also risks making you look picky and difficult (even if your complaint is legitimate). Send food back during important meetings only if it is completely inedible.

HOST MISTAKES

• **Choosing an inappropriate restaurant.** If possible, choose a place where you have dined previously so that you know it is appropriate. Also, provide guests with a specific reason why you selected this particular restaurant for them. This shows that you put some thought into the meeting.

Example: Send your dining companion's assistant an e-mail prior to the meal to find out about his food restrictions or preferences.

When your guest arrives, say, "I know you like steak, and this place has the best in town."

●**Letting guests handle their own problems.** It's your responsibility as host to look after your guests. If a guest is served the wrong meal or a meal that clearly is not properly prepared, say, "Let's have that taken care of," and—unless your guest declines your assistance—call over the waiter and politely explain what the problem is. If the guest's meal must be returned to the kitchen, stop eating your meal until the guest's food returns.

GUEST MISTAKES

●**Ordering one of the most expensive dishes on the menu.** Your host might consider this taking unfair advantage. It's acceptable only if the host himself orders a high-end item or specifically recommends one.

●**Being unprepared for light conversation.** Even if the purpose of the meal is to discuss an important topic, there's likely to be small talk, too. Flip through a newspaper before the meal for current events...check whether there's anything new going on in your dining partner's sector...and double-check the names of his/her spouse and kids.

Stay Positive...

At least 50% of your job is to get along with coworkers, customers, clients and management. Not maintaining a positive work atmosphere can cost you your job.

Hunter Lott, former senior course leader, America Management Association and owner of PleaseSueMe.com.

Nondrinkers at a Business Disadvantage

Many business deals are developed or closed over drinks, and professionals who abstain from alcohol often find that they are not included. Research shows that moderate drinkers earn more in corporate life than non-drinkers, on average—although heavy drinkers earn less than moderate drinkers.

For nondrinkers: Order a drink and leave it untouched...order something nonalcoholic in a glass usually used to serve alcoholic beverages.

The New York Times. www.NYTimes.com

Benefit of Being Bald...

Men with shaved heads are seen as being more masculine, dominant and better able to lead others than men with thinning hair or longer locks.

Results of three studies that tested people's perceptions of men with shaved heads by researchers at The Wharton School, University of Pennsylvania, Philadelphia, published online in *Social Psychological and Personality Science.*

The Power of Good Posture!

Sitting up straight is good for more than your back.

Finding: Standing and sitting tall increases *testosterone* in men and women...decreases the stress hormone *cortisol*...and makes people feel more powerful.

Amy Cuddy, PhD, assistant professor, negotiation, organizations and markets unit, Harvard Business School, Cambridge, Massachusetts.

Loneliness Reduces Productivity

Employees who are lonely are less productive both as individuals and in teams. Loneliness tends to increase hostility, negative thinking and anxiety, as well as reduces cooperation—all changes that can have a negative impact in the workplace.

Self-defense: Help yourself or a lonely colleague by connecting in small ways, such as taking time for a chat...asking for input on a project...or going out for coffee or lunch together. Talk to a manager or company counselor if your loneliness or that of another employee seems to be persistent and is having an effect on productivity.

Study of more than 650 workers by researchers at California State University, Sacramento, and The Wharton School, University of Pennsylvania, Philadelphia, reported in *The New York Times*.

Fun Way to Boost Productivity at Work

Checking your Facebook account at work can *increase* your productivity!

Recent finding: Employees who paused briefly during the workday to read news online, check Facebook or watch a YouTube video were 9% more productive than ones who worked straight through.

Study of 300 people led by researchers at University of Melbourne's department of management and marketing, published in *New Technology, Work and Employment*.

Office Buildings Linked to Headaches

In a recent finding, when exposed to an uncomfortable indoor environment, 38% of workers reported having a headache one to three days a month...18% had a headache one to three days a week...and 8% had headaches daily. An uncomfortable indoor environment was defined as one with abnormal levels of carbon monoxide, carbon dioxide, volatile organic compounds, light, humidity and/or temperature. Headaches ranged from mild to migraine, and women were more likely to report headaches than men.

Study of 4,326 office workers in 100 large office buildings led by researchers in the department of physiology and health science, Ball State University, Muncie, Indiana, published in *Annals of Indian Academy of Neurology*.

Don't Let Unemployment Hurt Your Heart

People who were jobless because they had been fired, laid off or quit a job earlier in life had a 35% higher risk for heart attack after age 50 than people who remained employed. Multiple job losses posed as much of a threat to heart health as smoking, high blood pressure and diabetes. Talk to your doctor about heart-health strategies, such as reducing stress.

Matthew Dupre, PhD, assistant professor of community and family medicine, Duke University, Durham, North Carolina, and leader of a study published online in *Archives of Internal Medicine*.

If an Employer Asks for Your Facebook Password...

Employer requests for Facebook passwords violate the site's terms of service, but not the law. Many employers regard Facebook postings as part of background checks, but many job seekers are uncomfortable giving out their passwords. You can try to divert the request by asking if the interviewer is looking for something specific. If the employer insists, decide how much you want the job.

Safest: Treat your Facebook postings as if they are public information.

Kiplinger's Personal Finance. www.Kiplinger.com

What a Stay-at-Home Parent Would Earn...

A stay-at-home parent would earn $112,962 per year if he/she were paid for all the things he does. That includes payment for the jobs of janitor, driver, cook, doing laundry, facilities manager, psychologist and household CEO. The average stay-at-home parent works almost 95 hours a week.

Analysis by the Web site Salary.com.

20

Safety Survey

Facebook Is Spying on You: 6 Ways Your Privacy Could Be Compromised

A billion people worldwide use Facebook to share the details of their lives with their friends. Problem is, they also might be unintentionally divulging matters they consider private—to friends...coworkers, clients and employers...marketing companies...and even to competitors, scammers and identity thieves.

Six ways Facebook could be compromising your private information and how to protect yourself...

1. The new Timeline format exposes your old mistakes. Timeline, introduced in late 2011, makes it easy for people to search back through your old Facebook posts, something that was very difficult to do in the past. That could expose private matters and embarrassing photos that you've long since forgotten posting.

What to do: To hide Timeline posts that you do not wish to be public, hold the cursor over the post, click the pencil icon that appears in the upper-right corner, then click "Hide from Timeline" or "Delete."

2. Facebook apps steal personal details about you—even details that you specifically told Facebook you desired to keep private. Third-party apps are software applications available through Facebook but developed by other companies. These include games and quizzes popular on Facebook such as *Farm-Ville* and *Words with Friends*, plus applications

John Sileo, president and CEO of The Sileo Group, a Denver-based identity theft prevention consulting and education provider that has worked with the Department of Defense, the Federal Reserve Bank and many other clients. He speaks internationally about online privacy, social-media exposure and digital reputation. He is author of *Privacy Means Profit: Prevent Identity Theft and Secure Your Bottom Line* (Wiley). *www.Sileo.com*

such as Skype, TripAdvisor and Yelp. Most Facebook apps are free—the companies that offer them make their money by harvesting personal details about users from their Facebook pages, then selling that information to advertisers.

Many apps collect only fairly innocuous information, such as age, hometown and gender, that probably is not secret. But others dig deep into Facebook data, even accessing information that you may have designated private, such as religious affiliation, political leanings and sexual orientation.

What to do: Read user agreements and privacy policies carefully to understand what information you are agreeing to share before signing up for any app. The free Internet tool Privacyscore is one way to evaluate the privacy policies of the apps you currently use (*www.Facebook.com/privacyscore*). You also can tighten privacy settings by clicking the lock icon in the upper-right-hand corner. Select "See More Settings," then choose "Apps" from the left menu. Under "Apps You Use," click "Edit" to see your privacy options.

3. Facebook "like" buttons spy on you—even when you don't click on them. Each time you click a "like" button on a Web site, you broadcast your interest in a subject not just to your Facebook friends but also to Facebook and its advertising partners.

But if you're a Facebook user and you visit a Web page that has a "like" button, Facebook will record that you visited that page even if you don't click "like." Facebook claims to keep Web-browsing habits private, but there's no guarantee that the information won't get out.

What to do: One way to prevent Facebook from knowing where you go online is to set your Web browser to block all cookies. Each browser has a different procedure for doing this, and you will have to re-enter your user ID and password each time you visit certain Web sites.

Alternatively, to eliminate cookies created during a specific browser session, you can use the "InPrivate Browsing" mode (Internet Explorer), "Incognito" mode (Google Chrome) or "Private Browsing" mode (Firefox and Safari).

There also are free plug-ins to stop Facebook from tracking you, such as Facebook Blocker (*www.Webgraph.com/resources/facebookblocker*).

4. "Social readers" tell your Facebook friends too much about your reading habits. Some sites, including *The Washington Post* and *The Huffington Post*, offer "social reader" Facebook tools. If you sign up for one, it will tell your Facebook friends what articles you read on the site.

Problem: The tools don't share articles with your Facebook friends only when you click a "like" button—they share everything you read on the site.

What to do: If you've signed up for a social reader app, delete it. Click the lock icon in the upper-right-hand corner, select "See More Settings," then choose "Apps" on the left. Locate the app, click the "X" and follow the directions to delete.

5. Photo and video tags can hurt you. They could let others see you in unflattering and unprofessional situations. If you work for a straight-laced employer or with conservative clients or you are in the job market, you already may realize that it's unwise to post pictures of yourself in unprofessional and possibly embarrassing situations. But you may fail to consider that pictures that other people post of you also can hurt you.

A Facebook feature called photo tags has dramatically increased this risk. These tags make it easy for Facebook users to identify by name the people in photos they post, then link these photos to the Facebook pages of all users pictured.

What to do: Untag yourself from unflattering photos. Hold your cursor over the post, and click the pencil icon. Select "Report/Remove Tag," then follow the directions to remove the tag. Enable review of all future photos you're tagged in before they appear on your Timeline. Click the lock icon in the upper right, then "See More Settings" and select "Timeline and Tagging." Then click "Edit" next to "Review posts friends tag you in before they appear on your Timeline," and click "Enabled" on the drop-down menu.

6. Your friends on Facebook—and those friends' friends—might reveal too much about you. Even if you're careful not to provide sensitive information about yourself on Facebook, those details could be exposed by the company you keep.

Example: A 2009 Massachusetts Institute of Technology study found it was possible to determine with great accuracy whether a man was gay. This was based on factors such as the percentage of his Facebook friends who were openly gay—even if this man did not disclose his sexual orientation himself.

If several of your Facebook friends indicate a potentially risky or unhealthy activity, such as smoking or bar hopping, among their interests—or include posts or pictures of themselves pursuing a risky interest—an insurer, college admissions officer, employer or potential employer might conclude that you likely enjoy this pursuit yourself.

What to do: Take a close look at the interests and activities mentioned by your Facebook friends. If more than a few of them discuss a dangerous hobby, glory in unprofessional behavior or are open about matters of sexual orientation or political or religious beliefs that you consider private, consider removing most or all of these people from your friends list or at least make your friends list private. Click your name in the upper right, then click "Friends," then "Edit" and select "Only Me" from the drop-down menu.

More from John Sileo...

How to Protect Your Wi-Fi

How secure is the wireless router that you use at home when sending online content through the air? Although it's commonly known that you need to protect a router with a password to prevent neighbors from borrowing your Internet connection, cyberthieves can easily circumvent these passwords if they are improperly configured.

If these cyberthieves—known as "sniffers" or "war drivers"—are within range of your Wi-Fi signal, typically 100 yards, they can send and/or download information over your connection once they breach your security. They also can use eavesdropping software to snoop through your e-mail...get the credit card numbers that you enter into Web sites...and get the user name and password you type in at your bank's Web site.

If your computer's hard drive isn't protected by special software, sniffers even can use your Internet connection to access your data files.

To protect yourself...

• **Consult the owner's manual for your wireless router or call your Internet provider** and ask for a technician to walk you through setting up a few security options. These options normally are left unactivated by the router's manufacturer, and most people don't bother to turn them on.

• **Turn on WPA2 encryption or better.** The old standard WEP encryption is easy to breach.

• **Set up MAC addressing.** This is a bit complicated, so if you can't figure it out through your owner's manuals, you may have to call a technician. This tool allows only computers that you specifically designate to access your wireless connection.

• **Protect your hard drive by enabling the firewall.** Both Windows-based and Apple Macintosh–based computers come with this software. It acts like an entryway lock that prevents other Internet users from accessing your hard drive.

What to Do If Your E-Mail Gets Hacked

Karen McDowell, PhD, information security analyst with the University of Virginia, Charlottesville. She has worked in computer security for more than 15 years and holds a GCIH certification as a certified incident handler trained to manage computer system attacks.

Have you ever received e-mails that appear to be from friends but aren't? Or have friends told you that they've received e-mails from you that you didn't send? These are signs of a "computer hijacking."

Here's how to limit the damage if you suspect that your computer has been hijacked and what you need to do to prevent it from happening again…

CORRECTIVE MEASURES

Update and run your antivirus program and a malware-removal program. (Malware is software that hijacks, disables and/or steals computer data.)

If you don't have an antivirus program—for PCs, purchase Norton Antivirus ($39.99,* *http://us.Norton.com*)…McAfee AntiVirus Plus ($34.99, *http://home.McAfee.com*)…or Microsoft Security Essentials (free, *http://Windows. Microsoft.com/mse*). For Macs, use Sophos Anti-Virus (free for home users, *www.Sophos.com*, click "Free security tools").

To find and eliminate hijack software on PCs, use Malwarebytes Anti-Malware (free, *www.MalwareBytes.org*) and Spybot Search & Destroy (free, *www.Safer-Networking.org*). I know of no similar programs for Macs.

Next, change your e-mail account password, and check the e-mail account's settings to make sure a hijacker does not have access to your account.

Example: In Gmail, click the gear icon in the upper right, then click "Settings," then "Accounts and Import," and check whether another account is listed in the "Grant access to your account" section.

If you no longer have access to the account, contact your company's IT department (if it's a corporate e-mail account) or follow the e-mail provider's procedure for a password reset.

Example: With Gmail, select "Can't access your account?" in the sign-in box, then "I'm having other problems signing in."

If your computer has been taken over by "scareware"—a pop-up claiming the computer has been infected by a virus and offering to sell you corrective software—don't touch any key or click any on-screen button. Disconnect the computer from the Internet quickly, perhaps by disconnecting its network cable or unplugging your wireless router.

With the computer still disconnected from the Internet, run a full system scan with your antivirus program and a separate anti-malware program. If this doesn't fix your pop-up problem, you may have to take the computer to a professional technician. The technician might have to completely erase your hard drive and reload your operating system to remove the malware, which could cost around $200.

PREVENTIVE MEASURES

To protect your computer from future attempted invasions…

•**Always use hard-to-guess passwords** for all your accounts, and use a separate password for each account. A good idea is to combine numbers and upper- and lowercase letters.

Example: Instead of just using the word "elephant," you might try "3l3ph4NT." It is relatively easy to remember but hard to crack. Or use a short phrase.

•**Make sure your computer's firewall is turned on.** Activating your computer firewall varies depending on your computer and operating system.

•**Don't click links in an e-mail unless you're very confident** that the message really comes from the person who appears to have sent it.

•**Never access your e-mail account from a public computer.**

Don't Get Skimmed

Karen Larson, editor, *Bottom Line/Personal*, 281 Tresser Blvd., Stamford, Connecticut 06901. *www.BottomLine Publications.com*

Patrons of a Citibank near me recently got "skimmed" using the ATMs in the bank's own lobby. Crooks installed hidden devices to capture information encoded on the magnetic strips of bank cards. They then used the information to steal funds from victims' accounts.

Few banks and gas stations are doing enough to protect their customers, says Robert Siciliano, CEO of Boston-based security company IDTheftSecurity.com. *His advice…*

•**Examine ATMs carefully.** If the card reader extends outward from the face of the

*Prices subject to change.

ATM, give the external portion a quick yank or twist. Do the same with the panel containing the keypad. Don't use the ATM if either feels loose. Be wary if the color of the plastic around the card reader or the keypad doesn't match the plastic elsewhere.

●**Don't assume that an ATM is safe because it is in a well-monitored location.** Last year, there was a rash of skimmings at ATMs near the registers inside busy supermarkets.

●**Look for tiny hidden cameras aimed at the keypad.** Crooks sometimes use these to learn victims' PINs. A camera could be hidden inside a bank brochure holder near the ATM keypad or in a fake speaker mounted on the ATM. To be safe, use your free hand to cover your typing hand.

●**Confirm that your card slides in and out of the card reader smoothly.** Jamming suggests a skimmer.

●**Be wary of gas pumps—you might be skimmed.** Use a credit card (or select "credit" when using a debit card)—laws protect credit card users from substantial losses.

●**Check your bank account regularly.** Contact the bank immediately if you notice any unexplained declines.

How to Delete Sensitive Info from Your Smartphone

Sensitive data may remain on your smartphone or computer even after you think you have erased it completely.

Recent finding: Of 30 used smartphones and computers purchased on Craigslist, 15 of the devices still had sensitive data, including bank account and Social Security numbers, work documents and court records. Android smartphones and Windows XP laptops and netbooks are particularly difficult to erase completely.

Self-defense: Instead of trying to sell a device that could contain personal information, smash it to bits. The iPad, iPhone and Black-Berry generally don't carry the same risk—but you should still wipe the device clean by reformatting multiple times and then reset it to the original factory settings before getting rid of it.

Robert Siciliano, identity-theft expert and CEO of IDTheftSecurity.com, Boston.

Guard Your Credit Card Number

Never give your credit card number to anyone who calls you. Thieves may pretend to be from your bank or utility company and read the last four or five digits that appear on your credit card receipt and the location where you used the card and claim to be looking into possible fraud or other issues. By giving out the rest of your card number, you enable the thief to charge items in your name.

If you think a call may be legitimate: Look up the number of the business, and call the firm on your own.

Also: Keep receipts until you get your credit card statement to check for accuracy and provide proof for any dispute.

Bill Hardekopf, CEO, LowCards.com.

Credit Card Interest Scam

Thieves use robocalls to offer you a reduced credit card interest rate—for a cost of $700 to $1,000.

What to do: Do not return the call. Instead, call your credit card issuer directly if you think that your interest rate is too high—depending on your credit standing, the issuer may reduce your interest rate at no extra charge to you.

Gerri Detweiler, personal-finance expert, Credit.com, quoted online at Money.MSN.com.

More from Gerri Detweiler...

Additional Protection Against Debt-Collector Abuses

In January 2013, the federal government's new Consumer Financial Protection Bureau stepped up its watchdog role when it comes to monitoring debt collectors.

Among the bureau's roles: Making sure that debt collectors identify themselves clearly and that they have a consumer complaint and dispute-resolution process in place...examining whether they use accurate information about the consumers they contact...and looking into whether consumers are being harassed.

Self-defense: When a debt collector calls, say that you want a written notice of the debt to be sent to you.

Beware...Debt Collectors

Debt collectors use prosecutors' letterheads to scare people into paying. District attorneys' offices allow this because the debt collectors also insist that debtors take a costly class on budgeting and financial responsibility—and the prosecutors' offices get a cut of the class fees. More than 300 district attorneys' offices work with debt collectors this way. Consumer lawyers are challenging the practice, saying that prosecutors are essentially renting out their stationery. But it is becoming more common as municipalities look for new revenue sources.

What to do: If a debt-collection company demands that you take a course in budgeting and claims that the district attorney insists on this, contact the prosecutor's office directly to investigate.

The New York Times. www.NYTimes.com

Debt Collection Con

Con artists try to collect phantom debt from consumers. Fraudulent companies have employees pose as government and law-enforcement officials who call and threaten people with arrest, lawsuits and/or job loss. Victims may become frightened and pay even if they do not owe the money.

Example: These companies demand payments for loans applied for but not made...or loans taken out by a former spouse...or ones that have already been repaid.

What to do: Insist that anyone who calls and claims that you owe a debt provides you with written notice of the amount owed, the names of creditors and your rights as a debtor. This information is required by law.

Los Angeles Times. www.LATimes.com

Scammed Again!

If you've been the victim of a scam, you may be targeted *again* by scammers who pose as government agents and promise to help you recover your lost money—for a hefty fee.

Self-defense: Ask for the person's or company's address and phone number—scammers are unlikely to provide these. Do a Web search using the company's name and include words such as "scam" or "rip-off." Also check the Better Business Bureau's Web site (*www.BBB.org*) to see if a report has been filed on the company.

Consumer Reports. www.ConsumerReports.org

Package-Delivery Scam

Victims receive an e-mail that appears to be from the US Postal Service stating that a package could not be delivered. The e-mail says to click on a link in the message to arrange delivery or pickup—but clicking on this link loads a malicious virus that can steal information from the victim's computer. Forward spam e-mails to Spam@USPIS.gov.

Note: If there is a package for you, the postal service will leave a notice in your mailbox rather than send an e-mail.

Margaret D. Williams, national public information representative with the US Postal Inspection Service. *http://PostalInspectors.USPIS.gov*

Sneaky Subscription Scam

Phony offers for subscription-renewals can cost many times what publishers charge for magazines—and the renewals may not even be processed. Dishonest companies notify subscribers that subscriptions are expiring and offer to renew them—but sending a check may or may not get your subscription continued and will likely cost far more than a direct renewal.

What to do: Read any renewal offer—if it does not come directly from the magazine itself, throw it out. If you are not sure, call the magazine to find out if the offer is legitimate and to ask for the best renewal price.

Los Angeles Times. www.LATimes.com

Check Your Phone Bill... You May Have Been "Crammed"

John Breyault, vice president of public policy, telecommunications and fraud at the National Consumers League, Washington, DC. *www.NCLnet.org*

You could end up being charged for a service on your monthly mobile phone bill even though you never asked for it. This practice, called "cramming," occurs when a provider other than your phone company supplies you with ringtones, sports scores, weather updates, horoscopes and/or other unwanted services, and your phone company adds a charge to your bill, typically several dollars. (With landlines, cramming will usually show up as a line item for "miscellaneous" or "enhanced" services.)

The phone company keeps a portion of the revenue. Although three major telephone companies—AT&T, CenturyLink and Verizon—agreed to cease most third-party billing for landlines by the end of 2012, they continue for wireless and smaller landline providers unless you opt out.

Self-defense: Call your phone company now, and request that all third-party providers be blocked. Review your phone bills every month for surprise charges, often listed as "service charge," "other fees," "calling plan" or "membership."

Also, avoid calling "900" numbers, accepting anonymous collect calls and signing up for contests online via your cell phone, all common methods that vendors use to cram you.

If you do get crammed, call your service provider and demand a refund.

Beware These 3 Area Codes

Area codes 284, 809 and 876 are for the British Virgin Islands, the Dominican Republic and Jamaica. Do not respond to letters, voice mails or e-mails that ask you to call one of these area codes to receive a prize. You will be charged $1.49 to $3.99 per minute. Scammers, who get a portion of the per-minute charge, try to keep you on the phone as long as possible.

Sid Kirchheimer, author of *Scam-Proof Your Life* (AARP Books/Sterling), writing in *AARP Bulletin*.

Health-Care Law Con

Scammers are using the *Affordable Care Act* to try and steal money and identities. Thieves claiming to be from the government call and ask for personal information—supposedly to verify a person's identity to be sure that he/she is eligible for coverage under the health-care law.

Example: A scammer might provide your bank's routing number and then ask for your account number.

Self-defense: Just hang up. No government employee will ever call to verify your personal information under the health-care law—there is no provision in the law to do this.

Federal Trade Commission, Washington, DC.

Scams That Target Investors

Crowdfunding scams: Using newly created Internet domains, scammers pretend to own small businesses to get people to invest in their fake stock offerings.

Self-directed IRAs: Scam artists pretend to own real estate or create fake businesses, then promote their fraudulent enterprises as great investments.

Investment-for-visa scams: Foreign investors who put at least $500,000 into a new business in the US can get a US visa under the Immigrant Investor Program. Unscrupulous promoters may seek to attract bond investments by touting a questionable or phony venture linked to this program.

A. Heath Abshure is president of the North American Securities Administrators Association, Washington, DC. *www.NASAA.org*

Tax Fraud Based on Identity Theft Is on the Rise

Criminals steal names and Social Security numbers from living or deceased people and use the information to defraud the government by filing phony returns claiming refunds. In 2012, the IRS investigated 650,000 identity theft cases. The IRS is developing new ways to screen for this fraud and is working harder to help victims.

What to do: If you suspect identity-theft tax fraud—for instance, if you receive an IRS notice that more than one return was filed in your name—go to *www.IRS.gov/identitytheft*, where a guide on preventing and dealing with fraud is posted. Or talk to your accountant.

Internal Revenue Service. *www.IRS.gov*

Alert: Tricky Apartment Rental Scams

Thieves commonly work online, promising extra-low rent for an apartment or no credit check. Some make up listings for places that are not for rent or do not exist. Others hijack legitimate listings by changing the e-mail address or other contact information. Scammers try to get victims to send money, often by saying that they are out of the country but will send keys upon receipt of a deposit. They then take the money and disappear.

What to do: Deal locally with people you meet in person...physically inspect any property before turning over any money—never wire funds...beware of any claims of no credit checks...and use a real estate agent who can verify that an offering is legitimate. Also, be realistic about rent—if an offer is substantially below the rents of similar properties in the neighborhood, it is likely to be a scam.

Los Angeles Times. www.LATimes.com

Tricks to Hide Valuables

Hollow out an old book or phone book with a utility knife, and store items inside. For jewelry and other small things, use an empty container from stick-type deodorant…or slit open the end of an empty toothpaste tube—clean the inside, insert valuables, then fold it a few times. The deodorant and toothpaste-tube approaches are especially good when traveling.

Jeff Yeager, author of *Don't Throw That Away!* and *The Cheapskate Next Door* (both from Three Rivers).

Pickpocket Prevention

Karen Larson, editor, *Bottom Line/Personal*, 281 Tresser Blvd., Stamford, Connecticut 06901. *www.BottomLine Publications.com*

My husband and I landed in Rome, jetlagged and luggage-laden, and rushed to catch the high-speed train to Florence. On the train, two young women offered to help us find our seats. I was pleased to have the assistance—until I heard my husband say, "Where's my wallet?"

The young women had been jostling us as we worked our way to our seats, a common pickpocket tactic. I grabbed the women by their wrists and demanded, "Where's my husband's wallet?" One of them pointed to the floor where she'd thrown it and said, "There it is."

Later I recognized that what I had done was not safe. Detective Kevin Coffey, a 31-year veteran of one of America's largest police forces and the founder of CorporateTravelSafety.com, agrees. Some pickpockets may become violent when cornered (though this is not common).

Prevention is the best course, says Coffey. Men should carry their wallets in their front pockets and avoid loose-fitting pants. Wrap a thick rubberband around the wallet, too—the rubber makes it harder for pickpockets to slide the wallet smoothly out of a front pocket.

Better yet, purchase a belt-loop wallet, sometimes called a hidden wallet or hidden pocket. This small pouch attaches to the belt and tucks inside the pants behind the front pocket, making it extremely difficult for pickpockets. It also is more convenient than a money belt because you don't have to untuck your shirt to gain access—just pull it out by its strap.

Women should carry purses that zip closed with a flap that folds over (the flap should face your body). For more travel safety tips, go to *www.CorporateTravelSafety.com/safety-tips*.

Crooks Are *Everywhere*!

Some thieves wait in the theater parking lots, then break into cars when moviegoers enter the theater, steal car registrations to get addresses and burglarize homes during the films.

What to do: Always carry your car registration with you.

Crooks steal library cards, then borrow DVDs from libraries and sell them—leaving the cardholders liable for late fees or replacement costs.

What to do: Treat a library card as you would a credit card—if you find that it is missing, contact the library and put a hold on your library account.

Phony casting agents ask for up-front fees for auditions.

What to do: Do not fall for the scam—legitimate talent agencies never charge in advance.

AARP.org

Deadly Headphone Hazard

In the seven-and-a-half years from January 2004 through June 2011 (most recent data available), 116 pedestrians were injured or killed while wearing headphones. More than half were hit by trains. Seventy percent of the accidents were fatal.

Study by researchers at University of Maryland, Baltimore, published online in *Injury Prevention*.

Hotel Rooms That Kill

Karen Larson, editor, *Bottom Line/Personal*, 281 Tresser Blvd., Stamford, Connecticut 06901. *www.BottomLine Publications.com*

Carbon monoxide leaking from a swimming pool heater exhaust pipe hospitalized 16 guests—and killed one—at a West Virginia Holiday Inn Express early in 2012. No carbon monoxide detector sounded because there were no carbon monoxide detectors in the hotel. While carbon monoxide detectors have become increasingly common in homes in the past decade—you usually don't see them in hotels. State and local fire codes rarely require them.

Learning that made me want to travel with a portable carbon monoxide detector.

"You certainly could do that," says Robert E. Solomon, division manager for Building and Life Safety Codes at the nonprofit National Fire Protection Association. "Another option is to call various hotels before making reservations to see if they have carbon monoxide detectors."

Two circumstances where hotel carbon monoxide detectors are particularly important…

•**In a room equipped with a fuel-burning device,** such as a wood-burning stove or gas fireplace. Don't let this fuel-burning device operate through the night if there's no carbon monoxide detector in the room.

•**In a motel room that opens onto an enclosed parking area.** You could be in danger if a vehicle is left running.

Carbon monoxide is colorless and odorless, so without a detector, victims often don't realize they are in danger. If a carbon monoxide alarm does sound—or symptoms such as headaches, dizziness, nausea, weakness and/or confusion suggest a possible carbon monoxide leak—get to fresh air quickly.

Emergency Alerts

A Wireless Emergency Alerts (WEA) service warns people via special text messaging about tornadoes, hurricanes, typhoons, blizzards and other dangerous conditions in their areas. Wireless carriers and the federal government launched the service, which is free, and consumers are automatically signed up.

USA Today. www.USAToday.com

What Does a Wind Advisory Mean?

A wind advisory means that there is, or will be, a period of at least an hour with winds of at least 30 miles per hour.

Forecasters issue a high-wind warning when winds are expected to exceed 40 miles per hour for one hour or more. *To protect yourself and your property when there is a wind advisory or high-wind warning…*

•**Secure outdoor furniture, trash cans, decorations and other objects**—or bring them indoors.

•**Park your vehicle in a protected area.** Winds may down trees and power lines.

•**Assume all downed wires are live.** Don't go near them. Report them to the utility company and police.

•**Keep flashlights and a battery-operated radio handy** in case of power outages.

•**Exercise special caution while driving.** Keep both hands on the wheel and slow down—especially on elevated roadways and bridges. Keep your distance from vans and trucks. A strong gust can cause them to swerve.

Eli Jacks, chief of fire and public weather services, National Weather Service, Silver Spring, Maryland. *www.Weather.gov*

Laptops and Lightning

Laptops and cell phones are safe to use during electrical storms—but landlines are not because their wired circuits can carry energy from lightning right to the handset.

Richard Kithil, Jr., founder and CEO, National Lightning Safety Institute, Louisville, Colorado.

Index